T0325023

Advanced Methods for Complex Network Analysis

Natarajan Meghanathan
Jackson State University, USA

A volume in the Advances in Wireless Technologies and Telecommunication (AWTT) Book Series

Published in the United States of America by
Information Science Reference (an imprint of IGI Global)
701 E. Chocolate Avenue
Hershey PA, USA 17033
Tel: 717-533-8845
Fax: 717-533-8661
E-mail: cust@igi-global.com
Web site: http://www.igi-global.com

Library of Congress Cataloging-in-Publication Data

Names: Meghanathan, Natarajan, 1977- editor.
Title: Advanced methods for complex network analysis / Natarajan Meghanathan, editor.
Description: Hershey, PA : Information Science Reference, [2016] | Includes bibliographical references and index.
Identifiers: LCCN 2015050776| ISBN 9781466699649 (hardcover) | ISBN 9781466699656 (ebook)
Subjects: LCSH: System analysis.
Classification: LCC QA402 .A295 2016 | DDC 003/.72--dc23 LC record available at http://lccn.loc.gov/2015050776

This book is published in the IGI Global book series Advances in Wireless Technologies and Telecommunication (AWTT) (ISSN: 2327-3305; eISSN: 2327-3313)

British Cataloguing in Publication Data
A Cataloguing in Publication record for this book is available from the British Library.

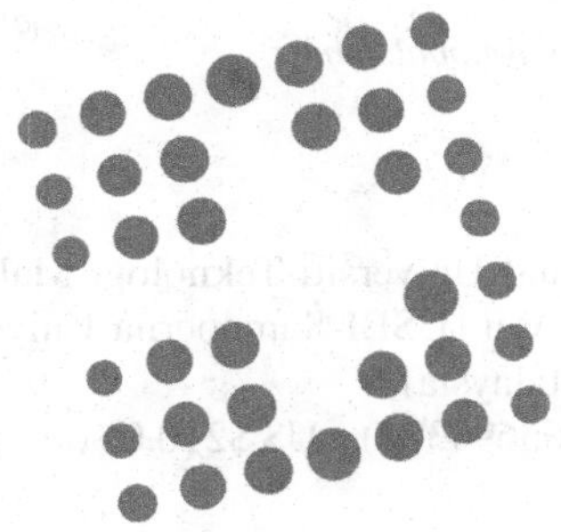

Advances in Wireless Technologies and Telecommunication (AWTT) Book Series

Xiaoge Xu
The University of Nottingham Ningbo China, China

ISSN: 2327-3305
EISSN: 2327-3313

Mission

The wireless computing industry is constantly evolving, redesigning the ways in which individuals share information. Wireless technology and telecommunication remain one of the most important technologies in business organizations. The utilization of these technologies has enhanced business efficiency by enabling dynamic resources in all aspects of society.

The **Advances in Wireless Technologies and Telecommunication Book Series** aims to provide researchers and academic communities with quality research on the concepts and developments in the wireless technology fields. Developers, engineers, students, research strategists, and IT managers will find this series useful to gain insight into next generation wireless technologies and telecommunication.

Coverage

- Network Management
- Cellular Networks
- Mobile Communications
- Wireless Broadband
- Grid Communications
- Wireless Sensor Networks
- Radio Communication
- Digital Communication
- Mobile Web Services
- Telecommunications

IGI Global is currently accepting manuscripts for publication within this series. To submit a proposal for a volume in this series, please contact our Acquisition Editors at Acquisitions@igi-global.com or visit: http://www.igi-global.com/publish/.

The Advances in Wireless Technologies and Telecommunication (AWTT) Book Series (ISSN 2327-3305) is published by IGI Global, 701 E. Chocolate Avenue, Hershey, PA 17033-1240, USA, www.igi-global.com. This series is composed of titles available for purchase individually; each title is edited to be contextually exclusive from any other title within the series. For pricing and ordering information please visit http://www.igi-global.com/book-series/advances-wireless-technologies-telecommunication-awtt/73684. Postmaster: Send all address changes to above address.

Titles in this Series

For a list of additional titles in this series, please visit: www.igi-global.com

Critical Socio-Technical Issues Surrounding Mobile Computing
Norshidah Mohamed (Prince Sultan University, Kingdom of Saudi Arabia and Universiti Teknologi Malaysia, Malaysia) Teddy Mantoro (USBI-Sampoerna University, Indonesia) Media Ayu (USBI-Sampoerna University, Indonesia) and Murni Mahmud (International Islamic University Malaysia, Malaysia)
Information Science Reference • copyright 2016 • 357pp • H/C (ISBN: 9781466694385) • US $210.00 (our price)

Handbook of Research on Next Generation Mobile Communication Systems
Athanasios D. Panagopoulos (National Technical University of Athens, Greece)
Information Science Reference • copyright 2016 • 604pp • H/C (ISBN: 9781466687325) • US $370.00 (our price)

Game Theory Framework Applied to Wireless Communication Networks
Chungang Yang (Xidian University, China) and Jiandong Li (Xidian University, China)
Information Science Reference • copyright 2016 • 502pp • H/C (ISBN: 9781466686427) • US $235.00 (our price)

Enabling Real-Time Mobile Cloud Computing through Emerging Technologies
Tolga Soyata (University of Rochester, USA)
Information Science Reference • copyright 2015 • 399pp • H/C (ISBN: 9781466686625) • US $195.00 (our price)

Emerging Perspectives on the Design, Use, and Evaluation of Mobile and Handheld Devices
Joanna Lumsden (School of Engineering and Applied Science, Aston University, UK)
Information Science Reference • copyright 2015 • 334pp • H/C (ISBN: 9781466685833) • US $205.00 (our price)

Technological Breakthroughs in Modern Wireless Sensor Applications
Hamid Sharif (University of Nebraska – Lincoln, USA) and Yousef S. Kavian (Shahid Chamran University of Ahvaz, Iran)
Information Science Reference • copyright 2015 • 417pp • H/C (ISBN: 9781466682511) • US $200.00 (our price)

Handbook of Research on Software-Defined and Cognitive Radio Technologies for Dynamic Spectrum Management
Naima Kaabouch (University of North Dakota, USA) and Wen-Chen Hu (University of North Dakota, USA)
Information Science Reference • copyright 2015 • 927pp • H/C (ISBN: 9781466665712) • US $505.00 (our price)

Interdisciplinary Mobile Media and Communications Social, Political, and Economic Implications
Xiaoge Xu (The University of Nottingham Ningbo China, China)
Information Science Reference • copyright 2014 • 409pp • H/C (ISBN: 9781466661660) • US $205.00 (our price)

www.igi-global.com

701 E. Chocolate Ave., Hershey, PA 17033
Order online at www.igi-global.com or call 717-533-8845 x100
To place a standing order for titles released in this series, contact: cust@igi-global.com
Mon-Fri 8:00 am - 5:00 pm (est) or fax 24 hours a day 717-533-8661

Editorial Advisory Board

List of Reviewers

Table of Contents

Foreword xvi

Preface xviii

Chapter 1
On Vertex Cover Problems in Distributed Systems 1
Can Umut Ileri, Ege University, Turkey
Cemil Aybars Ural, Ege University, Turkey
Orhan Dagdeviren, Ege University, Turkey
Vedat Kavalci, Izmir University, Turkey

Chapter 2
On k-Connectivity Problems in Distributed Systems 30
Vahid Khalilpour Akram, Ege University, Turkey
Orhan Dagdeviren, Ege University, Turkey

Chapter 3
Link Prediction in Complex Networks 58
Manisha Pujari, Université Paris 13, France
Rushed Kanawati, Université Paris 13, France

Chapter 4
Design of Structural Controllability for Complex Network Architecture 98
Amitava Mukherjee, IBM India Private Limited, India
Ayan Chatterjee, Jadavpur University, India
Debayan Das, Jadavpur University, India
Mrinal K. Naskar, Jadavpur University, India

Chapter 5
Triadic Substructures in Complex Networks 125
Marco Winkler, University of Wuerzburg, Germany

Chapter 6
Characterization and Coarsening of Autonomous System Networks: Measuring and Simplifying the Internet 148
Alberto Garcia-Robledo, Cinvestav-Tamaulipas, Mexico
Arturo Diaz-Perez, Cinvestav-Tamaulipas, Mexico
Guillermo Morales-Luna, Cinvestav-IPN, Mexico

Chapter 7
Connectivity and Structure in Large Networks 180
Rupei Xu, University of Texas at Dallas, USA
András Faragó, University of Texas at Dallas, USA

Chapter 8
A Study of Computer Virus Propagation on Scale Free Networks Using Differential Equations 196
Mohammad S. Khan, Texas A&M University – Kingsville, USA

Chapter 9
SNAM: A Heterogeneous Complex Networks Generation Model 215
Bassant Youssef, Virginia Tech, USA
Scott F. Midkiff, Virginia Tech, USA
Mohamed R. M. Rizk, Alexandria University, Egypt

Chapter 10
Social Network Analysis 237
Paramita Dey, Government College of Engineering and Ceramic Technology, India
Sarbani Roy, Jadavpur University, India

Chapter 11
Evolutionary Computation Techniques for Community Detection in Social Network Analysis 266
Abhishek Garg, Indian Institute of Technology (BHU) Varanasi, India
Anupam Biswas, Indian Institute of Technology (BHU) Varanasi, India
Bhaskar Biswas, Indian Institute of Technology (BHU) Varanasi, India

Chapter 12
Differential Evolution Dynamic Analysis in the Form of Complex Networks 285
Lenka Skanderova, VSB Technical University of Ostrava, Czech Republic
Ivan Zelinka, VSB Technical University of Ostrava, Czech Republic

Chapter 13
On Mutual Relations amongst Evolutionary Algorithm Dynamics and Its Hidden Complex Network Structures: An Overview and Recent Advances 319
Ivan Zelinka, VSB Technical University of Ostrava, Czech Republic

Chapter 14
Wireless Body Area Network for Healthcare Applications 343
Danda B. Rawat, Georgia Southern University, USA
Sylvia Bhattacharya, Georgia Southern University, USA

Chapter 15
Application of Biomedical Image Processing in Blood Cell Counting using Hough Transform....... 359
Manali Mukherjee, Government College of Engineering and Ceramic Technology, India
Kamarujjaman, Government College of Engineering and Ceramic Technology, India
Mausumi Maitra, Government College of Engineering and Ceramic Technology, India

Chapter 16
A Hybrid Complex Network Model for Wireless Sensor Networks and Performance Evaluation 379
Peppino Fazio, University of Calabria, Italy
Mauro Tropea, University of Calabria, Italy
Salvatore Marano, University of Calabria, Italy
Vincenzo Curia, University of Calabria, Italy

Chapter 17
A Network Analysis Method for Tailoring Academic Programs.. 396
Luis Casillas, University of Guadalajara, Mexico
Thanasis Daradoumis, University of the Aegean, Greece & Open University of Catalonia, Spain
Santi Caballe, Open University of Catalonia, Spain

Compilation of References 418

About the Contributors 452

Index 459

Detailed Table of Contents

Foreword xvi

Preface xviii

Chapter 1
On Vertex Cover Problems in Distributed Systems 1
Can Umut Ileri, Ege University, Turkey
Cemil Aybars Ural, Ege University, Turkey
Orhan Dagdeviren, Ege University, Turkey
Vedat Kavalci, Izmir University, Turkey

An undirected graph can be represented by G(V,E) where V is the set of vertices and E is the set of edges connecting vertices. The problem of finding a vertex cover (VC) is to identify a set of vertices VC such that at least one endpoint of every edge in E is incident to a vertex V in VC. Vertex cover is a very important graph theoretical structure for various types of communication networks such as wireless sensor networks, since VC can be used for link monitoring, clustering, backbone formation and data aggregation management. In this chapter, we will define vertex cover and related problems with their applications on communication networks and we will survey some important distributed algorithms on this research area.

Chapter 2
On k-Connectivity Problems in Distributed Systems 30
Vahid Khalilpour Akram, Ege University, Turkey
Orhan Dagdeviren, Ege University, Turkey

k-Connectivity detection and restoration are important problems in graph theory and computer networks. A graph is k-connected if it remains connected after removing k-1 arbitrary nodes. The k-connectivity is an important property of a distributed system because a k-connected network can tolerate k-1 node failures without losing the network connectivity. To achieve the k-connectivity in a network, we need to determine the current connectivity value and try to increase connectivity if the current k is lower than the desired value. This chapter reviews the central and distributed algorithms for detecting and restoring the k-connectivity in graphs and distributed systems. The algorithms will be compared from complexity, accuracy and efficiency perspectives.

Chapter 3
Link Prediction in Complex Networks 58
Manisha Pujari, Université Paris 13, France
Rushed Kanawati, Université Paris 13, France

This chapter presents the problem of link prediction in complex networks. It provides general description, formal definition of the problem and applications. It gives a state-of-art of various existing link prediction approaches concentrating more on topological approaches. It presents the main challenges of link prediction task in real networks. There is description of our new link prediction approach based on supervised rank aggregation and our attempts to deal with two of the challenges to improve the prediction results. One approach is to extend the set of attributes describing an example (pair of nodes) calculated in a multiplex network that includes the target network. Multiplex networks have a layered structure, each layer having different kinds of links between same sets of nodes. The second way is to use community information for sampling of examples to deal with the problem of class imbalance. All experiments have been conducted on real networks extracted from well-known DBLP bibliographic database.

Chapter 4
Design of Structural Controllability for Complex Network Architecture 98
Amitava Mukherjee, IBM India Private Limited, India
Ayan Chatterjee, Jadavpur University, India
Debayan Das, Jadavpur University, India
Mrinal K. Naskar, Jadavpur University, India

Networks are all-pervasive in nature. The complete structural controllability of a network and its robustness against unwanted link failures and perturbations are issues of immense concern. In this chapter, we propose a heuristic to determine the minimum number of driver nodes for complete structural control, with a reduced complexity. We also introduce a novel approach to address the vulnerability of the real-world complex networks, and enhance the robustness of the network, prior to an attack or failure. The simulation results reveal that dense and homogenous networks are easier to control with lesser driver nodes, and are more robust, compared to sparse and inhomogeneous networks.

Chapter 5
Triadic Substructures in Complex Networks 125
Marco Winkler, University of Wuerzburg, Germany

An important topological characteristic which has been studied on networks of diverse origin is the abundance of motifs – subgraph patterns which occur significantly more often than expected at random. We investigate whether motifs occur homogeneously or heterogeneously distributed over a graph. Analyzing real-world datasets, it is found that there are networks in which motifs are distributed highly heterogeneously, bound to the proximity of only very few nodes. Moreover, we study whole graphs with respect to the homogeneity and homophily of their node-specific triadic structure. The former describes the similarity of subgraphs in the neighborhoods of individual vertices. The latter quantifies whether connected vertices are structurally more similar than non-connected ones. These features are discovered to be characteristic for the networks' origins. Beyond, information on a graph's node-specific triadic structure can be used to detect groups of structurally similar vertices.

Chapter 6
Characterization and Coarsening of Autonomous System Networks: Measuring and Simplifying the Internet 148
Alberto Garcia-Robledo, Cinvestav-Tamaulipas, Mexico
Arturo Diaz-Perez, Cinvestav-Tamaulipas, Mexico
Guillermo Morales-Luna, Cinvestav-IPN, Mexico

This Chapter studies the correlations among well-known complex network metrics and presents techniques to coarse the topology of the Internet at the Autonomous System (AS) level. We present an experimental study on the linear relationships between a rich set of complex network metrics, to methodologically select a subset of non-redundant and potentially independent metrics that explain different aspects of the topology of the Internet. Then, the selected metrics are used to evaluate graph coarsening algorithms to reduce the topology of AS networks. The presented coarsening algorithms exploit the k-core decomposition of graphs to preserve relevant complex network properties.

Chapter 7
Connectivity and Structure in Large Networks 180
Rupei Xu, University of Texas at Dallas, USA
András Faragó, University of Texas at Dallas, USA

Graph models play a central role in the description of real life complex networks. They aim at constructing graphs that describe the structure of real systems. The resulting graphs, in most cases, are random or random-like; so it is not surprising that there is a large literature on various classes of random graphs and networks. Our key motivating observation is that often it is unclear how the strength of the different models compare to each other, e.g., when will a certain model class contain another. We are particularly interested in random graph models that arise via (generalized) geometric constructions. This is motivated by the fact that these graphs can well capture wireless communication networks. We set up a general framework to compare the strength of random network models, and present some results about the equality, inequality and proper containment of certain model classes.

Chapter 8
A Study of Computer Virus Propagation on Scale Free Networks Using Differential Equations 196
Mohammad S. Khan, Texas A&M University – Kingsville, USA

The SIR model is used extensively in the field of epidemiology, in particular, for the analysis of communal diseases. One problem with SIR and other existing models is that they are tailored to random or Erdos type networks since they do not consider the varying probabilities of infection or immunity per node. In this paper, we present the application and the simulation results of the pSEIRS model that takes into account the probabilities, and is thus suitable for more realistic scale free networks. In the pSEIRS model, the death rate and the excess death rate are constant for infective nodes. Latent and immune periods are assumed to be constant and the infection rate is assumed to be a function of the size of the total population and the size of the infected population. A node recovers from an infection temporarily with a probability p and dies from the infection with probability (1-p).

Chapter 9
SNAM: A Heterogeneous Complex Networks Generation Model 215
Bassant Youssef, Virginia Tech, USA
Scott F. Midkiff, Virginia Tech, USA
Mohamed R. M. Rizk, Alexandria University, Egypt

Complex networks are characterized by having a scale-free power-law (PL) degree distribution, a small world phenomenon, a high average clustering coefficient, and the emergence of community structure. Most proposed models did not incorporate all of these statistical properties and neglected incorporating the heterogeneous nature of network nodes. Even proposed heterogeneous complex network models were not generalized for different complex networks. We define a novel aspect of node-heterogeneity which is the node connection standard heterogeneity. We introduce our novel model "settling node adaptive model" SNAM which reflects this new nodes' heterogeneous aspect. SNAM was successful in preserving PL degree distribution, small world phenomenon and high clustering coefficient of complex networks. A modified version of SNAM shows the emergence of community structure. We prove using mathematical analysis that networks generated using SNAM have a PL degree distribution.

Chapter 10
Social Network Analysis 237
Paramita Dey, Government College of Engineering and Ceramic Technology, India
Sarbani Roy, Jadavpur University, India

Social Network Analysis (SNA) looks at how our world is connected. The mapping and measuring of connections and interactions between people, groups, organizations and other connected entities are very significant and have been the subject of a fascinating interdisciplinary topic . Social networks like Twitter, Facebook, LinkedIn are very large in size with millions of vertices and billions of edges. To collect meaningful information from these densely connected graph and huge volume of data, it is important to find proper topology of the network as well as analyze different network parameters. The main objective of this work is to study network characteristics commonly used to explain social structures. In this chapter, we discuss all important aspect of social networking and analyze through a real time example. This analysis shows some distinguished parameters like number of clusters, group formation, node degree distribution, identifying influential leader/seed node etc. which can be used further for feature extraction.

Chapter 11
Evolutionary Computation Techniques for Community Detection in Social Network Analysis 266
Abhishek Garg, Indian Institute of Technology (BHU) Varanasi, India
Anupam Biswas, Indian Institute of Technology (BHU) Varanasi, India
Bhaskar Biswas, Indian Institute of Technology (BHU) Varanasi, India

Community detection is a topic of great interest in complex network analysis. The basic problem is to identify closely connected groups of nodes (i.e. the communities) from the networks of various objects represented in the form of a graph. Often, the problem is expressed as an optimization problem, where popular optimization techniques such as evolutionary computation techniques are utilized. The importance of these approaches is increasing for efficient community detection with the rapidly growing networks. The primary focus of this chapter is to study the applicability of such techniques for community detection.

Our study includes the utilization of Genetic Algorithm (GA) and Particle Swarm Optimization (PSO) with their numerous variants developed specifically for community detection. We have discussed several issues related to community detection, GA, PSO and the major hurdles faced during the implication of evolutionary approaches. In addition, the chapter also includes a detailed study of how these issues are being tackled with the various developments happening in the domain.

Chapter 12
Differential Evolution Dynamic Analysis in the Form of Complex Networks 285
Lenka Skanderova, VSB Technical University of Ostrava, Czech Republic
Ivan Zelinka, VSB Technical University of Ostrava, Czech Republic

In this work, we investigate the dynamics of Differential Evolution (DE) using complex networks. In this pursuit, we would like to clarify the term complex network and analyze its properties briefly. This chapter presents a novel method for analysis of the dynamics of evolutionary algorithms in the form of complex networks. We discuss the analogy between individuals in populations in an arbitrary evolutionary algorithm and vertices of a complex network as well as between edges in a complex network and communication between individuals in a population. We also discuss the dynamics of the analysis.

Chapter 13
On Mutual Relations amongst Evolutionary Algorithm Dynamics and Its Hidden Complex Network Structures: An Overview and Recent Advances 319
Ivan Zelinka, VSB Technical University of Ostrava, Czech Republic

In this chapter, we do synthesis of three partially different areas of research: complex networks, evolutionary computation and deterministic chaos. Ideas, results and methodologies reported and mentioned here are based on our previous results and experiments. We report here our latest results as well as propositions on further research that is in process in our group (http://navy.cs.vsb.cz/). In order to understand what is the main idea, lets first discuss an overview of the two main areas: complex networks and evolutionary algorithms.

Chapter 14
Wireless Body Area Network for Healthcare Applications 343
Danda B. Rawat, Georgia Southern University, USA
Sylvia Bhattacharya, Georgia Southern University, USA

Wireless Body Area Network (WBAN) is an emerging field of research which has been progressing rapidly in recent years. WBAN is a network utilized for continuous monitoring of physiological state of the subject, where the patient can perform his regular activities while his body parameters get measured continuously and are accessed by the physician remotely. This chapter provides a thorough survey of current WBAN technologies in the healthcare sector. Besides the recording of physiological parameters, discussions have been provided on remote data transmission to a server called Virtual Doctor Server (VDS). During this transmission, WBAN network uses various technologies namely Ultra Wide Band WBAN, Technology Enabled Medical Precision Observation 3.1 (TEMPO 3.1), J2ME and Bluetooth. Details of several existing WBAN related projects have been discussed along with their applications. The next section of the chapter deals with the use and design of medical sensors in WBAN. Performance comparison between WBAN and WSN (Wireless Sensor Network) has also been provided.

Chapter 15
Application of Biomedical Image Processing in Blood Cell Counting using Hough Transform....... 359
Manali Mukherjee, Government College of Engineering and Ceramic Technology, India
Kamarujjaman, Government College of Engineering and Ceramic Technology, India
Mausumi Maitra, Government College of Engineering and Ceramic Technology, India

In the field of biomedicine, blood cells are complex in nature. Nowadays, microscopic images are used in several laboratories for detecting cells or parasite by technician. The microscopic images of a blood stream contain RBCs, WBCs and Platelets. Blood cells are produced in the bone marrow and regularly released into circulation. Blood counts are monitored with a laboratory test called a Complete Blood Count (CBC). However, certain circumstances may cause to have fewer cells than is considered normal, a condition which is called "low blood counts".This can be accomplished with the administration of blood cell growth factors. Common symptoms due to low red blood cells are:fatigue or tiredness, trouble breathing, rapid heart rate, difficulty staying warm, pale skin etc. Common symptoms due to low white blood cells are: infection, fever etc. It is important to monitor for low blood cell count because conditions could increase the risk of unpleasant and sometimes life-threatening side effects.

Chapter 16
A Hybrid Complex Network Model for Wireless Sensor Networks and Performance Evaluation 379
Peppino Fazio, University of Calabria, Italy
Mauro Tropea, University of Calabria, Italy
Salvatore Marano, University of Calabria, Italy
Vincenzo Curia, University of Calabria, Italy

This chapter proposes a new approach, based on Complex Networks modeling, to alleviate the limitations of wireless communications. In fact, many recent studies have demonstrated that telecommunication networks can be well modeled as complex ones, instead of using the classic approach based on graph theory. The study of Complex Networks is a young and active area of scientific research, inspired largely by the empirical study of real-world networks, such as computers and social networks. The chapter contributes to the improvement of distributed communication, quantifying it in terms of clustering coefficient and average diameter of the entire network. The main idea consists in the introduction of Hybrid Data Mules (HDMs) that are able to enhance the whole connectivity of the entire network. The considered HDMs are equipped by "special" wireless devices, using two different transmission standards. The introduction of special nodes contributes to the improvement of network scalability, without substantial changes to the structure of the network.

Chapter 17
A Network Analysis Method for Tailoring Academic Programs.. 396
Luis Casillas, University of Guadalajara, Mexico
Thanasis Daradoumis, University of the Aegean, Greece & Open University of Catalonia, Spain
Santi Caballe, Open University of Catalonia, Spain

Producing or updating an academic program implies a significant effort: involving people, academic units, knowledge elements, regulations, institutions, industry, etc. Such effort entails a complexity related to the volume of elements involved, the diversity of the origins of contributions, the diversity of formats, the representation of information, and the required granularity. Moreover, such effort is a common task performed by humans who collaborate for long periods of time participating in frequent meetings in order to achieve agreement. New educational approaches are heading to adaptive, flexible, ubiquitous, asynchronous, collaborative, hyper-mediated, and personalized strategies based on modern Information and Communication Technologies (ICT). We propose an approach for tailoring academic programs to provide a practical and automated method to discover and organize milestones of knowledge through the use of Complex Networks Analysis (CNA) techniques. Based on indicators from CNA, the act of tailoring an academic program acquires meaning, structure and even body elements.

Compilation of References 418

About the Contributors 452

Index 459

Foreword

It is my pleasure to write the foreword for the book entitled: "Advanced Methods for Complex Network Analysis," edited by Dr. Natarajan Meghanathan of Jackson State University for IGI Publishers. I have known the editor Dr. Meghanathan for the last four years. He has firmly established himself in the areas of Graph Theory and Complex Network Analysis. I have served on the editorial boards of journal issues/books and in the technical committees of the conferences that Dr. Meghanathan has organized.

The book falls under the area of "Network Science" - a rapidly emerging area of interest for both theory and practice. With the phenomenal growth of the Internet, web, social networks, information on biological networks, etc., it is imperative that we need advanced methods to analyze such large-scale networks and understand their underlying graph-theoretic models as well as be able to extract useful information (like communities in the networks, robustness to information diffusion, structural controllability and vulnerability of the network, etc.). The book provides a thorough description of the different aspects of the state-of-the-art research in Network Science and a comprehensive treatment of the various graph models, algorithms, analysis measures and tools that are available for Network Science research and practice. Furthermore each chapter includes a very good literature review that points to other advances in the area considered.

The book has a total of 17 chapters (authored by several leading researchers) covering a broad range of topics in the area of complex network analysis. I am very impressed with the contents of the chapters and the contributions they make to the literature. The chapters are technically strong and written in simple language. The first half of the book includes chapters on graph theory basics, generative models for complex networks and structural analysis and establish a strong foundation for any interested reader in this area. The second half of the book includes chapters on evolutionary dynamics and its use for complex network analysis, social network analysis and applications of methods for complex network analysis in the areas of health-care applications, wireless sensor networks and academic program design. The chapters have been written and organized in such a way that there is a smooth transition from one topic to another. This is a welcome feature in an edited book.

In conclusion the book on "Advanced Methods for Complex Network Analysis," stands out among its competing titles in the area of Network Science. The book would serve as an excellent reference for students and faculty as well as for industry practitioners who are interested in state-of-the-art advanced methods for complex network analysis and their applications.

Krishnaiyan Thulasiraman
University of Oklahoma, USA

Krishnaiyan "KT" Thulasiraman *has been professor and Hitachi chair in computer science at the University of Oklahoma, Norman, Oklahoma, since 1994 and holds the professor emeritus position in electrical and computer engineering at Concordia University, Montreal, Québec, Canada. His prior appointments include professorships in electrical engineering and computer science at the Indian Institute of Technology Madras, Chennai, India (1965–1981) and in electrical and computer engineering at the Technical University of Nova Scotia, Halifax, Nova Scotia, Canada (1981–1982), and at Concordia University (1982–1994). He has held visiting positions at several prestigious universities around the world. "KT" earned his bachelor's and master's degrees in electrical engineering from Anna University (formerly College of Engineering, Guindy), Chennai, India, in 1963 and 1965 respectively and a PhD in electrical engineering from the Indian Institute of Technology Madras, Chennai, India, in 1968. His research interests have been in graph theory, combinatorial optimization, and related algorithmic issues with a specific focus on applications in electrical and computer engineering. He has published extensively in archival journals and has coauthored two textbooks entitled "Graphs, Networks and Algorithms" and "Graphs: Theory and Algorithms", published by Wiley Inter-Science in 1981 and 1992 respectively. He has been editor-in-chief of a recently completed "Handbook of Graph Theory, Combinatorial Optimization, and Algorithms" for the Taylor and Francis/CRC Press. "KT" has received several honors and awards, including the Distinguished Alumnus Award of the Indian Institute of Technology Madras; IEEE Circuits and Systems Society Charles Desoer Technical Achievement Award; IEEE Circuits and Systems Society Golden Jubilee Medal; senior fellowship of the Japan Society for Promotion of Science; and fellowship of the IEEE, AAAS, and the European Academy of Sciences.*

Preface

Complex Network Analysis falls under the subject area of Network Science, a rapidly emerging area of interest for both theory and practice. With the phenomenal growth of the Internet, web, social networks, information on biological networks, etc., it is imperative that we need algorithms to analyze such large-scale networks, visualize and extract useful information (like communities in the networks, robustness to information diffusion, diameter of the network, etc). Network Science deals with the analysis and visualization of large complex network graphs and the development of efficient algorithms to study the characteristics of networks involving hundreds and thousands of nodes.

Network Science falls within the realm of "Big Data Computing" where the Big Data is the larger graphs that model complex real-world networks (like social networks, biological networks, Internet, web, citation networks, etc). The book includes chapters presenting research advances in the algorithms and measures for analyzing large-scale complex networks and the visualization of such networks. The book presents applications of the theoretical algorithms and graph models to analyze real-world networks and characterize the topology and behavior of these networks. The chapters also explore the use of network science paradigms (like centrality measures, community detection algorithms and etc) in some of the prominent types of computer networks such as wireless sensor networks, body area networks, etc as well as for health-care related applications.

The overall objective of this book is to provide a thorough description of the different aspects of the state-of-the-art research in complex network analysis and its applications to diverse network domains. Ours is the first such book to present a comprehensive discussion of the various state-of-the-art graph models, algorithms, analysis measures and tools that are available for network science research and practice. It will be a one-stop reference for both beginners and professionals in network science and will be a good guiding material for further research in academics as well as for implementing the theory, algorithms, models and analytical measures for practical applications.

We anticipate the target audience of the book to be both students and faculty pursuing research in academics as well as industry practitioners and business professionals. The book will be structured in such a way that it discusses both the theory as well as practical aspects of network science research for a wide variety of network domains, attracting audience from diverse quarters. Also, there are not many books that present the research advances in this area; most of the books in network science are like textbooks suited primarily for graduate-level and senior-level undergraduate courses and present information from a teaching perspective. The proposed book will present information from a research perspective and kindle interest in the mind of the reader to further extend an existing research work and/or develop innovative ideas. Nevertheless, all the basic background information that are needed by a reader to understand the research concepts and ideas will be covered in the beginning of the chapters as well as through certain stand-alone tutorial-style chapters that will present both the theory behind the graph models, algorithms and analysis measures as well as on the use of state-of-the-art tools and cyber infrastructure for network modeling, analysis and visualization. Hence, in terms of market value, we anticipate the proposed book to serve as a valuable source of reference for students pursuing research in undergraduate and graduate levels and be a recommended book for advanced elective/research-oriented special topics courses as well as be a good source of reference and citation for faculty and professionals in university and industry pursuing research in network science.

A high-level overview of the 17 chapters in this book are as follows. Chapters 1-2 focus on distributed graph theory algorithms for vertex cover and k-connectivity. Chapters 3-6 focus on structural analysis of complex networks from the points of view of link prediction, robustness to node failures, motifs, homophily and k-core decomposition. Chapters 7-9 focus on generative models for complex networks and their characteristics. While Chapters 7 and 8 focus on classical random network and scale-free network graph models, Chapter 9 proposes a novel generation model for heterogeneous complex networks. Chapters 10-11 focus on social network analysis and algorithms for community detection. Chapters 12-13 discuss the use of evolution dynamics and its applications for complex network analysis to unravel the hidden relations in these networks. Chapters 14-17 discuss the applications of the methods for complex network analysis for healthcare applications, wireless sensor networks and academic program design. We now briefly describe the contributions of each of the chapters.

A vertex cover for a graph is a set of vertices such that for every edge in the graph - at least one of its two end vertices are in the vertex cover. In Chapter 1 titled, "On Vertex Cover Problems in Distributed Systems," the authors Can Umut Ileri, Cemil Aybars Ural, Orhan Dagdeviren and Vedat Kavalci discuss the applications of vertex cover in various types of communication networks such as wireless sensor networks. The authors discuss the applications of vertex cover for link monitoring, clustering, backbone formation and data aggregation management. The authors also survey some important distributed algorithms to determine approximations to vertex cover for communication networks.

A graph is *k*-connected if it remains connected after the removal of *k*-1 nodes. It is imperative to analyze the k-connectivity of complex real-world networks and investigate measures to improve the k-connectivity of these networks. In Chapter 2 titled, "On K-Connectivity Problems in Distributed Systems," the authors Vahid Khalilpour Akram and Orhan Dagdeviren review the centralized and distributed algorithms for detection and restoration of *k*-connectivity in graphs and distributed systems. The authors compare these algorithms from the perspective of complexity, accuracy and efficiency.

In Chapter 3 titled, "Link Prediction in Complex Networks," the authors Manisha Pujari and Rushed Kanawati propose a new link prediction approach based on supervised rank aggregation and deals with the challenges in link prediction for real-world networks in two ways. While one of the approaches extends the set of attributes for any two nodes in a multiplex network that have a layered structure, with each layer having different kinds of links between the same set of nodes; the second approach is to use community information from sampling of existing links to deal with the problem of class imbalance. The experiments have been conducted based on networks extracted from the well-known DBLP bibliographic database.

Structural controllability deals with network robustness in the presence of node and link failures. In Chapter 4 titled, "Design of Structural Controllability for Complex Network Architecture," the authors Amitava Mukherjee, Ayan Chatterjee, Debayan Das and Mrinal Naskar propose an efficient heuristic to determine the minimum number of driver nodes that are needed for complete structural control. The authors also propose a novel approach to address the vulnerability of real-world complex networks and enhance the robustness of these networks, prior to an attack or failure. Simulation results in Chapter 4 reveal that dense and homogeneous networks are more robust and easier to control with fewer driver nodes, while the sparse and heterogeneous networks are relatively less robust and would need more driver nodes for structural control.

Motifs are small sub graph patterns that occur significantly more often than expected at random. In Chapter 5 titled, "Triadic Substructures in Complex Networks," the author Marco Winkler investigates whether motifs occur homogeneously or heterogeneously distributed over a graph, and observes that the distribution is more heterogeneous - bound to the proximity of only very few nodes. The authors also studies graphs with respect to homogeneity and homophily of their node-specific triadic structures, and these two features have been observed to be characteristic of the networks' origins. In addition, the chapter also explains that information on a graph's node-specific triadic structure can be used to detect groups of structurally similar vertices.

Graph coarsening is the problem of grouping vertices together and building condensed, smaller graphs from these groups. In Chapter 6 titled, "Characterization and Coarsening of Autonomous System Networks: Measuring and Simplifying the Internet," the authors Alberto Garcia-Robledo, Arturo Diaz-Perez and Guillermo Morales-Luna study the correlation between various well-known complex network metrics for the Internet and methodologically identify a subset of non-redundant and potentially independent metrics that can be used to coarse the Internet at the Autonomous System (AS) level. The authors present graph coarsening algorithms to exploit the k-core decomposition of graphs to preserve relevant complex network properties.

Graph models play a central role in the description and characterization of real-world complex networks. Among the various graph models, random network models have attracted considerable attention. In Chapter 7 titled, "Connectivity and Structure in Large Networks," the author Rupei Xu presents a general framework to compare the strength of various models for generating random network graphs and discusses results about the equality, inequality and proper containment of certain model classes. The chapter also focuses on random graph models that arise via generalized geometric constructions as these graphs can very well capture wireless communication networks.

The well-known SIR model (SIR - Susceptible, Infected, Removed) and other existing models for the analysis of spread of communal diseases (in the field of epidemiology) are more tailored to random network graphs. However, it is not possible to model varying probabilities of infection or immunity per node or random network graphs. In Chapter 8 titled, "A Study of Computer Virus Propagation On Scale Free Networks Using Differential Equations," the author Mohammad S. Khan presents an analysis of the computer virus propagation using the pSEIRS model that takes into account the probabilities of infection and is more suitable for the real-world scale-free networks. The pSEIRS model assumes the death rate and excess death rate to be constant for infective nodes as well as assumes the latent and immune period to be constant; on the other hand, the model assumes the infection rate to be a function of the size of the total population and the size of the infected population.

Complex networks are observed to exhibit the small-world phenomenon, scale-free power-law degree distribution, high average clustering coefficient and emergence of community structure. In Chapter 9 titled, "SNAM - A Heterogeneous Complex Networks Generation Model," the authors Bassant Youssef, Scott Midkiff and Mohamed Rizk observe that most of the complex network generative models that have been proposed in the literature do not incorporate the above statistical properties as well as neglect the heterogeneous nature of network nodes. The authors propose a novel "settling node adaptive model (SNAM)," that reflects the above statistical properties as well as reflects the heterogeneous nature of the network nodes. The authors also present a case study using a Facebook dataset to illustrate the potential use of SNAM in modeling online social networks.

Social network analysis looks at the mapping and measurement of connections and interactions between people, groups, organization and other connected entities in a social environment. However, the real-world social networks are typically dense connected graphs with huge volume of data. In Chapter 10 titled, "Social Network Analysis," the authors Paramita Dey and Sarbani Roy study network characteristics commonly used to explain social structures. The authors discuss all important aspect of social networking and analyze them through a real-time example. The analysis identifies some important parameters like the number of clusters, group formation, node degree distribution and seed nodes, etc that can be used further for feature extraction.

Community detection is a problem of great interest in complex network analysis. There is a strong need for efficient techniques for optimal community detection. In Chapter 11 titled, "Evolutionary Computation Techniques for Community Detection in Social Network Analysis," the authors Abhishek Garg, Anupam Biswas and Bhaskar Biswas study the applicability of evolutionary computation techniques such as Genetic Algorithm (GA) and Particle Swarm Optimization (PSO) as well as their numerous variants for community detection. The authors also identify various issues with community detection and discuss how the evolutionary computation techniques can handle these issues.

In Chapter 12 titled, "Differential Evolution Dynamic Analysis in the Form of Complex Networks," the authors Ivan Zelinka and Lenka Skanderova present a novel method for analysis of the dynamics of evolutionary algorithms in the form of complex networks. The authors discuss the analogy between individuals in populations in an arbitrary evolutionary algorithm and vertices of a complex network as well as between edges in a complex network and communication between individuals in a population. The authors also discuss the dynamics of the analysis.

In Chapter 13 titled, "On Mutual Relations Amongst Evolutionary Algorithm Dynamics, its Hidden Complex Network Structures: An Overview and Recent Advances," the author Ivan Zelinka explores mutual relations among evolutionary computation algorithms and their dynamics, deterministic chaos and complex networks. The objective of this chapter is to explore the applicability of evolutionary algorithms for complex network analysis and unravel their hidden structures in an efficient fashion.

In Chapter 14 titled, "Wireless Body Area Network for Healthcare Applications," the author Danda Rawat provides a thorough survey of current technologies for Wireless Body Area Networks (WBAN) in the healthcare sector. The chapter discusses details of several existing WBAN-related projects along with their applications. The chapter discusses the use and design of medical sensors in WBAN as well as provides a comparison of WBAN and WSN.

Chapter 15 titled, "Application of Biomedical Image Processing in Blood Cell Counting using Hough Transform," considers blood stream as a complex network of red blood cells (RBCs), white blood cells (WBCs) and platelets. The authors Manali Mukherjee, Kamarujjaman Sk and Mausumi Maitra discuss the use of the Hough Transform feature extraction technique to process microscopic images of blood cells for counting. The Hough transform technique finds imperfect instances of objects within a certain class of shapes by a voting procedure carried out in a parameter space to identify conditions leading to low blood counts.

Chapter 16 titled, "A Hybrid Complex Network Model for Wireless Sensor Networks and Performance Evaluation," models telecommunication networks as a complex network and quantifies the terms clustering coefficient and average diameter of the entire network for distributed communication. The authors Peppino Fazio, Mauro Tropea, Salvatore Marano and Vincenzo Curia propose the use of "Hybrid Data

Mules" to enhance the connectivity and scalability of the network. The mules are equipped with special wireless devices using two different transmission standards.

In Chapter 17 titled, "A Network Analysis Method for Tailoring Academic Programs," the authors Luis Casillas, Thanasis Daradoumis and Santi Caballe propose a complex network-based approach for tailoring academic programs to provide a practical and automated method to discover and organize knowledge milestones. The chapter explores the use of information and communication technologies that would create adaptive, flexible, ubiquitous, asynchronous, collaborative, hyper-mediated and personalized strategies for representation and visualization of information from a complex network point of view.

With the phenomenal growth of various state-of-the-art networking domains (social networks, wireless networks, web) and the enriched information available on classical networks (like biological networks), it becomes imperative that we need a comprehensive book to address the analysis of all of these networks from both theoretical and practical standpoint. The existing books in Network Science are primarily written by some of the prominent academic researchers in this area and hence these books focus mainly on their proposed algorithms and analysis for network science as well as applied only to a particular domain of networks like biological networks or social networks. Our book fills this void as it brings together chapters from a diverse set of researchers working on various domains of networks, and hence will be a good source of information for analysis of a variety of networks. Readers will become knowledgeable in the algorithms, methodologies and tools that are suitable for analyzing diverse categories of networks and will be able to appropriately apply them depending on the context of the network under study. We anticipate our book will be a highly cited one in future conference proceedings and journal articles in the area of Network Science and will be a valuable source of information for students, researchers, industry practitioners and business professionals.

Natarajan Meghanathan
Jackson State University, USA

Chapter 1
On Vertex Cover Problems in Distributed Systems

Can Umut Ileri
Ege University, Turkey

Orhan Dagdeviren
Ege University, Turkey

Cemil Aybars Ural
Ege University, Turkey

Vedat Kavalci
Izmir University, Turkey

ABSTRACT

An undirected graph can be represented by G(V,E) where V is the set of vertices and E is the set of edges connecting vertices. The problem of finding a vertex cover (VC) is to identify a set of vertices VC such that at least one endpoint of every edge in E is incident to a vertex V in VC. Vertex cover is a very important graph theoretical structure for various types of communication networks such as wireless sensor networks, since VC can be used for link monitoring, clustering, backbone formation and data aggregation management. In this chapter, we will define vertex cover and related problems with their applications on communication networks and we will survey some important distributed algorithms on this research area.

INTRODUCTION

In this section the vertex cover problems and the contributions of this chapter will be introduced.

Vertex Cover Problems

Given a graph $G(V, E)$ where V is the set of vertices and E is the set of edges between vertices, the problem to find a set of vertices $VC \in V$ such that for any edge $\{u,v\} \in E$, at least one of u and v is in VC is called *vertex cover problem*. V itself is a vertex cover and it may have numerous subsets satisfying the vertex cover conditions. Among all possible vertex covers of a given graph, the one(s) that have the minimum cardinality are called the *minimum vertex cover*. Finding the minimum vertex cover on an undirected graph is an NP-Hard problem. A *minimal vertex cover* is a vertex cover VC whose cardinality cannot be decreased, in other words, exclusion of any vertex from VC would break the vertex cover

DOI: 10.4018/978-1-4666-9964-9.ch001

conditions. Note that a minimal vertex cover is not required to have the minimum possible cardinality. Figure 1 illustrates such a case.

Several objective functions are used for vertex cover problem. In *minimum cardinality vertex cover problem*, the optimum vertex cover VC^* is the one (or possible ones) that has (or have) the minimum cardinality among all possible vertex covers. In a weighted graph where a weight w_v is assigned to each vertex $v \in V$, the objective could be to find a vertex cover VC^* in which the total weights of the vertices are the minimum among all possible vertex covers of the graph. This problem is called *minimum weighted vertex cover problem* and is also NP-Hard. Note that the vertex cover having the minimum weight may not be the one having the minimum cardinality. Figure 2 illustrates such a case.

Numbers on the vertices are the weights. In (a), solution size is 3 (the minimum cardinality) and total weight is 23; while in (b), total weight is only 19 (minimum weight), although the cardinality is doubled.

Another variation of the problem is the *connected vertex cover problem* in which the graph induced by the vertex cover is connected. Vertex cover can be used for link monitoring to provide secure communication in wireless ad hoc networks. To achieve this operation, nodes in *VC* set are trusted and can monitor the transmissions between nodes. Since every communication link will be under the coverage of one or more nodes. Other important applications are data aggregation management, backbone and cluster formations, hub or router location designation and traffic control on the information flow.

Figure 1. Minimal and Minimum Vertex Covers: Dark vertices are the ones in the VC solution set. Removal of any vertex from the VC solution in (b) breaks the VC conditions, that is, the solution is minimal. However its cardinality is 6, while there is a possible solution having less number of vertices (5) as shown in (c)

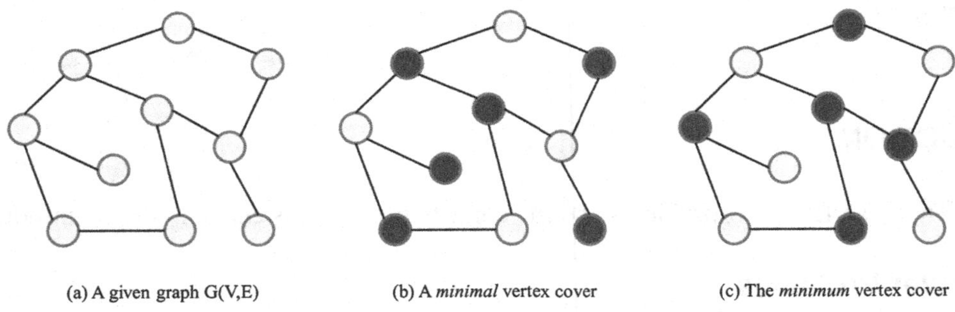

(a) A given graph G(V,E)
(b) A *minimal* vertex cover
(c) The *minimum* vertex cover

Figure 2. Minimal cardinality vs. Minimum Weight: Dark vertices are the ones in the solution set

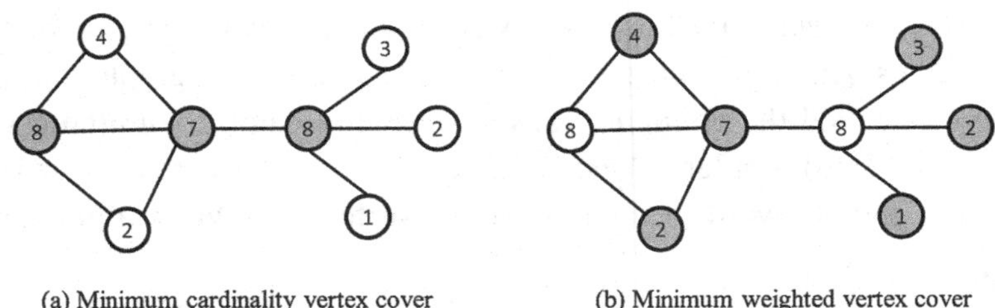

Contributions

The contributions of this chapter can be listed as follows:

- To the best of the authors' knowledge, this is the first study which reviews cardinality based distributed vertex cover algorithms, weighted distributed vertex cover algorithms and self-stabilizing distributed vertex cover algorithms in detail. The steps of each algorithm are given clearly by using simple primitives like send, receive and terminate. These are valuable for algorithm implementers working on real distributed environments such as wireless sensor networks, mobile ad hoc networks, grid computing and cloud computing.
- Each algorithm is theoretically analyzed and its time, bit and space complexities are provided for readers. Approximation ratios of some important algorithms are given. These theoretical studies are helpful to envision the resource consumptions and the qualities of produced vertex covers of the algorithms.
- Open research problems and possible future directions are identified in Section 3. This chapter is believed to be a roadmap work for researchers which are studying on the design and implementation of distributed vertex cover algorithms.

DISTRIBUTED MINIMUM CARDINALITY VERTEX COVER ALGORITHMS

Distributed Greedy Minimum Cardinality Vertex Cover Algorithm (MinCVC-Greedy)

This algorithm aims at attaining a vertex cover set on a network with minimum cardinality. The idea is to find the vertices having the highest degree within their neighborhood and place them in VC. This algorithm is inspired from the work of Parnas and Ron (2007). All vertices compare their degree with that of their neighbors, and if it is higher, they add themselves to the VC and delete themselves from the candidates' group. Coordination and collaboration are conveyed by means of a graph-wide round looping. This procedure goes on until the termination condition is satisfied. Briefly, it depends on the following assumptions:

- Each node is aware of the maximum degree (Δ) of the graph.
- Each node is aware of its neighbors.
- Each node has a guaranteed communication with its neighbors via messaging and by acknowledgements.
- A global (graph-wide) round count is known by each node.

Pseudocode of the Distributed Greedy Minimum Cardinality Vertex Algorithm is given in Algorithm 1. Figure 3 shows an example VC produced by this algorithm.

Theorem 1. *The time complexity of the Distributed Greedy Minimum Cardinality Vertex Cover Algorithm is* $O(\log_2(\Delta))$.

Figure 3. VC Produced by the distributed greedy minimum cardinality vertex cover algorithm

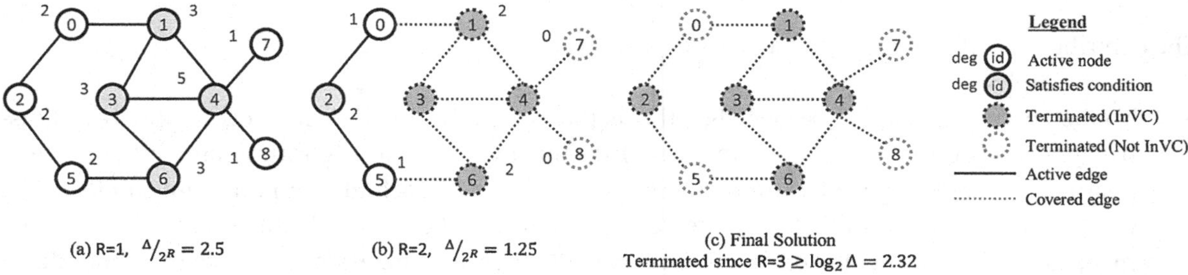

Algorithm 1. Distributed greedy minimum cardinality vertex cover algorithm

```
/* At each node */
Message types: DROP_ME
R ← 0 (round counter is set to zero)
At the start of a round
   R ← R+1
   if R > log2(Δ) then terminate
   if degree > (Δ / (2^R) then
      enter the VC
      send DROP_ME to all neighbors

When a message is received:
   if DROP_ME message is received,
      delete the appropriate node from the adjacency list
      degree ← degree-1
```

Proof. Due to the termination condition, the algorithm terminates at any node in at most $log_2(\Delta)$ rounds, where Δ is the maximum degree on the graph. In other words, a node certainly decides whether it is in (or out of) the solution set in at most $log_2(\Delta)$ round. □

Theorem 2. *The bit complexity of the Distributed Greedy Minimum Cardinality Vertex Cover Algorithm is* $O(|E|\ log_2(n))$.

Proof. At the worst case, a node can send a message to each of its neighbors. Hence, in the worst case message complexity is $O(\Delta)$ per node. Since each message is made up of $O(log_2(n))$ bits, the bit complexity is $O(n\ \Delta\ log_2(n))$ which is in $O(E\ log_2(n))$. □

Theorem 3. *The space complexity of the Distributed Greedy Minimum Cardinality Vertex Cover Algorithm is* $O(\Delta log_2(n)))$ *per node.*

Proof. Each node has to store its own neighbor list and the maximum degree *Δ* of the graph. Thus, the space complexity of this algorithm becomes $O(\Delta log_2(n))$ per node. □

This algorithm guarantees to find a $(2.log_2(\Delta)+1)$-approximate solution to the problem. (Parnas & Ron, 2007). Therefore the approximation ratio in the worst case is of $O(log_2(\Delta))$.

Distributed Vertex Cover Algorithm via Greedy Matching (MinCVC-Match)

This algorithm utilizes graph matching to construct a VC. On a given graph of $G(V, E)$, finding a set of edges $M \subseteq E$ such that no two edges in M are incident to the same vertex is called the *matching problem*. The distributed greedy weighted matching protocol by Hoepman(2004) greedily and asynchronously selects the edges with the locally highest weights and the end vertices of those edges (matched vertices) drop themselves from the graph. This algorithm is adapted to the vertex cover problem by adding all of the matched vertices to the vertex cover set, unless they are matched in the very first round, dropping all adjacent edges to the matched vertices from the graph, and then repeating the procedure until all edges are covered. Edge weights are neglected in order to yield a distributed vertex cover algorithm to be applied on unweighted graphs. This goes on until the termination condition is satisfied. This algorithm depends on the same assumptions with the Distributed Greedy Minimum Cardinality Vertex Cover Algorithm's assumptions with an exception that the nodes do not need to know Δ. Pseudocode of this algorithm is given in Algorithm 2.

A sample execution of the algorithm is shown in Figure 4. Each node determines their candidate and sends a PROPOSE message to it. Since nodes 2 and 5 proposed to each other, they are matched, as show in Figure 4(b). Nodes 4 and 8 are matched at the first round due to the same procedure, too. Procedure repeats until either all nodes are matched or they do not have an active neighbor. Final solution is given in Figure 4(d).

Theorem 4. *The time complexity of the MinCVC-Match is $O(n)$.*

Proof. At each two rounds, at least one edge is guaranteed to match, which means that 2 nodes are deactivated. Thus, algorithm is expected to terminate in n rounds. □

Theorem 5. *The bit complexity of the MinCVC-Match is $O(|E| \log_2(n))$.*

Proof. Each node sends at most one message having size of $\log_2(n)$ in each round. In a network of n nodes, $O(n^2)$ messages are sent in n rounds. The bit complexity of the algorithm is $O(n^2 \log_2(n))$. □

Theorem 6. *The space complexity of the MinCVC-Match is $O(\Delta \log_2(n))$ per node.*

Proof. Each node has to store the original and actual degrees of their neighbors, which requires $2\Delta \log_2(n)$ bits at the worst case. Other variables such as the id of the candidate and the status of the node require at $\log_2(n)$ bits each. Thus, space complexity is $O(\Delta \log_2(n))$. □

Distributed Vertex Cover Algorithm via Bipartite Matching (MinCVC-BipMM)

As presented in the previous section, once a maximal matching is given, it is easy to obtain a vertex cover solution, and more importantly, the time complexity of the vertex cover problem is determined by the maximal matching algorithm.

Besides, it is important to mention the fact that finding a maximal matching is relatively easier in 2-colored graphs (i.e. the graph is bipartite and each node is aware of its group) than it is in general graphs. If one group of nodes is allowed to make requests and the other group is only allowed to respond to this requests, a maximal matching can be obtained in at most Δ steps, where Δ is the highest degree in the network (marriage problem).

Hanckowiak et. al. (1998) proposed a distributed algorithm to exploit this fact in order to find a maximal matching in general graphs in $O(\Delta)$ time. Polishchuk & Suomela (2009) used this approach in a different manner to find a maximal matching in general graphs in $O(\Delta)$ time and then to use this

Algorithm 2. Distributed Vertex Cover Algorithm via Greedy Matching Algorithm

```
/* At each node */
Message types: PROPOSE, DROPME
cand ← null, inVC ← false, status ← ACTIVE
//Algorithm starts
Odd-numbered round
   //Select candidate
   learn degrees of neighbors and set d(j)'s accordingly
   C ← select neighbors with the lowest degree
   cand ← select the node having the highest id in C
   //Matching
   send PROPOSE to cand
   do until the end of the round
      receive PROPOSE message from j
      if j = cand // j and me proposed to each other
            if round = 1
                  if (d(me) > d(j)) OR (d(me) = d(j) AND id(me) > id(j))
                        inVC ← true
                  else
                        inVC ← false
            else
                  inVC ← true
            status ← INACTIVE
Even-numbered round
   if status = INACTIVE
      send DROPME message to all neighbors
      terminate
   do until the end of the round
      receive DROPME message from j
      remove j from neighborhood
      if there is no active neighbor
            status ← INACTIVE
            terminate
```

matching to obtain a vertex cover solution which is at most 3 times the optimum *VC* solution. Their algorithm, which is presented in this section, implements this reduction in the following way:

Given a general graph $G(V, E)$, one can obtain a bipartite graph $G'(V_1', V_2', E')$ such that:

- For each node $v \in V$, there will be $v_1' \in V_1'$ and $v_2' \in V_2'$, and
- For each edge $\{u,v\} \in E$, there will be two edges: $\{u_1', v_2'\} \in E'$ and $\{u_2', v_1'\} \in E'$

Figure 4. VC solution by the distributed vertex cover algorithm via greedy matching

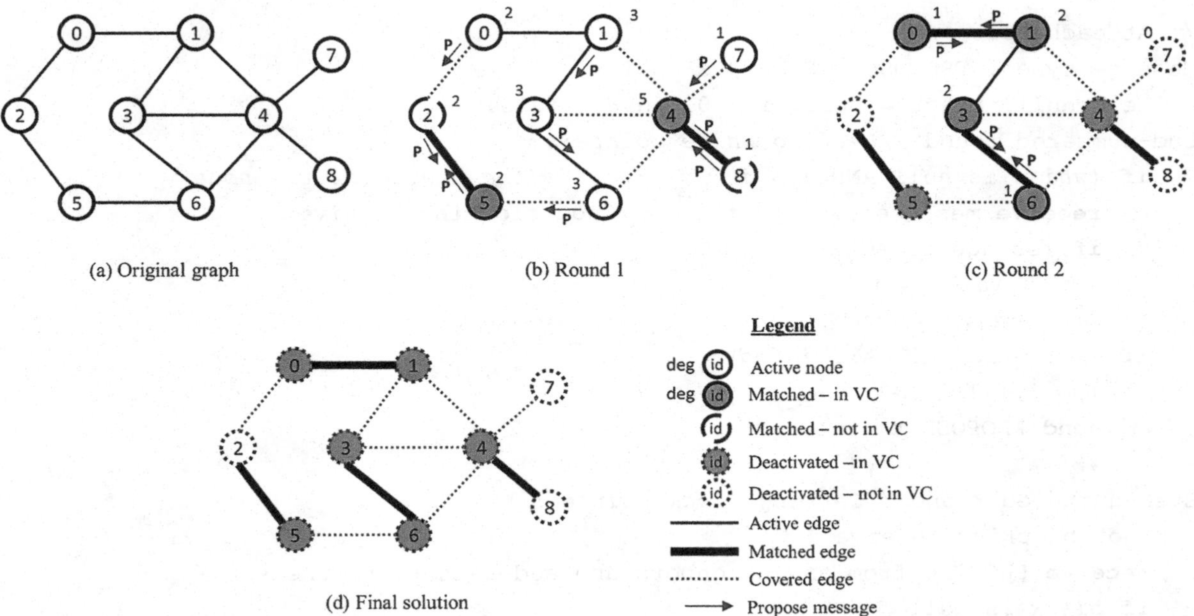

In other words, for each node in the general graph, two copies (namely black copy and white copy) are obtained in such a way that, if two nodes u and v are connected in the original graph, then the white copy of u will be connected to the black copy of v, and vice versa. An illustration of this reduction is in Figure 5.

After finding a maximal matching on the bipartite graph, vertex cover set can be obtained by a single decision: If any of the two copies of a node in the original graph is in the matching set of the bipartite graph, that node is included in the vertex set.

Procedure is shown formally in Algorithm 3. A node with degree d is assumed to have ports numbered from 1 to d. Each node has two pointers (black pointer and white pointer) which can point to a neighbor node. If a black pointer of a node u points to a neighbor node v, it means in a sense that the black copy of u is matched with the white copy of v.

Figure 5. Example illustration of reduction from a general graph to a bipartite graph and finding a vertex cover solution by solving maximal matching problem on the bipartite graph

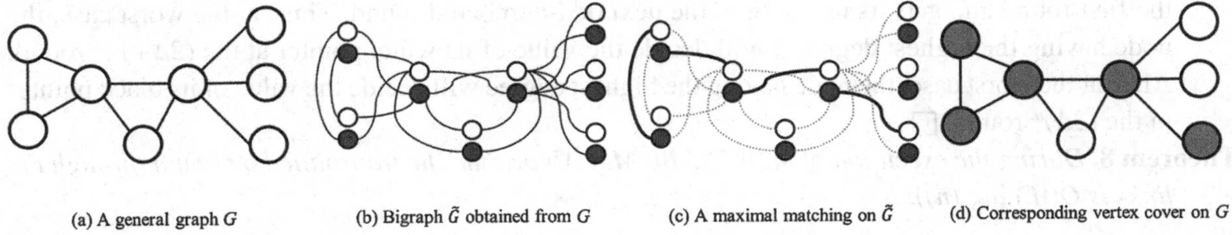

(a) A general graph G
(b) Bigraph $\tilde{G}$ obtained from G
(c) A maximal matching on $\tilde{G}$
(d) Corresponding vertex cover on G

Algorithm 3. Distributed vertex cover algorithm via bipartite matching

```
/* At each node */
Message types: PROPOSE, ACCEPT, REJECT
white ← null, black ← null, i ← 0, inVC ← false
Odd-numbered round //Setting white pointers
   if (white is null AND 1 ≤ i ≤ d) // d is the degree of the node
      receive message from port I    // not blocking receive
      if message is ACCEPT
            white ← i
            inVC ← true
   if (white is null AND i ≤ d)
      i ← i + 1
      send PROPOSE to the port i

Even-numbered round //Setting black pointers
  //not blocking receive
   receive PROPOSE from any neighbors and add senders to the set P
   if black is null
      select p ∈ P incoming from the lowest-numbered port
      send ACCEPT to p
      send REJECT to all in (P - {p})
      inVC ← true
   else
      send REJECT to all in P
```

An example execution of MinCVC-BipMM is illustrated in Figure 6. Original graph is shown in (a). Numbers on the outgoing edge of each node are the related port numbers. In the first round (b), each node sends a PROPOSE message through their ports numbered 1. In the second round, each node having received one or more PROPOSE message selects the one incoming from the lowest numbered port, sets its black pointer accordingly, enters the solution set and sends an ACCEPT message as a reply. All other proposers are responded with a REJECT message. In round 3 (in (d)), the nodes, which have received an ACCEPT message, set their white pointers accordingly and enter the solution set. Final solution is shown in (e).

Theorem 7. *MinCVC-BipMM Algorithm finds a vertex cover solution in $2\Delta+1$ rounds.*

Proof. Each node, in order to set its white pointer, sends a PROPOSE message through the first port at the first round and gets its response at the next odd-numbered round. Thus, at the worst case, the node having the highest degree Δ will decide the value of its white pointer at the $(2\Delta+1)^{th}$ round. Also, at the worst case, the node having the highest degree will decide the value of its black pointer in the $(2\Delta)^{th}$ round. □

Theorem 8. *During the execution of MinCVC-BipMM Algorithm, the transmitted bit count through the links is $O(|E| \log_2(n))$.*

Figure 6. Example execution of MinCVC-BipMM Algorithm

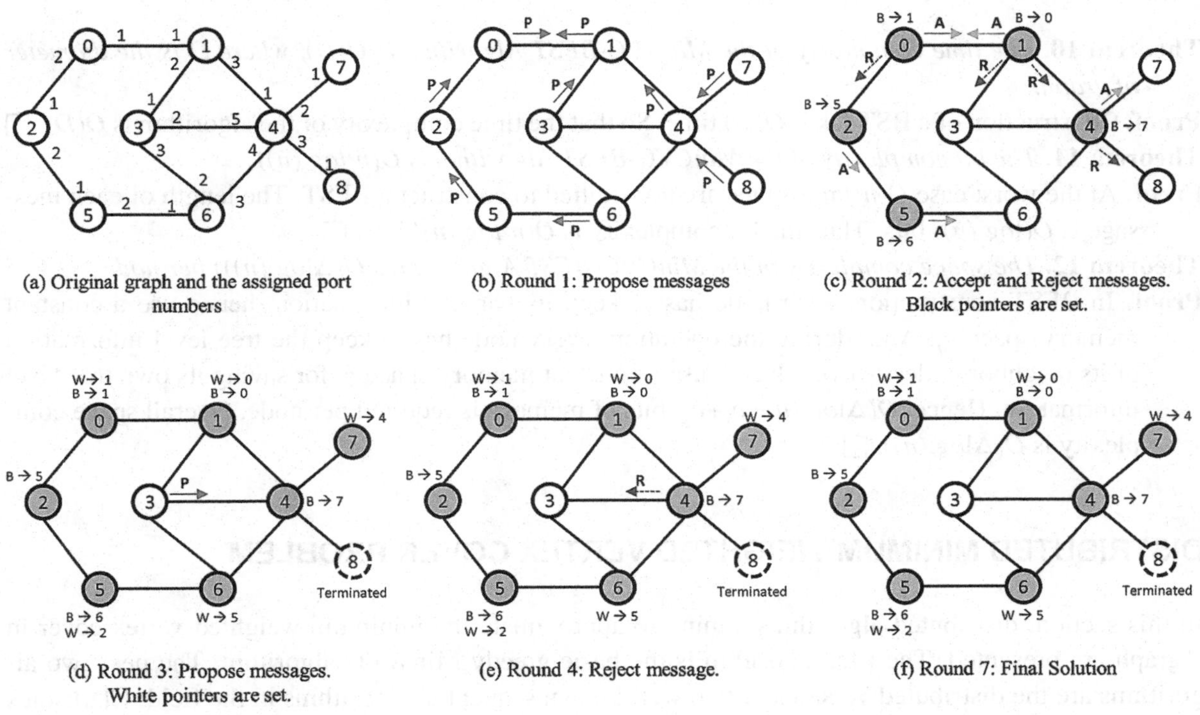

(a) Original graph and the assigned port numbers

(b) Round 1: Propose messages

(c) Round 2: Accept and Reject messages. Black pointers are set.

(d) Round 3: Propose messages. White pointers are set.

(e) Round 4: Reject message.

(f) Round 7: Final Solution

Proof. Each node may send at most one message through and receive at most one message from each of its port. In other words each port deals with at most two messages. Total number of ports on the graph is 2|E|. Total number of messages is 4|E|. The messages can be at most $log_2(n)$ bits. Thus, bit complexity of MinCVC-BipMM Algorithm is $O(|E| \log_2(n))$. □

Theorem 9. *Each node requires $O(\Delta \log_2(n))$ bits of memory space in order to execute MinCVC-BipMM Algorithm.*

Proof. Each node is assumed to have the set of ids of its neighbors, which require at most $\Delta \log_2(n)$ bits. □

Distributed Vertex Cover Algorithm via Breadth First Search Tree (MinCVC-BFST)

This algorithm builds a Breadth First Search Tree (BFST) and constructs a VC by using this BFST as the infrastructure. BFST formation is very important for wireless ad hoc networks since BFST provides a routing backbone. In a BFST, each vertex is associated with a level value which is its level-wise distance from the root (or sink) node (Kavalci et. al., 2014).

In the following algorithm each vertex advertises its level information to its neighbors. Afterwards, each of them decides whether it should participate within VC or not. If the level value of a vertex is even, then it will be directly in the set. If the level is odd and the vertex has a neighbor with an odd-level, then the vertex having the larger ID among them decides whether it is in the VC or not. This algorithm depends on the same assumptions with the Distributed Vertex Cover Algorithm via Greedy Matching and a root node should be selected before the execution of the algorithm.

Pseudocode and an example VC produced by this algorithm are given in Algorithm 4 and Figure 7.

Theorem 10. *The time complexity of the MinCVC-BFST Algorithm is O(D), where D is the diameter of graph.*

Proof. Construction of a BST takes *O(D)* time. So that the time complexity of the algorithm is *O(D)*. □

Theorem 11. *The bit complexity of the MinCVC-BFST Algorithm is* $O(n^3 log_2(n))$.

Proof. At the worst case $O(n^3)$ messages are transmitted to construct a BFST. The length of each message is $O(\log_2(n))$ bits. Thus the bit complexity is $O(n^3 log_2(n))$ bits. □

Theorem 12. *The space complexity of the MinCVC-BFST Algorithm is* $O(\Delta\log_2(n)))$ *per node.*

Proof. In BFST construction, each node has to keep its parent's information, hence use a constant memory space c_1. And, during the operation, every node has to keep the tree level information of its neighbor nodes. Also, it has to use a constant memory space c_2 for saving its own tree level information. Hence, $O(\Delta log_2(n)+c_1+c_2)$ bits of memory is required per node. Overall space complexity is $O(\Delta log_2(n))$. □

DISTRIBUTED MINIMUM WEIGHTED VERTEX COVER PROBLEM

In this section, distributed algorithms aiming to approximate the minimum weighted vertex cover in a graph are presented. The first algorithm is the basic greedy MinWVC algorithm. The next two algorithms are the distributed versions of two well-known sequential algorithms in the field: Clarkson's Algorithm (1983) and Bar-Yehuda&Even's Algorithm (1981). The last one is a distributed algorithm

Figure 7. VC Produced by the Distributed Vertex Cover Algorithm via Breadth First Search Tree

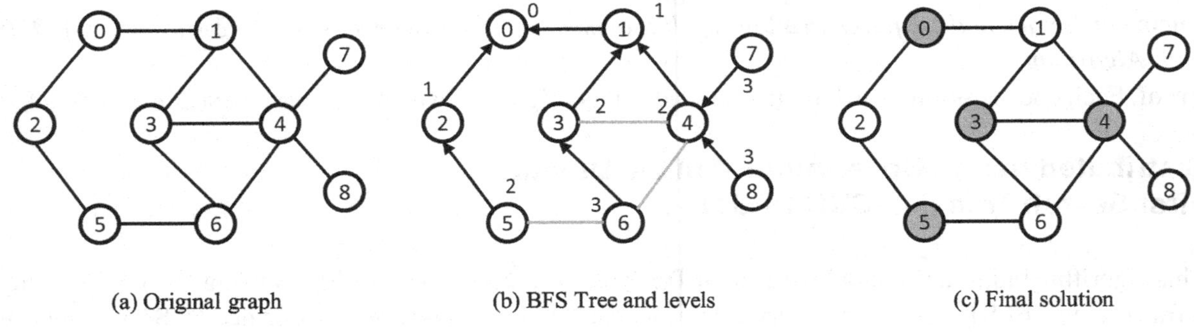

(a) Original graph
(b) BFS Tree and levels
(c) Final solution

Algorithm 4. Distributed Vertex Cover Algorithm via Breadth First Search Tree Algorithm

```
run a Distributed BFST algorithm and find the level
if level is even then
   inVC ← true
else if level is odd and the node has an odd level neighbor with a smaller id
   inVC ← true
```

due to Grandoni et. al. (2008) which is based on the fact that a 2-approximation solution to the vertex cover problem can be computed via a solution of maximal matching.

Greedy Distributed Minimum Weighted Vertex Cover Algorithm (GreedyWVC)

This algorithm is similar to the distributed greedy minimum cardinality vertex cover algorithm. The only difference is that this algorithm favors the nodes having the minimum weight instead of the ones having the maximum degree.

Assuming all the nodes have the information of the weights of their neighbors (this can be obtained in a single round), each node can easily determine if it is the locally lightest node. Once a node knows it is the locally lightest, it marks itself as being in the solution set VC, informs its neighbors by a COVER message and terminates its program. When a node receives a COVER message, it marks the sender as covered. Nodes remove their neighbors from which they have received a COVER message. This procedure repeats until all neighbors are inactive as given in Algorithm 5.

An execution of GreedyWVC Algorithm on a graph with 9 nodes is shown in Figure 8. Numbers on the vertices denote the weights. There are two locally-lowest weighted nodes, which are 5 and 13 (in (b)). They are included in VC and send COVER message to their neighbors. Deactivations of these nodes enable other nodes to be local leaders. Final solution to the problem is shown in Figure 8(e).

In this example, the greedy algorithm computes the minimum weighted vertex cover. However this algorithm does not guarantee a constant approximation to the optimal solution. For example, consider the star graph in Figure 9. Greedy algorithm for this example resulted with a solution which is almost n times the optimum.

Algorithm 5. Greedy distributed minimum weighted vertex cover algorithm

```
/* At each node */
Message types: COVER
// Initialization
send myweight to all my neighbors
receive their weights from all my neighbors
// Covering
while the node is not in the solution set OR it has at least one uncovered
edge, perform rounds as follows:
   if my weight is the lightest among my active neighbors
      inVC ← TRUE // The node is in the solution set
      send COVER message to all active neighbors
   else
      do until the end of the round
            receive COVER message
            // edge between me and the sender is covered
            mark the sender as inactive
            remove the sender from my active neighborhood
```

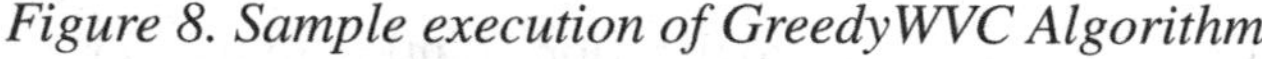
Figure 8. Sample execution of GreedyWVC Algorithm

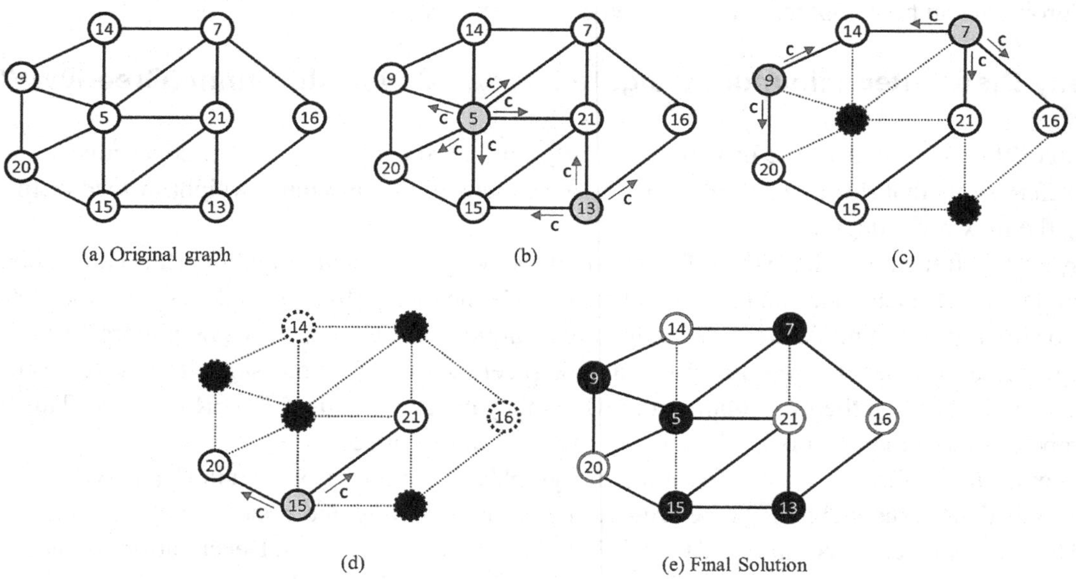

Figure 9. Illustration of a sample case where the greedy algorithm misses trivial solution

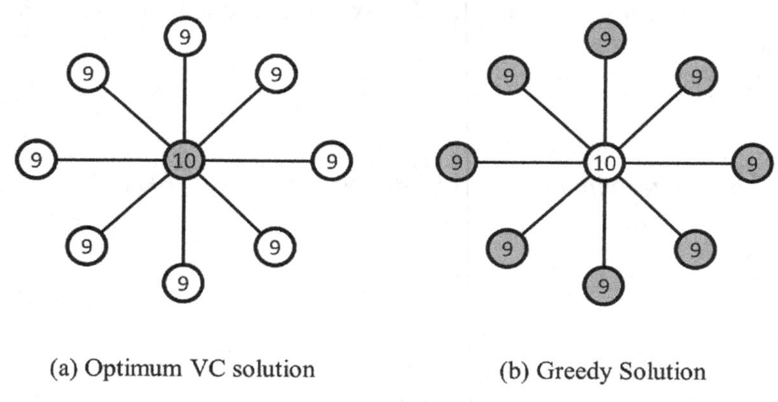

Theorem 13. *GreedyWVC Algorithm terminates in at most O(n) rounds.*

Proof. In any round, the graph has a globally lightest active node and it is guaranteed to be included in the solution set in that round. □

Theorem 14. *Total number of bits transmitted through the network during the execution of GreedyWVC is* $O(n^2 \log_2(n))$.

Proof. In each round, each node sends exactly one message having size of $O(\log_2(n))$ bits. In a single round, $O(n \log_2(n))$ bits are transmitted on the network. Assuming $O(n)$ rounds at the worst case, the bit complexity of the algorithm is $O(n^2 \log_2(n))$. □

Theorem 15. *GreedyWVC requires each node to have* $O(\Delta \log_2(n) + \log_2(w))$ *memory space where w is the maximum weight.*

Proof. Each node stores the identifier and weight of each of its neighbors, i.e. $(log_2(n)+ log_2(w))$ bits per neighbor. A node may have at most Δ neighbors. Total size of the required space is $O(\Delta\ (log_2(n)+ log_2(w)))$ bits per node. □

Distributed Version of Clarkson's Vertex Cover Algorithm (MinWVC-Cla)

As it has been presented above, the biggest reason why the greedy algorithm failed to perform well is that it did not take the degree of any vertex into consideration. Figure 9 shows a sample case where the greedy approach that ignores the degrees results in a "heavy" solution.

Clarkson's sequential 2-approximation weighted vertex cover algorithm (Clarkson, 1983) favors the nodes having higher degrees in forming the VC set, simply by using the weights in proportion to the degree of the node. It basically calculates, for each vertex v, the value $p(v) = W(v)/D(v)$ where W is the weight function and D is the degree function. The vertex v such that $p(v) \geq p(u)$ for all $u \in V$ and $(u,v) \in E$ is added to the solution set VC. For the next step of the algorithm, all of the edges incident to v are removed from the graph and weights of the neighbors of v are updated as follows, and the procedure repeats until all edges are covered:

$$W(u)' = W(u) - p(v) \text{ for all } u \in \Gamma(v)$$

This algorithm can be implemented in distributed settings. Each vertex can calculate its p value, since it knows its own weight and degree. All the nodes can get the knowledge of the p value of their neighbors in a single communication round. In Algorithm 6, this information sharing is realized with UPDATE messages. Then, as in the greedy distributed weighted vertex cover algorithm, each vertex can decide whether it has the locally lowest p value. If it does, it marks itself as being "in VC" and informs all their neighbors about it by means of a COVER message. When a vertex receives a COVER message, it decreases its weight by p value of the sender, decreases its degree by one and adjusts its own p value accordingly.

This procedure can be implemented as a synchronous distributed algorithm having odd- and even-numbered rounds, where the nodes share their p values in odd numbered rounds and make decisions on covering in the even-numbered rounds. This synchronous algorithm is shown in Algorithm 6.

On the graph given in Figure 10, each node firstly calculates its p value (blue numbers next to nodes). There are two nodes having the locally-lowest p values, namely 2 and 4. They are included in the solution set and inform their neighborhood. Observe that the neighbors of the locally-lowest nodes update their weights at the end of each round. When a node does not have any active neighbor, it terminates the algorithm (see the node at the bottom left in Figure 10(c)). Resulting vertex cover is shown in Figure 10(e), where the total weight of the solution is 77.

Theorem 16. *MinWVC_Cla Algorithm terminates in at most $O(n)$ rounds.*

Proof. There is at least one node having the locally-lowest p value at any round, and it is guaranteed to be included in the solution set at the next round. Thus, at the worst case, the algorithm will terminate at the $(2n)^{th}$ round, where n is the node count. □

Theorem 17. *Total number of bits transmitted through the network during the execution of MinWVC-Cla is $O(n^2 \log_2(n))$.*

Algorithm 6. Distributed version of Clarkson's weighted vertex cover algorithm (MinWVC-Cla)

```
/* At each node */
Message types: COVER, UPDATE
while the node is not in the solution set OR it has at least one uncovered
edge, perform rounds as follows:
   In an odd numbered round: //Information Sharing
      P ← W/D
            send P to all my neighbors
      do until UPDATE (j, P_j) message is received from all active neighbors
            receive UPDATE (j,P_j)
            update P_j
   In an even numbered round: // Covering
      if my P value is the lowest among my active neighbors
            inVC ← TRUE // I am in the solution set, i.e. I cover my edges
            send COVER message to all active neighbors
      do until the end of the round
            receive COVER message
            // edge between me and the sender is covered by the sender
            mark the sender as inactive
            W ← W - P_sender
            D ← D - 1
            remove the sender from my active neighborhood
```

Figure 10. Sample execution of MinWVC-Cla Algorithm

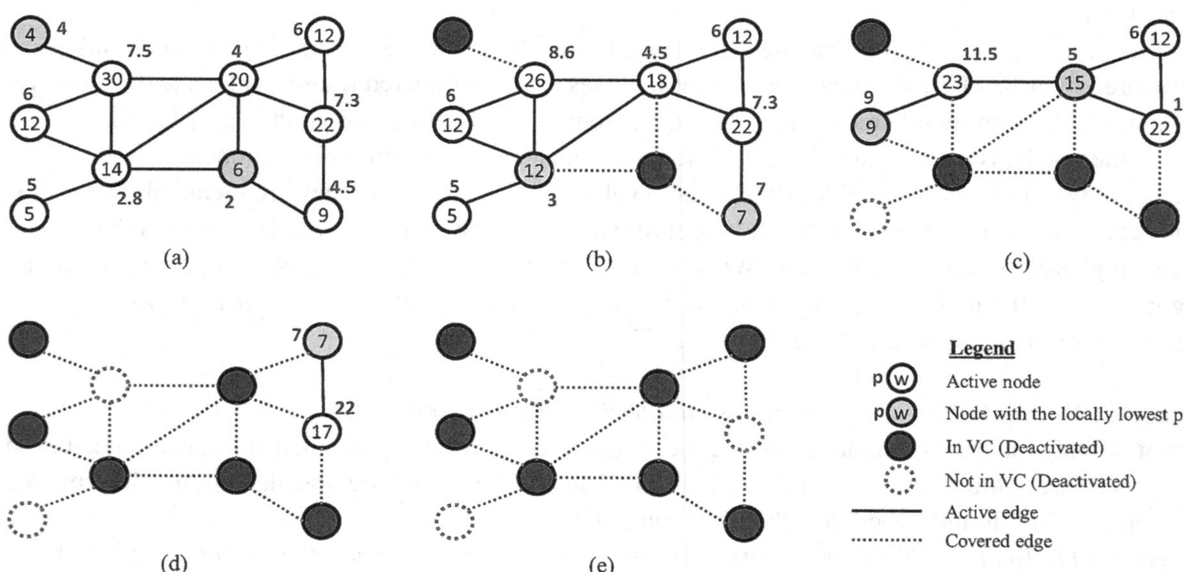

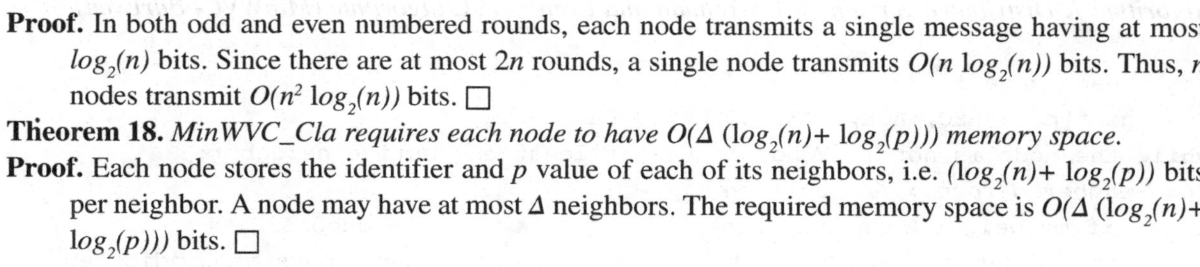

Proof. In both odd and even numbered rounds, each node transmits a single message having at most $log_2(n)$ bits. Since there are at most $2n$ rounds, a single node transmits $O(n\ log_2(n))$ bits. Thus, n nodes transmit $O(n^2\ \log_2(n))$ bits. □

Theorem 18. *MinWVC_Cla requires each node to have* $O(\Delta\ (\log_2(n)+\ \log_2(p)))$ *memory space.*

Proof. Each node stores the identifier and p value of each of its neighbors, i.e. $(log_2(n)+\ log_2(p))$ bits per neighbor. A node may have at most Δ neighbors. The required memory space is $O(\Delta\ (log_2(n)+\ log_2(p)))$ bits. □

Distributed Version of Bar-Yehuda and Even's Algorithm (MinWVC- BarEven)

Bar-Yehuda and Even's sequential algorithm (Bar-Yehuda & Even, 1981) arbitrarily selects an edge (u,v) where $w_u \leq w_v$, and includes its incident node having the smaller weight (u) into the vertex cover solution set *VC*. It then updates the weights of the incident node having the greater weight (v) by the following formula: $w_v \leftarrow w_v - w_u$. Node u and all edges incident to u are removed from the graph and the procedure iterates until all of the edges are covered.

This algorithm can be implemented as a synchronous distributed algorithm. As the sequential algorithm chooses an arbitrary edge at each step, it is required to decide which edges to consider first in the distributed algorithm. One way could be to rely on ids and to start with the nodes having the locally lowest or highest ids. In the implementation presented in this section, the weights of the nodes are used instead.

Algorithm 7 shows the implementation. The nodes having the locally-heaviest weight make decisions. (Local identifiers can be used for symmetry breaking in case of equal weights.) They decide which edge to consider first (randomly or deterministically) and send a REQ message to the node at the other end of this edge. On the receiver side, a node may receive more than one REQ messages, since it may be connected to more than one locally-heaviest nodes. In order to wait for all request messages, a round is devoted for requests.

At the subsequent round, there are three types of nodes: (1) the ones having received one or more REQ messages, (2) the ones having sent a REQ message (locally-heaviest nodes), and (3) the remaining nodes. The first group of nodes is included in VC since they are the lower-weighted part of the matching. Then, they set their own weights to zero, they choose a node k from the requesters, send an ACK message to k, NAK messages to other requesters and COVER messages to all other nodes. NAK and COVER mean that the new weight of the sender node is zero.

Nodes at the second group wait for a response for their REQ messages. If the response is an ACK, they reduce their weights by the matched node's weight and they remove the matched node from their active neighborhood. If the response is NAK, even though the proposal is rejected, it is known that the requested node has accepted a proposal of another node, thus it is to be removed from the neighborhood. In any case, they send UPDATE messages to their active neighborhood in order to inform their new weights.

All the other nodes wait for UPDATE or COVER messages and perform the related operations. Once a node is included in VC or all of its neighbors are deactivated: the algorithm terminates. The sum of weights of nodes in the resulting solution set VC is at most twice the optimum WVC solution (Bar-Yehuda & Even, 1981).

Figure 11. illustrates a sample execution of MinWVC-BarEven Algorithm. Given the graph in (a), nodes having weights 32 and 22 are the locally-heaviest and make their requests for the nodes having weights 12 and 2, respectively. At the second round, the requests are acknowledged. Lower-weighted nodes are deactivated and the weights of their neighbors are updated. Observe that this update causes

Algorithm 7. Distributed version of Bar-Yehuda and Even's WVC algorithm (MinWVC- BarEven)

```
/* At each node */
Message types: REQ, ACK, NAK, COVER, UPDATE
while the node is not in VC or it has at least one active neighbor:
 Odd-numbered round: // Decision
      if my weight W is the highest among my active neighbors
            set cand ← j∈ Γ(me) // select one of my neighbors as candidate
            send REQ to cand
      else
            till the end of the round
                  receive REQ message from j
                  add j to R // R is the set of requesters
   Even-numbered round: // Covering and Synchronization
      if R is not empty // I have received at least one REQ at the prev. round
 W ← 0 //Update my weight
            inVC ← TRUE
            choose one k from R
            send ACK to k
            send NAK to R - {k} //reject the other requestors
            send COVER(W(me)) to Γ(me)-R // Inform neighbors
      else if cand is not null // I sent a REQ at the previous round
            do until the end of the round
                  receive message from j
                  if received message is an ACK
                        W(me) ← W(me) - W(j)
                        remove j from the active neighborhood
                        send UPDATE(W(me)) to all active neighboors
                  else if received message is a NAK or COVER

                        remove j from the active neighborhood
      else
            do until the end of the round
                  receive message //either COVER or UPDATE message
                  if message is UPDATE
                        update W(j) ← message.w
                  else
                        remove j from active neighborhood
```

one of the nodes to lose its "locally-heaviest" status. In round 3 (in (c)), there are three deciders, two of which make request to the same node. This node arbitrarily selects one of the requesters and accepts its proposal. In round 4, two more nodes are included in *VC* and two nodes are deactivated due to not having an active neighbor (d). Algorithm terminates in the 6th round when all the nodes are deactivated. Final solution is shown in (g).

Theorem 19. *MinWVC_BarEven Algorithm terminates in at most O(n) rounds.*

Proof. There is at least one heaviest node in an odd numbered round. Then at least two nodes will match in an even-numbered node and one of them terminates. Thus, at the worst case, *n* nodes will be deactivated as of the $(2n)^{th}$ round.□

Theorem 20. *Total number of bits transmitted through the network during the execution of MinWVC_BarEven is* $O(n^2 \log_2(n))$.

Proof. In an odd-numbered round, there can be at most *n*/2 locally-heaviest nodes. Assuming each message carries the integer identifier, $O(n\log_2(n))$ bits are transmitted. In an even numbered round,

Figure 11. Sample execution of MinWVC-BarEven Algorithm

(a) Round 1

(b) Round 2

(c) Round 3

(d) Round 4

(e) Round 5

(f) Round 6

(g) Final Solution with original weights

Legend

- Active node with current weight w
- Node having the locally heaviest weight
- In VC (Deactivated)
- Not in VC (Deactivated)
- Active edge
- Covered edge

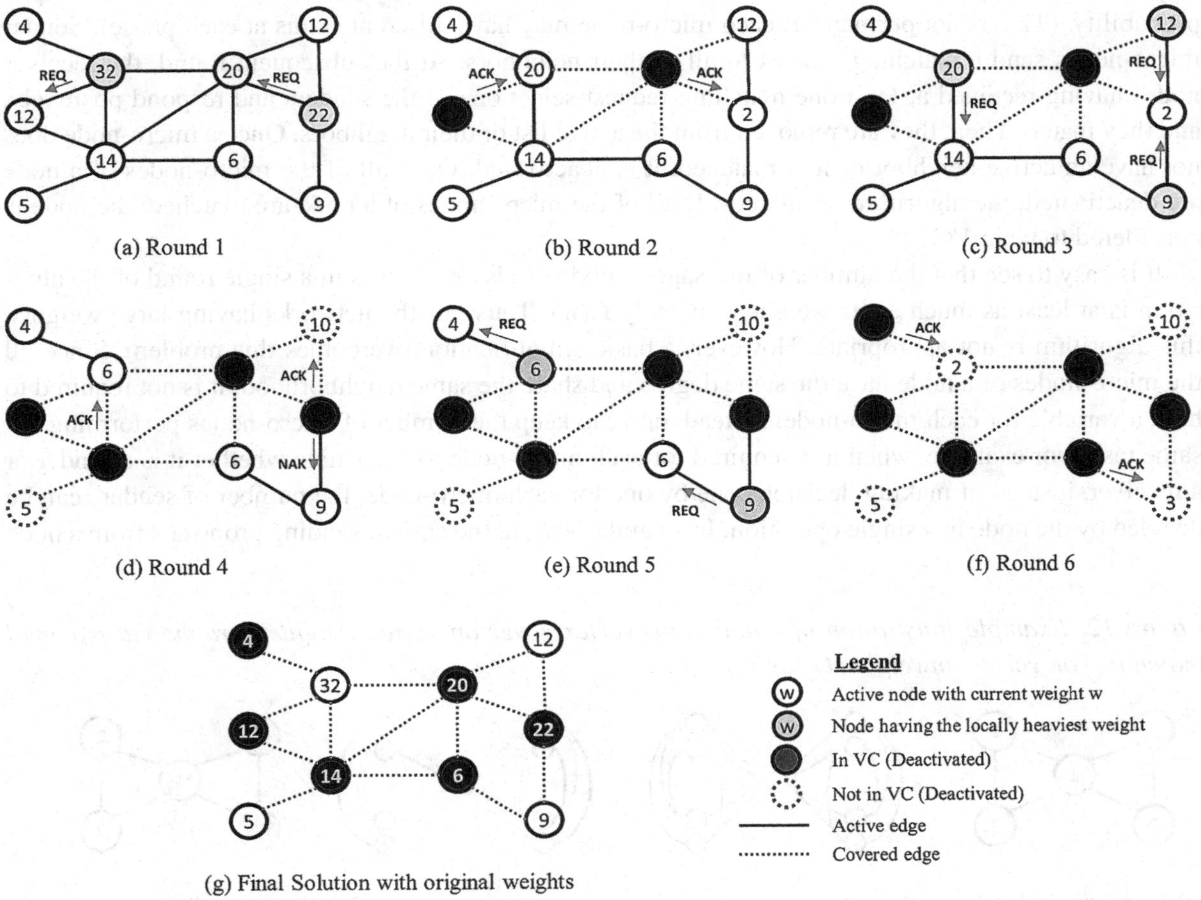

each node transmits exactly one message in size of $log_2(n)$ bits. Since there are most $2n$ rounds, $O(n^2 \log_2(n))$ bits are transmitted on the network. □

Theorem 21. *MinWVC_BarEven requires that each node to have $O(\Delta \log_2(n))$ memory space.*

Proof. See proof of Theorem 18.

Distributed Weighted Vertex Cover Algorithm via Maximal Matching (MinWVC-MM)

Consider a vertex-weighted graph $G(V,E)$ with each node v having an integer weight w(v). Using G, a vertex-unweighted graph G'(V',E') can be obtained in such a way that G' will include *w(v) micro-nodes* ($v_1', v_2', \ldots, v_{w(v)}'$) for each $v \in V$, and there will be an edge $(u_i, v_j) \in E'$ if and only if there is an edge $(u,v) \in E$. Figure 12 (a to b) shows such a reduction.

If a maximal matching M is found on G', a corresponding vertex cover set VC can be obtained in G by including a node $v \in V$ into VC if all of the micro-nodes of v are matched in G'. Figure 12(c) and 12(d) show an example correspondence. MinWVC-MM Algorithm (Grandoni et al., 2008) is a distributed algorithm based on this notion. Though they simplified and improved it, let us first describe the basic idea the algorithm is based on.

Each node on the distributed network is assumed to have as many micro-nodes as its weight. At the beginning of each phase of the algorithm, a micro-node becomes either a *sender* or a *receiver* with equal probability. (This is not permanent; each micro-node may have different status at each phase). Sender micro-nodes send a matching request to all of their neighbors. At the subsequent round, the receiver nodes having received at least one matching request select one of the senders and respond positively, and they match. Then, they are removed from the active list of their neighbors. Once a micro-node does not have an active neighbor or it is matched, it is deactivated. Once all of the micro-nodes of a node are deactivated, the algorithm terminates. If all of the micro-nodes of a node are matched, the node is considered to be in VC.

It is easy to see that the number of messages a node sends or receives in a single round of the algorithm is at least as much as its weight w, namely $\Omega(w)$. Thus, for the networks having large weights, this algorithm is not appropriate. However, a basic simplification overcomes this problem. Since all the micro-nodes of a node have the same degree and share the same neighborhood, it is not required to hold a variable for each micro-node. Instead, one can keep the number of micro-nodes performing the same task. For example, when it is required for each micro-node to determine whether it is a sender or a receiver, instead of making decisions one by one for each micro-node, the number of senders can be decided by the node in a single operation. In a similar way, in the case of sending proposals from a node

Figure 12. Example illustration of obtaining a vertex cover on vertex-weighted graphs via maximal matchings on vertex-unweighted graph

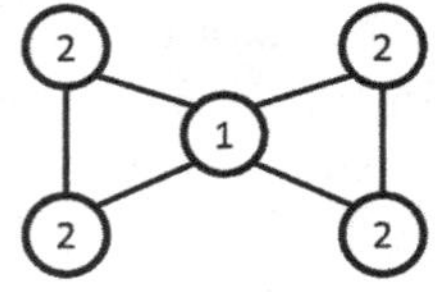

(a) A vertex-weighted graph G

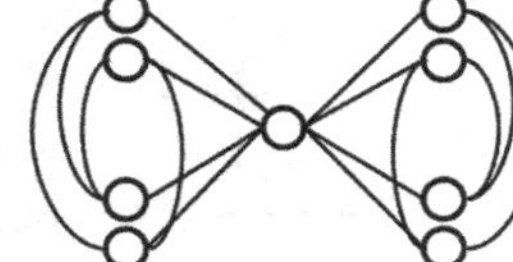

(b) Vertex-unweighted graph $\tilde{G}$

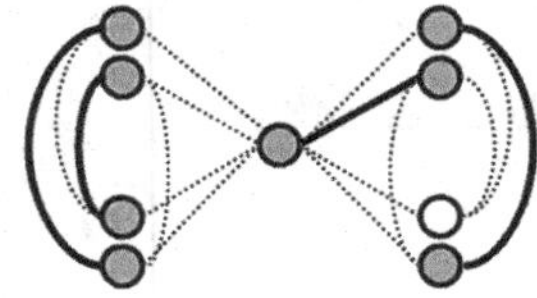

(c) Maximal matching on $\tilde{G}$

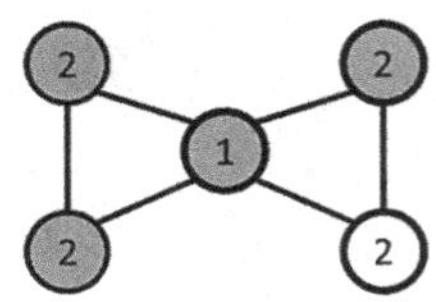

(d) Corresponding vertex cover on G

v to a neighbor u, instead of passing one message per each (v_i, u_j) micro-node pair, a single message (carrying information of the number of senders) can be sent from v to u.

Simplified and improved algorithm works as follows: Initially at each phase of the algorithm, each node decides on the number of senders (s_i) (so-called *sender micro-nodes*) and receivers (r_i) (so-called *receiver micro-nodes*) such that the total number will be equal to the weight ($s_i + r_i = w_i$). It then sends a proposal to any neighbors $j \in \Gamma(v)$ with a p_{ij} value such that the sum of p_{ij}'s will be equal to the number of senders ($\sum_{j \in \Gamma(v)} p_{ij} = s_i$).

When a node i receives a proposal p_{ji} from j, it means there are p_{ji} micro-nodes of j proposing to be matched with the micro-nodes of v. Since the number of receiver micro-nodes of v is limited to r_i, it sends back an acknowledgement with value $max(p_i, r_i)$. Then, it reduces its actual weight by the total number of acknowledged incoming proposals and acknowledged outgoing proposals. The residual weight of a node, in a sense, is the number of unmatched micro-nodes which will try to be matched at the next phase, if they still have active neighbors. This procedure is more formally demonstrated in Algorithm 8.

A sample execution of MinWVC-MM Algorithm is illustrated in Figure 13. At the proposing round of the first phase of the algorithm (a), each node decides number of senders and receivers, which are shown in parentheses in respective order. For example, the leftmost node having weight 8 decided to have 2 senders and 6 receivers, while the node, which has the weight of 5, assigned all of its micro-nodes as sender. Each node, then, distributes their senders among their neighbors. For example, the node having weight 12 decided that 3 of its senders will make matching proposals to the node having weight 9, 2 of its senders will propose to the leftmost node and its remaining senders will make proposal to the node having weight 5. All proposals are shown with a solid blue arrow.

The node, having received proposals, decides on their responses in the second round of the first phase (b). For example, the node having weight 9 decided to make a positive response to all 3 proposes of node having weight 12. Note that the number of positive responses cannot exceed the number of receivers. Observe that the bottom-left node responded none of the 3 proposes positively, because it does not have a receiver micro-node. All responses are shown with a dashed red arrow.

At the end of each phase, each node reduces its weight by the number of matched micro-nodes. See in Figure 13(b) that the top-right node has 3 of its receivers matched with senders of node 12, 1 of its receivers with senders of node 3, 1 of its senders with receivers of node 3, and 2 of its senders with receivers of node 7. Thus, it has 2 unmatched micro-nodes; in other words, a residual weight of 2. (Figure 13(c)). Since the right-most node has a residual weight of 0, it is included in *VC* and deactivated.

The sequence of assigning senders-receivers, making proposes and making responses are repeated until all nodes are deactivated. Final solution is a vertex cover with a total weight at most twice the optimum WVC solution.

Theorem 22. MinWVC-MM Algorithm halts in $O(log_2(n) + log_2(W))$ rounds, where W is weight of the heaviest node on the network.

Proof. The residual weight of the heaviest node is expected to decrease by at least a positive constant in each phase. Then, at the worst case, a node is expected to have a residual weight 0 in $O(log_2(n) + log_2(W))$ rounds. The formal proof is beyond the scope of this book. Interested readers are referred to (Grandoni et. al., 2008). □

Theorem 23. The bit complexity of MinWVC-MM Algorithm is $O(\Delta n\ (log_2(n) + log_2(W)))$.

Proof. In each phase, a node sends exactly one UPDATE, at most one PROPOSE and at most one RESPONSE message to each of its neighbors. Hence, it may send at most 3Δ messages in a single

Algorithm 8. Distributed weighted vertex cover algorithm via maximal matching (MinWVC-MM)

```
/* At each node */
Message types: PROPOSE, RESPONSE, COVER, UPDATE
States: ACTIVE, INVC, OUTVC
while status is ACTIVE, perform Phases as follows:
 //Phase starts
 //Synchronization round
   update my knowledge of neighborhood via sending/receiving UPDATE messages
   if I do not have an active neighbor
      set status ← OUTVC
   else
      decide number of senders s and receivers r
      distribute s among neighbors //(determine p_ij 's)
      // Proposing Round
      send PROPOSE to j if p_ij > 0
      till the end of the Propose round
            receive PROPOSE from j
            set p_ji
      // Acknowledgement Round
      Assign c_ij for each j where p_ji > 0 //Decide which neighbor will receive
what
      for each j where p_ji > 0
            send RESPONSE(c_ij) to j
            W ← W - c_ij
      till the end of the Propose round
            receive message from j
            if message is RESPONSE(c_ji)
                  set W ← W - c_ji
                  if W = 0 // I have all my micro-nodes matched
                        send COVER to all active neighbors
                        status ← INVC
            else if message is COVER
                  remove j from active neighborhood
```

phase. Accordingly, total number of messages in each round is at most $3\Delta n$. Since the algorithm takes $O(log_2(n) + log_2(W))$ rounds, bit complexity is $O(\Delta n\ (log_2(n) + log_2(W)))$. □

Theorem 24. Each node running MinWVC-MM Algorithm requires $O(\Delta\ (log_2(n) + log_2(W)))$ bits of memory space.

Proof. Each node stores its id and weight of its neighbors which take $O(\Delta\ (log_2(n) + log_2(W)))$, assuming integer identifiers. □

Figure 13. Sample execution of MinWVC-MM Algorithm

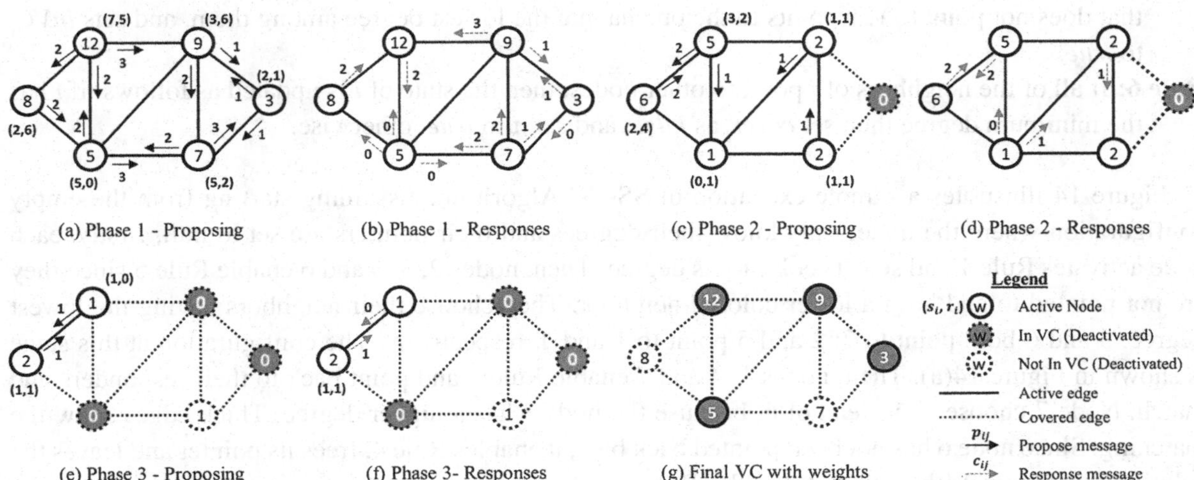

SELF-STABILIZING VERTEX COVER ALGORITHMS

Kiniwa's Self-Stabilizing Vertex Cover Algorithm (SS-VC)

Recall that the simple greedy approach to the minimum cardinality vertex cover problem presented in Section 2.1, which simply chooses the node having the maximum degree, removes it from the graph and iterates until all edges are covered; approximates the optimum solution by a factor of $O(log_2(n))$ in the worst case. On the other hand, recall also that the algorithm that finds the vertex cover via a maximal matching (described in Section 2.2) has a bounded approximation ratio and guarantees to find a solution which is at most twice the optimum solution.

Combining these two ideas, Kiniwa (2005) proposed both a sequential algorithm and its self-stabilizing distributed version. This algorithm constructs a maximal matching by favoring the edges connecting heaviest nodes with the lightest nodes on the graph and then covers the nodes on the basis of this matching.

The algorithm works under a distributed daemon, i.e., each node independently decides when it will change its state. Every node $v \in V$ has a pointer p_v that points to the matching candidate, an integer variable $degree_v$ holding the degree of v, another integer variable $color_v$ holding degree of the pointed node, and a boolean variable $inVC_v$ which is true when the node is in VC. Two nodes are considered *matched* if they point to each other. There are six rules determining the next state of the node.

For any node $v \in V$,

Rule 1: If v is not matched, its color must be equal to its degree.

Rule 2: If v is matched with a node $k \in \Gamma(v)$, its color should be the greater of $degree_v$ and $degree_k$.

Rule 3: If there are higher colored nodes pointing to the node v, then node v must point back to the one having the highest degree among them, namely k, it must set its color to the color of k, and removes itself from the solution set by setting $inVC_v$ to *false*.

Rule 4: If v points to a higher colored node which does not point back to v, then v must free the pointer, reset the color to its own degree and set $inVC_v$ to *false*.

Rule 5: If none of the higher colored neighbors points to v and there is at least one lower colored node that does not point to v, v points to the one having the lowest degree among them, and sets $inVC_v$ to *true*.

Rule 6: If all of the neighbors of i point to other nodes, then the state of i is updated as follows: if i has the minimum degree then set $cover_i$ as *false*; and set it to *true*, otherwise.

Figure 14 illustrates a sample execution of SS-VC Algorithm. Assuming starting from the empty configuration where the nodes only know their degrees and their pointers are set to null, firstly, each node activates Rule 1 and sets its color to its degree. Then, nodes 2, 3, 5 and 6 enable Rule 5 since they are not pointed to and have a lower colored neighbor. They choose their neighbors having the lowest degree. 3 and 6 both point to 7; 2 and 5 point to 1 and 4, respectively. The configuration at this stage is shown in Figure 14(a). Then, nodes 1, 4 and 7 enable Rule 3 and point back to their responders and match. Node 7 chooses 3 instead of 6, because the node 3 has a higher degree. Thick edges show the matching. Since node 6 has not been pointed back by 7, it enables Rule 4, frees its pointer and leaves the solution set (Figure 14(b)). Node 6 enables Rule 6 and re-enters to the solution set because it is not the node with the lowest degree in its neighborhood. Stabilized solution is shown in Figure 14(c).

In order to see the behavior of SS-VC Algorithm in case of a failure in the network, assume that node 7 is down due to any reason. In this case, node 3 starts to point 1 by means of Rule 5 (Figure 14(d)). Then node 1 breaks its matching and starts to point back the node 3 due to Rule 3. Node 2 consecutively enables Rules 4 and 6 and frees its pointer. It does not leave the solution because it does not have the lowest degree. However, node 6 also enables Rule 6 and leaves the solution set due to having the lowest degree. Though, in case a failure of a node, the remaining nodes are still a vertex cover, this example showed that SS-VC is able to lower the size of the VC set.

Theorem 25. SS-VC stabilizes in $O(n)$ rounds.

Figure 14. Sample execution of SS-VC Algorithm

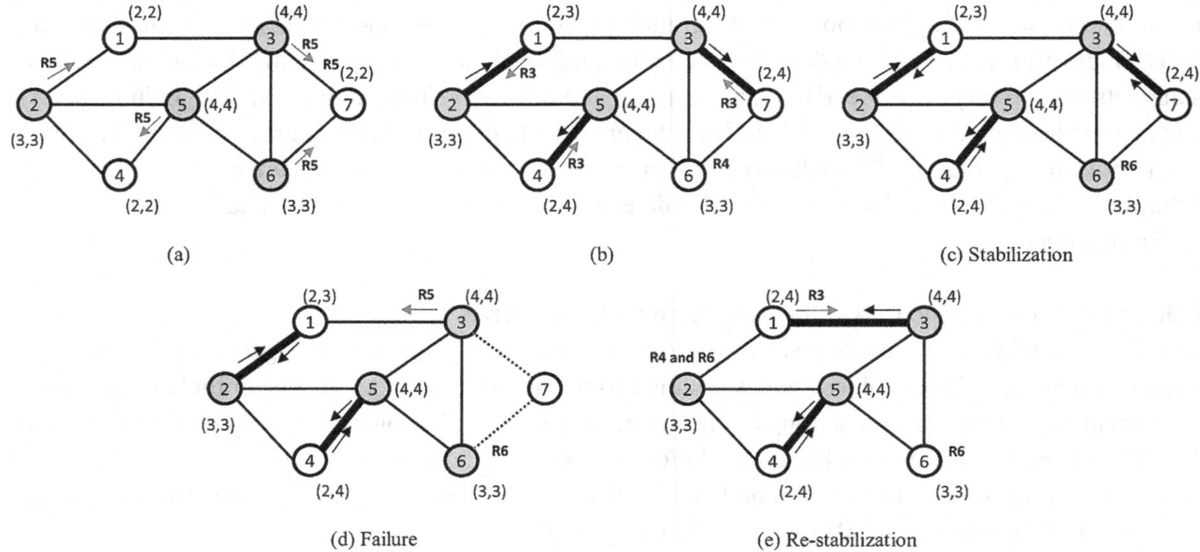

Proof. At the worst case, the network has only one highest degree in any round. Then, it is guaranteed that, in each round, at least one node will make a matching proposal and its proposal will be accepted at the next round. At round *t*, at least *t-1* nodes will be matched. A maximal matching may include n nodes, where *n* is the node count. Therefore, *n* nodes will be matched in at most n+1 rounds, i.e. $O(n)$. □

Approximation ratio of SS-VC is $2\text{-}1/\Delta$. Interested readers are referred to (Kiniwa, 2005).

Bipartite Matching Based Self-Stabilizing Vertex Cover Algorithm (SS-VC-Bip)

The algorithm to be presented in this section is the self-stabilizing version of Polishchuk and Suomela's distributed approximation Algorithm described in Section 2.1.3. Recall that this algorithm firstly treats the given graph as bipartite graph simply by assigning two pointers for each node, finds a maximal matching on that bipartite graph and adds the matched nodes into the solution set.

Turau (2009) implemented this idea as a self-stabilizing algorithm, in other words, it guarantees to obtain a vertex cover even in case of starting from an arbitrary state. The algorithm runs under a distributed daemon. Each node *v* has two pointers ($black_v$ and $white_v$) and two binary variables (*blackMatched* and *whiteMatched*). There are two rules to determine which node or nodes the pointers point to.

Rule 1 (Deals with the Value of White Pointer): If the white pointer of the node *i* points to a node *k* but the black pointer of *k* does not point back to *i*, the white pointer of *i* is set to null. If the white pointer of *i* does not point to any node and there is at least one node whose black pointer points to *i*, then set the white pointer to one of these nodes.

Rule 2 (Deals with the Value of Black Pointer): If the black pointer of node *i* points to a node *k* but the white pointer of *k* points to another node *m* where $m \neq i$, then frees the black pointer. If the black pointer is free and there is a node $k \in \Gamma(i)$ whose white pointer is free, then set the black pointer to *k*.

The behavior of these rules is illustrated in Figure 15.

Figure 15. Possible states and the behavior of SS-VC-Bip

	Guard			Action	
Rule 1	White pointer is free but there is a neighbor whose black pointer points to me		→	White pointer points to that node	
	White pointer points to a vertex whose black pointer points to another vertex		→	Free white pointer	
Rule 2	Black pointer points to a vertex whose white pointer points to another vertex		→	Free the pointer	
	Black pointer is free and there is a neighbor with a free white pointer		→ →	Black pointer points to that node	

A sample execution of the algorithm is illustrated in Figure 16. Though the algorithm works under distributed daemon, it is assumed for simplicity that the nodes take decision one by one in ascending order with respect to their unique identifiers. Also, each node is assumed to have an ordered list of their neighbors and to favor the one having the lower id when two or more candidates are available for pointing. The time period between the activation of the first node and the last node is called a round. Figure 16(b) shows the end of the first round. Pointers are illustrated as arrows. B is the black pointer and W is the white pointer. When a node has a null pointer, it is not shown on the graph. At the first iteration, black pointer of Node 1 was set to 2 according to Rule 2. Node 2 activated Rule 1 and responded to node 1 by setting its white pointer to 1. Similarly, nodes 5 and 7 activated Rule 2 and Rule 1, respectively and became matched. Nodes 3, 4, 6, 8 and 9 activated Rule 2 and pointed their neighbor having the lowest identifier among those which have a free white pointer. Matched nodes are shown in dark color. At the second round, node 1 executed Rule 1 and chose the node 3 among the set {3,4,6,9}, which is the set of nodes having black pointer that points to 1. It pointed node 3 via its white pointer. Since its white pointer is no longer null, nodes 4 and 6 freed their black pointer according to Rule 2. Similarly, node 5 pointed to node 8 with its white pointer, and finally, node 9 freed its black pointer since none of its neighbors has a null white pointer. The resulting configuration illustrated in Figure 16(c) is stable. As the algorithm suggests, all of the nodes are either matched or have both their pointers set to null. Matched nodes are in the solution set.

Just as Polishchuk and Suomela's Algorithm, SS-VC-Bip is a 3-approximation algorithm. Turau provides an improvement to this self-stabilizing algorithm by introducing 3 more rules which are used to eliminate the so called loose nodes on the solution set. Loose nodes are the nodes that are matched and have only one neighbor. For example, the nodes 3 and 8 in Figure 16(c) are loose nodes and can be removed from the solution set without breaking the vertex cover condition. Though this approach does not improve the theoretical approximation ratio on regular graphs, it decreases the size of the solution set. Interested readers are referred to (Turau, 2009).

Theorem 26. *The algorithm SS-VC-Bip stabilizes in $O(m+n)$ moves, assuming a distributed scheduler.*

Proof. A node running SS-VC-Bip points to each of its neighbors with its black pointer at most once. Then, at the worst case, a node i will change the value of its black pointer $2d(i)$ times, where $d(i)$ is the degree of i. Therefore, the total number of execution of Rule 2 is $4m$, since $\sum_{i \in V} d(i) = 2m$. Also, a node i can activate Rule 1 at most two times: when it starts pointing to a node which points to i with its black pointer, and when it frees its white pointer. Then, at the worst case, total number of execution of Rule 1 is $2n$. Therefore, total number of moves of the algorithm is bounded by $4m+2n$, i.e. $O(m+n)$. □

Figure 16. Sample Execution of SS-VC-Bip

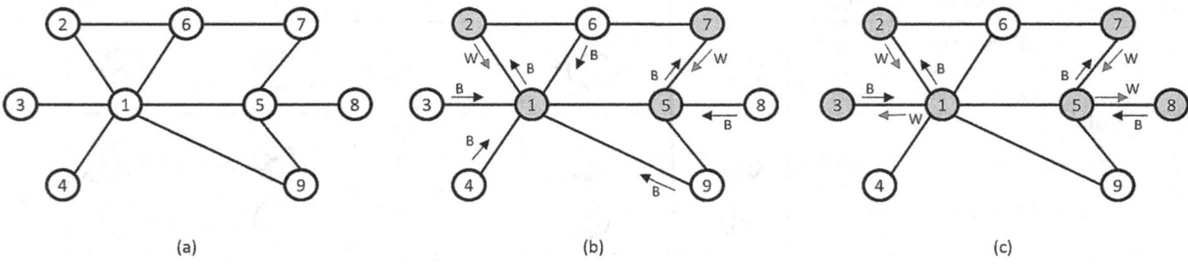

Self-Stabilizing Connected Vertex Cover Algorithm (SS-MConVC)

The only algorithm dealing with the self-stabilizing connected vertex cover problem was introduced by Delbot et al. (2014). The main idea of the algorithm is to firstly decompose a given graph *G(V, E)* into a set of cliques of maximal size, while securing that all cliques having a size greater than one are connected. Once this *connected minimal clique partition problem* is solved, one can obtain a connected vertex cover solution by putting the member nodes of the cliques having size at least one into the solution set.

First phase of the algorithm, which is a self-stabilizing connected minimal clique partition algorithm (*SS-MConCliq*), requires a root node $r \in V$. Also, all the other nodes should have the knowledge of their distances from the root node, namely dist_v. (A self-stabilizing BFS algorithm can be used for determining those values.) This distance, together with the identifier of the node, determines the clique construction priority of a node. Root node *r* has the highest priority. Thus, *r* constructs its own maximal clique and becomes the *local leader* of the clique. Other nodes in the clique know their leader by a variable $leader_v$. Then, among the nodes having not been included to any clique, the ones with the locally lexicographically-lowest $(dist_v, v)$ pair become local leaders and construct their own *candidate* maximal cliques. If the nodes in this candidate clique acknowledge being in this clique, then clique is considered a *finalized* clique. Also, in order for a node to construct its clique, it should have the knowledge of the neighborhood of its neighbors, in other words, it must be aware of its 2-hops neighborhood $N_v \subseteq V$.

Informal descriptions of the 4 rules of SS-MConCliq algorithm are listed below:

- **N-Action:** If a node *v* does not have the correct information of its 2-hops neighborhood, let it have. If it does not have the correct information of $dist_v$, update it.
- **C1-Action:** If a node *v* has not been selected by a leader yet and it is not a local leader, let *v* be a local leader and build its candidate clique by selecting candidate neighbors.
- **C2-Action:** If a node *v* has been selected as a candidate by a local leader and *v* is not the lexicographically smallest in its neighborhood, then assign the lexicographically smallest node in the clique as the $leader_v$, free the clique of *v* if it had one previously.
- **C3-Action:** If a node *v* has not been selected by a leader and *v* has already built a candidate clique, make the candidate clique a finalized clique.

A sample execution of the algorithm is illustrated in Figure 17. It is assumed that a self-stabilizing BFS algorithm has already run and stabilized and SS-MConCliq Algorithm has not been initiated yet. When algorithm runs, initially all the nodes activate the N-action and store the correct information about their distances from the root. Within the parentheses next to each node in Figure 17(a) is the pair $(dist_v, v)$ of each node. Note that, at this stage, none of the nodes but only the root can activate an action. *r* activates C1-action and selects the nodes 2 and 4 for its candidate clique. Once 2 and 4 are selected, they are enabled to execute C2-action. They assign *r* as their leader. *r* activates C3-action and finalize the clique. Figure 17(b) shows the clique. Leader of the clique is marked with a dashed outline. As the clique is finalized, nodes 1, 3 and 5 become local leaders, execute C1-action and build their candidate cliques. 1 and 3 construct trivial cliques ($|C|= 1$). 8 executes C2-action and 5 executes C3-action (Figure 17(c)). Other cliques are built similarly (Figure 17(d)).

Figure 17. Sample Execution of SS-MConCliq and SS-MConVC

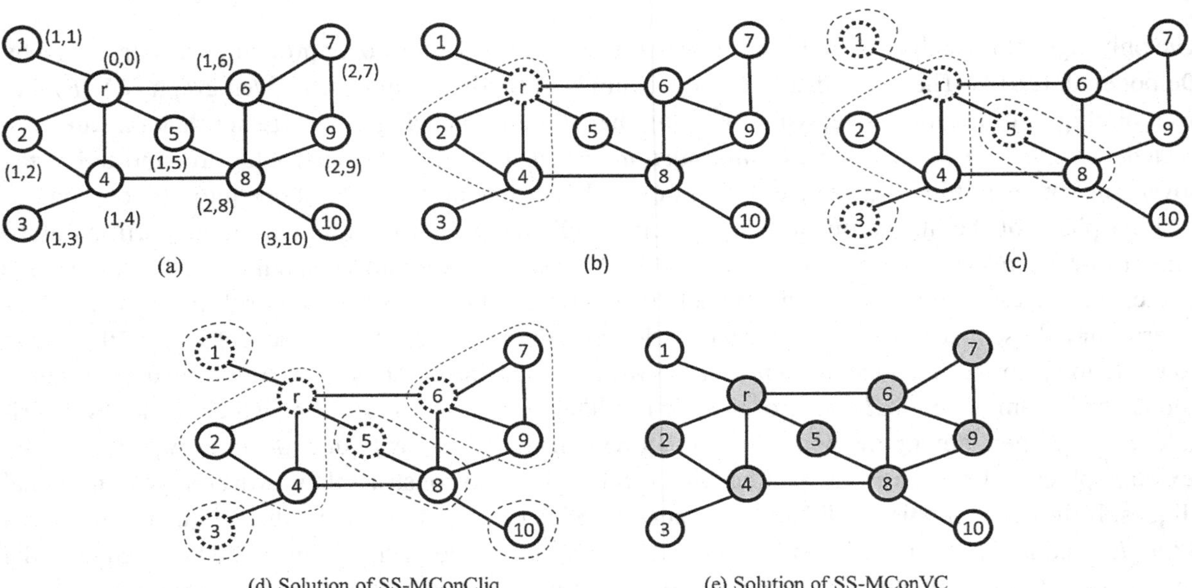

In order to find a vertex cover solution given the solution of SS-MConCliq, an additional binary variable $inVC_v$ and the following rule are used:

- **VC-Action:** If the node v is not a leader of any clique or it is the leader of a clique having cardinality greater than 1, then set the value of $inVC_v$ to *true*, and otherwise, to *false*.

In other words, VC-action guarantees that only the nodes which are leaders of a trivial clique ($|C|=1$) is removed from VC solution set, and all other nodes are put in VC. Vertices 1, 3 and 10 in Figure 17(d) are leaders of trivial cliques and they are not included in VC (Figure 17(e)).

Theorem 27. *Assuming each node knows its distance from the root, the algorithm SS-MConCliq stabilizes in $O(min(n_c Diam, n))$ rounds, where n_c is the maximum number of cliques in G, Diam is the diameter of G.*

Proof. Since r is the only local leader at the initial step, it can construct its clique in $O(1)$ rounds, executing only C1-action and C3-action. Once the root constructs its clique, there is exactly one local leader k having the lexicographically lowest pair $(dist_v, v)$ at distance 1 and it can build its clique in $O(1)$ rounds, too. By induction, it is proved that in at most $O(t)$ rounds, a clique is built at every local leader at a distance t from r. Since the distance of a local leader from r can be at most *Diam*, all cliques are built in $O(n_c Diam)$ rounds. Moreover, the maximum number of cliques a graph can have is n. Therefore, the bound can be written as $O(min(n_c Diam, n))$. □

Theorem 28. *Assuming a stabilized configuration of SS-MConCliq Algorithm, it takes O(1) rounds for SS-MConVC to stabilize.*

Proof. Once each node is assigned to a maximal clique and knows its leader, it updates its $inVC_v$ variable in a single instruction. □

CONCLUSION AND FUTURE RESEARCH DIRECTIONS

In this chapter, vertex cover algorithms for distributed systems has been reviewed. Firstly, cardinality based vertex cover, weighted vertex cover and connected vertex cover problems are identified. After that distributed vertex cover algorithms are categorized as follows: minimum cardinality vertex cover algorithms, minimum weighted vertex cover algorithms and self-stabilizing vertex cover algorithms. The first minimum cardinality distributed algorithm (MinCVC-Greedy) given in this chapter is greedy and inspired from Parnas and Ron's algorithm. MinCVC-Greedy has $O(log_2(n))$ time complexity, $O(n\Delta\ |E|\ log_2(n))$ bit complexity and $O(\Delta log_2(n)))$ space complexity. The approximation ratio of this algorithm is $O(log_2(\Delta))$. The second algorithm (MinCVC-Match) uses greedy matching to construct a vertex cover. The bit and space complexities of MinCVC-Match are same with those of MinCVC-Greedy. On the other side, although time complexity of MinCVC-Match is $O(n)$, its approximation ratio is 2. The third algorithm (MinCVC-BipMM) is derived from bipartite matching which needs $2\Delta+1$ rounds and has same space and bit complexities. The last algorithm (MinCVC-BFST) uses breadth-first search tree and has $O(D)$ time complexity, $O(n^3 log_2(n))$ bit complexity and $O(\Delta log_2(n)))$ space complexity. The approximation ratio obtained from the simulations of this algorithm varies from 1 to 2, in most cases not exceeding 1.5.

In the second category, minimum weighted vertex algorithms are investigated. The first algorithm that belongs to this category and given in this chapter is greedy distributed minimum weighted cover algorithm (GreedyWVC) where this algorithm is similar to MinCVC-Greedy and favors node weights instead of node ids. GreedyWVC has $O(n)$ time complexity, $O(n^2 log_2(n))$ bit complexity, $O(\Delta(log_2(n)+ log_2(w)))$ space complexity. The second weighted algorithm is distributed version of Clarkson's vertex cover algorithm. This algorithm uses weight ratios instead of solely weights and is a 2-approximation algorithm. The complexity values of this algorithm are similar with those of GreedyWVC. The third weighted algorithm is the distributed version of Bar-Yehuda and Even's algorithm that arbitrarily selects an edge, includes its incident node having the smaller and updates the weight of incident node having the greater weight. Algorithm continues this procedure until all edges are covered. The synchronous version of the algorithm has similar complexity values with those of former algorithms except that its space complexity is $O(\Delta(log_2(n))$. The last weighted algorithm reviewed in this chapter is distributed weighted vertex cover algorithm via maximal matching (MinWVC-MM). This algorithm introduces the idea of micro-nodes for each adjacent vertices and aims to a maximal matching on the newly constructed topology of micro-nodes. MinWVC-MM halts in $O(\log_2(n)+ \log_2(W))$ rounds, its bit complexity is $O(\Delta n(\log_2(n)+ \log_2(W)))$, and its space complexity is $O(\Delta(\log_2(n)+ \log_2(W)))$.

As the last category of vertex cover algorithms, self-stabilizing algorithms are studied. Self-stabilization is an important concept in the presence of failures. The first self-stabilizing algorithm given in this chapter is Kiniwa's self-stabilizing vertex cover algorithm (SS-VC). Kiniwa combined the greedy selection idea and maximal matching idea to construct an efficient vertex cover. Kiniwa's algorithm can be implemented with six rules under a distributed daemon where each node independently decides when it will change its state. This algorithm stabilizes in $O(n)$ rounds. The second self-stabilizing algorithm presented in this chapter is bipartite matching based self-stabilizing vertex cover algorithm (SS-VC-Bip). This algorithm is designed by Turau and it is the self-stabilizing version of Polishchuk and Suomela's distributed algorithm (MinCVC-BipMM). The algorithm runs under a distributed daemon and have two rules. The algorithm stabilizes in $O(n+m)$ rounds. The last self-stabilizing algorithm covered in this chapter is the self-stabilizing connected vertex cover algorithm which was introduced by Delbot et al

(SS-MConVC). The main idea of this algorithm is to firstly solve the connected minimal clique partition problem and obtain a connected vertex cover solution by selecting the member nodes of the cliques. SS-MConVC has 4 rules and stabilizes in $O(min(n_c Diam,n))$ rounds.

Finally, the open research issues and possible future directions related to the distributed vertex cover finding problem are listed in the following:

- Breadth-first search tree rooted at the sink node is a suitable routing infrastructure for wireless ad hoc and sensor networks. Besides that as aforementioned vertex cover is used to monitor links and to cluster nodes. Instead of constructing these two graph-theoretic structures separately Kavalci et al. proposed an integrated approach. The authors think that this approach can be further improved such as integrating distributed greedy vertex cover algorithm with the distributed breadth-first search tree algorithm.
- To the best of the authors' knowledge, the tight bounds for move count and round number at the worst case are not found for the self-stabilizing algorithms. Investigation of these tight bounds and the design of efficient algorithms which produce these bounds can be an important research objective.
- Another interesting open research problem related to the self-stabilization is the capacitated and self-stabilizing distributed vertex cover algorithm design and implementation. Capacitated vertex cover problem is a constrained version of vertex cover problem such that each node can cover edges with *c* predefined capacity of edges. For energy-efficient networks, this topic seems to be promising.
- Design and implementation of distributed vertex cover algorithms on graph models other than undirected graph and unit disk graph models are not well-studied research areas to the best of the authors' knowledge. These models include various structures such as quasi-unit disk graph model, unit ball graph model and double disk graph model.
- Using polynomial time evolutionary algorithms to approximate the solutions of vertex cover, weighted vertex cover and connected vertex cover is also a promising research area. Design and implementation of genetic algorithms, ant colony based algorithms, bee colony based algorithms and other bio-inspired artificial intelligence methods to solve vertex cover related problems are attractive research subjects nowadays.

REFERENCES

Bar-Yehuda, R., & Even, S. (1981). A linear-time approximation algorithm for the weighted vertex cover problem. *Journal of Algorithms*, *2*(2), 198–203. doi:10.1016/0196-6774(81)90020-1

Clarkson, K. L. (1983). A modification of the greedy algorithm for vertex cover. *Information Processing Letters*, *16*(1), 23–25. doi:10.1016/0020-0190(83)90007-8

Delbot, F., Laforest, C., & Rovedakis, S. (2014). Self-stabilizing algorithms for Connected Vertex Cover and Clique decomposition problems. *Principles of Distributed Systems*, 307-322.

Erciyes, K. (2013). *Distributed graph algorithms for computer networks*. London: Springer. doi:10.1007/978-1-4471-5173-9

Grandoni, F., Könemann, J., & Panconesi, A. (2005). Distributed weighted vertex cover via maximal matchings. *Computing and Combinatorics*, 839-848.

Hanckowiak, M., Karonski, M., & Panconesi, A. (2001). On the distributed complexity of computing maximal matchings. *SIAM Journal on Discrete Mathematics*, *15*(1), 41–57. doi:10.1137/S0895480100373121

Hoepman, J. H. (2004). *Simple distributed weighted matchings*. arXiv preprint cs/0410047

Kavalci, V., Ural, A., & Dagdeviren, O. (2014). Distributed Vertex Cover Algorithms For Wireless Sensor Networks. *International Journal of Computer Networks & Communications*, *6*(1), 95–110. doi:10.5121/ijcnc.2014.6107

Kiniwa, J. (2005). Approximation of self-stabilizing vertex cover less than 2. In *Self-Stabilizing Systems* (pp. 171–182). Springer Berlin Heidelberg. doi:10.1007/11577327_12

Parnas, M., & Ron, D. (2007). Approximating the minimum vertex cover in sublinear time and a connection to distributed algorithms. *Theoretical Computer Science*, *381*(1), 183–196. doi:10.1016/j.tcs.2007.04.040

Polishchuk, V., & Suomela, J. (2009). A simple local 3-approximation algorithm for vertex cover. *Information Processing Letters*, *109*(12), 642–645. doi:10.1016/j.ipl.2009.02.017

Turau, V., & Hauck, B. (2009). A self-stabilizing approximation algorithm for vertex cover in anonymous networks. *Stabilization, Safety, and Security of Distributed Systems*, 341-353.

KEY TERMS AND DEFINITIONS

Connected Vertex Cover: A variation of the vertex cover in which the graph induced by the vertex cover is connected.

Graph Matching: On a given graph of *G(V, E)*, graph matching is a set of edges $M \subseteq E$ such that no two edges in *M* are incident to the same vertex.

Minimal Vertex Cover: A minimal vertex cover is a vertex cover VC whose cardinality cannot be decreased, in other words, exclusion of any vertex from VC would break the vertex cover conditions.

Minimum Vertex Cover: Among all possible vertex covers of a given graph, the one(s) that have the minimum cardinality are called the minimum vertex cover.

Minimum Weighted Vertex Cover: In a weighted graph where a weight w_v is assigned to each vertex $v \in V$, *VC** is a minimum weighted vertex cover in which the total weights of the vertices are the minimum among all possible vertex covers of the graph.

Self-Stabilization: A self-stabilizing distributed system initially starts at any state and regain a legal state in a finite time without any external intervention.

Vertex Cover: Given a graph *G(V, E)* where *V* is the set of vertices and *E* is the set of edges between vertices, vertex cover is a set of vertices *S* such that for any edge $\{u,v\}$ in *E*, at least one of *u* and *v* is in *S*.

Chapter 2
On k-Connectivity Problems in Distributed Systems

Vahid Khalilpour Akram
Ege University, Turkey

Orhan Dagdeviren
Ege University, Turkey

ABSTRACT

k-Connectivity detection and restoration are important problems in graph theory and computer networks. A graph is k-connected if it remains connected after removing k-1 arbitrary nodes. The k-connectivity is an important property of a distributed system because a k-connected network can tolerate k-1 node failures without losing the network connectivity. To achieve the k-connectivity in a network, we need to determine the current connectivity value and try to increase connectivity if the current k is lower than the desired value. This chapter reviews the central and distributed algorithms for detecting and restoring the k-connectivity in graphs and distributed systems. The algorithms will be compared from complexity, accuracy and efficiency perspectives.

INTRODUCTION

The connectivity is one of the key properties in all networks. A network is said to be connected if there is at least one path between every node. Most of the computer networks such as LANs and WANs have communication infrastructures (e.g. cables, switches and routers) and provide high reliability from the connectivity perspective. However it is not possible to prepare a communication infrastructure in all environments, whereas using ad hoc or mobile wireless sensor networks is inevitable or affordable in some applications. In this kind of networks there is no communication infrastructure and all nodes communicate with each other using some intermediate nodes. These kinds of networks provide lower connection reliability, because failure in some nodes can cut off the packet flow in the network.

A network is called 1-connected if there is at least one path between every pair of nodes and there exists at least one node, which its removal, divides the network to separated segments. Such a node is called *cut vertex*. Having a 1-connected topology puts the network in high division risk. There are many

DOI: 10.4018/978-1-4666-9964-9.ch002

researches that have been made to find and resolve the cut vertices in a network (Atay & Bayazit, 2010) (Dagdeviren & Akram, 2014)(Tarjan, 1972). In ad hoc and wireless sensor networks, for example, the nodes typically are battery powered and it is possible that some nodes die due to energy consumptions caused by packet transmissions. A *k*-connected network can tolerate and remain connected if *k*-1 arbitrary nodes stop working. Figure 1 shows a network with *k*=2. The nodes that their removal from graph decrease *k* are referred as *MinCut* set. In Figure 1 the red nodes with thick circles belong to *MinCut* set and removing any of them can reduces the disjoint path count while a failure in normal (black) nodes does not affect *k*.

DEFINITIONS

The following symbols and terms have been used to explain and analysis the proposed algorithms in the next sections.

- The network is modeled as an undirected graph $G=(V,E)$ where V is the set of vertices that represents the nodes and E is the set of edges that indicates the links between nodes.
- d_v indicates the number of links connected to v or the degree of v in G.
- d is the minimum degree of G. It means that all nodes in G have at least d neighbors.
- D is the network diameter which is the length of the longest short path between two nodes.
- Δ is the maximum degree in G. So we have $\Delta=\max(d_v: v\in V)$.

CONCEPTS OF COMPLEX NETWORKS

Generally most of the networks in real systems do not follow neither a specific topology pattern nor a random graph model such as Erdos and Renyi model (Erdos,1959). These kinds of the networks, which are referred as complex networks, have the most frequency in the biological, social and technological networks (Newman, 2003). Although complex networks have no regular structure or randomness, they have some common properties which are used as metrics to analyze them. These properties provide a

Figure 1. A sample network with k=2

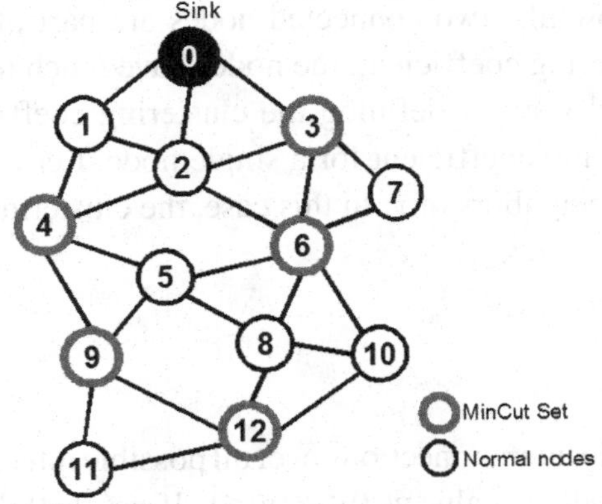

global view of the network structure and usually affect each other or network functionality in various ways. In this section some of the key properties of complex networks and their effect on connectivity are presented.

Degree Distribution

The degree of node v or d_v in any network is the number of links connected to v. The degree distribution provides general information about the structure of network. In a random network studied by Erdos and Renyi, most nodes have close degrees to each other. However, the degree distributions in complex networks are very different. In a complex network, some of the nodes have very small, while some others have very large degrees. The location and number of nodes with higher degrees affect other important properties such as D. Besides that increasing the number of nodes with higher degree may lead the increase of the network connectivity. Hence the degree distribution plays an important role in the performance of complex networks.

The degree distribution p_i is the probability that a uniformly chosen random node has exactly i links. Estimating the degree distribution in random (Bernoulli) or Erdos and Renyi models are simple but it is usually hard for complex networks. For example in a social network, calculating the probability that a randomly chosen person has 5 friends is hard because people may have very different number of friends. However, usually it is possible to estimate this value using other properties or application specific parameters.

Maximum and Minimum Degree

The minimum and maximum degrees of nodes in a complex network are other parameters that provide some useful information about the network. Generally the minimum and maximum degrees of nodes depend on the size of network. The value of maximum and minimum degrees of nodes highly depends on the degree distribution. The probability that a node has maximum degree is $1/n$. The minimum degree in every connected network is 1. This value highly depends on the application field. For example in WSNs the minimum degree can be estimated from other network characteristics including radio range of nodes, sensing area and node count.

Clustering Coefficient

Clustering coefficient shows how like two connected nodes are part of a larger group of nodes. In a network with high average clustering coefficient, the nodes have much more tendency to form a cluster of connected nodes. One typical way for defining the clustering coefficient of the entire network, is starting by declaration of clustering coefficient for a single node. Let v be a node in a network, and e_v be the number of links between neighbors of v. In this case, the clustering coefficient of node v will be:

$$cc(\mathrm{v}) = \frac{2\,e_v}{d_v\left(d_v - 1\right)}$$

$cc(v)$ is the fraction of available interconnections over all possible interconnections between neighbors of v. Clustering coefficient of node v is always $0 \leq cc(v) \leq 1$. If $cc(v)=0$ then none of the neighbors of v

is connected to each other and v is the center of a star topology. If $cc(v)=1$ then all neighbors of v are connected to each other and we have a clique around v. The clustering coefficient of the entire network is the average of clustering coefficient of all nodes:

$$cc = \frac{1}{n} \sum_{for\ all\ v} cc(v)$$

The clustering coefficient gives the probability of having a connection between two nodes u and v when both u and v are connected to another node x. For example in a social network it is the probability that two friends have another common friend.

The Small-World Property

Many researches have shown that in the most real biological and social networks, the average distance between each randomly selected pair of nodes is about $L=\log n$ where n is the number of nodes and most of the times L is less than 6 (Curia, et, al., 2014). These networks are known as small-world networks. The communication delays in small-world networks are generally small because there are only a few hops between each pair of nodes. A small-world network may have many nodes but the network diameter D always is small.

Fast delivery of packets is one of the most interesting and desirable feature of a network. Hence there are many researches that provide various models to construct a small-world WSN or an ad hoc network (Guidoni, et,al., 2008) (Luo & Yu, 2010). Generally in these models the network diameters are reduced by inserting new nodes, increasing degree of nodes or relocating the nodes in the network area. Reducing the diameters in the networks with high node count, increase the node density in the deployment areas. Despite many advantages of small-world complex networks, it may not be possible to establish these networks in all applications.

Scale-Free Structure

In a scale-free network the probability that the degree of randomly selected node be at least i, is $p_i=1/i^2$. The degree distribution of a scale-free network follows the power law distribution. Generally the distributions of a wide variety of real world events follow a power law function. The mathematical relation of power law distribution is:

$$f(x) = \frac{c}{x^{\alpha}}$$

where c is a constant value and $\alpha>1$ (typically $2<\alpha<3$). The major parts of nodes in a scale-free network have small degrees hence the probability that a randomly selected node has small degree is very high. Most of the social networks are scale free because generally people tend to have relationship with small groups of other people. For example in any social network finding a person who has a few friends is much easier than finding a person who has hundreds of friends.

Generally the nodes in scale-free networks are divided to dense groups where most of the nodes in each group are only connected to a single node referred as hub. Usually there are some nodes that are connected to more than one hub and in this way the entire network become connected. Failures in leaf nodes do not terminate the connectivity among other nodes. If we suppose the failure occurs randomly, the probability that a leaf fails is much more than the probability of failure in a hub. Hence most of the failures in a scale-free network do not lead to the termination of connections between other nodes and usually these networks are fault tolerant.

Average Path Length

Average path length is the average number of hops along the shortest paths between all pairs in the network. This is another parameter which helps to estimate the efficiency of communication in the network. Lower average path length leads to faster communications, lower energy lost and higher throughput. If $s(v_i, v_j)$ is the shortest path length between each pair of nodes then the average path length will be as follows:

$$L = \frac{1}{n(n-1)} \sum_{i \neq j} s(v_i, v_j)$$

L is not equal but highly affected with network diameter *D* and increasing *D* directly increments *L*. In the next section formal declaration of *k*-connectivity and its relation to mentioned properties of the complex networks are presented.

K-CONNECTIVITY PROBLEMS

The *k*-connectivity strongly related to other mentioned properties of complex networks. In any *k*-connected network each node has at least *k* disjoint paths to other nodes. Therefore each node should have at least *k* neighbors so the degree distribution $p_{i<k}$=0. Higher values for *k* directly increase the minimum node degree in complex networks. But the reverse is not true. A complex network with minimum degree *k* necessarily is not *k* -connected.

Star topologies have the smallest possible *k* value which is 1. On the other hand the connectivity value of a complete network is $k=n-1$ which is maximum possible value. Achieving higher connectivity values require more direct and indirect links between nodes which increase clustering coefficient. When *cc* goes to 1 the value of *k* goes to $n-1$. The reverse is also true.

The connectivity value *k* and the average path length are two complementary values which provide useful information about the number of paths and the length of each path between the nodes. The degree distributions of scale-free complex networks are usually low and this reduces the value of *k* in scale-free networks. On the other hand small diameter and high density in both scale-free and small-world networks generally increase the probability of having more disjoint paths between nodes which leads to higher *k* values. There are three major approaches for detecting the connectivity value of a graph:

- Approximating the connectivity value using probabilistic methods.
- Central algorithms.
- Distributed algorithms.

To restore the connectivity to a specific value of k there are two general approaches:

- Placing new nodes or activating reserved nodes.
- Moving mobile nodes to new locations.

Each of these approaches has some advantages and disadvantages that will be discussed in next sections.

THE *K*-CONNECTIVITY DETECTION

In the k-connectivity detection problem we need to find the current connectivity value of an arbitrary topology. The value of k in dense topologies is generally higher than the sparse topologies. Therefore it is reasonable that we define a probabilistic relation between density and connectivity of a topology. The most effective parameter on density is the number of nodes in the network and the area that the nodes placed in.

Probabilistic Approaches for Detecting *k*

The probability of being a k-connected graph has been studied on many researches (Bettstetter, 2002) (Ling & Tian, 2007)(Penrose, 1999)(Reif & Spirakis, 1985) (Xing et. al., 2009) (Zhao, 2014)(Zhao, et. al., 2014) The aim of all of these approaches is to find a relation between the probability of having a k-connected graph and other parameters such as minimum or maximum node degrees, number of nodes and the area that the nodes are distributed. For example Penrose (Penrose, 1999) proved that the probability of having a k-connected graph is equal to the probability that the value of d in that graph is equal or greater than k.

$$P(G \text{ is } k-\text{connected}) = P(d \geq k) \tag{1}$$

Bettstetter (Bettstetter, 2002) and Ling (Ling & Tian, 2007) proved that the probability of having a wireless sensor network with minimum degree d can be calculated as relation (2).

$$P(d \geq n_0) = \left(1 - \sum_{j=0}^{n_0-1} \frac{\left(\rho \pi r_0^2\right)^j}{j!} e^{-\rho \pi r_0^2} \right)^n \tag{2}$$

where $\rho = \frac{n}{A}$

In relation (2), n is the number of nodes, A is the area that the nodes are distributed and r is the range of each node. Using relations (1) and (2) it is possible to estimate a probabilistic value for the connectivity in a network. For example the probability of having a 5-connected network in a 100*100 area with n=50 and r=30 is:

$$P(G \text{ is } 5-\text{connected}) = P(d \geq 5)$$

$$P(d \geq 5) = \left(1 - \sum_{j=0}^{5-1} \frac{(0.005*3.14*900)^j}{j!} e^{-0.005*3.14*900}\right)^{50} = 0.92$$

However these formulas only provide a probability of having a k-connected network according to the area, number of nodes and range of each node and are not useful to find the exact k value.

Central Algorithms

Currently the only way to determine the exact value of k in a graph is to use a central algorithm. The simplest way to find k in a graph is to try all possible removal combinations of nodes and check the connectivity of the graph which leads to a brute force algorithm.

Brute Force Algorithm

In this algorithm we try to consider all possible removals of nodes and check whether the graph remains connected after removing any subset of nodes. The brute force algorithm generates the *power set* of nodes and removes each element in the power set from the graph and checks whether the remaining nodes in the graph are connected. The power set of any set S is the set of all possible subsets of S including S itself. For example the set of nodes in the graph of Figure 2 is V={0,1,2,3,4} and the power set of V is

$PS(V)$ = {{0}, {1},{2}, {3}, {4}, {0,1}, {0,2}, {0,3}, {0,4}, {1,2}, {1,3}, {1,4}, {2,3}, {2,4}, {3,4}, {0,1,2}, {0,2,3}, …, {0,1,2,3,4}}

In the graph of Figure 2, removing the sets {0}, {1}, {2}, {3}, {4}, {0,1}, {0,2}, {0,3}, {0,4}, {1,2}, does not divide the graph into disconnected parts. But by removing the set {1,3,) node 4 disconnects

Figure 2. A graph with k=2

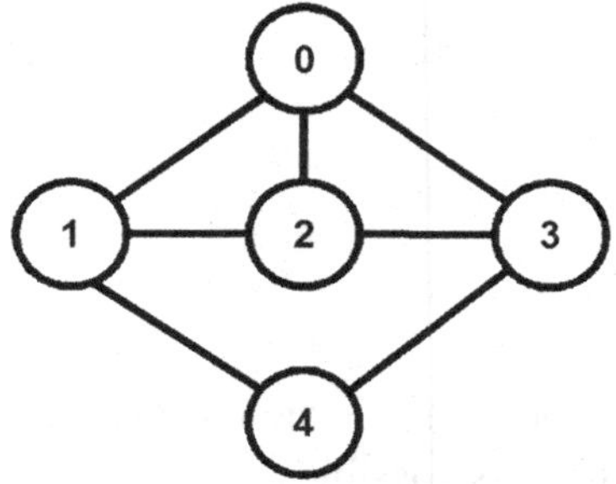

from nodes 1 and 2. Because the size of removed set is 2 the algorithm reports k=2 for this graph. The pseudo code of brute force algorithm is as follows.

Algorithm: BruteForce (Graph G)

```
Begin
        ps=powerSet(G.V)     //generates the power set of  nodes of G
        sort(ps)             //sort ps according to the size of subsets
        foreach s in ps do
            T=remove(s,G)     //remove all nodes in s from G
            if  isConnected(T)=false then
                     return | s |
        return |G.V|
End
```

The *isConnected* function checks connectivity of the graph and returns true if all nodes in the graph is connected and false otherwise. The DFS[1] or BFS[2] algorithms can be used to implement the *isConnected* function. If we have a complete graph the algorithm returns the number of nodes in the graph as the value of k, because removing the subsets in the power set does not divide the graph into disconnected partitions.

The brute force algorithm is a simple way to find the exact value of k in any graph. But obviously it is inefficient. The number of element in the power set of any set S is $2^{|s|}$. To generate all subsets of a set with n elements, any efficient power set generator algorithm will run at least with $O(2^n)$ time complexity. Also the time complexity of BFS or DFS algorithms (to check the connectivity of the graph after each removal) is $O(n+|E|)$. Consequently in the worst case the time complexity of brute force algorithm is $O(2^n(n+|E|))$ and it is impossible to use this algorithm practically.

Network Flow and Connectivity Testing

Network flow is one of the famous and widely used problems in graph theory. A flow network is a directed graph $G=(V,E)$ where each edge $e \in E$ has a non-negative capacity $c(e)$. The capacity $c(e)$ is the upper bound for the amount of the flow that can pass from e. In a flow network the amount of incoming flow into a node $v \in V/\{\text{source,sink}\}$ equals to the amount of flow that goes out from v. The *source* vertex has only outgoing flow and the *sink* has only incoming flow. A path with available capacity from *source* to *sink* is called an *augmenting path*.

A simple greedy approach can be used to find the maximum flow between two nodes in a network. We can find a path with highest capacity from source to sink and use the maximum possible flow of that path and continue to find further paths until there is no capacity left between source and sink. But this approach may lead to non-optimal results. For example consider the graph in Figure 3. The goal is to send as much flow as possible from node s to node t with respect to the rules that total passed flow from each edge must be lower than or equal to the edge capacity, and for any node except s and t, the in and out going flows must be equal.

Applying the greedy idea on the flow network of Figure 3 has been illustrated in Figure 4. The first detected path can be $s \to b \to a \to t$ (Figure 4-a) with flow=3 (the minimum capacity of edges in the path). In the second try we find $s \to a \to t$ with flow=1 because 3 amount of $a \to t$ has been used in the previous

Figure 3. An example flow network

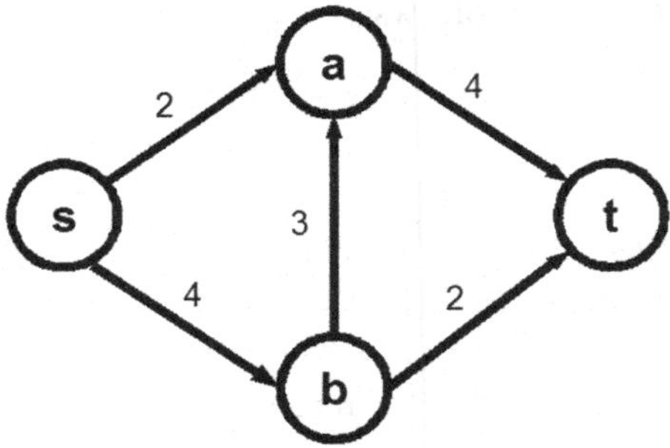

path and only 1 amount is left for new path (Figure 4-b). In the third iteration we find the path *s→b→ t* with flow=1 (Figure 4-c) and after this path there is no other path with positive flow between *s* and *t*. Therefore the maximum detected flow with greedy approach is 3+1+1=5, while the optimal value is 6. Selecting the path *s→ a→t*, *s→b→ t* and *s→b→a→t* with flow=2 for each path, provides optimal value 6 for the maximum flow in this network.

One of the first and efficient approaches that finds the maximum flow between two nodes has been provided by Ford–Fulkerson. The base idea of Ford–Fulkerson algorithm is similar to the greedy approaches: as long as there is a path from *s* to *t*, with unused capacity on all edges, transfer maximum possible flow from that path and try to find another path. The key point of Ford-Fulkerson algorithm is *Residual Graph*.

Residual Graph of a flow network shows the additional possible augmenting paths in each step of Ford–Fulkerson algorithm. If there is an augmenting path from source to sink in residual graph, then it is possible to increase the current detected maximum flow. Every edge of a residual graph has a capacity value called residual capacity which initially is equal to original capacity of the edges in the flow network graph.

The Ford-Fulkerson algorithm continuously finds an augmenting path *p* between *s* and *t* in residual graph and updates it as follows:

- Find an augmenting path *p* between source and sink.
- For each $e \in p$ decrease the capacity of *e* by *c(p)* where *c(p)* is the amount of flow that can be sent using path *p*. Formally $\forall e \in p$: $c(e) = c(e) - c(p)$ where $c(p)=\min(c(e))$.
- For each $e=(u,v) \in p$, add reverse edges $e' = (v,u)$ with the capacity *c(p)* to the residual graph.

Figure 4. Steps in greedy algorithm to find the maximum flow

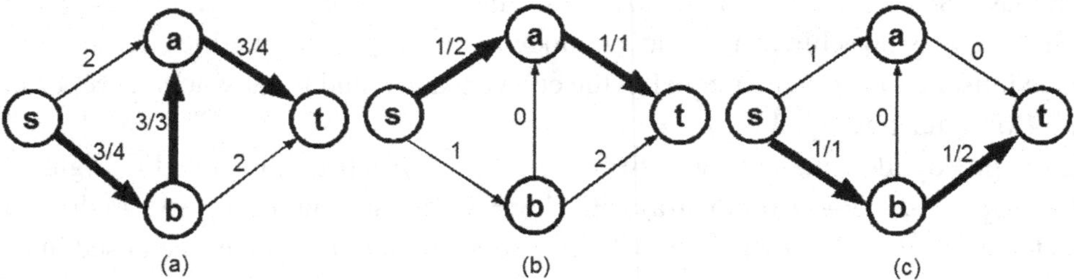

Figure 5. Steps in Ford-Fulkerson algorithm to find the maximum flow

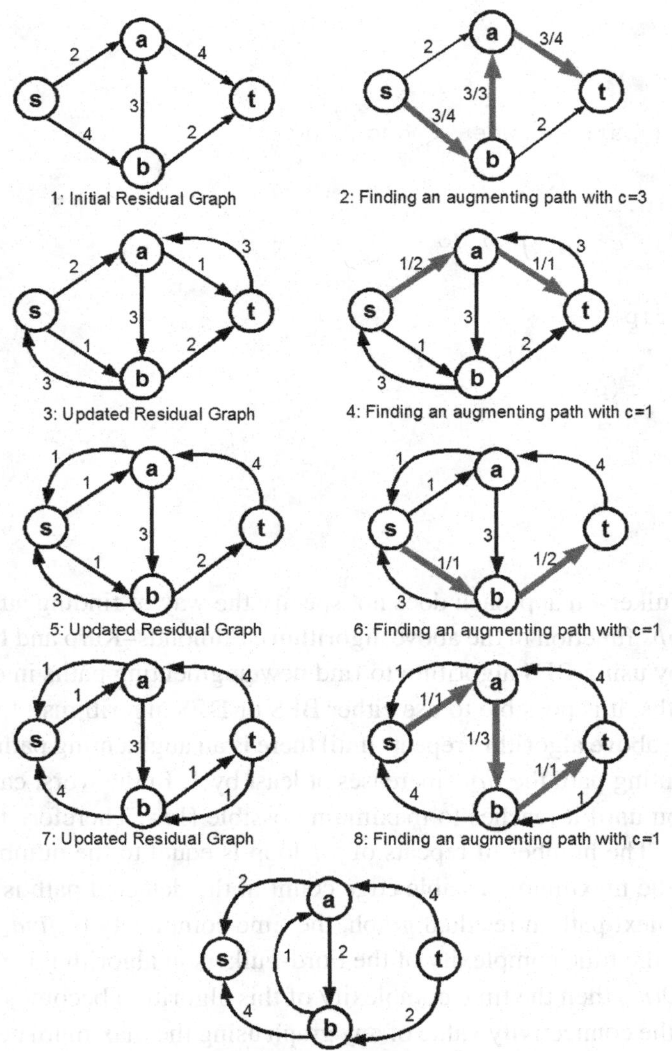

Figure 5 shows the steps of Ford-Fulkerson algorithm on the graph of Figure 3. The residual graph initially equals to original graph. Suppose that the first detected augmenting path is $s \to b \to a \to t$ with $f=3$. After sending the maximum possible flow from this path the residual graph is updated by adding reverse edges and decreasing the used flow from edges capacity as Step 3 in Figure 5. The next selected path is $s \to a \to t$ with $f=1$ which changes the residual graph as Step 5. The path $s \to b \to t$ is the next selected path to transfer 1 more flow from s to t. Selecting this path converts the residual graph to Step 7 in Figure 5. There is still another path $s \to a \to b \to t$ which increases the flow by 1. After using this path and updating the residual graph there is no more augmenting path left and the algorithm finds maximum flow in this network as 3+1+1+1=6 which is optimum. The Ford-Fulkerson algorithm for maximum flow problem is as follows:

Algorithm: Ford-Fulkerson (graph G, vertex s, vertex t)

```
Begin
    flow=0
    RG=G
    while there is a path between s and t do
    begin
        p=find_path(G,s,t)
        for each edge e=(u,v)∈p do
        begin
        c(e)=c(e)- f(p)
        addEdge (G, v, u, f(p)
        flow = flow+ f(p)
        end
    end
    return flow
End
```

The original Ford–Fulkerson approach does not specify the way of finding augmenting paths in the residual graph (*find_paths* function in the above algorithm). Edmonds–Karp and Dinic completed Fold-Fulkerson approaches by using BFS algorithm to find new augmenting paths in each step. However to find the augmenting paths, it is possible to use either BFS or DFS algorithms.

The *while* loop in the above algorithm repeats until there is an augmenting path in the residual graph. By finding each augmenting path the *flow* increases at least by 1. In the worst case, the flow increases one unit in each iteration until it reaches to maximum possible flow. Therefore the *while* loop repeats at most max flow times. The number of repeats of *for* loop is equal to the number of edges in the detected path. Obviously the maximum possible edge count in the detected path is $|E|$. If we use BFS or DFS algorithms to find next path in residual graph, the time complexity of *find_path* function will be $O(n+|E|)$. Consequently the time complexity of the Ford-Fulkerson algorithm is $O(\text{maxFlow}\times(n+|E|))$. If we consider $O(|E|)=O(n^2)$ then the time complexity of this algorithm becomes $O(\text{maxFlow}\times n^2)$.

It is possible to find the connectivity value of any graph using the maximum network flow algorithm (Even & Tarjan, 1975) (Galil, 1980). To do this we should create an initial residual graph G_R as follows:

- For any $v \in G$ add two vertices v_i and v_o to G_R
- Add a directed edge e from v_i to v_o with $c(e)=1$.
- For any incoming edge $e=(u,v)$, add $e=(u,v_i)$ to G_R and set $c(e)=\infty$.
- For any outgoing edge $e=(v,u)$, add $e=(v_o,u)$ to G_R and set $c(e)=\infty$.

If the initial graph is undirected we can create two directed edge for each undirected edge between nodes. Figure 6 shows the Residual graph of the undirected graph of Figure 2. In Figure 6 the capacity of edges that have no label is infinite.

If we set the capacity of all inner edges (v_i,v_o) in the G_R to 1, at most one flow can passes over each v in G and the maximum flow between two arbitrary vertices in G_R indicates the number of disjoint paths between them because the flow capacity of each node is 1. In this case if we have n nodes in the graph,

Figure 6. Residual graph of undirected graph of Figure 2

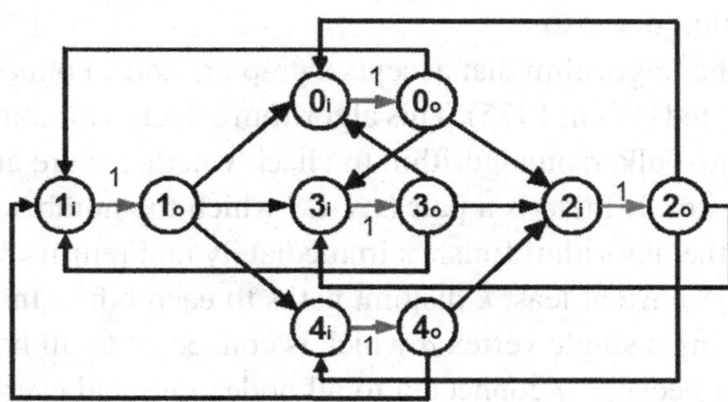

the maximum possible disjoint paths between two arbitrary nodes can be n-1 (in a complete graph each node has at most n-1 neighbors). Hence if the capacity of all nodes is 1 then the maximum possible flow between every pairs of nodes is n-1 and the time complexity of Ford-Fulkerson algorithm will be $O(n\times n^2) = O(n^3)$. To find the value of k in a graph we should find the disjoint path count between all pairs of nodes and select the smallest value as k. In a graph with n nodes there is $n(n-1)/2$ possible pairing among the nodes which leads to $O(n^2)$ time complexity. Consequently time complexity of finding the value of k using network flow algorithm is $O(n^2\times n^3)=O(n^5)$. The algorithm is as follows:

Algorithm: findConnectivityValue (Graph G)

```
Begin
        flow=0
        k=|V|
       GR=createResidualGraph(G)
       for each vertex v∈ V do
    for each vertex u∈ V do
          if  v ≠ u    then
begin
       flow=Ford-Folkerson(GR, v, u)
       if   flow < k    then
       k = flow
       end
       return  k
End
```

The above algorithm is base of several other connectivity detection algorithms that try to find the value of k faster. Various improvements have been made on the above algorithm which results significant reduction in time complexity. Even proposed an improved version of the above algorithm which finds the connectivity value of G with $O(|V|^{1/2}|E|^2)$ time complexity (Even & Tarjan, 1975). Gomory and Hu proved that it is possible to solve the multi terminal maximum network flow problem by considering only n-1 pairs of nodes instead of $n(n-1)/2$ possible pairs. Therefore the time complexity of above algorithm can be reduced to $O(n^4)$. Kleitman has improved the above algorithm and provided a method which can run in $O(k^2n^3)$ time complexity. Obviously we always have $k \leq n$ and Kleitman's algorithm runs faster than Gomory's algorithm if $k \leq \sqrt{n}$.

Also Even provided another algorithm that accepts a graph G and a connectivity value k and checks whether G is at least k-connected (Even, 1975). This algorithm selects a random subset $S \subseteq V$ where $|S|=k$. Then the algorithm runs Ford-Fulkerson algorithm to check whether there are at least k disjoint paths between all pairs $(u,v) \in S$ or not. If there is a pair $(x,y) \in S$ which the number of disjoint paths between them is smaller than k then the algorithm finishes immediately and returns false. The algorithm starts second phase if all nodes in S have at least k disjoint paths to each other. In the second phase a graph G' is created from G by adding a single vertex a which is connected to all nodes $u \in S$. Obviously each $u \in S$ has k disjoint paths to a because a connected to all nodes in S and every node in S has k disjoint paths to other nodes. The most important property of node a is that if any node $u \in V/S$ has k disjoint paths to a then it has k disjoint paths to each node $v \in S$ because a connected to other nodes only with k vertices in S and every node that has k disjoint paths to a must use one of the nodes in S. We can conclude that if each node $u \in V/S$ has k disjoint paths to a then it has a disjoint path to each node in $v \in S$ and because S is k-connected then each node $u \in V$ has k disjoint paths to all other nodes and G is k-connected. Figure 7 shows the main steps of Even algorithm for testing k=3.

In Figure 7-a we see the initial graph. Suppose that the algorithm is called with k=3 to check whether the graph is at least 3-connected. Hence a set with 3 vertices is selected. Suppose the selected vertices are the nodes 3,5 and 7 (Figure 7-b). In the next step the algorithm checks that the selected vertices have

Figure 7. Main steps in Even Algorithm for checking the graph connectivity

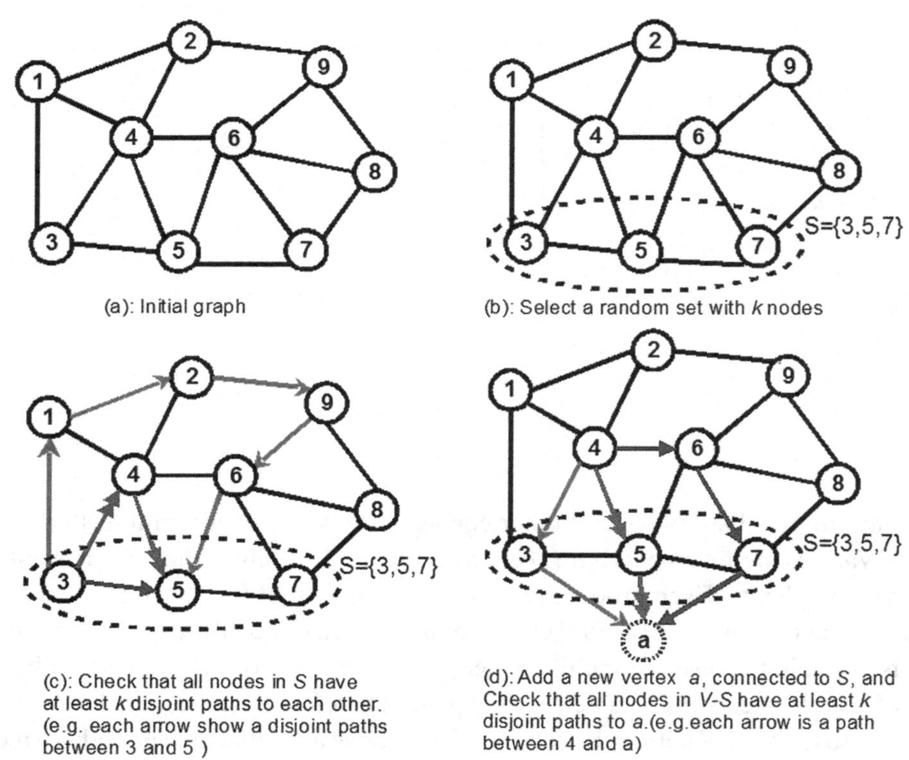

1
2
3
4
5
6
7
8
9
(a): Initial graph
S={3,5,7}
(b): Select a random set with k nodes
S={3,5,7}
(c): Check that all nodes in S have at least k disjoint paths to each other. (e.g. each arrow show a disjoint paths between 3 and 5)
S={3,5,7}
a
(d): Add a new vertex a, connected to S, and Check that all nodes in V-S have at least k disjoint paths to a.(e.g.each arrow is a path between 4 and a)

at least k disjoint paths to each other (Figure 7-c). If all nodes in S have k disjoint paths to each other, the algorithm starts second phase and adds a dummy vertex a to graph G and connects it to all nodes in S. After that if each vertices in V/S has k disjoint paths to a the algorithms returns true otherwise it return false.

To pseudo code of this algorithm is as follows:

Algorithm: checkConnectivity (Graph G, k)

```
Begin
    //step 1: create and test S
    GR=createResidualGraph(G)
    for i=1 to k  do
        for j=i+1 to k  do
        begin
                c= Ford-Fulkerson( GR, G.V[i],G.V[j] )
                if c < k then
          return false
end
    G' = (G.V ∪ a, G.E)
    for i=1 to k  do
        connect (G'.V[i],a)
    GR=createResidualGraph( G' )
    for i=k+1 to |G.V|  do
    begin
            c= Ford-Fulkerson(GR, G'.V[i], a )
            if c < k then
        return false
    end
        return  true
End
```

It is mentioned before that the Ford-Fulkerson algorithm finds the disjoint path count between two vertices with $O(maxFlow \times n^2)$ time complexity. Here *maxFlow* is at most k and we have two nested for loops which call Ford-Fulkerson algorithm. Hence the time complexity of step one is $O(k^2 \times k \times n^2)=O(k^3n^2)$. Also the *for* loop in step 2 repeats at most n times and each time calls Ford-Fulkerson algorithm with $O(kn^2)$ complexity. Hence the time complexity of step 2 is $O(kn^3)$ and the total time complexity of algorithm is $O(kn^3+k^3n^2)$. If we suppose $k < \sqrt{n}$ then we have:

$$k < \sqrt{n} \rightarrow \quad k^2 < n \quad \rightarrow \quad k^3 < kn \quad \rightarrow \quad n^2k^3 < kn^3$$

Therefore for $k \leq \sqrt{n}$ the time complexity of algorithm is $O(kn^3)$. However this algorithm needs an initial value for k and it cannot find the connectivity value of the graph. Henzinger has proposed a faster algorithm for both k-connectivity detection and testing problems (Henzinger & Gabow, 2000).

This algorithm combines the ideas of Even's connectivity detection algorithm and Hao's *MinCut* set detection algorithm (Hao & Orlin,1994). To pseudo code of this algorithm is as follows:

Algorithm: FastKdetection (Graph G)

```
begin
    i=0;
    k=n-1;
    repeat
            i=i+1;
            k=min( k   , minCut(x_i ,G) , minCut( x_i  ,G^R )   );
    until i>k
end
```

In the above algorithm *minCut* function finds the minimum nodes set that their removal disconnect *x* from *G*. Hao's algorithm finds this set with $O(n^3)$ time complexity. In each *k*-connected network after checking at most *k* nodes the minimum possible *minCut* set is detected. Let $C=\{c_1,c_2,\ldots,c_k\}$ be the minimum node set that their removal divides the network. So $k=|C|$ and finding *C* is sufficient to find *k*. The *minCut* set of each $v \notin C$ is equal to *C*. Hence finding the *minCut* of at most *k*+1 nodes determines the members of *C*. In the above algorithm the maximum repeat count of loop is *k* and consequently the time complexity of algorithm is $O(kn^3)$.

Extending the above algorithm to check the connectivity of a network is very simple. We can send a new parameter ***k*** (the value that we want to check) to the algorithm and compare the detected *k* in each iteration of loop with ***k***. If all of the detected *k* values are greater than ***k*** the algorithm returns true, otherwise it returns false. To pseudo code of this algorithm is as follows:

Algorithm: FastKtest(G, **k**)

```
begin
    i=0;
    k=n-1
    repeat
            i=i+1
            k=min( k   , minCut(x_i ,G)  , minCut( x_i , G^R)   )
            if k >k then   return   false
   until i> k
   return true
 end
```

The time complexity of the above algorithm is $O(min(k,k)n^3)$.

Central algorithms cannot be directly implemented in a distributed system. To apply a central *k*-connectivity detection algorithm on a distributed system, we must collect all information about the topology of the network in a single node which needs huge amount of data transmission in the network. In the other hand, finding the exact value of *k* using local information in a distributed system is a hard task.

Distributed Algorithms

To solve *k*-connectivity problem in a distributed system, all nodes should be able to start a distributed algorithm and find the value of *k* using local information or some message exchanges with other nodes. Currently all proposed algorithms estimate *k* according to local information. Most of the *k*-connectivity detection and restoration algorithms have been proposed for WSN infrastructure. WSNs can be considered as special instances of complex adaptive systems (Yan, & Hong, 2010). A complex adaptive system is a collection of adaptive agents that have some processing capabilities and interact with environment or other agents to achieve their local or global goals. The sensor nodes in WSNs satisfy required conditions for agents in complex adaptive systems (Yan, & Hong, 2010). They have processing and sensing capabilities and can interact with environment or other motes to perform their duties. Generally most of the complex networks can be modeled as complex adaptive systems. Hence usually it is possible to apply the algorithms for WSNs to other complex networks with some modifications.

Three Localized Distributed Algorithms

Jorgic presented three localized distributed algorithms to estimate the *k*-connectivity in a given WSN (Jorgic, et. al., 2007). In these algorithms the value of *k* is estimated using local neighborhood information. In the first algorithm named LND[3], each node finds the number of its neighbors and broadcasts it to *p*-hop away where *p* can be 1, 2 or 3. Therefore, each node learns the degree of its *p*-hop neighbors and sets the *k* to the minimum visited degree. In the start of algorithm each node broadcast a *Hello* message to find its degree. After finding local *d* each node broadcasts the *d* for *p* hop away and updates *k* each time it receives lower value for *d* from other nodes. The LND algorithm is as follows:

Algorithm: LND

```
Begin
     Broadcast a Hello message
     Find d by counting the number of received Hello messages.
    Broadcast d to p-hop away by setting the message ttl to p
    Set k to the minimum of local d and received degrees from other nodes,
End.
```

In the LND algorithm each node broadcasts exactly one *Hello* message and at most *p-hop* degree messages. Hence the upper bound of the total broadcasted messages in the entire network is *n (1+p-hop)*. The value of *p-hop* determines the level of locality in the algorithm. Higher values for *p-hop* increase the accuracy of estimation but causes to transmit more messages in the network. If we consider *p*=3, the number of exchanged messages in the network can increase up to *4n* messages. Each message carries a single number indicating the degree of a node. The maximum possible value for degree in a graph is Δ so the size of each message is $\log_2\Delta$ bits. Therefore the total bits of exchanged messages in LND are $O(n\log_2\Delta)$ which make LND an applicable approach from performance perspective. But in term of correctness, LND is not a favorable approach. The value of *k* in any graph is at most equal to the minimum degree of the graph. Hence even if the minimum degree of the graph reaches to all nodes after *p-hop* broadcast, the probability of correct estimation is low. Generally most of the times k is smaller than d and the detected value by LND is generally higher than the real k. In Figure 1, for example, the minimum degree of the graph is 3 while k is 2.

The second proposed algorithm by Jorgic is Local Subgraph Connectivity Detection (LSCD). In this algorithm each node finds its one hop neighbor list, by broadcasting a *Hello* message. In the second phase, each node broadcasts its one hop neighbor list to *p-hop* away. In this way each node learns its *p-hop* local sub-graph. Finally the nodes find the connectivity value of this sub-graph using a central algorithm and accept the result as an estimation of global k. The pseudo code of LSCD algorithm is as follows:

Algorithm: LSCD

```
Begin
    Find one hop neighbor list by broadcasting Hello messages.
    Construct p-hop local subgraph G^p by exchanging one hope neighbor list.
    Run a central algorithm to find the connectivity value of G^p.
    Set k to the connectivity value of G^p.
End
```

In LSCD algorithms all nodes need to exchange one-hop neighbor lists. Each item in the neighbor list is identifier of a node and consumes $\log_2 n$ bits in the message. The maximum possible neighbor count for each node is Δ. Hence the maximum size of each message is $\Delta \log_2 n$. Considering n nodes in the network which send one hop lists for the first time, the total exchanged bits in the network is $\Delta \log_2 n$ bits. Each message is rebroadcasted by the neighbors of the sender, *p-hop* times. If we set $p = 3$, the total size of exchanged bits in the network will be $O(n\Delta^3 \log_2 n)$.

Figure 8 shows an example graph and the *2-hop* local subgraphs of each node in LSCD algorithm. In this figure the black nodes are root nodes that run the algorithm. The one hop neighbors of root nodes are shown with solid circles and two hop neighbors are distinguished by dashed circles. The correct k value in the initial graph is 2, but only two nodes find the correct value of k.

Except the local subgraphs of nodes 4 and 6, all other subgraphs include cut edges and central algorithm running on them find k=1. Nodes 4 and 6 find k=2 which is correct. Generally the probability of having a cut edge in local subgraph of each nodes is high and hence the nodes may find k=1 in their local subgraphs.

The third algorithm is Local Critical Node Detection (LCND) which is very similar to LSCD. This algorithm exchange the neighbor list information just like LSCD and create local subgraphs but try to finds cut vertices in the subgraph by removing the nodes one by one. The connectivity value of a graph that has a cut vertex is 1 and there is no need to call a central k detection algorithm in such a graph. If there is no cut vertex in subgraph then the local subgraph is 2-connected and node remove itself from graph and recall the cut vertex detection algorithm. If the resulting graph has no cut vertex then k is 3. This process continues until finding a cut vertex in the local subgraph. After removing each node from local subgraph the nodes increase k by one. Although this approach may provide a different detection method for k, but it still has same problems as LSCD and exchange large amount of messages in the network without providing a correct estimation for k.

Figure 8. An example graph and its 2-hop local subgraphs

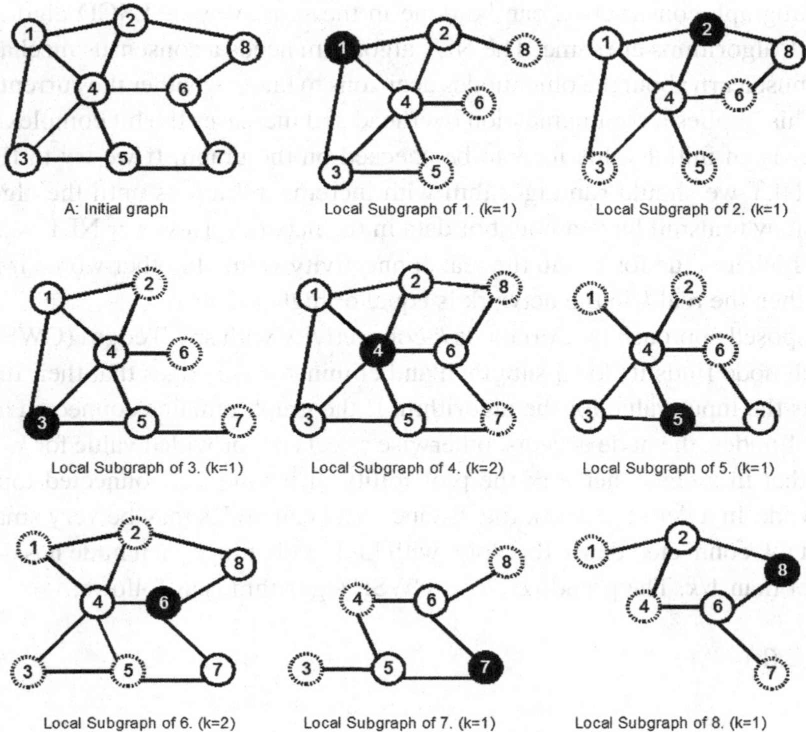

Safe Algorithms

Cornejo and Lynch provided two distributed algorithms for k-connectivity on unit disk graphs (Cornejo & Lynch, 2010) both algorithms are safe and need an initial value for k to test whether the topology of the network is at least k-connected. A safe algorithm never estimate higher values for k than the real connectivity value. The first algorithm is Natural Local Test (NLT) for k connectivity testing which is similar to LSCD algorithm. In NLT algorithm each node finds the local subgraph of the network and launches a central algorithm to accept or reject the provided k for the algorithm. If all nodes accept the given value, it is accepted as general k. The pseudo code of NLT algorithm is as follows:

Algorithm: Natural Local Test (k)

```
Begin
      Construct t hop local subgraph G' by exchanging one hop neighbor list.
      Run a central algorithm to find k(G'), the connectivity value of G'.
       if  k(G') < k   then
      accept
       else
      reject
End
```

In the above algorithm the network is considered as k-connected if all nodes accept the given value for k. The local subgraph construction can be done in the same way as LSCD algorithm and the bit complexity for both algorithms are same. The NLT algorithm needs a consensus mechanism among the nodes. All nodes must learn about the other nodes decisions to know whether the current k is accepted by all nodes or not. This implies a communication overhead and increases the bit complexity of algorithm. This algorithm needs an initial value for k to be checked on the graph. If we try to find an estimated value for k using NLT we should run algorithm with incremental inputs until the algorithm rejects a value for k which may transmit huge amount of data in the network. However NLT is a safe algorithm. It never estimates higher value for k than the real connectivity value. In other words if all nodes accept the input value x, then the real k in the network is equal or higher than x.

The second proposed approach by Cornejo is k-connectivity with small edges (CWSE) algorithm. In this algorithm each node finds its local subgraph and eliminates the edges that their distance is longer than $1/k$ where k is the input value for the algorithm. If the graph remains connected after elimination and has at least $k+1$ nodes, the node accepts, otherwise rejects the provided value for k. The idea behind this algorithm is that in a dense network the probability of having a k-connected topology is higher than a sparse network. In a dense network the distance between nodes may be very smaller than sparse network. Hence in a k-connected dense topology with high probability each node has a connected edge with length smaller than $1/k$. The pseudo code of CWSE algorithm is as follows:

Algorithm: CWSE (k)

```
Begin
       Construct t hop local subgraph G^t by exchanging one hope neighbor list.
       Remove all edges with length longer 1/k  from G^t.
      if  G^t is connected and N(G^t) > k+1 then
      accept
      else
      reject
End
```

Figure 9 shows an example network and the execution steps of CWSE algorithm in node 7. The 2-hop local subgraph of node 7 has been presented in Figure 9-b. After creating local subgraph all edges that are longer than $1/k$ must be removed from this graph. The resulting graph after removing these edges is Figure 9-c and the node 7 incorrectly rejects k=3. However for k=2 all nodes accept the given value because every node has at least one connected edge which its length is smaller than 0.5.

In the above algorithm $N(G^t)$ is the number of nodes in G^t. The bit complexity of this algorithm is exactly same as LSCD. Also just like the NLT, this algorithm needs consensus between nodes to flood all accept or reject decisions in the network. The algorithm is safe and never accepts a value higher than real k. It cannot find the connectivity value and needs an initial guess about the k to check the graph for that connectivity. Unlike the NLT or LSCD algorithms, CWSE uses two heuristics with lower time complexity instead of calling a central connectivity algorithm to decide about the given k, and this is the most important aspect which differs CWSE from previous algorithms.

Figure 9. The execution steps of CWSE in node 7 for k=3

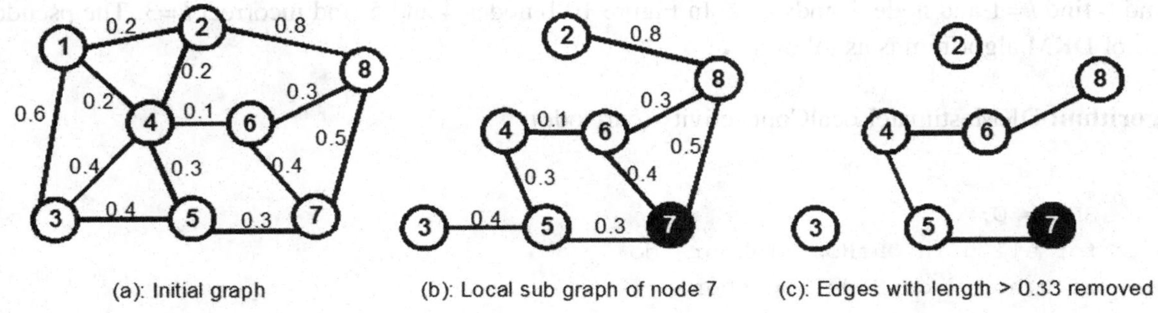

Distributed k-Connectivity Maintenance

Distributed *k*-Connectivity Maintenance (DKM) is another distributed algorithm which has two phases; detection and restoration (Szczytowski, et. al., 2012). In this algorithm each node estimates its disjoint path count to sink. This algorithm assumes that sink is a special reliable node which never stops working. If each node has *k* disjoint paths to sink then all nodes have *k* disjoint paths to each other and the network is *k*-connected. The hop count between sink and each other node is used to estimate the number of disjoint paths between sink and that node. To estimate the number of disjoint paths to sink all nodes find their Support Node Set (SNS). The support node set of node *v* is the set of one and two hop neighbors of *v* which are closer to sink. For example in Figure 10-a if we suppose the sink is node 0 then SNS(3)= {2,1}, SNS(4)=SNS(6)={3} and SNS(5)={4,6}. The support node set also includes the nodes that are in two hop neighbor list and connected by a node which have same hop number from the sink. For example, in Figure 10-b, SNS(5)={4,6,3} because node 6 has smaller hop value than node 5 and node 4 connected to node 3 with smaller hop value than node 5.

Figure 10. Two sample topologies

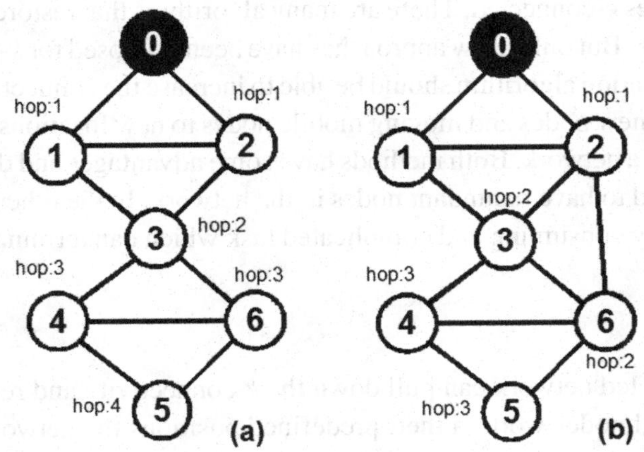

The size of *SNS*(*v*) is considered as local *k* estimation in node *v*. For example in Figure 10-a nodes 4 and 6 find *k*=1 and node 5 finds *k*=2. In Figure 10-b nodes 4 and 5 find incorrect *k*=3. The pseudo code of DKM algorithm is as follows:

Algorithm: DKMestimateLocalConnectivity (curNode)

```
Begin
     SNS = Ø;
     for all u in oneHopNeighbors do
     if u.hop < curNode.hop then
               SNS ← SNS ∪ u
          else if u.hop = curNode.hop then
               for all v  in twoHopNeighbors do
                    if v.hop < curNode.hop and v ∉ oneHopNeighbors then
                         SNS ← SNS ∪ v
               SNS ← SNS ∪ u
     return |SNS|
End
```

In the DKM algorithm each node must find and broadcast its one hop neighbor list. The one hop neighbor lists are rebroadcasted with other nodes one more time. Therefore we have $O(n\Delta^2\log_2 n)$ bit complexity. DKM provides an approximate value for the number of disjoint paths between each node and sink. It is quite possible that the algorithm overestimates or underestimates the disjoint path count.

THE *K*-CONNECTIVITY RESTORATION

Developing a strategy for connectivity restoration after or before a failure is one of the essential and unavoidable task in most of the networks. The connectivity restoration in a distributed system is the process of automatically detecting and resolving the connection lost between the nodes in the network. A *k*-connectivity restoration is the process of increasing or restoring the links in the network such that the resulting topology becomes *k*-connected. There are many algorithms that restore 1-connectivity between active nodes in the network. But only a few approaches have been proposed for *k*-connectivity restoration.

A *k*-connectivity restoration algorithm should be able to increase the connectivity of a network at least to *k*. Placing or activating new nodes and moving mobile nodes to new locations are two common way to restore the connectivity of a network. Both methods have some advantages and disadvantages. Placing or activating new nodes, need to have redundant nodes in the network. In the other hand, moving a node to a new position is an energy consuming and complicated task which can terminate some existence links.

Central Algorithm

Node failure in a *k*-connected network can pull down the *k*-connectivity and reduce the value of *k*. In a *k*-connected network, if all nodes work in their predefined positions the network remains *k*-connected. From another view if we only consider the location of nodes in a *k*-connected network, as long as we have working nodes in that locations the network is *k*-connected. Failure in some locations may not affect the connectivity value of the network but it is possible that a failure in a node which converts one of these locations to an empty slot reduce the value of *k*. So after each failure we have one of the following situations:

1. Remaining working nodes form a *k*-connected network.
2. Remaining working nodes do not form a *k*-connected network.

In case 1 we are lucky and the stopped node has no effect on connectivity value. In this case there is no need to do any restoration activity. In case 2 we should select and move a working node from its original location to the failed node location. Obviously we must select a node that its vacation does not affect the *k*-connectivity. We call the location of this node as safe location. Also to achieve the optimality we must select a node from a safe location which its moving consume lowest energy in the entire network. Wang (Wang et. al., 2011) proposed to use the maximum weighted matching algorithm on a bi-partite graph of active nodes and default locations of nodes to achieve an optimum solution. Let *P* be the set of default positions of all nodes, V be the set of all nodes, v_f be the failed node and p_f be the position of failed node. The Wang's algorithm first checks whether the resulting graphs $H=P/p_f$ is *k*-connected or not. If *H* is *k*-connected then the algorithm finishes immediately. Otherwise the algorithm removes one of the positions $p_i \in P$ from *P* and checks whether the resulting graph of P/p_i is *k*-connected and then runs a maximum weighted matching on a bi-partite graph of V/v_f and P/p_i. This process repeats for every $p_i \in P$ and finally the maximum weighted matching which produces a *k*-connected graph is selected as result. Obviously in selected matching the failed node position p_f has been matched with another position p_j which means that the node in p_j must moves to new location p_f. The weight of edges of bi-partite graph must have reverse relation with the cost of moving between locations.

This central algorithm provides an optimum solution for the *k*-restoration problem. The time complexity of the best central algorithm that can check the connectivity of a network with predefined candidate for *k* is $O(kn^3)$. Also the maximum weighted matching algorithm runs on $O((2n)^3)$ time complexity (we have $2n$ vertices in bi-partite graph). Hence each iteration of testing and matching has $O((2n)^3+kn^3)=O(kn^3)$ time complexity. Repeating this computation for all locations in the graph leads to $O(kn^4)$ time complexity for Wang's algorithm.

Distributed Algorithm

The only proposed distributed algorithm for *k*-connectivity restoration, that supports both detection and restoration phases is DKM. In the restoration phase, DKM algorithm increases the number of active resources in the nodes that estimate lower value for *k* than the desired connectivity. DKM assumes that there is unlimited number of resources (nodes) in the location of each node and every node can increase active resources to desired values to achieve the *k*-connectivity. In the restoration phase, the algorithm supposes that each node knows the desired value for *k*. Having this value, every node computes a *vote* value as follows:

$$vote = k_{desired} - k_{estimated}$$

Then each node v that has a positive *vote* sends this value to the nodes which are in $SNS(v)$. Each node in the network that receives at least one *vote* from their neighbors, calculates a response to the votes as follows:

$$responce.\ value = \sum_{i \in V} vote_i \quad responce.minVote = \min(vote_i)$$

$vote_i$ is the ith received vote by the node. In this way every node that receives some votes, collects them and broadcasts a response that includes the sum up of all votes and also the minimum received votes. After receiving response messages, node v selects node u which is the sender of biggest *response. value* and sends a *select* message to u. In this way, node u learns that it must activate at least $response_u$. *minVote* resources to increase the connectivity of at least one neighbor to k. The nodes that receive more than one *select* message for a *response,* just take into account one of them and ignore the others. In other words, if a node receives more than one *select* for a single *response* it just actives *minVote* number of its resources and waits for next *vote-response-select* cycle. The algorithm finishes if all nodes have at least k nodes in their support node set and do node broadcast any *vote*.

Algorithm: DKMresolveNode (curNode, $k_{desired}$)

```
begin
 k=estimateLocalConnectivity(curNode)
  while k < k_desired do
           vote = k_desired -k
           for all v in SNS do
                     sendVote(v, vote);
           responses= collectResponses( )
           maxResponse=0
           for each response r in  responses do
                 if r.sender.hop < curNode.hop and response.value > maxRe-
sponse then
                           maxResponse = response;
           sendSelection ( maxResponse.sender )
           k = estimateLocalConnectivity ( curNode )
end
```

In the above algorithm each node estimates a local value for k and repeats a while loop until the estimated k equals to desired k value. In the while loop a *vote* is calculated and sent to all nodes in SNS and *responses* are collected from them. Then the sender of highest *response* is selected and a *select* message is sent to that node. Finally the estimation process is called again to find the new connectivity value. To send appropriate response messages, each node runs the following algorithm.

Algorithm: voterResponce (curNode, k)

```
begin
votes = collectVotes( )
response.value=0
response.minVote = max
for all vote in votes do
begin
response.value += vote;
response.minVote = min(response.minVote, vote);
end
response.sender = curNode;
broadCastResponse(vote.sender, response)
s=collectSelections( maxDelay )
if |s|>0 then
   active more  response.minVote  resources
end
```

In the above algorithm each node collects votes and calculates the total and minimum received votes. Then a *response* message which includes the total and minimum of votes is broadcasted. After that the node waits for *maxDelay* time to receive select messages. If a *select* message arrives, the node activates more *minVote* resources. Activating these resources increases the number of connectivity of another node to *k*. This process continues until all nodes reaches to *k*-connectivity. The main drawback of restoration phase in DKM algorithm is the assumption about the unlimited number of resources in each node.

In another algorithm (Atay & Bayazit, 2010) introduced a new metric, named *k-redundancy*, which provides a criterion to identify critical parts of a network. The *k-redundancy* of node *v* is the minimum number of nodes that their removal disconnects two neighbors of *v*. This provides a measure to represent the importance of a node in keeping the connectivity of graph. With this definition the cut vertices in the topology are 0-redundant. It means that there are no supporting nodes for cut vertices in the network and if we lose a cut vertex the graph is divided to disconnected partitions. If we lose a 1-redundnunt node there is still one node that keeps the connectivity of all nodes in the network. In this way a 2-redundunt node has two supporting nodes and there is a reverse relation between redundancy value and the importance of node. With increasing the redundancy value of each node its importance from connectivity perspective decreases because the failure of that node can be easily tolerated by redundant nodes. Figure 11 shows a sample graph and the *k*-redundancy value of each node.

The authors provide two approaches, to maintain and repair the connectivity using *k*-redundancy information. The proposed methods do not support *k*-connectivity detection and restoration and only restore a disconnected network to 1-connected form. However using *k*-redundancy as a metric of importance of a node in connectivity is another application of *k*-connectivity which shows the importance of this issue in the networks.

Figure 11. k-redundancy of nodes in a sample graph

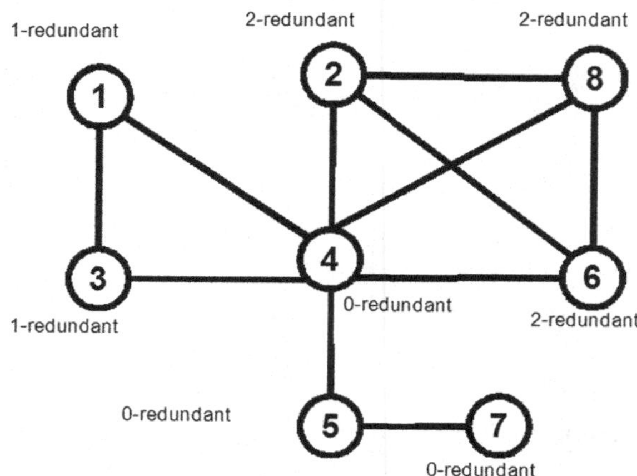

CONCLUSION

The k-connectivity is an appropriate property to measure the connectivity robustness of any network. Especially in complex networks that the intermediate nodes are used to deliver the packets, 1-connectivity put the network in high disconnection risk. In this chapter the proposed central and distributed algorithms for both k-connectivity detection and k-connectivity restoration were discussed. Generally the central algorithms use network flow algorithm to find the connectivity value. Currently the best central algorithm can find the value of k with $O(kn^3)$ time complexity. Distributed algorithms try to estimate the value of k using some local information such as nodes degree or one hop and two hop neighbor lists. Generally these estimations are not equal to the real k value.

To restore the connectivity of a network to a desired level of k, there are two major approaches: moving other active nodes and placing new nodes in the network. Adding new nodes is not possible in all environments. Moving active nodes is a very complicated task which can produce new link failure in the graph. There is a central algorithm which uses maximum matching algorithm to determine the best moving for optimal result. The time complexity of this algorithm is $O(kn^4)$. A distributed algorithm named DKM estimates the current value of k in the network and increases it to desired value by activating more resources in each node.

The main drawback of central algorithms is the need of gathering the entire topology in a single node which needs huge amount of data exchange in large networks. On the other hand distributed algorithms can only estimate the connectivity value of the network using local information.

ACKNOWLEDGMENT

Authors would like to thank to TUBITAK (The Scientific and Technological Research Council of Turkey) for supporting this study with ARDEB project number 113E470.

REFERENCES

Atay, N., & Bayazit, B. (2010). Mobile wireless sensor network connectivity repair with *k*-redundancy. *Algorithmic Foundation of Robotics*, *8*, 35–49.

Bai, X., Xuan, D., Yun, Z., Lai, T. H., & Jia, W. (2008). Complete optimal deployment patterns for full-coverage and *k*-connectivity ($k \leq 6$) wireless sensor networks. *Proceedings of the 9th ACM international symposium on Mobile ad hoc networking and computing* (pp. 401-410). ACM.

Bettstetter, C. (2002). On the minimum node degree and connectivity of a wireless multihop network. *Proceedings of the 3rd ACM international symposium on Mobile ad hoc networking & computing* (pp. 80-91). ACM. doi:10.1145/513800.513811

Cornejo, A., & Lynch, N. (2010). *Fault-tolerance through k-connectivity*. Workshop on Network Science and Systems Issues in Multi-Robot Autonomy.

Curia, V., Tropea, M., Fazio, P., & Marano, S. (2014). Complex networks: Study and performance evaluation with hybrid model for Wireless Sensor Networks. *IEEE 27th Canadian Conference on Electrical and Computer Engineering* (CCECE), (pp. 1-5). IEEE.

Dagdeviren, O., & Akram, V. K. (2014). An Energy-Efficient Distributed Cut Vertex Detection Algorithm for Wireless Sensor Networks. *The Computer Journal*, *57*(12), 1852–1869. doi:10.1093/comjnl/bxt128

Erdos, P., & R&WI, A. (1959). On random graphs I. *Publ. Math. Debrecen*, *6*, 290–297.

Even, S. (1975). An algorithm for determining whether the connectivity of a graph is at least *k*. *SIAM Journal on Computing*, *4*(3), 393–396. doi:10.1137/0204034

Even, S., & Tarjan, R. E. (1975). Network flow and testing graph connectivity. *SIAM Journal on Computing*, *4*(4), 507–518. doi:10.1137/0204043

Galil, Z. (1980). Finding the vertex connectivity of graphs. *SIAM Journal on Computing*, *9*(1), 197–199. doi:10.1137/0209016

Guidoni, D. L., Mini, R. A., & Loureiro, A. A. (2008). Creating small-world models in wireless sensor networks. *IEEE 19th International Symposium on Personal, Indoor and Mobile Radio Communications. PIMRC 2008* (pp. 1-6). IEEE. doi:10.1109/PIMRC.2008.4699823

Henzinger, M. R., Rao, S., & Gabow, H. N. (2000). Computing vertex connectivity: New bounds from old techniques. *Journal of Algorithms*, *34*(2), 222–250. doi:10.1006/jagm.1999.1055

Jorgic, M., Goel, N., Kalaichevan, K. A. L. A. I., Nayak, A., & Stojmenovic, I. (2007). Localized detection of *k*-connectivity in wireless ad hoc, actuator and sensor networks. *Proceedings of 16th International Conference on Computer Communications and Networks, ICCCN 2007* (pp. 33-38). IEEE. doi:10.1109/ICCCN.2007.4317793

Ling, Q., & Tian, Z. (2007). Minimum node degree and *k*-connectivity of a wireless multihop network in bounded area. *IEEE Global Telecommunications Conference. GLOBECOM'07* (pp. 1296-1301). IEEE. doi:10.1109/GLOCOM.2007.249

Luo, X. U., & Yu, H. (2010). Constructing wireless sensor network model based on small world concept. *3rd International Conference on Advanced Computer Theory and Engineering (ICACTE)*, (Vol. 5, pp. V5-501). IEEE.

Newman, M. E. (2003). The structure and function of complex networks. *SIAM Review*, *45*(2), 167–256. doi:10.1137/S003614450342480

Reif, J. H., & Spirakis, P. G. (1985). *k*-connectivity in random undirected graphs. *Discrete Mathematics*, *54*(2), 181–191. doi:10.1016/0012-365X(85)90079-2

Szczytowski, P., Khelil, A., & Suri, N. (2012). *DKM: Distributed k-connectivity maintenance. In Wireless On-demand Network Systems and Services (WONS)* (pp. 83–90). IEEE.

Tarjan, R. (1972). Depth-first search and linear graph algorithms. *SIAM Journal on Computing*, *1*(2), 146–160. doi:10.1137/0201010

Wang, S., Mao, X., Tang, S. J., Li, M., Zhao, J., & Dai, G. (2011). On "Movement-Assisted Connectivity Restoration in Wireless Sensor and Actor Networks". *IEEE Transactions on Parallel and Distributed Systems*, *22*(4), 687–694. doi:10.1109/TPDS.2010.102

Xing, X. Wang, G., Wu, J., & Li, J. (2009). Square region-based coverage and connectivity probability model in wireless sensor networks. *5th International Conference on Collaborative Computing: Networking, Applications and Worksharing*, (CollaborateCom 2009) (pp. 1-8). IEEE.

Yan, C., & Ji-Hong, Q. (2010). Application analysis of complex adaptive systems for WSN. *International Conference on Computer Application and System Modeling (ICCASM 2010)* (Vol. 7).

Zhao, J. (2014). Minimum node degree and *k*-connectivity in wireless networks with unreliable links. *IEEE International Symposium on Information Theory (ISIT)*, (pp. 246-250). IEEE. doi:10.1109/ISIT.2014.6874832

Zhao, J., Yagan, O., & Gligor, V. (2014). *Results on vertex degree and k-connectivity in uniform s-intersection graphs*. Technical Report CMU-CyLab-14-004. CyLab, Carnegie Mellon University.

KEY TERMS AND DEFINITIONS

Cut Vertex: A vertex which its removing divides the graph to at least two disconnected parts.

Degree: Number of connected links to a node.

Disjoint Paths: A set of paths between two arbitrary nodes that do not share any common vertex.

***k*-Connected Network:** A *k*-connected network remains connected if *k*-1 arbitrary nodes stop working.

***k*-Connectivity Detection:** Finding the current value of *k* in a network.

Min Cut Set: Minimum set of nodes that their removal divides the graph to disconnected parts.

Restoration: Reconnecting the separated parts in the network or increasing the number of disjoint paths between nodes to a specific value.

ENDNOTES

1 Depth-First Search
2 Breadth-First search
3 Local Neighborhood Detection

Chapter 3
Link Prediction in Complex Networks

Manisha Pujari
Université Paris 13, France

Rushed Kanawati
Université Paris 13, France

ABSTRACT

This chapter presents the problem of link prediction in complex networks. It provides general description, formal definition of the problem and applications. It gives a state-of-art of various existing link prediction approaches concentrating more on topological approaches. It presents the main challenges of link prediction task in real networks. There is description of our new link prediction approach based on supervised rank aggregation and our attempts to deal with two of the challenges to improve the prediction results. One approach is to extend the set of attributes describing an example (pair of nodes) calculated in a multiplex network that includes the target network. Multiplex networks have a layered structure, each layer having different kinds of links between same sets of nodes. The second way is to use community information for sampling of examples to deal with the problem of class imbalance. All experiments have been conducted on real networks extracted from well-known DBLP bibliographic database.

1. INTRODUCTION

Link prediction has attracted the attention of many researchers from different research fields. It consists of estimating the likelihood of existence or appearance of an edge between two unlinked nodes, based on observed links and attributes that contain information about the nodes, edges or the entire graph. It has important applications in many fields including social, biological and information systems etc. Link prediction has been widely used in biological networks like protein interaction network, metabolic networks, food web. It is used for finding missing links and thereby helps in reducing the experimental cost if the predictions are accurate. In social interaction and academic or commercial collaboration networks they can play an important role to predict new associations (new edges). This further has utility in recommendation task: a service provided by almost all social networks and majorly used in e-commerce

DOI: 10.4018/978-1-4666-9964-9.ch003

sites. Link prediction can also be helpful in finding hidden links in criminal networks, which is another critical field of research. Link prediction can be basically of two types: structural and temporal.

- Structural link prediction refers to the problem of finding missing or hidden links which probably exist in a network (Liben-Nowell & Kleinberg, 2007; Menon & Eklan, 2011; Taskar et al., 2003; Yin et al., 2011). It focuses on inferring the existence of links that are not directly visible, by using observable data of the network. It has direct application to find unobserved patterns of genes, protein interactions for the medical studies on various diseases like cancer, HIV, Alzheimer etc. (Airoldi et al., 2006; Eronen & Toivonen, 2012). It can also help to find existing criminal links which often remain hidden in a network (Clauset et al., 2008; Fire et al., 2013).
- Temporal link prediction refers to the problem of finding new links by studying the temporal history of a network (Benchettara, Kanawati, & Rouveirol, 2010; Hasan, Chaoji, Salem, & Zaki, 2006; Berlingerio et al., 2009; Hasan et al., 2006; Huang & Lin, 2008; Liben-Nowell & Kleinberg, 2007). So here we have information about the network till time t and the goal will be to predict a new link that may appear at some point of time in future say t+k. It has its application primarily in recommendation systems that are being used widely in e-commerce websites for product recommendations, in any search engines to help users with probably relevant terms they might be searching, for recommendation of tags in social resources sharing websites like Flickr[1], YouTube[2], De.li.ci.ous[3] etc. and very commonly used for recommendation of friends in many social networks like Facebook[4] and Twitter[5]. It has another significant use in predicting future collaborations between researchers for academic purposes (Benchettara et al., 2010a,b; Kunegis et al., 2010).

Rest of this chapter continues as follows. In section 2, there is a formal description of the problem of link prediction. Details about different evaluation methods for link prediction approaches is given in section 3. Section 4, has a detailed description of various link prediction approaches focusing mainly on topological and temporal link prediction methods. Section 5 summarizes some important challenges in link prediction especially faced by supervised classification based models. Section 6 presents details of our work in the field of link prediction. Section 7 concludes the chapter.

2. PROBLEM DESCRIPTION AND NOTATIONS

The problem of prediction of new links (or simply called link prediction problem) refers to a question of inferring the formation of links at a future time, by studying the history of appearance or disappearance of links in a network over a period of time. In topology based link prediction approaches, only structural properties of the network are used to implement learning methods and to find a model that will be used to predict links.

For prediction of new links at a certain point of time t_{n+1} having network information till time t_n, the network can be presented as a sequence of graphs representing different snapshots of the network at different points of time $\langle t_0,\ t_1,\ \ldots,\ t_n \rangle$. Suppose the temporal sequence of graphs $G = \langle G_0, G_1, \ldots, G_n \rangle$ each having their own sets of nodes and edges. The network can also be represented as a graph $G = \langle V, E \rangle$ such that $V = \bigcup_{i=0}^{n} V_i$ and $E = \bigcup_{i=0}^{n} E_i$. The goal of a link prediction approach is to find the likelihood of appearance of an edge between any two nodes u and v at a point of time t_{n+1} or t_{n+k}, k being any inte-

Table 1. Confusion matrix for link prediction

	Predicted Positive	Predicted Negative
Positive	True Positive (TP)	False Negative (FN)
Negative	False Positive (FP)	True Negative (TN)

ger to decide the duration of time for prediction, with conditions that $u,v \in V$ and $(u,v) \notin E$. This is equivalent to finding linking structure of graph G_{n+1} or G_{n+k} assuming that they contain same nodes that have already appeared in any of the graphs during the observation time period i.e. between t_0 and t_n.

Most of traditional link prediction approaches formulate the problem either as label propagation problem where existent and non-existent links are labelled as positive and negative respectively or as a problem of existence probability estimation, where links predicted to be existent can have higher existence probabilities (Zhang & Philip, 2014). Conventionally, if represented in terms of machine learning, a true positive case will be one where a link is classified or predicted as positive and it is actually positive. Same is for false positive case and so on. Table 1 presents this better.

A link prediction approach can provide either an ordered list of all unobserved and possible links (node pairs) or a score/probability of appearance for each unobserved and possible links. This output is finally used to evaluate the performance of the approach. Different ways for evaluation of link prediction approach is provided next.

3. EVALUATION

As mentioned above, most of the topological link prediction approaches provide, as output, either ranks of or scores for unlinked pairs of nodes in the concerned network. Out of this, pairs with top-k ranks or top-k highest scores will be considered as predicted new links. Alternatively, a binary classification like way can be used to label each pair as positive or negative. Many evaluation metrics can be applied on the outputs to measure the performance of an approach. Below is the list of metrics that can be used for such a purpose.

- **Accuracy:** Accuracy can be defined as the number of correctly predicted labels in the test network out of total numbers of possible instances of unobserved links.

$$Accuracy = \frac{TP + TN}{TP + TN + FP + FN}$$

- **Precision:** Precision is defined as the proportion of correctly predicted links out of total number predictions made.

$$Precision = \frac{TP}{TP + FP}$$

Alternatively where top-k ranks or scores are used as predicted links, the formula becomes:

$$Precision_k = \frac{TP}{k}$$

- **Recall:** Recall is defined as the proportion of correctly predicted links out of total number of actual new links:

$$Recall = \frac{TP}{TP + FN}$$

- **F1-Measure:** F1-measure is defined by the harmonic mean of both precision and recall. Formally it is given by:

$$F1 = \frac{2 * Precision * Recall}{Precision + Recall}$$

All these above mentioned methods use a fixed threshold (k) to calculate the performance that may not be necessarily available or be the most optimal one. It may be domain dependent and can show a wrongly quantified low or high performance if not selected correctly. To deal with such cases threshold curve based metrics can be used. They have mostly been used in binary classification task to show results. They are especially useful when class distribution is highly imbalanced. Below is the list of such metrics.

- **ROC Curves:** ROC curves are generated by plotting the true positive rate (TPR) against the false positive rate (FPR). It depicts the level of separation between two distributions, one corresponding to the true negatives, and the other corresponding to the true positives, given the scores from a classifier. Formally, $TPR = \frac{TP}{TP + FN}$ and $FPR = \frac{TP}{TN + FP}$

Area under ROC curve (AUC) is equivalent to the probability of a randomly selected positive instance appearing above a randomly selected negative instance (in terms of scores or ranks). Having a ranked list of all unobserved links (unlinked node pairs), if n independent comparisons are made, of which n_{high} times a true positive has higher score (or rank) and n_{same} times it has the same score (or rank) as the corresponding false positive one, then the AUC can also be computed as suggested in (Lü & Zhou, 2011)

$$AUC = \frac{n_{high} + 0.5 * n_{same}}{n}$$

Larger AUC correspond to better classification results. A value of 0.5 represents pure chance for an identical and independent distribution in a balanced dataset and hence the degree to which the value exceeds 0.5 shows how better a link prediction algorithm is.

- **Precision-Recall Curves:** In precision-recall (PR) curves, each point corresponds to a precision and recall value at different score (or rank) threshold. The x-axis is recall and y-axis is precision. Area under PR curve can also be used for the same purpose as AUC i.e. for evaluating a link prediction algorithm. A higher value shows better performance of a model. These curves can give a more discriminative view of performance of different models in presence of extreme class imbalance. Link prediction is such a case as we can have very few numbers of positive instances as compared to negative instances; hence they have a great utility in evaluating different link prediction algorithms.

The major difference between the two curves is that, a PR curve does not account for true negatives and thus is not very much affected by the relative imbalance in class, whereas ROC's measure of TPR and FPR will reflect the influence of heavy class imbalance since the number of negative examples dwarfs the number of positive examples. So in such scenarios, PR curves are much better in illustrating the difference between performances of algorithms especially for predicting true positive instances (minority class in context of link prediction). ROC and AUC will show a very small difference between algorithms. If a model needs to perform equally well on positive and negative classes then ROC is more preferable (Davis & Goadrich, 2006). A very good analysis on efficient methods to be used for evaluating link prediction approaches is provided in (Lichtenwalter & Chawla, 2012).

4. LINK PREDICTION APPROACHES

Many link prediction approaches have been proposed in recent years. Some of them use node features or node attributes and some use only the structural information of the graph. The former are known as node-features based approaches while the later are known as topological approaches. A few of the approaches may use both node-feature information and structural information. Such approaches may be termed as hybrid approaches.

In node-features based approaches, one has extra content information regarding the properties or characteristics of nodes. For example in protein interaction graphs, sometimes the features describing the biological properties of proteins are also available. This extra information can be helpful in predicting links between nodes by finding similarities between unlinked nodes. Topological approaches refer to those, which involve only exploitation of network structure. They are based on computing the linking probability for pairs of unlinked nodes based on only the graphical features of the network. They observe how the connections have been established between nodes and how they change over time. Based on former they try to predict a missing link or based on the later they predict a new link. Additional node features are more useful when the network graph is very sparsely connected and not much can be learned from graph topology. But content-based approaches necessarily need the presence of content description of the data. Whereas, topological approaches are efficient in the absence of content or feature information and are more generic in nature. Both have their own utility and at times a combination of both can come out to give a very good predictor. These kinds of approaches can be termed as hybrid approaches. In this paper, we are more focused on studying and developing topological link prediction approaches due to their generic nature.

There can be various ways of categorizing topological approaches. They can be categorized as *temporal* or *non-temporal/static* based on the fact that whether they take into consideration the dynamic aspect of the network or not. Another way to categorize them can be as *dyadic*, *community/subgraph based*, or *global* approaches based on level at which scores or probabilities are computed. The ones in which scores are locally computed for a pair of unlinked nodes are dyadic approaches. When the same is done in a community or subgraph, the approach can be a community/subgraph-based approach. And when the entire graph is taken into account for computing the scores it is a global approach. They can also be classified as *unsupervised*, *supervised* and *semi-supervised*, based on the kind of model learning method used. Unsupervised approaches involve ranking of unlinked node pairs based on some topological attribute scores. They do not necessarily need learning of a model to do prediction and hence do not really need labelled data. However, in link prediction ground truth about the network structure is available most of the time and so supervised methods can be easily implemented. Supervised approaches generate a model using many topological scores for unlinked node pairs and the available ground truth about structure of a network, to predict new links. Also there exist few approaches that use semi-supervised methods of learning where a model is generated by using partially labelled training data. In the sections below, we describe some of the prominent unsupervised, supervised and semi-supervised approaches.

4.1. Unsupervised Approaches

There are many unsupervised dyadic methods for predicting links where link scores are computed for unlinked node pairs based on the network structure. These scores represent some kind of similarities between two nodes that can indicate the possibility of having a link.

A seminal work on link prediction is the work of Liben-Nowell and Kleinberg (2007). They analyse co-authorship networks. Authors have shown that simple topological features representing relationships between pairs of unlinked nodes can be used for predicting formation of new links. They experimented with many different types of topological features or attributes to characterize unlinked node pairs, mostly concentrating on proximity based attributes. They rank unlinked node pairs by different attribute values and compute their individual performance in link prediction task by considering the top-k ranked node pairs as the predicted links.

Let's consider the case of applying numbers of common neighbours as a topological attribute. Common-neighbours index counts the numbers of nodes (i.e. neighbours) that are directly connected to both the nodes under observation. Formally it is given by:

$$CN(x,y) = \mid \Gamma(x) \cap \Gamma(y) \mid$$

Now let L be the list of unlinked node pairs. We have $L = \{(x,y) : x, y \in V \wedge (x,y) \notin E\}$. Common neighbour score for x and y can be represented by *CN(x,y)* and is computed as defined above. The list *L* is then sorted according to the values obtained by applying the common neighbors function to unlinked node pairs. The top k node pairs are then returned as the output of the prediction task. The assumption here is that, the more a pair of unlinked nodes share common neighbours, the more they are likely to have a link in the future. In Liben-Nowell and Kleinberg (2007), k is equal to the number of really appearing new links. This proximity or similarity between two unlinked nodes can be computed using many other types of topological features. In the following subsections, we describe some of the topological similarity metrics.

4.1.1. Neighbourhood Based Features

Many of the link prediction approaches are based on the idea that two nodes are similar and more likely to form a link in the future if they are connected to same or similar neighbours. That means their sets of neighbours have large overlap. Apart from common neighbours, there are many other measures based on local neighbourhood of the nodes. These are listed below.

- **Jaccard Coefficient:** Jaccard coefficient calculates the ratio of number of common neighbours to that of the total number of neighbours of the two nodes (Jaccard, 1901). Here they normalize the similarity score computed by common neighbours by dividing it with total number of neighbours of the two concerned nodes. This coefficient is defined as below:

$$JC(x,y) = \frac{|\Gamma(x) \cap \Gamma(y)|}{|\Gamma(x) \cup \Gamma(y)|}$$

- **Adamic Adar Coefficient:** This index was proposed by L. Adamic and E. Adar to compute similarity between two web pages (Adamic & Adar, 2003). For two web pages x and y, sharing a set of features z, this index is computed as:

$$AA(x,y) = \sum_{z \in F(x) \cap F(y)} \frac{1}{\log(frequency(z))}$$

where $F(x)$ denotes the set of features of x.

In a general sense it is a meta-measure that can be calculated for any two nodes in a network and for a variety of topological features. In the context of link prediction it was used by Liben-Nowell using common neighbours as a topological feature (Liben-Nowell & Kleinberg, 2007). This metric proposes to weight the common neighbours based on their connectivity while computing the score. It gives more weight to less connected neighbours increasing their contribution in the score. Formally it can be presented as:

$$AA(x,y) = \sum_{z \in \Gamma(x) \cap \Gamma(y)} \frac{1}{\log(|\Gamma(z)|)}$$

- **Resource Allocation:** This metric is based on resource allocation dynamics on complex networks (Ou et al., 2007). Like Adamic-Adar coefficient, this index also depresses the contribution of high-degree common neighbours. It is formally given as:

$$RA(x,y) = \sum_{z \in \Gamma(x) \cap \Gamma(y)} \frac{1}{|\Gamma(z)|}$$

- **Neighbour's Clustering Coefficient:** This metric computes the clustering coefficient for the common neighbours of any two nodes, which can then be aggregated using any functions like average, maximum, minimum etc. The assumption here is that, if the common neighbours of two unlinked nodes have a high clustering coefficient, it can imply a greater linking probability between the two nodes. A way of computing the coefficient is the following:

$$NCF(x,y)=\frac{\sum_{z\in\Gamma(x)\cap\Gamma(y)} Cc(z)}{|\Gamma(x)\cap\Gamma(y)|}$$

where $Cc(z)$ is the local transitivity or clustering coefficient of the node z. Such a measure has been used in a Naive Bayes based link prediction models as the conditional probability of having a pair of node linked (Liu et al., 2011; Tan et al., 2014).

4.1.2. Path Based Features

Path based features may use the lengths of path or the time required to cover those paths to reach from one node to another. The basic idea is that two nodes can be similar if they have less distance between them. There are two major categories in this: distance based features and random walk based features.

4.1.2.1. Distance Based

These features are mostly based on shortest paths or paths of specific lengths. They make use of either number or lengths of shortest paths to find the proximity of between two nodes.

- **Shortest Path Length:** It is equal to the number of edges in the shortest path between x and y in G. It is also known as the geodesic distance between nodes. More is the distance, lesser is the similarity between the nodes and also the chance of having a link between them.
- **Katz's Index:** This metric sums over a collection of paths and is exponentially damped by length to give shorter paths more weights (Katz, 1953). Mathematically it is defined as follows:

$$Katz(x,y)=\sum_{l=2}^{\infty}\beta^{l}x\mid path^{l}_{x,y}\mid$$

where *x* is the number of paths between *x* and *y* of length *l* and β<<1 is a positive parameter (i.e. damping factor) having value between (0, 1), which favours shortest paths. The same can be presented using adjacency matrix as:

$$Katz(x,y)=\sum_{i=1}^{\infty}\beta^{i}A^{i}[x,y]$$

where *A* is the binary adjacency matrix. Recall that A^i gives for a graph the number of paths of length I between any couple of nodes. A very small β leads to a score close to number of common neighbours because long paths contribute very little. So the matrix showing Katz score between all pairs of nodes can be found as: $K=(I-\beta A)^{-1}-I$.

β must be lower than the reciprocal of the largest eigenvalue of matrix A to ensure the convergence of above given equations demonstrated in (Lü & Zhou, 2011). The computational complexity of this measure in $O(N^3)$, due to which, sometimes it becomes difficult to use Katz coefficient especially in large networks. In such cases one can chose to stop after a certain length l_{max}. This is known as truncated Katz coefficient (Lü & Zhou, 2011) and is computed as:

$$TKatz(x,y)=\sum_{l=1}^{l_{\max}} \beta^l \mid path_{x,y}^l \mid.$$

In most cases l_{max} is set to 2 or 3 making the computation of this score much easier than the original Katz index.

4.1.2.2. Random Walk Based

These methods use paths of any length randomly chosen while traveling from one node to another.

- **Matrix Forest Index:** Matrix forest index computes the similarity between two nodes as the ratio of number of spanning rooted forests such that the two nodes belong to the same tree rooted at one of the nodes of all the spanning rooted forests of the network. It can be computed as $M=(I-L)^{-1}$, I being the identity matrix and L the Laplacian matrix of the network. (Chebotarev & Shamis, 1997).
- **Hitting Time and Commute Time:** Hitting time computes the time required by a random walker to go from node x to node y in a graph. It is defined as the expected number of steps required for a random walker to walk from one node to another. Shorter hitting time denotes nodes are similar. As this metric is not symmetrical, often for undirected graphs, average commute time is used instead. If $HT(x,y)$ is the hitting time to reach node y from node x, average commute time is given by:

$$CT(x,y)=HT(x,y)+HT(y,x)$$

A negated value of hitting or commute time can be used as a score for predicting links. A major disadvantage of using these measures is their sensitive dependence on parts of graph far away from nodes x and y even when x and y are connected by very short paths.

- **Rooted Pagerank:** PageRank denotes the importance of a node by summing up the importance of all other nodes linked to it. This feature can be altered to find a similarity score between two nodes and is termed as *rooted PageRank* in Liben-Nowell and Kleinberg (2007). The similarity between two nodes x and y is measured as the stationary probability of y in a random walk that returns to x with probability $1-\alpha$ in each step, moving to a random neighbor with probability α. Rooted PagerRank for all node pairs can be computed as follows:

$RPR = (1 - \alpha)(1 - \alpha N)^{-1}$

where $N=DA^{-1}$ is adjacency matrix with row sums normalized to 1 and D is the diagonal degree matrix.

- **PropFlow:** PropFlow captures the probability that a restricted random walk starting from one node x ends at another node y in l or less steps using link weights as the transition probabilities. The restriction is that a walk terminates on reaching y or on revisiting any node including x. The walk selects links based on their weights that produces a score to estimate likelihood of new links. This measure is a more localized measure of propagation and is insensitive to topological noise far from the source node (Lichtenwalter et al., 2010).

4.1.2.3. Aggregation of Node Topological Features

This category advocates the idea that two nodes can be similar if they have similar topological features. The individual node features can thus be aggregated to use them for link prediction. Various ways of aggregation can be used starting from simple min, max, sum and product to more complex ones. *Preferential attachment* is a very well-known metric that combines the degrees of the two nodes and was used in the context of analysing scaling in random networks (Barabasi & Albert, 1999). The work proposes that the probability of appearance of a new link is directly proportional to the degree of the observed nodes. It is computed as: $PA(x,y)=|k_x x k_y|$

For a simple undirected and unweighted graph the degree of a node is equal to the number of neighbours i.e. $k_x = |\Gamma(x)|$. Similarly many other aggregation-based measures that can be used for link prediction can be used such as:

- **Sum of Neighbours:** In the work of (Hasan, Chaoji, Salem, & Zaki, 2006), the authors have used sum of neighbours as a topological feature for characterizing unlinked node pairs. Formally, it can be defined as:

$$Sum_{CN}(x,y)=|\Gamma(x)|+|\Gamma(y)|$$

It represents the social connectivity of the nodes. It advocates the fact that the more connected two nodes are, the more will be their likelihood of forming new links.

4.2. Supervised Approaches

The ground truth about the existence or absence of links is almost always available from the history of the network that makes it suitable to be used with supervised algorithms. Also supervised algorithms are able to capture important inter-dependency relationships between topological properties (Lichtenwalter et al., 2010).

4.2.1. Supervised Machine Learning Approaches

Many of link prediction approaches attempt to combine the effects of individual topological metrics in order to enhance the overall prediction performance. Most of these works involve the application of Machine Learning algorithms. In machine learning language, the unlinked pairs of nodes are called examples or instances.

If the time aspect of the network is to be considered, then the examples can be generated as follows. Let $G = \langle G_0, G_1, \ldots, G_n \rangle$ be a temporal sequence of an evolving network. The whole sequence is divided into two parts: training and testing. Each part is then again divided into two sub-sequences one for generation of examples and another for labelling those examples. Thus, in training we shall have learning and labelling phases resulting in graphs namely G_{learn} and G_{label} generated by making union of the temporal sequences of the graphs for the corresponding time slots. The training data is constructed as follows. An example for learning is a couple of nodes (x,y) that are not linked in G_{learn} but both belonging to the same connected component. The class is obtained by checking whether the nodes are indeed connected in G_{label}. If such a connection exists then it will be a positive example and if no connection exists, it will be a negative example. These examples are also characterized by a given number of topological attributes computed on learning (or test) graphs. Figure 1 illustrates the process diagrammatically.

The first approach we studied converts the problem of link prediction into a binary classification problem where examples are unlinked node pairs and are characterized by a vector of topological attribute values (Hasan, Chaoji, Salem, & Zaki, 2006). Having a graph for generation of examples and computation of topological attributes and one for labelling as described before, we can construct set of instances to be fed to any classification algorithm to generate a model that can further be used to classify test instances with same attributes.

The work of Benchettara, Kanawati, and Rouveirol (2010) is a temporal approach for link prediction based on Decision tree algorithm with boosting. In this approach evolution of the network is also taken into account. Their work is mostly based on bipartite graphs and they introduce the concept of indirect topological measures computed using the projected graphs. For a bipartite graph $G = \langle V_1, V_2, E_{bip} \rangle$, the projected graphs will be $G_1 = \langle V_1, E_1 \rangle$ and $G_2 = \langle V_2, E_2 \rangle$. For any topological attribute $X(i,j)$, if it is directly computed on G_1 for any two nodes $i,j \in V_1$, it becomes a direct attribute for projected graph G_1 and we represent it as $X_{G_1}(i,j)$. The associated indirect attribute is computed on other projected graph G_2 as:

$$X_{indirect}(i,j) = f_{x \in \Gamma_G(i), y \in \Gamma_G(j)} X_{G_2}(i,j)$$

f is some aggregate function like min, max, average etc. and $x,y \in V_2$. Authors show how the use of indirect attribute greatly affects the final prediction result in a positive way.

Another work that uses supervised machine learning for classifying unlinked node pairs to predict missing links is the work proposed in (Fire, et al., 2011). In this paper, authors propose a set of simple and computationally efficient topological features to be used for link prediction in various social networks. They use various neighbourhood based features and their variants, edge subgraph features and shortest

Figure 1. Creation of examples/instances for supervised machine learning: (a) division of time for learning, labeling, and testing; (b) construction of labeling and learning graphs; (c) generation of examples from graphs

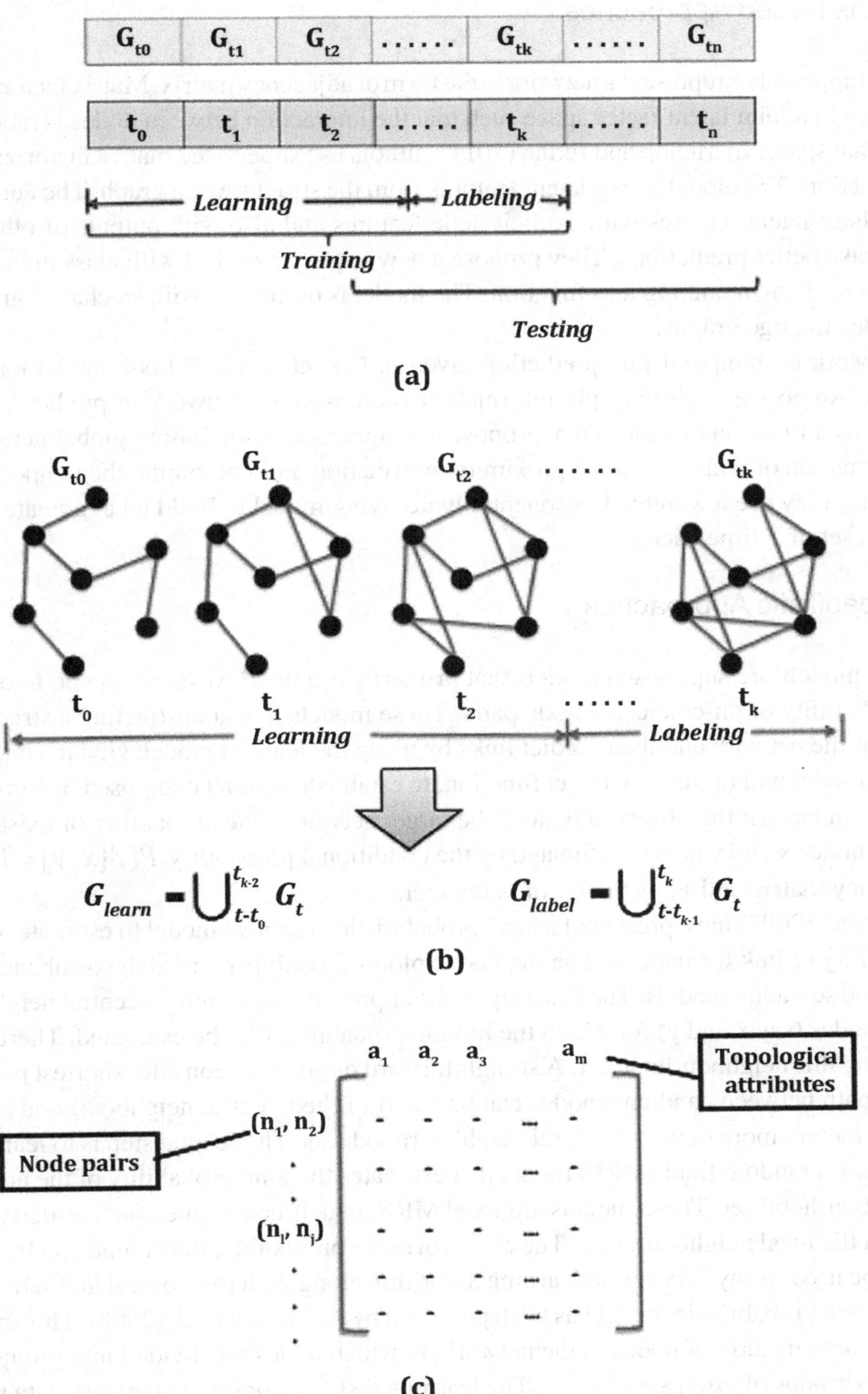

path length in both directed and undirected graphs. The authors apply various supervised machine learning algorithms to generate models and evaluate them using 10-fold cross validation.

4.2.2. Matrix Based Approaches

Matrix based approaches represent a network in the form of adjacency matrix. Matrix factorization models map the nodes to a joint latent factor space such that the interaction between nodes is modelled as inner products in that space. In Menon and Eklan (2011) authors use supervised matrix factorization approach for link prediction. The model learns latent features from the structure of a graph. The authors show that combining these latent features with explicit node features and also with outputs of other models can be used to make better predictions. They propose a new approach to deal with class imbalance problem by directly optimizing a ranking loss function. The model is optimized with stochastic gradient descent and also scales to large graphs.

Another work on temporal link prediction given in Gao et al. (2011) is a model based on matrix factorization. Authors exploit multiple information sources in the network to predict link occurrence probabilities as a function of time. They propose a unique model combining global network structure, content information of nodes and local proximity information. For combining the temporal information of the network, they use a weighted exponentially decaying model to build an aggregate weighted link matrix over a set of T time slices.

4.2.3. Probabilistic Approaches

Probabilistic models are supervised models that primarily use the Bayesian concept, to obtain a co-occurrence probability of un-connected node pairs. These models aim at abstracting a structure from observed data of the network and then predict links by using the learned model. Given a target network, a probabilistic model will optimize a target function, to establish a model composed of a group of parameters, which can best fit the observed data of the target network. The probability of existence of a link between two nodes x and y is then estimated by the conditional probability $P(A[x,y]=1\,|\,\Theta)$ where A is the adjacency matrix and Θ is the set of parameters.

C. Wang et al. (2007) have presented a local probabilistic graphical model to estimate joint co-occurrence probability of link formations. The method explores probabilistic models to enhance the result of topological and semantic models. The first step of the approach is to identify a central neighbourhood set for a pair of nodes (say x and y) for which the linking probability is to be estimated. There can be many ways of finding this neighbourhood set. A straightforward option is to consider shortest paths. All nodes in a shortest path between candidate nodes can be a part of their central neighbourhood set. So there is possibility of having more than one central neighbourhood sets. The second step is to learn a maximum entropy Markov's random field (MRF) model that estimates the joint probability of the nodes inside the central neighbourhood set. These models are local MRF models constrained on non-derivable frequent itemsets from the local neighbourhood. The co-occurrence probability, thus found can be used as a feature and can be used in any supervised learning algorithm along with topological and semantic features.

A hierarchical probabilistic model has been proposed by A. Clauset et al. (2008). This model involves a hierarchical organization of nodes in the network, in which nodes are divided into groups that further subdivide into groups of groups and so on. The learning task uses observed network data to fit the most likely hierarchical structure through statistical inference, to find missing links. In this work, statistical inference is obtained by using Maximum likelihood approach and Monte Carlo sampling algorithm. A Markov's chain Monte Carlo method is used to sample possible dendrograms and then, one of these sampled dendrogram that is most likely to explain the network structure, is selected for link prediction. Using the dendrogram thus obtained, for any two nodes, the number of links between the two is calculated, normalized by the total possible number of links. This value decides the probability of having a link between the two concerned nodes in the network. However there is no guarantee of accuracy in such approaches and also such methods are unsuitable for large networks due to the computational complexity of obtaining the hierarchical structures.

Another interesting approach is the stochastic block model (Lü and Zhou, 2011) based approach. It is one of the most general network model in which the nodes are partitioned into groups and the probability that two nodes are connected depends solely on the groups to which they belong. Let us consider a partition M where each node belongs to only one group. Say, for two groups α and β, the probabilities of two nodes within a group being connected is $P_{\alpha\alpha}$ and probabilities of two nodes in different groups is $P_{\alpha\beta}$. Also, $e_{\alpha\beta}$ is the number of edges between nodes in groups α and β. $n_{\alpha\beta}$ is the number of pairs of nodes such that one node is in α and another is in β. Then the likelihood of observed network structure will be: $L(A|M)=\prod_{\alpha\leq\beta} P_{\alpha\beta}^{e_{\alpha\beta}}\left(1-P_{\alpha\beta}\right)^{n_{\alpha\beta}-e_{\alpha\beta}}$

Another important approach is that of probabilistic relational models that provide a way to incorporate both node and edge attributes to model a joint probability distribution of a set of nodes and the links that associate them. These kinds of approaches are mostly based on either Bayesian networks considering relational links to be directed (Getoor et al., 2003) or Markov's networks that consider the links to be undirected (Taskar et al., 2003). These models represent a joint probability distribution over the attributes of a relational dataset. They allow the property of an object (node/link) to depend, in a probabilistic manner, both on other properties of that object and on properties of related objects. A typical probabilistic relational model uses three graphs: a data graph (G_D), a model graph (G_M), and an inference graph (G_I):

- The data graph represents the original target network. The data objects are represented as nodes and the relationships are edges. Both nodes and edges are associated with a set of attributes corresponding to their type.
- The model graph represents the dependencies among the attributes at the object level (node/edge) type. As mentioned earlier, an attribute of an object (node/edge) depends probabilistically on other attributes of same object as well as attributes of other related (or similar) objects in the data graph. A data graph can be decomposed into multiple parts corresponding to each type. Using this, a joint model of dependencies among type attributes can be built. Hence a model graph has two parts: A dependent structure of all type attributes and the conditional probability distribution associated with each node in the model graph.
- The inference graph represents probabilistic dependencies among all variables in a single test set. It can be instantiated by a rollout process of data graph and model graph. Each object-attribute pair in data graph gets a separate copy of corresponding conditional probability distribution from the model graph. The relations in model graphs determine the way data graph is rolled out to form the inference graph.

These probabilistic relational models are originally designed for attribute prediction problem for relational data. In case of link prediction, the existence or absence of links needs to be considered (assuming only the binary case for simplicity). B. Taskar et al. (2003) have proposed to consider a set of potential links between nodes. Each potential link is associated with a tuple of node attributes, but it may or may not actually exist. They denote this event of existence or absence of a link, using a binary attribute Exists, which is true if the link between the associated nodes exists and false otherwise. Then the link prediction task is reduced to the problem of predicting the existence attributes of these link objects.

4.3. Semi-Supervised Approaches

Semi-supervised learning is a type of learning that makes use of unlabelled instances along with a small amount of labelled instances. Traditional supervised learning methods require labelled data to train a model (especially in tasks of classification). Labelled instances however are often difficult, expensive, or time consuming to obtain, as they require the efforts of experienced human annotators. At the same time, unlabelled data may be relatively easy to collect, but there has been few ways to use them. Semi-supervised learning addresses this problem by using large amount of unlabelled data, together with the labelled data, to build better classifiers. Because semi-supervised learning requires less human effort and gives high accuracy, it is of great interest both in theory and in practice. We suggest readers to refer to the work of X. Zhu (2005) for a detailed survey on semi-supervised learning.

This type of learning has not been very well explored in the context of link prediction. To our knowledge only a few work exist, of which a prominent one is the work of H. Kashima et al. (2009). Authors have dealt with the problem of predicting the unknown (or future) parts of a network structure from the known part of the structure. It can also be seen as the problem of completing an adjacency matrix representing the network. The proposed method is a node-information based approach and uses the concept of label propagation (which was originally developed for node classification) to predict links between pairs of nodes. Authors extend the principle of label propagation to fit it for a pair of nodes. The principle is that if two pairs of nodes are similar to each other, they can share link pattern (absence or presence of a link) and link type. Kronecker sum and product similarity has been applied in this work to find similarities between any two triplets of the form ($node_1$, $node_2$, *link_type*). In the later part, authors have also proposed a conjugate gradient-based method to deal with scalability problem.

Another interesting work in this field is the work proposed by C. Brouard et al. (2011) that is based on Output Kernel Regression. The link prediction task that has been previously represented as a binary classification task, is converted to an output kernel learning task. A target output kernel is assumed to encode similarity between nodes in a graph. The function to find these similarities is to be approximated using appropriate input features. Once the output kernel is learned using kernel tricks, a threshold can be put on the kernel values of pairs of input nodes, to predict the presence or absence of links.

Although semi-supervised methods provide an interesting alternative for link prediction, their applicability is limited to prediction of missing links. Whether these kinds of approaches are equally useful for predicting new links, is an open issue. Moreover, both the above-mentioned approaches use node feature information for finding similarity between nodes. This does not assure their performance in a purely topology-based scenario.

5. CHALLENGES IN LINK PREDICTION TASK

Link prediction in complex networks comes with some important challenges especially when the problem is dealt as a supervised classification problem. These challenges are mostly due to the large size and sparsity of data available in real world networks. We describe a few important issues here based on the list presented in the work of Al Hasan and Zaki (2010) and Z. Bao et al. (2013).

5.1 Class Skewness

Class skewness is the problem of having imbalance in the ratio of instances belonging to different classes or class distribution in any dataset. In a typical case of supervised machine learning based classification task, the class ratio is balanced. It is expected to have the same probability of randomly choosing a positive or negative example. But, in link prediction problems, there is an extreme class imbalance owing to the fact that the number of actual new links is very small as compared to the number of possible links. Also, with the evolution of the network, the number of negative links grows quadratically while the number of positive links grows linearly (Rattigan & Jensen, 2005). Thus, in any supervised approach for link prediction, during learning of models and its validation, the number of negative examples is many times more than the number of positive ones. This makes it difficult for an algorithm to generate a good model with a good performance on the test data. Also, in presence of large class skew, the information carried by the positive examples gets diluted in the vast negative class. Moreover unlike classical classification problem in machine learning context where overall prediction accuracy is important, in link prediction, correct classifications of positive examples are more important. Another aspect is that the performance of a learning algorithm greatly depends on the variance in the model estimates. Even a low proportion of negative instances that are similar to positive instances can cause the model to end up with a large number of false positives. A solution to the problem of class imbalance is under-sampling of negative instances. M. Kubat et al. (1997) have proposed to selectively under-sample majority class while keeping all instances of the minority class. N. Chawla et al. (2002) propose to use over-sampling of minority class along with under-sampling of majority class. They use the product of number of positive examples and the length of attribute vector for increasing the number of positive examples for learning. However, over-sampling approaches can increase the size of dataset and also the training time. Other approaches include making the learning process active and cost sensitive (Al Hasan & Zaki, 2010). However, under-sampling comes with the risk of losing valuable information and so, careful selection should be made on the criteria deciding which examples are to be discarded. More details about class imbalance problem can be found in Al Hasan and Zaki (2010) and Lichtenwalter and Chawla (2012). In Lichtenwalter and Chawla (2012), there is a detailed description about how the predictor performance changes with sampling of test data. They also provide valuable information about which performance measure is to be used for evaluating different link prediction techniques.

5.2 Model Calibration

Sometimes calibrating a model is more crucial than finding the right algorithm to build a classification model (Al Hasan & Zaki, 2010). Model calibration is a process to find a function that transforms the output score of a model to label. Varying or biasing this function can control the ratio of false positive error and false negative errors. This will also depend on the requirements of the network on which a link prediction model is being developed. For example in a terrorist network missing a positive link is more serious than in online social networks where recommending a negative link can be a bigger mistake.

5.3 Selection of Attributes or Features

In network topology-based approaches, appropriate selection of attributes is very essential. They affect link prediction in two ways. First the performance of the prediction depends highly on the prediction capabilities of the attributes. And second the computational efficiency of the attributes will decide the overall computational complexity of the link prediction approach. Having a prior knowledge about the performance of the different topological predictors makes it easy to select the best performing ones as attributes and to have a good prediction result. But this is not the case in reality, as the performances of different topological predictors vary in function of the kind of networks to which they are being applied. So some methods to find the importance of these as attributes is needed. One way to cope with this issue is to apply principal component analysis (PCA) as in the work of Z. Bao et al. (2013). Authors propose a framework of three steps. First principal component analysis is done to determine principal components (PCs) out of all attributes. These components are statistically independent and are ranked in the decreasing order of their contribution to the variance of result. Then out of them only those m predictor variables are selected which have the highest eigenvalues and which are grouped into h clusters. From each cluster the attribute closest to the mean of the cluster is selected. In the third and final step, considering only the attributes selected in the previous step, multiple linear regression method is applied to find weights for the selected h components. Using these weights and selected features the link prediction is done.

5.4 Dynamic Update of Models

Complex networks are dynamic in nature. Hence for any link prediction approach one of the important challenges is to deal with the temporal aspects of the network. In such networks, with time more information may be added in the form of introduction of new nodes and links or disappearance of a few nodes and links. This information can play a crucial role to affect the prediction results. Hence in many works on link prediction this time aspect has been included (Acar et al., 2009; Benchettara et al., 2010b; Cooke, 2006; Dunlavy et al., 2011; Gao et al., 2011; Huang et al., 2008; Huang & Lin, 2008; Lahiri & Berger-Wolf, 2007; Ouzienko et al., 2010). Dynamic update of models is needed in order to adapt the model with changes that arrive with time. This aspect is more essential when a link prediction approach is to be implemented in a real evolving network like in applications such as recommender systems in various social networks. In such cases the trade-off between complete rebuilding and updating the model should be taken into consideration (Al Hasan & Zaki, 2010). A few works that propose such temporally adaptive models for online social networks are given in Aggarwal et al. (2012) and Song et al. (2009).

5.5 Heterogeneity

In general many of the link prediction approaches have dealt with only homogeneous networks that have same kind of nodes and links. But real networks are usually heterogeneous in nature. So in many of complex networks, link prediction task may include prediction of links between different types of nodes and also prediction of different kinds of links between same types of nodes. Considering heterogeneity in a complex network can also be helpful to improve the performance of a link prediction approach, owing to the fact that complex networks are very sparse and much more information can be added by using the linking patterns in different dimensions (Aggarwal et al., 2012; Davis et al., 2011, 2013; Eronen & Toivonen, 2012; Pujari & Kanawati, 2013; Wang & Sukthankar, 2013; Yu et al., 2012).

6. OUR WORK ON LINK PREDICTION

In our research, we were very much interested in devising topological approaches for link prediction because of its generic nature. While studying all these different topological approaches, we realized that none of the works try to combine the effects of different topological features using rank aggregation method. These are methods that combine rankings provided by different experts on a set of candidates and conceptually come from social choice theory. We already had an in-hand experience of working with rank aggregation methods, applying it in the context of tag recommendation on folksonomy (Pujari & Kanawati, 2012). So we were quite hopeful about its applicability in the context of link prediction. Hence we developed a supervised rank aggregation based link prediction approach. For experimentation we used scientific collaboration networks which are a part of bibliographical networks. Bibliographical networks come with a diverse kind of information. We saw that two authors in scientific collaboration network can be linked in many different ways. For example they can be linked if they publish papers in same conferences/journals or attend same conferences. Another way of linking them is based on the references they have used in their works. All this made us think that if we can exploit this heterogeneous link information, the prediction of co-authorship links may be improved. Thus we were inspired to work on multiplex networks. Multiplex networks are a form of heterogeneous networks where the network is represented as layers for graphs, each having same nodes but different kinds of edges. They have a simple structure with a possibility of applying existing topological measures without much difficulty. Moreover, there is not much work done in the field of link prediction in multiplex networks. So we developed a link prediction approach for multiplex network using simple topological attributes and their extended versions for a multiplex scenario. At the same time, another concept that caught our attention was that of existence of communities in social networks. We were highly interested to explore the utility of communities in the context of link prediction. So after studying few works on community detection approaches, we came up with our approach of using them for filtering of examples in link prediction. This sampling may provide a solution to deal with the problem of creating a better prediction model in presence of huge class imbalance in the data.

6.1. Supervised Rank Aggregation Based Link Prediction

After having an overview of the work done to solve the problem of link prediction, we came to a conclusion that none of the previous work attempt to combine the prediction power of individual topological measures by applying computational social choice algorithms or simple voting rules. These methods are a part of social choice theory and were mostly applied to election related problems (Black et al., 1998; de Borda, 1781; Young & Levenglick, 1978). A detailed description about voting methods and their history can be found in the work of C. Dwork et al. (2001), D. Black et al. (1998), and H.P. Young et al. (1978). These techniques were designed to ensure fairness among experts while combining their rankings and hence all experts are given equal weights. Expressing the link prediction problem in terms of a vote is straightforward: candidates are examples (pairs of unconnected nodes), while voters are topological measures computed for these pairs of unlinked nodes. Then we have a voting problem with quite huge set of candidates and rather a reduced set of voters. These settings are very similar to those encountered when considering the problem of ranking documents in a meta-search engines where voting schemes have also been applied with success (Dwork et al., 2001; Aslam & Montague, 2001; Montague & Aslam, 2002).

In our settings, prediction performances can be boosted by weighting differently the different applied topological measures (voters) in function of their individual performances in predicting new links. Weights are used in two different weighted rank aggregation methods: The first one is based on the classical Borda count approach (Borda, 1781), while the second is based on the Kemeny aggregation rule. The latter is known to compute the *Condorcet* winner of an election (if it exists): the candidate that wins each duel with all other candidates.

Before describing these approaches, here is a brief description about two of the well known classical rank aggregation methods.

- *Borda's method* (Borda, 1781) is a positional method as it is based on the absolute positioning of the ranked elements rather than their relative rankings. A Borda score is calculated for each element in the lists and based on this score the elements are ranked in the aggregated list. For a set of full lists $L=[L_1,L_2,...,L_n]$, the Borda's score for a element x and a list L_i is given by:

$$B_{L_i}(x)=\{count(y) \mid L_i(y)<L_i(x)\wedge y\in L_i\}$$

The total Borda's score for an element is then given by:

$$B(x)=\sum_{i=1}^{n} B_{L_i}(x)$$

- *Kemeny optimal aggregation* proposed in (Dwork et al., 2001), makes use of Kendall-Tau distance to find the optimal aggregation. Kendall-Tau distance counts the number of pairs of elements that have opposite rankings in the two input lists i.e. it calculates the pairwise disagreements.

$$K(L_1,L_2)=\{count((x,y)) \mid L_1(x)<L_1(y)\wedge L_2(x)>L_2(y)\}$$

The first step is to find an initial aggregation of input lists using any standard method. The second step is to find all possible permutations of the elements in the initial aggregation. For each permutation, a score is computed which is equal to the sum of distances between this permutation and the input lists. The permutation having the lowest score is considered as optimal solution. For example, for a collection of input rankings $\tau_1,\tau_2,\ldots,\tau_n$ and an aggregation π, the score is given by:

$$SK(\pi,\{\tau_1,...,\tau_n\})=\sum_{i\in(1,n)} K(\pi,\tau_i)$$

The main feature of Kemeny optimal aggregation is that it complies with *Condorcet principle,* which is not the case of positional methods such the Borda's algorithm. *Condorcet principle* (Young & Levenglick, 1978) states that if there exists an item that defeats every other item in simple pairwise majority voting then, it should be ranked above all other. In spite of all advantages Kemeny optimal aggregation is computationally hard to implement. So while looking for an alternative solution that gives similar kind of aggregation but is computationally feasible, we are led to another approach named *Local kemenization* (Dwork et al., 2001). A full list π is locally Kemeny optimal aggregation of partial lists $\tau_1, \tau_2, \ldots, \tau_n$, if there is no full list π' that can be obtained from π by performing a single transposition of a single pair of adjacent elements and for which

$$SK(\pi', \{\tau_1, \ldots, \tau_n\}) < SK(\pi, \{\tau_1, \ldots, \tau_n\})$$

In other words, it is impossible to reduce the total distance of an aggregation by flipping any adjacent pair of elements in the aggregation.

6.1.1. Supervised Rank Aggregation

Supervised rank aggregation refers to the same process of combining rankings but giving different weights to experts and these weights are learned in a due process of training. First let's define some basic functions used later in defining weighted aggregation functions. Let L_i be a ranked list of n candidates (a vote). Let $L_i(x)$ be the rank of element x in the list L_i. The basic individual Borda score of an element x for a voter i is then given by: $B_i(x) = n - L_i(x)$.

Let x and y be two candidates. We define the local preference function as follows:

$$pref_i(x, y) = \begin{cases} 1 : B_i(x) > B_i(y) \\ 0 : B_i(x) < B_i(y) \end{cases}$$

Introducing weights in Borda aggregation rule is rather straightforward: Let $w_1, w_2, \ldots, w_r$ be weights of r voters providing r ranked lists on n candidates. The weighted Borda score for a candidate x is then given by:

$$B(x) = \sum_{i=1}^{r} w_i \times B_{L_i}(x)$$

For approximate Kemeny aggregation we introduce weights into the definition of the non-transitive preference relationships between candidates. This is modified as follows. Let w_T be the sum of all computed weights i.e. $w_T = \sum_{i=1}^{r} w_i$. For each couple of candidates x,y we compute a score function as follows:

$$score(x,y) = \sum_{i=1}^{r} w_i \times pref_i(x,y)$$

The weighted preference relation $\succ_w$ is then defined as follows:

$$x \succ_w y : score(x,y) > \frac{w_T}{2}$$

This new preference relation is used to sort an initial aggregation of candidates in order to obtain a supervised Kemeny aggregation. The initial aggregation can be any of the input lists or an aggregation obtained by applying any other classical aggregation method like Borda. In our algorithm, we have applied merge-sort.

6.1.2. Link Prediction using Supervised Rank Aggregation

Each attribute of an example has the capacity to provide some unique information about the data when considered individually. The training examples are ranked based on the attribute values. So, for each attribute we will get a ranked list of all examples. Considering only the top *k* ranked examples and with an assumption that when we rank the examples according to their attribute values, the positive examples should be ranked on the top, we compute the performance of each attribute. This performance is measured in terms of either *precision* (maximization of identification of positive examples) or *false positive rate* (minimization of identification of negative examples) or a combination of both. Based on the individual performances, a weight is assigned to each attribute.

For validation, we use examples obtained from the validation graph characterized by same attributes and try to rank all examples based on their attribute values. So for *n* different attributes we shall have *n* different rankings of the test examples. These ranked lists are then merged using a *supervised rank aggregation* method and the *weights of the attributes* obtained during learning process. The top *k* ranked examples in the aggregation are taken to be the predicted list of positive examples. Using this predicted list, we calculate the performance of our approach. *k* in this case is equal to the number of positive examples in the validation graph.

6.1.2.1 Weights Computation

We propose to compute topological attributes weights based on their capability to identify correct elements in top *k* positions of their rankings. Weights associated to applied topological measures are computed based on the following criteria:

- **Maximization of Positive Precision:** Based on maximization of identification of positive examples the attribute weight is calculated as:

$$w_i = n \times precision_i$$

where *n* is the total number of attributes and $precision_1$ is the precision of an attribute a_i based on identification of positive examples. Just to remind, precision is defined as the fraction of retrieved instances that are relevant.

- **Minimization of False Positive Rate:** By minimizing the identification of negative examples we get a weight as:

$$w_i = n \times (1 - FPR_i)$$

where n is the total number of attributes and FPR_i is the false positive rate of attribute a_i based on identification of negative examples. False positive rate is defined as the fraction of non-relevant instances that are retrieved as relevant.

In both cases, we are multiplying it with a constant value n (which is totally optional) in order to enhance the numeric value of weights, which at times can be very little and close to zero. Also the weights are normalized by dividing them by the total weights of all topological attributes. Other criteria for weight computation can also be applied. For example in Subbian and Melville (2011), weights are computed based on AUC of node features on training data.

6.1.3. Experiments

We evaluate our approach using data obtained from DBLP[6] databases. Our network consists of authors as nodes and they are linked if they have co-published at least one paper during the observed period of time. The data corresponds to year between 1970- 1979. We create three graphs out of that. We generate examples from each of the graphs. Table 2 provides information about the training or test graphs while Table 3 summarizes information about the examples generated.

We have applied our approach to the datasets as described in Table 4. K is a parameter used in rank aggregation to decide the top k predictions and is equal to the number of actual positive links in the test data. For rank aggregation, we have used supervised Borda and supervised Kemeny methods. We wanted to experiment with a score based rank aggregation method as well as an order based one. For score based method Borda was obvious. Our second choice was Kemeny aggregation approach as it produces an optimal final aggregation, keeping in tact the preferences of all experts as much as possible. We compare our approach with link prediction approaches using supervised machine learning algorithms like Decision tree, Naive Bayes and k-Nearest neighbours algorithm. These methods are simple to implement and

Table 2. DBLP Co-authorship graphs used for generation of examples

Graphs	|V|	|E|	Density	Avg(Degree)	Avg(Cc)	Diameter	Avg(PathLength)
1970-1973	91	116	0.028	2.549	0.333	14	6.114
1972-1975	221	319	0.013	2.887	0.462	16	7.203
1974-1977	323	451	0.009	2.793	0.404	18	7.504

Table 3. Examples generated from co-authorship graphs

Learn/Test	Label	#Positive	#Negative
1970-1973	1974-1975	16	1810
1972-1975	1976-1977	49	12141
1974-1977	1978-1979	93	26223

represent three different concepts of classification. We name our approaches as Supervised Borda 1 and Supervised Borda 2 based on how the attribute weights are computed. 1 represents weights computed based on maximization of positive precision and 2 represents weights being computed based on minimization of false positive rates. We will follow the same convention to represent supervised Kemeny. The supervised machine learning algorithms are implemented using Orange[7], which is Python-based data analysis and visualization software. We selected the following topological attributes to characterize examples (i.e node pairs): Number of common neighbours (CN), Jaccard coefficient (JC), Preferential attachment (PA) Adamic Adar coefficient (AA), Resource allocation (RA) Shortest path length (SPL), Path betweenness centrality (PBC), Truncated Katz (TKatz) and Neighbour's clustering coefficient (NCF).

We compute the performance of our rank aggregation based link prediction methods and link prediction based on supervised machine learning algorithms. We use the three algorithms for supervised machine learning. We also compute the same using ensemble learning with decision tree. We have restricted the number of predictions made by machine learning algorithm to *K*, the parameter that is selected for rank aggregation based methods. This is done in order to have a justified comparison between the two kinds of approaches. Figure 2 and Figure 3 present the results we obtained in terms of precision and AUC for all methods. AUC is computed using the formula given in section 3 as proposed in (Lü and Zhou, 2011), but the difference is that instead of exact score we compare the ranks of negative and positive examples. So actually, we compute the probability of finding a positive example ranked above a negative example in the list of prediction that is the top k ranked lists provided by all link prediction algorithms. Also we are unable to take into account the equal ranks between negative and positive examples, as we are not treating ties for the moment. Ties are broken randomly whenever they appear in the score and dealing with ties during ranking can be added to future updates of our work.

While our method based on Borda and supervised Borda failed to provide any substantial results (due to which we have not listed them here), our approximate Kemeny and supervised Kemeny based methods outperform all the supervised machine learning and ensemble methods for both datasets in terms of precision. This shows the validity of our approach. Although in terms of AUC the result is slightly different, with decision tree giving the best AUC for dataset 1. But still the precision for the same is not very high. The low values of AUC can be attributed to the fact that we have used raw data without any sort of pre-treatment or refining. To ease the process of supervised Kemeny aggregation further, we make a selection of best performing attributes. We discard all attributes that have a zero weight during learning. That means these attributes failed to identify any of the positive examples in the top *k* positions during learning. So, the rankings provided by such topological attributes do not seem to be very useful for being used further during prediction of links on the test set. This step can be significant to select the best serving attributes for the prediction task and they also help the execution process.

Precision-recall curves are more indicative of the difference between the performances of algorithms in presence of a class imbalance, having a large number of negative examples as compared to positive examples. So we decided to use them, in order to compare different algorithms. Looking at the precision-recall curves in Figure 4 and Figure 5 created by varying the value of *K*, we can clearly see the difference between various algorithms. For dataset 1, *k* varies between 5 and 49 (the actual number of positive links in the test set) with an epoch of 5. For dataset 2, *k* varies from 10 to 93 with an epoch 10. The two figures show that, for both datasets, rank aggregation based methods perform better than the supervised machine learning based methods as their corresponding curves lie above covering greater area than those representing supervised machine learning methods. Also it is evident that our method

Table 4. Datasets for experiments

Datasets	Learning Year	Test Year	K
Dataset 1	1970-1973	1972-1975	49
Dataset 2	1972-1975	1974-1977	93

Figure 2. Results for all algorithms in terms of Precision

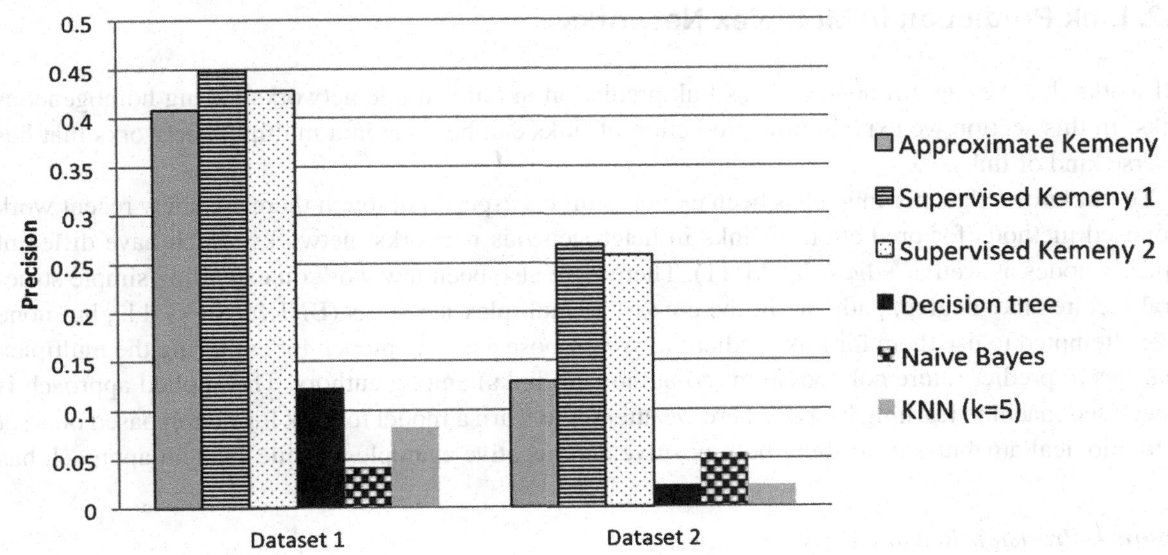

Figure 3. Results for all algorithms in terms of AUC

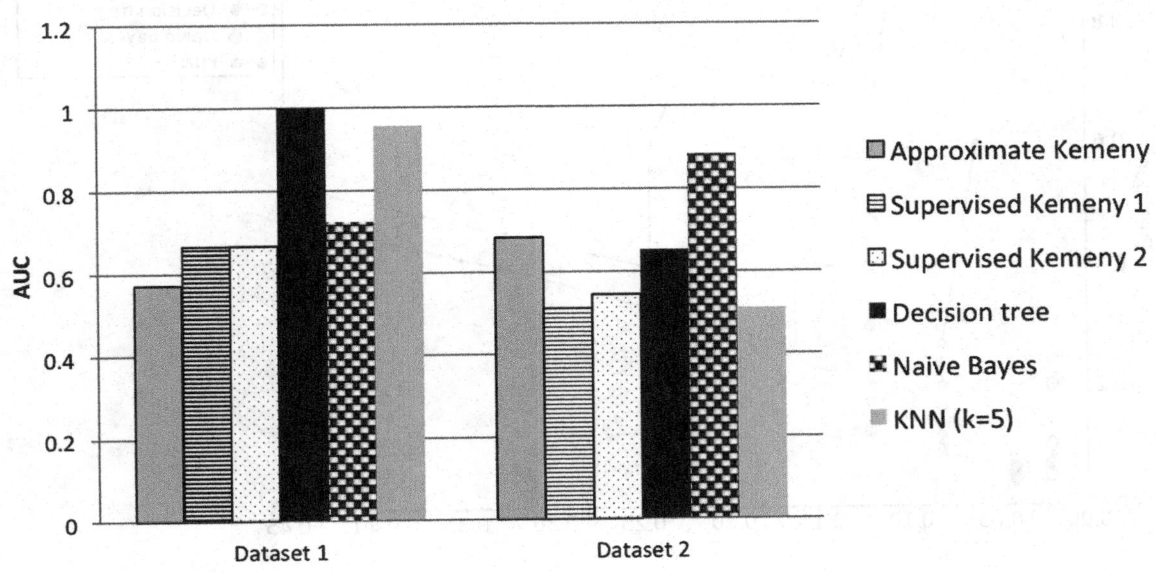

based on supervised Kemeny aggregation, where weights are computed based on precision outperform all other methods.

Although it is still early to say that rank aggregation based methods are better performing than the other approaches of link prediction, the preliminary results do show that rank aggregation especially with Kemeny method indeed adds some useful information which can enhance the result of prediction task. This is quite encouraging for us to continue this work further. Still, the fact remains that rank aggregation methods especially Kemeny based methods have a high computational complexity but some relaxation can be provided by using approximation of optimality.

6.2. Link Prediction in Multiplex Networks

All works that we saw till now, address link prediction in only simple networks having homogeneous links. In this section we explain how prediction of links can be done in a multiplex networks that has diverse kind of links.

To our knowledge, not much has been explored in this aspect. Although there are a few recent work proposed methods for prediction of links in heterogeneous networks, networks which have different types of nodes as well as edges (YRM+11). There have also been few work on extending simple structural features like degree, path etc. in the context of multiplex networks (BNL13, BCG+11), but none have attempted to use them for link prediction. We propose a new approach for exploring the multiplex relations to predict future collaboration (co-authorship links) among authors. The applied approach is supervised machine learning based, where we attempt to learn a model for link formation based on a set of topological attributes describing both positive and negative examples. While such an approach has

Figure 4. Precision-Recall curves on Dataset 1

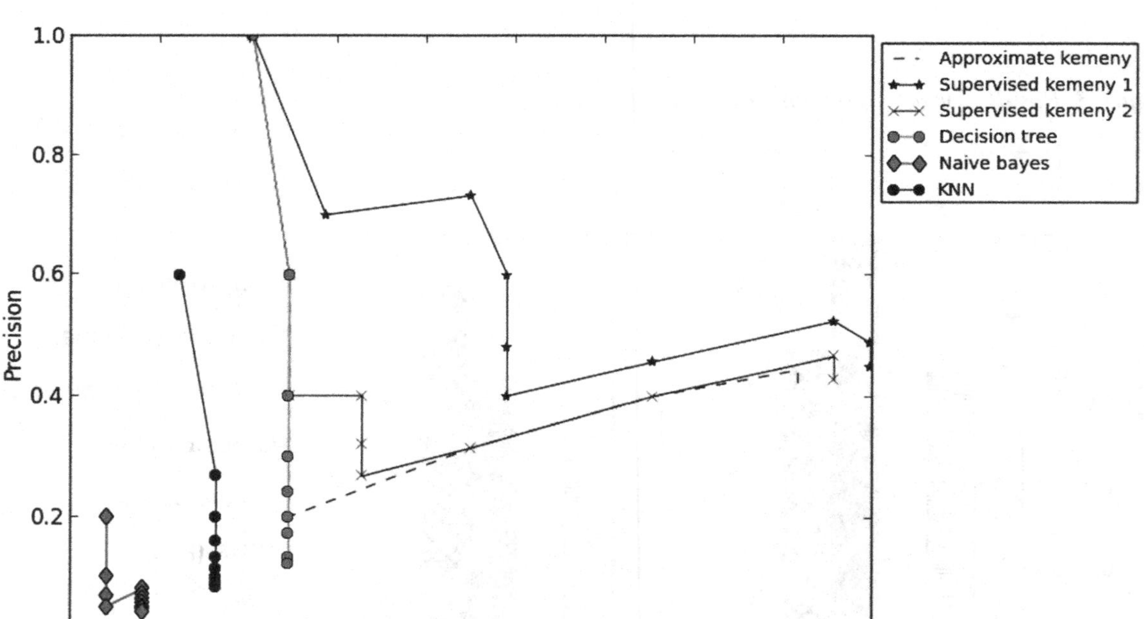

Figure 5. Precision-Recall curves on Dataset 2

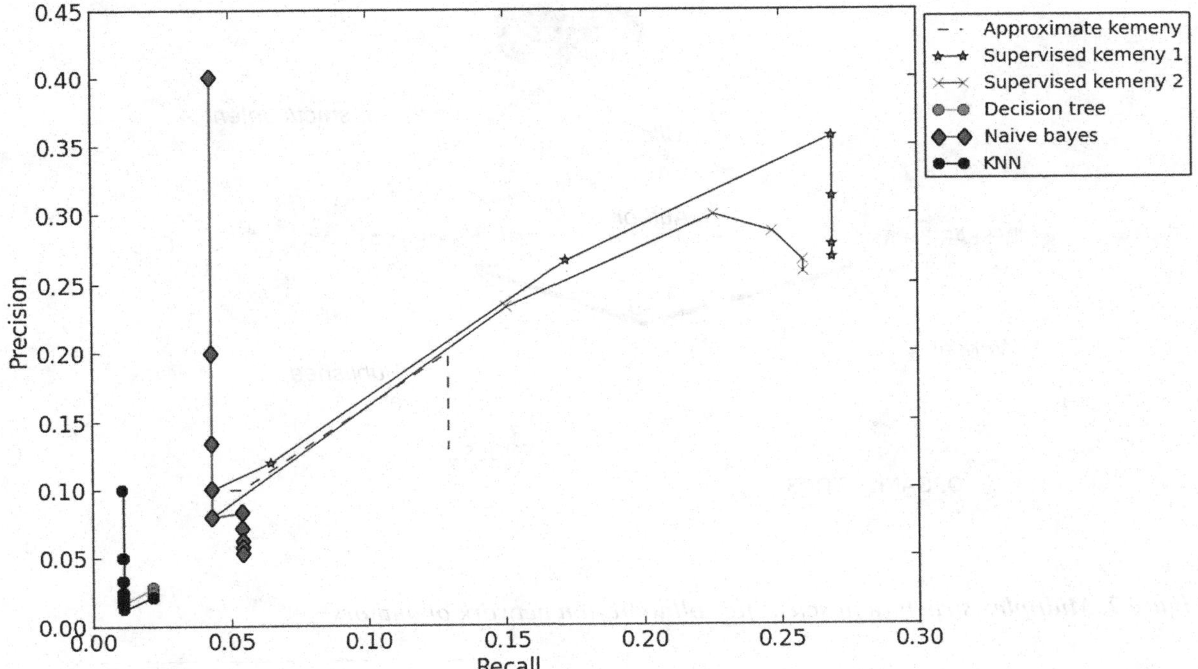

been successfully applied in the context of simple networks, different options can be used to extend it to the multiplex networks. One option is to compute topological attributes in each layer of the multiplex. Another one is to compute directly new multiplex-based attributes quantifying the multiplex nature of dyads (potential links). Both approaches will be discussed in the next section. Multiplex networks are a category of heterogeneous complex networks, which essentially have different kinds of links between same nodes. They can be represented as a set of simple networks, each having the same nodes but different sets of links.

A common example of multiplex network is a scientific collaboration network derived from bibliographical networks shown in Figure 6. These networks are composed of researchers or authors of scientific papers, who can be linked if they have co-published some articles or if they have published their articles in the same conferences or the domain of their research are the same. They can also be linked if they have referred to same works in their articles. Figure 7 shows a scientific collaboration network and how it can be represented by multiple layers, each having same nodes but different types of links or edges.

6.2.1. Proposed Approach

Our approach includes computing simple topological scores for unconnected node pairs in a graph. Then we extend these attributes to include information from other dimension graphs or layers. This can be done in three ways: First we compute the simple topological measures in all layers; second is to take the aggregation of the scores; and third we propose an entropy based version of each topological measures which gives importance to the presence of a non-zero score in each layer. In the end all these attributes

Figure 6. Bibliographic networks

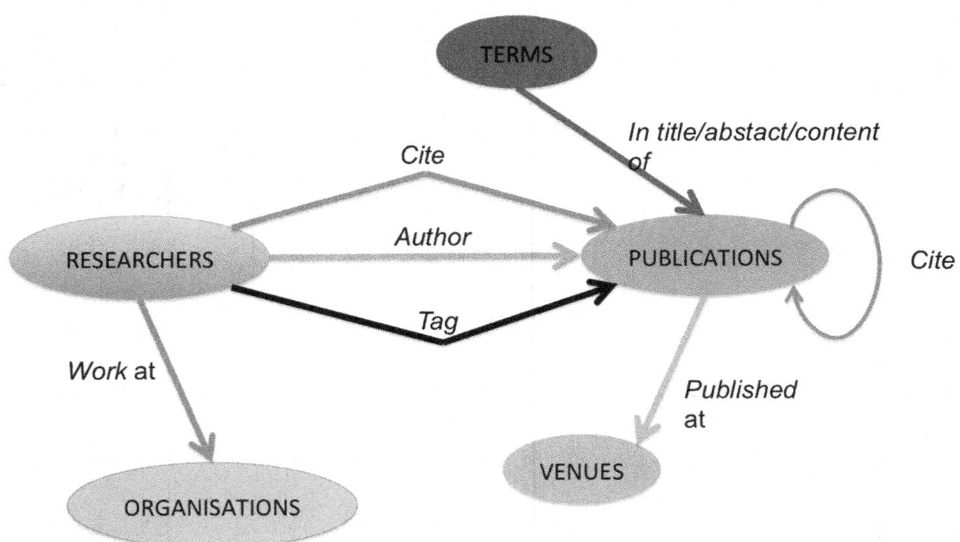

Figure 7. Multiplex structure in scientific collaboration network of authors

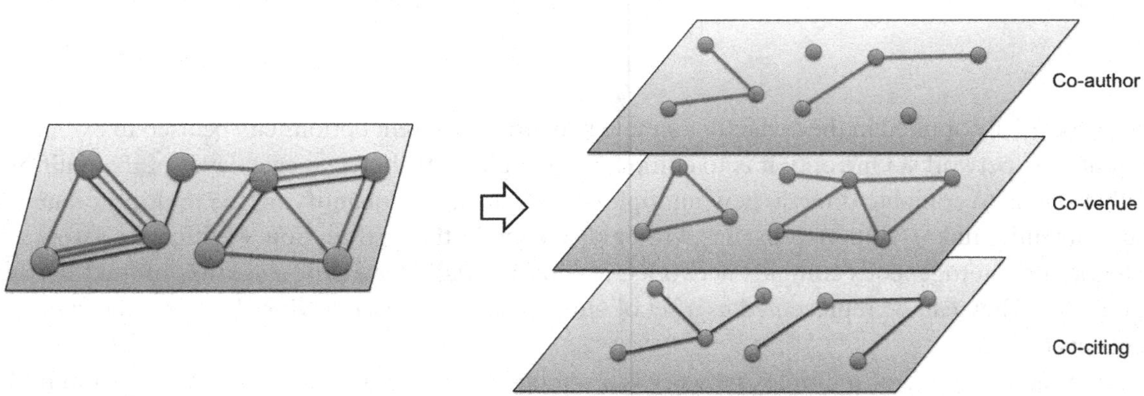

can be combined in various ways to form different sets of attribute values (vectors) characterizing examples or unconnected node pairs.

- **Direct and indirect attributes:** Formally, if we have a multiplex $G = < V, E_1, \ldots, E_m >$ which in fact is a set of graphs $< G_1, G_2, \ldots, G_m >$ and a topological attribute *X*. For any two unconnected nodes *u* and *v* in graph G_T (where we want to make a prediction), $X(u,v)^{[T]}$ computed on G_T will be *direct attribute* and the same computed on all other dimension graphs will be *indirect attributes*.
- **Multiplex Attributes:** The first category of multiplex attribute computes an *aggregation of the attribute* values over all layers. This can be done using any of the existing functions like *min*, *max*, *sum*, *average* etc. For example, we choose to use average, so our new attribute is given by:

$$X_{avg}(x,y) = \frac{\sum_{\alpha=1}^{m} X(x,y)^{[\alpha]}}{m}$$

where m is the number of types of relations in the network (dimensions or layers).

In the second category we propose a new attribute called *product of node degree entropy* (PNE) that is based on degree entropy, a multiplex property proposed by F. Battistion et al. (2013). If degree of node u is $k(u)$, the degree entropy is given by:

$$E(u) = -\sum_{\alpha=1}^{m} \frac{k(u)^{[\alpha]}}{k_{total}(u)} \log(\frac{k(u)^{[\alpha]}}{k_{total}(u)})$$

where $k_{total}(u) = \sum_{\alpha=1}^{m} k(u)^{[\alpha]}$ and we define product of node degree entropy as $PNE(u,v) = E(u)*E(v)$.

We also extend the same concept to define entropy of a simple topological attribute, and call them entropy-based attributes X_{ent}

$$X_{ent}(x,y) = -\sum_{\alpha=1}^{m} \frac{X(x,y)^{[\alpha]}}{X_{total}(u)} \log(\frac{X(x,y)^{[\alpha]}}{X_{total}(u)})$$

where $X_{total}(u) = \sum_{\alpha=1}^{m} X(u)^{[\alpha]}$.

The entropy-based attributes are more suitable to capture the distribution of the attribute value over all dimensions. A higher value indicates uniform distribution attribute value across the multiplex layers. We address average and entropy based attributes as multiplex attributes. Figure 8 illustrates our concepts using a simple example. We have three layers of graphs and we want to make prediction on the first layer, which we call target layer. We compute different versions of common neighbours topological metrics for the selected nodes u and v, excluding and including the multiplex information.

6.2.2. Experiment

We evaluate our approach using same data obtained from DBLP databases corresponding to year between 1970-1979. We create two datasets from three graphs, each corresponding to a different period of time. The examples are generated on the target layer on which we want to make the prediction. In this case it is the co-authorship layer and we predict the co-authorship links.

Table 5 summarizes the information about the graphs. Refer Table 3 and Table 4 for information regarding examples and datasets used for validating the approach.

We selected the following topological attributes: Number of common neighbors, Jaccard coefficient, Preferential attachment, Adamic Adar coefficient, Resource allocation and Shortest path length. All these topological measures were computed on the three graphs. Their average and multiplex versions are also added as additional attributes and we also used product of node entropy as one additional entropy based

Figure 8. An example of computing direct, indirect and multiplex attributes based on number of common neighbors

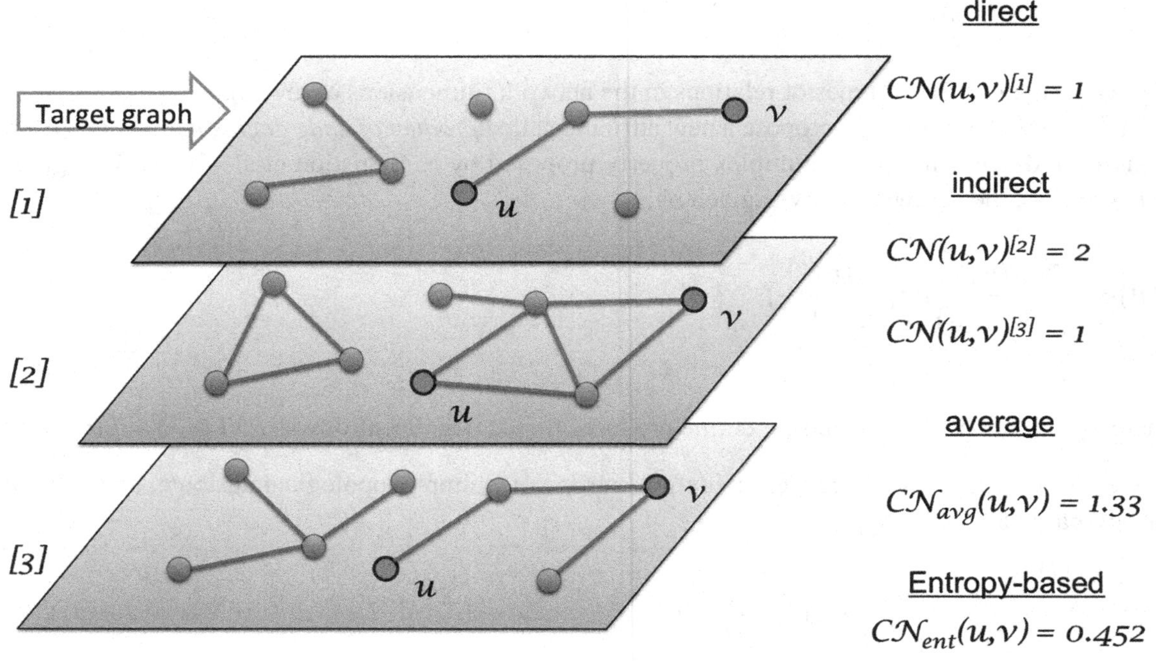

Table 5. Multiplex graphs

Graphs	Properties	Co-Author	Co-Venue	Co-Citation
1970-1973	$\|V\|$	91	91	91
	$\|E\|$	116	1256	171
	Density	0.028327	0.306715	0.041758
1972-1975	$\|V\|$	221	221	221
	$\|E\|$	319	5098	706
	Density	0.013122	0.209708	0.029041
1974-1977	$\|V\|$	323	323	323
	$\|E\|$	451	9831	993
	Density	0.008673	0.189047	0.019095

multiplex attribute. We applied decision tree algorithm on dataset 1 to generate a model and then tested it on another dataset 2. Decision tree was a quick choice owing to its simplicity and popularity. Also, we already had an in hand experience of using this algorithm for prediction task in simple co-authorship network. We are using data mining tool Orange for this. We use four types of combinations of the attributes creating five different sets namely:

- **Direct:** Attributes computed only in the co-authorship graph;
- **Direct + Indirect:** Attributes computed in co-authorship, co-venue and co-citation graphs;

- **Direct + Multiplex:** Attributes computed from co-authorship graph with average attributes obtained from three dimension graphs, and also entropy based attributes;
- **Direct + Indirect + Multiplex:** Attributes computed in co-authorship, co-venue and co-citation graphs, with average of the attributes, and also entropy based attributes; and
- **Multiplex:** Average of attributes and entropy based attributes.

In this experiment, our goal is to predict co-authorship links and the target layer is co-author layer. But the same procedure can be used for prediction of links in any other layer. Figure 9 and Figure 10 show the results obtained in terms of F1-measure and area under the ROC curve (AUC). We observe that the inclusion of indirect and multiplex attributes does not improve the prediction result in terms of F1- measure. However, we can see that there is slight improvement in the result when we use only multiplex attributes for learning and validating our model. This shows that there is indeed some useful information that can be captured by multiplex attributes and can be use in link prediction task. Also AUC increases for all the sets that include multiplex and indirect attributes for both datasets. This justifies our belief on the usefulness of indirect and multiplex attributes.

The reason for not having a very good result with indirect and multiplex attributes can be due to the fact that we have not really verified the edge overlaps between layers. We have used the co-citation layer which has links based on the common bibliographical references made by two authors in their papers and the co-venue layer has links if the authors have published in same conferences. It is possible that these two layers are just the super-graphs of the co-authorship layer. That means, they may contain all the links that are also found in the co-authorship layer plus some new links. So they may not explicitly represent the multiplexity in the network. We believe that considering edge overlap and other such correlation measures can lead to having some different result. Moreover we have made a naive attempt of defining the multiplex topological measures only based on entropy. Other such concepts can also be implemented for the same purpose after a detailed verification of importance and applicability of the concepts. This may also result in more distinct and better performances.

Figure 9. Result for experiment on different attribute sets in terms of F1-measure

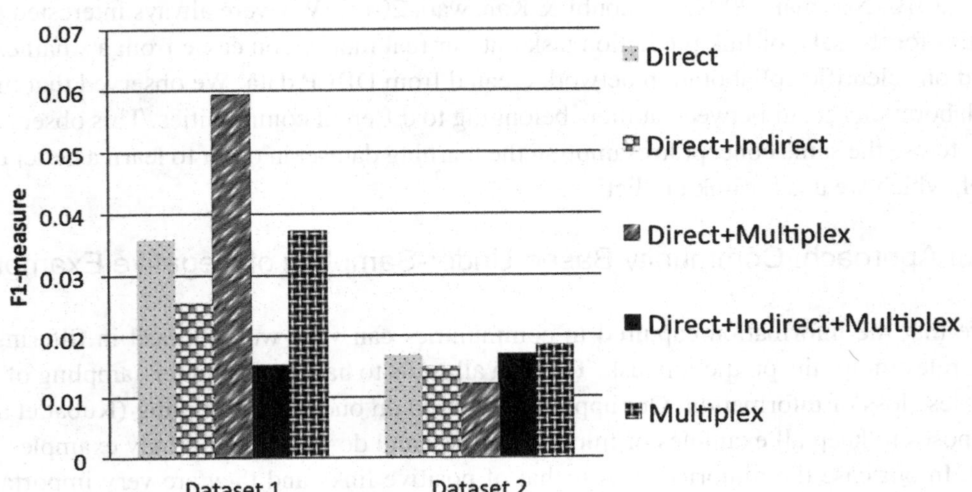

Figure 10. Result for experiment on different attribute sets in terms of AUC

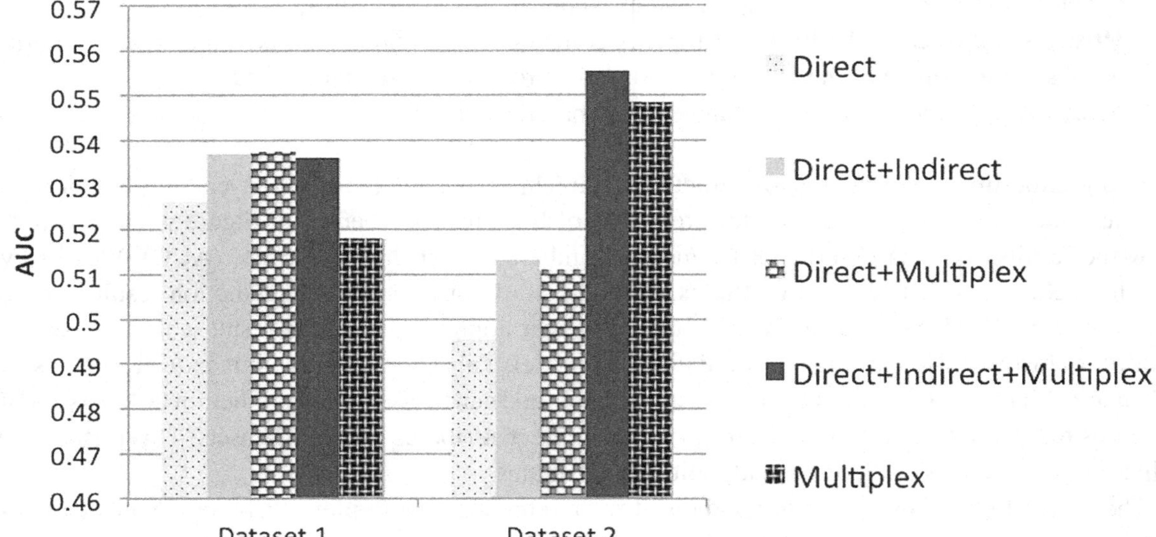

6.3. Link Prediction using Community Information

Community structures are very common in real world complex networks. Communities can be defined as groups of nodes in a network that are generally more connected within each other than with nodes exterior to the communities. Members of a community are supposed to have some common properties or play some kind of common roles in the network. The semantic interpretation of a community depends largely on the type of network or type of information presented by a network.

Community detection and link prediction are two important fields of research in complex network analysis. They have been running in parallel since long and it is very recently that researchers have come up with the thought of using community information for link prediction (Benchettara, 2011; Soundarajan & Hopcroft, 2012). However link and path information have been already in use for finding communities (Fortunato, 2010; Newman, 2004a; Yakoubi & Kanawati, 2014). We were always interested to explore communities for the sake of link prediction task but our real motivation came from a small experiment that we did on scientific collaboration network created from DBLP data. We observed that most of the future collaborations occur between authors belonging to different communities. This observation gave us the idea to use the same concept for sampling the learning dataset in order to learn a better classification model, which we use for link prediction.

6.3.1. Our Approach: Community Based Under-Sampling of Negative Examples

We believe that the information captured in communities can very well be used in filtering of node pairs more relevant for the prediction task. This can allow us to have a safe under-sampling of examples without or less loss of information. Our approach is based on one-sided sampling (Kubat et al., 1997), which proposes to keep all examples of minority classes and do sampling on only examples of majority classes. In our case the minority class is that of positive links and they are very important for the prediction task, so we keep all the positive examples. Out of negative examples that form the majority class, we propose to select the node pairs where both nodes do not belong to the same community. That means, they lie in the belt of inter-community links. This is the region where we observed the presence of most of the positive examples. Hence the negative examples that are found outside the communities can be more informative than those found inside the communities. These node pairs can better represent the negative class and can help to learn a better classification model.

Given a graph $G = \langle V, E \rangle$ on which examples have been generated, a community detection method $Algo_{com}$, and sets of positive and negative examples (*P,N*) generated from *G*, our algorithm has the following steps:

1. *com*←$Algo_{com}$(*G*) /* Computing the community structure */
2. For all (*x,y*)∈*N do*
   if ∃*c*∈*Com*: (*x,y*)∈*C then*
   N←*N*\{(*x,y*)}
3. Return *N*.

The algorithm ensures sub-sampling the negative examples set, while the positive set of examples remains unchanged.

6.3.2. Experiments

We implement our concept of under-sampling on the same data of DBLP co-authorship networks formed from data corresponding to year 1970-1979. The information about the three graphs and datasets can be found in Table 2, Table 3 and Table 4. We have used four community detection methods: Louvain (Blondel et al., 2008), Walktrap (Pons & Latapy, 2006), Infomap (Rosvall et al., 2009) and LICOD (Yakoubi & Kanawati, 2014). The numbers of communities found by each algorithm on different graphs is reported in Table 6. Also, we compute random samples and distance-based samples. For random sampling, we have selected *n* random negative examples, keeping *n* as close as possible to the numbers found by the community-based methods. For distance-based sampling we have used two values of distance between nodes of negative examples *d*≤5 and *d*≤10. The number of examples found from all these sampling techniques has been reported in Table 7.

Using all these examples we apply a supervised machine learning based classification using a simple decision tree algorithm. For this we use *TreeLearner* decision tree algorithm of data mining tool *Orange* with default parameters. Training of the model is done on sampled datasets whereas validation of the model is done on the original and complete dataset containing all negative examples. Figure 11 and Figure 12 shows the performance of the link prediction model in terms of F1-measure and AUC. Results of random sampling correspond to the average result of 10 random samples based models.

It can be observed from the figure that learning from a set of examples sampled using communities produces a model that outperforms models trained on original datasets, random samples and distance based samples. One can also notice that the training done on random samples produce better result than that of distance based samples. The failure of distance-based sampling may be due to the fact that nodes that are closer are theoretically more similar and have a greater tendency to form an edge. Thus removing the ones with distance greater than a threshold causes loss of some relevant information about

Table 6. Number of communities found in co-authorship graphs

Graphs	Louvain	LICOD	Walktrap	Infomap
1970-1973	9	9	8	16
1972-1975	14	29	17	37
1974-1977	17	25	27	47

Table 7. Original and sampled examples found in co-authorship graphs

Learn/Test	Label	#Positive	#Negative	Sampling Method	#Sampled Negative
1970-1973	1974-1975	16	1810	Louvain	1639
				Walktrap	1553
				LICOD	1507
				Infomap	1737
				Distance≤5	810
				Distance≤10	1767
				Random	1648
1972-1975	1976-1977	49	12141	Louvain	11122
				Walktrap	11569
				LICOD	11382
				Infomap	11941
				Distance≤5	3686
				Distance≤10	11030
				Random	11123
1974-1977	1978-1979	93	26223	Louvain	24833
				Walktrap	23835
				LICOD	25150
				Infomap	25839
				Distance≤5	7832
				Distance≤10	24222
				Random	24831

negative class. Within community based sampling we see that Louvain method does not give a good result on dataset 1 where as it is the best choice for dataset 2. The other three community algorithms have a comparative result in both datasets in terms of both F1-measure and AUC and their result is almost consistent on both datasets. Another important point that we notice here is that Walktrap performs quite well in both datasets whereas the performance of distance based sampling methods is not as good. The basic idea behind Walktrap is that if we perform random walk in a network, then these walks are likely to stay within same communities, as there are very few edges that lead outside a given community. The distance to be covered in random walks can be restricted to a certain length and the best modularity decides which level of partitions to choose from the dendrogram obtained. So, we can say that distance

Figure 11. Result in terms of F1-measure, using different sampled sets for learning

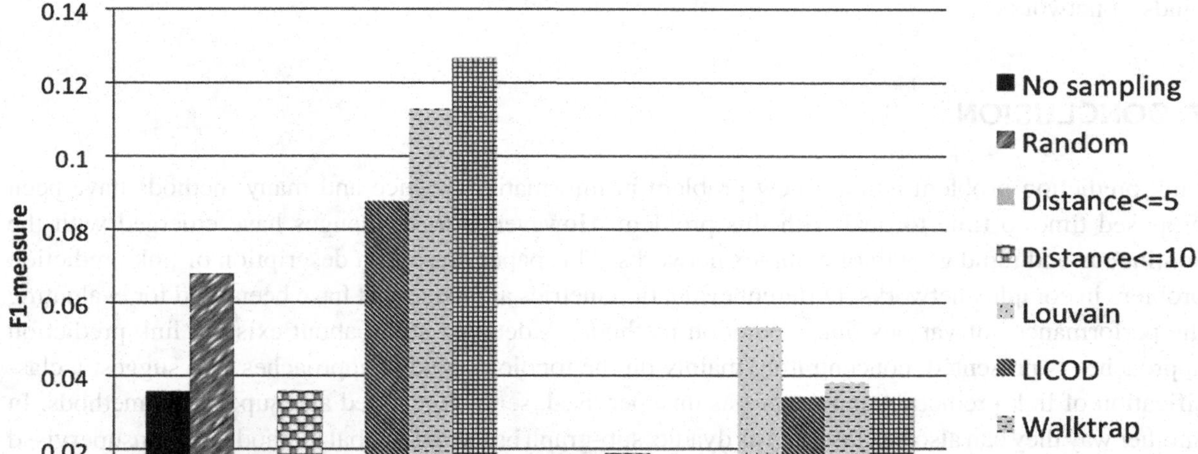

Figure 12. Result in terms of AUC, using different sampled sets for learning

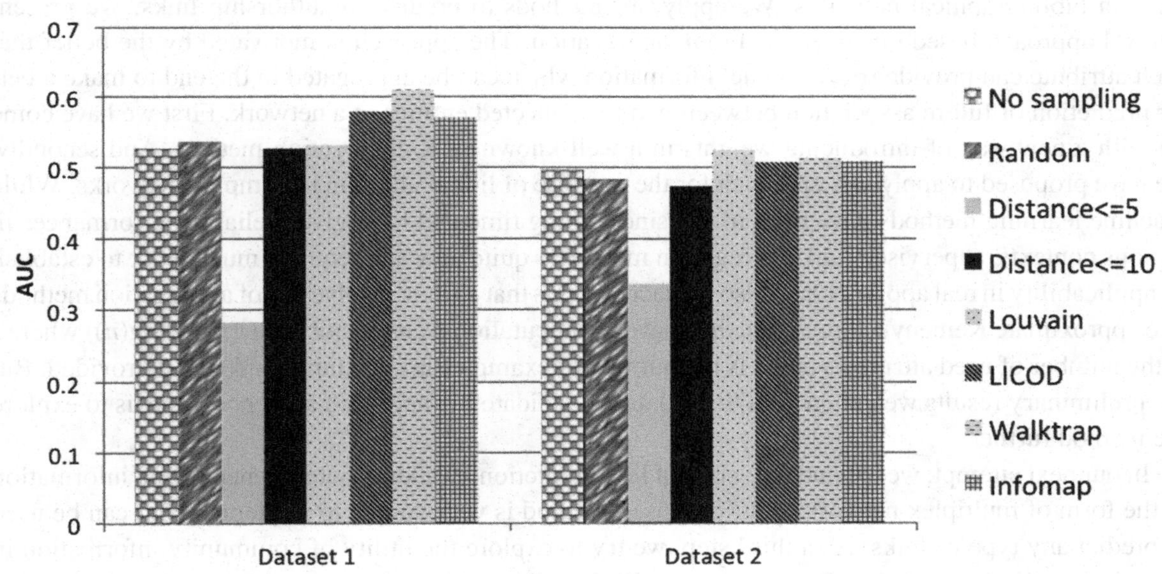

and path length can serve as a good criterion for under-sampling but careful selection of constraints are needed to make it useful for the task. We would like to specify here that this work of using communities for prediction co-authorship links is based on some experimental observations in particularly scientific collaboration network of DBLP data. So we cannot say at this stage if the same concept will work for other kinds of networks like social interaction networks, biological networks, geographical networks etc.

The behaviour of communities and distribution of links across communities can change with different kinds of networks.

7. CONCLUSION

Link prediction problem is not a new problem in information science and many methods have been proposed time to time to deal with this problem. However, new challenges have emerged with the continuous and rapid growth of complex networks. This paper presents a description of link prediction problem in complex networks. Different evaluation metrics are listed that have been used for evaluating the performances of various link prediction methods. A detailed study about existing link prediction approaches is presented, concentrating mainly on the topology guided approaches. We suggest a classification of link prediction approaches as unsupervised, semi-supervised and supervised methods. In another way they can also be classified as dyadic, sub-graph based and global methods. The unsupervised methods involve computation of scores for unlinked node pairs and ranking them based on the scores. In supervised approaches, especially machine learning based methods attempt is made to combine the effect of various topological attributes to generate a model which is then used to predict links on a test graph. There exist also some approaches that use semi-supervised methods for learning where a model is generated using partially labelled data.

We then present our own research work on link prediction. Our main focus is to analyse and predict links in bibliographical networks. We apply our methods to predict co-authorship links. We present a novel approach based on supervised rank aggregation. The approach is motivated by the belief that each attribute can provide some unique information which can be aggregated in the end to make a better prediction of future association between two unconnected entities in a network. First we have come up with a new way of introducing weights in a well-known rank aggregation method. And secondly, we have proposed to apply this approach for the purpose of link prediction in complex networks. While machine learning methods have been in use since a long time and have given reliable performances in various contexts, supervised rank aggregation method is quite new and requires much work to establish its applicability in real applications. Also the fact remains that as they involve use of aggregation methods like approximate Kemeny aggregation, they have a computational complexity of $O(r \times n \times \log(n))$ where r is the number of used attributes and n is the number of examples in each input ranked list provided. But the preliminary results we get on the DBLP datasets validate the approach and encourage us to explore the method further.

In our next attempt, we expand the scope of link prediction by adding heterogeneous link information in the form of multiplex networks. Our proposed method is very simple to implement and can be used to predict any type of links. As a third step, we try to explore the utility of community information in the context of link prediction. We use communities to filter out the list of candidate node pairs that are considered for prediction, but may not be very relevant for building a good model. This approach helps us to build a better prediction model in the presence of high class-imbalance. The result for community based filtering was better than the classical random filtering or distance based filtering. However, we would like to remind the readers that this was an experiment made specifically on bibliographic networks and the results may vary on other kinds of complex networks.

REFERENCES

Acar, E., Dunlavy, D. M., & Kolda, T. G. (2009). *Link prediction on evolving data using matrix and tensor factorizations.* ICDM Workshops. doi:10.1109/ICDMW.2009.54

Adamic, L., & Adar, E. (2003). Friends and neighbors on the Web. *Social Networks, 25*(3), 211–230. doi:10.1016/S0378-8733(03)00009-1

Aggarwal, C. C., Xie, Y., & Philip, S. Y. (2012). *On dynamic link inference in heterogeneousnetworks. In SDM* (pp. 415–426). SIAM.

Airoldi, E., Blei, D., Fienberg, S., Xing, E., & Jaakkola, T. (2006). Mixed membership stochastic block models for relational data with application to protein-protein interactions. *Proceedings of the International Biometrics Society Annual Meeting.*

Al Hasan, M., & Zaki, M. J. (2010). In C. C. Aggarwal (Ed.), *A survey of link prediction in social networks.* Social Network Data Analysis.

Aslam, J. A., & Montague, M. (2001). Models for metasearch. *Proceedings of the 24th annual international ACM SIGIR conference on Research and development in information retrieval* (pp. 276-284). New York: ACM.

Bao, Z., Zeng, Y., & Tay, Y. C. (2013). SonLP: Social network link prediction by principal component regression. *I Advances in Social Networks Analysis and Mining*, 364-371.

Barabasi, A.-L., & Albert, R. (1999). Emergence of scaling in random networks. *Science, 286*(5439), 509–512. doi:10.1126/science.286.5439.509 PMID:10521342

Battiston, F., Nicosia, V., & Latora, V. (2013). *Metrics for the analysis of multiplex networks.* arXive:1308.3182

Benchettara, N., Kanawati, R., & Rouveirol, C. (2010). *Supervised machine learning applied to linkprediction in bipartite social networks. International Conference on Advances in Social Network Analysis and Mining, ASONAM 2010.* doi:10.1109/ASONAM.2010.87

Berlingerio, M., Bonchi, F., Bringmann, B., & Gionis, A. (2009). Mining graph evolution rules. In W. L. Buntine, M. Grobelnik, D. Mladenic, & J. Shawe-Taylor (Ed.), ECML/PKDD (vol. 5781, pp. 115-130). Springer. doi:10.1007/978-3-642-04180-8_25

Berlingerio, M., Coscia, M., Giannotti, F., Monreale, A., & Pedreschi, D. (2011). Foundations ofMultidimensional Network Analysis. *Advances in Social Networks Analysis and Mining, 2011*, 485–489.

Black, D., Newing, R., McLean, I., McMillan, A., & Monroe, B. (1998). The Theory of Committees and Elections (2nd ed.). Kluwer Academic Publishing.

Blondel, V. D., Guillaume, J., & Lefebvre, E. (2008). Fast unfolding of communities in largen etworks. *Journal of Statistical Mechanics, 2008*(10), P10008. doi:10.1088/1742-5468/2008/10/P10008

Borda, J. D. (1781). *Mémoire sur les Elections au Scrutin.* Academic Press.

Brouard, C., D'Alché-Buc, F., & Szafranski, M. (2011). Semi-supervised penalized output kernel regression for link prediction. *Proceedings of the 28th International Conference on Machine Learning (ICML-11).*

Chawla, N. V., Bowyer, K. W., Hall, L. O., & Kegelmeyer, W. P. (2002). SMOTE: Synthetic minority over-sampling technique. *Journal of Artificial Intelligence Research, 16*(1), 321–357.

Chebotarev, P., & Shamis, E. (1997). The matrix-forest theorem and measuring relations in small social groups. *Automation and Remote Control, 58*(9), 1505–1514.

Clauset, A., Moore, C., & Newman, M. (2008). Hierarchical structure and the prediction of missinglinks in networks. *Nature, 453*(7191), 98–101. doi:10.1038/nature06830 PMID:18451861

Cooke, R. J. (2006). *Link prediction and link detection in sequences of large social networks using temporal and local metrics.* (Master Thesis). University of Cape Town.

Davis, D., Lichtenwalter, R., & Chawla, N. V. (2013). Supervised methods for multi-relational link prediction. *Social Network Analysis and Mining*, 1-15.

Davis, J., & Goadrich, M. (2006). The relationship between Precision-Recall and ROC curves. *Proceedings of the 23rd international conference on Machine learning.* doi:10.1145/1143844.1143874

Dunlavy, D. M., Kolda, T. G., & Acar, E. (2011). Temporal link prediction using matrix and tensor factorizations. *ACM Transactions on Knowledge Discovery from Data, 5*(2), 10. doi:10.1145/1921632.1921636

Dwork, C., Kumar, R., Naor, M., & Sivakumar, D. (2001). Rank aggregation methods for the web. *Proceedings of the 10th international conference on World Wide Web.* ACM.

Eronen, L., & Toivonen, H. (2012). Biomine: Predicting links between biological entities using network models of heterogeneous databases. *BMC Bioinformatics, 13*(1), 119. doi:10.1186/1471-2105-13-119 PMID:22672646

Fire, M., Tenenboim, L., Lesser, O., Puzis, R., Rokach, L., & Elovici, Y. (2011). Link prediction in social networks using computationally efficient topological features. *Proceedings of the 3rd IEEE Int. Conference on Social Computing.* doi:10.1109/PASSAT/SocialCom.2011.20

Fortunato, S. (2010). Community detection in graphs. *Physics Reports, 486*(3-5), 75–174. doi:10.1016/j.physrep.2009.11.002

Gao, S., Denoyer, L., & Gallinari, P. (2011*).* Temporal link prediction by integrating content and structure information. *Proceedings of the 20th ACM international conference on Information and knowledge management - CIKM '11* (p. 1169). New York: ACM Press. doi:10.1145/2063576.2063744

Getoor, L., Friedman, N., Koller, D., & Taskar, B. (2003). Learning probabilistic models of link structure. *Journal of Machine Learning Research, 3*, 679–707.

Hasan, M. A., Chaoji, V., Salem, S., & Zaki, M. (2006). *Link prediction using supervised learning.* Workshop on link analysis, Counter-terrorism and security, SIAM Data Mining Conference.

Huang, Z., & Lin, D. K. (2008). The time-series link prediction problem with applications in communication surveillance. *INFORMS Journal on Computing, 21*(2), 286–303. doi:10.1287/ijoc.1080.0292

Jaccard, P. (1901). Étude comparative de la distribution florale dans une portion des alpes et des jura. *Bulletin de la Société Vaudoise des Sciences Naturelles*, *37*, 547–579.

Kashima, H., Kato, T., Yamanishi, Y., Sugiyama, M., & Tsuda, K. (2009). Link propagation: A fast semi-supervised learning algorithm for link prediction. *SDM*, *9*, 1099–1110.

Katz, L. (1953). A new status index derived from socimetric analysis. *Psychmetrika*, *18*(1), 39–43. doi:10.1007/BF02289026

Kubat, M., & Matwin, S. et al. (1997). Addressing the curse of imbalanced training sets: One-sided selection. *ICML*, *97*, 179–186.

Kunegis, J., De Luca, E. W., & Albayrak, S. (2010). The Link Prediction Problem in Bipartite Networks. *Computational Intelligence for Knowledge Based Systems Design, 10.*

L, L., & Zhao, T. (2011). Link prediction in complex networks: A survey. *Physica A: Statistical Mechanics and its Applications, 390*(6), 1150-1170

Liben-Nowell, D., & Kleinberg, J. (2007). The link-prediction problem for social networks. *JASIST*, *58*(7), 1019–1031. doi:10.1002/asi.20591

Lichtenwalter, R., & Chawla, N. (2012). Link Prediction: Fair and Effective Evaluation. *Advances in Social Networks Analysis and Mining* (ASONAM), 376-383.

Lichtenwalter, R. N., Dame, N., Lussier, J. T., & Chawla, N. V. (2010). New perspectives and methods in link prediction. *Proceedings of the 16th ACM SIGKDD international conference on Knowledge discovery and data mining*. doi:10.1145/1835804.1835837

Liu, Z., Zhang, Q.-M., L, L., & Zhou, T. (2011). Link prediction in complex networks: A local naïve Bayes model. *EPL, 96*(4).

Menon, A. K., & Eklan, C. (2011). Link prediction via matrix factorization. Machine Learning and Knowledge Discovery in Databases, 6912, 437-452. doi:10.1007/978-3-642-23783-6_28

Montague, M., & Aslam, J. A. (2002). Condorcet fusion for improved retrieval. *Proceedings of the eleventh international conference on Information and knowledge management.* ACM.

Newman, M. E. (2004). Coauthorship networks and patterns of scientific collaboration. (PNAS). *Proceedings of the National Academy of Science of the United States*, *101*(Supplement 1), 5200–5205. doi:10.1073/pnas.0307545100 PMID:14745042

Ou, Q., Jin, Y. D., Zhou, T., Wang, B. H., & Yin, B. Q. (2007). Power-law strength-degree correlation from resource-allocation dynamics on weighted networks. *Physical Review E: Statistical, Nonlinear, and Soft Matter Physics*, 75. PMID:17358308

Ouzienko, V. A. (2010). Prediction of Attributes and Links in Temporal Social Networks. *ECAI*, 1121-1122.

Pons, P., & Latapy, M. (2006). Computing Communities in Large Networks Using Random Walks. *J. Graph Algorithms Appl.*, *10*(2), 191–218. doi:10.7155/jgaa.00124

Pujari, M., & Kanawati, R. (2012). *Link prediction in Complex Networks by Supervised Rank Aggregation*. ICTAI 2012: 24th IEEE International Conference on Tools with Artificial Intelligence. doi:10.1109/ICTAI.2012.111

Pujari, M., & Kanawati, R. (2012). *Tag Recommendation by link prediction based on supervised Machine Learning*. ICWSM.

Pujari M & Kanawati R. (n.d.). Link prediction in multiplex networks. *AIMS Networks & Heterogeneous Media Journal, 10*(1), 17-35. 782-789.

Puzis, R., Elovici, Y., & Fire, M. (2013). Link Prediction in Highly Fractional Data Sets. Handbook of Computational Approaches to Counterterrorism, 283-300.

Rattigan, M. J., & Jensen, D. (2005). The case for anomalous link discovery. *ACM SIGKDD Explorations Newsletter*, *7*(2), 41–47. doi:10.1145/1117454.1117460

Rosvall, M., Axelsson, D., & Bergstrom, C. T. (2009). The map equation. *The European Physical Journal. Special Topics*, *178*(1), 13–23. doi:10.1140/epjst/e2010-01179-1

Song, H. H., Cho, T. W., Dave, V., Zhang, Y., & Qiu, L. (2009). Scalable proximity estimation and link prediction in online social networks. *Proceedings of the 9th ACM SIGCOMM conference on Internet measurement conference*. doi:10.1145/1644893.1644932

Soundarajan, S., & Hopcroft, J. (2012). Using community information to improve the precision of link prediction methods. *Proceedings of the 21st international conference companion on World Wide Web*. doi:10.1145/2187980.2188150

Subbian, K., & Melville, P. (2011). Supervised rank aggregation for predicting influence in networks. *Proceedings of the IEEE Conference on Social Computing (SocialCom-2011)*.

Sun, Y., Barber, R., Gupta, M., Aggarwal, C., & Han, J. (2011). *Co-author relationship prediction in heterogeneous bibliographic networks. In Advances on social network Analysis and mining*. Kaohsiung, Taiwan: ASONAM.

Tan, F., Xia, Y., & Zhu, B. (2014). Link prediction in complex networks: A mutual information perspective. *PLoS ONE*, *9*(9), 1–8. doi:10.1371/journal.pone.0107056 PMID:25207920

Taskar, B., Wong, M., Abbeel, P., & Koller, D. (2003). Link prediction in relational data. In S. Thrun, L. K. Saul, & B. Schölkopf (Eds.), *NIPS. MIT Press*.

Wang, C., Satuluri, V., & Parthasarathy, S. (2007). Local probabilistic models for link prediction. In Y. Shi, & C. W. Clifton (Ed.), *Seventh IEEE International Conference on Data Mining (ICDM)*. doi:10.1109/ICDM.2007.108

Wang, X., & Sukthankar, G. (2013). Link prediction in multi-relational collaboration networks. *Proceedings of the 2013 IEEE/ACM International Conference on Advances in Social Networks Analysis and Mining*. doi:10.1145/2492517.2492584

Yakoubi, Z., & Kanawati, R. (2014). LICOD: A Leader-driven algorithm for community detection in complex networks. *Vietnam Journal of Computer Science*, 241-256.

Yin, D., Hong, L., & Davison, B. (2011). Structural link analysis and prediction in microblogs. *Proceedings of the 20th ACM international conference on Information and knowledge management - CIKM '11* (p. 1163). doi:10.1145/2063576.2063743

Young, H., & Levenglick, A. (1978). A consistent extension of Condorcet's election principle. *SIAM Journal on Applied Mathematics*, *35*(2), 285–300. doi:10.1137/0135023

Yu, X., Gu, Q., Zhou, M., & Han, J. (2012). Citation Prediction in Heterogeneous Bibliographic Networks. *SDM*, 1119-1130.

Zhang, J., & Philip, S. (2014). *Link prediction across heterogeneous social networks: A survey*. Chicago: University of Illinois.

Zhu, X. (2005). *Semi-supervised learning literature survey. Tech Report, Computer Sciences*. University of Wisconsin-Madison.

ENDNOTES

1 http://www.flickr.com
2 http://www.youtube.com
3 http://www.delicious.com
4 http://www.facebook.com
5 http://www.twitter.com
6 http://www.dblp.org
7 http://www.orange.biolab.si

Chapter 4
Design of Structural Controllability for Complex Network Architecture

Amitava Mukherjee
IBM India Private Limited, India

Debayan Das
Jadavpur University, India

Ayan Chatterjee
Jadavpur University, India

Mrinal K. Naskar
Jadavpur University, India

ABSTRACT

Networks are all-pervasive in nature. The complete structural controllability of a network and its robustness against unwanted link failures and perturbations are issues of immense concern. In this chapter, we propose a heuristic to determine the minimum number of driver nodes for complete structural control, with a reduced complexity. We also introduce a novel approach to address the vulnerability of the real-world complex networks, and enhance the robustness of the network, prior to an attack or failure. The simulation results reveal that dense and homogenous networks are easier to control with lesser driver nodes, and are more robust, compared to sparse and inhomogeneous networks.

1. INTRODUCTION

With the recent advances in network sciences and technology, we are compelled to recognize that nothing happens in isolation. Most of the phenomena occurring around us are connected with an enormous number of other pieces of a complex universal puzzle (Tanner, 2004; Barabasi, 2002; Strogatz, 2001). Our biological existence, religious practices and the social world, vividly depict a pellucid story of interrelatedness. With the Internet dominating our lives in the 21st century, we are witnessing a revolution in the making. But, the underlying critical question is: are we ready to embrace the importance of networks around us?

We should learn to appreciate the importance of networks, as part of our daily lives. Recent developments indicate that networks will dominate the next hundreds of years, to a much greater extent than most people are even prepared to acknowledge (Barabasi, 2002; Strogatz, 2001) this fact.

DOI: 10.4018/978-1-4666-9964-9.ch004

Complex networks are those real-world networks that are characterized by irregular non-trivial topological features, dynamically evolving with time (Strogatz, 2001; Dorogovtsev et al., 2003; Newman et al., 2006; Albert et al., 2002). Different neural networks in our body, various biological networks, the Internet, power-grid (Broder et al., 2000), World Wide Web, social networks etc., can effectively be modeled as complex networks (Strogatz, 2001; Dorogovtsev et al., 2003; Newman et al., 2006). Hence, complex networks form a crucial part of our daily lives (Dorogovtsev et al., 2003). Since the last decade, we have been witnessing a major surge of growing interest and research, with the main focus shifting from the analysis of small networks to that of systems with thousands or millions of nodes. Reductionism was the key driving force behind much of the research of the previous century (Barabasi, 2002). For decades, scientists and researchers have studied atoms and their constituents to understand the universe, molecules to comprehend life, individual gene to characterize and to examine human behavior. Now, relying on the results gathered from the research done in the previous century, we are close to knowing everything about the individual piece. We have successfully disassembled the nature by spending billions of research dollars. But now we are clueless as we run into the hard wall of complexity (Barabasi, 2002; Albert et al., 2002). Nature is not a well-designed puzzle with a unique solution. In complex systems, the components can reassemble in more ways than we can ever imagine. Nature exploits all-encompassing laws of self-organization, whose roots are still mysteries to us (Barabasi, 2002; Newman et al., 2006).

Networks with irregular and random topological behavior appear in almost all fields of modern science and economics. Focus of engineering analysis is based on controlling real-world systems. Similar analysis also holds for these networks. But existing classical control theory fails in case of complex networks for reasons described in later sections. Thus, the modern theory of structural controllability has gained prominence. Structural Control theory is the main tool in the analysis of large scale networks. Unlike classical control theory, structural control theory is based on graph theory. Dilation-free paths play a major role in this type of control and are discussed in details in this chapter. For any network, few certain nodes play the role of controllers. These nodes are known as the driver nodes. This is an implication of the famous Pareto Principle that the entire network can be structurally controlled by a smaller set of nodes (driver nodes). This chapter deals with the mathematical procedure of eliminating dilation in networks and thereby determining the driver nodes for more efficient control of complex network from the view point of structural controllability theory.

1.1. Motivation

Complete structural controllability of a complex network is a mandate for ubiquitous data flow through a complex network. By complete structural controllability it is meant that all nodes in a network either lie on some augmenting path controlled by a driver node or thenode itself is a driver node. Evaluating the structural controllability of any real-world complex network, requires the determination of maximum matching in the network (Chatterjee et al., 2013; Das et al., 2014). The notion of maximum matching has been elaborated in the later sections. The classical definition of controllability proposed by Kalman (Kalman, 1963), did not workfor complex networks, mainly due to the basic fact that the real-world networks were directed, whereas the definition held for undirected networks. Also, in most practical cases, as the networks tended to expand, it was almost impossible to compute the rank of the controllability state matrix Q_C (Luenberger, 1979). Hence, the classical control theory did not serve our purpose for complex networks. Thus, to control efficiently the complex networks, Lin proposed the structural controllability theorem (Lin, 1974). To evaluate the structural controllability of a network, we required evaluating the number of external inputs to control the entire network. For this purpose, the Minimum Inputs theorem was used to determine the maximum matching in a network (Liu, et al., 2011). Maximum matching in a unipartite graph was a two-stage process. In the first stage, the bipartite equivalent, and finally, the maximum matching was computed using the famous Hopcroft Karp algorithm (Hopcroft and Karp, 1973). The algorithm had the complexity of the order $n^{5/2}$, where n was the number of nodes in the complex network. Other proposed algorithms (Hanckowiak et al., 1998; Galil, 1980) also required the computation of the bipartite equivalent. The deduction of bipartite equivalent through clique covering was an problem of NP- complete class, as the solution could not be obtained in polynomial time. In this chapter, we propose a heuristic that gives the maximum matching directly from the unipartite graph, thereby making the problem solvable in real time, with a lesser worst case complexity of $O(n^2)$.

We proceed further to show that the obtained set of driver nodes and the corresponding augmenting paths are necessary, but not sufficient to provide any tolerance to the network over unwanted link failures and perturbations. Cascades are intrinsic characteristic of any complex network, which keeps on growing with the passage of time (Motter, 2004; K. Zhao, 2011; Newth & Ash, 2005). As the number of users keeps on increasing, the networks become susceptible to various external attacks (Cohen et al., 2000).

On August 14, 2003, the Northeastern and Midwestern United States and Canadian province of Ontario suffered a widespread power outage. The Northeast blackout was a vivid instance of a cascading failure as the alarms failed to detect the overloading in the transmission lines. The investigation report stated that it was the failure of the interconnected grid's reliability; organizations had to provide effective real-time diagnostic support. What could have been a manageable local blackout, cascaded into widespread distress on the electric grid (Barabasi, 2002).

Recently in 2014, the social networking service Facebook, suffered a major outage. Even after fixing the original issue, flow of queries continued. The databases had entered feedback loop and thus failed to recover. Thus, to stop this unwanted feedback cycle, they were forced to block the entire traffic to the database cluster, and hence the site was turned off for almost 2.5 hours. Hence, failures in the real-world networks are a very critical issue (Zhao et al., 2007), and in the final part of this chapter, we propose a model to mitigate those issues up to a certain degree of link failures.

1.2. Contribution

The key contributions of this chapter are:

- We propose our heuristic to determine the maximum matching of a real-world network with reduced complexity.
- We introduce a new network parameter 'R' to determine the tolerance of a network over unavoidable link failures. We define tolerance as the measure of the vulnerability of a network against perturbations and the unavoidable link failures.
- We study the change in the number of driver nodes with random link deletion of a directed network and determine the requisite number of driver nodes required to ensure complete controllability of the entire network with a specified degree of tolerance.
- Given the tolerance limit, we propose a model to build the architecture of a real-world complex network.

1.3. Chapter Organization

The remainder of the chapter is organized as follows. In section 2, we summarize the existing works on controllability of complex networks. Section 3 discusses the Kalman's classical control theory and its limitations in real-world complex networks. The Hopcroft Karp algorithm is also discussed. Section 4 deals with the structural control theory and the Lin's theorem. Various important concepts like maximum matching, driver nodes, augmenting paths are introduced, along with the Minimum inputs theorem. In section 5, we propose our heuristic for maximum matching in complex networks. Section 6 presents the simulation results of the proposed degree-first greedy search algorithm. Section 7 introduces the new parameter tolerance (R), and analyzes the behavior of a real-world directed complex network in qualitative terms. The simulation results of behavior of networks on unavoidable link failure are presented in section 8. Section 9 concludes the chapter, along with its future scope.

2. RELATED WORKS

Studying real-world complex networks is impossible without having sufficient knowledge of graph theory. The main section in the study of graphs is various algorithms that give solutions to graph related problems. Swiss mathematician Euler was pioneering in this field of mathematics. Solution to the Konigsberg's Bridge Problem by Euler laid the foundation of graph theory. Two large islands on both side of Pregel River in Prussia were connected by seven bridges. The problem was to travel through all the islands at least once while crossing all the bridges exactly once. Euler showed that this was not possible by considering the islands as nodes and the bridges as links (Euler, 1736). He proved that the inclusion of another bridge would make the problem solvable.

Many problems regarding graphs had been developed later on, which included Chinese Postman problem, Three-cottage problem, Traveling salesman problem and many more. Some of them were solvable, some of them were not. The main interest lies in the application of these ideas in real life problems, in economics, in network theory, in computer science, in biology. This chapter deals with the problem the maximum matching for the controllability of complex networks, mapped into the context of a graph theory problem.

Irrespective of the nature of the nodes and links, for our simplicity, we consider the networks as graphs. But, again simplifying Internet architecture into agraph poses certain challenges. The type of graph formed for Internet differs completely with that of the graph of cell architecture or brain architecture. Yet, the final aim of all researchers was to obtain the simplest possible explanation. Hence, in 1959, Erdős and Rényi proposed the Erdős-Rényimodel (Erdős & Rényi, 1960), which fundamentally treated each network as a random network. Thus, it predicted that most people had same number of connections in the society, i.e., we lived in a society of averages. This model never planned to provide a universal theory of network formation. It had been assumed that all the nodes were equivalent and that we had all the nodes present from its inception. Until recently, we had no alternative for describing the interlinked network universe. The discovery of network hubs, and the power laws describing them, compelled us to abandon assumptions of degree distributions to be Poisson (Barabasi, 2002). It was observed in the recent studies that complex networks followed the "small worlds" property, i.e., the degree of separation was very less (six) between two nodes (Tanner, 2004). To explain the ubiquity of clustering followed in the most real networks, Watts Strogatz model (cluster friendly extension of the previous model) was proposed in 1998. Both the models assumed a static network, which did not evolve with time (Strogatz, 2001).

Recently, Barabasi showed that real world networks were governed by two laws: growth and preferential attachment (Barabasi, 2009; see also Barabasi and Albert, 1999). Each network started from a small nucleus and grew with the addition of new nodes. Then, the existing nodes grew by the "rich gets richer" mechanism, i.e., they preferred to attach themselves to another node having more number of links. Since it was the first model to explain the hubs of nodes and the scale-free power law, it became popular as the scale-free model (Barabasi, 2009, Caldarelli, 2007; Faloutsos et al., 1999).

Controlling a complex network using minimum number of driver nodes was not a practical solution and the network was prone to external attacks and link failures. Robustness against attacks and failures were a mandate for real-world networks. Earlier, Barabasi et al. had proposed that, scale-free networks were more robust than random networks, against unwanted attacks and failures (Barabasi and Albert, 1999; Albert et al., 2000). But, when the hubs were preferentially attacked, the scale-free networks were also vulnerable. Crucitti et al. (Crucitti et al., 2004), concluded that robustness of a complex network against attacks and link failures, depended on its topology. Beygelzimer et al. (Beygelzimer et al., 2005), and Moreira et al. (Moreira et al., 2009) proposed modifications of network topologies to prevent damages due to an attack occurred in the network. But, in practical cases, we could not always rehash i.e., reorient an existing network topologically before an attack or a failure occurred. In 2005, Kuhn et al. (Kuhn et al., 2005) came up with a solution where the network reacted immediately in the case of disappearance of a node.

3. CLASSICAL CONTROL THEORY AND ITS LIMITATIONS

Let us discuss the problem that this chapter deals with. Controlling systems mean that the systems can reach a state from any other state on the application of finite inputs in finite time (Kalman, 1963; Luenberger, 1979; Slotine et al., 1991; Srikant, 2004; Chiang et al., 2007; Kelly et al., 1998). An example should clarify the definition. Controlling the steering wheel of a car allows us to take the car from one place to another in a finite time. Thus it is controllable. Similar definition is applicable for any network. State of a network is defined by a vector whose elements are various parameters of the networks at particular instant. Like state of a car can be defined with its position coordinates in a reference plane.

Checking controllability of any system in classical control theory invokes theKalman's controllability criterion(A. Lombardi, 2007; B. Liu, 2008). Consider the continuous linear time-invariant system,

$$\overset{\text{Ù}}{x}(t) = Ax(t) + Bu(t) \tag{1}$$

$$y(t) = Cx(t) + Du(t) \tag{2}$$

where x(t) is the state vector nX1, y(t) is output vector mX1 and u(t) is the input control matrix rX1. The system is said to be controllable iff$Q_C = [B\ AB\ A^2\ B\ \ldots\ A^{n-1}B]$ and rank(Q_C) = n, where A is the system matrix of dimension n X n, and B is the n X m input matrix (m ≤ n). Dealing with these state matrices for a large network with millions of nodes and links is not feasible at all. Moreover, the classical definition of controllability is only valid for undirected networks, whereas most of the complex networks in real-world are directed in nature. It does not give us any solution to determine the driver nodes, and to bring an uncontrollable system under control.

4. ADVENT OF STRUCTURAL CONTROLLABILITY

To define the controllability of complex networks, Lin proposed a new concept "Structural Controllability" in the year 1970.Any structurally controllable system could be shown to be completely controllable for almost every weight combination. Thus, the advent of structural controllability helped us to overcome our inherently incomplete knowledge of the link weights in the system matrix A.

From the classical definition of controllability, it can be said that a system can be controlled by external inputs if and only if the system is fully controllable, and from the definition of driver nodes, we can say that the number of driver nodes are always equal to the number of inputs to the system [Evans, 2004]. Eventually we summarize these two facts that if the minimum number of driver nodes for a digraph can be calculated then the number of inputs needed to control the system can be evaluated. We are mainly interested in identifying the minimum number of driver nodes, N_D, which is sufficient to control the system's dynamic.

Now, in the basic concept of *structural controllability*, it is considered that the system obeys the linear Equation (1) and that the matrices A and B are structured. (A, B) are structured - implies that the elements of A and B are either 0 (representing the absence of connection between two nodes) or are independent free parameters (weights of the connected links between the nodes). The system (A,B) is said to be *structurally controllable*, if it is possible to fix the independent free parameters of the matrix pair A and B to certain values for which A and B can pass the Kalman's controllability test (Kalman, 1963), that is, rank $(Q_C)= n$. When the system becomes controllable for any value of the independent free parameters of the matrix pair (A, B), then the system is said to be 'strongly structurally controllable' (Mayeda & Yamada, 1979).

4.1. Lin's Structural Controllability Theorem

In the structural controllability theorem proposed by Lin (Lin, 1974), two basic conditions were imposed on the complex network - a) inaccessibility and b) dilation. In a digraph, a node was said to be inaccessible if that node could not be influenced by an external input. For instance, as shown in Figure 1, an isolated node was an inaccessible node. In a digraph, if there was a driver node which was not the starting node of a directed path, then the nodes upstream to the driver node would-be the inaccessible nodes as those nodes could not be accessed by the external input connected to the driver node.

In a digraph, if there existed more number of subordinate nodes than that of superior nodes. Figure 2 represents inaccessibility due to dilation. Lin's structural controllability theorem stated that a digraph would-be fully structurally controllable, iff it did not contain any inaccessible nodes and dilation.

To evaluate the structural control of a certain digraph, we have to determine the number of external inputs needed to control the network completely. It will be economical if we are able to determine the minimum number of inputs to control it. For this purpose minimum inputs theorem can be used.

Figure 1. Inaccessibility due to Isolated Node

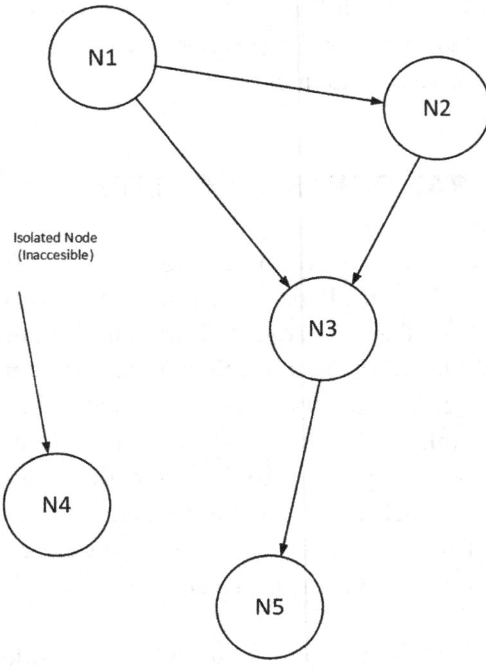

Figure 2. Dilation

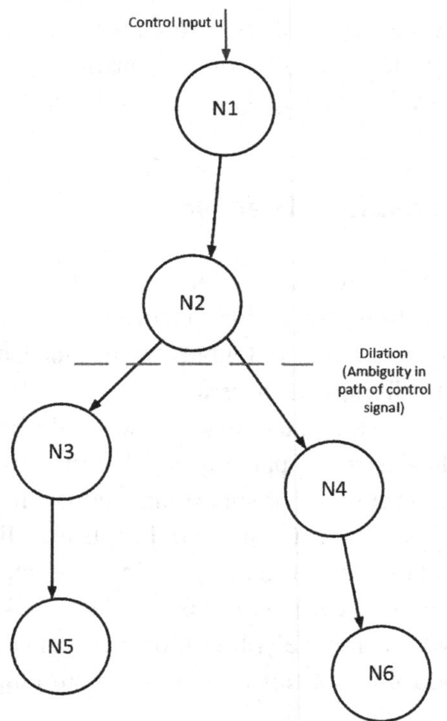

4.2. Minimum Inputs Theorem

The minimum inputs theorem states that, in a directed real-world controlled network, the minimum number of inputs equals to the minimum number of driver nodes needed to fully control the network (Liu et al, 2011). From Figure 3, we see that the minimum number of inputs required for complete structural control of the network is three. If the minimum number of driver nodes is one, i.e., only one input is necessary to control the network completely, then the controlled network is said to be perfectly matched (Lovasz & Plummer, 2009). In figure3, N5, N1 and N4 are the driver nodes, where three independent inputs are applied.

4.3. Maximum Matching in Directed Networks

A matching M_1 of the graph G_1 is an edge set such that no two edges of M_1 share their endpoints. Given a bipartite graph $G_1 = (V_1, E_1)$, the maximum matching is a matching that contains the largest possible set of edges. Maximum matching in directed networks refers to finding the smallest set of augmenting paths i.e., the linear paths without dilations. So that the maximum number of nodes lies on few linear paths with head (what is meant for) nodes acting as driver nodes. Maximum matching of a digraph introduces some linear paths, none of which share any interconnection. These paths are called *augmenting paths*. The start nodes of these paths are called *driver nodes*. Figure 3 shows a maximum matched network with three driver nodes, in which the external inputs are to be given, to control the entire network completely. If maximum matching of a network has only one start node and end node, then it is called complete matching (Zdeborova & Mezard, 2006).

Figure 3. Minimum number of inputs required here is 3

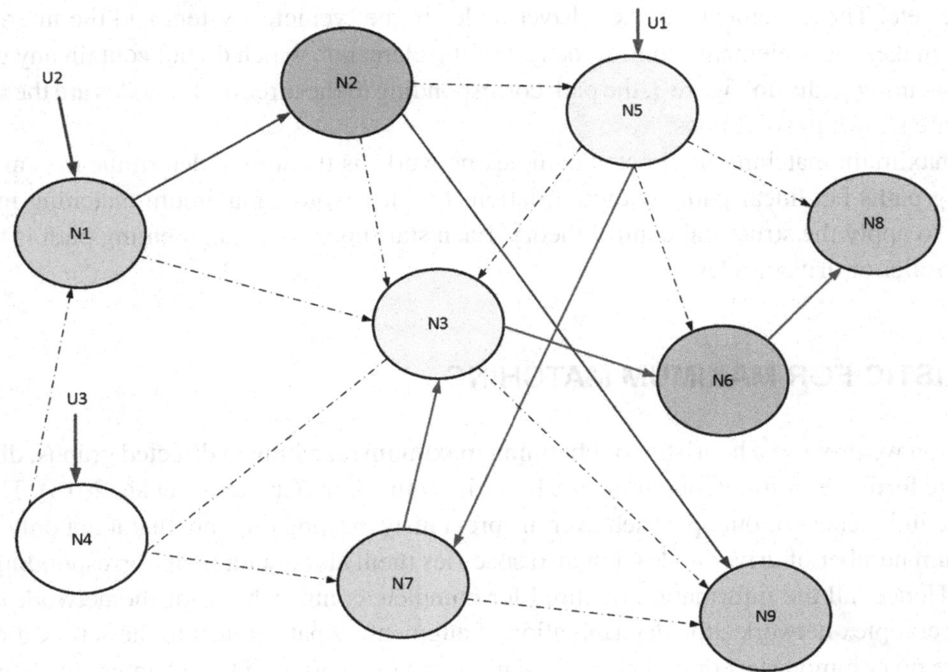

A bipartite graph represents a graph which has two disjoint sets of nodes. In a bipartite graph, maximum matching refers to the set of edges without common vertices (Guillaume & Latapy, 2004). A node is called matched, if it lies on either end of a matched edge. Solution to this problem was first proposed by Hopcroft and Karp (Hopcroft & Karp, 1973). It took a bipartite graph as an input (Guillaume & Latapy, 2004) and computed its maximum matching.

4.4. Driver Node and Augmenting Path

In a maximum matched undirected network, driver nodes are designated by the end points of matched paths, otherwise called the augmenting paths (Das et al., 2014). In directed networks, driver node is the starting node of the augmenting path, where the desired input is applied for controlling the whole path corresponding to it. From Figure 3, we see that N1, N4, N5 are the driver nodes to which the inputs U2, U3, U1 are applied. In Figure 3, the path corresponding to the three driver nodes are the augmenting paths and are shown in solid lines.

Take an example of a vehicle. Say it has around 5000 different mechanical, electrical and electronic elements (parts). But when we drive the vehicle, we only consider steering wheel, gear and clutches for controlling the whole vehicle. We have then not at all bothered about most of other unseen elements. These three controlling elements can take the vehicle from a place to another place in a finite time. Thus it is controllable by these three elements. These elements are key driver nodes in the 'vehicle' system and the internal connection which makes these elements control the rest of the elements, which do not contain any dilation, are called augmenting paths. This is a practical analogy of how structural control takes place in real life system like motor vehicle system.

Let us consider an example of a particular vehicle in the context of complex system. There are thousands of different mechanical, electrical and electronic elements (parts). We need not care about all those parts while driving the vehicle. We control only few parts like the steering wheel, the breaks, the clutches etc. These elements are key driver nodes in the 'vehicle' system and the internal connection which makes these elements control the rest of the elements, which do not contain any dilation, are called augmenting paths. In Figure 3, the path corresponding to the three driver nodes are the augmenting paths and are shown in solid lines.

Thus, maximum matching in directed complex networks is the tool to determine the smallest set of augmenting paths i.e. linear paths without dilation. In other words, maximum matching in a network enables us to apply the structural control theory. Each start node in an augmenting path is thus known as the controller or driver nodes.

5. HEURISTIC FOR MAXIMUM MATCHING

In this section we propose a heuristic for obtaining maximum matching in directed graphs, directly from its unipartite form, i.e., without obtaining the bipartite equivalent (Chatterjee et al., 2013). The main advantage and uniqueness of our approach over the previously existing ones are that it not only determines the minimum number of driver nodes, but also specifies them along with their corresponding augmenting paths. Hence, all the information required for complete controllability of the network is obtained. In directed complex networks, the determination of augmenting paths refers to the sets of directed links which share no common start or end point. The basic notations used in this chapter are shown in Table

Table 1. Notations

Notation	Description
N	Number of nodes in the complex network
L	Number of links in the complex networks
N_d	Number of driver nodes obtained from maximum matching
n_d	Driver node density
Nd_{eff}	Effective minimum number of driver nodes to control the entire network
R	Tolerance of the network

1. The steps given below are used in determining the maximum matching in directed networks using our algorithm. Table 1 shows the various notations used for parametric description of any network.

Steps of algorithm:

1. Determine the highest out-degree node in the entire network under consideration. Let this node be denoted as N_X. As discussed, this is a driver node of the corresponding augmenting path.
2. Now, determine the node connected to N_X with the highest out-degree. Let the node be denoted as N_Y.
3. Consider the link from node N_X to N_Y and discard all the links connected to N_X, thereby setting its degree as 1. Discard N_X in the augmenting path and discard it from further consideration.
4. Finally, assign node N_Y to N_X and repeat steps 2 and 3, till the degree of N_X becomes 1. After completion of step 4, the augmenting path having N_X (from step 1) as the driver node is obtained. Go to next step, when the last node in the augmenting path has 0 out-degree.
5. Repeating steps 1-4, the next augmenting path is obtained.
6. Repeat steps 1-5, till all the nodes of the network has been considered.

We explain our algorithm with a simple example.

Let us consider this network as given in Figure 4. Here N=9 and L=16. We use our algorithm on this unipartite network to find the maximum matching.

At first we find the highest out-degree node N5.

Consider Figure 5. N5 is the highest degree node. The outward links and inward links are marked by brown and blue respectively. Now, according to the algorithm, we check the out-degree of N3, N6, N8.

Now we see that the node N7 has the highest out-degree, connected with N5. All the links connected to N5 except the one connected to N7 are discarded virtually, as in Figure 6.

Consider Figure 7. This link, marked in brown, is included in the augmented paths. Now we repeat the same process for N7.

Again we check the highest out-degree node connected with N7, as shown in Figure 8.

Now, consider Figure 9. The highest out-degree node connected to N7 is N3. So we keep the link between N7 and N3 and discard all other links connected with N7.

As in Figure 10, we repeat the same process for N3. Highest out-degree node connected to it is N6.

Figure 4. Digraph with N=9 and L=16

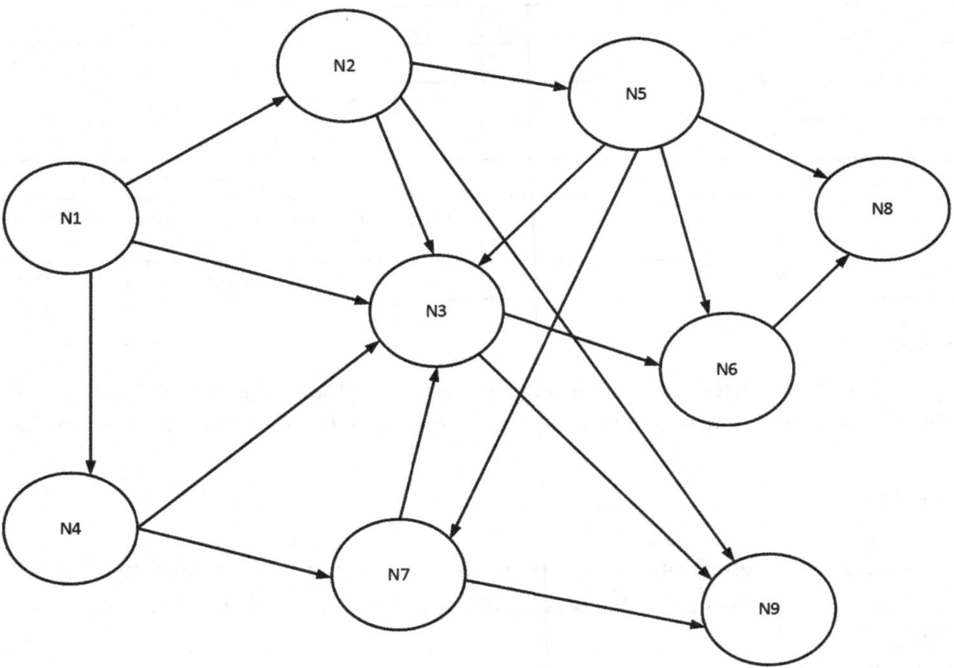

Figure 5. Highest out-degree node is marked blue

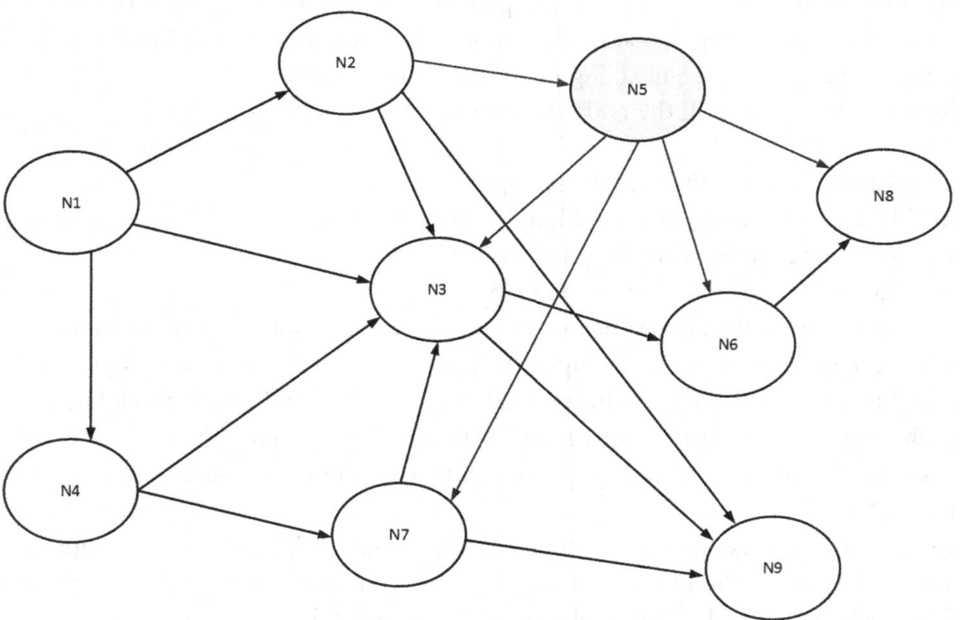

Figure 6. Highest out-degree node connected to N5 is colored green

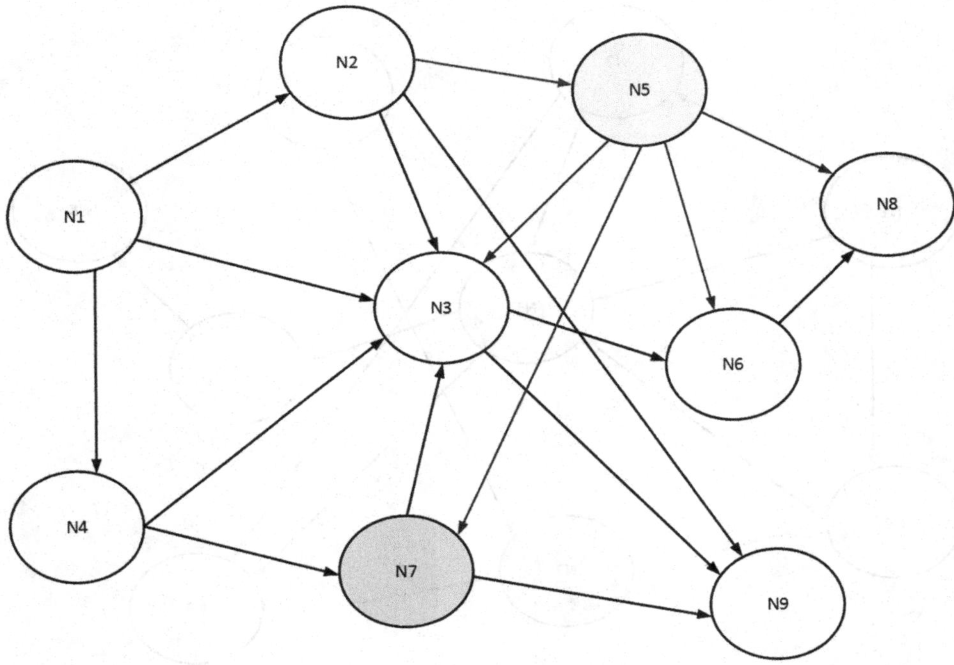

Figure 7. Links not lying on augmenting path are removed (virtually)

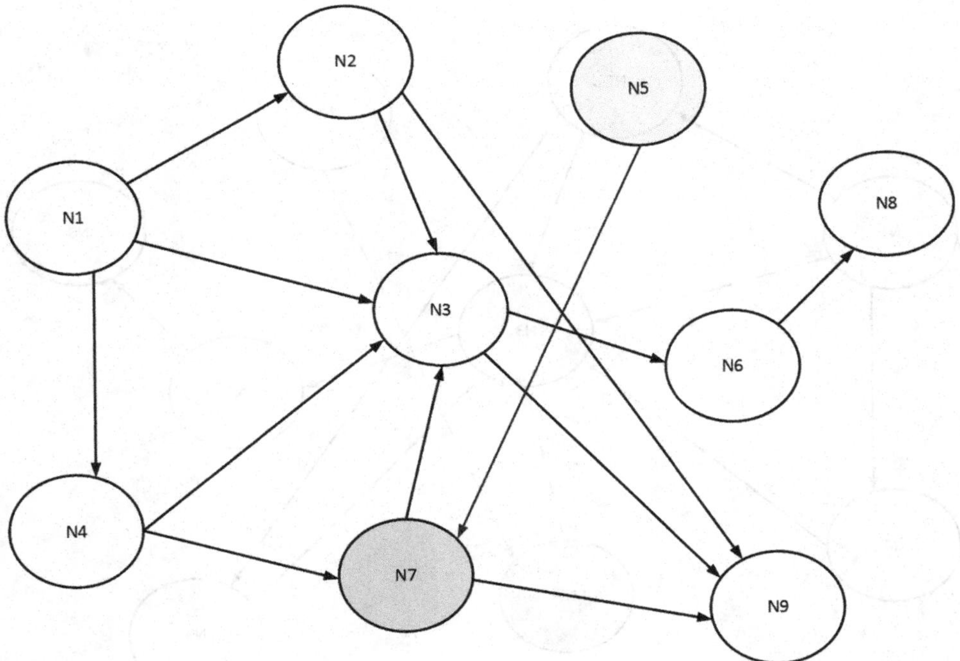

Figure 8. Highest out-degree node connected to N7 is marked

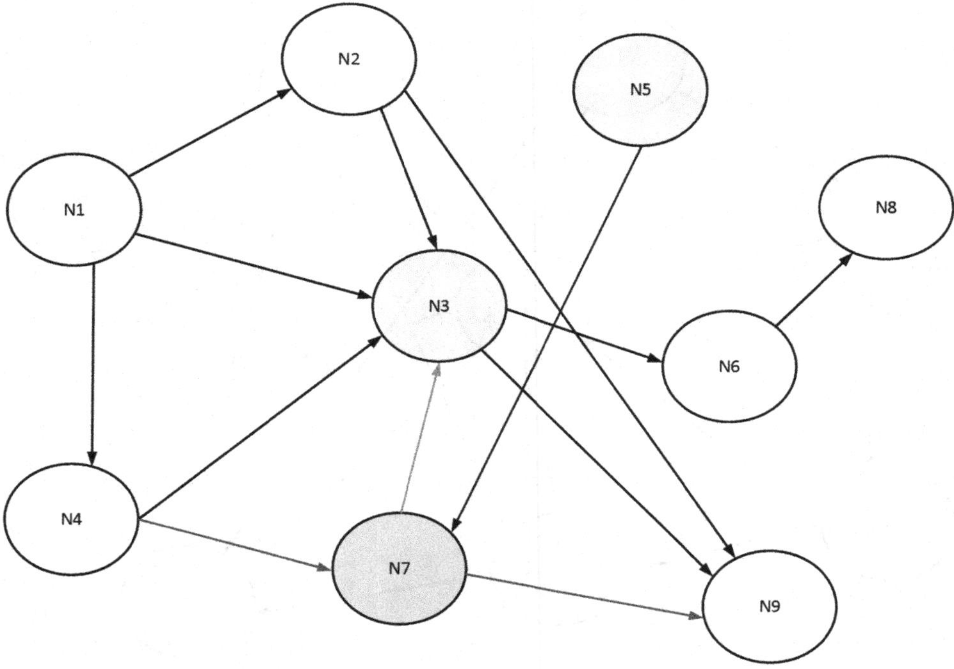

Figure 9. Links not lying on augmenting path are deleted

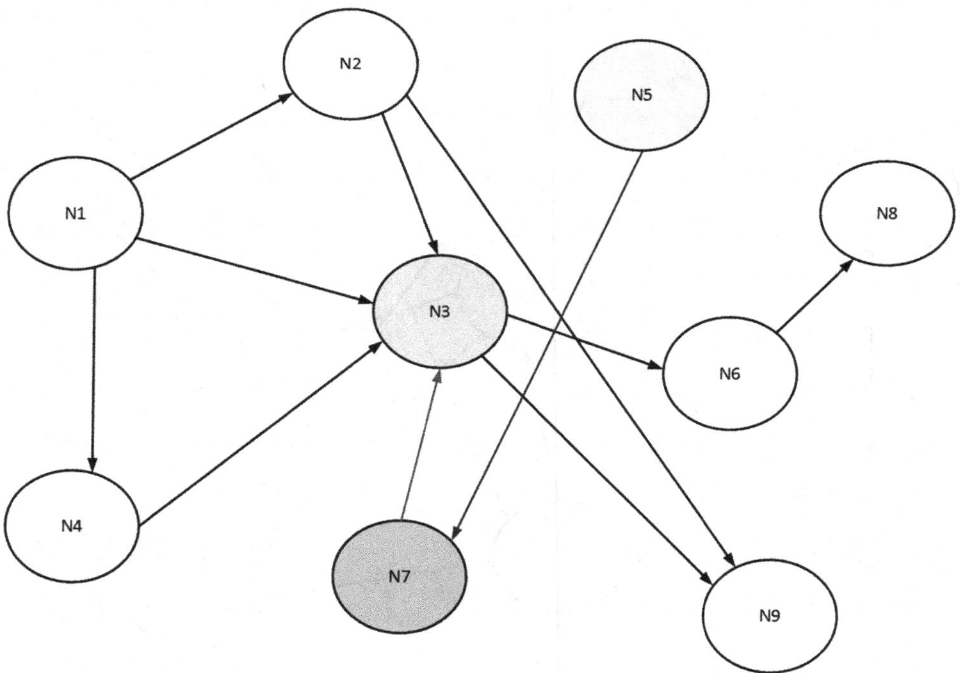

In a similar manner all other links connected to N3 are discarded, as shown in Figure 11. N5-N7-N3-N6-N8 is an augmenting path with driver node N5 as the last node N8 has zero out-degree.

We again repeat the same process for the rest of the network except the augmenting path found above. Now we get the new highest out-degree node to be N1, as seen from Figure 12.

Consider Figure 13. The highest-out degree node connected to N1 is N2. So link between N1 and N4 is discarded.

So, the next augmented path obtained is N1-N2-N9, with driver node N1. The isolated node remaining in the network is N4, as seen from Figure. 14. So it is treated as a driver node itself.

Hence, according to the proposed algorithm, the maximum matched network is as shown in Figure 15.

6. SIMULATION RESULTS OF THE DEGREE-FIRST GREEDY SEARCH HEURISTIC

6.1. Simulation Environment

The networks, we consider for running simulation, follow the Erdős-Rényi model (Erdős & Rényi, 1960; Bollobas, 2001). These networks are generated using simulator Cytoscape (Version 2.8.3). Cytoscape is an open source software platform for visualizing complex networks, as well as a bio-informatics software platform for visualizing molecular interaction networks, and integrating them with any kind of attribute

Figure 10. Highest out-degree node connected to N3 is marked

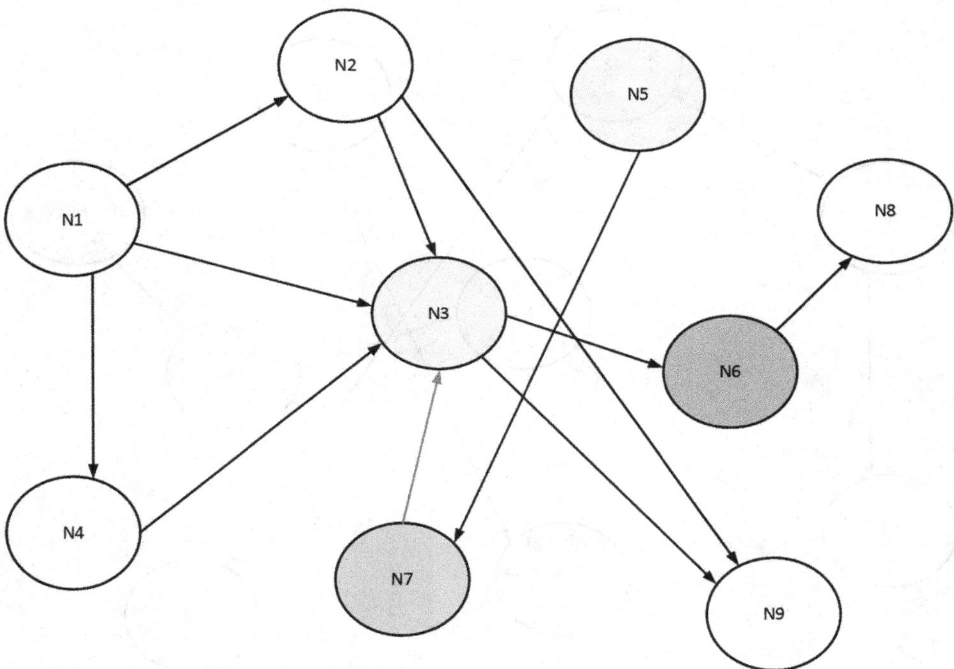

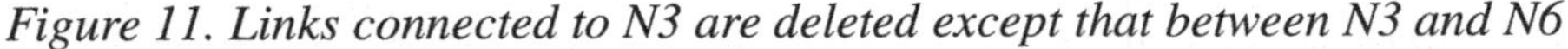

Figure 11. Links connected to N3 are deleted except that between N3 and N6

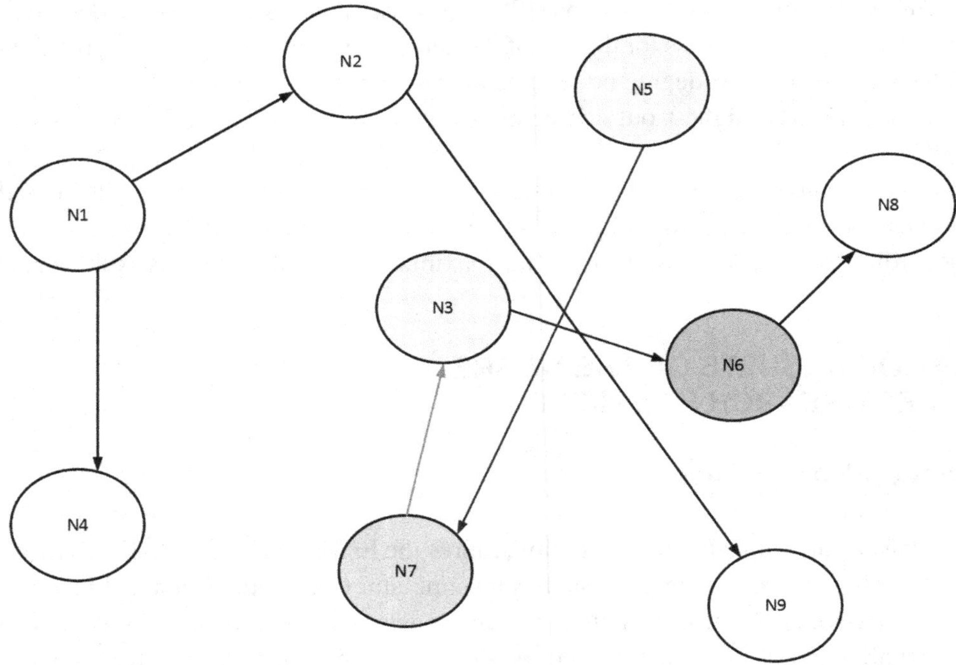

Figure 12. Highest out-degree node connected to N6 is marked

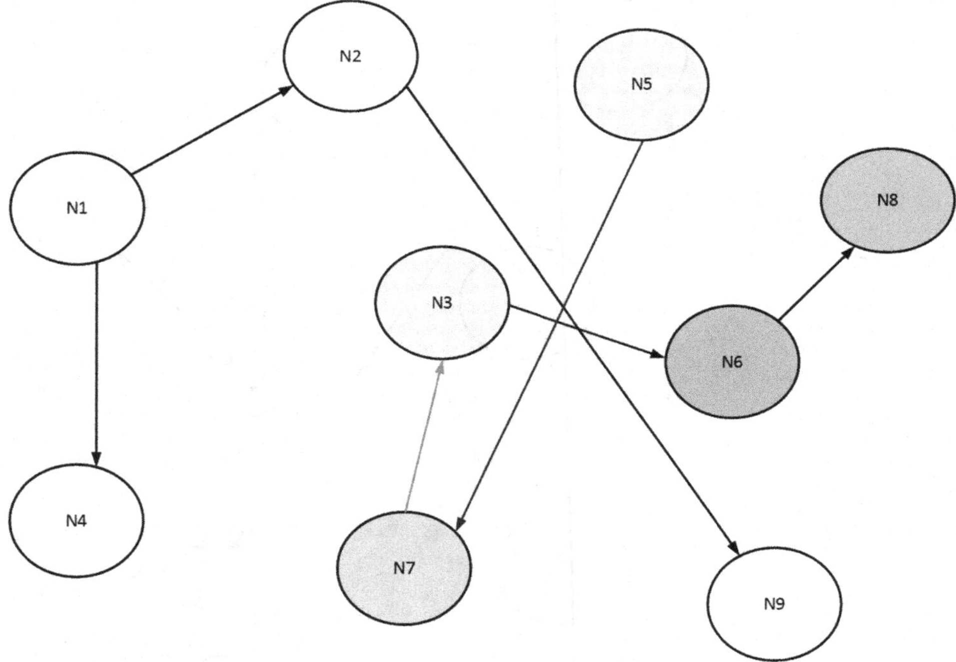

Figure 13. Highest out-degree node from remaining network (N1) is marked

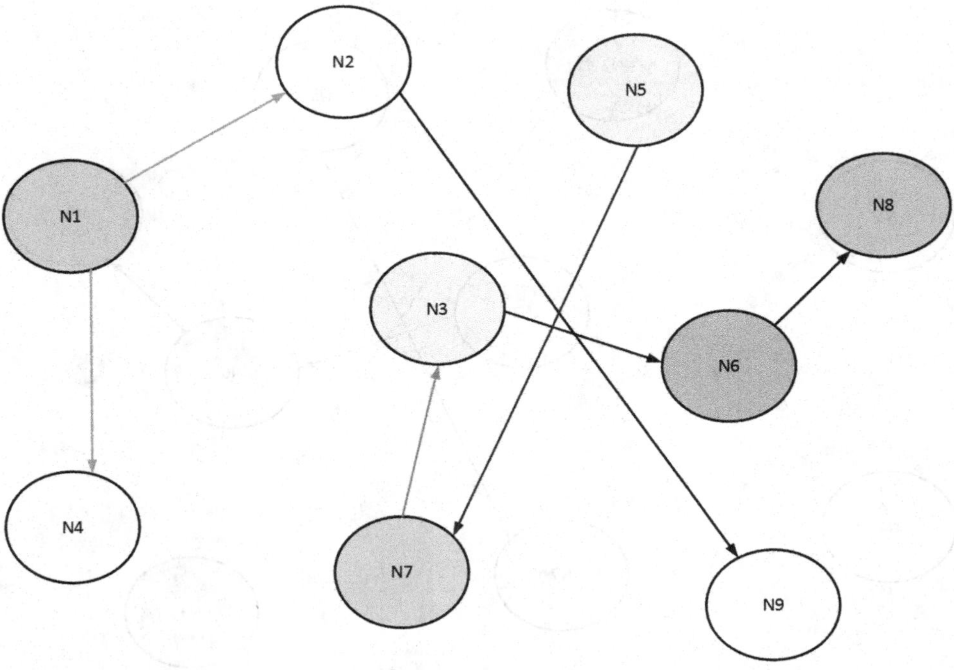

Figure 14. Highest out-degree node connected to N1 is marked green

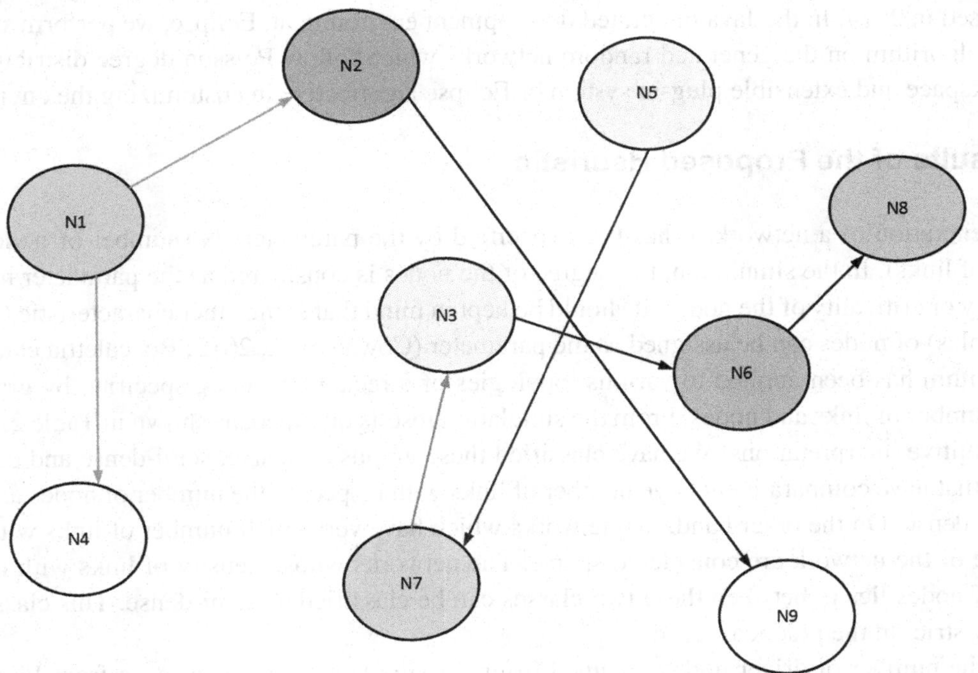

Figure 15. N9 is included in augmenting path and N4 becomes isolated

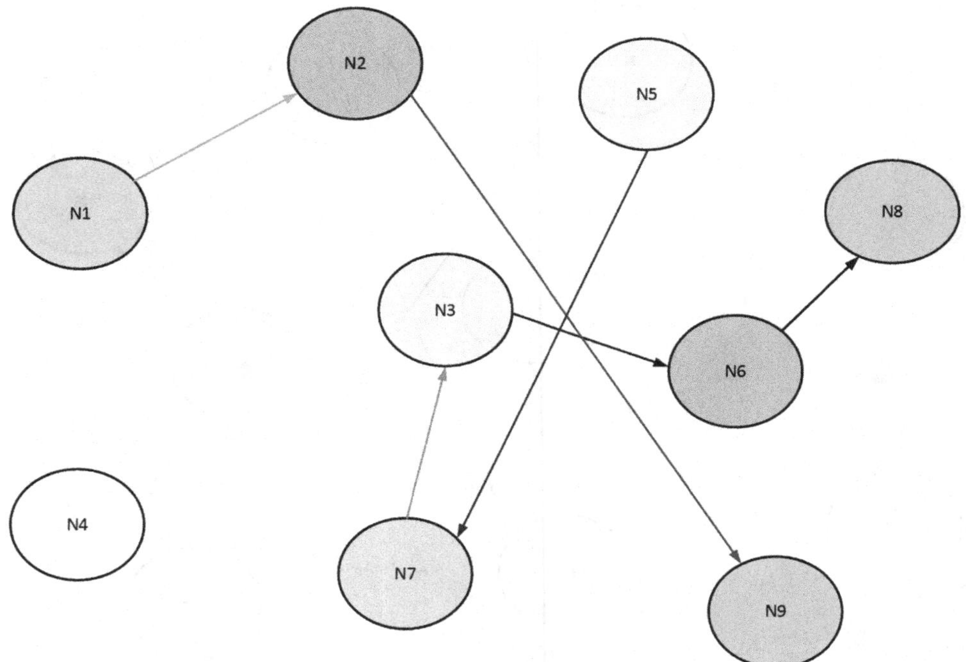

data. Here, the random network generation plug-in is used with the latest version of Cytoscape, which was released in 2014. In the Java integrated development environment, Eclipse, we perform simulation with our algorithm on the generated random networks which follow Poisson degree distribution. The base workspace and extensible plug-in system of Eclipse areeffective in customizing the environment.

6.2. Results of the Proposed Heuristic

During generation of a network, it has been specified by the parameters N (number of nodes) and L (number of links). In the simulation, the degree of the nodes is considered as the parameter measuring the priority or criticality of the nodes. It should be kept in mind that some other characteristic (attributes and variables) of nodes can be assigned as the parameter (Cowan et al., 2012; Boccalettia et al., 2006). Our algorithm has been applied to various topologies of directed networks, specified by graphs with varying number of links and nodes. From the simulation results obtained, as shown in Table 2, we reach certain intuitive interpretations. We have classified these graphs as sparse, semi-dense and dense. The networks that have comparatively large number of links with respect to the number of nodes are considered to be dense. On the other hand, the networks which have very small number of links with respect to the size of the network are considered sparse. The networks whose density of links with respect to number of nodes lies in between these two classes can be classified as semi-dense. This classification is not very strict in the practical sense.

From the number of driver nodes obtained from our simulation results, as seen from Figure 16, it is evident that lesser number of driver nodes is suffice to structurally control a denser network and the

Table 2. Driver node density obtained for various networks using our algorithm

Network Name	Total Number of Nodes (N)	Total Number of Links (L)	L/N	Number of Driver Nodes Obtained (N_d)	Driver Node Density Obtained (n_d)
Sparse Networks					
TRN-EC-2	418	519	1.241627	237	0.566985646
TRN-EC-1	1550	3340	2.154839	636	0.410322581
TRN-Yeast-2	688	1079	1.568314	347	0.504360465
S208	122	189	1.54918	67	0.549180328
S420	252	399	1.583333	128	0.507936508
Grassland	88	137	1.556818	51	0.579545455
Escherichia coli	2275	5763	2.533187	844	0.370989011
Saccharomyces cerevisiae	1511	3833	2.536731	539	0.356717406
Prison Inmate	67	182	2.716418	22	0.328358209
College Student	32	96	3	9	0.28125
P2p-2	8846	31839	3.599254	2388	0.269952521
P2p-3	8717	31525	3.616497	2493	0.285992887
P2p-1	10876	39994	3.677271	2926	0.269032733
Semi-Dense Networks					
Ythan	135	601	4.451852	25	0.185185185
Little Rock	183	2494	13.62842	15	0.081967213
Seagrass	49	226	4.612245	8	0.163265306
Caenorhabdituselegans	297	2345	7.895623	35	0.117845118
Ucloline	1899	20296	10.68773	176	0.092680358
Email Epoch	3188	39256	12.31368	252	0.079046424
Wikivote	7115	103689	14.5733	486	0.068306395
Dense Networks					
Political blogs	1224	19025	15.5433	76	0.062091503
Freemans-2	34	695	20.44118	2	0.058823529
Freemans-1	34	830	24.41176	1	0.029411765
TRN-Yeast-1	441	12873	29.19048	15	0.034013605

number of driver nodes increases as the network tends to become sparse. The L/N ratio of a network is the measure of the density of the network. It is intuitively clear that when the number of links in a network increases (that is, dense network), the number of augmenting paths should decrease, as the length of such paths increase with an increase in connectivity among the nodes. In a recent work (Liu et al., 2011), it had been shown that the driver node density$n_d$varied as $e^{-<k>}$, where k was the out-degree variable, P(k) represented the probability of a link to exist between two nodes and $n_d$was the density of driver nodes, obtained as the ratio of the minimum driver nodes required for complete control and the total number of nodes in the entire complex network. As the network became denser, <k> increased and thus n_d decreased, which led to similar result obtained from our simulation.

Figure 16. Exponential change of driver node density with network density

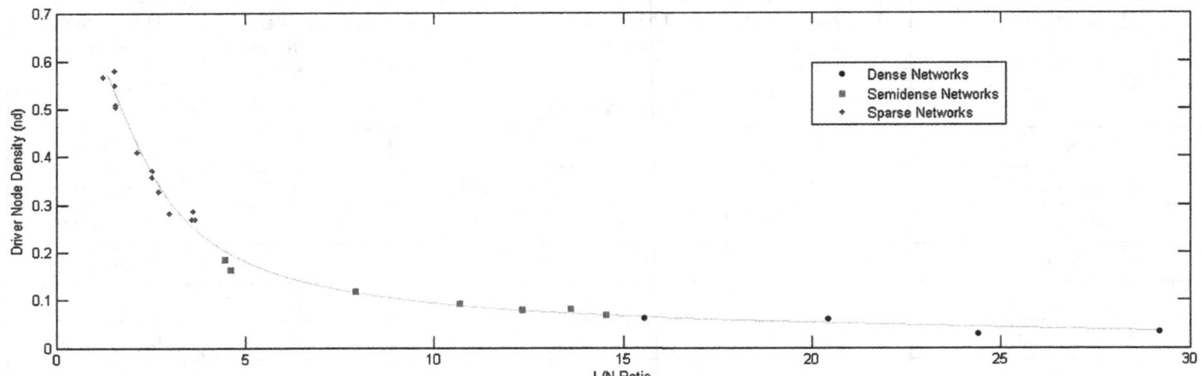

6.3. Complexity and Comparison with Some Existing Works

In the theory of computational complexity, NP (Non-deterministic polynomial time) class of problems may be defined as the set of decision problems that can be solved in polynomial time (Kalman, 1963) on a non-deterministic Turing machine. A problem *p* in NP is in NPC (NP Complete) if and only if every other problem in NP can be transformed into *p* in polynomial time. The available approaches, as discussed earlier for solving the problem of maximum matching in directed complex networks, belonged to this class of problems.

In the worst case, it may happen that all the n nodes are interlinked with each other. First, we search among n nodes to determine the node with the maximum out-degree. In the next step, we have to search among the remaining (n-1) nodes and so on, till the node number becomes 1.

Thus, required time complexity in the worst case, simply can be computed as,

$$1 + 2 + 3 + ... + n = \sum_{j=1}^{n} j = n\,(n + 1) / 2 = (n^2 + n)/2.$$

So time complexity of this algorithm is of the order of n^2.

Other existing algorithms for efficient computation of maximum matching lack either computational efficiency or are not applicable for directed networks. Hanckowiak et al. showed how to compute maximum matching in undirected synchronous, message-passing network without shared memory using Euler tours (Hanckowiak M., et al., 1998). They used the idea of spanners by means of a splitting procedure that cuts the degree of the vertices almost perfectly in half, which was proposed by Israeli and Shiloach. The fact that neither perfect splitters nor Euler circuits could be computed in O(n) rounds in the synchronous, message-passing model of computation inspired the above authors to compute approximate splitters instead of perfect splitters. Complexity of this process varied poly-logarithmically. The complexity of their algorithm was computed as T(Match, n) =O(log n ×T(BipartiteMatch, n)). Bipartite Match included separation of even and odd indexed nodes. However this proposal was not a general one. It is only applicable for certain kind of networks which are synchronous and do not use shared memory.

Again Galil in his classical paper (Galil Z., 1980) had discussed various problems, which constituted different cases of maximum matching: (1) Max cardinality matching in bipartite graphs, (2) Max cardinality matching in general graphs, (3) Max weighted matching in bipartite graphs, and (4) Max weighted matching in general graphs. The last one corresponded to structural control theoretical analysis of complex networks. Unlike problem (3), the final one could not be solved using duality of linear programming problems. The linear program obtained by dropping the integrality constraints from the integer program might have no integer optimal solution. Edmond also proposed a polynomial time algorithm for this problem (J. Edmonds, 1965). This solution was obtained by adding an exponential number of constraints over the problem-$\sum x_{ij} \leq$ [mod(B)/2] for every odd subset of the vertices 'B' and (i,j)∈(B,E) (E is the set of edges). Under this constraint, only an integral optimal solution was obtained with computational complexity of $O(n^3)$.

Comparison with the $O(n^{5/2})$ algorithm proposed by John Hopcroft and Richard Karp combined with classical process of obtaining bipartite equivalent of complex networks, reveals the primary advantage of our heuristic. From the proposed heuristic, we are able to determine uniquely the driver nodes and corresponding augmenting paths, and thus efficiently achieve structural control over any network.

After identifying the driver nodes and the corresponding augmenting paths, we apply control (input) signals to those driver nodes, which is proper retrieval indicate the accessibility and continuity of the augmenting paths corresponding to certain specific retrieving technique for the applied traffic signals. Any minor defect in the network can thus be efficiently tracked and detected, thereby reducing the down time of the entire network. This increases the robustness of the complex network against unwanted link failures and breakdowns.

7. CHARACTERIZATION OF NETWORK PERTURBATIONS

In this section, we discuss about the robustness issues in case of a complex network. Robustness is the critical attribute of any complex system, which gives the measure of the ability of the network to withstand link failures and perturbations. Robustness of a network evaluates the resilience of infrastructure networks such as the Internet or power grids.Most of the existing studies focussed on resolving the network to a stable state after it had encountered an attack. There had been several self-repairing solutions for the resilience of networks to combat failures. We address this lacuna in this section. We propose to build a more fault-tolerant architecture for a complex network. We observed, that increasing the number of driver nodes to a slight extent, than that obtained from maximum matching, could oppose link failures to a larger extent (Das et al., 2014).

An important aspect of failures in many complex networks is that one single failure of a node might induce failures in the neighboring nodes of the network. When a small number of failures induce more failures, thereby resulting in a large number of failures relative to the network size, a cascading failure is said to have occurred. There were various works to model cascading failures (Guillaume et al., 2005; Pastor-Satorras & Vespignani, 2001).These models differed in many details, and modeled different physical propagation phenomenon from power failures to information flow over Facebook or Twitter, but had some common principles. For each model there was a certain threshold, to determine when a node would fail or activate and contribute towards any cascading breakdown or propagation, and there was some mechanism defined by which propagation would-be directed when nodes activated or failed.

All these models interestingly predicted that some critical state, in which the distribution of the size of potential cascades followed the power law and the exponent, was uniquely determined by the degree exponent of the underlying complex network.

Using the degree-first greedy search algorithm, we obtain the minimum number of driver nodes and apply control signals to only those driver nodes to structurally control the entire network. The idea is valid in the ideal case and may not be applicable for real world networks, due to the unwanted attacks, which are otherwise termed as perturbations. We model these perturbations, by random link deletion; thereby resulting in the failure of a network, corresponding to the breakdown of the complex network due to these perturbations. In this model, with such random deletion of links from the network, we use the maximum matching algorithm dynamically and infer the desired number of driver nodes required to control the network, against such perturbations.

Tolerance (R) of a complex network is defined as the ability of the network to withstand attacks and unavoidable link failures. It is analogous to the robustness of the network. Thus, a network is said to possess high tolerance, if the number of driver nodes remains more or less unchanged, or changes rather in negligible, even with considerable amount of link deletion. It can be expressed as

$$R = - 1/(dn_d/dL) \tag{3}$$

Thus, greater the tolerance of a network more is its robustness against perturbations. We present a dynamic analysis of link failures and perturbation, using the Erdos-Renyi model. We observe that, the change in the number of driver nodes is negligible, compared to its initial value, up to a certain limit of link failure. We call this region of network behaviour as the stable region of operation of the network as shown in Figure 17. Beyond that, with the number of link failures increasing, the number of driver nodes starts to increase exponentially to protect the network from breaking down. We term this region as the breakdown region of operation (Das et al., 2014), as shown in Figure 17.

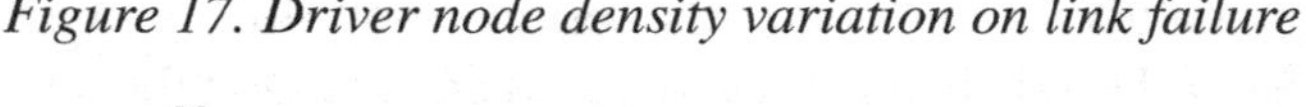

Figure 17. Driver node density variation on link failure

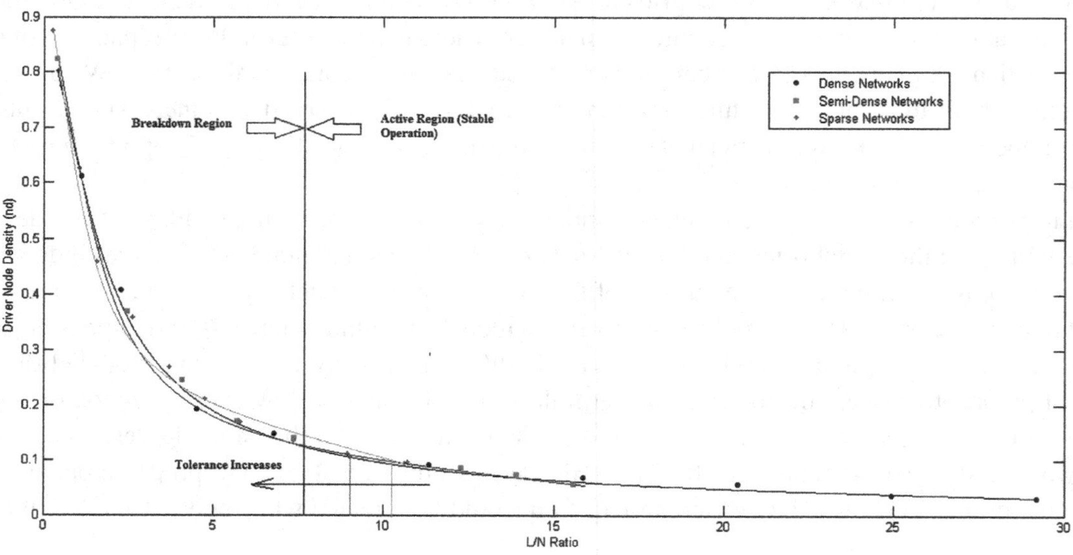

Active or stable region of operation of a network is defined as the threshold limit up to the network can withstand link failures without significant change in the number of driver nodes. This region can be approximated as a linear region, as seen from Figure 17.

Breakdown region of operation of a network is the region, where the network cannot withstand any attack or link failures any further. In this region of operation, the number of driver nodes exponentially increases with link failures.

Effective number of driver nodes (Nd_{eff}) is the number of driver nodes required to instil stability in the Complex network, by ensuring its operation in the stable region, up to the specified tolerance limit (R). Graphically, it corresponds to the boundary between the stable and breakdown region.

8. SIMULATION RESULTS OF BEHAVIOR OF NETWORKS ON LINK FAILURE

It is clear from the definition stated above that this classification of the networks as dense or sparse or semi-dense networks, is relative, and not strict in the practical sense. Now, we study the behaviour of different dense, semi-dense and sparse networks with random link deletion. With random deletion of links, we use the maximum matching algorithm dynamically on the networks and study the effective number of driver nodes required to control the network, as in Table 3. Figure17 shows the behaviour of World Wide Web (Political blogs), a real-world dense network (marked in red), in presence of random perturbations. The network originally consists of 1224 nodes and 19025 links. From Table 3, we observe that the number of driver nodes required increases negligibly and uniformly, up to a certain limit of link failures (deletion). Beyond which, the number of driver nodes tends to increase exponentially and the network enters the undesirable breakdown region of operation. From Figure 17, we obtain that the network remains stable up to 10700 links, which corresponds to an effective driver node densityn_{deff}= 0.11. Thus 134 effective driver nodes (approximately) are required practically to control the complex network structurally, instead of 76 driver nodes as obtained from maximum matching algorithm (Das et al., 2014). Using, Equation (3), we get tolerance R = 2 * 10^5 for the stable operating region.

Figure 17. also shows the behaviour of a social communication network - UCIonline, a real-world semi-dense network (marked in blue), in presence of random perturbations. The network originally consists of 1899 nodes and 20296 links. From Table 3, we observe that the number of driver nodes required increases negligibly and uniformly, up to a certain limit of link failures (deletion); beyond which, the number of driver nodes tends to increase exponentially and the network is said to penetrate into the undesirable breakdown region. From Figure 19, we obtain that the network remains stable up to 11200 links, which corresponds to an effective driver node density = 0.17. Thus 320 effective driver nodes (approximately) are required practically to control the complex network structurally. Using, Equation (3), we get tolerance R = 1.65 * 105 for the stable operating region.

Also, from Figure19, we see the behaviour of internet - p2p - 1 network, a real-world sparse network (marked in green), in presence of random perturbations. The network originally consists of 10876 nodes and 39994 links. From this figure, we obtain that the network remains stable up to 27000 links, which corresponds to number of driver nodes (approximately) that is required practically to control the complex network structurally, instead of 2926 driver nodes as obtained from maximum matching (Das et al., 2014).Using, Equation (3), we get tolerance R = 1.2 * 10^5 for the stable operating region. From the above results, we observe that tolerance is maximum for dense networks and minimum for sparse networks. Thus, it can be inferred that dense and homogeneous networks are easier to control, compared to sparse networks. Hence, the dense networks are more robust, whereas sparse networks are more vulnerable to attacks and link failures i.e., perturbations.

Table 3. Behavior of various networks on link failure

N	L	L/N	N_d	n_d
Dense Network: TRN-Yeast-1 Regulatory				
441	12873	29.19	14	0.032
441	11000	24.94	16	0.036
441	9000	20.41	25	0.057
441	7000	15.87	30	0.068
441	5000	11.34	40	0.091
441	3000	6.8	65	0.147
441	2000	4.53	85	0.193
441	1000	2.27	180	0.408
441	500	1.13	270	0.612
441	200	0.45	354	0.803
441	12873	29.19	14	0.032
Semi-Dense Network: Political Blogs				
1224	19025	15.541	68	0.056
1224	17025	13.91	90	0.074
1224	15000	12.25	105	0.086
1224	13000	10.62	115	0.094
1224	11000	8.99	130	0.106
1224	9000	7.35	169	0.138
1224	7000	5.71	208	0.169
1224	5000	4.08	300	0.245
1224	3000	2.45	450	0.368
1224	2000	1.63	591	0.483
1224	1000	0.82	850	0.694
1224	500	0.41	1010	0.825
1224	19025	15.541	68	0.056
Sparse Network: UCI Online				
1899	20296	10.69	175	0.095
1899	17000	8.95	210	0.111
1899	14000	7.37	255	0.134
1899	11000	5.79	320	0.169
1899	9000	4.74	400	0.211
1899	7000	3.69	510	0.269
1899	5000	2.63	681	0.358
1899	3000	1.58	930	0.458
1899	2000	1.05	1190	0.627
1899	1000	0.53	1470	0.774
1899	500	0.26	1665	0.876
1899	20296	10.69	175	0.095

9. CONCLUSION AND FUTURE WORKS

First, we have seen that the number of driver nodes for a complex network, compared to the total number of nodes in the network increases with the density of the network. Second, we have inferred from our simulation that the controllability of a system is mainly determined by the degree distribution, P (k_{in}, k_{out}) of the underlying network.

Till now, algorithm available for the computation of maximum matching in networks was the classical Hopcroft-Karp algorithm (Hopcroft and Karp, 1973), and some other algorithms (Hanckowiak et al., 1998; Galil, 1980), but all of them required the determination of the isomorphic bipartite equivalent of the network needed to obtain. Again, the bipartite equivalent of all complex networks could not be determined, as it was an NP-Complete problem. Neither did an algorithm exist to determine the bipartite equivalent of any unipartite complex network. Hence, this proposed algorithm discussed in this chapter has served the purpose of determining the maximum matching, and thus completely controlling a directed real-world complex network. In addition this algorithm may be modified to solve other max-flow problems.

The approach described in this article has been relevant in the real-life complex networks like various biological networks (in nervous system or in brain) etc. Using this algorithm, we can recognize the set of driver nodes, the time–dependent control of which can guide the entire network dynamics. From the results, which have been shown in this chapter we can conclude that for a dense and homogeneous network the number of driver nodes is the least. The number of driver nodes has increased as the number of links in the networks has tended to decrease in the network. So the number of driver nodes is larger for semi-dense and sparse networks compared to the dense network. Clearly, the networks that has required the less number of driver nodes are easier to control. The developed approach has provided a reliable framework to deal with the controllability issue of any arbitrary directed network, and can be envisioned as a fundamental step towards the ultimate control strategy of real-world complex systems.

Understanding nature is the greatest matter of concern of science. It has two steps- first, how nature works and second, how it is created. How natural systems grow is a topic of immense interest to the scientists and philosophers over centuries. Many theories had been developed throughout decades on how everything grows, but all of them had their own flaws. Proper degrees of separation, clustering coefficient, paradox of heterogeneity were observed in natural networks. Incorporating these characteristics in artificially grown networks was not at all easy task (Batagelj & Brandes, 2005). Again the most interesting thing was how nature achieved utmost controllability. How it prevented, avoided breakdown, tried to keep everything under control. On the other hand all these properties were achieved against cost of denser connection, higher cost. The nature is so dazzling it also balances this side.

Again, the breakdown of networks has been a significant issue of concern, from users' end, as well as from service providers' point of view. Maintaining a higher level of tolerance for any real world complex network is always desirable. Complex networks like social networks, power grids, optical communication networks etc., had all succumbed to link failures and random attacks in the recent past. The approach described in this chapter is relevant to these real-world networks. A system uptime of 99.999%, for the premium users is a real challenge to handle, and unavoidable failures and perturbations are the main hindrance towards achieving it. Various other papers (Moreira, 2009; Crucitti, 2004) had emphasized on bringing back a network to a stable state, using different rewiring strategies, after it had encountered an attack. All of those are definite requisites, but foremost, the networks must be able to combat the attacks, prior to facing the perturbations. In this chapter, we have proposed a novel concept to build the network architecture, in a way so as to withstand the unwanted attacks and perturbations. Using the proposed maximum matching algorithm, we have obtained the minimum number of driver nodes to control the network. With the fault-tolerant model, we have shown that using a slightly greater number of driver nodes, we can build the architecture of complex networks, using the preferential attachment algorithm with better stability against random attacks and perturbations.

REFERENCES

Albert, R., & Barabasi, A.-L. (2002). Statistical mechanics of complex networks. *Reviews of Modern Physics*, *74*(1), 47–97. doi:10.1103/RevModPhys.74.47

Albert, R., Jeong, H., & Barabasi, A.-L. (2000). Error and attack tolerance of complex networks. *Nature*, *406*(6794), 378–382. doi:10.1038/35019019 PMID:10935628

Barabasi, A. L. (2002). Linked: The New Science of Networks. Academic Press.

Barabasi, A. L. (2009). Scale-Free Networks: A Decade and Beyond. *Science*, *325*(5939), 412–413. doi:10.1126/science.1173299 PMID:19628854

Barabasi, A. L., & Albert, R. (1999). Emergence of scaling in random networks. *Science*, *286*(5439), 509–512. doi:10.1126/science.286.5439.509 PMID:10521342

Batagelj, V., & Brandes, U. (2005). Efficient generation of large random networks. *Physical Review E: Statistical, Nonlinear, and Soft Matter Physics*, 71. PMID:15903499

Beygelzimer, A., Grinstein, G., Linsker, R., & Rish, I. (2005). Improving network robustness by edge modification. *Physica A*, *3*(3-4), 593–612. doi:10.1016/j.physa.2005.03.040

Boccalettia, S., Latorab, V., Morenod, Y., Chavezf, M., & Hwanga, D.-U. (2006). Complex networks: Structure and dynamics. Elsevier. *Physics Reports*, *424*(4-5), 175–308. doi:10.1016/j.physrep.2005.10.009

Bollobas, B. (2001). *Random Graphs*. Cambridge Univ. Press. doi:10.1017/CBO9780511814068

Broder, A., Kumar, R., Maghoul, F., Raghavan, P., Rajagopalan, S., Stata, R., & Wiener, J. et al. (2000). Graph structure in the web. *Computer Networks*, *33*(1-6), 309–320. doi:10.1016/S1389-1286(00)00083-9

Caldarelli, G. (2007). *Scale-Free Networks: Complex Webs in Nature and Technology*. Oxford Univ. Press. doi:10.1093/acprof:oso/9780199211517.001.0001

Chatterjee, A., Das, D., Naskar, M. K., Pal, N., & Mukherjee, A. (2013). Heuristic for maximum matching in directed complex networks. *International Conference on Advances in Computing, Communications and Informatics (ICACCI)*. doi:10.1109/ICACCI.2013.6637339

Chiang, M., Low, S. H., Calderbank, A. R., & Doyle, J. C. (2007). Layering as optimization decomposition: A mathematical theory of network architectures. *Proceedings of the IEEE*, *95*(1), 255–312. doi:10.1109/JPROC.2006.887322

Cohen, R., Erez, K., ben-Avraham, D., & Havlin, S. (2000). Resilience of the internet to random breakdowns. *Physical Review Letters*, *85*(21), 4626–4628. doi:10.1103/PhysRevLett.85.4626 PMID:11082612

Cowan, N. J., Chastain, E. J., Vilhena, D.A., Freudenberg J. S., & Bergstrom, C. T. (2012). *Nodal dynamics, not degree distributions, determine the structural controllability of complex networks*. Academic Press.

Crucitti, P., Latora, V., Marchiori, M., & Rapisarda, A. (2004). Error and attack tolerance of complex networks. *Physica A*, *340*(1-3), 388–394. doi:10.1016/j.physa.2004.04.031

Das, D., Chatterjee, A., Bandyopadhyay, B., & Ahmed, S. J. (2014). Characterizing behaviour of Complex networks against perturbations and generation of Pseudo-random networks. *India Conference (INDICON), 2014 Annual IEEE*. doi:10.1109/INDICON.2014.7030428

Das, D., Chatterjee, A., Pal, N., Mukherjee, A., & Naskar, M. (2014). A degree-first greedy search algorithm for the evaluation of structural controllability of real world directed complex networks. *Network Protocols and Algorithms*, *6*(1), 1–18. doi:10.5296/npa.v6i1.4756

Dorogovtsev, S. N., & Mendes, J. F. F. (2003). *Evolution of Networks: From Biological Nets to the Internet and WWW*. Oxford Univ. Press. doi:10.1093/acprof:oso/9780198515906.001.0001

Edmonds, J. (1965, April-June). Maximum matching and a polyhedron with0,1 vertices. *J. Res. NBS*, *698*, 125–130.

Erdős, P., & Rényi, A. (1960). On the evolution of random graphs. *Publ. Math. Inst. Hung. Acad. Sci.*, *5*, 17–61.

Evans, T. S., (2004). Complex Networks. *Contemporary Physics*.

Faloutsos, M., Faloutsos, P., & Faloutsos, C. (1999). On power-law relationships of the internet topology. *Computer Communication Review*, *29*(4), 251–262. doi:10.1145/316194.316229

Galil, Z. (1980). Efficient Algorithms for finding Maximum Matching in Graphs. *ACM Computing Surveys*.

Guillaume, J.-L. (2004). *MatthieuLatapy*. Bipartite Graphs as Models of Complex Networks. CAAN.

J.-L. Guillaume, M. Latapy, & C. Magnien, (2005). Comparison of failures and attacks on random and scale-free networks. In *OPODIS* (LNCS), (pp. 186 – 196). Berlin: Springer.

Hanckowiak, M., Karonski, M., & Panconesi, A. (1998). *On the Distributed Complexity of Computing Maximal Matchings*. ACM-SIAM SODA.

Hopcroft, J. E., & Karp, R. M. (1973). An n5/2 algorithm for maximum matchings in bipartite graphs. *SIAM Journal on Computing*, 2.

Kalman, R.E., (1963). Mathematical description of linear dynamical systems. *J. Soc Indus. Appl. Math Ser., A1*, 152-192.

Kelly, F. P., Maulloo, A. K., & Tan, D. K. H. (1998). Rate control for communication networks: Shadow prices, proportional fairness and stability. *The Journal of the Operational Research Society*, *49*(3), 237–252. doi:10.1057/palgrave.jors.2600523

Kuhn, F., Schmid, S., & Wattenhofer, R. (2005). A self-repairing peer-to-peer system resilient to dynamic adversarial churn. *LNCS*, *3640*, 13–23.

Lin, C. T. (1974, June). Structural controllability. *IEEE Transactions on Automatic Control, 19*(3), 201–208. doi:10.1109/TAC.1974.1100557

Liu, B., Chu, T., Wang, L., & Xie, G. (2008). Controllability of a Leader–Follower Dynamic Network With Switching Topology. *IEEE Transactions on Automatic Control, 53*(4), 1009–1013. doi:10.1109/TAC.2008.919548

Liu, Y. Y., Slotine, J. J., & Barabasi, A. L. (2011). Controllability of complex networks. *Nature, 473*(7346), 167–173. doi:10.1038/nature10011 PMID:21562557

Lombardi, A., & Hornquist, M. (2007). Controllability analysis of networks. *Physical Review E: Statistical, Nonlinear, and Soft Matter Physics*, 75. PMID:17677136

Luenberger, D. G. (1979). *Introduction to Dynamic Systems: Theory, Models, & Applications*. Wiley.

Mayeda, H., & Yamada, T. (1979). Strong structural controllability. *SIAM Journal on Control and Optimization, 17*(1), 123–138. doi:10.1137/0317010

Moreira, J. A. J. A. A., Herrmann, H., & Indekeu, J. (2009). How to make a fragile network robust and vice versa. *Physical Review Letters*, 102. PMID:19257248

Motter, A. (2004). Cascade control and defense in complex networks. *Physical Review Letters*, 93. PMID:15447153

Newman, M., Barabasi, A.-L., & Watts, D. J. (2006). The Structure and Dynamics of Networks. Princeton Univ. Press.

Newth, D., & Ash, J. (2005). Evolving cascading failure resilience in complex networks. *Complexity International, 11*, 125–136.

Pastor-Satorras, R., & Vespignani, A. (2001). Epidemic spreading in scale-free networks. *Physical Review Letters, 86*(14), 3200–3203. doi:10.1103/PhysRevLett.86.3200 PMID:11290142

Slotine, J.-J., & Li, W. (1991). *Applied Nonlinear Control*. Prentice-Hall.

Srikant, R. (2004). *The Mathematics of Internet Congestion Control (Birkhauser)*. American Mathematical Society. doi:10.1007/978-0-8176-8216-3

Strogatz, S. H. (2001). Exploring complex networks. *Nature, 410*(6825), 268–276. doi:10.1038/35065725 PMID:11258382

Tanner, H. G. (2004). On the controllability of nearest neighbor interconnections. *43rd IEEE Conference on Decision and Control (CDC)*, 3. doi:10.1109/CDC.2004.1428782

Zdeborova, L. & Mezard, M., (2006). *The number of matchings in random graphs*. Academic Press.

Zhao, K., Kumar, A., Harrison, T., & Yen, J. (2011). Analyzing the resilience of complex supply network topologies against random and targeted disruptions. *IEEE Systems Journal, 5*(1), 28–39. doi:10.1109/JSYST.2010.2100192

Zhao, L., Park, K., Lai, Y.-C., & Cupertino, T. (2007). Attack induced cascading breakdown in complex networks. *Journal of the Brazilian Computer Society, 13*(3), 67–76. doi:10.1007/BF03192546

Chapter 5
Triadic Substructures in Complex Networks

Marco Winkler
University of Wuerzburg, Germany

ABSTRACT

An important topological characteristic which has been studied on networks of diverse origin is the abundance of motifs – subgraph patterns which occur significantly more often than expected at random. We investigate whether motifs occur homogeneously or heterogeneously distributed over a graph. Analyzing real-world datasets, it is found that there are networks in which motifs are distributed highly heterogeneously, bound to the proximity of only very few nodes. Moreover, we study whole graphs with respect to the homogeneity and homophily of their node-specific triadic structure. The former describes the similarity of subgraphs in the neighborhoods of individual vertices. The latter quantifies whether connected vertices are structurally more similar than non-connected ones. These features are discovered to be characteristic for the networks' origins. Beyond, information on a graph's node-specific triadic structure can be used to detect groups of structurally similar vertices.

1. INTRODUCTION

Elucidating the relationship between a network's function and the underlying graph topology is one of the major branches in network science. The mining of graphs in terms of their local substructure is a well-established methodology to analyze their topology (Shen-Orr et al., 2002; Milo et al., 2004; Alon, 2007, Berlingerio et al., 2009; Rahman et al. 2014). It was hypothesized that *motifs* – subgraph patterns which appear significantly more often than expected at random – play a key role for the ability of a system to perform its task (Milo et al., 2002; Mangan & Alon 2003; Alon, 2006). Yet, the framework commonly used for motif detection averages over the occurrences of subgraphs in the local environments of all nodes. It therefore remains unclear whether motifs are overrepresented homogeneously in the whole system or only in certain regions. If motifs were indeed critical for a network's function, but at the same time bound to specific parts of the graph, a failure of only very few important nodes could severely disable the whole system. Furthermore, especially for larger networks composed of different functional components, there may be areas in which *one* structural pattern is of importance, whereas in

DOI: 10.4018/978-1-4666-9964-9.ch005

different regions *other* patterns are relevant. On the system level, the abundance of these patterns may average out and hence, their importance may not even be recognized.

In this chapter, this issue will be investigated in more detail by mining *node-specific* patterns. More specifically, instead of detecting frequent subgraph patterns of the whole system, the neighborhood of every single node is investigated separately, i.e., for every vertex only the subgraphs it participates in are considered. This will facilitate to localize the regions of a graph in which the instances of a motif predominantly appear. Thus, it is possible to identify and remove the nodes and links which eventually make a certain pattern a motif of the network. This approach will permit future investigations to assess whether it is actually the presence of a motif which enables a system to perform its task or whether other structural aspects are more relevant.

After reviewing node-specific Z scores and the framework of node-specific triad pattern mining, as introduced in (Winkler & Reichardt, 2014), systems of various fields will be investigated. It will be found that, for many of them, motifs are distributed highly heterogeneously. Furthermore, node-specific triad pattern mining provides for a set of features for each node. These features will be utilized to cluster the vertices of a neural network.

2. RELATED WORK AND MOTIVATION

In the context of local subgraph analysis, most attention has been devoted to the investigation of triadic subgraphs (Milo et al., 2002; Shen-Orr et al., 2002; Milo et al., 2004; Sporns & Kötter, 2004; Albert & Albert, 2004). Apart from node permutations, there are 13 distinct connected triad patterns in directed unweighted networks as shown in Figure 1. It was found that certain patterns of third-order subgraphs occur significantly more frequently than expected in an ensemble of networks with the same degree distributions as the original network. Over- and underrepresentation of each pattern i in a graph is quantified through a Z score,

$$Z_i = \frac{N_{original,i} - \langle N_{rand,i} \rangle}{\sigma_{rand,i}}.$$

$N_{original,i}$ is the number of appearances of pattern i over all possible 3-tuples of nodes in the original network. Sampling from the ensemble of randomized networks yields the average occurrence $\langle N_{rand,i} \rangle$ of that pattern and the respective standard deviation $\sigma_{rand,i}$. Thus, the Z scores represent a measure for the significance of an over- or underrepresentation for each pattern i shown in Figure 1.

Figure 1. All 16 possible non-isomorphic triadic subgraphs (subgraph patterns) in directed unweighted networks

1 2 3 4 5 6 7 8 9 10 11 12 13 14 15 16

Hence, every network can be assigned a vector $\vec{Z}$ whose components comprise the Z scores of all possible triad patterns. Significant patterns are referred to as *motifs* (Milo et al., 2002). Further, one commonly refers to the normalized Z vector as the *significance profile*,

$$\overrightarrow{SP} = \vec{Z} / \sqrt{\sum_{i=4}^{16} Z_i^2}.$$

This normalization makes systems of different sizes comparable with each other (Milo et al., 2002).

A multitude of real-world systems has been examined in terms of their triadic Z score profiles and it was found that systems with similar tasks tend to have similar Z score profiles and thus exhibit the same motifs. Therefore, it was conjectured that their structural evolution may have been determined by the relevance of these motif patterns. Investigating isolated subgraphs, it has been reported that some patterns enhance the reliability of modeled information-processing dynamics in the presence of noise (Klemm & Bornholdt, 2005), and that there are patterns which stabilize the steady states of certain simulated dynamical processes (Prill et al., 2005). Moreover, it was found that the reliability and stability associated with triadic subgraphs coincided with their overrepresentation in real-world systems in which the respective measures are assumed to be essential. Furthermore, synthetic networks have been optimized, e.g. in order to make them robust against link failure. In the resulting graphs, motifs have been detected that are also abundant in real-world networks corresponding to the modeled processes (Kaluza et al., 2007; Burda et al., 2011). It was even suspected that motifs, rather than independent links, may serve as the basic entities of complex network structure (Milo et al., 2002; Shen-Orr et al., 2002; Alon, 2007). In particular, the role of the 'feed-forward loop' pattern (number 8 in Figure 1) has been discussed intensively in the field (Shen-Orr et al., 2002; Mangan & Alon 2002; Alon, 2007). It has been alleged to play a key role for systems to reliably perform information-processing tasks. However, there has also been ongoing discussion about the expressive power of the subgraph-analysis described above (Artzy-Randrup et al., 2004; Fretter et al., 2012).

This chapter aims to further unravel the role of triad motifs in complex networks. Utilizing the recently introduced methodology for *node-specific pattern mining* (Winkler & Reichardt, 2014) it is possible to localize the regions of a graph in which the instances of a motif predominantly appear. Thus, it is possible to identify and remove the nodes and links which eventually make a certain pattern a motif without altering the rest of the graph structure. This will enable future investigations to assess whether it is actually the presence of a motif which enables a system to perform its task or whether other structural aspects are more relevant.

3. NODE-SPECIFIC TRIADIC *Z* SCORES

In (Winkler & Reichardt, 2014), *node-specific*, triadic Z-score profiles have been introduced. For every node α in a graph, the abundance of all structural patterns in α 's neighborhood is evaluated. The patterns in α 's *neighborhood* or *environment* shall be defined as those patterns in which α participates in. The frequency of occurrence of patterns in the system under investigation is compared to the expected frequency in a randomized ensemble of the original network. In the randomization, both individual in- and out degrees of all nodes, and the number of unidirectional and bidirectional links are the same as in the original network.

In principle, the framework of node-specific subgraph mining can be realized for patterns composed of an arbitrary number of nodes, n. Nevertheless, with increasing n, the number of non-isomorphic subgraphs also increases rapidly. The remainder of this work will focus on triad patterns ($n = 3$).

One strives to evaluate the abundance of triad patterns from a particular node α 's point of view. Therefore, the symmetry of most patterns shown in Figure 1 is now broken and the number of connected *node-specific* triad patterns increases from 13 to 30. These are shown in Figure 2. To understand the increase in the number of patterns, consider the ordinary subgraph number 6 in Figure 1. From the perspective of one particular node, it splits into the three node-specific triad patterns 3, 8, and 22 in Figure 2. Some patterns are included in others, e.g. pattern 1 is a subset of pattern 3. In order to avoid biased results, it is not double counted, i.e. an observation of pattern 3 will only increase its corresponding count and not the one associated with pattern 1.

For every node α in a graph, one can compute Z scores for each of the 30 node-specific patterns, *i*, shown above,

$$Z_i^\alpha = \frac{N_{original,i}^\alpha - \left\langle N_{rand,i}^\alpha \right\rangle}{\sigma_{rand,i}^\alpha}.$$

$N_{original,i}^\alpha$ is the number of appearances of pattern i in the triads node α participates in. Accordingly, $\left\langle N_{rand,i}^\alpha \right\rangle$ is the expected frequency of pattern i in the triads node α is part of in the randomized ensemble. $\sigma_{rand,i}^\alpha$ is the corresponding standard deviation.

4. NODE-SPECIFIC TRIAD PATTERN MINING (NoSPaM$_3$)

In (Winkler & Reichardt, 2014), **No**de-**S**pecific **Pa**ttern **M**ining (NoSPaM) has been suggested. NoSPaM is an algorithm to compute the *node-specific* Z-score profiles described above. The particular focus will be on *triad* patterns (NoSPaM$_3$).

Figure 2. All possible connected, non-isomorphic triadic subgraph patterns in terms of a distinct node (here: lower node)

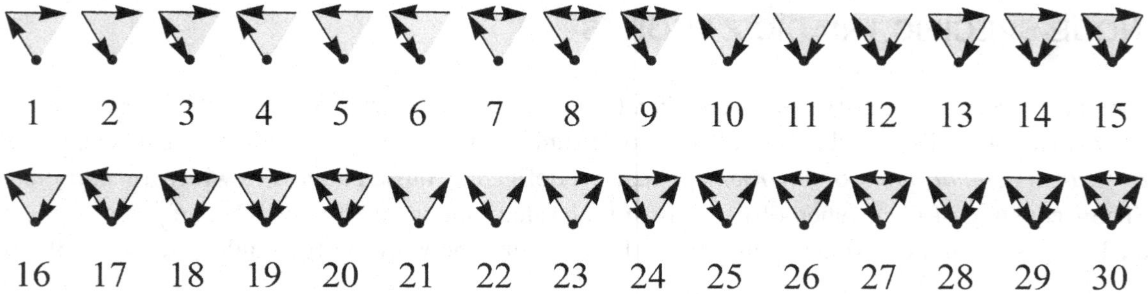

4.1. Algorithm

The algorithm for node-specific triad pattern mining consists of three parts. The first part is a degree-preserving randomization defined in Figure 3. Pairs of links are drawn uniformly at random from the graph structure and – if possible – are rewired such that the individual node degrees of all affected vertices are conserved. For details on the randomization process see, e.g., (Winkler & Reichardt, 2014). Further, Algorithm 2 performs the counting process for the appearances of triad patterns in a graph.

Because it is computationally expensive to test all triads in the system (the complexity is of order $O(N^3)$, it is rather iterated over pairs of adjacent edges in the graph. Since real-world networks are usually sparse, this is much more efficient.

Using the functions defined in Figure 3 and Figure 4, one can eventually formulate the routine of node-specific triad pattern mining (NoSPaM$_3$). Figure 5 describes its formalism. It computes the node-

Figure 3. Performs a degree-preserving randomization of a graph

Algorithm 1 Degree-preserving randomization of a graph

```
function RANDOMIZE(Graph G(V, E), no. of required steps)
    s = 0
    while s < number of required rewiring steps do
        pick a random link e1 ∈ E
        if e1 is unidirectional then
            pick a 2nd unidirectional link e2 ∈ E at random
        else
            pick a 2nd bidirectional link e2 ∈ E at random
        end if

        if e1 and e2 do not share a node then
            rewire according to the pair-switch rules in Fig. 3.3
            if one of the new links already exists then
                undo the rewiring
            end if
        else if e1 and e2 participate in a loop then
            rewire according to the loop-switch rule in Fig.3.3(a)
        end if

        s++
    end while
    return randomized instance of G
end function
```

specific Z scores, $\vec{Z}^{\alpha}$. The definition of the standard deviation over all I randomized instances involves the corresponding mean value,

$$\left(\sigma_{rand,i}^{\alpha}\right)^2 = \frac{1}{I}\sum_{k=1}^{I}\left(N_{rand,i,k}^{\alpha} - \left\langle N_{rand,i}^{\alpha}\right\rangle\right)^2.$$

Using this equation, it would be necessary to store all $N \times 30 \times I$ values $N_{rand,i,k}^{\alpha}$, since they all contribute to both σ_{rand}^{α} and $\left\langle N_{rand,i}^{\alpha}\right\rangle$. However, one can easily evaluate the standard deviation in one sweep utilizing

$$\left(\sigma_{rand,i}^{\alpha}\right)^2 = \left\langle \left(N_{rand,i}^{\alpha}\right)^2\right\rangle - \left\langle N_{rand,i}^{\alpha}\right\rangle^2$$

and therefore saving a factor I of storage consumption. All operations on the arrays $N_{original}$, N_{rand}, $N_{sq,rand}$, and Z in Figure 5 shall be defined to be performed element wise.

Figure 4. Counts the node-specific triad patterns in a graph

Algorithm 2 Counting of node-specific triad patterns

```
function NspPatternCounter(Graph 𝒢(V, E))
    𝒩: N × 30-dimensional array storing the pattern counts for every node of 𝒢
    for every edge e ∈ E do
        i, j ← IDs of e's nodes with i < j
        𝒞 ← {} be list of candidate nodes to form triad patterns comprising e
        𝒞 ← all neighbors of i
        𝒞 ← all neighbors of j
        for all c ∈ 𝒞 do
            if i + j < sum of IDs of all other connected
                            dyads in triad (ijc) then
                increase the counts in 𝒩 for i, j, and c for
                their respective node-specific patterns
            end if
        end for
    end for
    return 𝒩
end function
```

Figure 5. implements the procedure for node-specific triad pattern mining using Figure 3 and Figure 4

Algorithm 3 Node-specific triad pattern mining (NoSPaM_3)

```
function NoSPaM(Graph 𝒢, # required rewiring steps, # randomized instances)
    𝒩_original ← NspPatternCounter(𝒢)
    𝒩_rand ← {}
    𝒩_sq,rand ← {}
    for # randomized instances do
        𝒢 ← Randomize(𝒢, # required rewiring steps)
        counts ← NspPatternCounter(𝒢)
        𝒩_rand ← 𝒩_rand + counts
        𝒩_sq,rand ← 𝒩_sq,rand + counts * counts
    end for
    𝒩_rand ← 𝒩_rand/(#randomized instances)
    𝒩_sq,rand ← 𝒩_sq,rand/(#randomized instances)
    σ_rand ← √(𝒩_sq,rand − (𝒩_rand * 𝒩_rand))
    𝒵 ← (𝒩_original − 𝒩_rand)/σ_rand
    return 𝒵
end function
```

4.2. Performance

The computational cost of Algorithm 1, C_1, scales with the number of required randomization steps per instance, which should be chosen proportionally to the number of edges $M = |E|$ in graph **G**, i.e. $C_1 = O(M)$.

Algorithm 2 iterates over all edges of **G** and their adjacent edges. Therefore, it is $C_2 = O(M \times k_{\max}) \leq O(M^2)$ where $k_{\max}$ is the maximum node degree in **G**. In real-world networks, $k_{\max}$ is usually much smaller than M.

Finally, the total computational cost of NoSPaM_3, i.e. of Algorithm 3, depends on the desired number of randomized network instances, I. Algorithm 2 is invoked $(1+I)$ times; Algorithm 1 is invoked I times. Hence, the total computational cost is

$$C_{NoSPaM_3} = O(I \times M \times k_{\max}).$$

Furthermore, NoSPaM_3 is parallelizable straightforwardly since the evaluations in terms of the randomized network instances can be executed independently of each other. An implementation of the pattern-mining program is made publicly available online at www.mwinkler.eu.

5. REAL-WORLD NETWORK GRAPHS

The following section will focus on the analysis and comparison of multiple graphs with respect to their local triadic structure. This section provides for a brief description of the datasets. More details on the data can be obtained from the cited references. All networks are directed.

- **Ecoli Transcriptional (Alon, 2012; Mangan & Alon, 2003):** 424 nodes, 519 edges. Nodes are operons, each edge is directed from an operon that encodes a transcription factor to an operon that it directly regulates (an operon is one or more genes transcribed on the same mRNA).
- **Yeast Transcriptional (Alon, 2012; Costanzo et al. 2001):** 688 nodes, 1,079 edges. Transcriptional network of the yeast S. cerevisiae. Nodes are genes, edges point from regulating genes to regulated genes. It is not distinguished between activation and repression.
- **Neural Network of C. Elegans (Varshney et al., 2011;** http://www.wormatlas.org**):** 279 nodes, 2,194 edges. Nodes are the neurons in the largest connected component of the somatic nervous system of the nematode C. elegans. Edges describe the chemical synapses between the neurons.
- **Scientific Citations (Gehrke et al., 2003; Leskovec et al., 2005; Leskovec & Krevl, 2014):** 27,700 nodes, 352,807 edges. Nodes are high-energy physics papers on the arXiv, submitted between January 1993 and April 2003. Edges from node A to B indicate that paper A cites paper B. Although it may seem unintuitive, there are papers citing each other. This may happen as papers can be updated continuously in time.
- **Political blogs (Newman, 2012; Adamic & Glance, 2005):** 1,224 nodes, 19,025 edges. Largest connected component of a network where the nodes are political blogs. Edges represent links between the blogs recorded over a period of two months preceding the 2004 US Presidential election.
- **Leadership Social Network (Alon, 2012; Milo et al., 2004):** 32 nodes, 96 edges. Social network of college students in a course about leadership.
- **Prisoners Social Network (Alon, 2012; Milo et al., 2004):** 67 nodes, 182 edges. Social network of inmates in prison.
- **English Book (Alon, 2012; Milo et al., 2004):** 7,381 nodes, 46,281 edges. Word-adjacency network of an English book. Nodes are words; an edge from node A to node B indicates that word B directly follows word A at least once in the text.
- **French Book (Alon, 2012; Milo et al., 2004):** 8,325 nodes, 24,295 edges. Word-adjacency network of a French book.
- **Japanese Book (Alon, 2012; Milo et al., 2004):** 2,704 nodes, 8,300 edges. Word-adjacency network of a Japanese book.
- **Spanish Book (Alon, 2012; Milo et al., 2004):** 11,586 nodes, 45,129 edges. Word-adjacency network of a Spanish book.
- **Airport-Connections Network:** 3,438 nodes, 34,775 edges. Nodes are airports, an edge from airport A to airport B indicates a direct flight connection from A to B. Data processed from http://openflights.org/.
- **Electronic Circuit s208 (Alon, 2012; Milo et al., 2002):** 122 nodes, 189 edges. Network of electronic circuits. The nodes in these circuits represent electronic components, e.g., logic gates in digital circuits and resistors, capacitors, or diodes in analogic circuits. Edges are directed connec-

tions between the elements. Parsed by Milo et al. from the ISCAS89 benchmark set of sequential logic electronic circuits.

- **Electronic Circuit s420 (Alon, 2012; Milo et al., 2002):** 252 nodes, 399 edges. Network of electronic circuits.
- **Electronic Circuit s838 (Alon, 2012; Milo et al., 2002):** 512 nodes, 819 edges. Network of electronic circuits.
- **Triadic Random Graph FFL-1:** 49 nodes, 126 edges. Synthetic random network generated with the triadic random graph model (Winkler & Reichardt 2013) which allows to induce triadic motifs. The network is composed exclusively of unidirectional edges and has the feed-forward loop (pattern 8 in Figure 1) as a motif.
- **Triadic Random Graph FFL-2:** 147 nodes, 713 edges. The network is composed of both unidirectional and bidirectional edges and has the feed-forward loop (pattern 8 in Figure 1) as a motif.

6. NODE-SPECIFIC TRIAD PATTERNS IN REAL-WORLD NETWORK GRAPHS

In this section, results obtained from the application of NoSPaM_3 to various peer-reviewed real-world datasets of various origin will be presented. All networks are directed and edges are treated as unweighted.

6.1. Node-Specific vs. Ordinary Triadic Z-Score Profiles

Figure 7. shows the node-specific, triadic *Z*-score profiles for various systems, averaged over 1000 instances of the randomized ensemble. Note that there is one curve for *every* node in the graph. The node-specific patterns on the horizontal axis are oriented the way that the node under consideration is the lower one.

It can be observed that systems from similar fields have similar node-specific triadic *Z*-score profiles. Figures 7(a) and 7(b) show biological transcriptional networks, Figures 7(c) and 7(d) show data from a social context, specifically a social network of prisoners and the network of hyperlinks between political blogs. Figures 7(e) and 7(f) show word-adjacency networks in French and Spanish language, respectively. The observation that systems from a similar context exhibit similar local structural characteristics fosters the hypothesis that the latter are strongly linked to the systems' function.

The fact that NoSPaM_3 provides *localized* data facilitates to identify the areas of a graph where certain subgraph patterns primarily occur. Particularly, it allows to test whether motifs of a system are overabundant throughout the entire network or if they are restricted to limited regions or the proximity of few nodes. In order to explore this issue, for each node, its *node-specific* *Z* scores will be mapped to a score for the *regular* triad patterns (shown in Figure 1). This is realized by taking the mean over the *Z* scores of all node-specific triad patterns corresponding to a regular triad pattern. The mapping is shown in Figure 6. The vector composed of the mean node-specific *Z* scores of a node α is denoted as $\vec{M}^{\alpha}$. The measure for the contribution of a node α 's environment to the regular pattern 14 is then, for instance, $\vec{M}_{14}^{\alpha} = \left(\vec{Z}_{17}^{\alpha} + \vec{Z}_{26}^{\alpha}\right)/2$. Hence, one obtains a 13-dimensional, mapped node-specific *Z*-score profile, $\vec{M}^{\alpha}$, for *every node* in a graph.

The gray, thin curves in Figure 8 show the mapped *M* scores of each node for the networks presented in Figure 7. In addition, the red, thick curve shows the regular *Z*-score profile over the whole network obtained by the commonly used motif-detection analysis. Although the gray and the red curves are not

Figure 7. Node-specific Z-score profiles of various real-world networks: transcriptional networks of (a) the yeast S. cerevisiae and (b) E. coli, socially related networks such as (c) a social network of prisoners and (d) hyperlinks between political blogs, and word-adjacency networks of (e) French books and (f) Spanish books. The node-specific patterns on the horizontal axis are oriented the way that the node under consideration is the lower one. Figures as appeared in (Winkler, 2015)

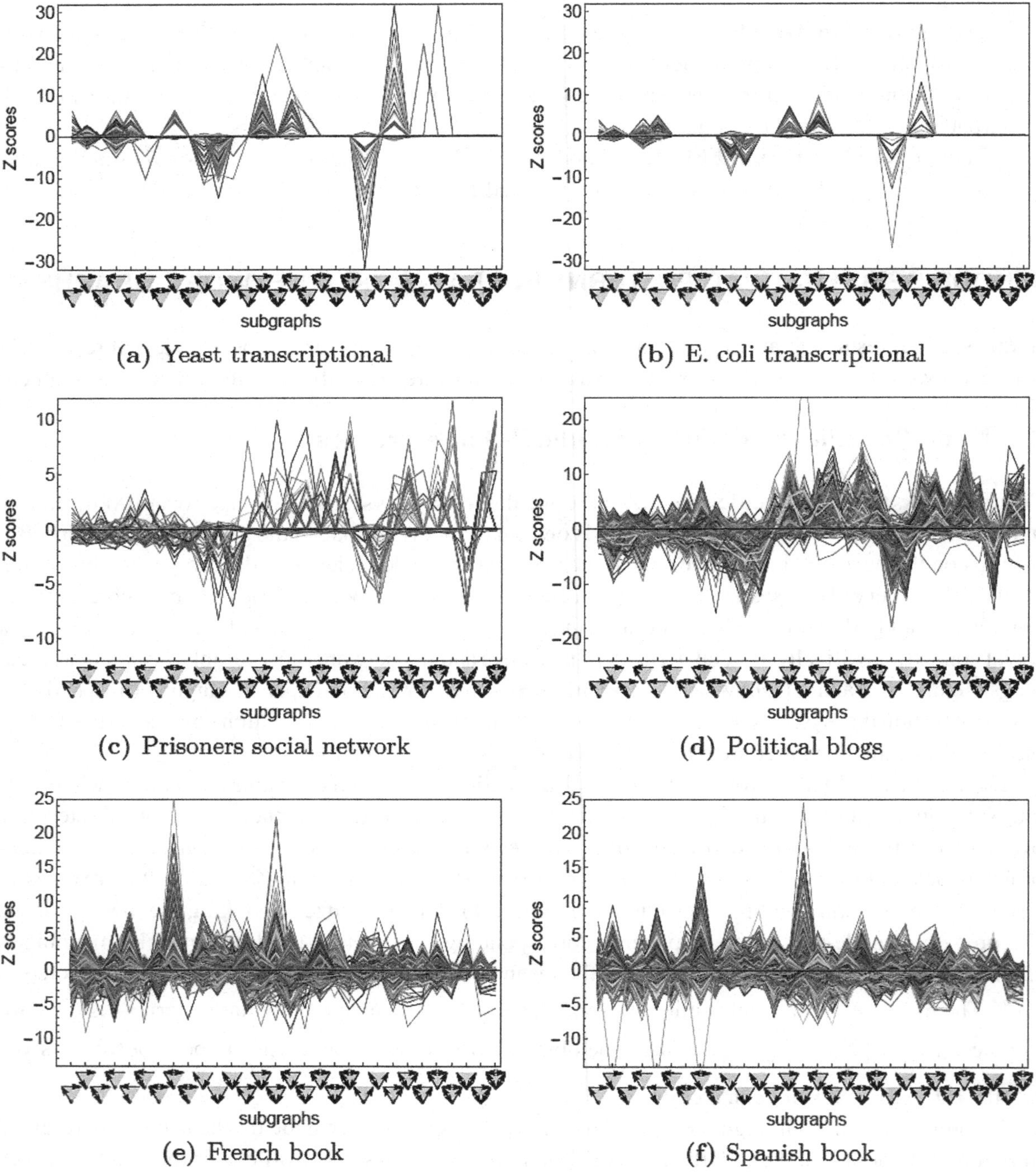

(a) Yeast transcriptional

(b) E. coli transcriptional

(c) Prisoners social network

(d) Political blogs

(e) French book

(f) Spanish book

Figure 6. Mapping of node-specific triad patterns to their corresponding regular triad patterns

Node-specific triad patterns

Regular triad patterns

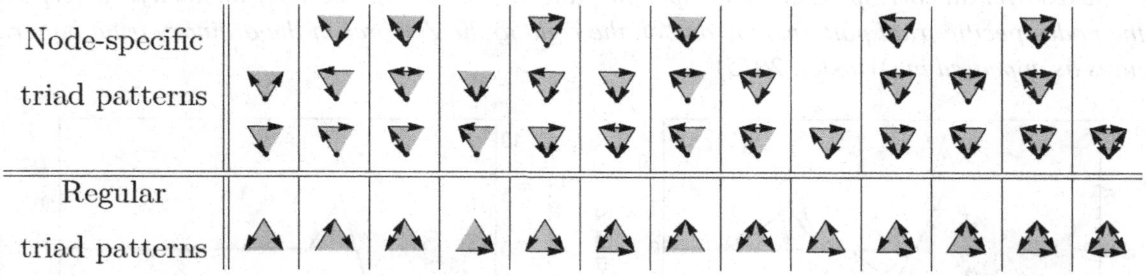

independent of each other, it shall be noticed that the regular *Z*-score profile cannot be computed from the gray curves directly. In particular, it is not the mean of the latter.

It can be observed that even though a pattern may be overrepresented in terms of the system as a whole, it may still be underrepresented in the neighborhood of certain nodes. Moreover, there are patterns with a rather low regular *Z* score, while there are both nodes with a strong positive and nodes with a strong negative contribution to the pattern. These contradictory effects seem to compensate each other on the system level. The described phenomenon can be particularly observed in the word-adjacency networks in Figures 8(e) and 8(f), especially for the loop pattern, number 12.

6.2. Heterogeneous Abundance of the Feed-Forward Loop

To further investigate whether regular motifs appear homogenously distributed over a graph, consider the feed-forward loop (FFL) pattern, number 8 in Figure 1. The FFL is one of the patterns that has been studied most intensively in terms of its relevance for guaranteeing systems to reliably perform their functions (Shen-Orr et al., 2002; Mangan & Alon, 2003; Alon, 2007). Specifically in transcriptional regulation networks, it was argued that the FFL pattern might play an important role for facilitating information-processing tasks (Shen-Orr et al., 2002).

For two of those transcriptional regulation networks, Figures 9(a) and 9(b) show histograms of the magnitude of the averaged node-specific *Z* scores of the three patterns corresponding to the FFL, i.e. the histograms reflect the contribution of individual nodes to the FFL pattern. In both of them the FFL is a motif (compare Figures 8(a) and 8(b)). Figure 9(a) shows the histogram of S. cerevisiae, Figure 9(b) the one of E. coli. Apparently, there are no nodes in the networks with a significant negative contribution to the FFL. Yet, neither is the pattern homogenously overrepresented throughout the whole system, even though it is a motif. In fact, for most nodes the FFL-subgraph structure does not seem to play any role whatsoever. This is reflected by the fact that both histograms exhibit a strong peak around zero, indicating that most nodes do not participate in FFL structures more frequently or less frequently than expected at random. In contrast, only very few nodes have a large mean node-specific *Z* score, M^{α}_{8}, for the patterns corresponding to the FFL. Hence, there are few nodes with a rather strong contribution to the FFL eventually making it a motif of the entire system.

There are two potential implications which can be derived from these observations: One conclusion could be that the FFL motif is actually not that important for the systems to work reliably. The second consequence could be that, in fact, very few nodes are critical for the systems to work the way they are supposed to. In the second case, the systems would be very prone to the failure of these crucial vertices.

Figure 8. Node-specific triadic Z scores mapped to the patterns of Figure 1. For each pattern, the average is taken over all corresponding node-specific patterns (Figure 6). The scale on the left corresponds to the node-specific triad patterns, the one on the right to the Z scores of the ordinary triad patterns. Figures as appeared in (Winkler, 2015)

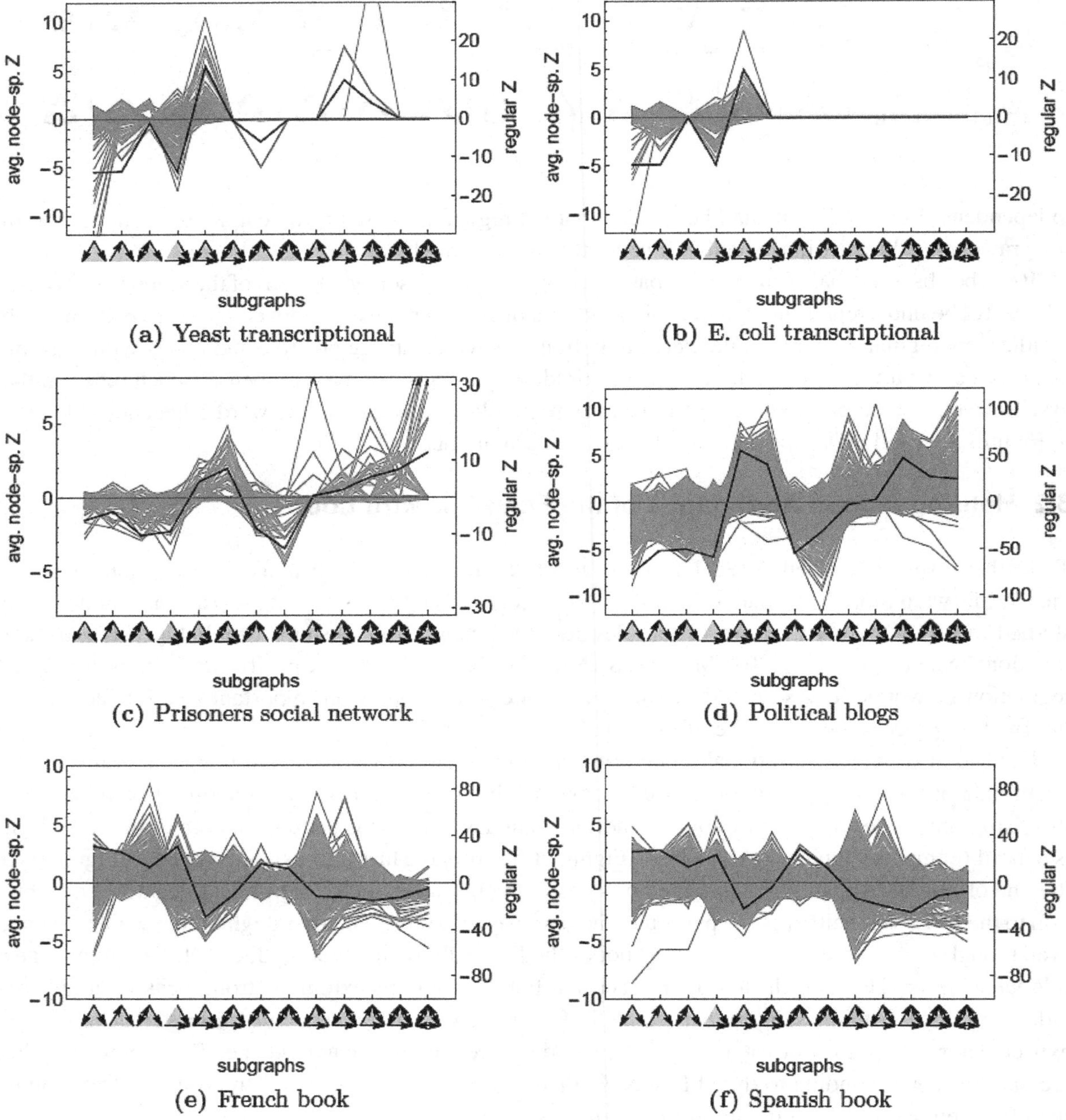

Figure 9. Histograms for the mean node-specific triadic Z scores corresponding to the feed-forward loop pattern (numbers 14, 16, and 23 in Figure 2). In all four networks the FFL is a motif. Figures as appeared in (Winkler, 2015)

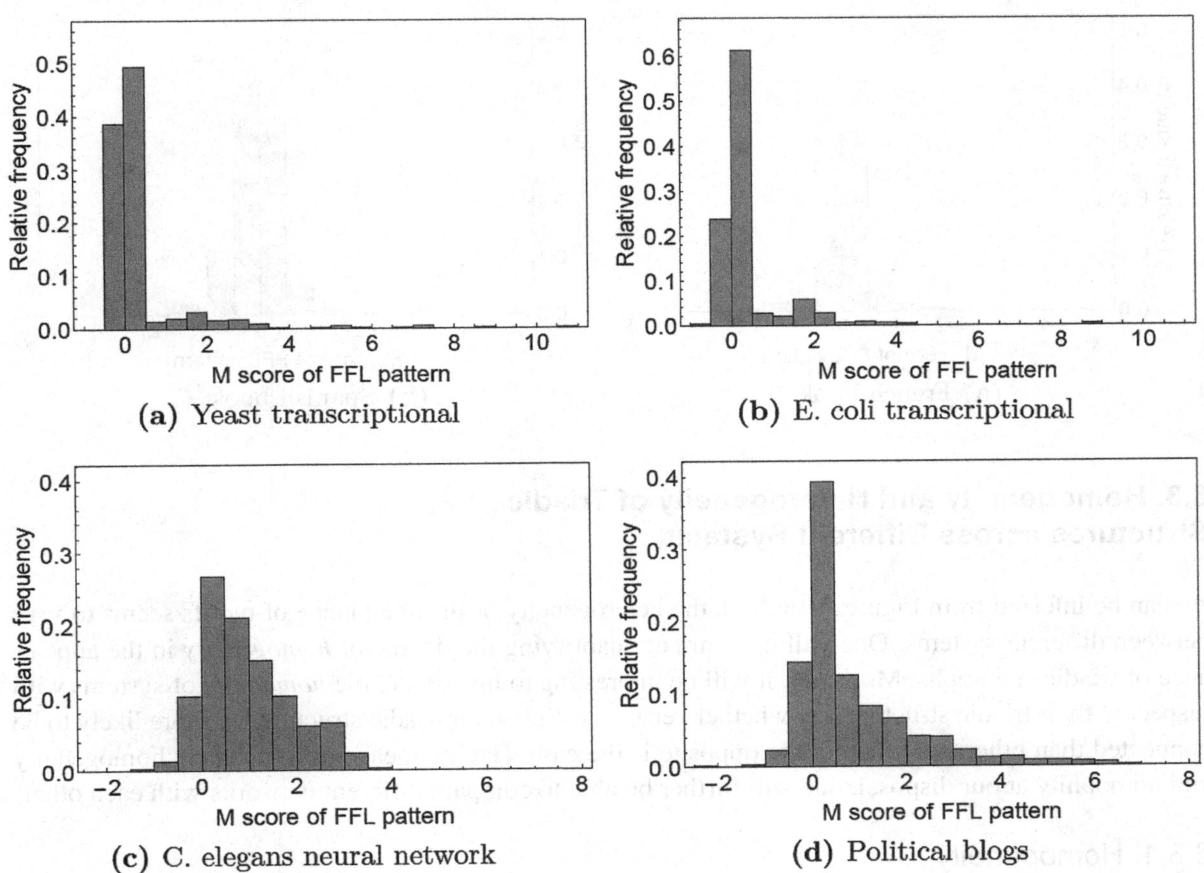

(a) Yeast transcriptional

(b) E. coli transcriptional

(c) C. elegans neural network

(d) Political blogs

It may be subject of future research to further investigate these possible implications for dynamical processes on different topologies and under node failure. Investigating the functional relevance of triadic motifs in terms of dynamical processes may be subject to future research.

The feed-forward loop is also a motif in the neural network of C. elegans and the network of hyperlinks between political blogs. Histograms of their mean node-specific *Z* scores corresponding to the FFL are shown in Figures 9(c) and 9(d), respectively. Although their M_8^α distributions also peak around zero, there are many more nodes with positive contributions to the FFL in comparison to the transcriptional regulation networks. This suggests a more homogeneous appearance of the pattern.

Furthermore, Figure 10 shows M_8^α histograms of two word-adjacency networks. The feed-forward loop is a motif in neither of them. In accordance, their distributions are narrowly centered around zero.

Figure 10. Histograms for the mean node-specific triadic Z scores corresponding to the feed-forward loop pattern (numbers 14, 16, and 23 in Figure 2). In neither of the networks the FFL is a motif. Figures as appeared in (Winkler, 2015)

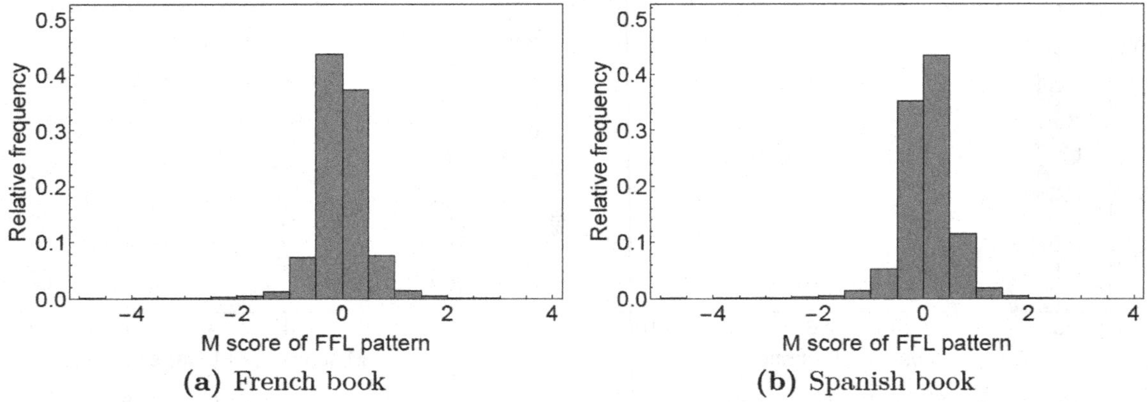

6.3. Homogeneity and Heterogeneity of Triadic Structures across Different Systems

As can be inferred from Figures 9 and 10, the heterogeneity of the abundance of motifs seems to vary between different systems. One will now aim at quantifying the degree of *homogeneity* in the appearance of triadic subgraphs. Moreover, it will be interesting to investigate the *homophily* of systems with respect to their triadic structure, i.e. whether vertices with similar triadic structure are more likely to be connected than others, or whether the opposite is the case. Having measures to quantify homogeneity and homophily at our disposal, one will further be able to compare different networks with each other.

6.3.1. Homogeneity

The mean correlation of the mapped node-specific Z scores, $\vec{M}^{\alpha}$, with the regular Z-score profile, $\vec{Z}$, be defined as a measure for the *homogeneity* of a graph **G**(V,E), in terms of its triadic substructure,

$$\left\langle C\left(\vec{M}^{\alpha},\vec{Z}\right)\right\rangle_{\alpha} = \frac{1}{|V|}\sum_{\alpha=1}^{|V|} C\left(\vec{M}^{\alpha},\vec{Z}\right).$$

A large homogeneity of a network indicates a similar triadic neighborhood of its vertices.

6.3.2. Homophily

Furthermore, one can define a measure for the *homophily* in terms of a network's triadic structure, i.e., a quantity to evaluate whether connected vertices are more similar to each other than unconnected ones. The similarity between the topological triadic environment of two nodes can be quantified by the correlation of their node-specific Z scores, $C\left(\vec{Z}^{\alpha},\vec{Z}^{\beta}\right)$. Hence, we define the homophily of a graph,

G(V,E), as the deviation of the mean pairwise correlation over the *connected pairs* of nodes, from the mean correlation over *all* pairs of nodes,

$$\left\langle C\left(\vec{Z}^{\alpha},\vec{Z}^{\beta}\right)\right\rangle_{\alpha NN\beta}-\left\langle C\left(\vec{Z}^{\alpha},\vec{Z}^{\beta}\right)\right\rangle_{\alpha,\beta}=\sum_{\alpha=1}^{|V|-1}\sum_{\beta=\alpha+1}^{|V|}\left(\frac{1}{\binom{|E|}{2}}A_{\alpha\beta}-\frac{1}{|V|}\right)C\left(\vec{Z}^{\alpha},\vec{Z}^{\beta}\right).$$

A large, positive homophily indicates that *connected* nodes tend to have much more similar structural environments than unconnected ones. A strongly negative homophily means that connected nodes tend to have more dissimilar neighborhoods. A homophily of zero implies that the alikeness of the surrounding structure of two vertices does not depend on whether they are connected or not.

6.3.3. Results

Analyses of a multitude of networks of diverse origin in terms of their homogeneity and homophily are presented in Figure 11. The horizontal axis represents the homophily; the vertical axis indicates the homogeneity. Figure 11 suggests that the position of a graph in the homogeneity-homophily space is strongly linked to the corresponding network's function. For the transcriptional-regulatory networks, a and b, the homogeneity is slightly positive while the homophily is slightly negative. For the word-adjacency networks, $d-g$, the homogeneity is zero and their homophily is slightly positive. Both a positive homogeneity and homophily can be observed for the electronic circuits, $h-j$ (shown in orange), and the social networks, $m-o$, with the latter being even more homogeneous. The positive homophily suggests that nodes with similar structural environment – and hence a similar structural role – are often directly linked to each other. For the triadic random graphs, k and l, the homogeneity of approximately 0.7 is quite large with a slightly negative homophily. The five groups mentioned above appear clearly separated in the homogeneity-homophily space of Figure 11, potentially reflecting typical structural aspects of graphs representing systems from the corresponding fields. Moreover, Figure 11 indicates a rather large homogeneity for the neural network of C. elegans, c, the citation network between scientific articles, p, and the airport-connection network, q. The last two furthermore exhibit a large homophily, i.e., connected nodes are structurally more similar than non-connected ones.

Our definition of homogeneity in averages over the similarity of $\vec{M}^{\alpha}$ and the overall Z score for all nodes α in the graph. To see whether this distribution itself is homogeneous, let us consider the standard deviation corresponding to the mean value in the definition of the homogeneity. Figure 12 displays the two measures plotted against each other for the systems of Figure 11. Again, the five groups are separated from each other in the two-dimensional plane. As in Figure 11, we can draw non-intersecting borders around the instances of every single group. The standard deviation itself is a measure for the heterogeneity of the distribution. In accordance with this fact, with decreasing standard deviation, the systems in Figure 12 show increasing homogeneity.

6.4. Clustering Based on Node-Specific Z-Score Profiles

Beyond allowing for a detailed investigation of the homogeneity of the appearance of motifs, with the triadic node-specific Z-score profiles, NoSPaM$_3$ provides for a whole new set of features for every node.

Figure 11. Comparison of multiple systems in terms of the homogeneity and homophily of their triadic substructure. a: E. coli transcriptional network; b: yeast transcriptional network; c: C. elegans neural network; word-adjacency networks of d: English book, e: French book, f: Spanish book, and g: Japanese book; electronic circuits h: s208, i: s420, and j: s838; triadic random graphs with FFL being a motif and k: unidirectional links only, l: both uni- and bidirectional links; m: political blogs; n: leadership social network; o: prisoners social network; p: scientific-citations between articles; q: airport-connections. Figure as appeared in (Winkler, 2015)

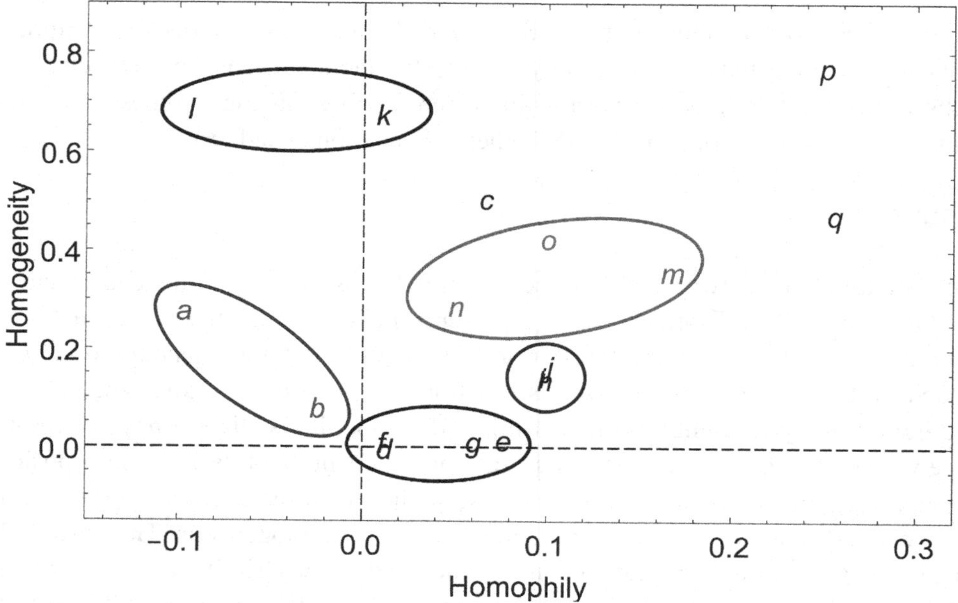

This new, 30-dimensional feature vector may be used for clustering and classification purposes. We will now utilize the node-specific *Z* scores, $\vec{Z}^{\alpha}$, to detect groups in the neural network of C. elegans by means of *complete-link clustering*.

6.4.1. Complete-Link Clustering

Complete-link clustering is a hierarchical, agglomerative clustering methodology. Following a bottom-up approach, for a system consisting of *N* units, agglomerative clustering algorithms initially assign every unit to its own cluster. Subsequently, using a *distance*, or *dissimilarity function*, $\delta\left(C_{\mu},C_{\nu}\right)$, between two clusters, C_{μ} and C_{ν}, the two most similar ones are merged. For the remaining *N*-1 clusters, the merging process is iteratively repeated until either the desired number of clusters is reached, or the smallest dissimilarity between two clusters exceeds a certain threshold.

For clustering nodes in terms of their local triadic substructure, we use the Euclidean distance between their node-specific triadic *Z*-score profiles, i.e.,

$$\delta(\alpha,\beta)=\sum_{i}\left(Z_i^{\alpha}-Z_i^{\beta}\right)^2,$$

Figure 12. Comparison of multiple systems in terms of the homogeneity of their triadic substructure. The vertical axis shows the correlation between the mapped node-specific Z scores, $\vec{M}^{\alpha}$, with the regular Z-score profile, $\vec{Z}$, averaged over all nodes of the systems. The horizontal axis represents the respective standard deviation. The presented systems correspond to those of Figure 11. Figure as appeared in (Winkler, 2015)

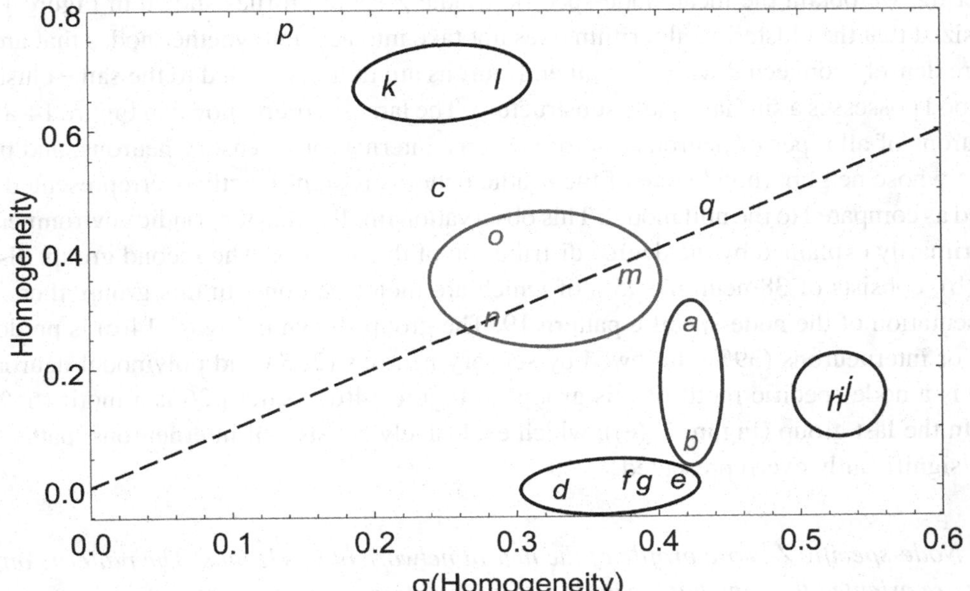

as the dissimilarity function between two nodes α and β.

However, given a distance function, $\delta(\alpha,\beta)$, between two *nodes*, α and β, there are multiple ways to define a distance function, $\delta(C_\mu,C_\nu)$, between two *clusters*, C_μ and C_ν, each consisting of more than one node. For complete-link clustering this distance between two clusters is defined as the maximum distance between any node in C_μ and any node in C_ν,

$$\delta_{complete\text{-}link}(C_\mu,C_\nu) = \max\left\{ d(N_\alpha,N_\beta) \,\middle|\, N_\alpha \in C_\mu, N_\beta \in C_\nu \right\}.$$

6.4.2. Clusters in the Neural Network of C. Elegans

The tiny roundworm *Caenorhabditis elegans (C. elegans)* has been studied intensively over the last decades and detailed data on its neural network is publicly available at www.wormatlas.org. On the one hand, with approximately 300 nodes, its neural network has a manageable size and can thus be examined in great detail. On the other hand, it can serve as a model organism for more complex animals. We will now consider the largest connected component of the graph representing the somatic nervous system of C. elegans. This neural network is composed of 279 neurons and 2,194 chemical synapses between them. The neurons of C. elegans are particularly suitable for cluster analysis, since existing expert classifications are available for comparison with our findings. The neurons are, for instance, classified into motor neurons, interneurons, and sensory neurons.

All 279 node-specific triadic Z-score profiles of C. elegans' neural network are displayed in Figure 13. There is a multitude of peaks in both positive and negative direction. Yet, not all peaks are present in the $\vec{Z}^{\alpha}$ profiles of *all* nodes simultaneously. Partitioning the neurons into five groups via complete-link clustering, we obtain the mean node-specific triadic Z-score profiles shown in Figure 14. It shall be emphasized that the clustering algorithm does not take into account whether nodes that are grouped together are densely connected with each other. Neurons are rather assigned to the same cluster if their neighborhood possesses a similar triadic substructure. The largest group, shown in Figure 14(a), consists of 172 neurons of all types of neurons (motor neurons, interneurons, sensory neurons, and polymodal neurons) in whose neighborhood none of the triadic patterns is significantly overrepresented or under-represented as compared to the null model. This observation implies that the triadic environment of these nodes is primarily explained by the degree distribution of the network. The second group, displayed in Figure 14(b), consists of 38 neurons, 95% of which are motor neurons. In this group, there is a clear overrepresentation of the node-specific pattern 19. The group shown in Figure 14(c) is predominantly composed of interneurons (39%), followed by sensory neurons (25%) and polymodal neurons (25%). Pattern 30 is a node-specific motif of this group. In Figure 14(d), pattern 26 is a motif (65% sensory neurons). In the last group (Figure 14(e)), which exclusively consists of interneurons, patterns 17, 24, and 30 are significantly overrepresented.

Figure 13. Node-specific Z-score profile of the neural network of C. elegans. The patterns on the horizontal axis are oriented the way that the node under consideration is the lower one. Figure as appeared in (Winkler, 2015)

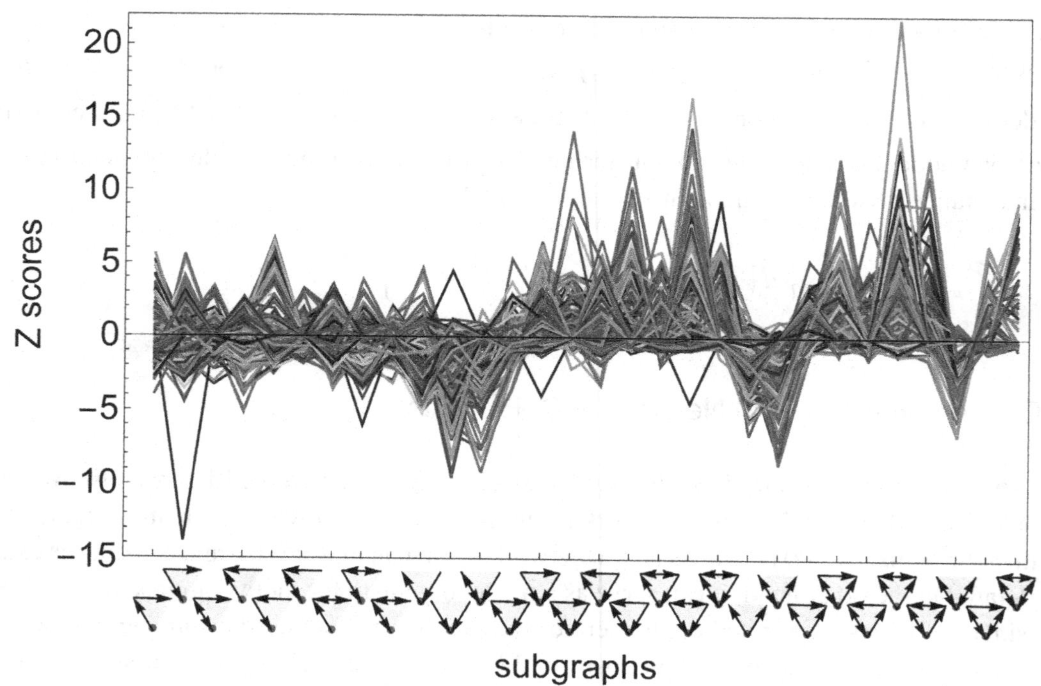

Figure 14. Averaged Z-score profiles over groups of neurons detected by means of a complete-link clustering of nodes in terms of their node-specific triadic Z-score profiles. (a) comprises all kinds of neuron types, the majority in (b) are motor neurons, (c) and (e) are dominated by interneurons, and (d) by sensory neurons. Error bars indicate one standard deviation. Figures as appeared in (Winkler, 2015)

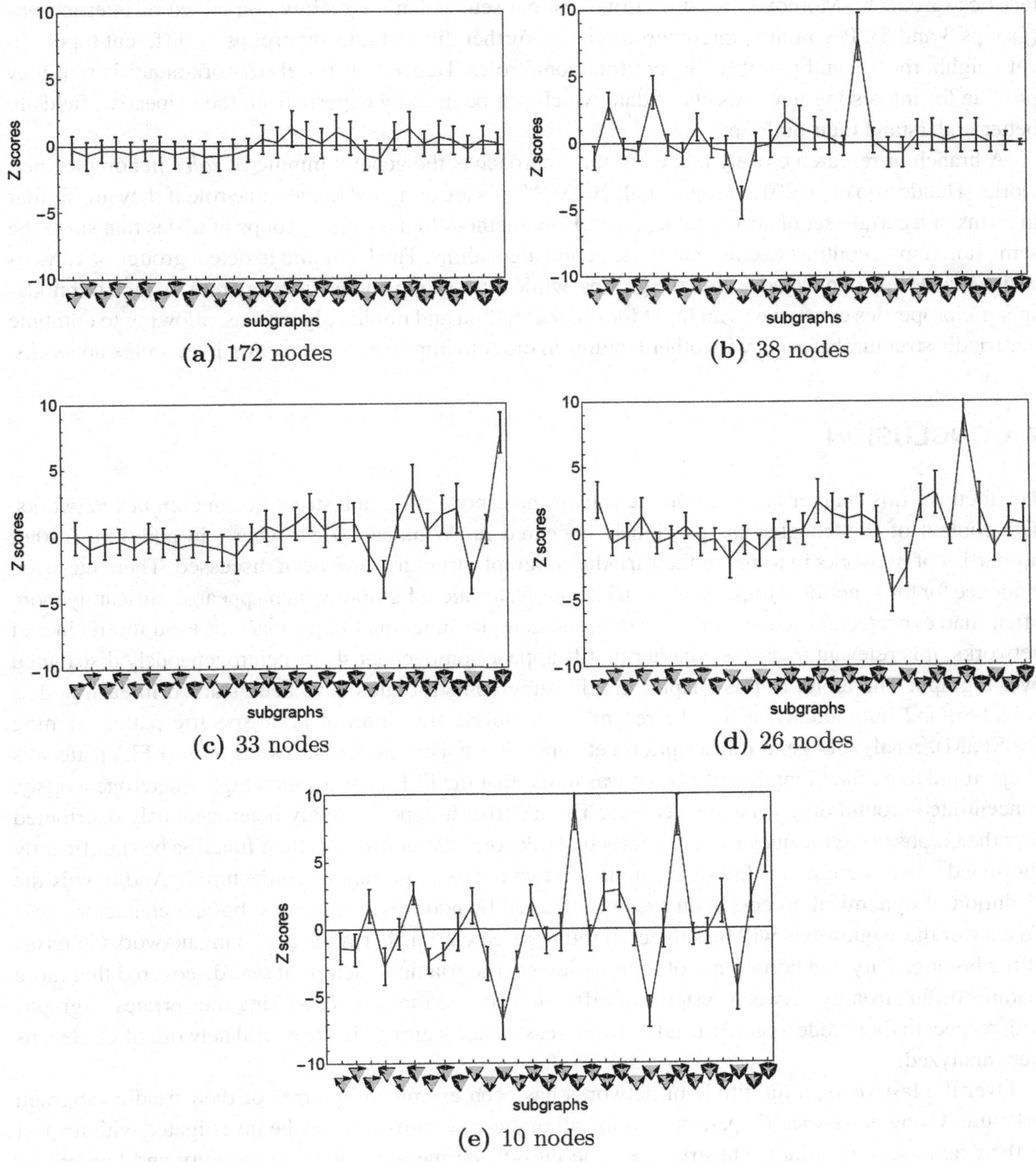

The analysis shows that, on the one hand, our clustering is, to great extent, in agreement with expert classifications in which neurons were assigned to be motor, sensory, or interneurons based on their structural and functional embedding in the graph structure. On the other hand, our clustering sorted out many neurons which, apparently, do not contribute strongly to the network's local structural characteristics (group 1). Moreover, we detect two distinct sets which are mainly comprised of interneurons (groups 3 and 5). Potentially, interneurons can be further divided into subgroups of different topological neighborhoods and possibly distinct functional roles. Hence, our novel network-analysis tool may provide for interesting new aspects of data which can be used by experts from the respective fields to better understand their buildup.

A branch of research closely related to this approach is the general mining of *roles* in complex networks (Henderson et al, 2012; Gilpin et al, 2013). Nodes are assigned to the same role if they are similar in terms of a certain set of structural features. Both methodologies detect groups of nodes that share the same function in contrast to community-detection algorithms. The latter aim to detect groups of vertices which are closely connected within the groups, while inter-group connections are rare. In fact, our node-specific properties can serve as an input for role-extraction and mining algorithms, allowing to combine our triadic structural aspects with other features in order to improve role detection in complex networks.

7. CONCLUSION

The focus of this chapter has been on the role of three-node subgraph structures in complex networks. The content of this chapter has previously appeared in (Winkler, 2015), where, in addition, further properties of networks in terms of their triadic subgraph structure have been discussed. There has been evidence for the functional importance of triad motifs, triadic subgraphs which appear significantly more often than expected at random. In order to investigate the functional importance of triad motifs in real networks, it is relevant to assess whether motifs appear homogeneously or heterogeneously distributed over a graph. Therefore, in this chapter, triadic subgraph structures have been studied in each node's neighborhood individually, using the recently introduced algorithm of node-specific pattern mining (NoSPaM). Analyzing gene-transcription networks – in which the feed-forward loop (FFL) pattern is conjectured to be functionally critical – it was found that the FFL is distributed highly heterogeneously, concentrated around only very few vertices. The fact that it appears highly heterogenously distributed over the graphs raises the question about its actual role for the systems. Will their function be significantly shortened when these nodes fail or are motifs in fact not as important as conjectured? And how is the evolution of dynamical processes on systems affected by nodes with certain subgraph characteristics? To answer these questions will be subject to future research. Furthermore, analyzing networks in terms of the homogeneity and homophily of their node-specific triadic structure, it was discovered that these features differ strongly between systems of different origin. Moreover, clustering the vertices of graphs with respect to their node-specific triadic structure, structural groups in the neural network of C. elegans were analyzed.

Over the last years, a multitude of networks has been examined in terms of their triadic subgraph structure. Using node-specific pattern mining, all of these systems can now be investigated with respect to their node-specific triadic substructure. The introduced measures for homogeneity and homophily will further allow to compare the detailed structure of different systems with each other and to extend the illustration in Figures 11 and 12. The analysis may unveil structural differences, even for those networks with similar ordinary triadic *Z*-score profiles. Furthermore, NoSPaM can also be applied to signed networks in order to investigate issues related to social balance research.

REFERENCES

Adamic, L. A., & Glance, N. (2005). The political blogosphere and the 2004 US election: divided they blog. In *Proceedings of the 3rd international workshop on Link discovery* (pp. 36-43). ACM. doi:10.1145/1134271.1134277

Albert, I., & Albert, R. (2004). Conserved network motifs allow protein–protein interaction prediction. *Bioinformatics (Oxford, England)*, *20*(18), 3346–3352. doi:10.1093/bioinformatics/bth402 PMID:15247093

Alon, U. (2006). *An introduction to systems biology: design principles of biological circuits*. CRC press.

Alon, U. (2007). Network motifs: Theory and experimental approaches. *Nature Reviews. Genetics*, *8*(6), 450–461. doi:10.1038/nrg2102 PMID:17510665

Alon, U. (2012). *Collection of complex networks*. Retrieved from http://www.weizmann.ac.il/mcb/UriAlon/

Artzy-Randrup, Y., Fleishman, S. J., Ben-Tal, N., & Stone, L. (2004). Comment on "Network motifs: Simple building blocks of complex networks" and" Superfamilies of evolved and designed networks. *Science*, *305*(5687), 1107–1107. doi:10.1126/science.1099334 PMID:15326338

Bastian, M., Heymann, S., & Jacomy, M. (2009). Gephi: An open source software for exploring and manipulating networks. *ICWSM*, *8*, 361–362.

Berlingerio, M., Bonchi, F., Bringmann, B., & Gionis, A. (2009). Mining graph evolution rules. In *Machine learning and knowledge discovery in databases* (pp. 115–130). Springer. doi:10.1007/978-3-642-04180-8_25

Burda, Z., Krzywicki, A., Martin, O. C., & Zagorski, M. (2011). Motifs emerge from function in model gene regulatory networks. *Proceedings of the National Academy of Sciences of the United States of America*, *108*(42), 17263–17268. doi:10.1073/pnas.1109435108 PMID:21960444

Costanzo, M. C., Crawford, M. E., Hirschman, J. E., Kranz, J. E., Olsen, P., Robertson, L. S., & Garrels, J. I. et al. (2001). YPD™, PombePD™ and WormPD™: Model organism volumes of the BioKnowledge™ Library, an integrated resource for protein information. *Nucleic Acids Research*, *29*(1), 75–79. doi:10.1093/nar/29.1.75 PMID:11125054

Fretter, C., Müller-Hannemann, M., & Hütt, M. T. (2012). Subgraph fluctuations in random graphs. *Physical Review E: Statistical, Nonlinear, and Soft Matter Physics*, *85*(5), 056119. doi:10.1103/PhysRevE.85.056119 PMID:23004833

Gehrke, J., Ginsparg, P., & Kleinberg, J. (2003). Overview of the 2003 KDD Cup. *ACM SIGKDD Explorations Newsletter*, *5*(2), 149–151. doi:10.1145/980972.980992

Gilpin, S., Eliassi-Rad, T., & Davidson, I. (2013). Guided learning for role discovery (glrd): Framework, algorithms, and applications. In *Proceedings of the 19th ACM SIGKDD international conference on Knowledge discovery and data mining* (pp. 113-121). ACM. doi:10.1145/2487575.2487620

Henderson, K., Gallagher, B., Eliassi-Rad, T., Tong, H., Basu, S., Akoglu, L., & Li, L. et al. (2012). Rolx: structural role extraction & mining in large graphs. In *Proceedings of the 18th ACM SIGKDD international conference on Knowledge discovery and data mining* (pp. 1231-1239). ACM. doi:10.1145/2339530.2339723

Klemm, K., & Bornholdt, S. (2005). Topology of biological networks and reliability of information processing. *Proceedings of the National Academy of Sciences of the United States of America, 102*(51), 18414–18419. doi:10.1073/pnas.0509132102 PMID:16339314

Leskovec, J., Kleinberg, J., & Faloutsos, C. (2005). Graphs over time: densification laws, shrinking diameters and possible explanations. In *Proceedings of the eleventh ACM SIGKDD international conference on Knowledge discovery in data mining* (pp. 177-187). ACM. doi:10.1145/1081870.1081893

Leskovec, J., & Krevl, A. (2014). *SNAP Datasets: Stanford Large Network Dataset Collection*. Retrieved from http://snap.stanford.edu/data

Mangan, S., & Alon, U. (2003). Structure and function of the feed-forward loop network motif. *Proceedings of the National Academy of Sciences of the United States of America, 100*(21), 11980–11985. doi:10.1073/pnas.2133841100 PMID:14530388

Milo, R., Itzkovitz, S., Kashtan, N., Levitt, R., Shen-Orr, S., Ayzenshtat, I., & Alon, U. et al. (2004). Superfamilies of evolved and designed networks. *Science, 303*(5663), 1538–1542. doi:10.1126/science.1089167 PMID:15001784

Milo, R., Shen-Orr, S., Itzkovitz, S., Kashtan, N., Chklovskii, D., & Alon, U. (2002). Network motifs: Simple building blocks of complex networks. *Science, 298*(5594), 824–827. doi:10.1126/science.298.5594.824 PMID:12399590

Newman, M. E. J. (2012). *Network Data*. Retrieved from http://www-personal.umich.edu/~mejn/netdata/

Prill, R. J., Iglesias, P. A., & Levchenko, A. (2005). Dynamic properties of network motifs contribute to biological network organization. *PLoS Biology, 3*(11), e343. doi:10.1371/journal.pbio.0030343 PMID:16187794

Rahman, M., Bhuiyan, M. A., & Al Hasan, M. (2014). GRAFT: An efficient graphlet counting method for large graph analysis. *IEEE Transactions on Knowledge and Data Engineering, 26*(10), 2466–2478. doi:10.1109/TKDE.2013.2297929

Shen-Orr, S. S., Milo, R., Mangan, S., & Alon, U. (2002). Network motifs in the transcriptional regulation network of Escherichia coli. *Nature Genetics, 31*(1), 64–68. doi:10.1038/ng881 PMID:11967538

Sporns, O., & Kötter, R. (2004). Motifs in brain networks. *PLoS Biology, 2*(11), e369. doi:10.1371/journal.pbio.0020369 PMID:15510229

Varshney, L. R., Chen, B. L., Paniagua, E., Hall, D. H., & Chklovskii, D. B. (2011). Structural properties of the Caenorhabditis elegans neuronal network. *PLoS Computational Biology*, *7*(2), e1001066. doi:10.1371/journal.pcbi.1001066 PMID:21304930

Winkler, M. (2015). *On the Role of Triadic Substructures in Complex Networks*. Berlin: epubli.

Winkler, M., & Reichardt, J. (2013). Motifs in triadic random graphs based on Steiner triple systems. *Physical Review E: Statistical, Nonlinear, and Soft Matter Physics*, *88*(2), 022805. doi:10.1103/PhysRevE.88.022805 PMID:24032881

Winkler, M., & Reichardt, J. (2014). Node-Specific Triad Pattern Mining for Complex-Network Analysis. In *ICDMW, 2014 IEEE International Conference on Data Mining* (pp. 605-612). IEEE. doi:10.1109/ICDMW.2014.36

Chapter 6
Characterization and Coarsening of Autonomous System Networks:
Measuring and Simplifying the Internet

Alberto Garcia-Robledo
Cinvestav-Tamaulipas, Mexico

Arturo Diaz-Perez
Cinvestav-Tamaulipas, Mexico

Guillermo Morales-Luna
Cinvestav-IPN, Mexico

ABSTRACT

This Chapter studies the correlations among well-known complex network metrics and presents techniques to coarse the topology of the Internet at the Autonomous System (AS) level. We present an experimental study on the linear relationships between a rich set of complex network metrics, to methodologically select a subset of non-redundant and potentially independent metrics that explain different aspects of the topology of the Internet. Then, the selected metrics are used to evaluate graph coarsening algorithms to reduce the topology of AS networks. The presented coarsening algorithms exploit the k-core decomposition of graphs to preserve relevant complex network properties.

INTRODUCTION

Recent years have witnessed the rise of Network Science, defined *as the study of network representations of physical, biological, and social phenomena leading to predictive models of these phenomena* (Committee on Network Science for Future Army Applications, 2005), thanks to: (1) the modernization and automation of data acquisition techniques using computer systems, (2) the growing availability of ever-increasing computing resources that enable the analysis of large volumes of data, (3) the availability

DOI: 10.4018/978-1-4666-9964-9.ch006

and openness of rich databases in different disciplines, and (4) the growing interest in holistic approaches to explain the behavior of complex systems as a whole (Albert & Barabási, 2002). Complex networks have been used to model the macroscopic structure of massive technological phenomena, including the topology of the Internet at the Autonomous System (AS) level.

An AS is a group of host IP addresses, known as routing prefixes, that share common routing policies. AS's interact with each other through a massive network of links to form an AS Network (ASN) that communicates dozens to millions of hosts around the world. From a technological perspective, the measurement of the Internet can be considered a Big Data problem that typically involves the analysis of the Internet topology for the discovery (and inference) of AS connections. ASN links, viewed as a whole, reveal important details of the functional organization and evolution of the Internet (Cho, 2012). As the Internet has evolved, it has achieved the characteristics of a complex network, which can be used to model the macroscopic structure of massive technological phenomena.

A variety of existing Internet measurement initiatives propose complex network metrics to characterize different topological aspects of ASN's for a wide variety of purposes (Angeles et. al., 2007). Unfortunately, the selection of a definitive set of metrics is hampered by the existence of a wide variety of redundant metrics that unintentionally explain the same aspects of complex networks. There are efforts that study the pair-wise correlation between metrics to select a subset of non-redundant metrics (Costa et. al., 2010; Li et. al., 2011; Jamakovic & Uhlig, 2008; Bounova & de Weck, 2012; Filkov et. al., 2009). However, it is not clear if existing results based on complex network datasets from different domains are valid for the characterization of ASN's. The characterization of an ASN should be performed in terms of non-redundant metrics, i.e. metrics that hold little correlation, inferred from measurements on ASN datasets characterized through size-independent metrics, as the authors will later observe in this Chapter.

On the other hand, the massive size of complex networks like the Internet topology introduces the need for mechanisms that reduce the size of real-world graphs for faster processing. Given a complex network, can the graph be quickly zoomed out? Is there a smaller equivalent representation of a large graph that preserves its topological properties, such as its degree distribution and its average degree? Graph coarsening methods combine nodes to shrink large graphs while preserving topological properties of interest.

It has been reported that the topology of the Internet shows a core (Carmi et. al., 2007), integrated of well-connected hubs that represent the backbone of the Internet. The k -core decomposition defines a hierarchy of nodes that enables the differentiation between core and non-core components of a network. The authors will take advantage of this differentiation to design a new graph coarsening framework that preserve relevant complex network properties.

The objective of this Chapter is two-fold: (1) to present a data-driven methodology to obtain non-redundant complex networks metrics, and (2) to apply the methodology on a practical scenario: the simplification of the Internet graph at the AS level.

The rest of this Chapter is organized as follows. First, the graph coarsening and metrics selection problems are defined, and their relationship is discussed. Later, a variety of degree, clustering, distance, centrality, and scaling complex network metrics are reviewed. Then, the correlations among the presented metrics on evolving Internet networks are presented. Non-redundant complex network metrics should provide roughly the same amount of information about ASN's than the full set of metrics. To test this claim, the researchers assess clusters of ASN's through Principal Component Analysis (PCA).

Later, the authors exploit non-redundant complex network metrics, the concept of node centrality and the coreness of graphs, to develop and evaluate coarsening algorithms based on the k-core decomposition of ASN's. Several criteria for the exploitation of the *k*-core hierarchy of ASN's are described, as well as experimental results on a variety of non-redundant complex network metrics.

THE GRAPH COARSENING AND METRICS SELECTION PROBLEMS

Let $G=(V,E)$ be an undirected graph, integrated of a non-empty set V of nodes or vertices and a set E of links or edges, such that there is a mapping between the elements of E and the set of unordered pairs $\{i,j\}$, $i,j \in V$. Let $n=|V|$ be the number of nodes and $m=|E|$ be the number of edges of G. Let $M(G)=(\mu_1(G),\mu_2(G),...,\mu_q(G))$ denote the values of a set $M=(\mu_1,\mu_2,...,\mu_q)$ of q complex network metrics μ_i. Starting from the original graph G, the graph coarsening problem is to construct a hierarchy of h graphs $G_1,G_2,...,G_h$ of decreasing size $n>n_1>...>n_h$ and $m>m_1>...>m_h$ by edge contractions, such that $M(G_i)\approx M(G_{i-1})$. The idea is that the solutions of a problem for G_i can be "efficiently" extended to that for G_{i-1} and vice versa.

However, how to decide on the set of metrics M that best characterize the properties of the original network G and the coarse networks G_i? Currently, there is no a consensus on a definitive set of metrics that provide a "complete" characterization of real-world complex networks like the Internet. Nonetheless, there are methodological efforts (Costa et al., 2007; Li et al., 2011; Jamakovic & Uhlig, 2008; Bounova & de Weck, 2012; Filkov et al., 2009) that, given an initial set of potentially redundant metrics, allow us to obtain a subset of potentially non-redundant metrics with similar "descriptive capacity" than the initial set.

The metrics selection problem is to get a subset of non-redundant metrics $M'\subseteq M$ such that any pair of metrics $\mu_i,\mu_j\in M'$ hold little or no redundancy. Current efforts to solve the complex network metrics selection problem (Costa et al., 2007; Li et al., 2011; Jamakovic & Uhlig, 2008; Bounova & de Weck, 2012) conclude that many widely-used metrics are strongly correlated.

Throughout this Chapter it is presented the application of a data-driven methodology based on a metrics correlation analysis, in order to reveal pairwise metrics correlation patterns on different ASN datasets and to select a set of non-redundant metrics. Some of the selected metrics are then used to characterize the topology of ASN's and evaluate the quality of coarsening algorithms that simplify the topology of the Internet while preserving non-redundant complex network properties of interest.

METRICS FOR ANALYZING ASN'S AS COMPLEX NETWORKS

Much of the work in Network Science have been devoted to the statistical characterization of real-world graphs in terms of complex network metrics (Costa et. al., 2007). In this Section a list of a collection of structural and scaling complex network metrics is presented.

Structural Complex Network Metrics

Complex network metrics can be roughly grouped into two classes: structural and scaling metrics. On the one hand, structural metrics summarize information about the global structure of the graph, or the local organization or importance of vertices. On the other hand, the scaling of some structural metrics with the degree of vertices can reveal non-trivial high-level properties of graphs, such the scale-free form of the graph degree distribution, a hierarchy of clusters of nodes, or the existence of vertex degree correlations.

Structural metrics can be divided, in turn, into degree, clustering, distance and centrality, as shown in Table 1:

- **Degree Metrics:** These are directly derived from the degree of vertices, the degree distribution, and the vertex degree correlations. Connectivity metrics include: the degree of a vertex k_i, the degree distribution $P(k)$, the average degree $\langle k \rangle$, and the maximum degree k_{max}. Another example is the assortative coefficient as_r that measures the degree-degree vertex correlation.
- **Clustering Metrics:** The clustering coefficient CC_i allows the study the cyclic structure of a graph, by measuring the cohesion among the nearest neighbors of a vertex. Consider the set of neighbors $R_d(i)$, defined by those vertices at distance d from a vertex i. The hierarchical clustering coefficient of i at distance d, denoted as $hcc_d(i)$, is the number of edges in the ring $R_d(i)$ divided by the maximum possible number of edges among the vertices in $R_d(i)$. Another clustering metric, the rich-club coefficient $\phi(k)$, resembles the clustering coefficient in that it expresses how close are the vertices of the rich-club (vertices with degree $>k$) to form a complete graph.
- **Distance Metrics:** Distance between vertices is an important property that depends on the global structure of a complex network. The average path length $\langle L \rangle$, defined as the average of all the shortest paths lengths in the graph, is a well-known global distance metric, as well as the diameter D, defined as the length of the longest shortest path in the graph.
- **Centrality Metrics:** Centrality metrics try to quantify the intuitive idea that some vertices or edges are more "important" than others. For example, the betweenness centrality nBc_u expresses the proportion of shortest paths in which a vertex participates. The edge betweenness centrality mBc_e extends the same centrality concept to links. The closeness centrality Cc_i is inversely proportional to the sum of the distances of a vertex i to every other vertex in the graph. The central point dominance CPD measures the importance of the most influential node in terms of the betweenness centrality. The eigenvector centrality x_i is based on the intuition than the centrality of a vertex i is the result of the combination of the centralities of its neighbors, encoded in the eigenvalues of the graph adjacency matrix.

The definitions of the above mentioned metrics are listed in Table 1, which uses the following notation. Letters $i,j,k,u,v \in V$ represent vertices in G and e represents an edge in G. Let k_i be the degree of i, N_i be the neighborhood of i, $\{e_{jk}\}$ be the edges connecting the neighbors j,k of i, and $m{>}k$ be the number of edges connecting the $n{>}k$ vertices that have degree greater than k. Let $n_d(i)=|R_d(i)|$ be the number of nodes in the ring $R_d(i)$, and $m_d(i)$ be the number of edges in $R_d(i)$. Let d_{ij} be the length of the shortest path between i,j. Let $\sigma(i,u,j)$ and $\sigma(i,e,j)$ be the number of shortest paths between i,j that pass throughu vertex u and edge e, respectively, and $\sigma(i,j)$ be the total number of shortest paths between i,j. Let $Bc_{\max}$ be the maximum vertex betweenness centrality of a graph and λ be a constant. Let COR(X,Y) denote the the Pearson correlation coefficient between tuples X and Y. Finally, let K be the tuple of different vertex degrees in $G$and let $\log(S) = (\log(y)|y \in S)$ be the function that returns a set with the logarithm of each element in S.

Table 1. Definition of the degree, clustering, distance, centrality, and scaling complex network metrics used in this work

Metric μ	Symbol	Type	Equation
Avg. degree	$\langle k \rangle$	Degree	$\frac{1}{n}\sum_{v \in V} k_v$
Max. degree	k_{max}	Degree	$\max_{v \in V}\{k_v\}$
Assortativity coefficient	as_r	Degree	$\frac{m^{-1}\sum_{\{i,j\}\in E} k_i k_j - \left[m^{-1}\sum_{\{i,j\}\in E}\frac{1}{2}(k_i+k_j)\right]^2}{m^{-1}\sum_{\{i,j\}\in E}\frac{1}{2}(k_i^2+k_j^2) - \left[m^{-1}\sum_{\{i,j\}\in E}\frac{1}{2}(k_i+k_j)\right]^2}$
Clustering coefficient	CC_i	Clustering	..
Rich-club coefficient	$\phi(k)$	Clustering	$\frac{2m_{>k}}{n_{>k}(n_{>k}-1)}$
Hierarchical clustering coef. at distance *d*	$hcc_d(i)$	Clustering	$\frac{2m_d(i)}{n_d(i)(n_d(i)-1)}$
Avg. path length	$\langle L \rangle$	Distance	$\frac{1}{n(n-1)}\sum_{i,j\in V: i\neq j} d_{ij}$
Diameter	D	Distance	$\max_{i,j\in V: i\neq j}\{d_{ij}\}$
Vertex betweenness centrality	nBc_u	Centrality	$\sum_{i,j\in V: i\neq j}\frac{\sigma(i,u,j)}{\sigma(i,j)}$
Edge betweenness centrality	mBc_e	Centrality	$\sum_{i,j\in V: i\neq j}\frac{\sigma(i,e,j)}{\sigma(i,j)}$
Central point dominance	CPD	Centrality	$\frac{1}{n-1}\sum_{i\in V}(Bc_{max} - nBc_i)$
Closeness centrality	Cc_i	Centrality	$\frac{1}{\sum_{j\in V} d_{ij}}$
Avg. neighbor degree	$\langle k_n \rangle$	Centrality	$\frac{k_u}{k_i} : u \in N_i$
Eigenvector centrality	x_i	Centrality	$\frac{1}{\lambda}\sum_{j=1}^{n} A_{ij} x_j$

continued on following page

Table 1. Continued

Metric μ	Symbol	Type	Equation
Scaling of the degree distribution	$\langle P(k)\rangle_k$	Scaling	$\text{COR}\left(\log(K),\log\left(\left(P(k)\mid k\in K\right)\right)\right)$
Scaling of the avg. neighbor connectivity	$\langle k_{nn}(k)\rangle_k$	Scaling	$\text{COR}\left(\log(K),\log\left(\left(\langle k_{nn}(k)\rangle\mid k\in K\right)\right)\right)$
Scaling of the rich-club coefficient	$\Phi(k)_k$	Scaling	$\text{COR}\left(\log(K),\log\left(\left(\phi(k)\mid k\in K\right)\right)\right)$
Scaling of the clustering coefficient	$\langle CC(k)\rangle_k$	Scaling	$\text{COR}\left(\log(K),\log\left(\left(\langle CC(k)\rangle\mid k\in K\right)\right)\right)$

Scaling of Complex Network Metrics

The scaling of local metrics with the degree of vertices can be used to characterize the scale-freeness, the degree correlations, the cohesiveness of the rich-club, and the hierarchical structure of ASN's (Angeles et. al., 2007):

- A graph is scale-free if the probability of finding a node of degree k, $P(k)$, decreases when increasing the degree k, following a power-law form (Barabási et. al., 2000).
- A graph is disassortative if the average neighbor connectivity $\langle k_{nn}(k)\rangle$ decreases when increasing the degree k (Pastor-Satorras et. al., 2001).
- The level of cohesiveness between the members of a rich-club can be assessed by looking at the $\phi(k)$ scaling curve with the degree of vertices (Zhou and Mondragón, 2007).
- Let $CC(k)$ denote the average clustering coefficient of nodes with degree k. The hierarchical nature of networks is captured by the $CC(k)$ curve, which can reveal a hierarchy of nodes having different degrees of clustering (Ravasz and Barabási, 2003).

These scalings are not trivially correlated (Colizza et. al., 2006). For example, an assortative network does not always have a rich-club structure. Likewise, disassortative networks may have a strongly connected rich-club, and only a few of the rich-club edges are needed to provide strong connection to other hubs (Zhou & Mondragón, 2004). Uncorrelated scale-free networks are always small-world, but this is not necessarily true for correlated scale-free graphs (Small et. al., 2008). Furthermore, the well-known model of Albert-Barabási (Barabási et. al., 2000) produces scale-free graphs that are neither assortative nor disassortative (Newman, 2002).

CORRELATIONS PATTERNS ON COMPLEX NETWORK METRICS

The investigation of complex network metrics correlations has been successfully applied in fields like Biology and Air Traffic Management (ATM). For example, Roy and Filkov (2009) related several microbe characteristics and phenotypes to the topology of their networks. To achieve this, a correlation analysis of network metrics was carried out, revealing that the identified metrics agree with the studied biological characteristics. On the other hand, Li et. al. (2011) performed a correlation analysis of network metrics for the characterization of functional brain networks of healthy subjects. Li et. al. (2011) found that the correlation patterns on the brain networks were similar to the patterns found on Erdös-Rényi random graphs. Finally, Sun and Wandelt (2014) identified functional dependencies and non-linear relationships among complex network metrics through regression analysis, with the objective of identifying and removing redundant metrics as a preprocessing step to assess the structural similarity of the air navigation route systems in different countries.

There is evidence that many of the metrics used for the study of the evolution, modeling, and reduction of ASN's could be redundant. For example, Costa et. al. (2007) found that many metrics are highly correlated on Barabási-Albert networks. These networks are generated by a widely-known preferential attachment process used to replicate the scale-free topology of the Internet. Likewise, Jamakovic and Uhlig (2008) and Filkov et. al. (2009) investigated metric correlations in a variety of technological, social, biological, and linguistic networks, and sets of highly correlated metrics were found.

Unfortunately, it is not completely clear if the metric correlations found by Jamakovic and Uhlig (2008) and Filkov et. al. (2009) on ensembles of networks with very heterogeneous structure can be directly applied to ASN datasets. Costa et. al. (2007) show that correlation patterns for a network model do not necessarily agree with the patterns that arise when different models are put together. Likewise, Bounova and de Weck (2012) advice against mixing network ensembles from different applications domains to extract global metric correlation patterns. Moreover, Li et. al. (2011) presented analytical results on metric correlations on Erdös-Rényi, Barabási-Albert, and Watts-Strogatz random networks, and it is concluded that the degree distribution have influence on the metric correlations.

On the other hand, Li et. al. (2011) showed that metric correlation patterns change with the size and density of graphs. Likewise, Bounova and de Weck (2012) conclude that size-dependent metrics distort the correlations between metrics. ASN datasets are composed of snapshots of the same complex phenomena taken at different dates. This introduces the need for the normalization of size-dependent metrics in order to analyze ensembles of networks with varying size. However, Jamakovic and Uhlig (2008), Filkov et. al. (2009), and Costa et. al. (2007) ignore that some of the studied metrics are size-dependent.

The authors presented an experimental study on the linear correlations among widely used complex network metrics to identify potentially independent metrics that explain different aspects of the ASN's on a single ASN dataset (García-Robledo, Diaz-Perez and Morales-Luna, 2013). A PCA analysis showed that different ASN datasets require separated correlation analyses. In this work the authors realize such studies, with the objective of discovering common correlation patterns inherent to the dynamics of the Internet topology.

ASN Datasets

Let the term *ASN dataset* denote an ensemble of s graphs $(G_1, G_2, \ldots, G_s)$, each graph representing an ASN which, in turn, models a snapshot of the topology of the Internet at a given date. In this study ASN's from three real-world Internet datasets were characterized: RV/RIPE (Dhamdhere and Dovrolis, 2011), CAIDA (CAIDA, 2014), and DIMES (Shavitt and Shir, 2005). For comparison purposes, synthetic ASN's generated by INET-3.0 (Winick and Jamin, 2002) were also characterized:

- **RV/RIPE Dataset:** It includes Border Gateway Protocol (BGP) AS-paths obtained from raw BGP table dumps from two major publicly available collectors: Route Views (RV) and RIPE. RV/ RIPE ASN's include large/small transit providers, content/access/hosting providers and enterprise networks AS's; and focuses on the modeling of customer-provider links. The dataset includes 51 ASN's corresponding to the evolution of the Internet from January 1998 to January 2010. The smallest ASN contains 3,247 nodes and 5,646 edges, while the largest one has 33,796 nodes and 94,394 edges[1]. The study of the RV/RIPE dataset is interesting because it models a very specific ASN phenomenon: the Internet growth settlement since 2001 due to the telecoms market crash.
- **CAIDA Dataset:** It includes ASN's derived from RV BGP table snapshots. The CAIDA dataset models customer-provider, peer-to-peer, and sibling-to-sibling AS relationships. It is composed of 61 networks that include ASN's from January 2004 to November 2007. The smallest ASN has 8,020 nodes and 18,203 edges, while the largest one has 26,389 nodes and 52,861 edges.
- **DIMES Dataset:** Mid-level modeling of the Internet where each node represents a small AS or a Point of Presence (PoP) of a large/medium size AS. The dataset was built by exploiting a distributed approach where a large community of host nodes run lightweight measurement agents in background. The DIMES dataset is composed of 60 networks that include ASN's from January 2007 to April 2012. The smallest giant component has 16,029 nodes and 27,620 edges, while the largest one has 28,035 nodes and 108,373 edges.
- **INET3 Dataset:** INET3 is an Internet topology generator that produces random networks that resemble the topology of the Internet from November 1997 to Feb 2002, and beyond, according to raw BGP tables from The National Laboratory for Applied Network Research (NLANR) and the RV project (University of Michigan, 2002). For the INET3 dataset 51 ASN's were generated with approximately the same number of vertices than the ASN's in the RV/RIPE dataset, and the default values were used for the model parameters. The number of edges is decided by the generator.

Table 2 contains some statistics on important complex network properties of the ASN's contained in each dataset. Note that $\langle L \rangle \ll n$ and $1/n \ll \langle CC \rangle < 1$ hold in average for the RV/RIPE, DIMES, and the CAIDA datasets. This means that these ASN's show the small-world phenomenon. In contrast, even when $\langle L \rangle \ll n$ holds in average for the INET3 dataset, their average clustering coefficient $\langle CC \rangle$ is several orders of magnitudes lower than the $\langle CC \rangle$ of the other datasets. This is caused by the absence of a high clustering between the large-degree nodes (Winick and Jamin, 2002) that compose the backbone of the Internet. This agrees with the low rich-club coefficient $\phi(k)$ shown by the INET3 ASN's.

Also, note that $\langle P(k) \rangle_k > 0.9$ holds in average for the RV/RIPE, DIMES, and CAIDA datasets. This means that these ASN's are very likely to show a scale-free degree distribution. Additionally, note that $as_r<0$ holds for the RV/RIPE, DIMES, and CAIDA datasets, meaning that these ASN's are slightly disassortative, i.e. that there is a tendency of the large-degree nodes to be connected with the low-degree nodes. In contrast, the INET3 ASN's are less likely to be scale-free, and they seem to lack of any degree correlation.

Table 2. Statistics on the number of nodes n and edges m, the average path length $\langle L \rangle$, the average clustering coefficient $\langle CC \rangle$, the rich-club coefficient $\phi(k)$, the cumulative degree distribution scaling $\langle P(k) \rangle_k$, and the assortativity coefficient as_r for the ASN's in each ASN dataset

Metric μ	Statistics	RV/RIPE	DIMES	CAIDA	INET3
n	Min.	3,247	16,029	8,020	6,887
	Max.	33,796	28,035	26,389	33,796
	Avg.	**17,879**	**23,496**	**22,442**	**18,696**
	Std. dev.	9,421	3,310	3,152	8,366
m	Min.	5,646	27,620	18,203	7,679
	Max.	94,394	234,125	53,231	150,264
	Avg.	**45,548**	**83,140**	**45,543**	**67,730**
	Std. dev.	27,924	37,268	6,339	43,616
$\langle L \rangle$	Min.	3.5630	2.7859	3.3059	4.4515
	Max.	3.8258	3.7501	4.0297	15.2086
	Avg.	**3.7260**	**3.2746**	**3.8389**	**5.8987**
	Std. dev.	0.0729	0.1672	0.0802	2.3568
$\langle CC \rangle$	Min.	0.3184	0.4203	0.2771	0.0000
	Max.	0.4705	0.7043	0.4094	0.0023
	Avg.	**0.4094**	**0.6372**	**0.3494**	**0.0010**
	Std. dev.	0.0336	0.0406	0.0187	0.0005
$\phi(k)$	Min.	0.0206	0.0158	0.0061	0.0013
	Max.	0.0517	0.1432	0.0471	0.0052
	Avg.	**0.0295**	**0.0305**	**0.0122**	**0.0029**
	Std. dev.	0.0074	0.0267	0.0048	0.0011
$\langle P(k) \rangle_k$	Min.	-0.9654	-0.9568	-0.9438	-0.7256
	Max.	-0.9003	-0.8403	-0.8999	-0.4147
	Avg.	**-0.9449**	**-0.9058**	**-0.9278**	**-0.5152**
	Std. dev.	0.0163	0.0327	0.0092	0.0842
as_r	Min.	-0.1019	-0.1359	-0.0621	-0.0208
	Max.	-0.0202	0.0161	-0.0060	0.0927
	Avg.	**-0.0735**	**-0.0225**	**-0.0191**	**0.0627**
	Std. dev.	0.0207	0.0329	0.0087	0.0225

Table 3. Normalization functions f_μ of size-dependent complex networks metrics: Average neighbor degree $\langle k_n \rangle$, average degree $\langle k \rangle$, diameter D, node betweenness centrality $\langle nBc_u \rangle$, edge betweenness centrality $\langle mBc_e \rangle$, maximum degree k_{max}, and path length $\langle L \rangle$, where n is the number of vertices of an ASN, and the averages are over all vertices (or all edges for $\langle mBc_e \rangle$) (Bounova and de Weck, 2012)

Metric μ	Symbol	f_μ
Avg. neighbor degree	$\langle k_n \rangle$	$(n-1)$
Avg. degree	$\langle k \rangle$	$(n-1)$
Diameter	D	$(n-1)$
Avg. node betweenness centrality	$\langle nBc_u \rangle$	$2/(n-1)\ (n-2)$
Avg. edge betweenness centrality	$\langle mBc_e \rangle$	$2/n(n-1)$
Maximum degree	k_{max}	$(n-1)$
Avg. path length	$\langle L \rangle$	$(n-1)$

Metrics Correlation Patterns on ASN's

Let $M = (\mu_1, \mu_2, \ldots \mu_q)$ be the vector of the complex network metrics listed in Table 1. The metrics correlation study in this Section considers the average of the vertex betweenness $\langle nBc_u \rangle$, the clustering coefficient $\langle CC \rangle$, the closeness $\langle Cc \rangle$, the neighborhood degree $\langle k_n \rangle$, and the eigenvector centrality $\langle x \rangle$ metrics over all vertices, as well as the average of the edge betweenness centrality $\langle mBc_e \rangle$ over all edges. This study also considers the average of the hierarchical clustering coefficient $\langle hcc_2(i) \rangle$ and $\langle hcc_3(i) \rangle$ over all vertices at distances 2 and 3, respectively; and the rich-club coefficient $\phi(k)$ of the 5% of the richest vertices.

Recall that $\mu(G)$ is the value of the metric μ evaluated on the graph G. ASN datasets are composed of Internet topologies of different sizes. Size-dependent metrics measurements can alter the metrics correlation patterns (Bounova and de Weck, 2012). In this study, measurements for a size-dependent metric μ are normalized by dividing the value $\mu(G)$ of size-dependent metrics by a metric-specific normalization function $f_\mu(n)$. Studied size-dependent metrics and the used normalization functions are listed in Table 3.

Recall that s is the number of graphs in the dataset. Let X be the sxq feature matrix; where the ith row of X is the feature vector $X_{i,*} = (\mu_1(G_i), \mu_2(G_i), \ldots, \mu_q(G_i))$ that characterizes the ith ASN G_i in the dataset. X is standarized by subtracting to each matrix value the corresponding column mean (centering) and then by dividing each matrix value by the corresponding column standard deviation (normalization). Let $X_{*,j} = (\mu_j(G_1), \mu_j(G_2), \ldots, \mu_j(G_s))$ be the jth column of X, i.e. the values of the metric μ_j evaluated on every ASN in the dataset. The degree of pairwise dependence between the metrics is assessed

Figure 1. Heat maps of absolute pairwise metric correlations on each experimented dataset. White cells denote an absolute correlation of C=0. Cells in dark denote an absolute correlation of C=1

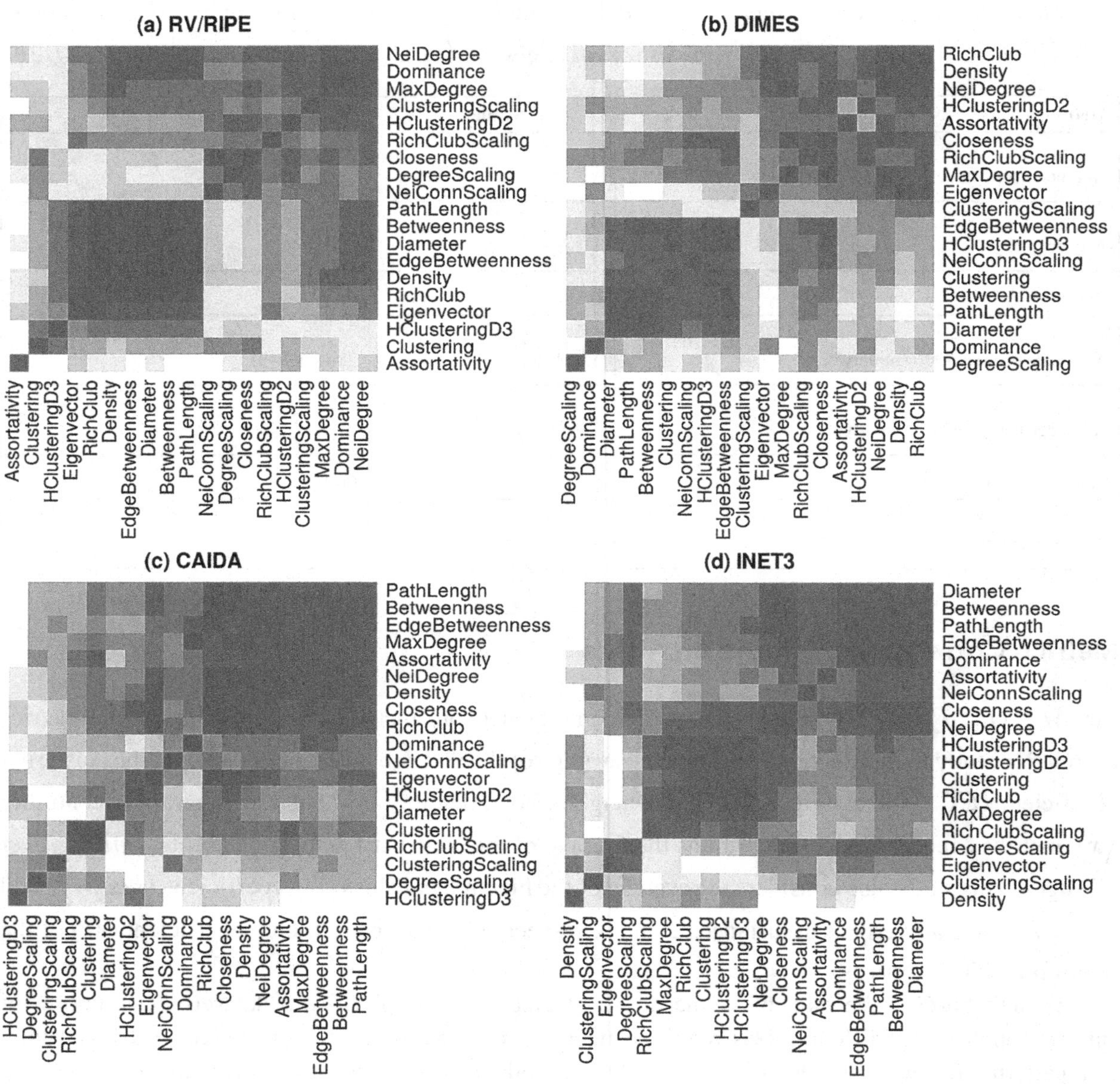

by calculating the $q \times q$ symmetric correlation matrix C; where the matrix value $C_{j,j'} = |\,\mathrm{COR}(X_{*,j}, X_{*,j'})\,|$ is the absolute Pearson correlation between the columns X_{*j} and $X_{*,j'}$.

Figure 1 contains heat map visualizations of the correlation matrix C for the four datasets. By using a hierarchical clustering algorithm, rows and columns of the heat map are permuted in such a way that the most correlated metrics are placed close together. Note that each dataset shows clusters of highly correlated metrics. Figure 2, on the other hand, contains the graph representation of the four heat maps in Figure 1. Nodes represent metrics and links represent high correlations $0.9 \le C \le 1.0$.

Figure 2. Graph representation of absolute pairwise metric correlations on the experimented datasets, for correlation values $0.9 \leq C_{ij} \leq 1$. Vertices represent metrics and edges are weighted with pairwise correlations. The vertex size is proportional to the average weight of incident edges

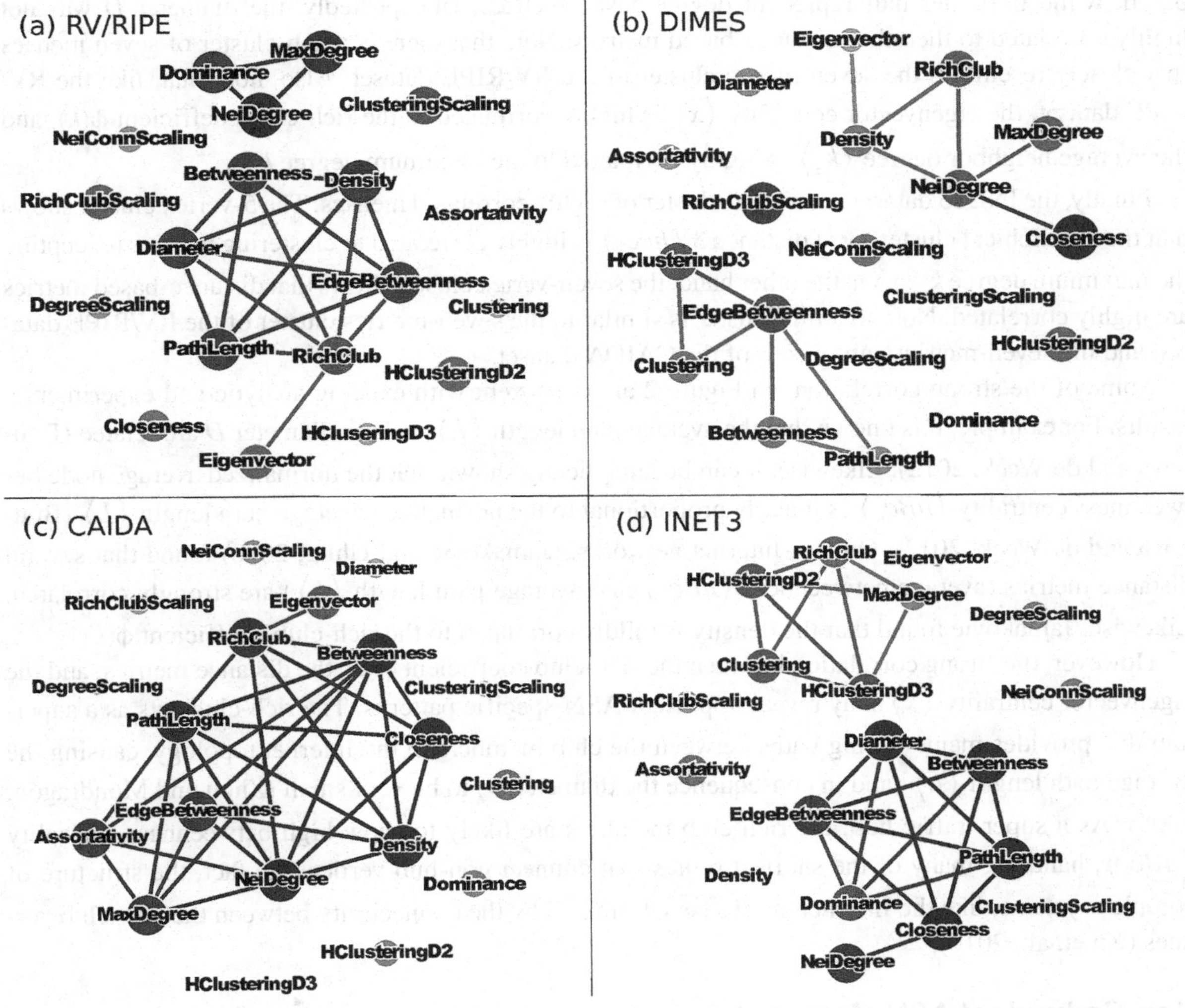

For the RV/RIPE dataset, the three-vertex cluster in Figure 2 represents metrics related to the most central vertex of ASN's. Most of the metrics in the seven-vertex cluster describe either density or shortest-path properties of ASN's. This is in contrast to existing results (Bounova & de Weck, 2012) that conclude that density and distance metrics form two orthogonal groups of highly correlated metrics.

The six-vertex cluster in the DIMES dataset shows that the average neighborhood degree $\langle k_n \rangle$ is highly correlated to other degree-based and neighborhood-based metrics. Additionally, it is also highly correlated to the closeness centrality $\langle Cc \rangle$, a distance-based metric. The eigenvector centrality $\langle x \rangle$ showed to be highly correlated to the graph density $\langle k \rangle$. The five-vertex cluster shows that the edge betweenness centrality $\langle mBc_e \rangle$ is highly correlated not only to distance-based metrics but also to clustering metrics.

The CAIDA dataset shows a large cluster of 10 metrics. Half of the metrics in the cluster are distance-based, while the other half repredent degree-based metrics. Unexpectedly, the diameter D was not highly correlated to the other distance-based metrics. Note that there is a sub-cluster of seven metrics that closely resembles the seven-metric cluster of the RV/RIPE dataset. Also, note that, like the RV/RIPE dataset, the eigenvector centrality $\langle x \rangle$ is highly correlated to the rich-club coefficient $\phi(k)$, and the average neighbor degree $\langle k_n \rangle$ is highly correlated to the maximum degree k_{max}.

Finally, the INET3 dataset shows two cluster of highly correlated metrics. The 5-vertex cluster shows that the hierarchical clustering at distance 3 $\langle hcc_3 \rangle$ is highly correlated to clustering metrics (excepting the maximum degree k_{max}). On the other hand, the seven-vertex cluster shows that distance-based metrics are highly correlated. Note that this cluster is similar to the seven-metrics cluster of the RV/RIPE dataset, and the seven-metrics sub-cluster of the CAIDA dataset.

Some of the strong correlations in Figure 2 are consistent with existing analytic and experimental results. For example, it is known that the average path length $\langle L \rangle$ and the diameter D are related (Bounova and de Weck, 2012). Likewise, it can be analytically shown that the normalized average node betweenness centrality $\langle nBc_u \rangle$ is linearly proportional to the normalized average path length $\langle L \rangle$ (Bounova and de Weck, 2012). On non-Internet networks, (Jamakovic and Uhlig, 2008) found that several distance metrics (average betweenness $\langle nBc_u \rangle$ and average path length $\langle L \rangle$) are strongly correlated. Likewise, Jamakovic found that the density is mildly correlated to the rich-club coefficient $\phi(k)$.

However, the strong correlation between the rich-club coefficient $\phi(k)$, the distance metrics, and the eigenvector centrality $\langle x \rangle$ may reveal important ASN-specific patterns. The rich-club acts as a super-hub that provides many routing paths between the club members in the Internet topology, causing the average path length $\langle L \rangle$ (and in consequence the diameter D) to be very small (Zhou and Mondragón, 2004). As a super-traffic hub, the rich-club members are likely to show high betweenness centrality $\langle nBc_u \rangle$, handling many of the shortest routes that connect non-hub vertices. In fact, the structure of complex systems, like the Internet, might be determined by the connectivity between the rich-club vertices (Xu et. al., 2010).

Non-Redundant ASN Metrics Selection

Let us call *isolated metric* any metric showing not a high correlation ($C<0.9$) to any other metric. Isolated metrics appear as isolated vertices in Figure 2.

For each dataset $\delta \in \{$rvripe, dimes, caida, inet3$\}$, a reduced list of non-redundant metrics $M_\delta \subset M$ can be obtained as follows. First, select from Figure 2 all isolated metrics. Then, from each metric cluster, select the metric that (1) shows the highest average correlation and (2) that is connected to most of the vertices in its cluster, according to Figure 2. Finally, select those metrics hanging from a cluster of metrics, according again to Figure 2.

Figure 3 contains the frequency of selection and isolation of each metric across ASN datasets after following the above-described metrics selection method. Note that the rich-club coefficient $\phi(k)$, the

Figure 3. Bar plots with: (a) the frequency of selection of metrics as non-redundant, and (b) the frequency of occurrence of metrics as isolated (not highly correlated to any metric) in the four experimented datasets

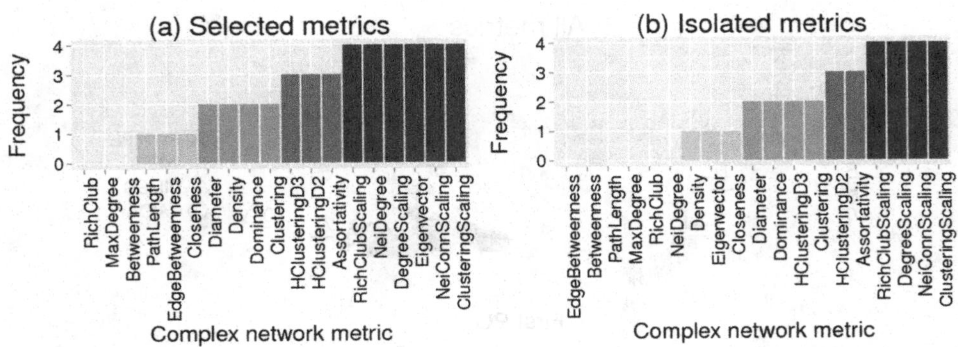

maximum degree k_{max} and the betweenness centrality $\langle nBc_u \rangle$ consistently appear as highly correlated to other metrics across the four datasets, suggesting a high level of redundancy.

On the contrary, note that the four scaling metrics appear as isolated in the four datasets, along with the neighbor degree $\langle k_n \rangle$ and the eigenvector centrality $\langle x \rangle$. This suggests that the scaling metrics, along with $\langle k_n \rangle$ and $\langle x \rangle$, consistently explain different aspects of the topology of ASN's, and that they can be particularly useful for encoding the Internet topology at the AS level.

PCA Projection of ASN Datasets

PCA (Jolliffe, 2002) is a non-supervised machine learning technique for reducing the number of features (dimensions) of a dataset while retaining most of the original variability in the data. Features are linearly combined into orthogonal variables called principal components (PCs). PCA is an useful tool to visualize multivariate data in two or three dimensions. Descriptive non-redundant metrics should allow us to discriminate among different ASN datasets, and this should be verifiable by inspecting PCA visualizations.

Let M_δ denote the selected non-redundant complex network metrics for a given ASN dataset δ, obtained by following the metrics selection method presented in the previous Section. Recall that *X* denotes the feature matrix. Let $X_\delta = X_{*,M_\delta}$ denote the sub-matrix of *X* that includes only the columns of *X* corresponding to the metrics in M_δ. Let X_δ be named the reduced feature matrix for the dataset δ. Non-redundant metrics in M_δ should provide roughly the same amount of information about ASN's than the full set of metrics *M*.

Figure 4 contains the PCA projection into the first two PCs of all datasets by using *X* (the full set of metrics). The datasets grouped into separated clusters of ASN's. Note that the artificial INET-3.0 ASN's appears as the most separated cluster. The organization of the ASN datasets into separated clusters suggests that the combination of ASN's from different sources might not represent a good statistical ensemble of complex networks (Bounova and de Weck, 2012). An exception might be the RV/RIPE and the CAIDA ASN's, that shows some degree of overlapping.

Figure 5 contains the PCA projection into the first two PCs of all dataset by using X_δ, this is, by using the reduced set of metrics found in each dataset, separately. Figure 5 shows that the PCA projection using X_δ successfully preserves the cluster organizations induced by the two first PCs when using

Figure 4. Visualization of the RV/RIPE, DIMES, CAIDA, and INET3 datasets using the first two PCs obtained with X, i.e. the full set of metrics

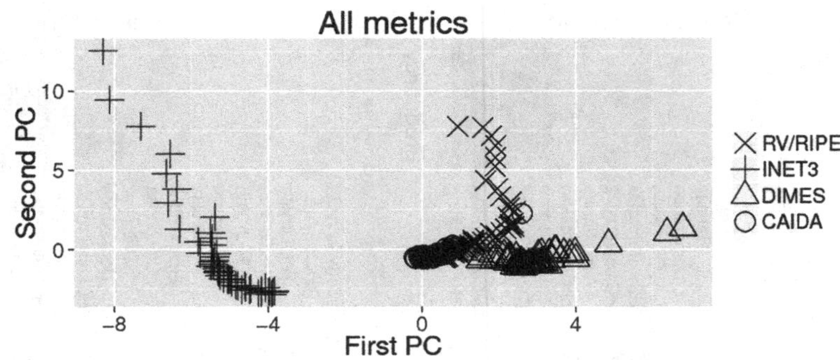

X. Note that the artificial INET-3.0 ASN's remains as the most separated cluster in all cases. The most notorious difference with regard to X is that the overlapping between the RV/RIPE and CAIDA is lost to some degree by using X_{rvripe} and X_{inet3}. This might be useful for studies where the differentiation of the datasets is relevant.

The AS-level Internet has gone through two growth phases: an initial exponential phase up to mid/late-2001, followed by a slower exponential growth thereafter (Dhamdhere and Dovrolis, 2011). This

Figure 5. Visualization of the RV/RIPE, DIMES, CAIDA, and INET3 datasets using the first two PCs obtained with X_g, i.e. with the set of non-redundant metrics for each dataset

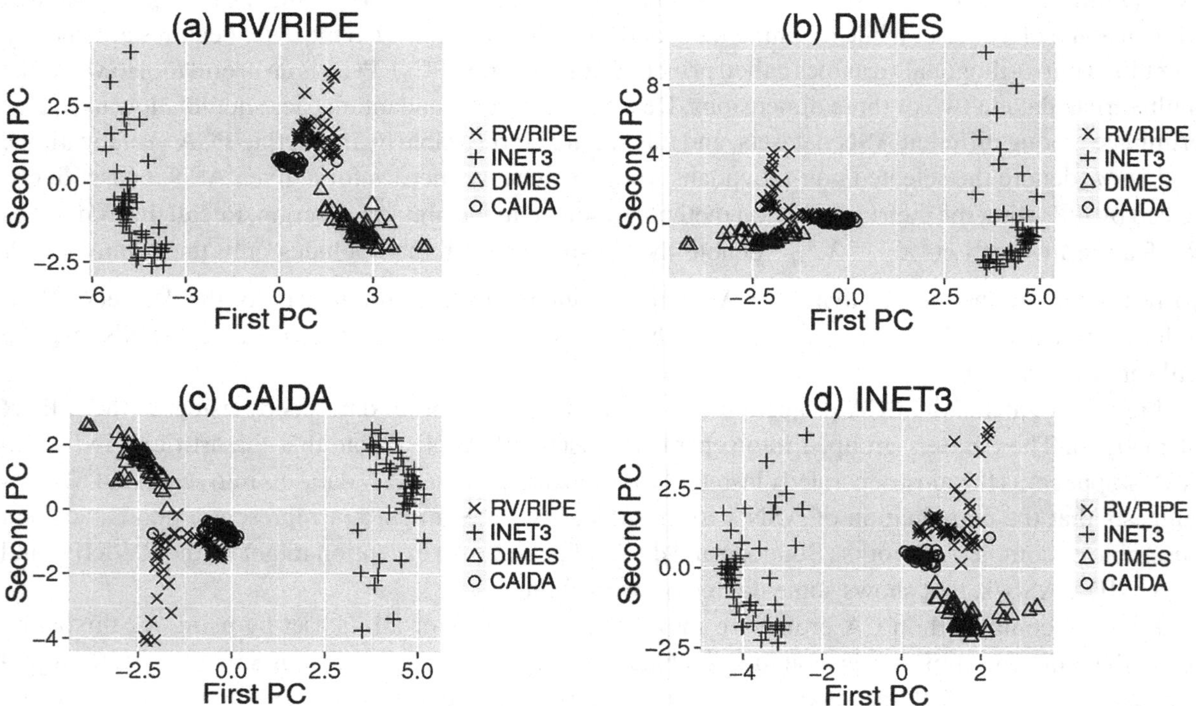

trajectory change, caused by the well-known telecoms market crash in 2001 (The great telecoms crash, 2002), can be observed in the PCA visualization of the RV/RIPE dataset. Figure 6 shows that the PCA projection using X_8 successfully preserved the pre-2001 and post-2001 differentiation of the RV/RIPE ASN's.

On the other hand, Figure 6 suggests that the differentiation between ASN's that belong to different years was mostly preserved in the RV/RIPE, DIMES, and CAIDA datasets. For example, note how the ASN's from different years (2004, 2005, 2006, and 2007) are grouped in different clusters in the CAIDA dataset when using both the X and the X_{caida} feature matrices.

Figure 6. Visualization of the RV/RIPE, DIMES, and CAIDA datasets using the first two PCs obtained with X (left) and X_r (right). ASN's are identified by their year

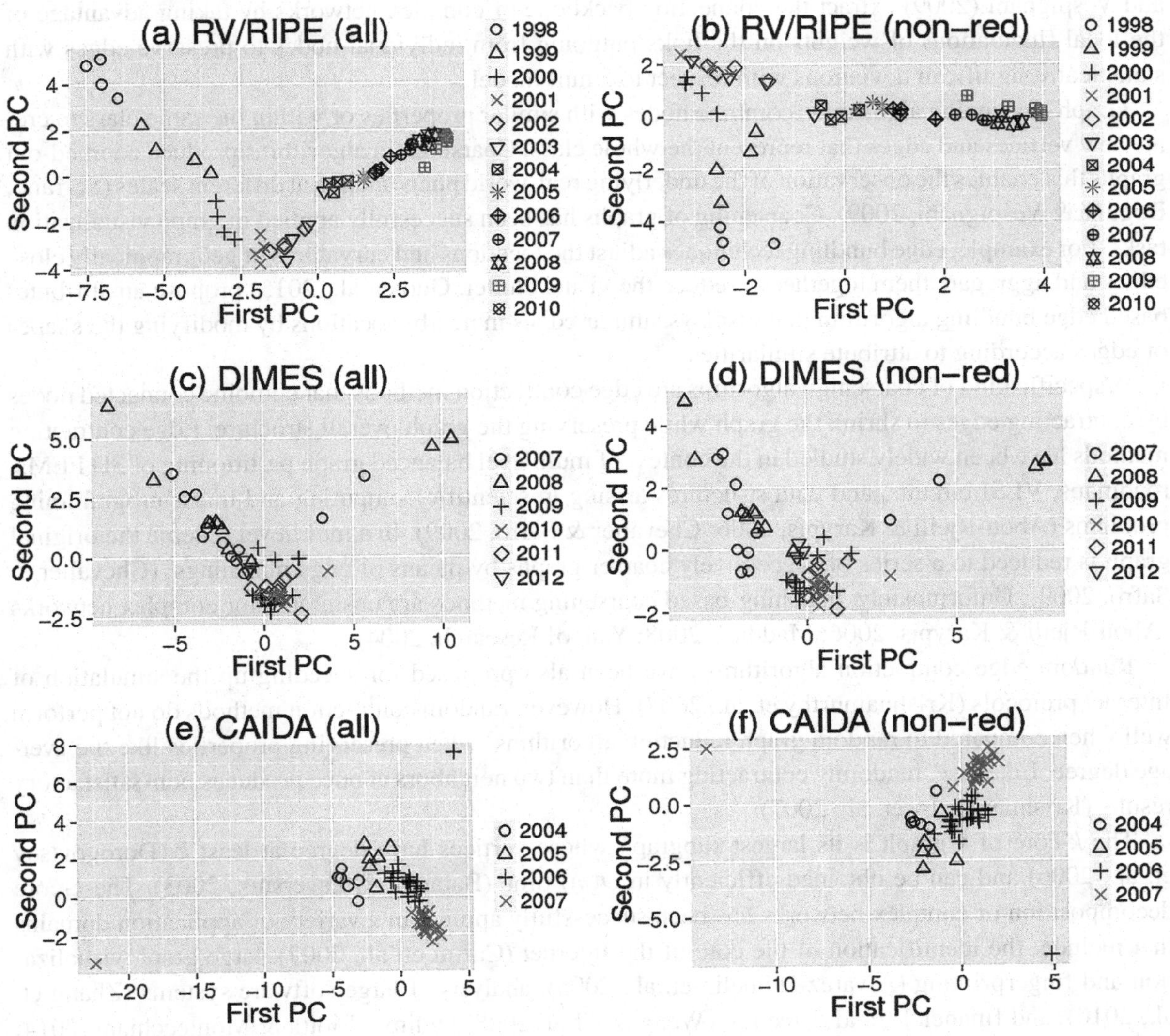

K-CORE-BASED SIMPLIFICATION OF THE INTERNET TOPOLOGY

The massive size of complex networks introduces the need for graph reduction mechanisms that decrease the size of real-world graphs for faster processing, in order to gain insight into the structure of graphs, and to assist the visualization process when the sizes of graphs are too large for a meaningful graphical representation.

Graph reduction schemes can be roughly divided into two categories: filtering/pruning and coarsening algorithms (Serrano, Boguñá & Vespignani, 2009).

Filtering/prunning algorithms fix the scale of networks and discard nodes or edges that do not encode relevant information about the network structure. For example, the simplification algorithm of Hennessey et. al. (2008) consists of two steps: the calculation of the importance metrics and pruning. The objective is to maintain the overall graph connectivity while providing a clearer visual representation of the graph topology. Zhou, Mahler and Toivonen (2012) provide an edge pruning algorithm that keeps the graph maximally connected by measuring the average connectivity over all pairs of nodes. Serrano, Boguná and Vespignani (2009) extract the connection backbone of complex networks by taking advantage of the local fluctuations of weights on the links outgoing from individual nodes to preserve edges with statistically significan deviations with respect to a null model.

Graph coarsening algorithms combine nodes with similar properties or within the same class to create new vertices and edges that represent the whole class. Coarse grain algorithms produce zoomed-out graphs that enables the observation of the underlying real-world phenomenon at different scales (Serrano, Boguñá & Vespignani, 2009). Coarsening of graphs has been succesfully applied in graph visualization tasks. For example, edge bundling techniques adjust the locations and curvatures of geographically close edges and aggregate them together to reduce the visual clutter. Guo et. al. (2015) propose an attribute-based edge bundling algorithm that displays similar edges in nearby locations by modifying the shapes of edges according to attribute similarities.

A specific kind of coarsenign algoritms are edge contraction methods that combine connected nodes by contracting edges to shrink the graph while preserving the graph overall structure. Edge contracting methods have been widely studied in the context of multilevel balanced graph partitioning of 3D FEMs, roadmaps, VLSI circuits, and data structures arising in scientific computing and linear programming problems (Abou-Rjeili & Karypis, 2006; Chevalier & Safro, 2009). In a multilevel scheme the original graph is reduced to a series of successively coarser graphs by means of edge matchings[2] (Chevalier & Safro, 2009). Unfortunately, matching-based coarsening methods are unsuitable for complex networks (Abou-Rjeili & Karypis, 2006; Madduri, 2008; Yahoo! Research, 2004).

Random edge contraction algorithms have been also proposed for speeding up the simulation of Internet protocols (Krishnamurthy et. al., 2007). However, random contraction methods do not perform well when compared to random graph reduction algorithms[3] when preserving properties like the average degree. Likewise, randomly contracting more than two neighbors at once produces non-satisfactory results (Krishnamurthy et. al., 2007).

The k-core of a graph is its largest subgraph whose vertices have degree at least k (Dorogovtsev et. al., 2006) and can be obtained efficiently in $O(m)$ time (Batagelj & Zaversnik, 2003). The k-core decomposition of complex networks has been successfully applied in a variety of application domains that include: the identification of the core of the Internet (Carmi et. al., 2007), large graph visualization and fingerprinting (Alvarez-Hamelin et. al., 2005), analysis of large software systems (Zhang et. al., 2010), and financial fraud detection (Wang & Chiu, 2008; Didimo, Liotta & Montecchiani, 2014; Wang, Li & Ji, 2015).

Intuitively, if one has to remove or to combine vertices to obtain reduced and coarse versions of graphs, an idea is to select edges whose contraction cause the minimum impact on the global graph topology. In the case of graph coarsening, contracted edges would likely to be incident to the least "core" vertices, i.e. those that lie on the "peripheries" of a complex network. The contraction of an edge connecting a core vertex to a peripheral one would result in the same core vertex with some extra edges incident to it.

Can the topological properties of complex netowrks be exploited to obtain a graph coarsening algorithm that perform better than a random one on ASN's? Can the notions of *k*-core decomposition, graph "coreness", graph "periphery", and edge contractions be exploited to reduce the size of large complex networks while keeping a selection of graph properties almost unaltered? The following sections further develop these questions.

Random Coarsening of ASN's

Let us consider first the behaviour of a simple coarsening algorithm that contracts edges at random.

Formally, the contraction of an edge $e \in \{u, v\}$ is the replacement of vertices *u* and *v* with a new vertex v_{new} such that edges incident to v_{new} are the edges that were incident to vertices *u* and *v*. Parallel edges, resulting from the combination of two vertices with common neighbors, are removed to keep the graph simple.

A simple random coarsening algorithm selects an edge uniformly at random from *E*, contract the edge, and repeat the same procedure until the graph has no edges.

The root-mean-square deviation (RMSD) can be used to measure the average deviation of a metric from its original value during a graph reduction process. Given the RMSD, the RMSD percentage (RMSDP) of deviation from the original metric value is calculated to quantify how much a given metric has deviated up to a given point of the graph coarsening process. The RMSDP is defined as follows:

$$RMSDP = \frac{RMSD \times 100}{\text{original metric value}}. \tag{1}$$

Figure 7 shows the average evolution curve for the value, RMSD and the RMSDP of three non-redundant topological metrics during 350 random coarsenings in a 2001 Oregon ASN graph, an AS peering topology inferred from the Oregon Route-Views project BGP dumps (Leskovec, Kleinberg and Faloutsos, 2005). It can be observed that random contractions produce a steady change of the values for distance, scaling and degree metrics during the reduction process, an undesirable behavior. Also, error bars in Figure 7 suggest that a single run of a simple random coarsening algorithm is not likely to produce representative graphs.

K-Core Decomposition of ASN's

A *k*-core of a graph $G=(V,E)$ is a subgraph $H=(C,E|C)$, induced by the set $C \subseteq V$, if and only if $\forall v \in C$: $k_v \geq k$ and *H* is a maximum subgraph with this property (Batagelj & Zaversnik, 2003). A node $v \in V$ is said to belong to the *k*-shell if and only if it belongs to the *k*-core but not to the $(k+1)$ -core. If *v* is in the *k*-shell then *v* has a shell index *k*.

Figure 7. Evolution of the value, RMSD and the RMSDP of three non-redundant topological metrics during random coarsenings in the Oregon ASN. Curves in (a), (c) and (e) are the average values for 350 random coarsenings +/- a standard deviation. Curves in (b), (d) and (f) are RMSD's calculated from the average curves

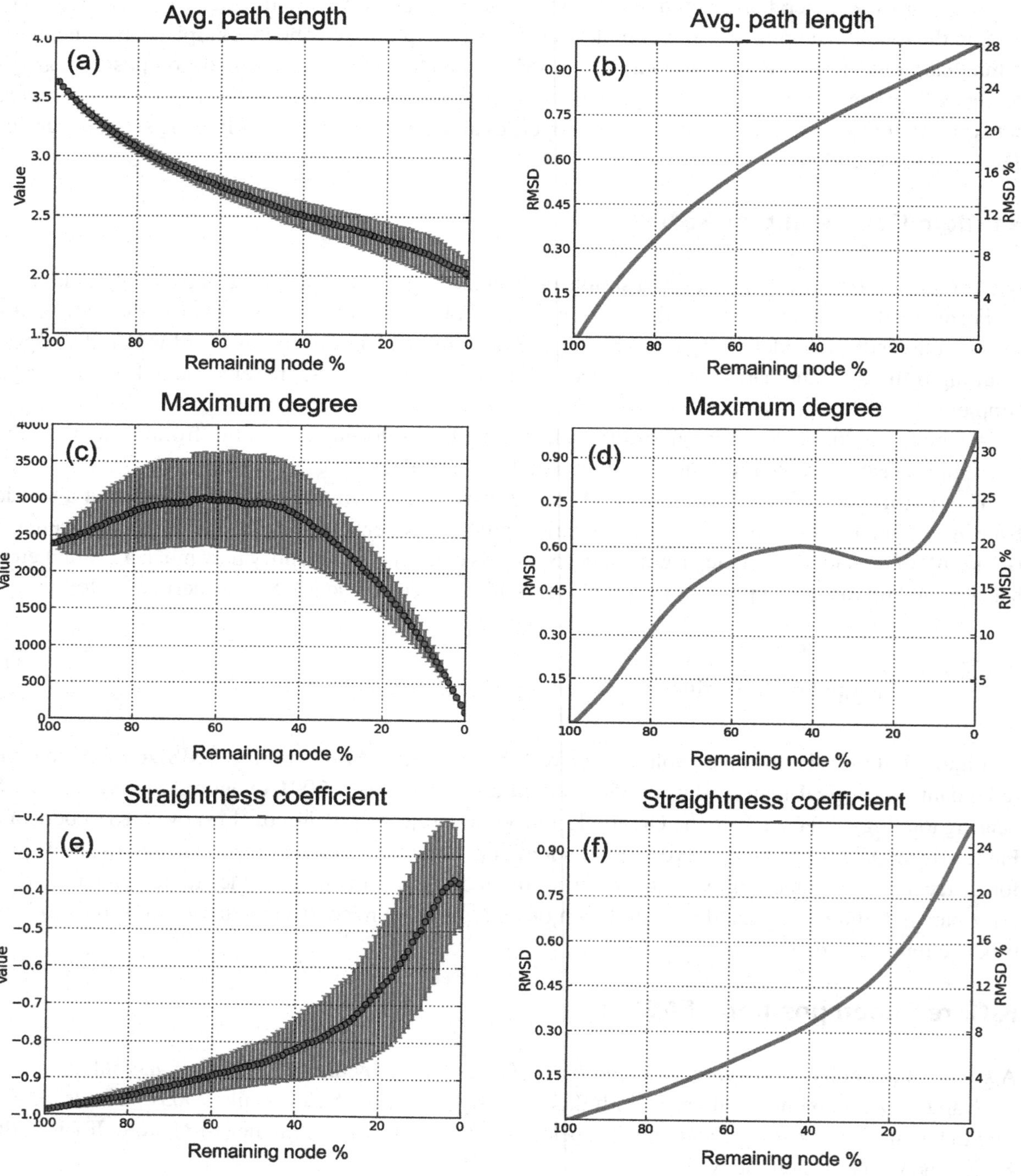

Figure 8. k-core decomposition of the Oregon AS graph (left) and the RV/RIPE AS graph (right)

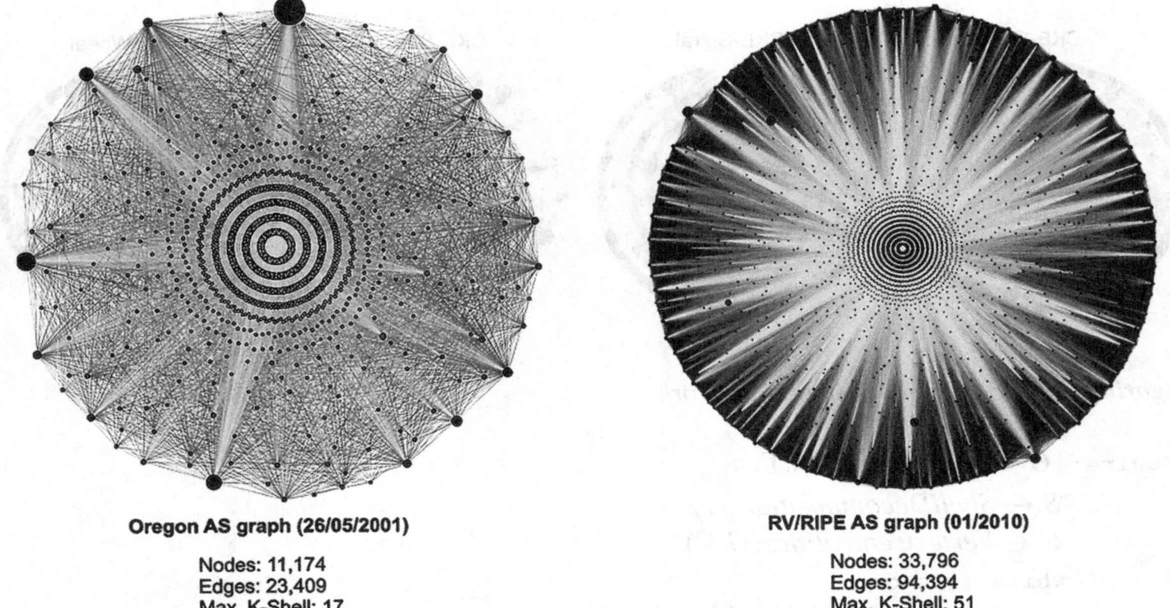

Figure 8 shows the k-core decomposition of an Oregon ASN and an RV/RIPE ASN. Vertices at the outer rings, that belong to the higher k-shells, are represented with stronger color tones. Size of nodes is proportional to the node degree. "Spines" whose vertices represent highly connected vertices at different k-shells reveal a hierarchy of hubs that are connected to the most inner nodes. Nodes at low k-shells represent peripheral nodes (Carmi et. al., 2007). Both the Oregon and the RV/RIPE ASN's show a high percentage of edges connecting nodes at very different k-shells, which can be partially explained by the scale-free distribution of the graphs. Note in Figure 8 that both ASN's show the same "urchin"-like structure, but at different scales.

The Contract K-shell Edge Coarsening Framework

This Section describes the Contract k-shell Edge (CKE) graph coarsening framework that exploit the urchin-like structure induced by the k-core decomposition (see Figure 9). The term *framework* is used here to denote a coarsening strategy where components such as the centrality and the k-shell visitation algorithms can be substituted to obtain different CKE coarsening algorithms. The CKE framework exploit the following intuition: contracting edges connecting nodes at very different k-shells should not impact the global properties of complex networks.

Algorithm 1 contains the main CKE coarsening framework algorithm. The input is a graph G, the k-shell visitation algorithm A, a vertex centrality algorithm Γ, and the final number of nodes n_{final}. Algorithm 1 returns the coarsened graph with n_{final} nodes. In each iteration, the CKE framework visits a single node at a given k-shell. Each time a vertex v is visited, a neighbor u of v located at the farthest k-shell is selected, and the edge $\{u,v\}$ is contracted. The CKE framework keep visiting vertices and contracting edges until the number of nodes reaches n_{final}.

Figure 9. Depiction of the four k-core-based CKE algorithms that exploit the k-shell decomposition of vertices in ASN's

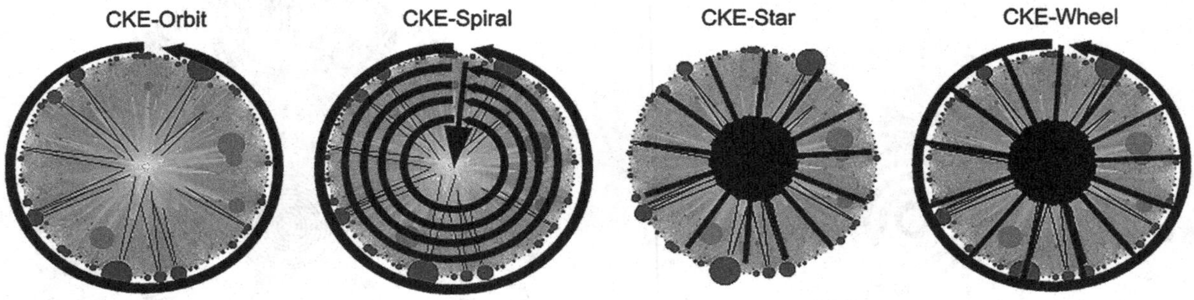

Algorithm 1. The CKE coarsening framework

Require: $G = (V(G), E(G)), \mathrm{A}, \Gamma, n_{final}$
$S \leftarrow ShellDecomposition(G)$
$C \leftarrow VertexCentralities(G, \Gamma)$
while True **do**
$k \leftarrow SelectNextShell(S, \mathrm{A})$
$v \leftarrow SelectNextVertexAtShell(k, S, C)$
$u \leftarrow SelectNeighbor(v, G, S, C)$
$G, S, C \leftarrow ContractEdge(\{u, v\}, G, S, C)$
if $|V(G)| = n_{final}$ **then**
return G
end if
end while

The invoked functions by the CKE framework are:

- $S \leftarrow ShellDecomposition(G)$: given *G*, returns the *k*-shell decomposition set *S*, where S_i denotes the *k*-shell index of vertex *i*.
- $C \leftarrow VertexCentrality(G, \Gamma)$: given *G* and a vertex centrality algorithm Γ, returns the vertex centrality set *C*, where C_i denotes the centrality of vertex *i*.
- $k \leftarrow SelectNextShell(S, \mathrm{A})$: given *S*, returns the next non-empty *k*-shell index, according to the *k*-shells visitation algorithm A.
- $v \leftarrow NextVertexAtShell(k, S, C)$: given *S*, it returns the next vertex *v* at the *k*-shell. Given *C*, vertices are returned cyclically, as if they were arranged in a circular list, sorted in increasing order of their centrality.
- $u \leftarrow SelectNeighbor(v, G, S, C)$: given *v*, *G* and *S*, returns the neighbor $u \in N_v$ of *v* at the farther *k*-shell, so that $u = \max \arg_{u \in N_v} \{|S_v - S_u|\}$. If there is a tie between different neighbors of *v*, the neighbor with the lowest centrality is returned, given *C*.

- $G',S',C' = ContractEdge(\{u,v\},G,S,C)$: given G, returns a new graph G' with $|V(G)|-1$ vertices, where the edge $\{u,v\}\in E(G)$ has been contracted. G' is simplified. Given S and C, it also returns the updated S' and C' sets, with the k-shell index and the centrality of the new combined vertex $v_{new} \in V(G')$. Let w be the vertex $w = \max \arg_{w\in\{u,v\}}\{S_w\}$, i.e. the vertex with the largest k-shell index among u and v. v_{new} acquires the k-shell index and the centrality of w, such that $S'_{v_{new}} = S_w$ and $C'_{v_{new}} = C_w$.

Let k_{max} be the highest k-shell index in G. Four different CKE algorithms based on the CKE framework are studied in this Section: CKE-Orbit, CKE-Spiral, CKE-Star, and CKE-Wheel. The difference among the CKE algorithms is the k-shells visitation algorithm A, that defines the order in which k-shells are explored:

- **CKE-Orbit:** It visits all the nodes at the k_{max} -shell. Then, it starts all over again by visiting all the nodes at the k_{max} -shell one more time, repeating the procedure until the number of nodes reaches n_{final}.
- **CKE-Spiral:** It starts by visiting all the nodes at the k_{max} -shell. Then, it visits all the nodes at the $(k_{max} - 1)$ -shell, and so on. When CKE-Spiral reaches the 1-shell, it starts all over again at the k_{max} -shell, repeating the procedure until the number of nodes reaches n_{final}.
- **CKE-Star:** It starts by visiting a single node at the k_{max} -shell. In the next iteration, it visits a single node at the $(k_{max} - 1)$ -shell, and so on. When CKE-Star reaches the 1-shell, it starts all over again by visiting the next node at the k_{max} -shell, repeating the procedure until the number of nodes reaches n_{final}.
- **CKE-Wheel:** It starts by visiting all the nodes at the k_{max} -shell. Then, it visits a single node at the remaining k-shells, in decreasing order of the k-shells. When CKE-Wheel reaches the 1-shell, it starts all over again and visits all the nodes at the k_{max} -shell again, repeating the procedure until the number of nodes reaches n_{final}.

CKE-Orbit only visits nodes at the highest k-shell. CKE-Spiral is similar to CKE-Orbit, but it visits nodes at every k-shell, in decreasing order of k. CKE-Wheel represents a combination of CKE-Orbit and CKE-Star. CKE-Spiral, CKE-Star and CKE-Wheel are motivated by the empirical observation that some metrics might be better preserved by contracting edges going not only from hubs at the k_{max} -shell but from hubs at different k-shells.

The most compute intensive functions are $ShellDecomposition(G)$ and $VertexCentralities(G,\Gamma)$. Recall that the k-core decomposition can be done in $O(m)$. Time of the centrality calculation depends on the centrality metric Γ (e.g. $O(nm)$ for the vertex betweenness centrality nBc_u or $O(n+m)$ for the eigenvector centrality x). Note that both the k-core decomposition and the centrality calculation are performed only once, at the beginning of the CKE algorithms. $ContractEdge(\{u,v\}, G,S,C)$ makes sure that the new vertex "inherits" the k-shell index and the centrality of one of the contracting vertices, so there is no need to calculate the decomposition and the centrality again. The inheritance of the k-shell index also guarantees that there will be always at least a non-empty k-shell.

Assuming that a $O(n+m)$ centrality metric is used, CKE algorithms are able to perform up to $n-1$ contractions[4] in $O(n+m+n(z+g))$ time, where $O(z)$ is the time for an edge contraction and $O(g)$ is the time for a vertex neighborhood query.

Simplifying the Internet Topology as of January 2010

This Section shows experiments with the CKE algorithms by coarsening the RV/RIPE ASN as of January 2010, the largest ASN instance of the RV/RIPE dataset with 33,976 AS's connected by 94,394 links. Table 4 contains the actual measurement values for a variety of complex network metrics on the mentioned ASN. The January 2010 ASN is scale-free, as it shows a high and negative straightness coefficient $\langle P(k)\rangle_k$, a large maximum degree k_{max}, and a small average degree $\langle k\rangle$. It is also small-world, showing a small average path length $\langle L\rangle$ and a high average clustering coefficient $\langle CC\rangle$. It is slightly disassortative, with a negative assortative coefficient as_r, and it presents a rich-club of core vertices. Finally, the ASN shows central nodes with high central point dominance *CPD*, high average betweenness centrality $\langle nBc_u\rangle$, and high average neighbor degree $\langle k_n\rangle$.

Seven variations of the four CKE strategies, listed in Table 5, are defined to study: (1) whether the ordering of the nodes at the higher *k*-shell is important, and (2) whether the ordering of the neighbors at the lower *k*-shells is important.

Figure 10. shows the evolution of five non-redundant and *size-independent* metrics when the 2010 ASN is coarsened by a run of the seven coarsening algorithms in Table 5. The size-independant metrics

Table 4. Values for different complex network metrics evaluated on the RV/RIPE January 2010 ASN graph

Metric μ	Symbol	Value μ(G)
Nodes	N	33,796
Edges	m	94,394
Avg. degree	$\langle k\rangle$	5.59
Maximum degree	k_{max}	2,634
Cum. degree distribution scaling	$\langle P(k)\rangle_k$	–0.93
Avg. path length	$\langle L\rangle$	3.82
Avg. clustering coefficient	$\langle CC\rangle$	0.38
Assortativity coefficient	as_r	–0.02
Rich-club coefficient	$\phi(k)$	0.74
Central point-dominance	*CPD*	0.14
Avg. vertex betweenness centrality	$\langle nBc_u\rangle$	47,668.27
Avg. neighbor degree	$\langle k_n\rangle$	504.71

Table 5. Variations of the four CKE coarsening algorithms

Algorithm	Visiting nodes	Selected neighbor
CKE-Orbit-1	Unsorted	Farther *k*-shell
CKE-Spiral-1	Unsorted	Farther *k*-shell
CKE-Spiral-2	Unsorted	Farther *k*-shell and minimum centrality
CKE-Spiral-3	Unsorted	Minimum centrality
CKE-Star-1	Unsorted	Farther *k*-shell
CKE-Star-2	Sorted by centrality	Farther *k*-shell
CKE-Wheel-1	Unsorted	Farther *k*-shell

are the straightness $\langle P(k)\rangle_k$, assortativity as_r and rich-club coefficient $\phi(k)$, the central point dominance *CPD*, and the average clustering coefficient $\langle CC\rangle$.

The straightness coefficient $\langle P(k)\rangle_k$ was best preserved up to 20% nodes by CKE-Orbit-1, with an RMSDP of only 0.8%; meaning that the ASN remained scale-free during most of the reduction process. Likewise, the rich-club coefficient $\phi(k)$ was best preserved up to 8% of nodes by CKE-Star-2, with an RMSDP of 36%. Additionally, the central point dominance *CPD* was best preserved up to 30% of nodes by CKE-Orbit-1, with an RMSDP of 9%. At 18% of nodes CKE-Spiral-3 and CKE-Orbit-1 intersect, with an RMSDP of 20%. Then, CKE-Spiral-3 shows a lower RMSDP than CKE-Orbit-1, ending with an RMSDP of 25%. This means that the influence of the vertex with the highest betweenness centrality is mostly preserved during the whole reduction process.

On the other hand, the clustering coefficient $\langle CC\rangle$ was best preserved up to 40% of nodes by CKE-Orbit-1, showing an RMSDP of 30%. At that point it is matched and superseded by CKE-Spiral-3, that terminates with an RMSDP of 35.8%. This means that the ASN remained with a clustering that is significantly larger than the clustering of a random network. The most difficult property to preserve was the assortativity coefficient as_r. It was best preserved up to 74% of nodes by CKE-Spiral-3, with an RMSDP of 23%. However, after that point, it started to deviate significantly and CKE-Spiral-3 was unable to preserve the ASN disassortative[5]. Nonetheless, while the other CKE algorithms shows significantly larger deviations, they were able to preserve the disassortativity of the original ASN until the end of the reduction.

Figure 11 shows the evolution of three non-redundant and *size-dependent* metrics during the ASN coarsenings: the maximum degree k_{max}, the average path length $\langle L\rangle$ and the average node neighbor degree $\langle k_n\rangle$. In addition, Figure 11 also shows the evolution of the average degree $\langle k\rangle$ and the betweenness centrality $\langle nBc_u\rangle$ that hold a degree of redundancy with the average path length $\langle L\rangle$.

Size-dependency suggests that these metrics are harder to preserve that size-independent metrics, due to the effect of the reduction of the graph size during the coarsening process. However, CKE algorithms shows to be useful for preserving size-dependent metrics as well. The average degree $\langle k\rangle$ was best preserved by CKE-Wheel during the whole coarsening process, ending with a 22% RMSDP. CKE-Wheel was followed by CKE-Orbit-1, showing a higher RMSDP from 60% of nodes onwards, but ending with the same RMSDP as CKE-Orbit-1. Likewise, the average node neighbor degree $\langle k_n\rangle$ was best preserved by CKE-Orbit-1 during the whole coarsening process, ending with an RMSDP of only 22%.

Figure 10. Evolution of the RMSDP of five non-size-dependent topological metrics during k-core-based coarsenings. Horizontal axis represents the percentage of remaining nodes during the graph coarsening execution

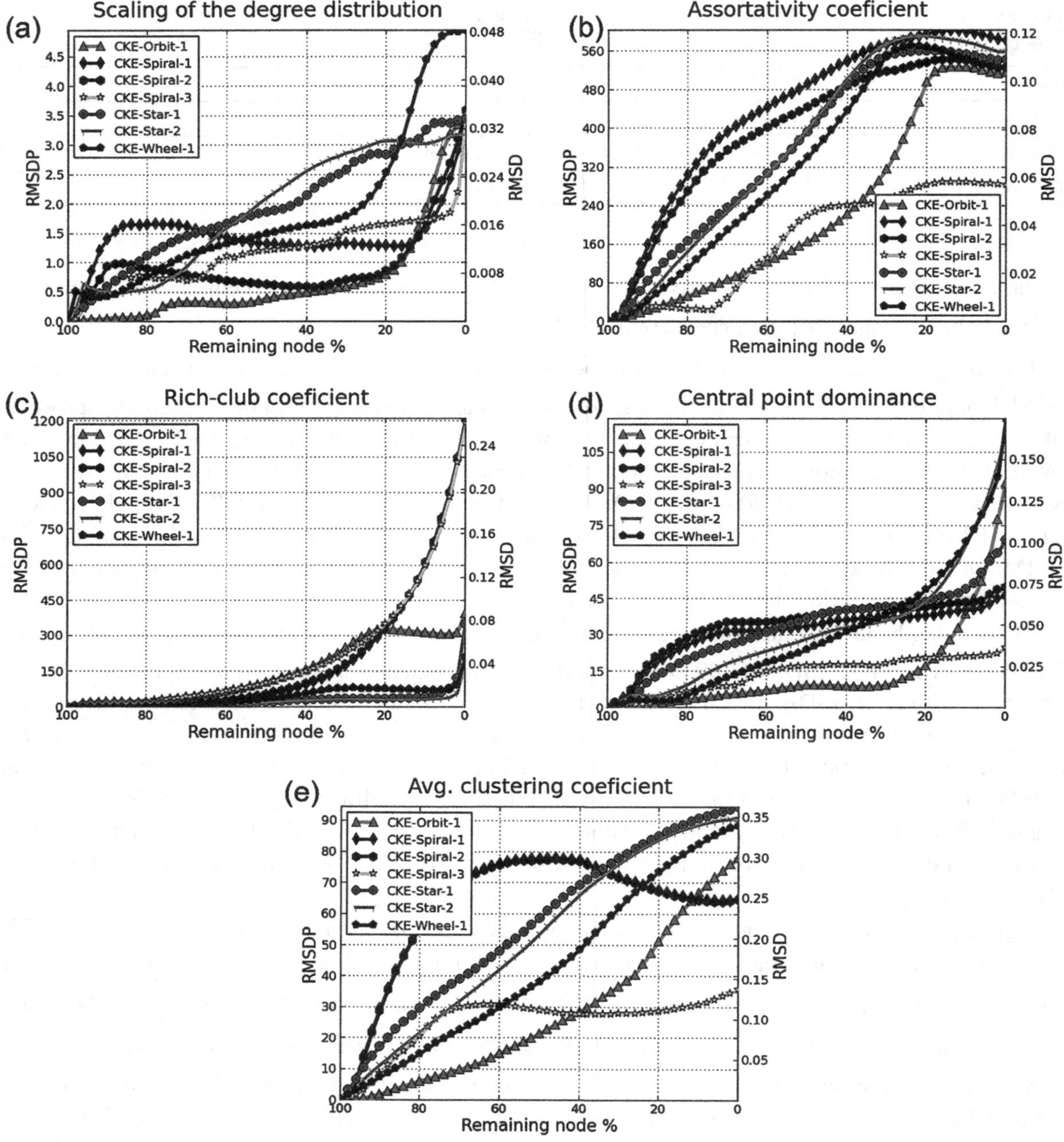

Additionally, the maximum degree k_{max} was best preserved up to 34% of nodes by CKE-Wheel-1,

Figure 11. Evolution of the RMSDP of five size-dependent topological metrics during k-core-based coarsenings. Horizontal axis represents the percentage of remaining nodes during the graph coarsening execution

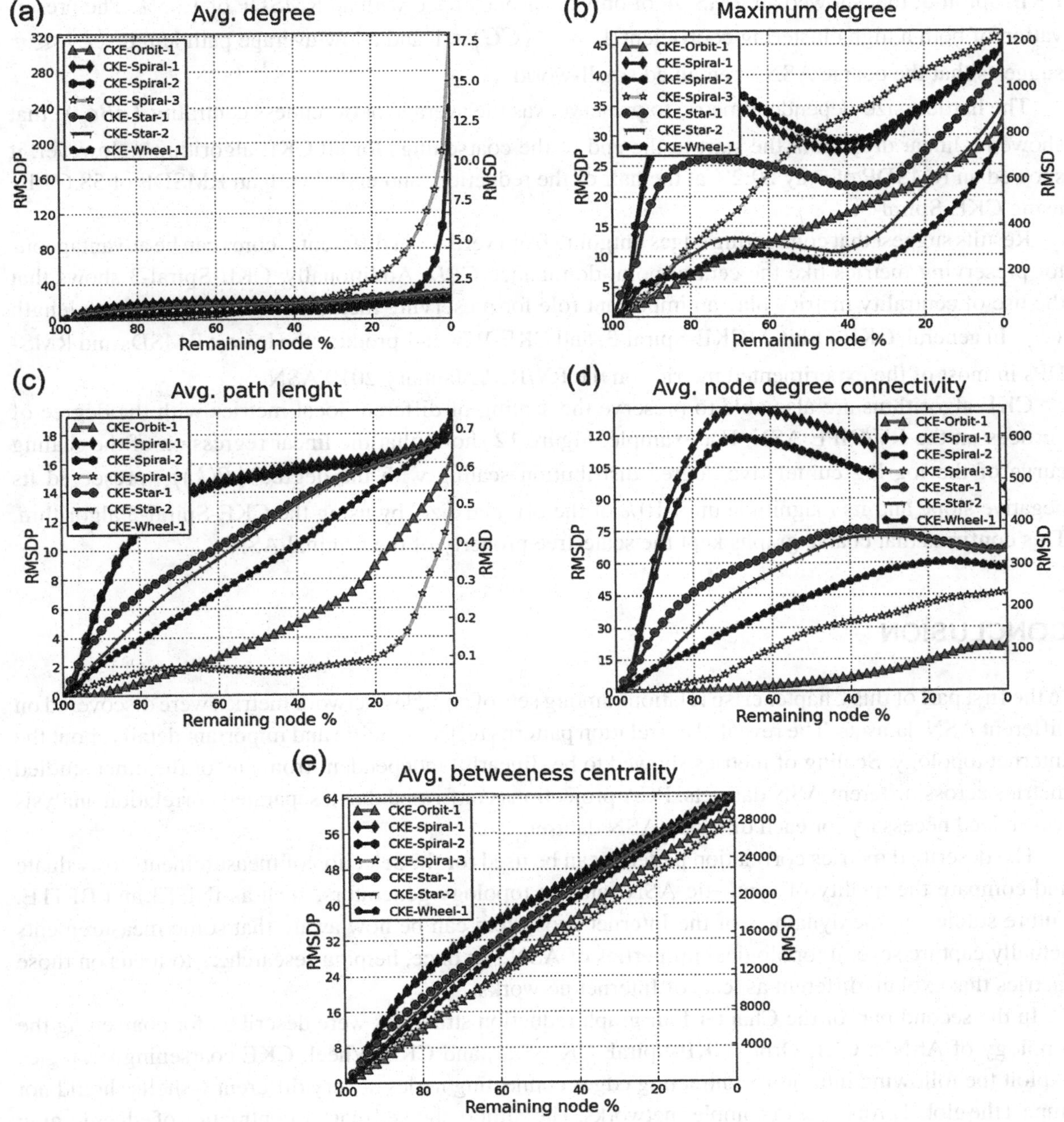

with an RMSDP of only 9%, and ending with an RMSDP of 30%. The preservation of both the maximum degree k_{max} and the central point dominance *CPD* suggests that the influence of the most central node remains in the coarser graphs. The average path length $\langle L \rangle$ was best preserved up to 22% of nodes by CKE-Spiral-3, that showed an RMSDP of only 2.3% and ended with an RMSDP of 13.5%. The preservation of both a high clustering coefficient $1/n \ll \langle CC \rangle < 1$ and a low average path length $\langle L \rangle \ll n$ suggests that the coarse ASN's remained small-world.

The hardest size-dependent metric to preserve was the average betweenness centrality $\langle nBc_u \rangle$, that showed a linear drop from the start to the end of the coarsenings for all CKE algorithms. However, it showed an RMSDP of only 29.2% at the half of the reduction, and ended with an RMSDP of 58.6% by using CKE-Spiral-3.

Results suggest that contracting edges outgoing from vertices at different k-cores can be advantageous for preserving metrics like the central point dominance *CPD*. Additionally, CKE-Spiral-3 shows that the use of centrality metrics play an important role for preserving metrics like the average path length $\langle L \rangle$. In general, CKE-Orbit-1, CKE-Spiral-3, and CKE-Wheel-1 produce the lowest RMSDs and RMSDPs in most of the experimented metrics on the RV/RIPE January 2010 ASN.

CKE algorithms are also able to preserve the scaling of different local metrics with the degree of vertices on the RV/RIPE ASN. For example, Figure 12 shows that the linear regression of the scaling curve of the log-log cumulative degree distribution scaling with the degree $\langle P(k) \rangle_k$ preserved its negative slope and its magnitude until 10% of the original size, by using the CKE-Spiral-3 algorithm. This confirms that coarse graphs kept the scale-free property of the original ASN.

CONCLUSION

In the first part of this Chapter crisp relations among sets of complex network metrics were discovered on different ASN datasets. The revealed correlation patterns reflect specific and important details about the Internet topology. Scaling of metrics showed to be (linearly) independent from any of the other studied metrics across different ASN datasets. PCA projections confirmed that a separated correlation analysis was indeed necessary for each different ASN dataset.

The described metrics correlation patterns can be used for the selection of measurements to evaluate and compare the quality of synthetic ASN random topology generators, such as INET3 and BRITE. Future studies on the dynamics of the Internet ecosystem can be now aware that some measurements actually capture several topological properties of ASN's at once, helping researchers to focus on those metrics that explain different aspects of Internet networks.

In the second part of the Chapter four graph reduction strategies were described for coarsening the topology of ASN's: CKE-Orbit, CKE-Spiral, CKE-Star, and CKE-Wheel. CKE coarsening strategies exploit the following intuition: contracting edges connecting nodes at very different k-shells should not impact the global properties of complex networks. The authors showed that the contraction of edges joining core and peripheral vertices is a powerful tool to reduce ASN's while preserving size-independent and size-dependent complex network metrics alike, as well as high-level properties of real-world networks, such as the scale-free distribution.

Figure 12. Scaling of the cumulative degree distribution with the degree of vertices at different points of a CKE coarsening execution, when using CKE-Spiral-3. The Pearson correlation coefficient between the degree and the cumulative degree distribution shows little variation, starting at -0.93 (100%) and ending at -0.86 (10%)

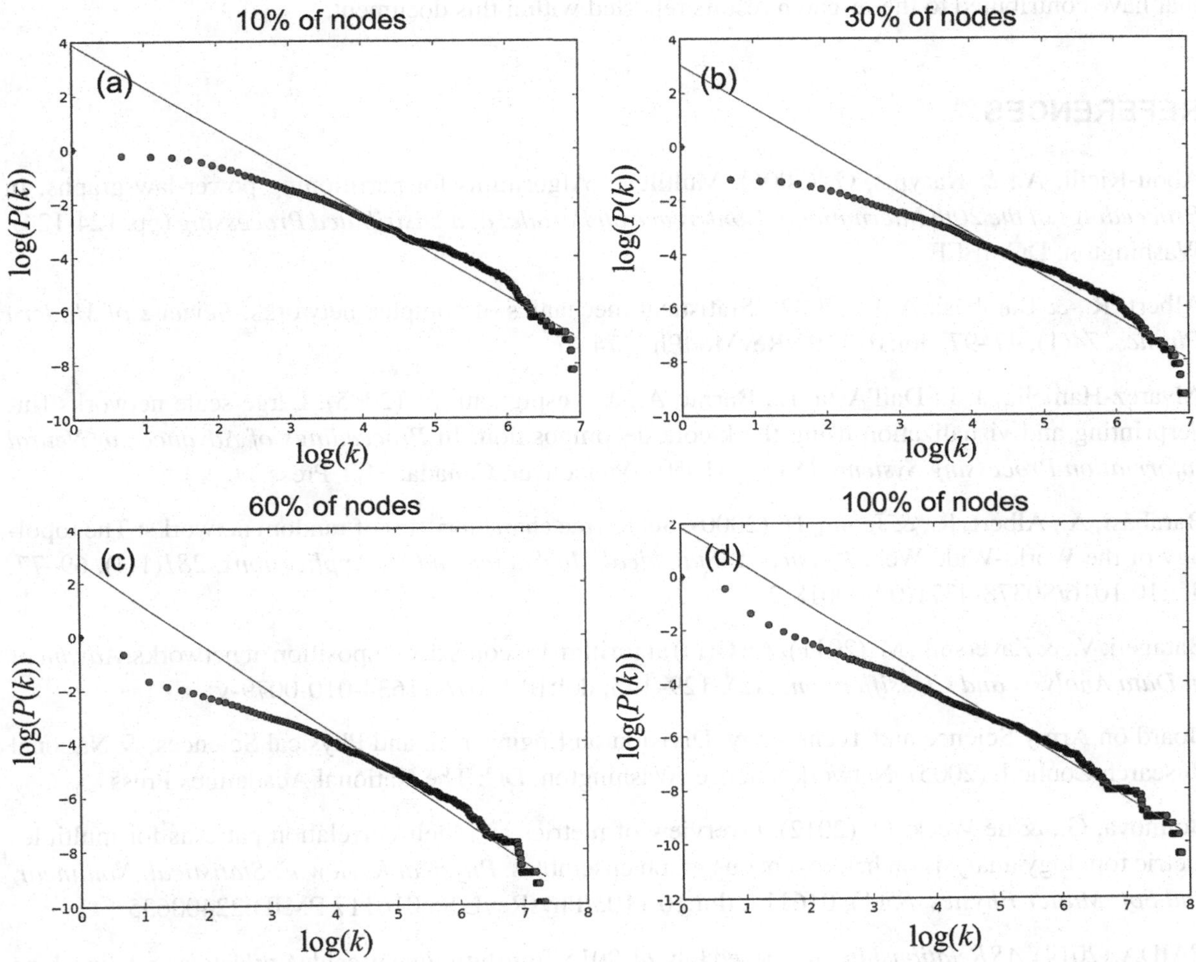

Unlike simple random coarsening algorithms, the CKE approach is able to produce representative coarse graphs in a single run. The presented results on a collection of size-independent and size-dependent non-redundant metrics can be useful to select the appropriate CKE algorithm when it is desired to preserve a specific complex network metric or topological property.

Future works that need to sample the topology of ASN's for simulation purposes can take into account the presented metrics correlation patterns and the k-core-decomposition-based coarsening algorithms to correctly assess the quality of the reduced networks and accelerate simulations on large Internet complex networks.

ACKNOWLEDGMENT

The authors acknowledge to the General Coordination of Information and Communications Technologies (CGSTIC) at Cinvestav for providing HPC resources on the Hybrid Cluster Supercomputer "Xiuhcóatl", that have contributed to the research results reported within this document.

REFERENCES

Abou-Rjeili, A., & Karypis, G. (2006). Multilevel Algorithms for partitioning power-law graphs. In *Proceedings of the 20th International Conference on Parallel and Distributed Processing* (pp. 124-124). Washington, DC: IEEE.

Albert, R., & Barabási, A. L. (2002). Statistical mechanics of complex networks. *Reviews of Modern Physics*, *74*(1), 47–97. doi:10.1103/RevModPhys.74.47

Alvarez-Hamelin, J. I., Dall'Asta, L., Barrat, A., & Vespignani, A. (2005). Large scale networks fingerprinting and visualization using the k-core decomposition. In *Proceedings of Advances in Neural Information Processing Systems 18* (pp. 41–50). Vancouver, Canada: MIT Press.

Barabási, A., Albert, R., & Jeong, H. (2000). Scale-free characteristics of random networks: The topology of the World-Wide Web. *Physica A. Statistical Mechanics and Its Applications*, *281*(1-4), 69–77. doi:10.1016/S0378-4371(00)00018-2

Batagelj, V., & Zaversnik, M. (2011). An O(m) algorithm for cores decomposition of networks. *Advances in Data Analysis and Classification*, *5*(2), 129–145. doi:10.1007/s11634-010-0079-y

Board on Army Science and Technology, Division on Engineering and Physical Sciences, & National Research Council. (2005). Network Science. Washington, DC: The National Academies Press.

Bounova, G., & de Weck, O. (2012). Overview of metrics and their correlation patterns for multiple-metric topology analysis on heterogeneous graph ensembles. *Physical Review E: Statistical, Nonlinear, and Soft Matter Physics*, *85*(1), 016117. doi:10.1103/PhysRevE.85.016117 PMID:22400635

CAIDA. (2014). *AS Relationships*. Retrieved July 24, 2015, from http://www.caida.org/data/as-relationships

Carmi, S., Havlin, S., Kirkpatrick, S., Shavitt, Y., & Shir, E. (2007). A model of Internet topology using k-shell decomposition. *Proceedings of the National Academy of Sciences of the United States of America*, *104*(27), 11150–11154. doi:10.1073/pnas.0701175104 PMID:17586683

Chevalier, C., & Safro, I. (2009). Comparison of coarsening schemes for multilevel graph partitioning. In *Including Subseries Lecture Notes in Artificial Intelligence and Lecture Notes in Bioinformatics)* (pp. 191–205). Springer. doi:10.1007/978-3-642-11169-3_14

Cho, K. (2012). Internet measurement and Big Data. *Internet Infrastructure Review*, *15*, 31–34.

Colizza, V., Flammini, A., Serrano, M. A., & Vespignani, A. (2006). Detecting rich-club ordering in complex networks. *Nature Physics*, *2*(2), 110–115. doi:10.1038/nphys209

Costa, L., Rodrigues, F., Travieso, G., & Villas Boas, P. (2007). Characterization of complex networks: A survey of measurements. *Advances in Physics*, *56*(1), 167–242. doi:10.1080/00018730601170527

Costa, L., Villas Boas, P., Silva, F., & Rodrigues, F. (2010). A pattern recognition approach to complex networks. *Journal of Statistical Mechanics*, *2010*(11), P11015. doi:10.1088/1742-5468/2010/11/P11015

Dhamdhere, A., & Dovrolis, C. (2011). Twelve years in the evolution of the Internet ecosystem. *IEEE/ACM Transactions on Networking*, *19*(5), 1420–1433. doi:10.1109/TNET.2011.2119327

Didimo, W., Liotta, G., & Montecchiani, F. (2014). Network visualization for financial crime detection. *Journal of Visual Languages and Computing*, *25*(4), 433–451. doi:10.1016/j.jvlc.2014.01.002

Dorogovtsev, S., Goltsev, A., & Mendes, J. (2006). K-core organization of complex networks. *Physical Review Letters*, *96*(040601), 1–4. PMID:16486798

Filkov, V., Saul, Z., Roy, S., D'Souza, R., & Devanbu, P. (2009). Modeling and verifying a broad array of network properties. *Europhysics Letters*, *86*(2), 28003. doi:10.1209/0295-5075/86/28003

García-Robledo, A., Díaz-Pérez, A., & Morales-Luna, G. (2013). Correlation analysis of complex network metrics on the topology of the Internet. In *Proceedings of the 10th International Conference and Expo on Emerging Technologies for a Smarter World* (pp.1-6). *Melville, NY*. IEEE Society. doi:10.1109/CEWIT.2013.6713749

Guo, L., Zuo, W., Peng, T., & Adhikari, B. K. (2015). Attribute-based edge bundling for visualizing social networks. *Physica A: Statistical Mechanics and its Applications*, *438*, 48-55.

Hennessey, D., Brooks, D., Fridman, A., & Breen, D. (2008). A simplification algorithm for visualizing the structure of complex graphs. In *Proceedings of the IEEE 12th International Conference on Information Visualisation* (pp. 616-625). London. doi:10.1109/IV.2008.37

Jamakovic, A., & Uhlig, S. (2008). On the relationships between topological measures in real-world networks. *Networks and Heterogeneous Media*, *3*(2), 345–359. doi:10.3934/nhm.2008.3.345

Jolliffe, I. (2002). *Principal Component Analysis*. New York, NY: Springer.

Krishnamurthy, V., Faloutsos, M., Chrobak, M., Cui, J., Lao, L., & Percus, A. (2007). Sampling large Internet topologies for simulation purposes. *Computer Networks*, *51*(15), 4284–4302. doi:10.1016/j.comnet.2007.06.004

Leskovec, J., Kleinberg, J., & Faloutsos, C. (2005). Graphs over time: densification laws, shrinking diameters and possible explanations. In *Proceedings of the 11th ACM SIGKDD International Conference on Knowledge Discovery in Data Mining* (pp. 177-187). New York, NY. ACM. doi:10.1145/1081870.1081893

Li, C., Wang, H., de Haan, W., Stam, C., & Van Mieghem, P. (2011). The correlation of metrics in complex networks with applications in functional brain networks. *Journal of Statistical Mechanics*, *2011*(11), P11018. doi:10.1088/1742-5468/2011/11/P11018

Madduri, K. (2008). *A high-performance framework for analyzing massive complex networks*. (PhD thesis). Georgia Institute of Technology.

Mirzasoleiman, B., Babaei, M., Jalili, M., & Safari, M. (2011). Cascaded failures in weighted networks. *Physical Review E: Statistical, Nonlinear, and Soft Matter Physics*, *84*(4 Pt 2), 046114. doi:10.1103/PhysRevE.84.046114 PMID:22181234

Newman, M. (2002). Assortative mixing in networks. *Physical Review Letters*, *89*(20), 208701. doi:10.1103/PhysRevLett.89.208701 PMID:12443515

Pastor-Satorras, R., Vázquez, A., & Vespignani, A. (2001). Dynamical and correlation properties of the Internet. *Physical Review Letters*, *87*(25), 258701. doi:10.1103/PhysRevLett.87.258701 PMID:11736611

Ravasz, E., & Barabási, A. (2003). Hierarchical organization in complex networks. *Physical Review E: Statistical, Nonlinear, and Soft Matter Physics*, *67*(2), 026112. doi:10.1103/PhysRevE.67.026112 PMID:12636753

Roy, S., & Filkov, V. (2009). Strong associations between microbe phenotypes and their network architecture. *Physical Review E: Statistical, Nonlinear, and Soft Matter Physics*, *80*(4), 040902. doi:10.1103/PhysRevE.80.040902 PMID:19905265

Serrano, M. A., Boguñá, M., & Vespignani, A. (2009). Extracting the multiscale backbone of complex weighted networks. *Proceedings of the National Academy of Sciences of the United States of America*, *106*(16), 6483–6488. doi:10.1073/pnas.0808904106 PMID:19357301

Shavitt, Y., & Shir, E. (2005). DIMES: Let the Internet measure itself. *SIGCOMM Computer Communication Review*, *35*(5), 71–74. doi:10.1145/1096536.1096546

Small, M., Xu, X., Zhou, J., Zhang, J., Sun, J., & Lu, J. A. (2008). Scale-free networks which are highly assortative but not small world. *Physical Review E: Statistical, Nonlinear, and Soft Matter Physics*, *77*(6 Pt 2), 066112. doi:10.1103/PhysRevE.77.066112 PMID:18643341

Sun, X., & Wandelt, S. (2014). Network similarity analysis of air navigation route systems. *Transportation Research Part E, Logistics and Transportation Review*, *70*, 416–434. doi:10.1016/j.tre.2014.08.005

The Great Telecoms Market Crash. (2002, July 18). *The Economist*. Retrieved from http://www.economist.com

University of Michigan. (2002). *INET-3.0: Internet topology generator*. Technical report. Author.

Wang, J. C., & Chiu, C. C. (2008). Recommending trusted online auction sellers using social network analysis. *Expert Systems with Applications*, *34*(3), 1666–1679. doi:10.1016/j.eswa.2007.01.045

Wang, P., Li, J., & Ji, B. (2015). Online fraud detection model based on social network analysis. *Journal of Information and Computational Science*, *12*(7), 2553–2562. doi:10.12733/jics20105690

Xu, X., Zhang, J., & Small, M. (2010). Rich-club connectivity dominates assortativity and transitivity of complex networks. *Physical Review E: Statistical, Nonlinear, and Soft Matter Physics*, *82*(4), 046117. doi:10.1103/PhysRevE.82.046117 PMID:21230355

Yahoo Research. (2004). Finding good nearly balanced cuts in power law graphs. Technical report. Pasadena, CA: Author.

Zhang, H., Zhao, H., Cai, W., Liu, J., & Zhou, W. (2010). Using the k-core decomposition to analyze the static structure of large-scale software systems. *The Journal of Supercomputing*, *53*(2), 352–369. doi:10.1007/s11227-009-0299-0

Zhou, F., Mahler, S., & Toivonen, H. (2012). Simplification of networks by edge pruning. In *Bisociative Knowledge Discovery* (pp. 179–198). Springer-Verlag Berlin. doi:10.1007/978-3-642-31830-6_13

Zhou, S., & Mondragón, R. (2004). The rich-club phenomenon in the Internet topology. *IEEE Communications Letters*, *8*(3), 180–182. doi:10.1109/LCOMM.2004.823426

Zhou, S., & Mondragón, R. (2007). Structural constraints in complex networks. *New Journal of Physics*, *9*(6), 173–173. doi:10.1088/1367-2630/9/6/173

ENDNOTES

1 Only the giant component of ASN's was considered.

2 A matching $E^{'} \subseteq E$ is a subset of the edges of G that does not share any common vertices.

3 Graph simplification algorithms that remove vertices or edges at random.

4 The maximum possible number of edge contractions in a simple connected graph.

5 A graph is disassortative if it has a negative assortativity coefficient.

Chapter 7
Connectivity and Structure in Large Networks

Rupei Xu
University of Texas at Dallas, USA

András Faragó
University of Texas at Dallas, USA

ABSTRACT

Graph models play a central role in the description of real life complex networks. They aim at constructing graphs that describe the structure of real systems. The resulting graphs, in most cases, are random or random-like; so it is not surprising that there is a large literature on various classes of random graphs and networks. Our key motivating observation is that often it is unclear how the strength of the different models compare to each other, e.g., when will a certain model class contain another. We are particularly interested in random graph models that arise via (generalized) geometric constructions. This is motivated by the fact that these graphs can well capture wireless communication networks. We set up a general framework to compare the strength of random network models, and present some results about the equality, inequality and proper containment of certain model classes.

INTRODUCTION

Large real life complex networks are often modeled by various random graph constructions, see, e.g. Bornholdt and Schuster (2006), Franceschetti and Meester (2008), Penrose (2003) and hundreds of further references therein. In many cases it is not at all clear how the modeling strength of differently generated random graph model classes relate to each other. We would like to systematically investigate such issues. Our approach was originally motivated to capture properties of the random network topology of wireless communication networks. We started some investigations in Faragó (2007, 2009, 2011), but here we elevate it to a more general level that makes it possible to compare the strength of different classes of random network models.

Specially, we introduce various classes of random graph models that are significantly more general than the ones that are usually treated in the literature, and show relationships among them. One of our

DOI: 10.4018/978-1-4666-9964-9.ch007

main results is that no random graph model can fall in the following three classes at the same time: (1) random graph models with bounded expected degrees; (2) random graph models that are asymptotically almost connected; (3) an abstracted version of geometric random graph models with two mild restrictions that we call locality and name invariance. In other words, in a mildly restricted, but still very general, class of generalized geometric-style models the requirements of bounded expected degrees and asymptotic almost connectivity are incompatible.

The rest of the paper is organized as follows. Section 2 introduces the various considered classes of random network models. Section 3 presents and proves the theorems about them. Section 4 shows an application example, which will (hopefully) convince the reader about the usefulness of elevating the approach to a higher level of abstraction. It allows to cut through a lot of complexity that would otherwise arise in the practically motivated example that is presented here. Finally, Section 5 concludes the paper by presenting some open problems.

CLASSES OF RANDOM GRAPH MODELS

General Random Graph Models

Let us first explain what we mean by random graphs and a random graph model in the most general sense. In full generality, by a random graph on n vertices we mean a random variable that takes its values in the set of all undirected graphs. on n vertices. (We use the words vertex and node interchangeably.) Let us denote a random graph on n nodes by G_n. At this point, it is still completely general, it can be generated by any mechanism, with arbitrary dependencies among its parts, it is just any graph-valued random variable, taking its values among undirected graphs on n nodes.

Definition 1. General Random Graph Model: A random graph model is given by a sequence of graph valued random variables, one for each possible value of n:

$$M = (G_n; n \in N).$$

The family of all such models is denoted by GEN.

Geometric Random Graph Models

Let us now introduce a model class that reflects a typical feature of geometric random graph models. This feature is that in geometric random graphs the primary random choice is picking random nodes from some domain and then the edges are already determined by some geometric property (typically some kind of distance) of the random nodes. We elevate this approach to an abstract level that, as will be shown later, actually turns out to be no less general than the totally unrestricted model. Our model is built of the following components:

- **Node Variables:** The nodes are represented by an infinite sequence $X_1, X_2, \ldots$ of random variables, called node variables. They take their values in an arbitrary (nonempty) set S, which is called the domain of the model. When a random graph on n nodes is generated, then we use the first n entries of the sequence, that is, $X_1,\ldots,X_n$ represent the nodes in G_n. It is important to note that we do not require the node variables to be independent.

- **Edge Functions:** We denote by $Y_{ij}^{(n)}$ the indicator of the edge between nodes X_i, X_j in the random graph G_n. Since loops are not allowed (which is typically the case in geometric random graph models), we always assume $i \neq j$, without repeating this condition each time. The (abstract) geometric nature of the model is expressed by the requirement that the random variables $Y_{ij}^{(n)}$ are determined by the nodes $X_i,\ldots,X_n$, possibly with additional independent randomization. Specially, we assume that there exist functions $f_{ij}^{(n)}$, $1 \leq i, j \leq n$; such that

$$Y_{ij}^{(n)} = f_{ij}^{(n)}\left(X_i,\ldots,X_n,\xi_{ij}\right)$$

where ξ_{ij} is a random variable that is uniformly distributed on [0,1] and is independent of all the other defining random variables of the model (i.e, the node variables and all the other ξ_{kl} variables). Henceforth the role of ξ_{ij} is referred to as independent randomization[1]. The undirected nature of the graph is expressed by the requirement $Y_{ij}^{(n)} = Y_{ji}^{(n)}$, which can simply be enforced by computing all values for $i<j$ only and defining the $i>j$ case by exchanging i and j.

We use the following notational convention: whenever a function is distinguished by certain parameters within some family of functions, such as $f_{ij}^{(n)}$ above, then it is assumed that the function "knows" its own parameters. In other words, the parameter values can be used in the definition of the function. Conversely, whatever information is used in computing the function should occur either as a variable or an explicitly shown parameter.

Definition 2. Abstract Geometric Model: The class of all models that have the structure explained above is called GEOM.

A model $\mathcal{M} \in \boldsymbol{GEOM}$, no matter how general it can be, still has a restricted structure. Therefore, one may ask whether every model in GEN can be represented in such a way. To make it precise when two models or model classes are considered equivalent, let us introduce the following definition.

Definition 3. Equivalence: Two random graph models $\mathcal{M} = \left(G_n;\ n \in N\right)$ and $\tilde{\mathcal{M}} = \left(\tilde{G}_n;\ n \in N\right)$ are called equivalent, denoted by $\mathcal{M} \sim \tilde{\mathcal{M}}$, if for any graph G on n vertices

$$Pr\left(G_n = G\right) = Pr\left(\tilde{G}_n = G\right)$$

holds, where equality of graphs means that they are isomorphic.

Definition 4. Containment, Equivalence, Intersection and Disjointness of Model Classes: Let C_1, C_2 be two classes of random graph models. We say that C_2 contains C_1, denoted by $C_1 \preceq C_2$, if for every $\mathcal{M}_1 \in C_1$, there is an $\mathcal{M}_2 \in C_2$, such that $M_1 \sim M_2$. If $C_1 \preceq C_2$ and $C_2 \preceq C_1$ both hold, then the two classes are called equivalent, denoted by $C_1 \simeq C_2$. The intersection of C_1 and C_2, denoted by $C_1 \wedge C_2$, is the set of models $\mathcal{M}$ with the property that there exist models $\mathcal{M}_1 \in C_1$ and $\mathcal{M}_2 \in C_2$, such that $\mathcal{M} \sim \mathcal{M}_1$ and $\mathcal{M} \sim \mathcal{M}_2$. If no model $\mathcal{M}$ has this property, then the classes C_1, C_2 are called disjoint.

Now we may ask whether **GEOM** $\simeq$ **GEN** holds or not. We show later that it does, even with more restrictions on GEOM. To this end, we introduce some restricting conditions to the model class GEOM. As a simple notation, whenever some restrictions $R_1,\ldots,R_k$ are applied, the arising class is denoted by $\mathbf{GEOM}(R_1,\ldots,R_k)$.

Subclasses of GEOM

The first considered restriction is called locality. Up to now we allowed that an edge in G_n can depend on all the nodes, and the dependence expressed by the $f_{ij}^{(n)}$ functions can be arbitrary and different for each edge. To get a little closer to the usual geometric random graph model (see, e.g., Penrose, 2003), we introduce the condition of locality. Informally, it restricts the dependence of an edge to its endpoints, in a homogeneous way, but still via an arbitrary function.

Definition 5. Locality: A model $\mathcal{M} \in$ **GEOM** is called local, if for every n and i, $j \le n$ the existence of an edge between X_i, X_j depends only on these nodes. Moreover, the dependence is the same for every i,j, possibly with independent randomization. That is, there are functions $f^{(n)}$ such that the edge indicators are expressible as

$$Y_{ij}^{(n)} = f^{(n)}\left(X_i, X_j, \xi_{ij}\right)$$

where ξ_{ij} represents the independent randomization. The set of local models in **GEOM** is denoted by GEOM(loc).

Note: with our notational convention $f^{(n)}$ can depend on its variables and on n. On the other hand, it has no access to the value of i and j, unless they are somehow contained in X_i, X_j, in a way that makes it possible to extract them without using anything else than the explicitly listed information.

Another restriction that we consider is a condition on the distribution of the vertices. To introduce it, let us first recall a concept from probability theory, called exchangeability.

Definition 6. Exchangeable Random Variables: A finite sequence $\xi_1,\ldots\xi_n$ of random variables is called exchangeable if for any permutation σ of $\{1,\ldots n\}$, the joint distribution of $\xi_1,\ldots\xi_n$ is the same as the joint distribution of $\xi_{\sigma(1)},\ldots\xi_{\sigma(n)}$. An infinite sequence of random variables is called exchangeable if every finite initial segment of the sequence is exchangeable.

Exchangeability can be equivalently defined such that when taking any $k \ge 1$ of the random variables, say, $\xi_{j1},\ldots\xi_{jk}$, their joint distribution does not depend on which particular k of them are taken, and in which order. Note that independent, identically distributed (i.i.d.) random variables are always exchangeable, but the converse is not true, so this is a larger family.

Now let us introduce the condition that we use to restrict the arbitrary dependence of node variables.

Definition 7. Name Invariance: A random graph modelM2 GEOM is called name invariant, if its node variables are exchangeable. The class of such models is denoted by GEOM(inv).

We call it the name invariance of the model because it means the names (the indices) of the nodes are irrelevant in the sense that the joint probabilistic behavior of any fixed number of nodes is invariant to renaming (reindexing) the nodes. In particular, it also implies that each single node variable X_i has the same probability distribution (but they do not have to be independent).

A simple example for a dependent, yet still name invariant, node generation process is a "clustered uniform" node generation. As an example, let *S* be a sphere in 3-dimensional space, i.e., the surface of a 3-dimensional ball. Let *R* be the radius of the ball. Let us first generate a pivot point *Y* uniformly at random from *S*. Then generate the nodes $X_1, X_2, \ldots$ uniformly at random and independently of each other from the neighborhood of radius $r \ll R$ of the random pivot point *Y* (within the sphere). It is directly implied by the construction that exchangeability holds. Moreover, any particular X_i will be uniformly distributed over the entire sphere, since *Y* is uniform over the sphere. On the other hand, the X_i are far from independent of each other, since they cluster around *Y*, forcing any two of them to be within distance 2*r*. The example can be generalized to applying several pivot points and non-uniform distributions, creating a more sophisticated clustering.

It is worth mentioning that any finite sequence $X_1, \ldots, X_n$ of random variables can be easily transformed into an exchangeable sequence by taking a random permutation σ of {1,…,*n*} and defining the transformed sequence by $\tilde{X}_i = X_{\sigma(i)}$. The resulting joint distribution will be

$$\Pr\left(\tilde{X}_1 = x_1, \ldots, \tilde{X}_n = x_n\right) = \frac{1}{n!} \Pr\left(X_{\sigma(1)} = x_1, \ldots, X_{\sigma(n)} = x_n\right)$$

where σ in the summation runs over all possible permutations of {1,…*n*}. Even though this simple construction does not work for infinite sequences, in many practically relevant cases there is vanishing difference between a very long finite and an actually infinite sequence.

A stronger restriction is if we want the node variables to be independent, not just exchangeable.

Definition 8. Free Geometric Model: A random graph model $\mathcal{M} \in \boldsymbol{GEOM}$ is called free, if its node variables are mutually independent. The class of such models is denoted by GEOM(free).

Other Model Classes

We define some other classes of random graph models, relating to some properties that are important in the applications of these models.

Definition 9. Bounded Expected Degree Model: A random graph model $\mathcal{M} \in \mathbf{GEN}$ is called a bounded expected degree model if there exists a constant C such that

$$\bar{d}(n) = \frac{2E(e(G_n))}{n} \leq C$$

for every n, where $e(G_n)$ denotes the number of edges in G_n, and E stands for the expected value. The class of bounded expected degree models is denoted by BD.

Since $2e(G_n)/n$ is the average degree in G_n, therefore, $d(n) = 2E(e(G_n))/n$ is the expected average degree. It can be interpreted as the expected degree of a randomly chosen node. Often the expected degree of each individual node is also equal to $\bar{d}(n)$, but in a general model it may not hold. Note that even if the expected degree of each node is equal to the expected average degree, it does not mean that the actual (random) degrees are also equal, so G_n may be far from regular.

Another important property of random graph models is asymptotically almost sure (a.a.s.) connectivity.

Definition 10. Connected Model: A random graph model $\mathcal{M} = (G_n;\ n \in N) \in GEN$ is called connected if

$$\lim_{n\to\infty} Pr(G_n \text{ is connected}) = 1.$$

The class of connected models is denoted by CONN.

Often the requirement of full connectivity is too strong, so we define a relaxed version of it and the corresponding model class.

Definition 11. β-Connectivity: For a real number 0≤β≤1, a graph G on n vertices is called β-connected if G contains a connected component on at least βn nodes.

When we consider a sequence of graphs with different values of n, then the parameter β may depend on n. When this is the case, we write β_n-connectivity. Note that even if $\beta_n \to 1$, this is still weaker then full connectivity in the limit. For example, if $\beta_n = 1 - 1/\sqrt{n}$, then we have $\beta_n \to 1$, but there can be still $n - \beta_n n = \sqrt{n}$ nodes that are not part of the largest connected component.

Definition 12. βn Connected Model: A random graph model $\mathcal{M} = (G_n;\ n \in N) \in GEN$ is called β_n-connected if

$$\lim_{n\to\infty} Pr(G_n \text{ is } \beta_n - \text{connected}) = 1.$$

The class of β_n -connected models is denoted by β_n --CONN.

It is clear from the definitions that with $\beta_n \equiv 1$, the class 1-CONN is the same as CONN. But if we only know that $\beta_n \to 1$, then β_n ---CONN becomes a larger class.

Finally, let us define some classes that restrict the independence structure of the edges. Let e be a (potential) edge. We regard it as a 0-1 valued random variable, indicating whether the edge is in the random graph or not. The probability that an edge e exists is $Pr(e=1)$, but we simply denote it by $Pr(e)$. We similarly write $Pr(e_1,\ldots,e_k)$ instead of $Pr(e_1=1,\ldots,e_k=1)$.

Definition 13. Independent Disjoint Edges: A random graph model $\mathcal{M}=(G_n;\ n\in N)\in GEN$ is said to have independent disjoint edges if any set $e_1,\ldots,e_k$ of pairwise disjoint edges are independent as random variables. That is, $Pr(e_1,\ldots,e_k)=Pr(e_1)\ldots Pr(e_k)$ holds whenever $e_1,\ldots,e_k$ are pairwise disjoint. The class of models with independent disjoint edges is denoted by **IDE**.

Definition 14. Positively Correlated Edges: A random graph model $\mathcal{M}=(G_n;\ n\in N)\in GEN$ is said to have positively correlated edges if any set $e_1,\ldots,e_k$ of distinct edges are positively correlated in the sense of $Pr(e_1,\ldots,e_k)\geq Pr(e_1)\ldots Pr(e_k)$. The class of models with positively correlated edges is denoted by POS.

RESULTS

Let us first address the question how the various restrictions influence the modeling strength of GEOM. The motivation is that one might think that a concept like locality imposes a significant restriction on the model. After all, it severely restricts which node variables can directly influence the existence of an edge. For example, it seems to exclude situations when the existence of an edge between X_i and X_j is based on whether one of them is among the k nearest neighbors of the other, according to some distance function (often called k-nearest neighbor graph).

Surprisingly, it turns out that locality alone does not impose any restriction at all on the generality of the model. Not just any model in GEOM can be expressed by a local one, but this remains true even if we want to express an arbitrary random graph model in GEN.

Theorem 1: Let $\tilde{\mathcal{M}}=(\tilde{G}_n;\ n\in N)\in GEN$ be an arbitrary random graph model. Then there exists another model $\mathcal{M}=(G_n;\ n\in N)\in GEOM(loc)$ such that $\mathcal{M}\sim\tilde{\mathcal{M}}$.

Proof: Let $\tilde{Y}_{ij}^{(n)}$ denote the edge indicators in $\tilde{\mathcal{M}}$. We show that a $\mathcal{M}\in\boldsymbol{GEOM}(loc)$ can be chosen such that its edge indicators $Y_{ij}^{(n)}$ satisfy $Y_{ij}^{(n)}=\tilde{Y}_{ij}^{(n)}$, which implies that the two models are equivalent.

Let Q be the set of all 0-1 matrices of all possible finite dimensions. For the domain S of $\mathcal{M}$ we choose the set of all infinite sequences with entries in Q. Let us define the node variable X_i such that $X_i=(Z_i^{(1)},Z_i^{(2)},\ldots)$, where $Z_i^{(n)}$ is an $(n+1)\times n$ sized 0-1 matrix with entries $Z_i^{(n)}[k,l]=\tilde{Y}_{k,l}^{(n)}$ for $k\neq l$ and $k,\ l\leq n$, $Z_i^{(n)}[k,k]=0$ and the last row $Z_i^{(n)}[n+1]$ contains the binary encoding of i. Then the edge functions for $\mathcal{M}$ can be defined as

$$f^{(n)}(X_i,X_j;\xi_{ij})=Z_i^{(n)}[i,j].$$

This indeed defines $f^{(n)}$, since knowing n the matrix $Z_i^{(n)}$ can be obtained as the nth component of X_i. The value of i can be read out from the last row of $Z_i^{(n)}$. Similarly, the value of j can be read out from the last row of $Z_j^{(n)}$, which is the nth component of X_j. Then the value of $Z_i^{(n)}[i,j]$ can be looked up. (The functions do not use the independent randomization). This definition directly implies that $\mathcal{M}$ is local, as $f^{(n)}$ does not use node variables other than X_i, X_j and the same function applies to any pair of nodes. Furthermore,

$$Y_{ij}^{(n)} = f^{(n)}\left(X_i, X_j, \xi_{ij}\right) = Z_i^{(n)}[i,j] = \tilde{Y}_{ij}^{(n)}$$

holds, completing the proof. **END.**

Next we show that a similar result holds for the restriction of name invariance.

Theorem 2: Let $\tilde{\mathcal{M}} = \left(\tilde{G}_n;\ n \in N\right) \in GEN$ be an arbitrary random graph model. Then there exists a another model $\mathcal{M} = \left(G_n;\ n \in N\right) \in GEOM(inv)$ such that $\mathcal{M} \sim \tilde{\mathcal{M}}$.

Proof: We show that the name invariant model $\mathcal{M} \in \boldsymbol{GEOM}(inv)$ can be chosen such that its edge indicators $Y_{ij}^{(n)}$ satisfy $Y_{ij}^{(n)} = \tilde{Y}_{ij}^{(n)}$, where the $\tilde{Y}_{ij}^{(n)}$ denote the edge indicators in $\tilde{\mathcal{M}}$.

Let $Z_n = \left[\tilde{Y}_{ij}^{(n)}\right]$ be an nxn matrix, containing all edge indicators of $\tilde{G}_n$. Define X_i as an infinite sequence $X_i = (Z_1, Z_2, \ldots)$.

Since X_i is defined without using the value of i, we have that all the X_i are equal, which is a trivial case of name invariance. (All random node variables being equal, re-indexing clearly cannot change anything.) Then, following the edge function format of **GEOM**, we can define the edge functions by

$$f_{ij}^{(n)}\left(X_1, \ldots, X_n, \xi_{ij}\right) = Z_n[i,j].$$

(The independent randomization is not used.) This edge function is well defined, since, knowing n, the array Z_n can be read out from any of the X_i and in the general **GEOM** model the functions can directly depend on i and j. As, by definition, $Z_n[i,j] = \tilde{Y}_{ij}^{(n)}$, we obtain

$$Y_{ij}^{(n)} = f_{ij}^{(n)}\left(X_1, \ldots, X_n, \xi_{ij}\right) = Z_n[i,j] = \tilde{Y}_{ij}^{(n)}$$

which completes the proof. **END**

Since we know by definition $\mathbf{GEOM}(\text{loc}) \preceq \mathbf{GEOM}$ and $\mathbf{GEOM}(\text{inv}) \preceq \mathbf{GEOM}$, as well as $\mathbf{GEOM} \preceq \mathbf{GEN}$, the theorems immediately imply the following corollary.

Corollary 3: $\mathbf{GEOM}(\text{loc}) \simeq \mathbf{GEOM}(\text{inv}) \simeq \mathbf{GEOM} \simeq \mathbf{GEN}$.

We have seen above that neither locality nor name invariance can restrict full generality. Both restrictions, if applied alone, still allow that an arbitrary random graph model is generated. This situation naturally leads to the question: what happens if the two restrictions are applied together? At first, one might think about it this way: if the set of local models and the set of name invariant models are both equal to the set of general models, then their intersection should also be the same. This would mean that even those models that are both local and name invariant are still fully general.

The above argument, however, is not correct. Although Corollary 3 implies

$$\mathbf{GEOM}(\mathrm{loc}) \wedge \mathbf{GEOM}(\mathrm{inv}) \simeq \mathbf{GEN}$$

(see Definition 4 for the $\wedge$ operation), it does not imply that

$$\mathbf{GEOM}(\mathrm{loc},\ \mathrm{inv}) \simeq \mathbf{GEOM}(\mathrm{loc}) \wedge \mathbf{GEOM}(\mathrm{inv})$$

also holds. In fact, the latter does not hold, which will be obtained as a consequence of the following theorem. The theorem proves the surprising fact that joint locality and name invariance, without any further restriction, makes it impossible that a model satisfies bounded expected degree and (almost) connectivity at the same time.

Theorem 4: Let $\beta_n \to 1$ be a sequence of positive reals. Then

$$\mathbf{BD} \wedge \beta_n - \mathbf{CONN} \wedge \mathbf{GEOM}(\mathrm{loc},\ \mathrm{inv}) = \varnothing$$

holds.

Proof: Consider a model $\mathcal{M} = (G_n;\ n \in N) \in \mathbf{GEOM}(\mathrm{loc},\ \mathrm{inv})$. Let I_n denote the (random) number of isolated nodes in G_n. First we show that

$$E(I_n) \geq n\left(1 - \frac{\overline{d(n)}}{n-1}\right)^{n-1} \tag{1}$$

holds[2]. Note that since our model is abstract and does not involve any real geometry, one has to be careful to avoid using such intuition that may appeal geometrically, but does not follow from the abstract model.

First, observe the following: name invariance implies that for any function g of the node variables and for any permutation σ of $\{1,\ldots,n\}$ we have

$$E(g(X_1,\ldots,X_n)) = E\left(g\left(X_{\sigma(1)},\ldots,X_{\sigma(n)}\right)\right).$$

Since the probability that a particular node has any given degree k is also expressible by such a function, therefore, the probability distribution of the node degree must be the same for all nodes (but the degrees, as random variables, may not be independent). As a consequence, the expected degree of each node is the same, which then must be equal to the expected average degree $\bar{d}(G_n)$.

Let us pick a node X_i. We derive a lower bound on the probability that X_i is isolated, i.e., that its degree is 0. Due to the above symmetry considerations, it does not matter which node is chosen, so we can take i=1. Let $\mathcal{I}_n$ be the (random) set of isolated nodes in G_n. What we want to compute is a lower bound on $\Pr(X_1 \in \mathcal{I}_n)$. Then we are going to use the fact that

$$E(I_n) = E(|\mathcal{I}_n|) = \sum_{i=1}^{n} \Pr(X_i \in \mathcal{I}_n)$$

Note that, due to the linearity of expectation, this remains true even if the events $\{X_i \in \mathcal{I}_n\}$ are not independent, which is typically the case. Then, by the symmetry considerations, we can utilize that $\Pr(X_i \in \mathcal{I}_n)$ is independent of i, yielding $E(I_n) = n\Pr(X_1 \in \mathcal{I}_n)$.

In order to derive a lower bound on $\Pr(X_1 \in \mathcal{I}_n)$, we need a fundamental result from probability theory, called de Finetti's Theorem[3]. This theorem says that if an infinite sequence $\xi_1, \xi_2, \ldots$ of 0-1 valued random variables[4] is exchangeable, then the following hold:

1. The limit

$$\eta = \sum_{N \to \infty} \frac{\xi_1 + \ldots + \xi_N}{N} \tag{2}$$

exists[5] with probabilit

2. For any N and for any system $a_1, \ldots, a_N \in \{0,1\}$ of outcomes with $s = \sum_{i=1}^{N} a_i$.

$$\Pr(\xi_1 = a_1, \ldots, \xi_N = a_N) = \int_0^1 x^s (1-x)^{N-s} \, dF_\eta(x)$$

holds, where F_η is the probability distribution function of η.

3. The ξ_i are conditionally independent and identically distributed (conditionally i.i.d.), given η, that is,

$$\Pr(\eta_1 = a_1, \ldots, \eta_N = a_n \mid \eta) = \prod_{i=1}^{N} \Pr(\xi_i = a_i \mid \eta).$$

Informally, de Finetti's theorem says that exchangeable 0-1 valued random variables, even if they are not independent, can always be represented as a mixture of Bernoulli systems of random variables. It is important to note, however, that even though the statements (ii) and (iii) refer to finite initial segments of the sequence $\xi_1,\xi_2,\ldots,$ it is necessary that the entire infinite sequence is exchangeable. For finite sequences the theorem may not hold, counterexamples are known for the finite case (Stoyanov, 2013).

Let us now define the infinite sequence of 0-1 valued random variables

$$e_j = f^{(n)}\left(X_1, X_j, \xi_{1j}\right), j = 2,3\ldots$$

Of these, $e_1,\ldots,e_n$ are the indicators of the edges with one endpoint at X_1. But the function $f^{(n)}$ is defined for any $(x,y,z)\in S\times S\times[0,1]$, so nothing prevents us to define the infinite sequence e_j; j=2,3,…, by taking more independent and uniform $\xi_{1j} \in [0,1]$ random variables.

Observe now that the sequence e_j; j=2,3,…, is an infinite exchangeable sequence of 0-1 valued random variables. Only the exchangeability needs proof. If we take any k indices $j_1,\ldots,j_k$, then the joint distribution of $e_{j_1},\ldots,e_{j_k}$ depends only on the joint distribution of $X_{j_1},\ldots,X_{j_k}$, plus the independent randomization. If we replace $j_1,\ldots,j_k$ by other k indices, then it will not change the joint distribution of the k node variables, due to their assumed exchangeability. The independent randomization also does not change the joint distribution, since the ξ_{1j} are i.i.d, so it does not matter which k are taken. Furthermore, the locality of the model implies that each e_j depends on one X_j (besides X_1) so taking another k cannot change how many node variables will any subset of the e_j share. Thus, for any k, the joint distribution of $e_{j_1},\ldots,e_{j_k}$ does not depend on which k indices are chosen, proving that e_j; j=2,3,…, is an infinite exchangeable sequence of 0-1 valued random variables.

Now, by de Finetti's Theorem, there is a random variable $\eta\in[0,1]$, such that the e_j are conditionally i.i.d, given η. Then we can write

$$\Pr\left(X_1 \in \mathcal{I}_n\right) = \Pr\left(e_2 = \ldots = e_n = 0\right) =$$
$$E\left(\Pr\left(e_2 = \ldots = e_n = 0 | \eta\right)\right) = E\left(\prod_{j=2}^{n}\left(\Pr\left(e_j = 0 | \eta\right)\right)\right) = E\left(\prod_{j=2}^{n}\left(1 - \Pr\left(e_j = 1 | \eta\right)\right)\right). \quad (3)$$

Notice that $\Pr(e_j = 1 | \eta)$ is the probability that an edge exists between X_1 and X_j, conditioned on η. Consequently, $\xi = \Pr(e_j = 1 | \eta)$ is a random variable, depending on η. At the same time, it does not depend on j, as by de Finetti's theorem, the ej are conditionally i.i.d, given η, so it does not matter which j is taken in $\eta = \Pr(e_j = 1 | \eta)$. Thus, we can continue (3) as

$$\Pr\left(\left(X_1 \in \mathcal{I}_n\right)\right) = E\left(\prod_{j=2}^{n}(1-\xi)\right) = E\left((1-\xi)^{n-1}\right). \quad (4)$$

We can now observe that $\xi\in[0,1]$ and the function $g(x)=(1-x)^n$ is convex in [0,1], so we may apply Jensen's inequality. Jensen's well known inequality says that for any random variable ζ and for any convex function g the inequality $E(g(\zeta))\geq g(E(\zeta))$ holds, which is a consequence of the definition of convexity. Thus, we can further continue (4), obtaining

$$\Pr\left(X_1 \in \mathcal{I}_n\right) = E\left(\left(1-\xi\right)^{n-1}\right) \geq \left(1-E\left(\xi\right)\right)^{n-1}.$$

Note that $E\left(\xi\right) = E(\Pr(e_j = 1 \mid \eta)) = \Pr\left(e_j = 1\right)$ is the probability that an edge exists between X_1 and X_j. By name invariance, this is the same probability for any two nodes, let p_n denote this common value. Thus,

$$\Pr\left(X_1 \in \mathcal{I}_n\right) \geq \left(1-p_n\right)^{n-1}$$

follows. We know that there are $n-1$ potential edges adjacent to each node, each with probability p_n. Therefore, despite the possible dependence of edges, the linearity of expectation implies the expected degree of each node under our conditions is $(n-1)p_n$, which is also equal to $\overline{d}\left(n\right)$. We can then substitute $p_n = \overline{d}\left(n\right)/\left(n-1\right)$, which yields

$$\Pr\left(X_1 \in \mathcal{I}_n\right) \geq \left(1-\frac{\overline{d\left(n\right)}}{n-1}\right)^{n-1},$$

Implying

$$E\left(I_n\right) = n\Pr\left(X_1 \in \mathcal{I}_n\right) \geq n\left(1-\frac{\overline{d\left(n\right)}}{n-1}\right)^{n-1}.$$

Assume now there is a model $\mathcal{M}' \in \mathbf{BD}$ with $\mathcal{M}' \sim \mathcal{M}$. This means, there is a constant C with $d(n) \leq C$ for every n. Then

$$\left(1-\frac{\overline{d\left(n\right)}}{n-1}\right)^{n-1} \geq \left(1-\frac{C}{n-1}\right)^{n-1} \to e^{-C},$$

so there exist constants $a>0$ and $n_0 \in N$, such that $E(I_n) \geq an$ holds for every $n \geq n_0$.

Now take a sequence $\beta_n \in [0,1]$ with $\beta_n \to 1$. We are going to show that the probability Pr(G_n is β_n-connected) cannot tend to 1, meaning that for any model $\mathcal{M}''$ with $\mathcal{M}'' \sim \mathcal{M}$ it holds that $\mathcal{M}'' \notin \beta_n - \mathbf{CONN}$.

Set $s_n = \Pr\left(I_n \leq \left(1-\beta_n\right)n\right)$. Then $\Pr\left(G_n \text{ is } \beta_n - connected\right) \leq s_n$ must hold, since β_n-connectivity implies that there may be at most $(1-\beta_n)n$ isolated nodes. Consider now the random variable $\gamma_n = n - I_n$. The definition of γ_n implies $\gamma_n \geq 0$ and $E\left(\gamma_n\right) = n - E\left(I_n\right)$. Therefore, $E\left(\gamma_n\right) \leq \left(1-a\right)n$ holds for $n \geq n_0$. Moreover, the definition also directly implies that the events $\left\{I_n \leq \left(1-\beta_n\right)n\right\}$ and $\gamma_n \geq \beta_n n$ are equivalent. Thus, we can write, using Markov's inequality for nonnegative random variables:

$$s_n = \Pr\left(I_n \le (1-\beta_n)n\right) = \Pr\left(\gamma_n \ge \beta_n n\right) \le \frac{E(\gamma_n)}{\beta_n n} \le \frac{(1-a)n}{\beta_n n} = \frac{1-a}{\beta_n}.$$

Since we know that $a>0$ is a constant and $\beta_n \to 1$, therefore, there must exist a constant $b<1$, such that $s_n \le b$ holds for all large enough n. This, together with $\Pr\left(G_n \text{ is } \beta_n - connected\right) \le s_n$, proves that the assumptions we made, that is, $\mathcal{M} \in \mathbf{GEOM}(\text{loc}, \text{inv})$ and $\mathcal{M} \sim \mathcal{M}' \in \beta_n - \mathbf{CONN}$, together imply that there is no $\mathcal{M}'' \sim \mathcal{M}$ with $\mathcal{M}'' \in \boldsymbol{BD}$, proving the theorem. **END.**

As a corollary, we obtain that $\mathbf{GEOM}(\text{loc}, \text{inv})$ is smaller than $\mathbf{GEOM}(\text{loc})$ and $\mathbf{GEOM}(\text{inv})$.

Corollary 5: $\mathbf{GEOM}(\text{loc}, \text{inv}) \simeq \mathbf{GEOM}(\text{loc})$ and $\mathbf{GEOM}(\text{loc}, \text{inv}) \simeq \mathbf{GEOM}(\text{inv})$.

Proof: Let $\mathcal{M} = (G_n;\ n \in N)$ be a model in which G_n is chosen uniformly at random from the set of all connected graphs with maximum degree at most 3. It follows from this construction that $\mathcal{M} \in \mathbf{BD} \wedge \mathbf{CONN}$, implying $\mathcal{M} \in \mathbf{BD} \wedge \beta_n - \mathbf{CONN}$ for any β_n. Then Theorem 4 implies $\mathcal{M} \notin \mathbf{GEOM}(\text{loc}; \text{inv})$. Since, naturally, $\mathcal{M} \in \mathbf{GEN}$, therefore, it follows that $\mathbf{GEOM}(\text{loc}, \text{inv}) \ne \mathbf{GEN}$. As we know from Corollary 3 that $\mathbf{GEOM}(\text{loc}) \simeq \mathbf{GEOM}(\text{inv}) \simeq \mathbf{GEN}$, we obtain $\mathbf{GEOM}(\text{loc}; \text{inv}) \ne \mathbf{GEOM}(\text{loc})$ and $\mathbf{GEOM}(\text{loc}; \text{inv}) \ne \mathbf{GEOM}(\text{inv})$ **END.**

AN APPLICATION

In this application example we model a mobile wireless ad hoc network, that is, a network in which wireless nodes communicate to each other directly, without a supporting infrastructure. The initial position of each node is chosen in the following way. Let P be a probability measure over a planar domain D. First we choose k pivot points independently at random, using P. Then the actual node positions are generated such that each potential node is chosen independently at random from P, but it is kept only if it is within a given distance 0 is index to at least one of the random pivot points, otherwise it is discarded. Note that this way of generating the nodes makes them dependent, as the non-discarded ones cluster around the random pivot points, thus modeling a clustered, non-independent node distribution.

The mobility of the nodes in this example is modeled in the following way. Over some time horizon T_n, that may depend on n, the number of nodes, each node moves along a random curve from its initial position with a constant speed v_0. The curve is chosen from a set C of available potential trajectories in D. For simplicity, it is assumed that each curve can be identified by a real parameter. This parameter is chosen using a probability distribution $Q_{x,y}$ that depends on the initial position (x,y) of the node. Then the randomly obtained curve is shifted so that its start point coincides with the random initial position of the node and then the node will move along this random trajectory.

Let $d(x,y)$ be a nonnegative real valued function over $D \times D$, with the only restriction that $d(x,x)=0$ holds for any x. This function is intended to measure "radio distance" in D. The assumption is that whenever $d(x,y)$ is small enough, then two nodes positioned at x and y can receive each other's transmissions. The function $d(x,y)$, however, does not have to satisfy the usual distance axioms, it may reflect complex radio propagation characteristics, such as expected attenuation and fading, it may account for the heterogeneity of the terrain, for propagation obstacles etc. We may also include random effects, making $d(x,y)$ a random variable, reflecting special conditions of interest, such as the random presence of eavesdroppers that can trigger the inhibition of certain links. We assume, however, that if there is randomness in $d(x,y)$, then it is independent of the other random variables in the model.

Let t_n and r_n be further parameters that may also depend on the number n of nodes. We now define the links of the network, as follows. Consider two nodes with initial position vectors $X_1(0)$, $X_2(0)$, respectively. As they move along their random trajectories, their positions at time t is denoted by $X_1(t)$, $X_2(t)$, respectively. The two nodes are considered connected by a link, if there is a closed subinterval of length at least t_n within the time horizon $[0,T_n]$, such that $d(X_1(t), X_2(t)) \leq r_n$ holds for every time t within the subinterval[6], with the possibly complicated radio distance.

Now the question is this: for given P, D, C, $Q_{x,y}$ and $d(x,y)$, and for the described way of dependent node generation, can we somehow choose the model parameters k, d_0, v_0, T_n, t_n, and r_n, such that the arising random graph is asymptotically almost surely connected, while the expected average degree in the graph remains bounded?

We believe that it would be rather hard to answer such a question with a direct analysis for arbitrary complex choices of P, D, C, $Q_{x,y}$ and $d(x,y)$. On the other hand, with our general results it becomes quite straightforward, showing the strength of the results.

Let us choose the model domain S as a 3-dimensional phase space, in which each node is represented by a point such that the first two coordinates describe the initial position of the node and the last coordinate encodes which random trajectory was chosen from C for the node. Let X_1, X_2, ... be the representations of the nodes in this phase space.

We can now check that, for any n, the joint distribution of $X_1, \ldots, X_n$ is invariant to re-indexing them. The reason is that both the initial positions and the trajectory choices are generated by processes in which the indices do not play any role. Therefore, the model is name invariant. Interestingly, this remains true despite having a lot of dependencies among the nodes: the initial positions of different nodes are not independent (due to clustering), and the trajectory of a given node is also not independent of its initial position, as it is drawn from a probability distribution that may depend on the location. Through this, the trajectories and initial positions of different nodes also become dependent, making their whole movement dependent. Yet, the model is still name invariant.

Let us now consider the links. As defined above, two nodes are considered connected if during their movement over the time horizon $[0,T_n]$ there is a subinterval of time, of length at least t_n, such that they remain within "radio distance" $\leq r_n$ during the entire subinterval. The radio distance, however, may be very different from the Euclidean distance, it may be described by an arbitrary function that may account for complex propagation characteristics, attenuation, obstacles, and it may also contain independent randomness.

Given some possibly complicated radio distance $d(x,y)$ and the node generation and movement process with possibly complex trajectories, it may not be easy to compute whether a link actually exists between two nodes according to the above definition. On the other hand, for us it is enough to note that once the phase space representations X_i, X_j of any two nodes are given, plus the realization of the independent randomness of the distance, they together determine whether a link exists between the two nodes or not. The reason is that the initial positions and the trajectories, given in the phase space representation, fully determine the movement of the nodes. Once this is known, it determines, along with the realization of the independent randomness of the distance function, whether the link definition is satisfied, i.e., if there is a subinterval of length $\geq t_n$ in $[0,T_n]$, such that the nodes stay within radio distance $\leq r_n$ during the entire subinterval. To actually compute it may not be easy for a sophisticated case, but for our purposes it enough to know that it is determined by the listed factors, without knowing anything about the other nodes. This implies that the model is local.

Thus, we have established that, for any choice of the parameters, the problem can be described by a model that is in $\mathbf{GEOM}(\text{loc}, \text{inv})$. Then this model cannot be in $\mathbf{BD} \wedge \mathbf{CONN}$, since we know from Theorem 4 that $\mathbf{BD} \wedge \beta_n - \mathbf{CONN} \wedge \mathbf{GEOM}(\text{loc}, \text{inv}) = \varnothing$ holds for any choice of $\beta_n \to 1$, including $\beta_n \equiv 1$. Thus, in our example it is impossible to keep the expected average degree bounded and achieving asymptotically almost sure connectivity at the same time. With this we could cut through a lot of complexity that would otherwise arise with the direct analysis of the specific model.

CONCLUSION AND OPEN PROBLEMS

Our research has been motivated by the fact that many different random graph constructions are used to model large real life networks, but often it is unclear how the strength of the different models compare to each other, e.g., when will a certain model property imply another. We have set up a general framework to compare the strength of various random graph model classes, and presented some results about the equality, inequality and proper containment of these classes. There are many research issues, however, that remain open. Let us mention some examples that seem interesting. They could lead to nontrivial representation theorems for various model classes, and could clarify the relative strength of these classes.

Open Problem 1: One can easily see from the definition that $\mathbf{GEOM}(\text{loc,free}) \preceq \mathbf{IDE}$. That is, in local geometric models with independent node variables the disjoint edges are independent. Is the converse true, i.e., can we represent any $\mathcal{M} \in \mathbf{IDE}$ by a local geometric model with independent node variables?

Open Problem 2: Is it true that in every local and name invariant geometric model the edges are positively correlated? In other words, does $\mathbf{GEOM}(\text{loc,inv}) \preceq \mathbf{IDE}$ hold? Or does at least $\mathbf{GEOM}(\text{loc,free}) \preceq \mathbf{IDE}$ hold? Or else, what additional condition should be imposed to imply positive edge correlations?

Open Problem 3: Is it true that $\mathbf{GEOM}(\text{loc,inv}) \preceq \mathbf{IDE}$? if not, what restrictions need to be added to POS to make it true?

Open Problem 4: It is not hard to show via small examples that ide and pos are incomparable, that is, neither $\mathbf{IDE} \preceq \mathbf{POS}$ nor .. hold. Can the class $\mathbf{IDE} \wedge \mathbf{POS}$ be characterized in a nontrivial way? How does it relate to $\mathbf{GEOM}(\text{loc,inv})$?

ACKNOWLEDGMENT

The authors gratefully acknowledge the support of NSF Grant CNS-1018760.

REFERENCES

Bornholdt, S., & Schuster, H. G. (Eds.). (2006). *Handbook of graphs and networks: from the genome to the internet*. John Wiley & Sons.

De Finetti, B. (1931). *Funzione caratteristica di un fenomeno aleatorio*. Academic Press.

Faragó, A. (2007). On the fundamental limits of topology control in ad hoc networks. *Algorithmica*, *49*(4), 337–356. doi:10.1007/s00453-007-9078-6

Faragó, A. (2009). Scalability of node degrees in random wireless network topologies. Selected Areas in Communications. *IEEE Journal on*, *27*(7), 1238–1244.

Faragó, A. (2011). Asymptotically optimal trade-off between local and global connectivity in wireless networks. *Performance Evaluation*, *68*(2), 142–156. doi:10.1016/j.peva.2010.08.024

Franceschetti, M., & Meester, R. (2008). *Random networks for communication: from statistical physics to information systems* (Vol. 24). Cambridge University Press. doi:10.1017/CBO9780511619632

Kallenberg, O. (2006). *Probabilistic symmetries and invariance principles*. Springer Science & Business Media.

Penrose, M. (2003). *Random geometric graphs* (Vol. 5). Oxford, UK: Oxford University Press. doi:10.1093/acprof:oso/9780198506263.001.0001

Stoyanov, J. M. (2013). *Counterexamples in probability*. Courier Corporation.

ENDNOTES

1 Note that the specified distribution of ξ_{ij} does not impose a restriction, since the functions $f_{ij}^{(n)}$ are arbitrary.

2 It is worth noting that even when $E(I_n)\to\infty$ is the case, this fact alone may not a priori preclude the possibilityof a.a.s. β_n-connectivity, even with $\beta_n\equiv 1$. For example, if G_n is connected with probability $1-1/\sqrt{n}$ andconsists of n isolated nodes with probability $1/\sqrt{n}$,then $E(I_n)=n/\sqrt{n}\to\infty$, but $\Pr(G_n \textit{ is connected})=1-1/\sqrt{n}\to 1$.)

3 It was first published in De Finetti (1931). Being a classical result, it can be found in many advanced textbooks on probability.

4 Various extensions exist to more general cases (see, e.g., Kallenberg, 2006) but for our purposes the simplest 0-1 valued case is sufficient.

5 Note that exchangeability implies that all ξ_i have the same expected value, so in case they were independent, then the strong law of large numbers would apply and the limit would be the common expected value, with probability 1. Since, however, the ξ_i are not assumed independent (only exchangeable), therefore, the average may not tend to a constant, it can be a non-constant random variable in [0,1].

6 The motivation is that the nodes should be within range at least for the time of sending a packet.

Chapter 8
A Study of Computer Virus Propagation on Scale Free Networks Using Differential Equations

Mohammad S. Khan
Texas A&M University – Kingsville, USA

ABSTRACT

The SIR model is used extensively in the field of epidemiology, in particular, for the analysis of communal diseases. One problem with SIR and other existing models is that they are tailored to random or Erdos type networks since they do not consider the varying probabilities of infection or immunity per node. In this paper, we present the application and the simulation results of the pSEIRS model that takes into account the probabilities, and is thus suitable for more realistic scale free networks. In the pSEIRS model, the death rate and the excess death rate are constant for infective nodes. Latent and immune periods are assumed to be constant and the infection rate is assumed to be a function of the size of the total population and the size of the infected population. A node recovers from an infection temporarily with a probability p and dies from the infection with probability (1-p).

1. INTRODUCTION

The growth of the internet has created several challenges and one of these challenges is cyber security. A reliable cyber defense system is therefore needed to safeguard the valuable information stored on a system and the information in transit. To achieve this goal, it becomes essential to understand and study the nature of the various forms of malicious entities such as viruses, trojans, and worms, and to do so on a wider scale. It also becomes essential to understand how they *spread* throughout computer networks.

A computer virus [1]is a malicious computer code that can be of several types, such as a trojan, worm, and so on (Aron, O'Leary, Gove, Azadegan, & Schneider, 2002; Perdisci, Lanzi, & Lee, 2008). Although

DOI: 10.4018/978-1-4666-9964-9.ch008

each type of malicious entity has a different way of spreading over the network, they all have common properties such as infectivity, invisibility, latency, destructibility and unpredictability (Kafai, 2008).

More recently, we have also started witnessing viruses that can spread on social networks. These viruses spread by infecting the accounts of social network users, who click on any option that may trigger the virus's takeover of the user's sharing capabilities, resulting in the spreading of these malicious programs without the knowledge of the user. While their inner coding might be different and while their triggering and spreading mechanisms (on physical vs. virtual social networks) may be different, both traditional viruses such as worms and social network viruses share, in common, the critical property of proliferation via spreading through a network (physical or social).

These malicious programs behave similarly to an infection in a human population. This, in turn, allows us to draw comparisons between the study of epidemiology, in particular the mathematical aspect of infectious diseases(Bailey, 1987) and the behavior of a computer virus in a computer network. This is generally studied via mathematical models of the spread of a virus or disease. Any mathematical model's ability to mimic the behavior of the infection largely depends on the assumptions made during the modeling process.

Most of the existing epidemiology models are modified versions of the classical Kermack and McKendrick's (W.O.Kermack & McKendrick, 1927) model, more commonly known as the SIR (Susceptible/Infected/Recovered) model. For example, Hethcote (Hethcote, 1976) proposed a version of the SIR model, in which it was assumed that the total population was constant. But in real world scenarios, the population will change in time. Thus, this model was later improved by Diekmann and Heersterbeek(Diekmann & Heesterbeek, 2000) by assuming that:

1. The population size changes according to an exponential demographic trend.
2. The infected individuals cannot reproduce.
3. The individuals acquire permanent immunity to further infection when removed from the infected class.

The eigenvalue approach has recently emerged as one of the popular techniques to analyze virus or malicious entity propagation in a computer network. Wang et al. (Yang, Chakrabarti, Chenxi, & Faloutsos, 2003) have associated the epidemic threshold parameter for a network with the largest eigenvalue of its adjacency matrix. This technique works only with the assumption that the eigenvalues exist. There are also certain restrictions on the size of the adjacency matrix, since calculating eigenvalues may not be easy or even possible for large matrices.

In this paper, we apply the malicious object transmission model (Mishra & Saini, 2007) in complete and scale free networks, that assumes a variable population and with constant latent and immune periods. The current model extends the classical SIR model proposed in (Lloyd & May, 2001) to a *probabilistic* SEIRS (Mishra & Saini, 2007) {Mishra, 2007 #38}type model in several directions:

1. It includes an *Exposed* class in addition to the *Susceptible*, *Infected* and *Recovered* classes.

   It furthermore includes a constant exposition period ω and a constant latency period τ.

2. When a node is removed from the infected class, it recovers with a temporary immunity with a probability p and dies due to the attack of the malicious object with probability (1-p).

The rest of this paper is organized as follows. In section 2, we introduce the classical SIR model and implement it on a small network. After presenting simulation and statistical results, we conclude that the SIR model does not capture the realistic nature of the virus propagation in a computer network. Thus, we consider the more realistic scale free network in section 3 and give some historical background about such networks. A system of delay differential equations is then presented that includes a probabilistic temporary immunity with probability p. A complete mathematical justification follows the introduction of pSEIRS model. Section 4 discusses the mathematical conditions for an infection free equilibrium. We also discuss the stability analysis of the proposed model using the phase plane plots. We then present simulation experiments to validate the scalability aspect of the proposed model and compare it with the classical SEIRS model. Section 5 presents our conclusion, then discusses some limitations of compartment type mathematical models, and finally closes with some possible directions for future work in this area.

2. THE CLASSICAL SIR MODEL

The SIR (Susceptible/Infected/Recovered) model (W.O.Kermack & McKendrick, 1927) is used extensively in the field of epidemiology, in particular, for the analysis of communal diseases, which spread from an infected individual to a population. So it is natural to divide the population into the separate groups of susceptible (S), infected (I) and those who have recovered or become immune to a type of infection or a disease (R). These subdivisions of the population, which are also different stages in the epidemic cycle, are sometimes called *compartments*. A total population of size N is thus divided into three stages or compartments:

$$N = S + I + R.$$

Since the population is going to change with time (t), we have to express these stages as a function of time, i.e., $S\ (t)$, $I\ (t)$ and $R\ (t)$. Here β (infection rate) and α (recovery rate) are the transition rates between $S \rightarrow I$ and $I \rightarrow R$, respectively, and are both in [0, 1].

The underlying assumption in the traditional SIR model is that the population is homogenous; that is, everybody makes contact with each other randomly. So from a graph theoretical point of view, this population represents a complete graph, which would be the case of a computer network that is totally connected. In this situation, the classical SIR model may be sufficient enough to understand the malicious object's propagation. The dynamics of the epidemic evolution can be captured with the following homogenous differential equations:

$$\begin{aligned} \frac{dS}{dt} &= -\beta IS \\ \frac{dI}{dt} &= \beta IS - \alpha I \\ \frac{dR}{dt} &= \alpha I\ . \end{aligned} \tag{1}$$

Based on (1), we define a basic reproduction rate as

$$R_0 = \frac{\beta}{\alpha}$$

R_0 is a useful parameter to determine if the infection will spread through the population or not. That is, if $R_0 > 1$ and $I(0) > 1$, the infection will be able to spread in a population, to a stage that is called *Endemic Equilibrium* and is given by

$$\lim_{t\to\infty}(S(t),I(t),R(t)) \to \left(\frac{N}{R_0},\frac{N}{\beta}(R_0-1),\frac{\alpha N}{\beta}(R_0-1)\right) \tag{2}$$

If $R_0 < 1$, infection will die out in the long run. This is called *disease free equilibrium* and is represented as

$$\lim_{t\to\infty}\left(S(t),I(t),R(t)\right) \to (N,0,0) \tag{3}$$

2.1. Simulation Results of the SIR Model with a Small Complete Network

The simulation results of the SIR model in a K_{12} network (complete graph with 12 nodes) are presented in Figure 1 and 2 with different values of β and α.

In Figure 1, $R_0 = 0.6 < 1$. So, the infection will not spread through the entire network.

In Figure 2, $R_0 = 2 > 1$. In this case, infection will spread to most of the nodes and the network will be in an endemic stage.

We gleam useful information about the virus propagation from Figures 1 and 2 in a K_{12} type network and make an analysis based on these simulations. Two obvious observations are the long-term behavior of the infection and the speed at which the population gets infected. Also, we can determine the rate at which the population is getting immune to the infection, i.e., the removal rate from the susceptible

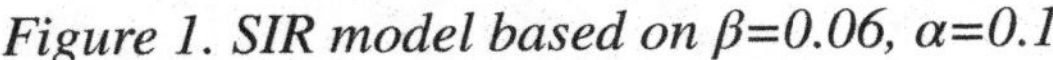

Figure 1. SIR model based on β=0.06, α=0.1

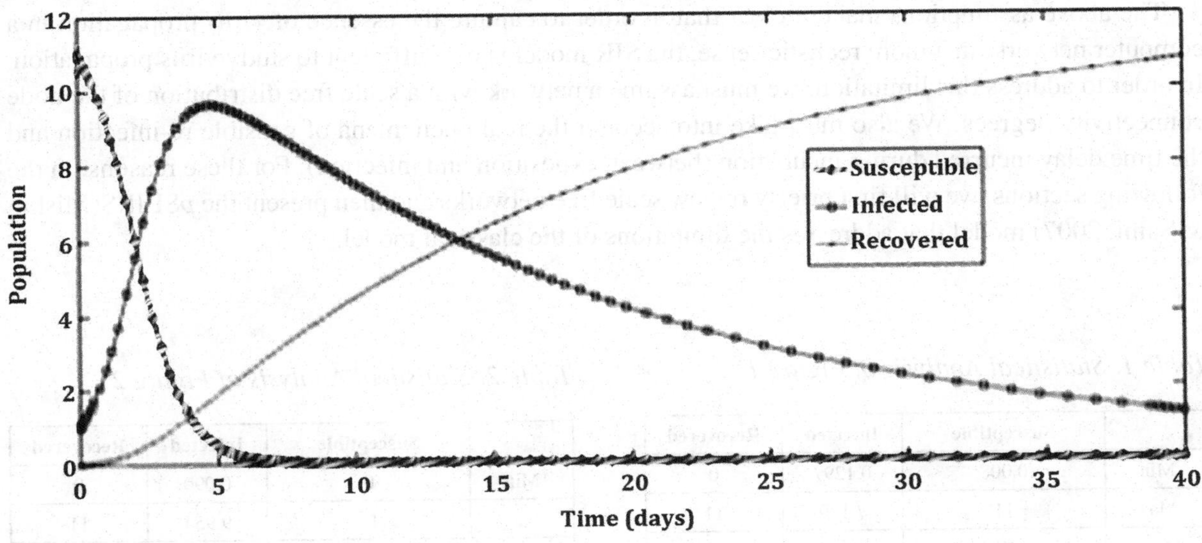

Figure 2. SIR model based on β=0.1, α=0.2

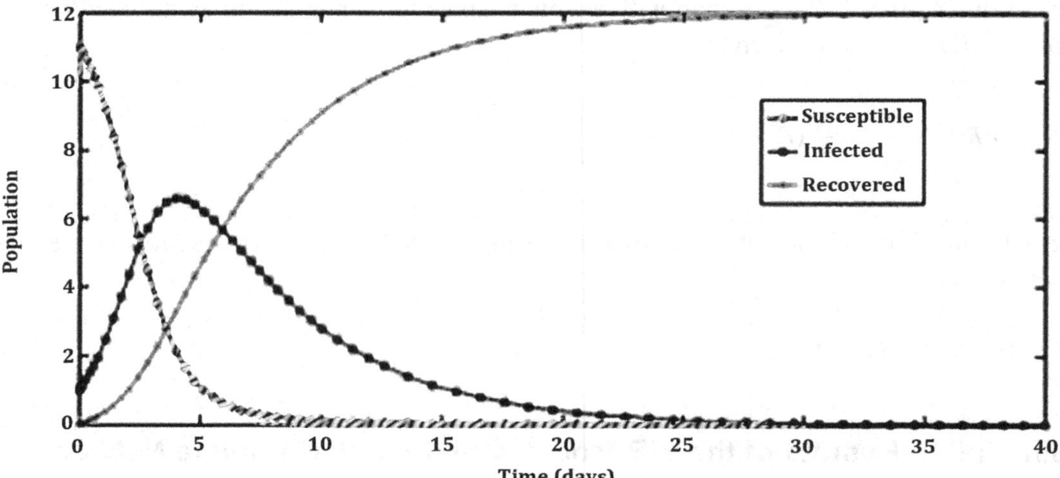

group. Information such as the maximum, minimum, and mean rate of the infected population can also be determined in each class. A statistical analysis of the cases in Figures 1 and 2 are presented in Table 1 and Table 2.

This analysis is based on some crucial assumptions, such as:

- Once a node is removed or recovered from the infection, it develops immunity and it cannot be infected again.
- The population is homogenous and well mixed.
- There is no latency, i.e., there is no time delay between exposure to the infection and actually getting infected.

The above assumptions make it clear that in order to capture the essence of virus propagation in a computer network, in a more realistic sense, the SIR model is not sufficient to study virus propagation. In order to address this limitation, we must assume a network with a scale free distribution of the node connectivity degrees. We also must take into account the real phenomena of possible re-infection and the time delay incurred during incubation (between exposition and infection). For these reasons, in the following sections, we will first briefly review scale free networks and then present the *p*SEIRS(Mishra & Saini, 2007) model that addresses the limitations of the classical model.

Table 1. Statistical Analysis of Figure 1

	Susceptible	Infected	Recovered
Min	0.008	0.1297	0
Max	11	7.189	11
Mean	3.619	2.522	5.859

Table 2. Statistical Analysis of Figure 2

	Susceptible	Infected	Recovered
Min	0	0.090	0
Max	11	9.954	11
Mean	1.965	4.832	5.203

3. APPLICATION OF PROBABILISTIC SEIRS MODEL

3.1. Scale Free Networks

Scale free networks were first observed by Derek de Solla Price in 1965, when he noticed a heavy-tailed distribution following a Pareto distribution or Power law in his analysis of the network of citations between scientific papers. Later, in 1999, the work of Barabasi and Albert (Barabási & Albert, 1999) reignited interest in scale free networks.

For example, Lloyd and May (Lloyd & May, 2001) generated the scale free network, depicted in Figure 3, using the network generating algorithm of Barabasi and Albert (Barabási & Albert, 1999). There are 110 nodes that are colored according to their connectivity degree in red, green, blue, and yellow, with the most highly connected nodes colored in blue. It is worth noting that there are only a few highly connected nodes, while the majority of the nodes have only a few connections. Thus, in a classical scale free network, the connectivity of a node follows a power law distribution (Lloyd & May, 2001).

3.2. Probabilistic SEIRS Model: *p*SEIRS

In the time delay model, parameter, γ, represents the probability of spreading the infection in one contact. It is obvious that the rate of propagation is proportional to the connectivity of the node. The propagation rate does not change in time throughout the network.

In order to capture more realistic dynamics within real world scale free networks, several more variables compared to the classical SIR model are used and to capture more realistic behavior, delay is consider on the network. An additional stage (*Exposed*) in the model represents the phenomenon of incubation, leading to a delay between susceptibility to infection and actual infection. The Exposed stage makes

Figure 3. Example of a scale free network

the model a SEIR model instead of a SIR model. Furthermore, the *p*SEIRS model is different from the classical SEIRS model (the latter is obtained for an immunity probability $p = 1$). The resulting model is described in terms of the following variables and constants:

$N(t)$: Total Population size
$S(t)$: Susceptible Population
$E(t)$: Exposed Population
$I(t)$: Infected Population
$R(t)$: Recovered Population
β: Birth rate.
μ: Death rate due to causes other than an infection by a virus.
ε: Death rate due an infection by a virus, it is constant.
α: Recovery rate which is constant.
γ: Average number of contacts of a node, also equal to the probability of spreading the virus in one contact.
ω: Latency period or time delay, which is a constant i.e., the time between the exposed and infected stages.
τ: Period of temporary immunity, which is a positive constant.
p: Probability of temporary immunity of a node after recovery.

Once an infection is introduced into a network, its nodes will become *susceptible* to the infection and, in due course, will get *infected*. Once a node is *exposed*, an incubation period is observed, which is captured by the new time delay parameter, which therefore models reality better: any infection goes through an incubation period before it propagates. After infection, anti-virus software may be executed to treat an infected node, thus providing it with *temporary immunity*. It is important to realize that there is no permanent immunity in a real network, thus an immune node may revert to the *susceptible* stage again. All these stages of infection from *susceptible* to *recovered*, and the phases in between, are shown in Figure 4.

The *p*SEIRS model in Figure 4 works under the following assumptions:

Figure 4. Flow of infection in a SEIRS model

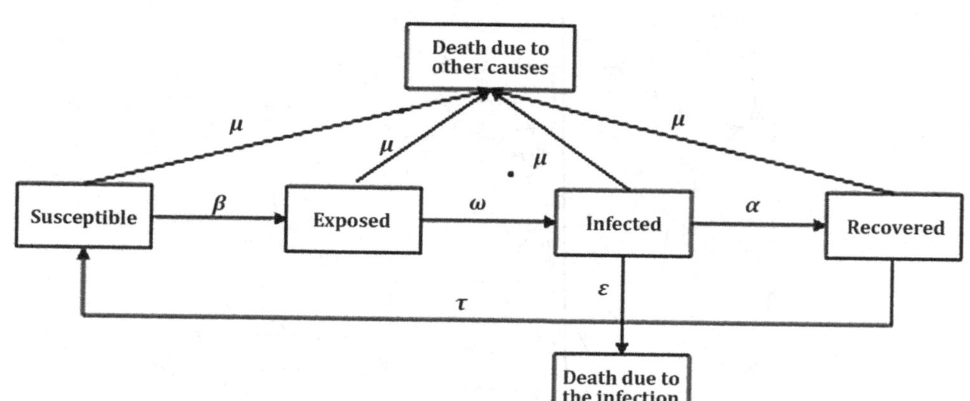

- Any new node entering the network is susceptible.
- The death rate of a node, when the death is due to other reasons that are separate from virus infection, is constant throughout the network.
- The death rate of a node due to infection is also constant.
- The latency period and immune period are constant.
- The incubation period for the exposed, infected and recovered nodes is exponentially distributed.
- Once infected, a node can either (i) recover and become immune with probability of temporary immunity p, or (ii) die from the infection with probability (1-p).

Once a network is attacked (some initial nodes become infective), any node that is in contact with the infective nodes becomes exposed, i.e., infected but not infectious. Such nodes remain in the incubation period before becoming infective and have a constant period of temporary immunity, once an effective anti-virus treatment is run. The total population size is expressed as

$$N(t) = S(t) + I(t) + E(t)\,R(t) \tag{4}$$

Also, it is important to understand that the infection remains in the network for at least $\kappa = max\,(\tau, \omega)$, so that we have an initial perturbation period. The model in Figure 3, has the following form for $t > \tau$:

$$\frac{dS(t)}{dt} = \beta N(t) - \mu S(t) - \gamma \frac{S(t)I(t)}{N(t)} + \alpha I(t-\tau)e^{-\mu\tau}$$

$$R(t) = \int_{t-\tau}^{t} p\alpha I(x)e^{-\mu(t-x)}dx$$

$$E(t) = \int_{t-\omega}^{t} \gamma \frac{S(x)I(x)}{N(x)} e^{-\mu(t-x)}dx,$$

$$\frac{dI(t)}{dt} = \gamma \frac{S(t-\omega)I(t-\omega)}{N(t-\omega)} e^{-\mu\omega} - (\mu + \varepsilon + \alpha)I(t)$$

$$\frac{dE(t)}{dt} = \gamma \frac{S(t)I(t)}{N(t)} - \gamma \frac{S(t-\omega)I(t-\omega)}{N(t-\omega)} e^{-\mu\omega} - \mu E(t)$$

$$\frac{dR(t)}{dt} = p\alpha I(t) - \alpha I(t-\tau)e^{-\mu\tau} - \mu R(t).$$

Equations (5) - (8) are called an integro-differential equation system. On differentiating (6) and (8), we get the following:

The system of differential equations (5), (7), (8) and (10) is collectively called a differential difference equation system and we will refer to it as M1. That is

$$\left.\begin{aligned}
\frac{dS(t)}{dt} &= \beta N(t) - \mu S(t) - \gamma \frac{S(t)I(t)}{N(t)} + \alpha I(t-\tau)e^{-\mu\tau} \\
\frac{dE(t)}{dt} &= \gamma \frac{S(t)I(t)}{N(t)} - \gamma \frac{S(t-\omega)I(t-\omega)}{N(t-\omega)} e^{-\mu\omega} - \mu E(t) \\
\frac{dI(t)}{dt} &= \gamma \frac{S(t-\omega)I(t-\omega)}{N(t-\omega)} e^{-\mu\omega} - (\mu+\varepsilon+\alpha)I(t) \\
\frac{dR(t)}{dt} &= p\alpha I(t) - \alpha I(t-\tau)e^{-\mu\tau} - \mu R(t).
\end{aligned}\right\} M1$$

It is important for the continuity of the solution to M1 to have

$$R(0) = \int_{-\tau}^{0} p\alpha I(x) e^{\mu x} dx$$

It is worth noting that M1 is different from the model by Cooke and Driessche (Cooke & van den Driessche, 1996) because they do not discuss the probability of immunity when a node recovers from the infection. M1, on the other hand, is a probabilistic model; here, a node acquires a temporary immunity with probability p and dies with probability 1-p. M1 is also different from Yan and Liu (Yan & Liu, 2006) because their model assumes that a recovered node acquires *permanent* immunity, which may not be the case in real networks.

Theorem 1(W.O.Kermack & McKendrick, 1927): A solution of the integro-differential equations system (5-8) with $N(t)$ given by (4) satisfies (9) and (10). Conversely, let $S(t)$, $E(t)$, $I(t)$ and $R(t)$ be a solution of the delay differential equation system (M1), with $N(t)$ given by (4) and the initial condition on [-τ,0]. If in addition,

$$E(0) = \int_{-\omega}^{0} \gamma S(x)I(x)e^{\mu x}dx \quad \text{and} \quad R(0) = \int_{-\tau}^{0} p\alpha I(x)e^{\mu x}dx,$$

then this solution satisfies the integro-differential system in (5-8).

4. INFECTION FREE EQUILIBRIUM

Let D be a close and bounded region such that

$$D = ((S,E,I,R)\colon S,E,I,R \geq 0,\ S + E + I + R = 1) \qquad (13)$$

In (13), we consider the equilibrium of M1, when the infection $I = 0$, then $E = R = 0$ and $S = 1$. This is the only equilibrium on the boundary of D and we also have the threshold parameter for the existence of the interior equilibrium:

$$R_0 = \frac{\gamma e^{-\beta\omega}}{\varepsilon + \beta + \alpha} \tag{14}$$

The threshold parameter R_0 is a measure of the strength of the infection. The quantity $\frac{1}{\beta + \varepsilon + \alpha}$ is the mean waiting time in the infection class, thus R_0 is the mean number of contacts of an infection during the mean time in the infection class. Asymptotically, as time $t \rightarrow \infty$, we get an infection free equilibrium (Cooke & van den Driessche, 1996).

The system of equations in M1 will always reach a disease free equilibrium if $R_0 < 1$, thus all the solutions starting in D will approach the disease free equilibrium. On the other hand, when $R_0 > 1$, we have an endemic equilibrium meaning that the infection will not die off in the long run.

4.1. Simulation Results with the *p*SEIRS Model

The dynamic behavior of the system M1 is presented in Figure 5, with the following values: β=0.330, μ=0.006, ε=0.060, α=0.040, γ=0.308, ω=0.15, τ=30, p=1.

Under the above assumption, we find that the threshold parameter is $R_0 = 7.77$. Hence, the system is in the endemic state. We also have p=1, thus assuming that all the recovered nodes have permanent immunity. In Figure 6, we present the overall impact on the population with the above-mentioned parameters.

Figure 5. pSEIRS model

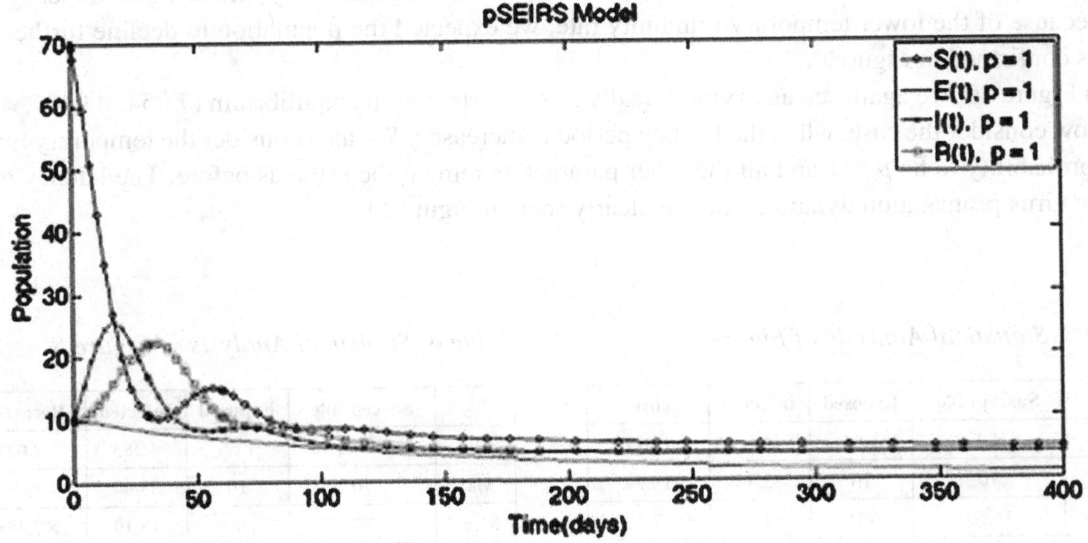

Figure 6. Population propagation under the pSEIRS model with p =1

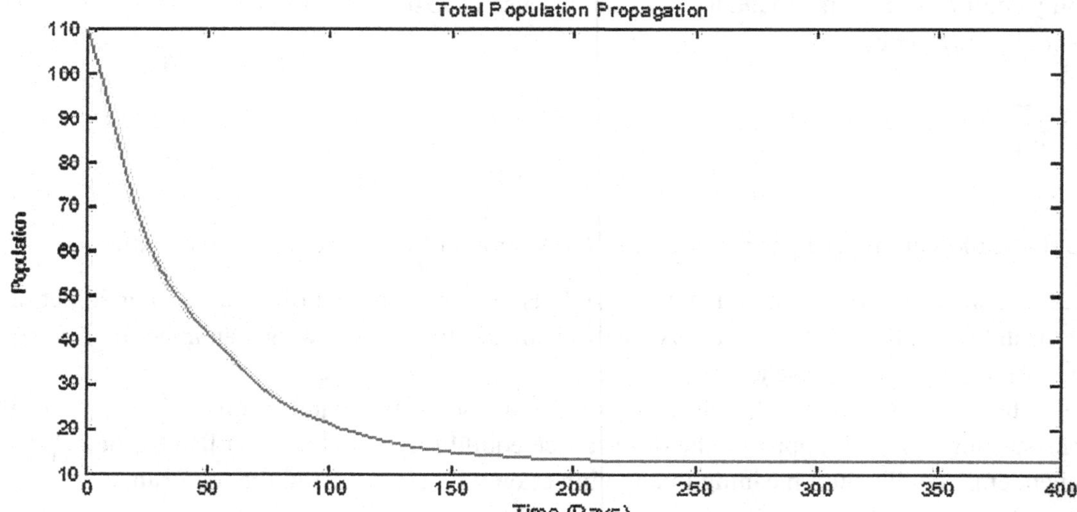

We notice from Table 3, that there are 33 nodes, which will get infected, and that the mean rate of infection is 12.37 nodes, while the number of recovered nodes is 20.00 with a mean recovery rate of 7.5 nodes.

Stability is an important issue with any dynamical system. In Figure 7, we present the phase plane portrait of our proposed model, which shows that we have an endemic equilibrium; hence our modeled system is asymptotically stable at the equilibrium (4.511, 0.9362, 4.161).

We now look at the dynamics with the temporary immunity probability $p = 0.4$. We can clearly notice that the recovery R (t) has declined in Figure 7 compared to Figure 4, since we have chosen a lower probability for temporary immunity.

We also notice from Table 4, that 34 nodes will get infected and the mean rate of infection is 13.00 nodes while the number of recovered nodes is 14.00, with a mean recovery rate of 7.255 node.

Because of the lower temporary immunity rate, we expected the population to decline further, and this is confirmed in Figure 9.

In Figure 10, we again see an asymptotically stable system at the equilibrium (7.054, 0.9407, 4.05).

Now consider the case, when the latency period is increased. We also consider the temporary immunity probability to be $p = 1$ and all the other parameters remain the same as before. The latency effect on the virus propagation dynamics can be clearly seen in Figure 11.

Table 3. Statistical Analysis of Figure 5

	Susceptible	Exposed	Infected	Recovered
Min	4.4	1.64	4.1	1.027
Max	70	10	33.46	19.94
Mean	16.59	6.16	12.37	7.5

Table 4. Statistical Analysis of Figure 8

	Susceptible	Exposed	Infected	Recovered
Min	4.216	1.66	4.283	2.027
Max	70	10	33.94	13.94
Mean	17.71	6.405	13.19	7.255

Figure 7. Phase Plan Portrait for temporary immunity probability p = 1 and latency period ω=0.15

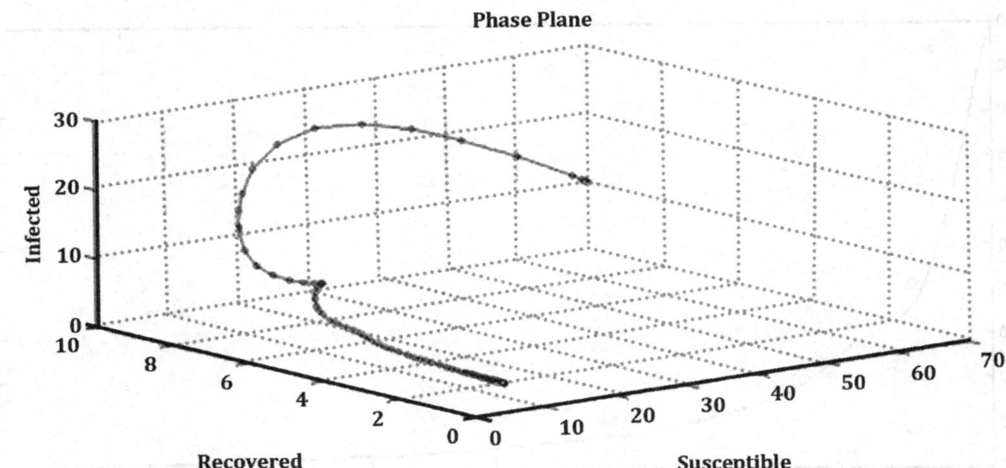

Figure 8. pSEIRS model

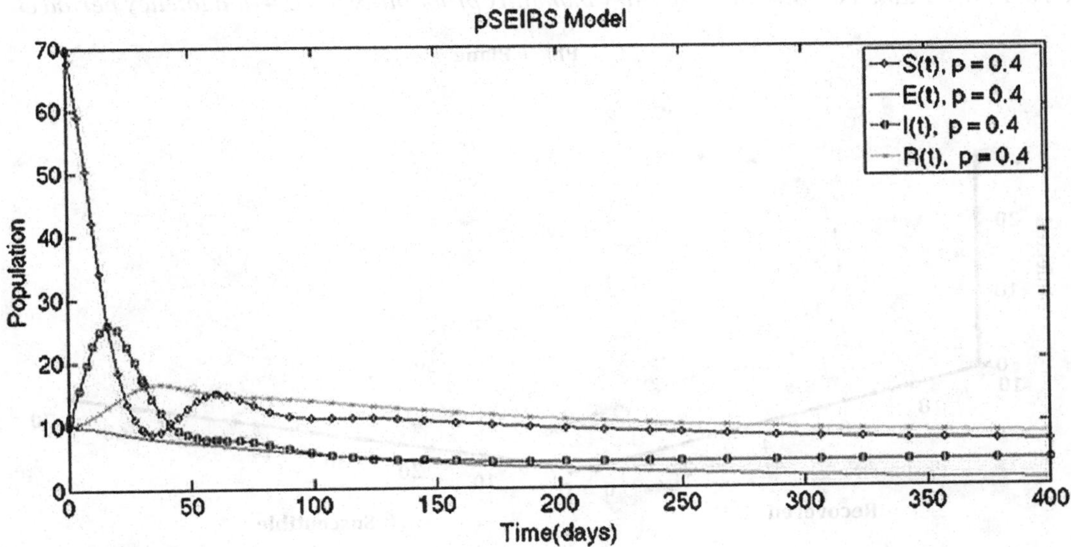

Infection is less likely to become an endemic in this case because $R_0 = 0.3703 < 1$. Instead, we expect to have an asymptotically stable system at a disease free equilibrium (1.118e-006, 20.63, 11.65), as shown in Figure 12.

4.2. Scalability of the pSEIRS Model

So far, we have used relatively speaking a small network of 110 nodes in a scale free network. We now consider a larger network of 5000 nodes, as shown in Figure 13. The network was generated in the Matlab environment using the Barabasi-Albert graph generation algorithm (Barabási & Albert, 1999).

Figure 9. Population propagation under the pSEIRS model with p = 0.4

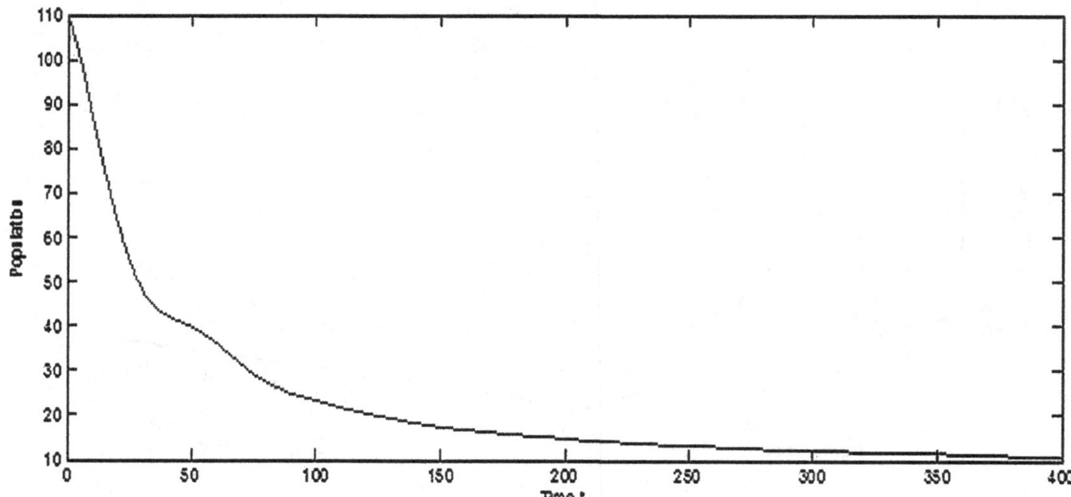

Figure 10. Phase Plane Portrait for temporary immunity probability p = 0.4 and latency period $\omega = 0.15$

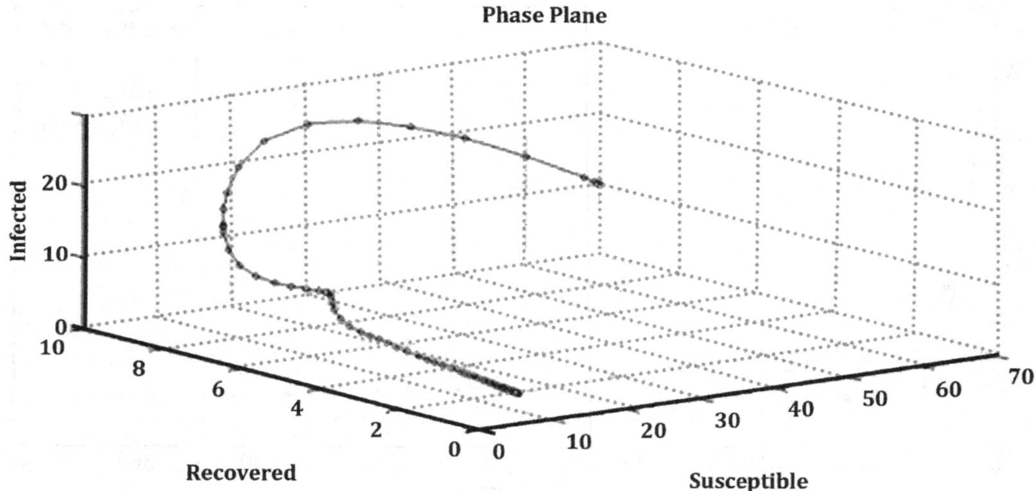

It is important to realize that it is very typical for most of the networks arising from social networks, World Wide Web links, biological networks, computer networks and many other phenomena, to follow a power law in their connectivity. Thus, networks are conjectured to be scale free(Clauset, Shalizi, & Newman, 2009). Here, the immunity probability is $p = 0.5$ and the rest of the parameters remain the same as before. So, under these assumptions, $R_0 = 8.621329079589127\text{e-}001 < 1$, meaning that the infection is less likely to become endemic. The global behavior of the proposed model is presented in Figure 14.

Moreover, we have an asymptotically stable system at a disease free equilibrium of (5.778, 2.51, 4.158). This can be seen in Figure 15.

The overall population propagation is presented in Figure 16, with $p = 0.5$.

Figure 11. pSEIRS model with ω=30

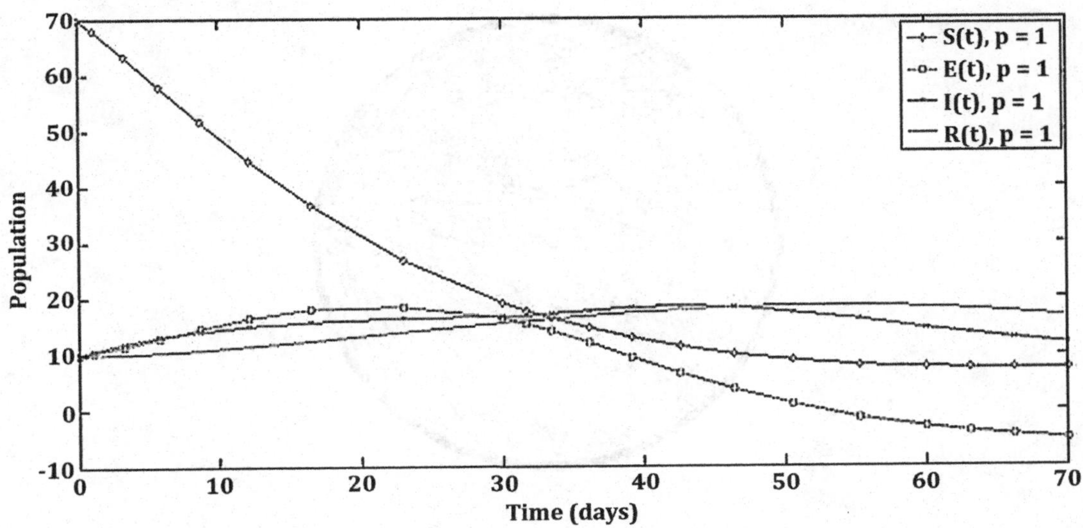

Figure 12. Phase Plane Portrait for temporary immunity probability p = 1 and a longer latency period (ω=30)

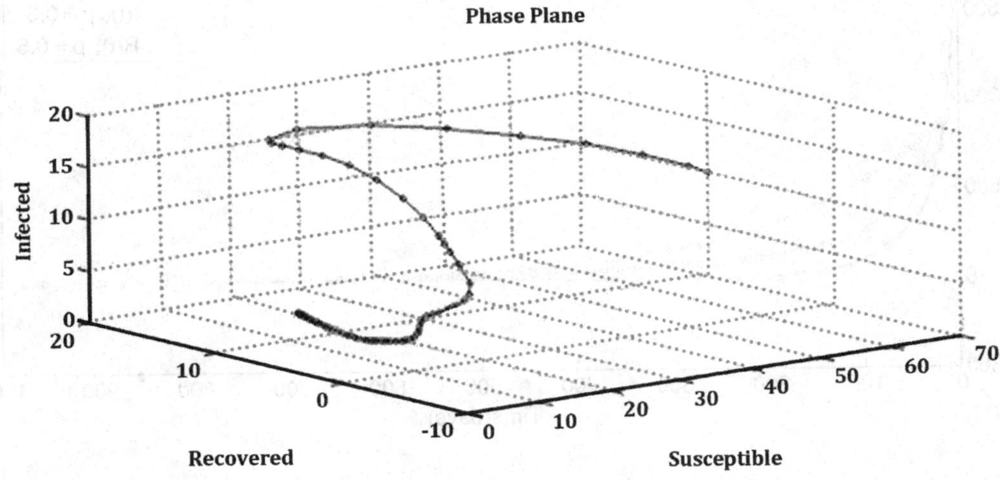

We now compare the *p*SEIRS model and the classical SEIRS model (the latter is obtained for an immunity probability $p = 1$). In Figure 17 and Figure 18, we can clearly see the difference between the recovery rates *R*(t) for the different models

In Table 5, we present a comparison of the model under different choices of the immunity probability *p*. The *p*SEIRS model gives a more realistic picture of the scale free network of 5000 nodes since it is unrealistic for all nodes to develop permanent immunity from getting infected with viruses, trojans and similar entities.

Figure 13. Scale free network of 5000 nodes

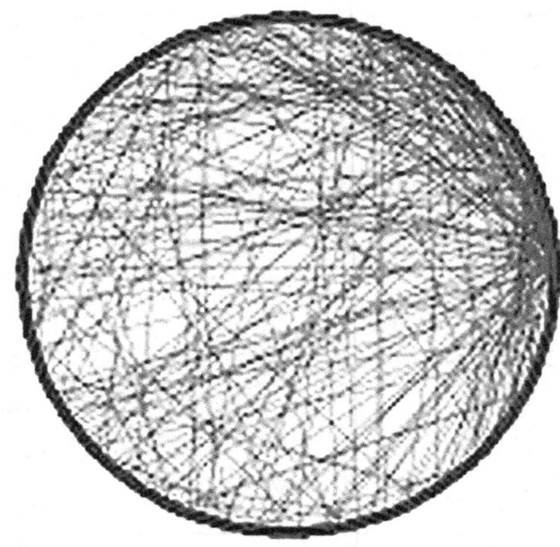

Figure 14. pSEIRS Model with 5000 nodes

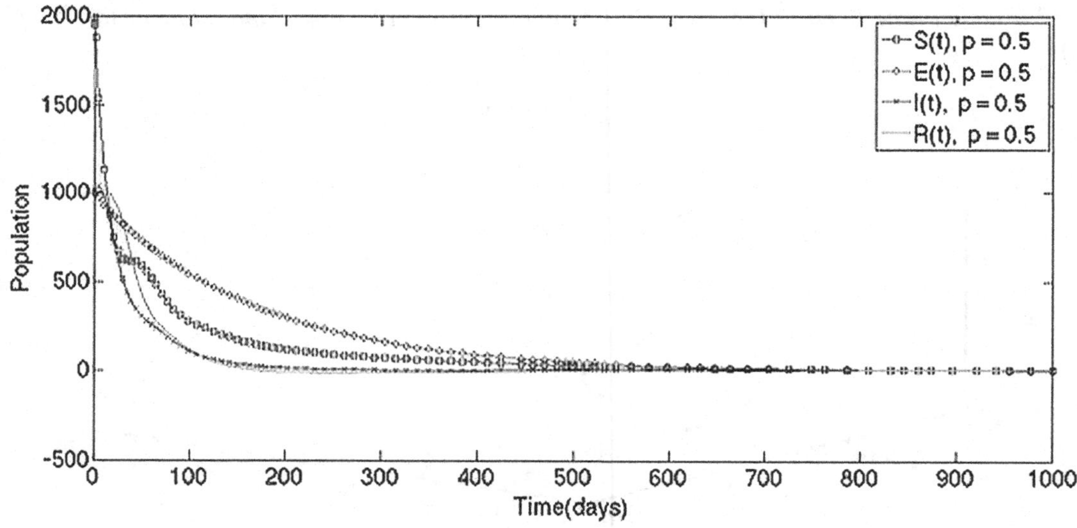

5. CONCLUSION AND DISCUSSION OF FUTURE DIRECTIONS OF RESEARCH

We have applied a variable population malicious object transmission model in complete and scale free networks, with constant latent and immune periods. The applied model extends the classical

SIR model proposed in (Lloyd & May, 2001) to a *probabilistic SEIR* type model in several directions: (i) it includes an *Exposed* class in addition to the *Susceptible*, *Infected* and *Recovered*, (ii) it furthermore includes a constant exposition period ω and constant latency period τ, (iii) when a node is removed from the infected class, it recovers with a temporary immunity with a probability p and dies due to the attack of the malicious object with probability (1-p). This is in contrast with Yan and Liu's model (Yan & Liu, 2006) which assumed that the node recovers with *permanent* immunity.

Figure 15. Phase plane portrait

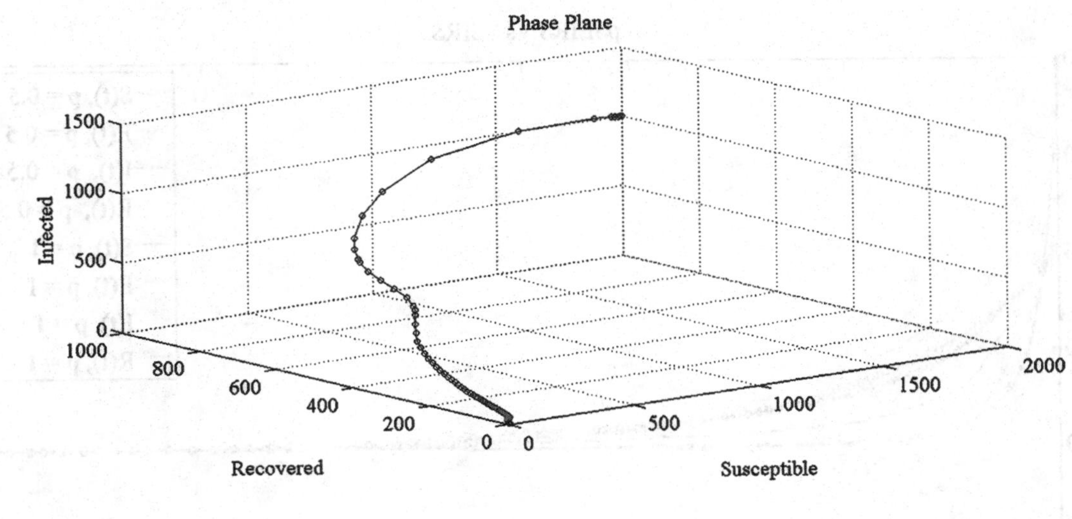

Figure 16. Population propagation under the pSEIRS model with p = 0.5 and 5000 nodes

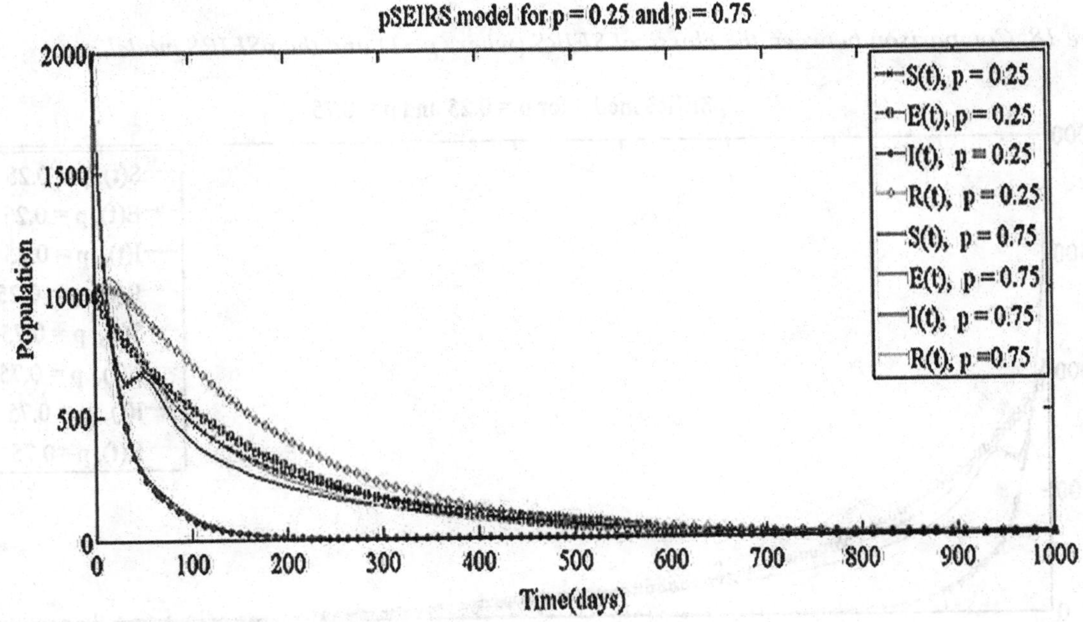

The model will be in an endemic state if the threshold parameter $R_0 > 1$. As ω increases, R_0 decreases and the condition of permanent infection will become less likely to be satisfied. Thus, the longer the exposure period of a system, the less likely it is that it will become endemic in the long run.

Another important information that we can gleam from the proposed model is the maximum number of nodes that will be infected. Knowing this number, we can assume that the most connected nodes are

Figure 17. pSEIRS model with p = 0.25 and p =0.75

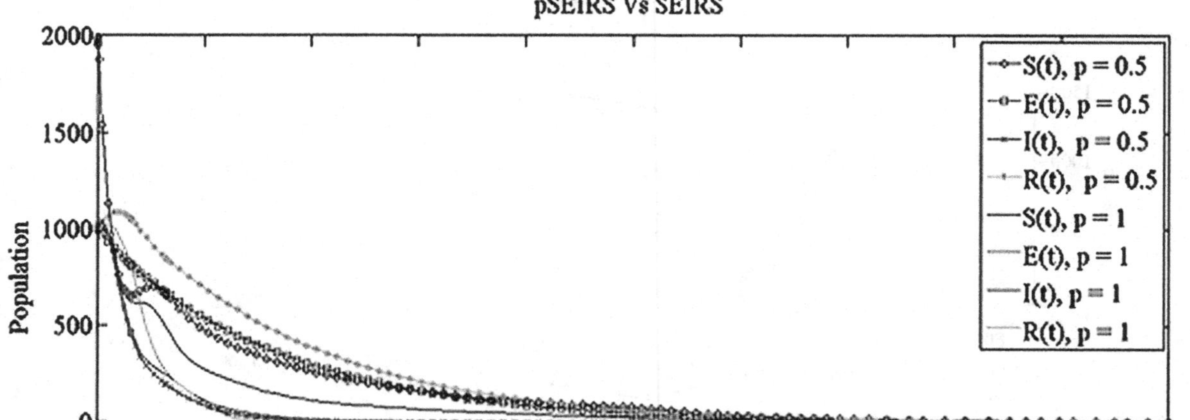

Figure 18. Comparison between the classical SEIRS (where p=1) and the pSEIRS model

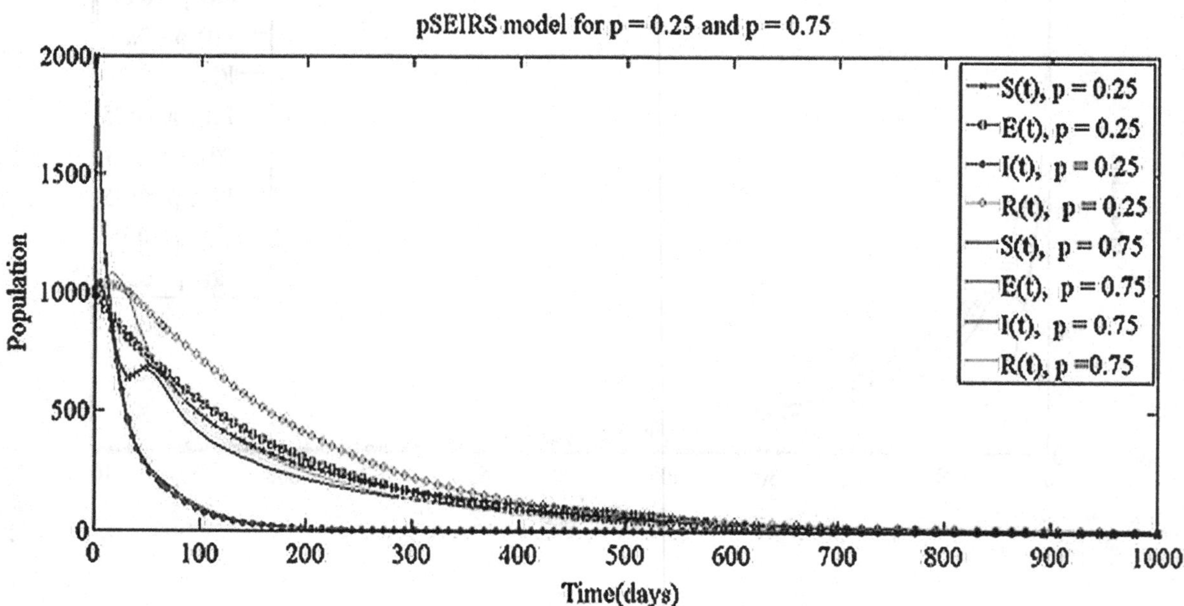

Table 5. Statistical Analysis of Figure 17 and Figure 18

Compartment	Probability	Min	Max	Mean
Susceptible	$p = 0.25$	8.008	2000	345.9
	$p = 0.5$	5.379	2000	327.1
	$p = 0.75$	8.41	2000	346.4
	$p = 1$	5.797	2000	318.3
Exposed	$p = 0.25$	2.509	1000	296.6
	$p = 0.5$	2.515	1000	322
	$p = 0.75$	2.504	1000	320.2
	$p = 1$	2.506	1000	349.1
Infected	$p = 0.25$	0.5927	1039	144.5
	$p = 0.5$	1.799	1040	163
	$p = 0.75$	1.212	1038	159.4
	$p = 1$	3.047	1039	175
Recovered	$p = 0.25$	8.63	1027	364.7
	$p = 0.5$	3.497	1000	253.9
	$p = 0.75$	9.491	1075	324.4
	$p = 1$	0.154	1018	196.5

the most vulnerable to an attack; thus special attention should be paid to these nodes. This information is of great importance to network administrators. Moreover, one can get the global dynamic behavior of the network under certain assumptions, as illustrated in our simulations.

The SEIRS and other related compartment models are good tools to study the global behavior of an epidemic in a network or a population dynamic. They are relatively simple to implement, yet they can still give valuable information about the network dynamics. One of the major issues for these types of models is setting the right set of values for the parameters, thus making them highly restricted in terms of their behavior. To make these models more realistic, it is important to make them as robust as possible.

Some of the possible ways in which future work in this topic can expand is to consider a dynamic rate of change, i.e., dynamic death rate, transmission rate, and latency period. Demirci et al. (Demirci, Unal, & zalp, 2011) considered only one such parameter. Ozalp and Demirci (Özalp & Demirci, 2011) also considered a non-constant population within their SEIRS model. This is a good starting point to improve the existing SEIRS model (Özalp & Demirci, 2011). Choosing a nonlinear incident rate in a SIERS model is also another direction. Though Ning and Junhong (Cui & Li, 2012) have done some work on this, one can think of improving their work.

REFERENCES

Aron, J. L., O'Leary, M., Gove, R. A., Azadegan, S., & Schneider, M. C. (2002). The Benefits of a Notification Process in Addressing the Worsening Computer Virus Problem: Results of a Survey and a Simulation Model. *Computers & Security*, *21*(2), 142–163. doi:10.1016/S0167-4048(02)00210-9

Bailey, N. T. (1987). *The Mathematical Theory of Infectious Diseases* (2nd ed.). Oxford University Press.

Barabási, A.-L., & Albert, R. (1999). Emergence of Scaling in Random Networks. *Science*, *286*(5439), 509–512. doi:10.1126/science.286.5439.509 PMID:10521342

Clauset, A., Shalizi, C. R., & Newman, M. E. J. (2009). Power-Law Distributions in Empirical Data. *SIAM Review*, *51*(4), 661–703. doi:10.1137/070710111

Cooke, K. L., & van den Driessche, P. (1996). Analysis of an SEIRS epidemic model with two delays. *Journal of Mathematical Biology*, *35*(2), 240–260. doi:10.1007/s002850050051 PMID:9008370

Cui, N., & Li, J. (2012). An SEIRS Model with a Nonlinear Incidence Rate. *Procedia Engineering*, *29*(0), 3929–3933. doi:10.1016/j.proeng.2012.01.596

Demirci, E., & Unal, A., & Zalp, N. (2011). A fractional order Seir model with density dependent death rate. *Hacettepe Journal of Mathematics and Statistics*, *40*(2), 287–295.

Diekmann, O., & Heesterbeek, J. A. P. (2000). *Mathematical epidemiology of infectious diseases: Model building, analysis and interpretation*. Chichester, UK: John Wiley & Sons Ltd.

Hethcote, H. W. (1976). Qualitative analyses of communicable disease models. *Mathematical Biosciences*, *28*(3–4), 335–356. doi:10.1016/0025-5564(76)90132-2

Kafai, Y. (2008). Understanding Virtual Epidemics: Children's Folk Conceptions of a Computer Virus. *Journal of Science Education and Technology*, *17*(6), 523–529. doi:10.1007/s10956-008-9102-x

Kermack, W. O., & McKendrick, A. G. (1927). A Contribution to the Mathematical Theory of Epidemics. *Proc. R. Soc., 115*, 700-721.

Lloyd, A. L., & May, R. M. (2001). How Viruses Spread Among Computers and People. *Science*, *292*(5520), 1316–1317. doi:10.1126/science.1061076 PMID:11360990

Mishra, B. K., & Saini, D. K. (2007). SEIRS epidemic model with delay for transmission of malicious objects in computer network. *Applied Mathematics and Computation*, *188*(2), 1476–1482. doi:10.1016/j.amc.2006.11.012

Özalp, N., & Demrc, E. (2011). A fractional order SEIR model with vertical transmission. *Mathematical and Computer Modelling*, *54*(1–2), 1–6. doi:10.1016/j.mcm.2010.12.051 PMID:21076663

Perdisci, R., Lanzi, A., & Lee, W. (2008). Classification of packed executables for accurate computer virus detection. *Pattern Recognition Letters*, *29*(14), 1941–1946. doi:10.1016/j.patrec.2008.06.016

Yan, P., & Liu, S. (2006). SEIR epidemic model with delay. *The ANZIAM Journal*, *48*(01), 119–134. doi:10.1017/S144618110000345X

Chapter 9
SNAM: A Heterogeneous Complex Networks Generation Model

Bassant Youssef
Virginia Tech, USA

Scott F. Midkiff
Virginia Tech, USA

Mohamed R. M. Rizk
Alexandria University, Egypt

ABSTRACT

Complex networks are characterized by having a scale-free power-law (PL) degree distribution, a small world phenomenon, a high average clustering coefficient, and the emergence of community structure. Most proposed models did not incorporate all of these statistical properties and neglected incorporating the heterogeneous nature of network nodes. Even proposed heterogeneous complex network models were not generalized for different complex networks. We define a novel aspect of node-heterogeneity which is the node connection standard heterogeneity. We introduce our novel model "settling node adaptive model" SNAM which reflects this new nodes' heterogeneous aspect. SNAM was successful in preserving PL degree distribution, small world phenomenon and high clustering coefficient of complex networks. A modified version of SNAM shows the emergence of community structure. We prove using mathematical analysis that networks generated using SNAM have a PL degree distribution.

1. INTRODUCTION

Complex networks are comprised of sets of numerous interconnected nodes that interact in different ways. Complex networks are large, containing from a thousand to several million or more nodes which are connected by edges. In addition to being large, the structure of complex networks is neither completely regular nor completely random. The structure of a complex network results from the fact that complex systems are self-organizing. As a complex system evolves, interactions, usually represented as

DOI: 10.4018/978-1-4666-9964-9.ch009

edges, among its many constituent units, usually represented as nodes, result in an emergent structure with unforeseen properties. While complex networks do share common characteristics with respect to size, structure, and emergent behavior, there is no single general, precise, and accepted definition of network complexity(Boyd, D. M. and Ellison N. B,2007). Therefore, differentiating complex networks from other types of networks is difficult given this lack of an accepted definition. Network nodes and links can represent different entities and relations depending on the analyzed network. For example, in social networks the users engage with each other for various purposes, including business, entertainment, citation, movies, transport, banking, knowledge sharing, and many other activities. The widespread use of complex networks as models in different fields has made the study of complex networks and their structure an important research topic.

The study and analysis of data extracted from complex networks has revealed a number of distinct features and behavioral patterns that distinguish these networks. Awareness of these features can lead to an improved understanding of the network's structure and dynamics. Such knowledge can be utilized in different fields to answer questions such as: How can the current World Wide Web (WWW) structure be used to predict future connections between websites? How can one deduce new relationships or reveal potential networks' vulnerabilities? We might have perfect knowledge of the parts constituting the network, but its large-scale structure and dynamics may not be immediately obvious. Analysis of complex networks analysis can provide insight into the ties and relations linking nodes and an improved understanding of a network's dynamics. Such analysis can help enhance decision-making dealing with network management and resource allocation in different applications. Analysis indicates that certain statistical properties are common to a large number of these networks (Barabási, A.-L. and R. Albert,1999, Newman, M. E. J., 2003, Barabási, A.-L. and R. Albert, 2002). These are only some of the motivations that make complex networks an important research topic.

Recent enhancements in computational and storage capabilities have made it feasible to pursue these three areas of study. Researchers are now able to gather and analyze large databases resulting from interactions between different nodes in real world networks. These developments allow researchers to identify the properties of complex networks. Real-world network datasets are often proprietary and hard to obtain. Thus, researchers often study networks using synthetic datasets generated via mathematical models. Knowledge of the properties of complex networks is essential in modeling these networks. Additionally, altering the parameters in a network model leads to the generation of datasets with different properties. These datasets can be used for thorough exploration and evaluation of network analysis algorithms (Barabási, A.-L. and R. Albert,1999, Newman, M. E. J., 2003).

The study of complex network draws on concepts from graph theory. In graph theory, a network is represented as a set of vertices joined by edges. An edge implies the existence of a relation between the connected vertices. Networks or graphs are of different types. Graphs may be static (for a constant network size) or dynamic (where network size changes with time) (Newman, M. E. J.,2003).

Networks can also be classified as heterogeneous or homogeneous. A heterogeneous network is a network with different types of vertices, while a homogeneous network is a network that has only one type of vertices. Edges in a network or a graph can be weighted (each edge is assigned a different weight) or un-weighted. Furthermore, edges can be directed (where edges have a direction associated with them) or undirected (Newman, M. E. J., 2003).

Using graph theory concepts, researchers have modeled the structure of complex networks and investigated how different structures can affect interactions in complex networks. Empirical studies of the statistical properties of complex real-world networks represented as graphs have led to the discovery of several common real networks properties.

1.2 Common Statistical Properties of Complex Networks

Complex networks represented as graphs have been shown to exhibit several common statistical properties, including degree distribution, average path length, clustering coefficient, and community structure. Recently, it was determined that some real-world networks, such as social networks, also exhibit the emergence of community structure (Barabàsi, A.L, R. Albert 2002). Of course, there may be other statistical properties that are important when analyzing or describing complex networks. (Newman, M. E. J, 2003) states that these additional measures can differ according to the type of the network and the topic being investigated. Thus, for the purpose of our work, we focus on the three statistical properties listed above and the emergence of community structure.

Small world effect means that for a certain fixed value of the nodes' mean degree, the value of the average path length scales logarithmically, or slower, with network size. A node's clustering coefficient C can be defined as ——the average fraction of pairs of neighbors of a node that are also neighbors of each other(Cutillo L.A., Molva, R. and Strufe, T.,2009), where C lies between 0 and 1. The average clustering coefficients in real complex network tend to have high values. Community structure emerges when nodes in a community have denser connections within themselves than to vertices of different communities (Barabasi, A.-L,R. Albert 2002). Degree distribution which is the fraction of vertices in the network with degree k follows a scale free power law distribution in real complex networks. Scale free power law distributions, P (k) ~ $k^{-\gamma}$, have a power law (PL) exponent γ independent of the size of the network and its values are in the range of $1 < \gamma < \infty$, (Boyd, D. M. and Ellison, N. B. 2007).

1.2.1 The Need for Mathematical Models of Complex Networks

There is an important need for devising a mathematical model that facilitates performing mathematical analysis on complex networks (Cutillo L.A., Molva, R. and Strufe, T.,2009),. Such mathematical models can be used to observe and/or predict how the complex network behaves under different scenarios. Mathematical models can also be used when real datasets are impossible or expensive to gather to generate synthetic datasets that may be used for network analysis. A good mathematical model should successfully mimic the modeled network's statistical properties. Several mathematical models have been proposed to mimic complex networks. The proposed models have been assessed to find out which of the observed real world network characteristics are incorporated into each model. The validation method for any of these models is based on performing simulations and statistical analysis of the networks generated based on the model and/or using theoretical approaches, such as continuum theory, the master-equation approach or the rate equation approach (Barabàsi,A.L, R. Albert 2002). .

The next section summarizes the three most influential models that have been presented for complex networks.

1.3 Most Influential Models for Complex Networks

Various models tried to find a faithful model for complex networks. The most influential models in the complex-network modeling field are: Erdo s and Re nyi (ER), Watts and Strogatz (WS), and Barabási and Albert (BA). Networks generated according to the ER random graph model have small average path length but they have Poisson degree distributions and are characterized by having clustering coefficients lower than that found in real complex networks (Newman, M. E. J., 2003, Barabàsi,A.L, R. Albert, 2002). Networks generated by WS small-world network model have a short average path length and a high clustering coefficient. However, it lacks modeling the scale free property for the networks' degree distribution (Newman, M. E. J. 2003, Barabàsi, A.L, R. Albert 2002). Thus, the scale-free power-law degree distribution of real complex networks was not represented in the ER or the WS models, rendering both models to be inaccurate in modeling the four characteristics of real complex-networks. This motivated Barbasi and Albert to induce the scale free property for node-degree distribution in their highly acclaimed model (Barabàsi, A.L, R. Albert 1999). The BA model uses a Preferential Attachment (PA) connection algorithm that reflects the belief that nodes usually prefer to connect to higher-degree structurally-popular nodes (Barabàsi,A.L, R. Albert 1999). . BA model succeeded in preserving the PL degree distribution and small world phenomenon of real complex-networks. Networks generated by the BA model show a power-law heavy-tail degree distribution, if and only if, the model has the following two properties; growth (where new nodes are continuously added to the network) and preferential attachment (PA). The BA model starts with a small number of nodes (m0), which is referred to as the seed network. A new node is added at each time step. The new node preferentially attach to other m nodes, (where m $\leq$ m0) using a connection function based on the old nodes' normalized degrees. Thus, new node i connects preferentially to an old node i having degree ki using a connection function (CF) based on the normalized degree of the node i given by,

$$\Pi\left(ki\right) = \frac{k_i}{\sum_j k_i}.$$

Networks generated using the BA model have a scale-free power-law degree-distribution and their average path lengths exhibit the small world phenomenon. However, BA model generates networks with a constant PL exponent value of $\gamma = 3$, unlike real networks where the exponent values differ according to the network type and ranges between $1 < \gamma < \infty$. Additionally, BA modeled network average clustering coefficient is lower than that observed in real complex networks of the same size (Barabási, A.-L. and R. Albert,1999, Newman, M. E. J., 2003, Barabási, A.-L. and R. Albert, 2002.

The ER, WS, and BA network models (Newman, M. E. J. 2003, Barabási, A.-L. and R. Albert, 2002). all fail to incorporate the emergence of the community structure property. Thus, none of the three models were successful in representing all characteristics observed in real world networks, namely, the small world phenomenon, scale-free degree distribution, a high clustering coefficient, and the emergence of community structure(Barabási, A.L, Bianconi, GL. 2001). Several models were introduced to remedy the shortcomings of the previous three models, as well as propose new network evolution algorithms. When evaluating these proposed models, the main focus was whether or not they succeed in incorporating the four properties of real world networks (Barabási, A.-L. and R. Albert, 2002). Since the BA model with PA (preferential attachment) was the only model that demonstrated a power law degree distribution, most researchers have adopted the BA model as their starting point and tried to modify the PA scheme used in BA model.

The purpose of many complex network models, especially earlier models, is to develop a mathematical model that preserves statistical properties of real-world networks. However, many more recent models focus on modeling the assembly, growth, or evolution of the network. The approach of modeling network evolution investigates how certain statistical properties emerge in real-world networks (Barabási, A.-L. and R. Albert, 1999). For example, the BA model investigates the mechanism responsible for the existence of a power law degree distribution. Many other models use another modeling approach which targets capturing the dynamics of an evolving network and allow observation of the statistical properties of these evolved networks. This modeling approach is based on the principle that if the model correctly captures the dynamics that occur during the network evolution, then it will capture the network topology correctly as well.

We observe the fact that nodes in complex networks differ from each other. Specifically, nodes, or entities, in real-world complex networks have different profiles and characteristics. We argue that nodes having different characteristics influence the density and the pattern of connections within a network.

Thus, our proposed models use the growth mechanism and incorporate the heterogeneity of nodes. This enables investigation of the effect of adding heterogeneity in our models on the properties of the generated network. We believe that adding heterogeneity to network generation models will succeed in generating networks that preserve the statistical properties common to real-world networks, unlike the BA, ER, and WS models. With our models, we try to generate networks with characteristics that resemble as much as possible the statistical properties common to some of the few real-world networks that have received attention from the research community.

Additionally, including heterogeneity of node properties or connection standards in the connection algorithms of our models makes them more suitable for generating the subset of complex networks that exhibit selective linking. Such networks are said to exhibit assortative mixing or homophily (Barabási, A.-L. and R. Albert, 1999). Thus, our research scope is focused on generating mathematical models for real-world networks that exhibit assortative mixing.

Assortative mixing is defined as a bias in favor of connections between network nodes with similar characteristics (Barabási, A.-L. and R. Albert, 1999). In other words, nodes tend to connect with nodes that are similar to them in some aspect. Assortative mixing is found in online social networks, webs of human sexual contacts, the WWW, the movie actor collaboration network, science collaboration graphs, and citation networks (Barabási, A.-L. and R. Albert, 1999). In online social networks, users tend to connect with users who are similar to them in some way, for example sharing interests or located in the same geographic area. Age, race, cultural similarities, and location are factors in choosing partners in webs of human sexual contacts. Language and subject matter play significant roles in the connections between WWW pages. Networks of collaborations between scientists or actors are affected by their interests, such as their research areas and genres of movies, respectively, location, and, language.

We expect that assortative mixing has a direct effect on the emergence of community structure, a not so frequently discussed statistical property of complex networks. Communities or groups of vertices that are similar in some way tend to have dense connections among each other and less dense connections with nodes belonging to different communities.

Although some heterogeneous complex network generation models were presented in prior work, these models rely on some assumptions about the exact nature of heterogeneity parameter. Examples of the heterogeneity parameters assigned for network nodes in prior work are attraction, age, and capacity(Newman, M. E. J., 2003, Barabási, A.-L. and R. Albert, 1999).). A few models (Barabási, A.L, Bianconi, 2001, Tao, S., Yue, X 2010,Y. Li, X. Jin,F. Kong; and J.Li, 2009) define general attributes for the network nodes. However, none of these models preserved all four of the defined statistical properties common to most real-world complex networks. Moreover, even the models that have been proposed for heterogeneous complex networks do not integrate the heterogeneity of nodes with other structural properties of the network in the analysis and connection algorithms for generating such networks. Also, many existing models are specific for the generation of certain types of complex networks and, therefore, are not general.

Thus, a general model for generating undirected heterogeneous complex networks with characteristics of real-world networks showing assortative mixing has yet to be found. Such a model should preserve the four statistical properties of complex networks. Additionally, the model should be capable of reflecting the fact that each node possesses many different characteristics. The different characteristics of the node should be represented as multiple attributes per node in the mathematical model.

2. RELATED WORK

Several researchers have proposed mathematical models that address the heterogeneous nature of the nodes composing a network. The success of these models in generating networks that mimic real complex-networks was examined by observing the statistical properties of these networks. This section will review a subset of these attempts.

Bianconi and Barabási in (Barabási, A.L, Bianconi, 2001) introduced the term node fitness to represent a node's ability to obtain connections. Their work was motivated by the observation that anode's ability to attract connections does not depend only on its degree (based on the node's age). WWW nodes that provide good content are likely to acquire more connections irrespective of their ages. In citation networks, a new paper with a breakthrough is likely to have more connections than older papers. Thus, each node should be assigned a parameter that describes its competitive nature to attain connections. In their model, node j upon birth is assigned a fitness factor η_j, following some distribution $\rho(\eta)$, which represents its intrinsic ability to attain connections. Bianconi and Barabási model followed the BA PA connection algorithm with a modified PA function. The model has the PA function value for connecting an old node j to a new added node i depending on the old-node degree Dj, and old-node fitness value η_j. Thus the PA function is independent of the new node parameters. When $\rho(\eta)$ follows a uniform distribution, the network degree distribution is a generalized power law, with an inverse logarithmic correction. The average clustering coefficient and average path length values of networks generated by this model were not calculated in Bianconi and Barabási's paper.

Taoa,*et al.*(Tao, S and Yue, X. 2010) observed that nodes with common traits or interests tend to interact. They introduced an evolving model based on attribute-similarity between the nodes. Each of the network nodes has an attribute set. Node attributes can be described by a true or false function as in fuzzy logic. Tao,*et al.* used fuzzy similarity rules to define a similarity function between attribute sets of two nodes. A connection is established between two nodes if their attributes similarities fall within a certain sector. Despite that this model satisfies the small world property; its degree distribution does not follow a power law.

Li,*et al.*(Li, Y, Jin, X, Kong .F and Li, J, 2009) argued that every vertex is identified with a social identity represented by a vector whose elements represent distinctive social features. The new node added at each time step connects with probability p to the group closest to its social identity and to the other groups with probability (1-*p*). The higher degree node is attached to the new node within a group using PA. Random linking to neighbours of the previously attached old node is repeated until the new node establishes its m links. Their generated network follows power-law degree distribution and used triad formation to produce high average clustering coefficients. The authors claimed that using triad formation produced high average clustering but they did not present values for it and they did not measure their generated networks' average path length. Additionally, the model did not increase the length of the attribute vector to more than one.

While (Balakrishnan, Hand Deo, N, 2006, G. Barabási,A.L,Bianconi, G, 2001,Tao and Yue, X 2010)based their connection algorithm on the PA attachment algorithm, some authors experimented with models that were not based on the BA PA algorithm such as those presented in (Kleinberg, J. M., Kumar, . S. R, Raghavan, P, Rajagopalan,S, and Tomkins, A, 1999) and (Krapivsky P.L and Redner, S, 2001). Kleinberg,*et al.*(Kleinberg, J. M., Kumar, . S. R, Raghavan, P, Rajagopalan,S, and Tomkins, A, 1999) used a copying mechanism which entails randomly choosing a node then connecting its m links to neighbours of other randomly chosen nodes. The model was found to preserve power-law distributions using heuristics only. They argued that analytical tools were unable to prove this conclusion, because the copying mechanism generated dependencies between random variables. Krapivsky, *et al.*in (Krapivsky P.L and Redner, S, 2001) argued that an author, in a citation network, citing a paper is most likely going to cite one of its references as well. In their model, when a new node i is added to the network, its edge attaches to a randomly chosen node j with probability (1-r). Then with probability r this edge from the new node i is redirected to the ancestor node o of the previous randomly chosen node j. The rate equations of the model show that it has a power-law degree distribution with degree exponent magnitude decreasing with the increase of the probability r value. Other statistical properties were not studied. These models were able to generate networks having a power-law degree distribution without using the PA algorithm of BA. However, their algorithm, where the node is copying its connections from a random node or connecting to the ancestor of a node previously connected to it, is not applicable for some types of complex networks. Additionally, the choice of the nodes from which the links are copied or the choice of the ancestors of the node is made randomly without regards to nodes-heterogeneous characteristics or their heterogeneous connection-standards.

Our paper (Youssef, B and Hassan, H, 2014) introduced the integrated attribute similarity models or IASM. IASM is a growing network model. It uses a preferential attachment algorithm to connect the nodes. The connection function, CF, in IASM depends on the attribute similarity between newly arriving nodes and old network nodes as well as the structural popularity of old nodes. Two different structural popularity measures are used in IASM simulation. In IASM_A, a node degree structural popularity measure based on the number of connections that the node has is used. In IASM_B, the structural popularity measure is based on the node's Eigen vector centrality. IASM preserves the power law degree distribution and the small world phenomenon, but it does not reflect the high average clustering coefficient and the emergence of community structure. We enhance both IASM models by adding a triad formation step which results in increasing the clustering coefficient values.

The present work introduces a general heterogeneous complex networks generation modelthat are capable to mimic different complex networks such as the Internet, the WWW, social networks, and food web networks. We present two concepts of node heterogeneity in these models, which are heterogeneity of node attributes and heterogeneity of node connection-standard. Heterogeneity of node connection standard is defined as the difference in each node's requirements to make a connection. Differences in the properties or the attributes of network nodes reflect heterogeneous node characteristics.

3. SETTLING NODE ADAPTIVE MODEL (SNAM)

As previously concluded, a general model for the generation of heterogeneous complex networks generation exhibiting selective linking is still to be devised. Thus, our goal in this research is to introduce mathematical models that accurately mimic the structure, dynamics, and evolution of heterogeneous complex networks. The proposed models are dynamic growing network models where nodes are added to the network at each time step as in the BA model. The models should be able to reflect the four common statistical properties of complex networks. To achieve this goal, we turn to the fact that nodes in complex networks are different from each other. Specifically, nodes, or entities, in real complex-networks have different profiles and characteristics. We argue that nodes having different characteristics influence the density and the pattern of connections within a network. The notion of node-attributes is used to highlight the node-distinct characteristics. The attribute set of each node is extracted from the characteristics or profiles of that network node. In our model, attributes are assigned randomly to each node upon its birth in (arrival to) the network.

Accordingly, the network graph G in our research is defined by a three-element set G ={V, E, A}, where V is the set of nodes in the network, E is the set of edges, and A is the set of attribute vectors defining the profiles/characteristics of all the network nodes. The idea of node attributes has been attempted before, but the proposed models in this work are novel in the following ways.

1. The models present a systematic way of defining attributes by incorporating the attribute set in the graph definition.
2. The proposed models are general and do not make any assumptions about the type of the network with assortative mixing.
3. To the extent of our knowledge, our models are the first to integrate the attribute similarity measure and one of the topological popularity measures in the computation of the connection function, CF. The connection algorithms uses values of CF to establish links between each new arriving node and the old network nodes.
4. In contrast to other efforts that considered node attributes, each node in the proposed model is assigned an attribute vector having more than one element. Each element in the attribute vector stands for one of node's attributes and their values are assumed to be statistically independent.
5. Our model, SNAM, introduces another aspect of node heterogeneity which is the nodes connection-standard requirement defined above. This concept of heterogeneity was not previously included in prior network generation models.
6. Through the proper choice of SNAM control parameters, the required values of network statistical characteristics can be achieved.
7. Modifying the function used in the connection algorithm of both models results in the generation of networks showing the presence of community structure.

SNAM departs from the classic PA connection algorithm presented in BA and proposes a new settling node adaptive model, referred to as "SNAM". SNAM reflects the idea that nodes are not only differentiated by their attributes, but also according to their connection-standard requirements. The connection-standard requirement of node x is its minimum acceptable value of CF for establishing a connection with another node. This minimum CF depend on both the value of the structural popularity measure of the old node and/or the value of attribute similarity measure between new added node and other network old existing nodes.

All of the proposed IASM models assume that all the arriving nodes have the same requirements for the existing nodes to which they connect. In real life this is not always true as some new arriving nodes can have lower connection requirements to existing nodes than others. Two newly-arriving nodes may have different connection standards, thus one node might accept an obtained CF value and make a connection to an existing node, while the other node might reject the same CF value and refuse the connection to the same existing node.

To reflect this behavior in our SNAM model, each new arriving node is assigned the value of its own intrinsic connection standard upon birth. This connection standard is used by the node only upon arrival to make a decision about which connection to make with randomly chosen old network nodes. If the *CF* value is equal to or higher than the standard of that arriving node and the arriving node has not yet established all its m connections, then the two nodes are connected. If the *CF* value is below the standard of that arriving node, no connection is made. Then the new node must test other old existing nodes to find the ones satisfying its standard. This is repeated for a finite number of tests. After this finite number of tests, the node must lower its standard if it did not complete all its m connections.

Thus, an arriving node *x* calculates its connection function value, CF_1, with an existing node *z*. If CF_1 is equal to or higher than the arriving node's *x* connection standard, then node *x* makes a connection to node *z*. If another arriving node *y* calculates its connection function, CF_2 with the same test node z and finds CF_2 lower than its connection standard. Then, node *y* refuses to connect to the same existing node *z*. The *CF* used in our SNAM model depends on the structural popularity of the tested existing node and its attribute similarity with the new node as defined for the IASM_A model.

To evaluate our models, we generate networks based on each model using MATLAB. For each of the generated networks, values for the power law exponent, the average path length and the average clustering coefficients are measured and assessed against values reported for a variety of real complex networks (.Barabâsi, A.L R, and Albert,1999, Newman, M. E. J., 2003). These statistical properties are the three metrics that validate that the three features of real complex networks are preserved in our models. Our mathematical models are general and apply for any complex network. Upon establishment of the mathematical model, we apply it to social networks as a proof of concept. Our choice of online social network is mainly due to their prevalence and their currently wide application in fields such as marketing, information, diffusion of epidemic diseases, and recommendation and trust analysis.

3.1 Model Assumptions

SNAM introduces the idea of heterogeneous connection-standard requirements of nodes. As previously defined, the connection-standard requirements of nodes represent the different requirements of the nodes when establishing connections. For example, two new users in a social network can have different standards for making a connection. One of these users can accept making connections with only very popular users while the other is satisfied with making connections with less popular users.

To the extent of our knowledge, all previously proposed models assumed that all new arriving nodes have the same connection requirements when linking to existing nodes. In reality, nodes may have different views of the same value of a connection-function (*CF*) that is calculated based on attribute similarity and/or structural popularity of the old node with which to connect. For example, a user in a social network can consider a *CF* value of 0.5 too low, while another user will consider the same value,

0.5, sufficient for establishing a connection. Thus, in SNAM, each arriving node, upon birth is assigned a value representing its own connection standard value *S* derived from a uniform distribution. An arriving node will calculate its *CF* values with old existing nodes. Hence, the *CF* values obtained will not be used to deploy the preferential attachment algorithm, but will be used to examine if the randomly chosen existing nodes will meet the arriving node's standards. A newly arriving node calculates the *CF* corresponding to randomly chosen nodes. This characteristic parameter *S*, $0 \leq S \leq 1$, represents the minimum acceptable value of the *CF* for the new node. All old pre-existing nodes whose *CF* values for the new node are below its standard cannot attach to that new node. An arriving node must then test other pre-existing nodes to find the ones that satisfy its connection standard. The new node establishes connections with the existing nodes whose *CF* values are equal to or higher than its connection-standard value, *S*. Similar to the IASM_A, the *CF* that is used depends on the normalized degree values and/or attribute similarity.

3.2 Simulation Setup and Parameters

The network starts with a seed network m_o. A new node arrives at each time step and each new node *i* is assigned a random connection-standard value S_i, where $0 < S_i$ 1. If, for a chosen existing node *j*, the CF_{ij} value exceeds or is equal to S_i, then node *i* establishes a connection to *j*. Otherwise, *i* rejects the connection to *j* and another existing node is tested.

This testing of other existing nodes continues until the new node achieves its predefined *m* connections or reaches its maximum number of tests, *NoT*. If node *i* reaches its maximum number of tests, *NoT*, and it still did not make its *m* connections, then arriving node *i* reduces its connection standard by a certain percentage and the testing of randomly chosen existing nodes is resumed. The reduced standard-connection value, $S_{i,reduced}$, is determined as follows.

$S_{ireduced} = S_i \times (1\text{-}€)$, where $€ < 1.0$

In the SNAM model, we experiment with the maximum number of tests *NoT* allowed for the arriving node *i* before it has to lower its connection-standard if node *i* has not established its *m* connections during the *NoT* tests. The models starts with a seed network of size $m_o = 5$. The network size grows as new nodes arrive to the network, until reaching a predetermined final size of N nodes. In our simulation N= 1000. Each newly arriving node has to establish m links with the existing network nodes, where m=m_o=5. Each new node in the network is randomly assigned an attribute vector of length $L = 10$, whose elements are derived from a uniform distribution. Simulation parameter values used are summarized in Table 1 and $€ = 0.1$. We choose this value for € because higher € values would make the nodes reduce their standard more rapidly. This will decrease the effect of the presence of the node's connection-standard on the generated network. Thus, when € approaches the value of one, the generated network approaches a network generated with no connection standards. The algorithm is shown in the flow chart in Figure 1.

Table 1. Simulation parameter values

m_o	m	L	N
5	5	10	1000

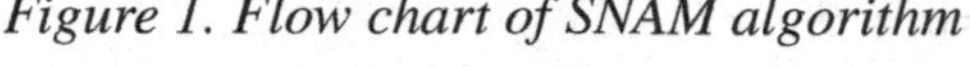

Figure 1. Flow chart of SNAM algorithm

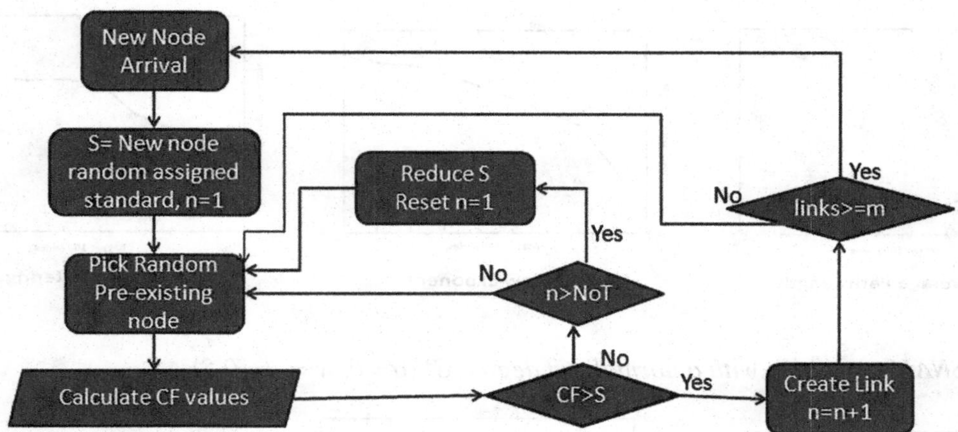

Number of trials *NoT*, as shown in flowchart, is a very important SNAM parameter having an integer value, *NoT*>1whose maximum is the current size of the network. This maximum implies testing the *CF* values for all network-nodes. Thus, the value of *NoT* depends on the current size (*CS*) of the network. The *NoT* is increased by one whenever the (*CS*) of network reaches certain predefined milestones. The value of the CS at which these milestones occur depends on the final size of the network (*N*) and the number of milestones (*NM*) occurring during network evolution. The number of milestones (NM) has two extreme values. The smallest number of milestones is one which is reached when the network reaches its final size *N*, implying use of constant NoT during network growth. The largest number of milestones occurs when we consider each node arrival to the network as a milestone. Thus, *NM* ranges between 1 and *N*. The higher the value of *NM*, the more rapid is the increase in *NoT*.

Our experimentation with the *NoT* parameter indicated that a rapid increase of *NoT* with network growth results in the presence of irregularities in the statistical characteristics of the generated network. Here, the number of milestones occurring during the arrival of every 100 nodes to the network is varied between 1 and 10. Thus, an *NM* value of 5 means that the *NoT* is increased by one 5 times during the arrival of 100 nodes to the network (i.e *NoT* increased by one each time 20 new nodes arrive to the network). This choice was made to avoid irregular statistical properties and has proven to give satisfactory results as shown in Figure 2a-c, Figure 3a-c, Figure 4a-c, and Figure 5a-c. The same values for parameters m_o, m, L, and N as used for the simulation IASM_A are used for the simulation of SNAM. The initial value of *NoT* in this simulation is 2 and $1 \leq NM \leq 10$. The connection function *CF* depends on the existing node degree D_i as in IASM_A, namely:

$$CF = (\alpha) + (\beta) + (w), \text{ where } \alpha + w + \beta = 1.0,\ 0 \leq \alpha \leq 1,\ 0 \leq w \leq 1, \text{ and } 0 \leq \alpha \leq 1. \quad (1)$$

3.3 Simulation Results

Results for three combinations of coefficients α, β and w are shown in Figures 2 through 4.

Figure 2. SNAM algorithm with a normalized degree CF (α =w = 0, β=1)

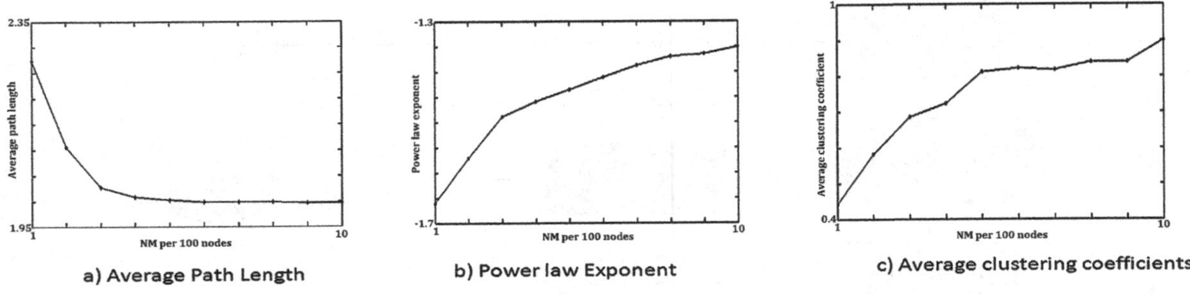

a) Average Path Length

b) Power law Exponent

c) Average clustering coefficients

Figure 3. SNAM algorithm with a normalized degree CF(α= 0, w = β= 0.5)

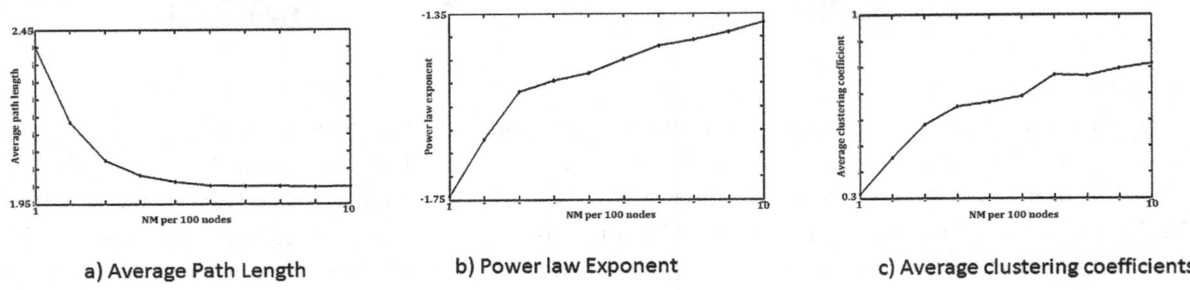

a) Average Path Length

b) Power law Exponent

c) Average clustering coefficients

Figure 4. SNAM algorithm with a normalized degree CF(α =1, w = β= 0)

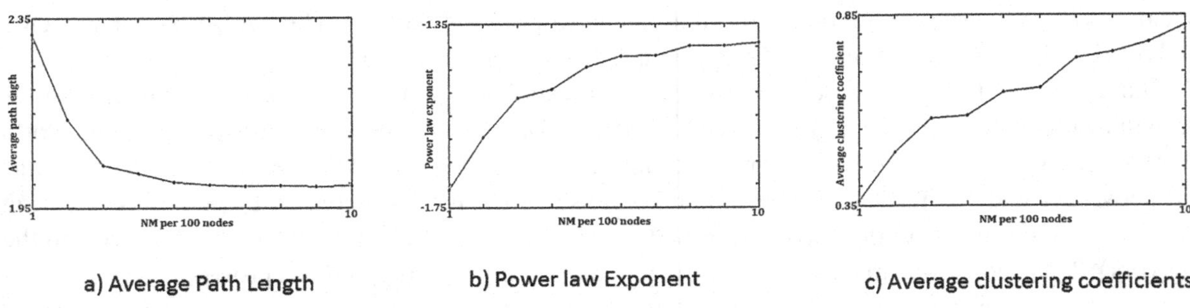

a) Average Path Length

b) Power law Exponent

c) Average clustering coefficients

Figure 5. Networks generated using SNAM algorithm with varying CF coefficient values

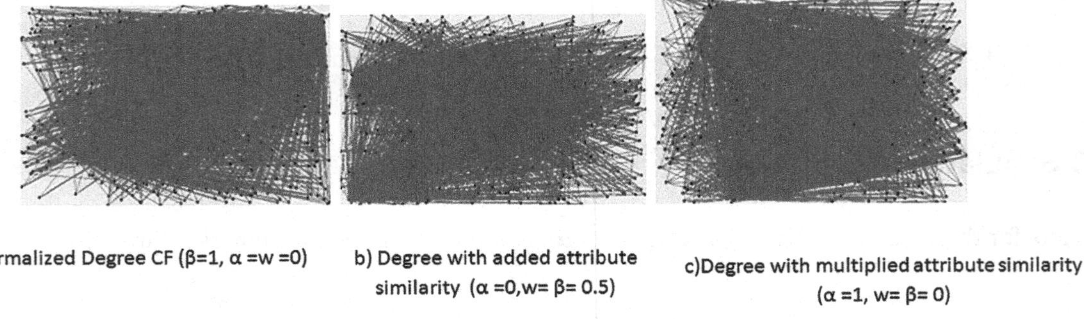

a) Normalized Degree CF (β=1, α =w =0)

b) Degree with added attribute similarity (α =0,w= β= 0.5)

c)Degree with multiplied attribute similarity (α =1, w= β= 0)

3.4 Analysis of Results

Figures 2a, 3a, and 4a show the average path length. The results indicate that the small world effect is preserved for the three combinations of α, β and w. The average path length decreases with increasing *NM*. The average path length saturates at the value of 2 when *NM*>4 for the three combinations of α, β and w. The resultant average path length for '*N*' sized network generated by SNAM is less than that for the same sized network generated by IASM. The lower average path length of SNAM makes the networks generated using it more reliable and fault tolerant.

Figures 2b, 3b, and 4b show that the magnitude of the PL exponents(γ) for the three variations remains in the range of $1.35 \leq \gamma \leq 1.75$, which is consistent with values found in real networks (Cutillo, A, and Molva, R. and Strufe, T, 2009),, R. Albert and A.L. Barabàsi,2002). At *NM* =1, *NoT*'s value remains constant, the PL exponent values are 1.68, 1.72, and 1.69 for 2(b), 3(b), and 4(b) respectively. Additionally, the magnitudes of the PL exponent saturates at values close to γ = 1.35 with increasing *NM*. This leads us to believe that the variation of the *CF* terms here had a minor effect on the obtained PL exponent values. However, increasing the *NM* values has led to the decrease of γ magnitudes,

The average clustering coefficient values increase with increasing *NM* for the three CF variations as shown in Figures 2c, 3c, and 4c. The average clustering coefficient reaches much higher values than those of the BA model or our IASMs. The clustering coefficients in Figure 2c, when the *CF* depends on the test-nodes normalized degree value, achieve higher values than those shown in Figures 3c and 4c when the *CF* integrates the attribute similarity measure with the normalized degree. The choice of the *CF* coefficient values has a direct effect on the obtained average clustering coefficients unlike when we used TFS for increasing the average clustering coefficients in IASM.

Generally, the increase of *NM* led to the increase of higher degree nodes(hubs) which is reflected by the decrease of γ magnitudes. Additionally, the formation of hubs increases the triples in the network which can affect the obtained values of the average clustering coefficient. Results indicate that the number of average clustering coefficient values increases with the increase of *NM*. Also, having hubs in the network can be beneficial in decreasing the APL as upon reaching a hub a network can reach many other nodes easily.

The SNAM generation model has preserved the PL degree distribution, has a small average path length, and has high clustering coefficient values. The value of parameter *NM* value can be used to generate a variety of complex networks with specific values of the clustering coefficient, the average path length, and the PL exponent. . For example using the *CF* depending solely on the normalized degree, we can generate networks with different statistical properties. For *NM*= 2, the average path length equals 2.1, the PL exponent has the magnitude of 1.56, and the average clustering coefficient has the value of 0.68. Increasing *NM* to 4 gives the values of 2, 1.4, and 0.82 for the average path length, PL exponent, and the average clustering coefficient respectively. Thus, we can change the used '*NM* 'value to generate a complex network with specific statistical properties.

Examples of the generated networks using SNAM are shown in Figure 5 for the three combinations of the coefficients α, β and w used in simulation, Figures 2, 3, 4 but for final node size N=500 and NM= 10.

As previously mentioned, node's connection-standard is reduced by a step of value €. When € is increased, the connection standard is reduced at a faster rate. Thus, we experiment with the effect that changing the connection-standard reducing step € would have on the generated networks statistical properties. A 500 nodes network with CF coefficient depending on normalized degree (β=1) is generated with € taking the values of 0.1, 0.25, 0.5 and 0.9. From Figure 6a, b and c, we can conclude that at

€ =0.9, the presence of the connection-standard becomes less effective. The average path length AvPL values increases with increase €. The average clustering coefficient ACC decreases with the increase of €. The power law exponents PLexp becomes unstable at €=0.9. High € values would make the nodes reduce their standard more rapidly. This will decrease the effect of the presence of the node's connection-standard on the generated network. Thus, when € approaches the value of one, the generated network approaches a network generated with no connection standards.

The Figure 7 shows effect of final node size on its statistical characteristics. Figures show that for a specific value of the parameter '*NM*', the power law exponent and the average clustering coefficient are not affected by the increase of network size. Thus, the generated network follows a scale free power law degree distribution. Additionally, the average clustering coefficients does not change with the increase of the final generated network size which is a desired property.

Additionally, we investigate if the initial seed size m_0 has an effect on the statistical properties of the generated networks. As we can see from Figure 8a, b and c, showing statistical averages versus *NM* per 100 nodes, that the average path length is almost unaffected by the initial seed size. The effect of the initial seed size is more evident for the power law exponent and the average clustering coefficient values.

Figure 6. Effect of varying SNAM parameter € on grown network statistical averages

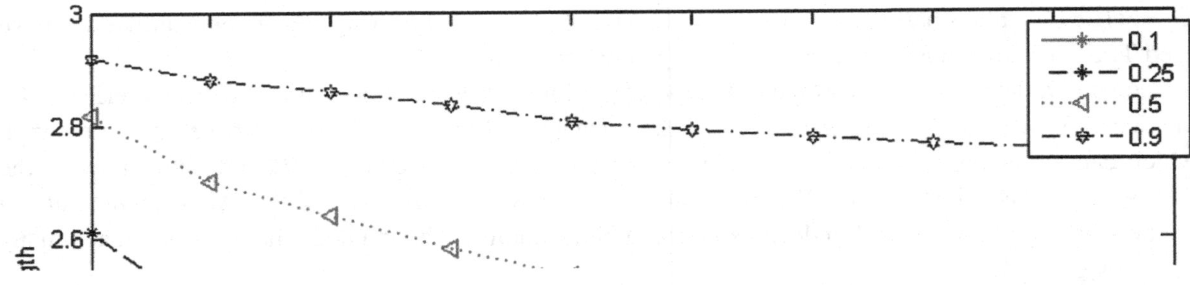

Figure 7. Effect of network size N on grown network statistical averages

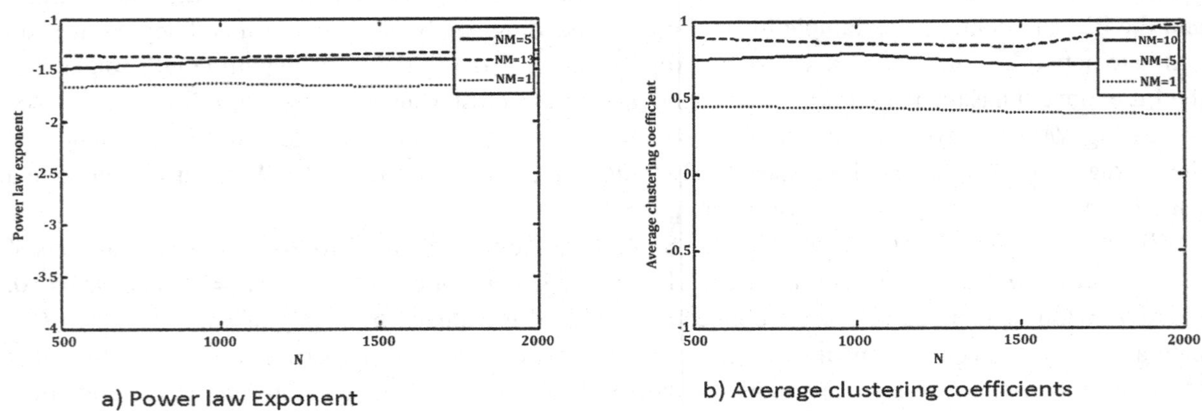

Figure 8. Effect of seed size m_o on grown network statistical averages

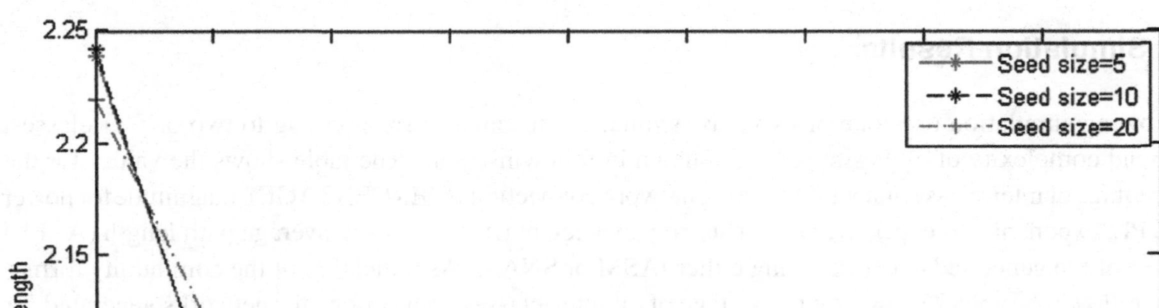

4. COMMUNITY STRUCTURE IN IASM AND SNAM

4.1 Model Assumptions

One of the characteristics of a real world network node is its belonging to a certain class. A node belonging to a certain class usually prefers to connect to nodes of a similar class. This preference leads to the existence of communities in the network where each community contains nodes of the same specific class. For example, users' age in a social network can affect their social circle as most of their connections are made within their age group. Another example is the users' gender where females or males prefer to connect to users of the same gender.

We argue that including this preference in our network generation model can lead to the existence of community structure as found in real social networks. The community structure characteristic is present when actors have most of their connections with actors of their same class while only few connections link actors of different classes together. We deploy this in our model by including a parameter CS_{ij} that describes the class similarity between the added new node '*i*' and the old test node '*j*' in the connection function. This class similarity parameter takes the value of 1 if the arriving node and the test node belong to the same class and is zero otherwise. This gives nodes belonging to the same class a higher probability to get connected. Nodes from different classes can still be connected but with a lower probability.

4.1.1 Simulation Setup and Parameters

This community structure models are modifications of IASM and SNAM models. The connection function, *CF*, of the modified models includes the added terms for normalized node degree, for normalized attribute similarity and for their normalized product in addition to a class similarity term. One, two or more nodes' attributes are used to compute class similarity between the nodes. This means having two, four, eight,,,,, or more classes. For arriving node *i* to form a connection with node *j*, the connection function *CF* is computed as:

$$\begin{aligned} CF = &\left(\alpha\right) \times Normalized[(degree\ of\ node\ j) \times (Attribute\ Similarity\ between\ nodes\ i,j)] \\ &+(\beta) \times Normalized\left(degree\ of\ node\ j\right) \\ &+(w) \times Normalized(Attribute\ Similarity\ between\ nodes\ i,j) \\ &+\left(\mu\right) \times (Class\ Similarity\ between\ nodes\ i,j) \end{aligned} \quad (2)$$

where, $\alpha + w + \beta + \mu = 1.0$, $0 \leq \alpha \leq 1$, $0 \leq w \leq 1$, and $0 \leq \beta \leq 1$.

4.2 Simulation Results

Following simulation uses one or two class similarity attributes corresponding to two or four classes, to avoid complexity of class similarity as shown in following table. The table shows the values for the percentage of inter-class connections among network connections (PERCENTAGE), magnitude for power law, PL, exponent (PL exp.), average clustering coefficient (AvClustr) and average path length (Av.PL) values of the generated networks using either IASM or SNAM. As indication of the community formation, following Table-2 shows the percentage of all inter-classes connections for networks generated for a subset of *CF* coefficients values, μwhere $\alpha + w + \beta + \mu = 1.0$

4.3 Analysis of Results

Increasing the weight of the class similarity coefficient μ in the *CF* has the following effects on the statistical properties of generated network:

- Decreases the percentage of inter-class connections between users belonging to different classes). Thus, enforcing the connections made between members of the same class (community). This emphasizes the presence of community structure within the network.
- Shows a small variation on the values of the generated PL exponent but the values are still within the exponent values range reported in (Cutillo, A,and Molva, R and Strufe, T, 2009, Newman, M. E. J., 2003, . Barabasi, A.L, R. Albert, 2002).
- Large values of class similarity coefficient μ increases the average path length to values slightly larger than 3, still smaller than 6, so the small world property is not lost. This increase in average path length can be explained to be due to addition of more constrains on the connections made between different users.

Table 2. Statistical properties values for 4 class generated networks using SNAM and IASM

CF Coeff. Values				SNAM				IASM			
Α	W	β	μ	Percentage	PL exp.	Av.PL	AvClustr	Percentage	PLexp	Av.PL	AvClustr
1.0	0	0	0	36.2531	-1.3294	1.994	0.7627	37.0709	-1.6691	3.256	0.0142
.975	0	0	.025	24.9397	-1.3453	2.057	0.6598	22.4373	-1.6671	3.272	0.0162
.95	0	0	.05	2.3933	-2.9327	2.957	0.2172	17.6844	-1.7010	3.285	0.0189
0	0	1	0	37.4496	-2.3210	1.998	0.7061	37.5077	-1.8169	3.200	0.0171
0	0	.99	.01	35.3781	-2.7901	2.017	0.7054	32.006	-1.8059	3.211	0.0165
0	0	.98	.02	33.7287	-2.1602	2.029	0.7295	27.9235	-1.7345	3.228	0.0161
0	0	.93	.07	14.7526	-3.4720	2.315	0.3577	17,1202	-1.7429	3.268	0.0204
0	0	.9	.1	1.0760	-2	3.409	0.1232	14.0462	-1.7036	3.297	0.0228
0	.5	.5	0	37.4497	-1.6435	2.000	0.6328	35.3259	-1.7244	3.247	0.0144
0	.47	.47	.06	0.4928	-2.3661	3.5973	0.1131	31.8473	-1.7276	3.2485	0.0150

- Increase magnitude of Pl exponent gamma (γ) which implies the decrease in number of higher degree nodes or hubs. This decrease in the number of hubs can cause an increase in the path lengths between nodes trying to reach each other. As the hub could act as a relay for shorter connection between multiple nodes. Thus, the increase in average path length can be a result of the decrease in number of hubs formed in the network.
- Decreases the average clustering coefficient of the generated network. We can see here further proof that the community structure and the average clustering coefficient are two different statistical properties unlike what some authors assume. Here, we can see that increasing the weight of the class similarity coefficient strengthens the community structure and decreases the average clustering coefficient of the whole generated networks.

The decrease in average clustering coefficient could also be tied to the decrease in the number of network-hubs. This decrease in number of hubs has an effect on the number of triplets formed in the network which is reflected in the value of the resultant average clustering coefficient of the network.

- Additionally, including the attribute similarity whether multiplicative (α) or additive (β) led to a faster decrease in the percentage of inter-class connections with increasing μ. This can be the result of our choice of dividing the network to different classes according to some (1, 2, or more) of the 10 nodes' attributes used in the simulation.
- Also, it is clear from different results that to reach same level of community structure, IASM requires higher values of class similarity coefficient than those required by SNAM.

Our SNAM community structure model preserved PL degree distribution, characteristic of the real world networks. Small world property is also still preserved. The model shows community structure as most of the connections are made between nodes belonging to the same class with only a small percent of the connections made between nodes of different classes .representing weak ties.

5. MATHEMATICAL ANALYSIS OF SNAM

5.1 Introduction

Simulation results that were previously presented show that SNAM preserves the power law degree distribution found in real-world complex networks. It was also shown that the exponent of SNAM's power law degree distribution depends on the model parameters, especially *NoT* which represents the number of tests performed to establish each of the m new links. This gives SNAM the capability to generate complex networks with different statistical properties depending on the value of *NoT* used during network evolution. To verify the power law dependence found through simulation and to better understand SNAM, here we analytically derive an expression for the nodes' degree distribution using the rate equation analysis method.

5.1.1 SNAM Analysis

To make SNAM analysis tractable, we need to make some modifications to previously described SNAM. For convenience, 'SNAM' refers to the version of SNAM as implemented and described previously and the modified version of SNAM used for the analysis is referred to as 'SNAM*'.

These modifications include the following:

1. In SNAM, the value of the number of tests, n_t or*NoT*, changes during the evolution of the network such that its value is incremented when reaching some predefined milestones during network evolution. Whereas in SNAM*, n_t has a constant value during entire network evolution. This assumption is made to facilitate the mathematical analysis to be able to reach a closed form equation for the degree distribution of the generated network. Having n_t incremented when reaching predefined milestones would not alter the power law degree distribution form of variation and its precise dependence on the value of n_t that is used. Thus, if the degree distribution power law dependence exists in SNAM*, it would still exist in SNAM, but in a more complex form. In particular, the value of the overall power law exponent for SNAM depends on the initial value of n_t and the number of network growth milestones. In SNAM*, the assumption that n_t is constant simplifies the power law exponent dependence to a dependence on a constant parameter n_t.
2. In SNAM, if node l reaches its maximum number of tests, *NoT*, and it still has not established its m connections, then arriving node l reduces its connection standard by a certain constant parameter €. The testing of randomly chosen existing nodes is resumed using this new reduced connection standard for the same maximum number of tests n_t. This sequence is repeated until the arriving node l completes its m connections. In SNAM*, we assume that the arriving node never has to decrease its connection standard. Thus, it is assumed that the probability of the arriving node failing to make its m connections during n_t trials is negligible. In the present analysis, it is assumed that the values of the arriving nodes connection standard are sufficiently low and that n_t is sufficiently large such that the assumption that the new node will establish all its m connections during n_t tests per link is valid and, thus, SNAM*approximates SNAM.
3. Whereas, *CF* for 'SNAM' depends on the normalized degree value and/or attribute similarity. The connection standard *CF*, used for 'SNAM*'in this analytic solution depends only on the normalized degree, similar to the BA model, for simplification of mathematical analysis. Note that, here, we are not modifying the connection algorithm. Making the *CF* dependent on the normalized degree only simplifies the calculation method of the connection parameter *CF*, but the connection algorithm is not affected.

5.1.2 SNAM*

SNAM* model starts with a seed network with m_o nodes connected by e_o edges given that $m_o \geq 2$ and $e_o \geq 1$. At each time step, a new node l is added to the network with m links to be connected to the existing network, one by one, where m $\leq m_0$. The connection function used here is as in the BA model, where a new node l will be connected to existing node I depends on the connectivity k_i of node i and is given by.

In SNAM, each of the arriving new nodes has its connection standard S_l which describes its minimum requirement when making connections to existing nodes. We perform a test to see if the randomly chosen old existing node connection function value exceeds or equals the connection standard of the arriving node. We note here that existing nodes are chosen randomly with replacement as finding a closed form for the probability density function after excluding previously tested existing nodes would prove to be challenging or impossible.

This test is repeated n_t times for each of the new node's m links, which is the number of independent tests used to find suitable exiting nodes to be connected to the new node, where $2 \leq n_t \leq$ number of existing nodes in the network.

The connection to a node can take place in any of consecutive tests.

1. Connection established on first test with probability p, or
2. Connection fails on first test and is then established on the second test with probability $(1-p)p$, or
3. Connection fails on first two tests and is then established on the third test with probability $(1-p)^2p$, and so on until
4. Connection fails on $(n_t\text{-}1)$ tests and is then established on test n_t with probability $\left(1-p\right)^{\left(n_t-1\right)} p$.

Since the tests are mutually exclusive, this link from new node will be made to an old existing test node i with probability $\boldsymbol{P}$.

$$\boldsymbol{P} = p + \left(1-p\right)p + \left(1-p\right)^2 p + \left(1-p\right)^3 p + \ldots + \left(1-p\right)^{\left(n_t-1\right)} p$$
$$= n_t + f\left(p^2, p^3, \ldots\right)$$

Since $p \ll 1$ is normalized, the higher orders of p terms can be neglected w.r.t. the value of $n_t p$. Therefore $\boldsymbol{P} \cong n_t p$.

Additionally, as explained above, we take small enough values of the node connection standards and high enough values of n_t so that it can be assumed that a connection will be made during the n_t tests.

Since this process is repeated for each of the m links to be established per unit step, the rate equation representing the rate at which the node i acquires edges can be written as follows.

$$\frac{\partial k_i\left(t\right)}{\partial t} = m\left[n_t p\right] = m\left[n_t \frac{k_i}{\sum_j k_j}\right] = \frac{m n_t k_i\left(t\right)}{2e_o + 2mt} \cong \frac{n_t}{2t} k_i\left(t\right) \, for \; t >>>$$

Therefore

$$\frac{\partial k_i\left(t\right)}{k_i\left(t\right)} = \frac{n_t}{2} \frac{\partial t}{t}$$

and by integrating both sides of the equation

$$\ln k_i(t) = \ln(t)^{\frac{n_t}{2}} + c,$$

where c is a constant

Since$k_i(t_i)=m$, since t_i is the time at which node i was added to the system

$$\ln m = \ln(t_i)^{\frac{n_t}{2}} + c$$

Therefore

$$\ln\frac{k_i(t)}{m} = \ln\left(\frac{t}{t_i}\right)^{\frac{n_t}{2}} \text{ or } k_i(t) = m\left(\frac{t}{t_i}\right)^{\frac{n_t}{2}}$$

To get the cdf of $k_i(t)$= the probability that a node i has a connectivity smaller than k,

$$P\left[k_i(t) < k\right] = P\left[m\left(\frac{t}{t_i}\right)^{\frac{n_t}{2}} < k\right] = P\left[t_i > \left(\frac{m}{k}\right)^{\frac{2}{n_t}} t\right]$$

Therefore

$$P\left[k_i(t) < k\right] = 1 - P\left[t_i \le \left(\frac{m}{k}\right)^{\frac{2}{n_t}} t\right]$$

Since seed size is m_o and one new node is added uniformly at each time step, $P(t_i) = \frac{1}{m_o + t}$. Therefore

$$P\left[k_i(t) < k\right] = 1 - \frac{\left(\frac{m}{k}\right)^{\frac{2}{n_t}} t}{m_o + t}$$

Probability density of node having degree k, $P[k]$ can be obtained from $P[k]$ as

$$P[k] = \partial P\left[k_i(t) < k\right] / \partial k,$$

$$P\left[k\right]=\frac{\partial P[k_i\left(t\right)<k]}{\partial k}=\frac{2}{n_t}\frac{\left(m\right)^{\frac{2}{n_t}}t}{m_o+t}\left(k\right)^{-\left(\frac{2}{n_t}+1\right)}.$$

Since at long times (stationary solution) $t >>> m_o$, $m_o+t \cong t$ and

$$P\left[k\right]=\frac{2}{n_t}\frac{\left(m\right)^{\frac{2}{n_t}}t}{t}\left(k\right)^{-\left(\frac{2}{n_t}+1\right)}=\frac{2}{n_t}\left(m\right)^{\frac{2}{n_t}}\left(k\right)^{-\gamma}$$

Therefore, $P[k]$ follows a power law distribution with $exponent \gamma=\frac{2}{n_t}+1$ for $n_t \geq 2$.

5.1.3 Discussion

We note that the BA model has produced a power law distribution given by Thus; the BA model has a constant exponent, γ, of value 3 which is different from what is found in real-world complex networks where γ ranges from 1 . SNAM (actually SNAM*) produced a network with power law distribution given by, where for . This gives SNAM an advantage over BA as SNAM is capable of generating complex networks with various statistical properties. In SNAM, changing the number of tests, yields different types of complex networks with different statistical properties.

Hence, we conclude from this analysis that SNAM is successful in preserving the power law degree distribution found in real-world complex networks and that the value of the power law exponent depends on the value of used in network generation. SNAM introduces a new concept of node heterogeneity which is the heterogeneity of the nodes' requirements to establish a connection. SNAM, as far as we know, is the only model for complex network generation that considers individual differences between nodes by assigning this heterogeneous connection standard parameter to the arriving nodes. Additionally, SNAM excels in its capability of generating specific types of complex networks by varying the model parameters.

REFERENCES

Albert, R., & Barabasi, A. L. (1999). Emergence of scaling in random networks. *Science*, *286*(5439), 509–512. doi:10.1126/science.286.5439.509 PMID:10521342

Albert, R., & Barabasi, A. L. (2002). Statistical mechanics of complex networks. *Reviews of Modern Physics*, *74*(1), 47–97. doi:10.1103/RevModPhys.74.47

Balakrishnan, H., & Deo, N. (2006). Discovering Communities in Complex Networks. *Proceedings of the ACM Southeast Regional Conference*. ACM Press.

Barab'asi, A.-L., & Bianconi, G. (2001). Competition and multiscaling in evolving networks. *Europhysics Letters*, *54*(4), 436–442. doi:10.1209/epl/i2001-00260-6

Boyd, D. M., & Ellison, N. B. (2007). Social network sites: Definition, history, and scholarship. *Journal of Computer-Mediated Communication*, *13*(1), 210–230. doi:10.1111/j.1083-6101.2007.00393.x

Cutillo, L. A., & Molva, R. (2009) Privacy Preserving Social Networking Through Decentralization. In *Proceedings of the Sixth International Conference on Wireless On-Demand Network Systems and Services*. doi:10.1109/WONS.2009.4801860

Kleinberg, J. M., Kumar, S. R., Raghavan, P., Rajagopalan, S., & Tomkins, A. (1999). The Webas a graph: Measurements, models and methods. In *Proceedings of the International Conference on Combinatorics and Computing* (LNCS), (vol. 1627, pp. 1–18). Springer.

Krapivsky, P. L., & Redner, S. (2001). Organization of Growing Random Networks. *Physical Review E: Statistical, Nonlinear, and Soft Matter Physics*, *63*(6), 066123. doi:10.1103/PhysRevE.63.066123 PMID:11415189

Li, Y., Xiaogang, J., Kong, F., & Li, J. (2009). *Linking via social similarity: The emergence of community structure in scale-free network.*1st IEEE Symposium on WebSociety, SWS '09. doi:10.1109/SWS.2009.5271769

Newman, M. E. J. (2003). The structure and function of complex networks. *SIAM Review*, *45*(2), 167–256. doi:10.1137/S003614450342480

Tao, S., & Yue, X. (2010). The attributes similar-degree of complex networks. *2nd International Conference on Future Computer and Communication (ICFCC)*. doi:10.1109/ICFCC.2010.5497519

Youssef, B., & Hassan, H. (2014). IASM: An Integrated Attribute Similarity for Complex Networks Generation. In *Proceedings of the 28th IEEE International Conferenceon Information Networking (ICOIN)*. doi:10.1109/ICOIN.2014.6799745

Chapter 10
Social Network Analysis

Paramita Dey
Government College of Engineering and Ceramic Technology, India

Sarbani Roy
Jadavpur University, India

ABSTRACT

Social Network Analysis (SNA) looks at how our world is connected. The mapping and measuring of connections and interactions between people, groups, organizations and other connected entities are very significant and have been the subject of a fascinating interdisciplinary topic . Social networks like Twitter, Facebook, LinkedIn are very large in size with millions of vertices and billions of edges. To collect meaningful information from these densely connected graph and huge volume of data, it is important to find proper topology of the network as well as analyze different network parameters. The main objective of this work is to study network characteristics commonly used to explain social structures. In this chapter, we discuss all important aspect of social networking and analyze through a real time example. This analysis shows some distinguished parameters like number of clusters, group formation, node degree distribution, identifying influential leader/seed node etc. which can be used further for feature extraction.

1. INTRODUCTION

In recent few years, there is a huge trend of using online social networks (OSNs) that drawn attention from all corner of the world and show an explosive growth trends.With the advent of earlier online networking communities like Friendster and Orkut along with the popularization of the notions of six degrees of separation, small world network and the Kevin Bacon's game, the concept of a social network takes hold in popular culture. In recent, OSN like Facebook, Twitter and linkedIn play a significant role for analysing the social behaviour as a group or community.Each user in social network required a user profile that contains basic information like name, date of birth, male/female to complex information like group formation, personal, educational or professional information, connection with different social communities and area of interest like hobbies, games etc. (Benevenuto et al, 2009; Wilson et al, 2012). It becomes analogous of real life where people interact, keep in touch and exchange data within the group. Facebook, a popular social network service, has attracted over 1.23 billion monthly active users as of January, 2014 (source: facebook.com). The huge user base of these OSNs provides huge scopes

DOI: 10.4018/978-1-4666-9964-9.ch010

for the researcher for characterise social network characteristics including user behaviour, statistics, social interaction pattern recognition and studies of information propagation. The main objective of this chapter is to study the network formation topologyand dynamics of different parameters required for social network analytic (Scott, 1998; Valiant and Leslie, 1990).

2. RELATED RESEARCH WORK

In 1950 social network analysis evolved as a research subjects for the sociologists and social anthropologists. But in late 80s the techniques are gradually evolved for the analysis of data for inference of the characteristics inherent between the social networks (Wasserman, 1994). As it is easier to save the social network in the form of a graph, different topologies are evolved for the proper representation of the data. It is started with random graph and evolved to more specialise one. As the data of OSN is a huge one and the number of users increased day by day, graph sampling algorithm was evolved which is based on the idea of clustering coefficient and node degree distribution will face a very little change at the time of sampling. Wang et al (2011) elaborate this in their paper and make a comparative study of different graph sampling techniques. A large research work was done for finding the centrality measures, especially between centrality for finding important nodes (Wayne and Oellermann, 2011). Small world network, which is based on the notion of six degree separation, is now becoming an interesting research option of the researcher (Kleinberg, 1998). Now in today's world where big data and cloud computing is the buzzword, instead of doing the graph sampling, research is moving on in the trends towards distributed computing environment.

2.1 Social Network Topology

Network topology formation, as discussed by Bonato (2005), Albert and Barabasi (2002) and many other researchers, started with simple random graph generation like Erdos-Reyni graph generation where edge generation is independent of the other nodes interaction. For social network analysis, where there are huge number of nodes and edges, it is important to have dynamic algorithms for formation of graphs (Bonato, 2005). Force Atlas 2 (used in GEPHI software), can be downloaded from gephi.github.io (GEPHI official website) integrates different algorithms such as Barnes Hut simulation, degree-dependent repulsive force, local and global adaptive temperatures for the network formation. The main criterion of that simulation is the repulsive force between the nodes and the attraction of edges. In these topology, all nodes are considered as unbiased node but in actual scenario all users that is considered as nodes are biased i.e. they have personal choices to choose their friends which is equivalent to the edge connection. Therefore in recent network formation (Morris et al, 2013) like Schelling's model is based on game theoretic approach. The evolution of these network topologies is discussed in this section. Figure 1 represents a series of topology from basic to the most recent one.

1. **Star-Shaped Networks:** Here seed nodes are acted as central nodes or hub and other nodes are connected to the hubs in the form of star. Central denotes the key nodes of the network and acts as the hub of the network.
2. **Hypercube Graph:** The graph is in the form of hypercube. Nodes are represented as the vertex of the hypercube as shown in Figure 1B.

3. **Complete Graph:** Complete graph is a simple undirected network topology where each node is connected to all other vertices with unique edges as represented in Figure 1C.
4. **Erdos-Reyni Random Graph:** This algorithm is based on two closely related network models for generating random graphs. This algorithm is named after Paul Erdos and Alfred Reyni, who introduced this model in 1959.The Erdos-Reyni graph can be defined as G(n,p) with two parameters n and p, where it is defined as n nodes on random graph G, where the edge between each pair of nodes is represented with the probability p . This probability factor of any edge of this model is independent to the all other edges of the network.

In a complete network, if G(*n*, e), a sub graph is chosen randomly in a uniform manner from the collection of all graphs which have *n* nodes and *e* edges. Then let we considered as n= 3 and e=2. Now

Figure 1. Topology of network formation

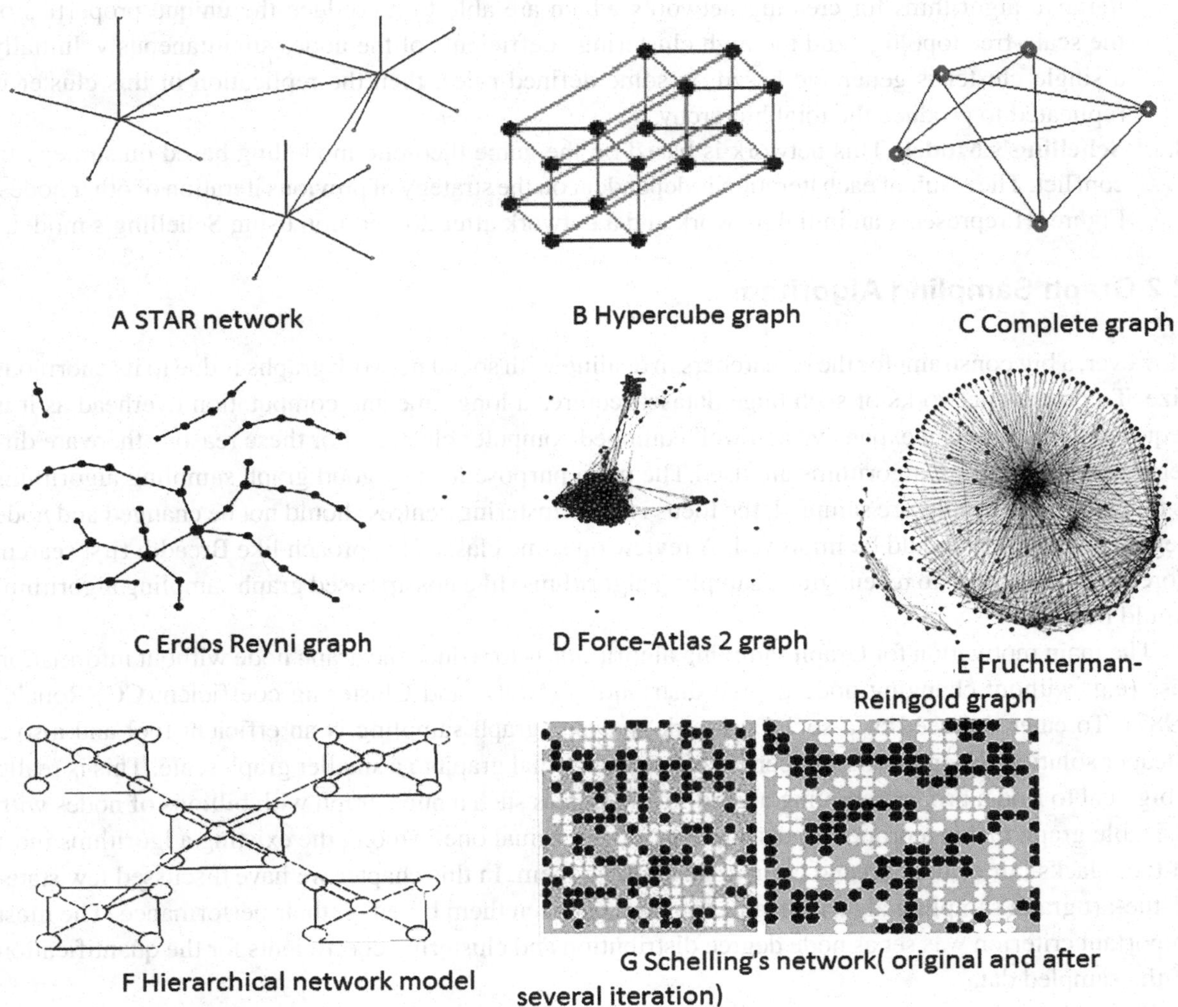

from that model we would find that, each of the three possible graphs on three vertices and two edges will have a probability of 1/3. A graph generated through this model is represented in Figure 1D.

5. **Force Atlas 2:** Force Atlas 2, presented by Bastian et al (2009) and Jacomy et al (2010), considered different graph generation techniques like Barnes Hut simulation, degree-dependent repulsive force, local and global adaptive temperatures etc. for simulate the network. The main criterion is that the nodes of the network face repulsive force and the edge faces the attraction. It is a continuous force directed layout of a network. After running the Force Atlas 2 simulation on the sampled data, we get the graph as Figure 1E.
6. **Fruchterman-Reingold Model:** According to this model designed by Fruchterman and Reingold (1991), continuous network modeling was done depending on eveb distribution of the vertices in the frame, making edge lengths uniform and reflect inherent symmetry. Figure 1F represents a topology based on *Fruchterman-Reingold model.*
7. **Hierarchical Network Graph:** Hierarchical network models (as represented in Figure 1G) use iterative algorithms for creating networks which are able to reproduce the unique properties of the scale-free topology and the high clustering coefficients of the nodes simultaneously. Initially a single cluster is generated based on some defined rules, then the replication of this cluster is replicated to produce the total hierarchy.
8. **Schelling's Model:** This network is based on the game theoretic modelling based on strategy of conflict. The result of each iteration is dependent on the strategy of previous iteration of other nodes. Figure1H represents an initial network and a network after 20 iteration using Schelling's model.

2.2 Graph Sampling Algorithm

However, a big constraint for the researchers in dealing with social network graphs is due to its enormous size. To process networks of such huge dataset requires a long time and computation overhead as it is required to maintain an expensive and well equipped computer clusters. For these reasons there are different graph sampling algorithms are used.The main purpose for any good graph sampling algorithms is that whenever graphs are sampled, the focus is that clustering centres should not be changed and node degree distribution should be improved. A review on some classical approach like Breadth first search, Forest Fire algorithm to recent graph sampling algorithms (like gossip based graph sampling algorithm) would be done.

The main motivation for Graph sampling algorithms is to reduce the graph node without information loss (e.g. without changing node degree distribution (NDD) and Clustering coefficient(CC)(Ronald, 1987). To cater the need of a social network analysis, graph sampling is an efficient tool and also a cheaper solution to capture the properties of original social graph to a smaller graph scale. This is really a big deal to find a proper sampling algorithm to address such a huge graph with billions of nodes with a sizable graph that is a proper representative of the original one. Among the existing a lgorithms most of them lacks fair evaluation and comparison among them. In this chapter we have discussed few state-of-the-art graph sampling algorithm and compare between them based on their performance. The most important criterion was set as node degree distribution and clustering coefficients for the quantification of the sampled data.

Some state of the art algorithms are discussed in the chapter.

2.2.1 Breadth-First Sampling (BFS)

Breadth-first search (BFS) is an algorithm for traversing or searching tree or graph data structures (as referred in Figure 2). It starts at the seed node which is selected randomly and try to explore the neighbor nodes first based on the shortest distance among them, before moving to the next level neighbors. In the late 1950s E. F. Moore, first propose the algorithms of BFS, used it to find the shortest path out of a maze, and the same is proposed independently by C. Y. Lee for using in wire routing algorithm in 1961.

It is observed that BFS is biased to the nodes with high degree and can be localised in local maxima. In BFS, nodes with a higher degree would be traversed more frequently. BFS generally characterised with higher local clustering coefficient than the original network clustering coefficient due to this reason.

BFS is most studied and applied in finding user behavior pattern of OSNs, measurement and topological characterization of OSNs.

2.2.2 Random Walk

A *random walk* is an algorithm to find the path that combines a succession of random steps. It is analogous to the path traced by a molecule when it traversed through a liquid or a gas. The search path of an animal, the fluctuating price of a stock or the financial status of a gambler, are all resemble with the model *of* random walks. In 1905 Karl Pearson was first introduced the term Random Walk. These algorithm is not only used in the field of social networking, but have many applications in the applied area like ecology, economics, psychology, computer science, physics, chemistry, and biology.

Random walks are primarily assumed to be based on Markov chains or Markov processes or Markov model, but other complicated random walks are also possible. Some random walks are working on graphs, others on the line, in the plane, in higher dimensions, or even curved surfaces, while some random walks can be applied in a group. Random walks also vary with the time parameter. Often, the walk is in discrete time, and indexed by the natural numbers, as in X_0, X_1, X_2,…

A random walk of length *k* on a possibly infinite graph *G* with a root 0 is a stochastic process with random variables X_1, X_2,........,X_k such that $X_1 = 0$ and X_{i+1} is a vertex chosen uniformly at random from

Figure 2. Breadth-first sampling

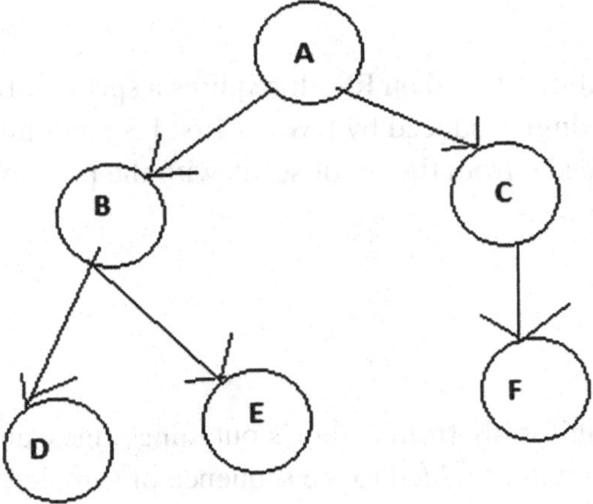

the neighbors of X_i . Then the number $p_{v,w,k}(G)$ is the probability that a random walk of length k starting at v ends at w. In other words, if G is a graph with root 0, $p_{0.0.2k}$ is the probability that a 2K step random walk returns to 0.

A random walk on a graph is generally follows the rule of a Markov chain. Unlike a general Markov chain, random walk on a graph enjoys a property called *time symmetry* ir*reversibility*. This property, also known as the principle of detailed balance, means that the probabilities to traverse a given path in one direction or in the other have a very simple connection between them (if the graph is regular, these paths would be equal). This property has a significance impact in the analysis of graph.

Starting in the 1980s, much research has gone into connecting properties of the graph to random walks.If the transition kernel p(x,y) is itself random (based on an environment ω) then the random walk is called a "random walk in random environment". When the law of the random walk includes the randomness of ω, the law is called the annealed law; on the other hand, if ω is considered as fixed, the law is called a quenched law. We can think about choosing every possible edge with the same probability as maximizing uncertainty, i.e., entropy locally. It could also be done globally – in maximal entropy random walk (MERW) it is optimized so that all paths to be equally probable, or in other words for each two vertexes, each path of given length is equally probable. This random walk has much stronger localization properties, shown by Wang et al (2011).

2.2.3 MHRW

MHRW is a Markov-Chain Monte Carlo (MCMC) algorithm to obtain random node samples based on the degree probability distribution of the nodes. Suppose we have a proposal function Q(v) = kv, which is the degree of vertex v. From node v's neighbors, MHRW randomly chooses a node w, and then generates a random number p from uniform distribution U(0; 1). If p _Q(v)=Q(w), the proposal is accepted and the sampling process will transit to w; otherwise, it stays at the original node v. If it stays at node v, it does not spend a cost as the node's profile has been downloaded already. If the degree of w (Q(w)) is small, The proposal function changes the transition probabilities although w will have a small chance to be chosen as the candidate, there will be a high probability that the proposal will be accepted once it occur previously. Thus the proposal function rectified the bias towards high-degree nodes. MHRW ends the recursion when the budget is reached (Wang et al, 2011).

2.2.4 FS

FS is an edge sampling algorithm is based on RW. It requires a specialestimator function to estimate the matrices for removing the biasingintroduced by RW. At first FS randomly chooses a set of nodes, S, as seeds. Then FS will select a seed v from the set of seeds with the probability defined as

$$P(v) = \frac{k_v}{\sum_{u \in S} k_u}$$

An edge (v,w) is selected uniformly from node v's outgoing edges, and v will be replaced with w in the set of seeds and edge (v,w) will be added to the sequence of sampled edges.

FS repeats these steps until the previously decided budget of the scheme is reached.

FS algorithm requires that at least one of the in degree or out degreeof the nodes. Otherwise the node has neither incomingnor outgoing edges, which means; this node is isolated and not connected with the other nodes of the network. It is the drawback of that algorithm. Inreal OSNs the number of isolated nodes is small and in mostnetworks isolated nodes are not considered. Otherwise it improves RW algorithm as it was not biased to the high degree nodes like Markov based RW (Wang et al, 2011).

2.3 Network Centrality

In graph theory and network analysis, centrality refers to indicators which identify the most important vertices within a network. Similarly, in a social network, it is used to identify the most influential person(s) in a social network. Different centrality measures, discussed by Freeman (1978/1979, 1979) are briefly discussed in this section.

1. **Degree Centrality:** Social network researchers measure network activity for a node by using the degrees, i.e., the number of direct connections a node has. A node with higher degree is considered as most influential in the network (Newman, 2001).
2. **Betweenness Centrality:** The node that has many direct connections, fewer than the average in the network, plays a powerful role in the network. This node has one of the best locations in the network, (may be most visited node in the shortest path connections between other nodes), between important constituencies. Thus, a node with high betweenness has great influence in the network. But the disadvantage is that this node is a single point of failure (Freeman et al, 1991).
3. **Closeness Centrality:** The nodes that have fewer connections, yet the pattern of their direct and indirect ties allow them to access all the nodes in the network more quickly than other. They have the shortest paths to all others, close to everyone else (Wayne and Oellermann, 2011). These nodes are in an excellent position to monitor the information flow in the network and they have the best visibility into what is happening in the network. The nodes with higher centrality plays a significant role in the network and the relation between high centrality nodes plays an important role in the characterization of overallnetwork structure. A network, which is highly centralized, is dominated by one or a few central nodes. If these nodes are omitted or damaged, the network quickly fragments into disjoint sub-networks. A node, with large central value can become a single point of failure. If one network is centralized around a well-connected hub (nodes with high degree and betweeness centrality) can fail certainly in abrupt way if that particular hub is disabled or removed from the network and makes that network very much unstable in nature. On the other hand, a less centralized network has no single point of failure. It can sustain in the context of many intentional attacks or random failures in the network. Many nodes or links can fail while allowing the remaining nodes to still connect to each other through other network links. For a sustainable network, network with low centrality is always preferred. But, if we consider influencing a network, centralized network has a special significance in context of social networking.
4. **PageRank Centrality:** It works by counting the number and quality of links to a page to determine a rough estimate of how important the website is. The underlying assumption is that more important nodes are likely to receive more links from other nodes. Eigenvector centrality is a measure of the centrality of an influential node in a network. It assigns relative scores to all nodes in the network

based on the assumption that connections to high-scoring nodes contribute more to the score of the node in question than equal connections to low-scoring nodes.

2.4 Community Structure and Clustering

2.4.1 Community Detection

It is the problem of identifying community structure in social network analysis. Community structure or module is denoted as the grouping of nodes in the network such that the grouping demonstrates property of high coupling and low cohesion, i.e., the number of edges within a group is maximized and the number of edges among groups is minimized. Detecting community structure in a graph is a well-studied problem in social network analysis. Communities, also known as clusters or modules, are groups of vertices that probably share common properties and/or play similar roles within the graph. In Figure 3. a schematic example of a community detection graph is shown.

In social studies, four metrices are identified for community detection, a. complete mutuality i.e. all members in the group share direct relation between them, b. reachability i.e. it is easier to reach a member in a group than members of other groups, c. vertex degree and d. comparison of internal versus external cohesion. Community structures depend on the cliques present in the graph. It denotes the membership/ affiliation of the different community. Two cliques can be overlapping in nature i.e., one user can be a member of different communities. It denotes the belongingness of nodes to some particular clusters of nodes. Community distribution denotes different communities where maximum interaction takes place (Fortunato and Castellano, 2007). Figure 4 represents a community detected users profile based on the sex of the profile.

Figure 3. Community detection
Fortunato and Castellano, 2007.

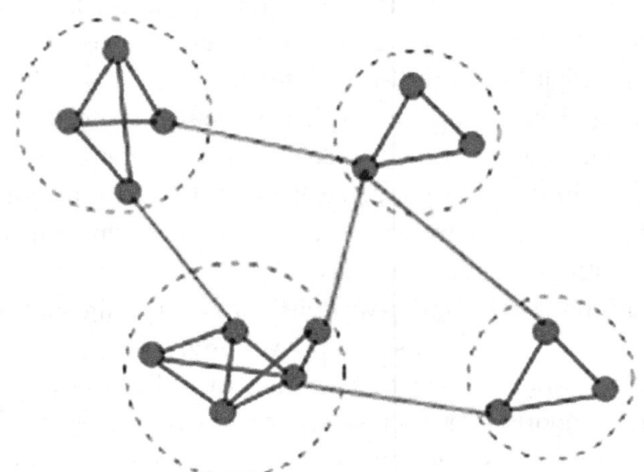

Figure 4. Community detection based on the sex of the user (light denotes male, dark denotes female)

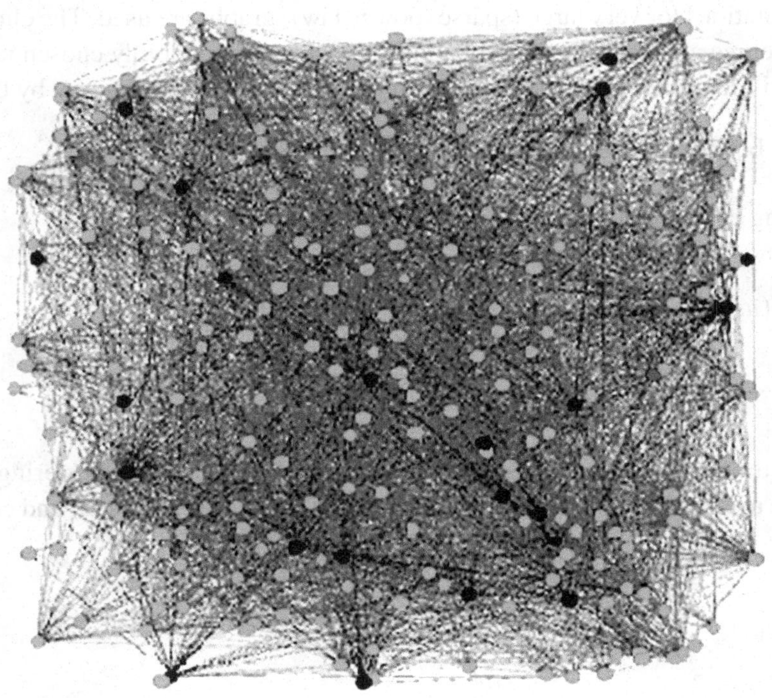

2.4.2 Clustering Coefficient (CC)

Clustering coefficient denotes the centres of different communities as discussed by Wang et al (2011). One have to be made sure whatever may be the change of network, clustering centres should not be changed.

Clustering Coefficient (CC) is a measure of the degree to which nodes in a graph tend to cluster together. The local clustering coefficient for node u in undirected graphs is given by

$$C_u = \begin{cases} \dfrac{2\,|E_{v,w}|}{k_u(k_u-1)} & if\ k_u > 1 \\ 0 & otherwise \end{cases}$$

where Ev,w is the set of edges among node u's neighbours. The average clustering coefficient is the network average clustering coefficient (NACC) of all nodes in the graphs can be expressed as

$$\overline{C} = \frac{1}{n}\sum_{i=1}^{n} C_i$$

where n is the total number of nodes in the graphs (Wang et al, 2011).

Another approach, proposed by Latapy (2008), for finding clustering coefficients is the main-memory triangle computations for very large (sparse (power-law)) graphs are used. The clustering coefficient of a vertex v (of degree at least 2) is the probability that any two randomly chosen neighbours of v are linked together. It is computed by dividing the number of triangles containing v by the number of possible edges $\binom{d(v)}{2}$ between its neighbours.

So the clustering coefficient can be defined as

$$\mu(G) = \frac{1}{\binom{n}{2}} \sum_{u,v \subset V} d(u,v) \,.$$

If d(v) denotes the number of neighbours of v. One may then define the clustering coefficient of the whole graph as the average of this value for all the vertices (of degree at least 2) and can be expressed as

$$\sigma(G) = \binom{n}{2} \mu(G) \,.$$

Applying the approaches of main memory triangle computation, clusters are shown in Figure 5 (records are based on information from ESPN crickinfo).

2.5 Small World Network

Small world network is an interesting criterion of social network which shows the properties that any two nodes, even in a very large network show that the minimum distance, based on minimum spanning tree algorithm, and is not very large apart in terms of hop count between them. Six degree separation is also based on that phenomenon. Erdos number project is a very well example of that. How to generate small world network and optimisation of that network is a well discussed research problem. Contagion

Figure 5. Clustering based on the player of the IPL players in cricket playing country

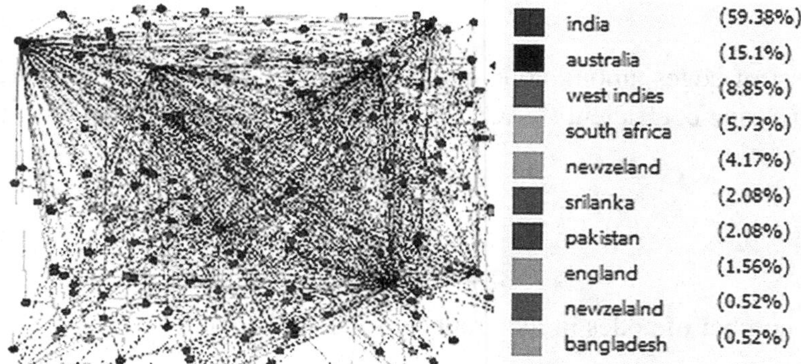

or spreading, also known as diffusion/ percolation in the network is the important criterion for influencing the network. For positive and negative gossiping, several approaches and algorithms are present.

2.5.1 Properties of Small-World Networks

The main property of a small world network is based on high clustering coefficient and small average shortest path. Small-world networks tend to contain cliques or highly connectedcommunity, and near-cliques, i.e. sub-networksthose are connections between almost any two nodes within them. This property results in the defining property of a high clustering coefficient. Secondly, most pairs of nodes will be connected by at least one short path. This results from the defining property that the mean-shortest path length be small. Several other properties are often associated with small-world networks. Typically there is an over-abundance of *hubs* - nodes in the network with a high number of connections (known as high degree nodes). These hubs/nodes act as the common connections mediating the short path lengths between other nodes. It is analogous to the small-world network of travelling salesman has a small mean-path length (i.e. between any two cities he is likely to have to move to three or fewer cities) because many paths are routed through hub cities. This property is often analyzed by considering the fraction of nodes in the network that have a particular number of connections going into them (the node degree distribution of the network). Networks with a greater than expected number of hubs will have a greater fraction of nodes with high degree, and consequently the degree distribution will be enriched at high degree values. This is commonly known as a long-tailed distribution. Graphs of very different topology qualify as small-world networks as long as they satisfy the two requirements as discussed above.

2.5.2 Small World Network Model

2.5.2.1 Watts-Strogatz Model

A *small-world network* represents a mathematical graph in which most nodes are not neighbours of one another (i.e. not directly connected), but most nodes can be reached from other nodes by a small number of hops. Specifically, a small-world network is defined to be a network where the distance betweenany two randomly chosen nodes (i.e. the required number of steps to reach the nodes) denoted by L, grows proportionally to the logarithm of the number of nodes N in the network, and can be defined as: $L \propto \log N$

In the context of a social network, this results in the small world criterion of strangers being linked by a mutual acquaintance. Many empirical graphs are well-modelled by the properties of small-world networks. Social networks, the connectivity of the Internet, wikis such as Wikipedia, andgene networks are all examplesof small-world network.

Duncan Watts and Steven Strogatz proposed this algorithm in 1998.They classified the graphsbased on two independent structural features, clustering coefficient (CC) and average shortest path length. This random graphs is formed according to the Erdos-Reyni (ER) model, based on small average shortest path length (generally proportionate to the logarithm of the number of nodes) along with small clustering coefficient. Watts and Strogatz showed that most of the real-world networks have a small average shortest path length, but clustering coefficient is significantly quiet high rather than expected by random selection. Watts and Strogatz then proposed a novel graph model, currently named the Watts and Strogatz model, with small average shortest path length, and large clustering coefficient. Barthelemy and Amara showed this crossover in the Watts–Strogatz model between a "large world" (such as a lattice) and a small world was first 1999. Further work was followed by a large number of papers, like Barrat and Weigt in 1999; Dorogovtsev and Mendes; Barmpoutis and Murray in 2010.

2.5.2.2 Cohen and Havlin Scale Free Network

Small-world criterion has been quantified by comparing clustering and path length of a given network to an equivalent random network with same degree distribution (as discussed above). Another method for quantifying network showing properties of small-world to utilize the original definition of the small-world network comparing the clustering of a given network to an equivalent lattice network and its path length to an equivalent random network. The small-world measure (ω) is defined as

$$\omega = \frac{L_{\Gamma}}{L} / \frac{C}{C_{\Gamma}}$$

Cohen and Havlin proved analytically that scale-free networks are ultra-small worlds. In this case, due to hubs, the shortest paths become significantly smaller. The network formation is discussed in the Figure 6. The rate of proportion in which it grows is

$$L \propto \log \log N$$

Figure 6. Small world network formation

(a)Rewindinding of edges in small world network

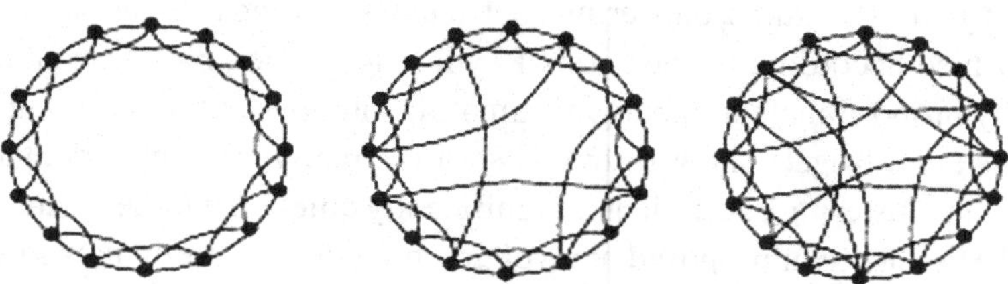

(b) Addition of links in the small world network

In small world network formation, for the Rewiring of edges, it is required to select a fraction p of edges reposition one of their endpoints. For the addition of links, a fraction p of additional edges leaving underlying lattice intact.

Figure 6 represents the process of Rewiring and Addition of links in a small world network shown in two subfigures respectively.

2.6 A Case Study of Facebook Profile Showing All Network Parameters

Figure 7 shows how the users of facebooks are really connected in a facebook profile. Three real time facebook profiles are used to show all the parameters of social network analysis. The profiles are extracted from facebook using Netviz, designed by Rieder(2013)and analysed through GEPHI.A comparative study between these three profiles has been done by Dey et al (2015). In social network analysis, people deal with relational data of the user. In this context, network visualization assumes key features. The main objective of this comparative study is to understand the basic features of the social network, extract and analysing the important parameters that characterized the social network. As open source tools are used and external module can be added to them, these data can be further characterized. Extracted information can be used for designing graph sampling, game theory based network design etc (Perar,2006).

Hadoop, Netvizz and Gephi, HivQl are used for data extraction and graph analysis from social networking site facebook. All the tools are free and open source. Netvizz is a software tool used for extracting data from different sections of the facebook profiles (personal profile, group, pages etc.) for research and non- commercial purposes. Gephi is an open source tool for graphical and network analysis for the usage of people for exploring and understanding graphs or data represented as graphs.

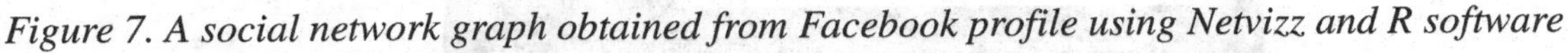

Figure 7. A social network graph obtained from Facebook profile using Netvizz and R software

2.6.1 Result Extracted from Facebook Profile using Netvizz

To find profile identity, group identity, liked pages etc. open Facebook real time profile then copy own profile URL, and go through the netvizz application which uses hadoop internally and optimize the searches gives the final output(refer to Figure 8).

Searching for the keyword Jagriti which was a group created in Facebook for student and jagriti Tech fest organized in Government college of Engineering & Ceramic Technology 2015. People who took part in Tech fest is connected via this group (as represented in second profile in Figure 8).

Figure 8. Profile identification through Netvizz

(a) Identity of individual profile in facebook.

(b) Identity of group in facebook.

(c)Identity of public group in facebook.

(d)Identity of private group in facebook can not be revealed.

For searching a public group, we can access its member name id. Everything there representing lots of people connected to each other via this group (as referred in third subfigure of Figure 8).

Now Looking for M.Tech group but it shows message like that (as shown in fourth profile of Figure 8) it cannot be open.

Because it is not a public group, hence we conclude that we get information only for public group private group is inaccessible due to security purpose (as referred in Figure 8).

Now we are going to search Narendra Modi, the prime minister of INDIA. We extract information number of pages created by his name, number of posts, like, country he belongs, and much useful information by using netvizz tool.

Go through the netvizz click on the drop down lists – go to the page and then go to the checkbox search for Narendra Modi (as referred in Figure 9).

506 pages exists by the name Narendra Modi in Facebook, identity, name of group, likes of group, category and description etc. (as referred in Figure 10 and Figure 11).

Figure 9. Netvizz pop up block for searching

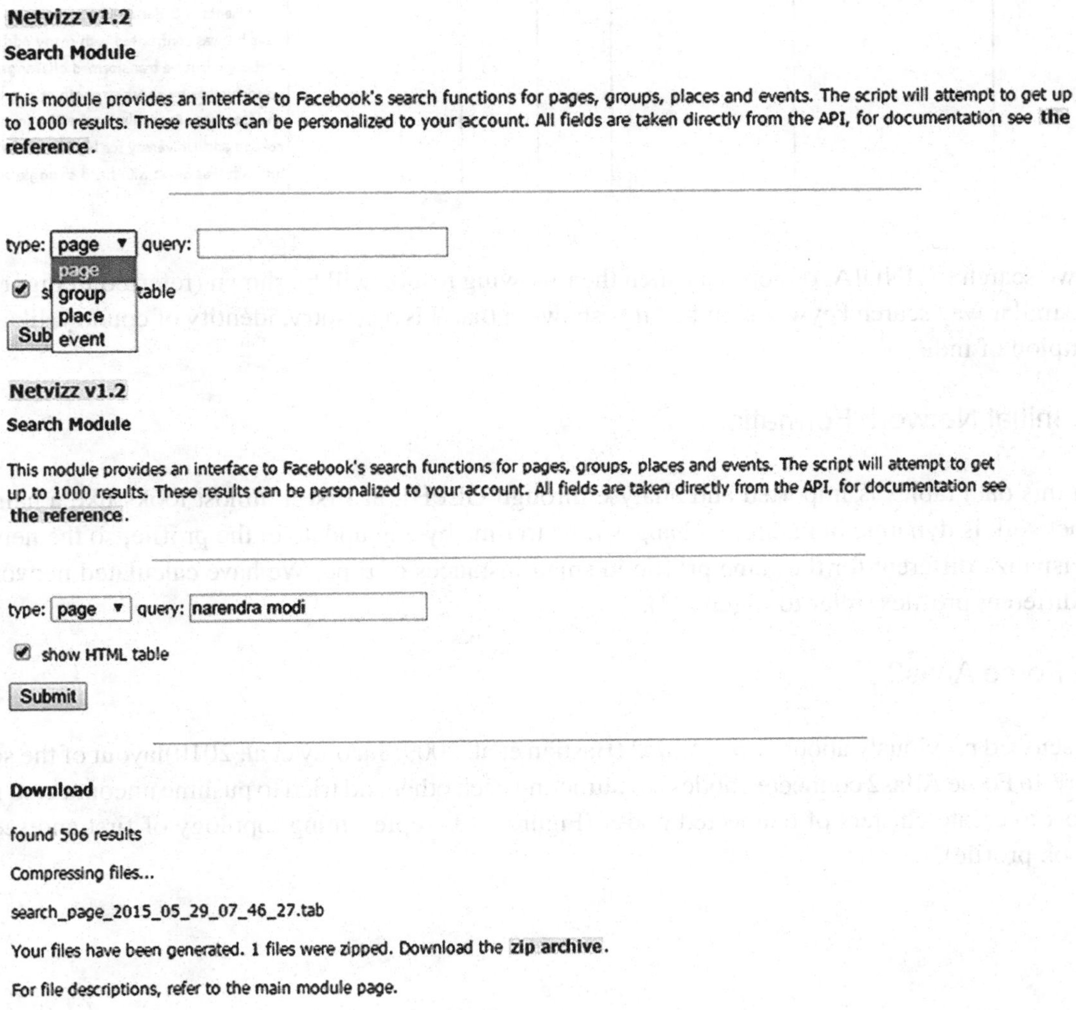

Netvizz v1.2

Search Module

This module provides an interface to Facebook's search functions for pages, groups, places and events. The script will attempt to get up to 1000 results. These results can be personalized to your account. All fields are taken directly from the API, for documentation see **the reference**.

type: page ▾ query:

page
group
place
event

table

Sub

Netvizz v1.2

Search Module

This module provides an interface to Facebook's search functions for pages, groups, places and events. The script will attempt to get up to 1000 results. These results can be personalized to your account. All fields are taken directly from the API, for documentation see **the reference**.

type: page ▾ query: narendra modi

show HTML table

Submit

Download

found 506 results

Compressing files...

search_page_2015_05_29_07_46_27.tab

Your files have been generated. 1 files were zipped. Download the **zip archive**.

For file descriptions, refer to the main module page.

Figure 10. Netvizz result for the searching parameter as text data on NarendraModi, prime minister of India

id	name	category	likes	checkins	talking_about_count	description
177526890164	Narendra Modi	Politician	31454352	0	2403190	
						Born on 17th September, 1950 at Vadnagar, a small town in Mehsana district of North Gujarat, Modi grew up in a culture that instilled in him the values of generosity, benevolence and social service. During the Indo-Pak war in the mid sixties, even as a young boy, he volunteered to serve the soldiers in transit at railway stations. In 1967, he served the flood affected people of Gujarat. Endowed with excellent organizational capability and a rich insight into human psychology, he was elected as the student leader of Akhil Bhartiya Vidhyarthi Parishad (All India Students' Council) and played a prominent role in various socio-political movements in Gujarat. Right from his boyhood days he was confronted with many odds and obstacles, but he transformed challenges into opportunities by sheer strength of character and courage. Particularly when he joined college and University for higher education, his path was beset with hard struggle and

If we search for INDIA, our country then the following results will be shown (referred in Figure 12) In similar way search keyword "india" it is showing that it is a country, identity of country, likes and descritpion of india.

2.6.2 Initial Network Formation

When this data tables is imported and analyse through GEPHI, at first it almost looks like a hairball. This network is dynamic in nature, it changes time to time by any update in the profile, so the network may visualize different for the same profile in small instances of time. We have calculated network of three different profiles (refer to Figure 13).

2.6.3 Force Atlas2

It is discussed previously about *Force Atlas2* (Bastian et al, 2009; Jacomy et al, 2010)layout of the social network.In Force Atlas2 connected nodes are attracting each other and tried to pushthe unconnected node far apart to create clusters of connected nodes (Figure 14 is representing topology of first and second facebook profile).

Figure 11. Netvizz result for the searching parameter as pictures of NarendraModi, prime minister of India

cover	link
	https://www.facebook.com/narendramodi
	https://www.facebook.com/namo1950
	https://www.facebook.com/ModiforPMOrg
	https://www.facebook.com/pages/Narendra-Modi-Team-Bangal/544651359001588
	https://www.facebook.com/narendramodiindiafirst

Figure 12. Netvizz result for the searching parameter as text documents on India

id	name	category	likes	checkins	talking_about_count	description
109524955741121	India	Country	874370	11430717	591053	India, officially the Republic of India, is a country in South Asia. It is the seventh-largest country by area, the second-most populous country with over 1.2 billion people, and the most populous democracy the world. Bounded by the Indian Ocean o the south, the Arabian Sea on the south-west, and the Bay of Bengal on the south-east, it shares land borders with Pakistan to the west; China, Nepal, and Bhutan to the north-east; and Burma (Myanmar) and Bangladesh to the east. In the Indian Ocean, India is in the vicinity of Sri Lanka and the Maldives; in addition, India's Andaman and Nicobar Islands share a maritime border with Thailand and Indonesia.Home to the ancient Indus Valle Civilisation and a region of historic trade routes and vast empires, the Indian subcontinent was identified with its commercial and cultural wealth for much of its long history. Four religions—Hinduism, Buddhism, Jainism, and Sikhism—originate here, whereas Zoroastrianism and the Abrahamic religions of Judaism, Christianity and Islam arrived in the 1st millennium CE and also helped shape the region's diverse culture. Gradually annexed by and brough

Figure 13. Initial network of three Facebook profile

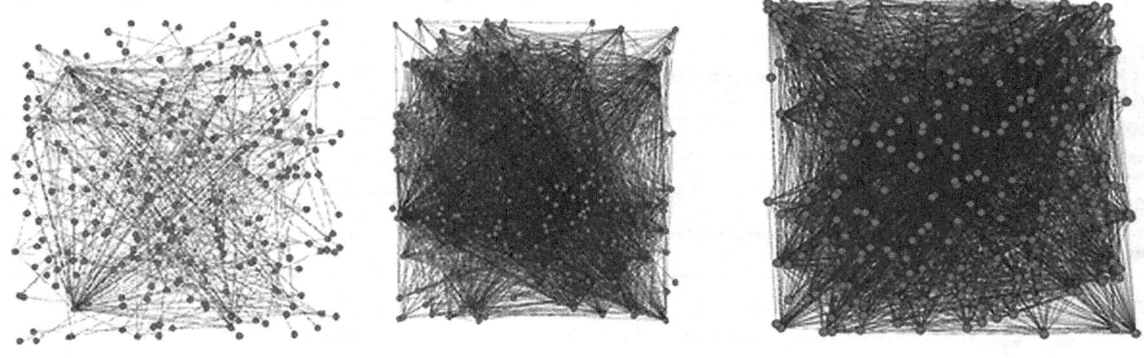

Figure 14. Network formation using Force Atlas2

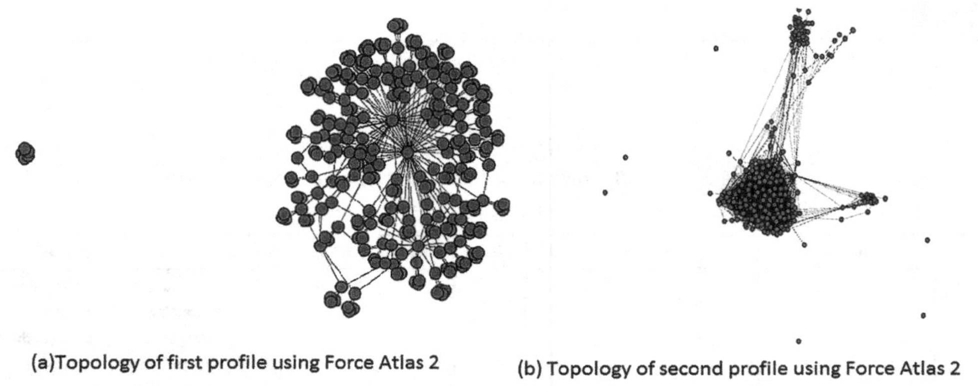

(a)Topology of first profile using Force Atlas 2

(b) Topology of second profile using Force Atlas 2

2.6.4 Fruchterman-Reingold

It is another way, proposed by Fruchterman and Reingold (1991), representation of node in network. It is also known as Force directed layout algorithm, Force directed algorithm means a force between every two node or the force of interaction between each and every pair of nodes. The users are represented in the form of steel rings and the edges are considered as the spring between vertices. The force of attraction is analogous to the force of spring and the repulsive force is analogous to the electric force working in the field, the algorithm is mainly used to minimize the energy through moving the node related to the change of energy. In the meantime the energy associated with each node is minimum because the separation between each node is constant and has minimum energy. Figure 15 represents networks of all profiles using this topology.

Figure 15. Topology of all profiles using FruchermanReingold

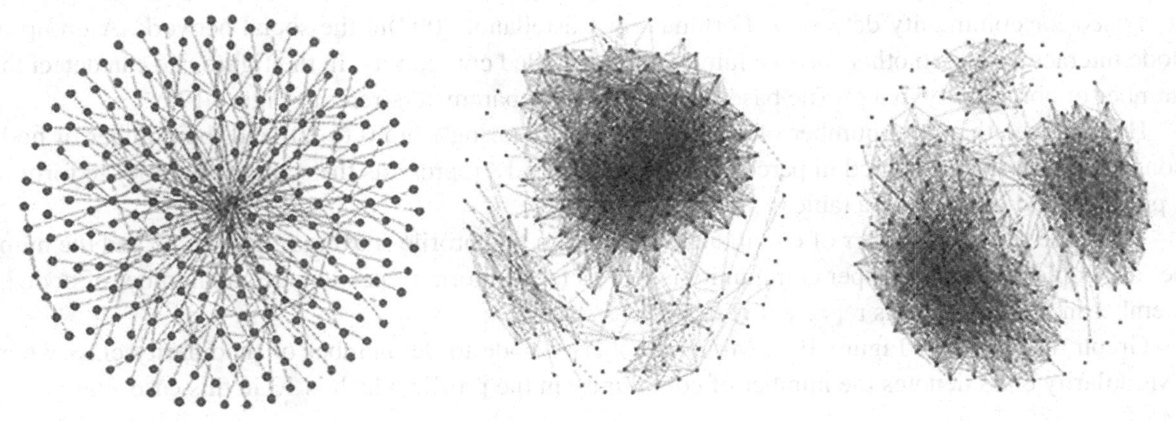

2.6.5 Ranking

Ranking means the number of connection between all nodes.Higher rank implies higher node degree connectivity. In the figure,bright colours use to represent highest degree of the most connected nodes in the network(as referred in Figure 16).

Figure 16. Ranking of profile1

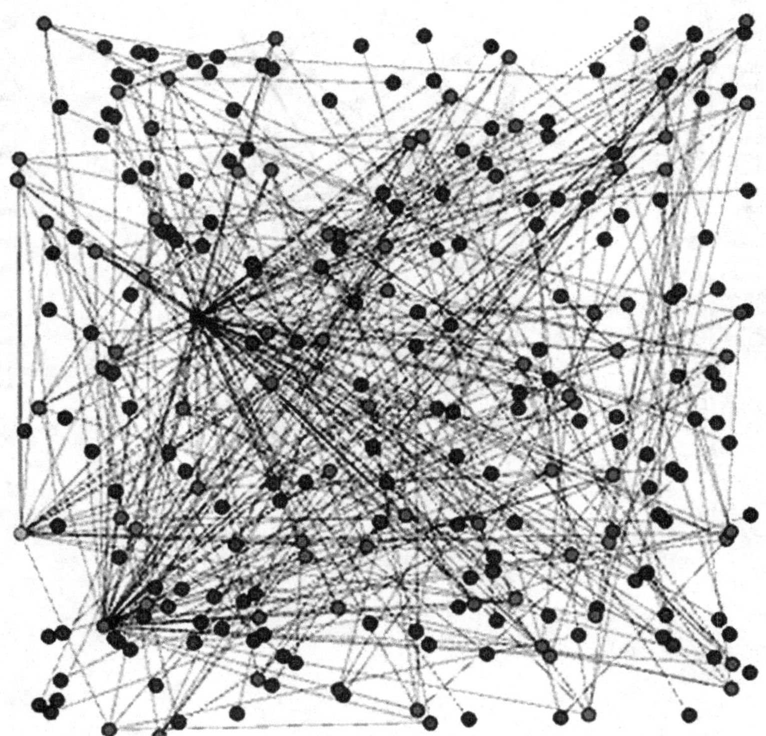

2.6.5.1 Modularity Distribution

It is used for community detection (Fortunato & Castellano, 2007)in the social network. A group of node interact with each other forms a family of node called community. In the figure, we can detect the number of community in a profile based on the different parameters(refer to Figure 17).

Here we see that total number of community is 21 (staring from 0 to 20) and the number of node connected to it is represented in percentage form. Figure 18 represents the same modularity in form of a pie chart and in forms of a table.

There are thirteen number of community detected in this profile starting from 0 to 12 and the number of people joined the proper community is represented in form of percentage and number of node or member in a community is representedin graph as shown.

Graph (as shown in Figure 19) exhibits number of node to the number of modularity class whereModularity class denotes the number of community in the profile which is 13 in this case.

2.6.6 Community Detection

As discussed in earlier section, Community distribution, which represents a clique in a network, is represented in Figure 20 and Figure 21(for absolute and percentage value respectively).

Figure 17. Modularity distribution for profile1

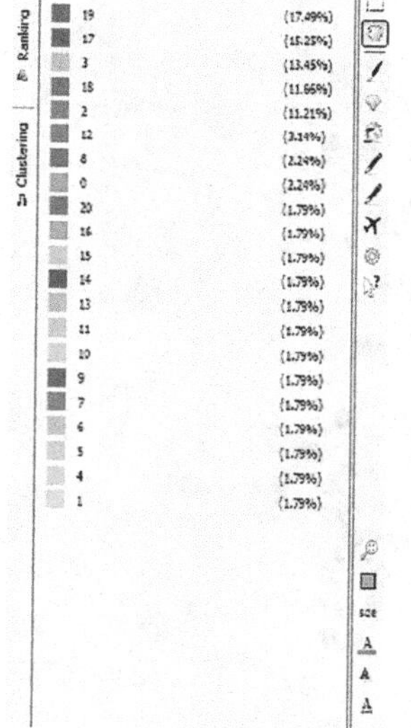

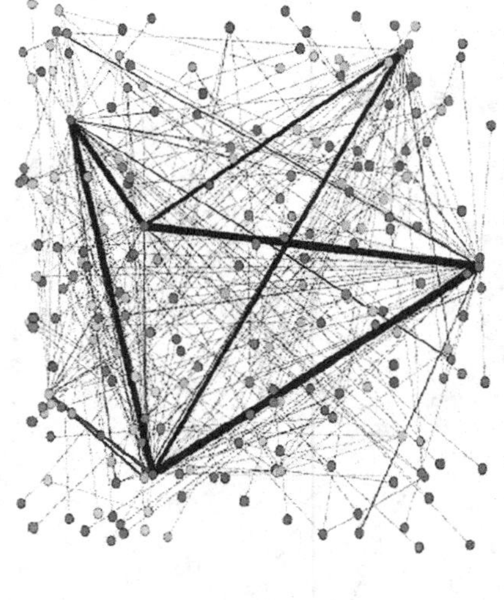

Figure 18. Modularity distribution in form of pie chart and table

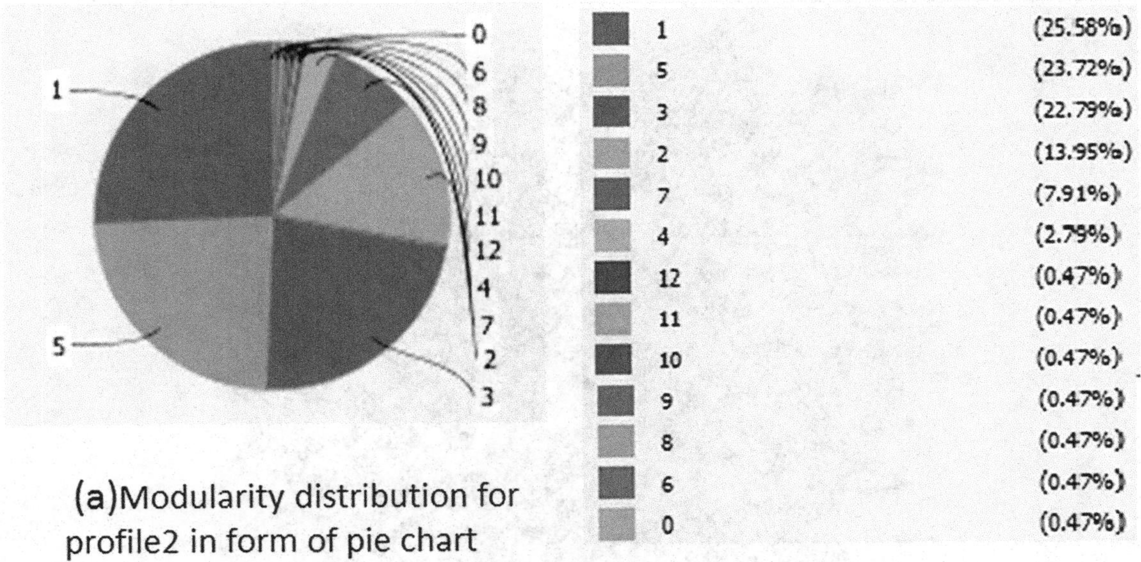

(b) Modularity distributionfor p in form of a table

Figure 19. modularity distribution

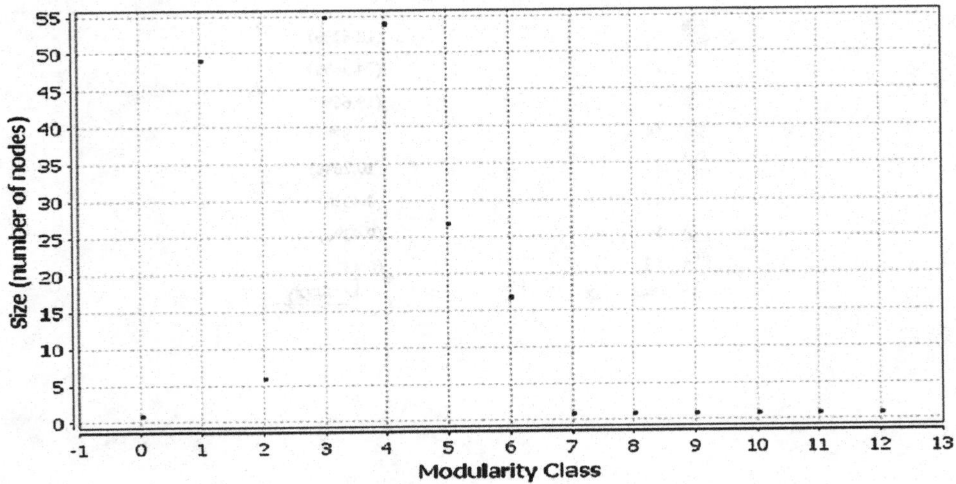

Figure 20. Community distribution of profile3

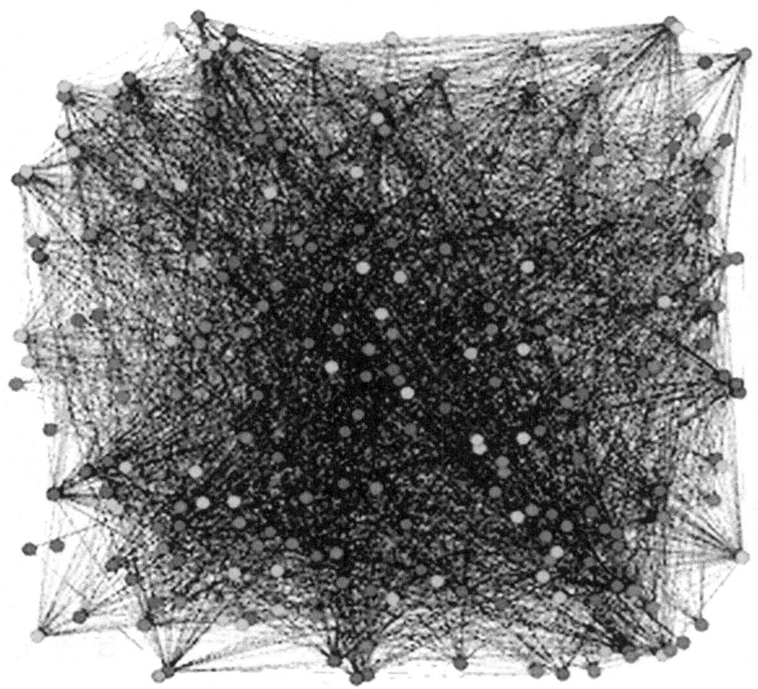

Figure 21. Community distribution of profile3 (in percentage)

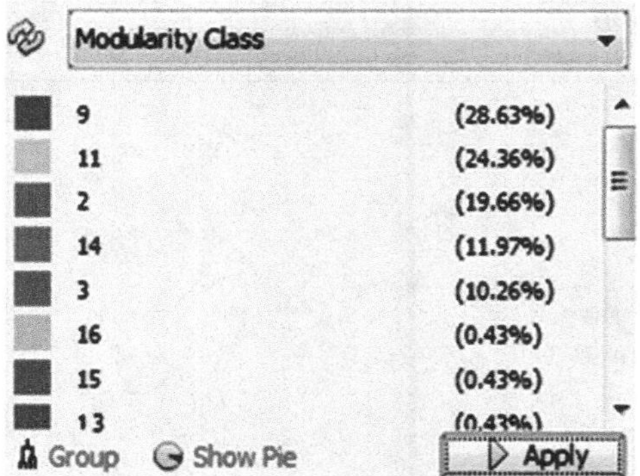

2.6.7 Sex Detection of a Node

One can detect the number of males and the number of females in the communicating group based on the data in the table (as referred in Figure 22).

Here we see that 76.74 percent of the people are male and 23.26 are female (as represented in Figure 23).

Figure 22. Male female identification of profile2

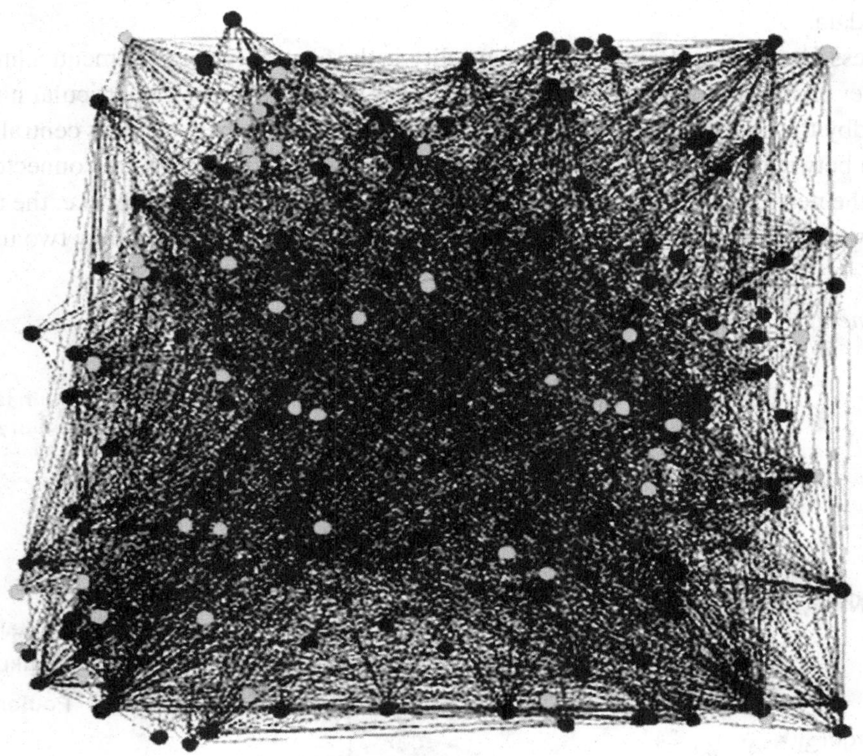

Figure 23. Male female identification ofprofile2 (in percentage)

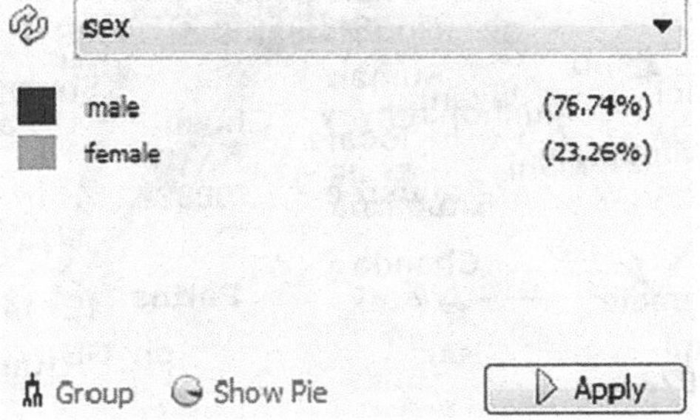

2.6.7.1 Detection of Name of Each Node

We can extract information of each and every node in a network sort by name their identity in the network etc. Using simple R program, we can find the profile pictures also (as shown in Figure 24)

Tabular representation of profile: It is the representation of name, identity, label, sex, locale, agerank in table form so it is called tubular representation and these information can be export from SVG or gdf file. It can also be put in the table directly. Figure 25 represents a data table.

- **Statistics:** It can determine average degree, average weighted degree, Network diameter, Graph Density, PageRank, connected component from the Statistics of the graph. Diameter, Radius, Node degree distribution, Clustering coefficient etc. can be calculated using the statistics obtained from the data.
- **Betweeness Centrality:** Betweenness centrality is the centrality measurementtechnique based on the number of shortest paths between any two nodes that pass through a particular node. Nodesthat connectedby the edge of a network would generally have a low betweenness centrality. The nodes with high betweenness centrality generally refer to the individuals that are connected to the other nodes in the network and play a significant role. We can calculate diameter (i.e. the maximum distance between any two users), radius (i.e. the minimum distance between any two users), Average

Figure 24. Name detection profile1

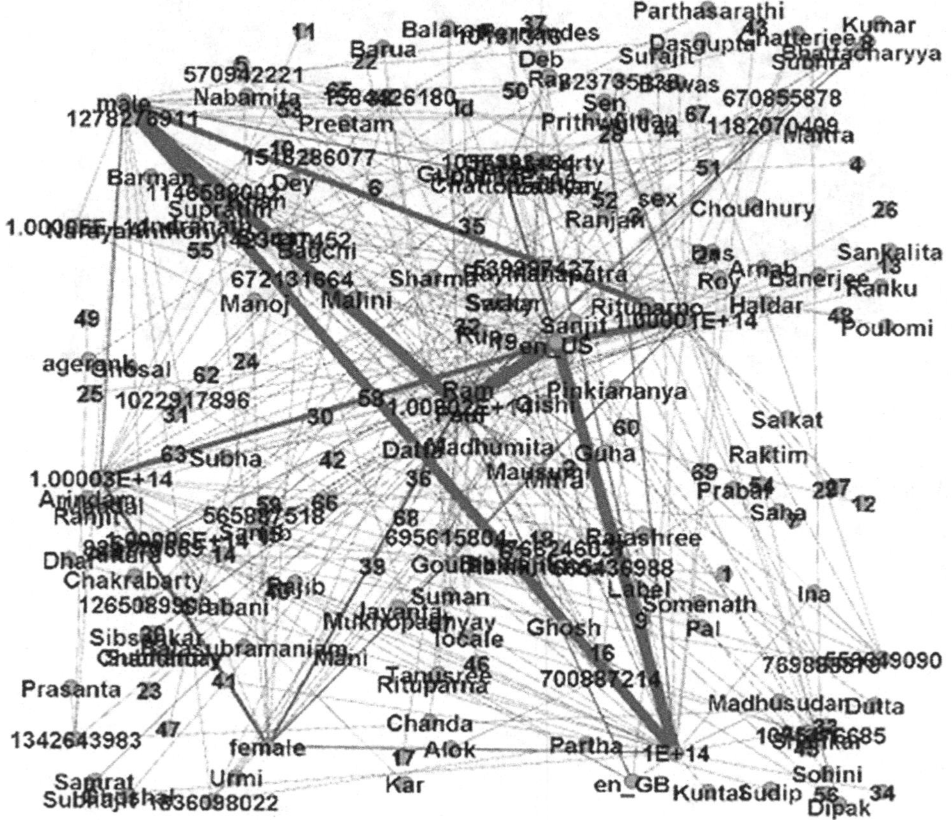

Figure 25. Data table

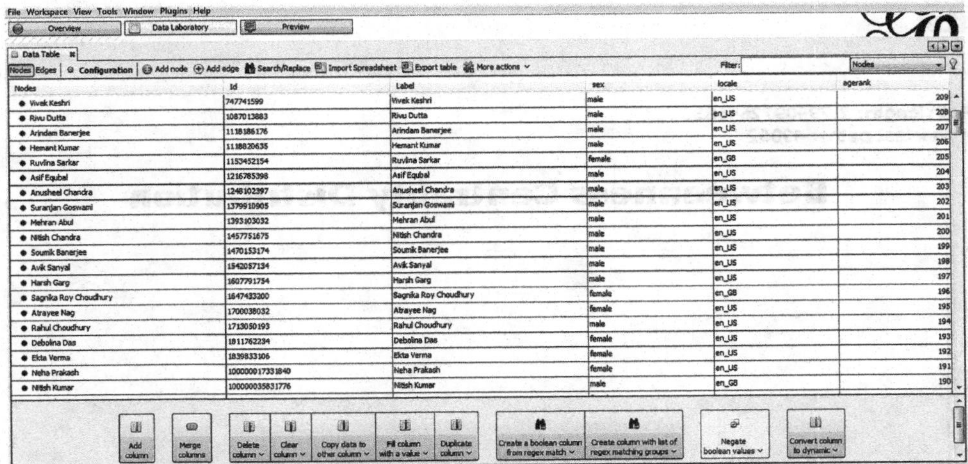

Nodes	Id	Label	sex	locale	agerank
Vivek Keshri	747741599	Vivek Keshri	male	en_US	209
Rivu Dutta	1087013883	Rivu Dutta	male	en_US	208
Arindam Banerjee	1118186176	Arindam Banerjee	male	en_US	207
Hemant Kumar	1118820635	Hemant Kumar	male	en_US	206
Ruvlina Sarkar	1153452154	Ruvlina Sarkar	female	en_GB	205
Asif Equbal	1216785398	Asif Equbal	male	en_US	204
Anusheel Chandra	1248102397	Anusheel Chandra	male	en_US	203
Suranjan Goswami	1379910905	Suranjan Goswami	male	en_US	202
Mehran Abul	1393103032	Mehran Abul	male	en_US	201
Nitish Chandra	1457751675	Nitish Chandra	male	en_US	200
Soumik Banerjee	1470153174	Soumik Banerjee	male	en_US	199
Avik Sanyal	1542057134	Avik Sanyal	male	en_US	198
Harsh Garg	1607791754	Harsh Garg	male	en_US	197
Sagnika Roy Choudhury	1647433200	Sagnika Roy Choudhury	female	en_GB	196
Atrayee Nag	1700038032	Atrayee Nag	female	en_US	195
Rahul Choudhury	1713050193	Rahul Choudhury	male	en_US	194
Debolina Das	1811762234	Debolina Das	female	en_US	193
Ekta Verma	1839833106	Ekta Verma	female	en_US	192
Neha Prakash	100000017331840	Neha Prakash	female	en_US	191
Nitish Kumar	100000035831776	Nitish Kumar	male	en_GB	190

path length (Rodriguez and Yebra, 1999) and number of shortest paths can be calculated from the distribution(as referred in Figure 26).

- **Closeness Centrality:** Closeness centrality (as discussed earlier) is a measure that indicates how close a particular node in the network is to the all other nodes in the network, whether or not the node is existing on a connecting shortest path within other nodes.A high closeness centrality refers to a less average distance between other nodes in the network. So a large closeness centrality means there is a small average distance to all other nodes in the network. A closeness centrality distribution is shown in Figure 27.
- **Eccentricity Distribution:** The eccentricity measure denotes the distance between a node and thefurthest nodefrom that node. So a node with high eccentricity refers to the maximum distant node in the network and a low eccentricity means that the furthest away node is actually not so distant. Figure 28 represents aeccentricity distribution of profile 3.

3. ANALYSIS AND COMPARATIVE STUDY

In Table 1, the value of all the parameters obtained from all three profiles are summarised in a tabular from and characterise the respective profiles.

4. CONCLUSION

The parameters of social network analysis represent the important characteristics of a groupand thus help to understand different aspects. The focus of this chapter is to discuss all important aspects and parameters of social network analysis. With the example of real-time profileparameters are tried to be explained and analysed. Each of the subtopics represent the overview of most focussed research area of social network analysis.

Figure 26. Betweenness centrality of profile3

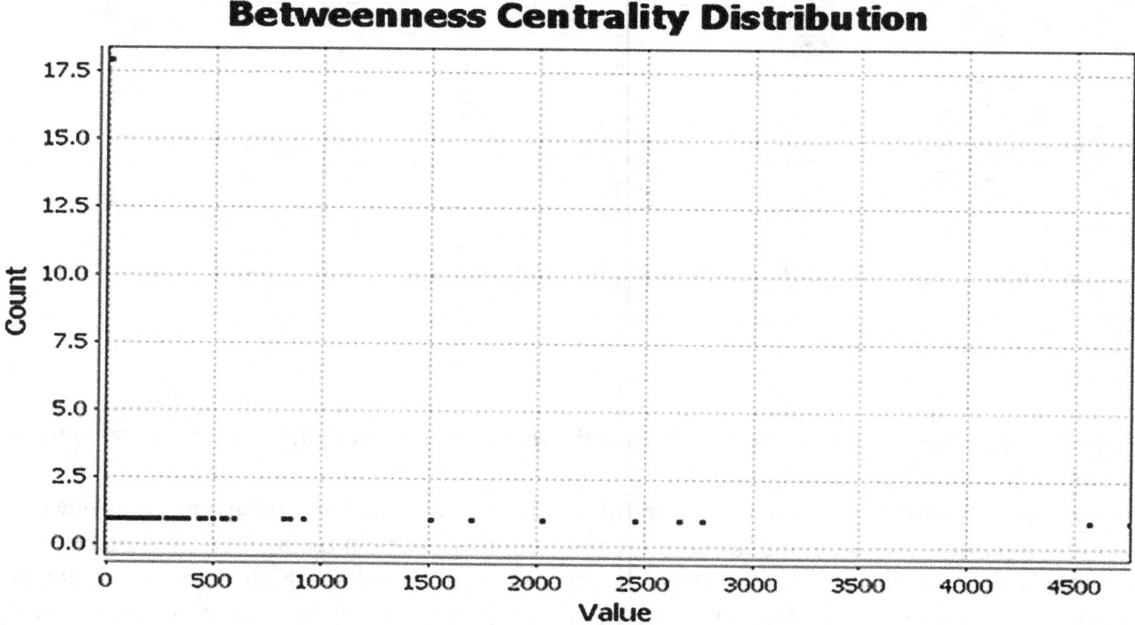

Figure 27. Closeness centrality of profile 2

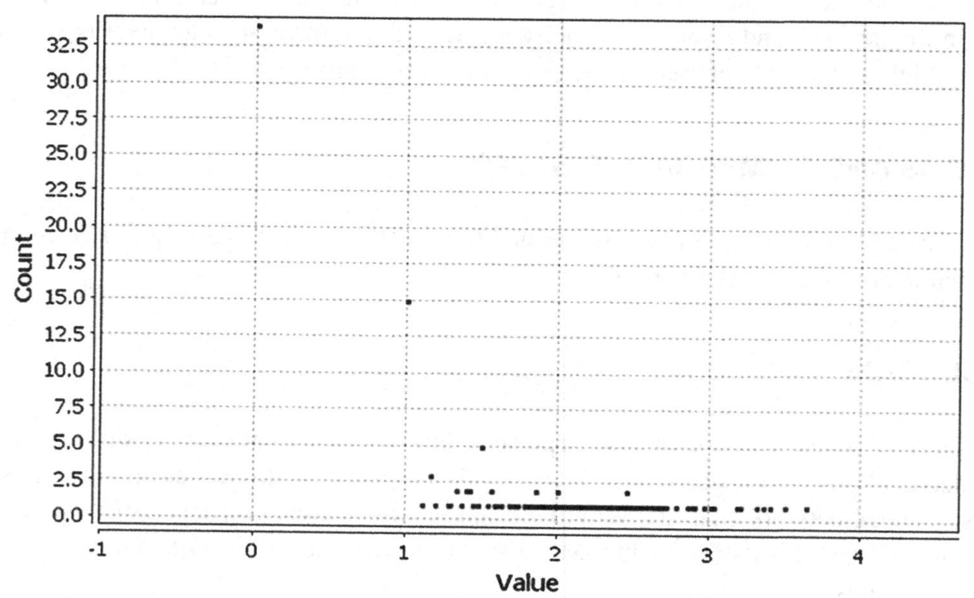

Figure 28. Eccentricity Distribution of profile3

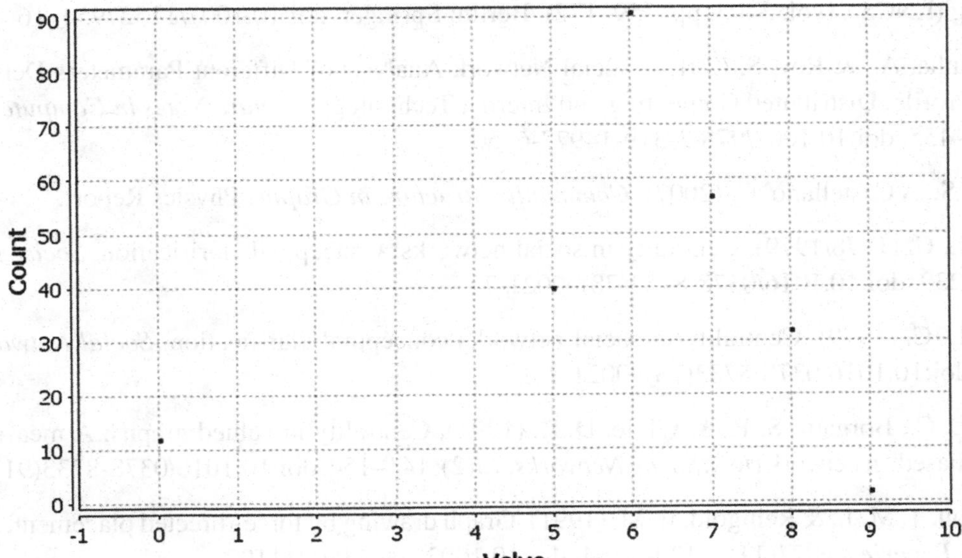

Table 1. A comparative study of parameters of three Facebook profiles

	Profile 1	Profile 2	Profile 3
No. of nodes	69	215	234
No. of edges	357	3114	3310
Diameter	6	8	7
Average path length	3.492	2.45	2.538
Number of communities	21	13	17
Density	0.012	0.135	0.061
Average weighted degree	3.202	28.967	14.145
Clustering Coefficient	0	0.561	0.592
Average path length (after clustering)	3.492	2.45	2.538

REFERENCES

Albert, R., & Barabasi, A. L. (2002). Statistical mechanics of complex networks. *Reviews of Modern Physics*, *74*(1), 47–97. doi:10.1103/RevModPhys.74.47

Bastian, M., Heymann, S., & Jacomy, M. (2009). *Gephi: An Open Source Software for Exploring and Manipulating Networks*. Association for the Advancement of Artificial Intelligence.

Benevenuto, F., Rodrigues, F., & Cha, M. (2009). Characterizing User Behaviour in Online Social Networks. *Proceedings of ACM IMC*.

Bonato, A. (2005). A survey of models of the web graph,Combinatorial and algorithmic aspects of networking (LNCS), (vol. 3405, pp. 159–172). Berlin: Springer. doi:10.1007/11527954_16

Dey, P., Sinha, A., & Roy, S. (2015). Social Network Analysis of Different Parameters Derived from Realtime Profile. Distributed Computing and Internet Technology. *Lecture Notes in Computer Science*, *8956*, 452–455. doi:10.1007/978-3-319-14977-6_50

Fortunato, S., &Castellano, C. (2007). *Community Structure in Graphs*. Physics Report.

Freeman, L. C. (1978/1979). Centrality in social networks: Conceptual clarification. *Social Networks*, *1*(3), 215–239. doi:10.1016/0378-8733(78)90021-7

Freeman, L. C. (1979). Centrality in social networks conceptual clarification. *Social Networks*, *1*(3), 215–239. doi:10.1016/0378-8733(78)90021-7

Freeman, L. C., Borgatti, S. P., & White, D. R. (1991). Centrality in valued graphs: A measure of betweenness based on network flow. *Social Networks*, *13*(2), 141–154. doi:10.1016/0378-8733(91)90017-N

Fruchterman, T. M. J., & Reingold, E. M. (1991). Graph drawing by force-directed placement. *Software, Practice & Experience*, *21*(11), 1129–1164. doi:10.1002/spe.4380211102

Jacomy, M., Heymann, S., Venturini, T., & Bastian, M. (2010). Force Atlas2, A Continuous Graph Layout Algorithm for Handy Network Visualization. *PLoS ONE*, *9*(6).

Kleinberg, J. (1998). Authoritative sources in a hyperlinked environment. *Proceedings of 9th ACM-SIAM Symposium on Discrete Algorithms*.

Latapy, M. (2008). Main-memory triangle computations for verylarge (sparse (power-law)) graphs. *Theoretical Computer Science, 407*(1-3), 458-473.

Morris, J. F., O'Neal, J. W., & Deckro, R. F. (2013). A random graph generation algorithm for the analysis of social networks. J. Defence Model. Simulation Appl. Methodology. *Technology (Elmsford, N.Y.)*, 1–12.

Newman, M. E. (2001). Scientific collaboration networks. II. Shortest paths, weighted networks, and centrality. Physics Review E, 64(1).

Perer, S. (2006). Balancing systematic and flexible exploration of social networks. *Visualization and Computer Graphics. IEEE Transactions on*, *12*(5), 693–700.

Rieder, B. (2013). *Studying Facebook via Data Extraction: The Netvizz Application*. ACM.

Rodriguez, J. A., & Yebra, J. L. A. (1999). It bounding the diameter and the mean distance of a graph from its Eigenvalues: Laplacian versus adjacency matrix methods. *Discrete Mathematics*, *196*(1-3), 267–275. doi:10.1016/S0012-365X(98)00206-4

Ronald, S. B. (1987). Social contagion and innovation: Cohesion versus structural equivalence. *American Journal of Sociology*, *92*(6), 1287–1335. doi:10.1086/228667

Scott, J. (1998). Social Network Analysis. *Sociology*, *22*(1), 109–127. doi:10.1177/0038038588022001007

Valiant, & Leslie, G. (1990). A bridging model for parallel computation. *Communications of the ACM*, *33*(8), 103-111.

Wang, T., Chen, Y., Zhang, X. T., Jin, L., Hui, P., Deng, B., & Li, X. (2011). Understanding Graph Sampling Algorithms for Social Network Analysis. Simplex'11. IEEE.

Wasserman, S. (1994). *Social network analysis: Methods and applications*. Cambridge University Press. doi:10.1017/CBO9780511815478

Wayne, G., & Oellermann, R. O. (2011). *Distance in Graphs, structural Analysis of Complex Networks*. Springer.

Wilson, R. E., Gosling, S. D., & Graham, L. T. (2012). A Review of Facebook Research in the Social Sciences Perspectives. *Psychological Science*, *7*(3), 203–220.

Chapter 11
Evolutionary Computation Techniques for Community Detection in Social Network Analysis

Abhishek Garg
Indian Institute of Technology (BHU) Varanasi, India

Anupam Biswas
Indian Institute of Technology (BHU) Varanasi, India

Bhaskar Biswas
Indian Institute of Technology (BHU) Varanasi, India

ABSTRACT

Community detection is a topic of great interest in complex network analysis. The basic problem is to identify closely connected groups of nodes (i.e. the communities) from the networks of various objects represented in the form of a graph. Often, the problem is expressed as an optimization problem, where popular optimization techniques such as evolutionary computation techniques are utilized. The importance of these approaches is increasing for efficient community detection with the rapidly growing networks. The primary focus of this chapter is to study the applicability of such techniques for community detection. Our study includes the utilization of Genetic Algorithm (GA) and Particle Swarm Optimization (PSO) with their numerous variants developed specifically for community detection. We have discussed several issues related to community detection, GA, PSO and the major hurdles faced during the implication of evolutionary approaches. In addition, the chapter also includes a detailed study of how these issues are being tackled with the various developments happening in the domain.

1. INTRODUCTION

Nowadays, representation of links among various objects present within the data in the form of network is very common in many domains. Such network representation in modern-day data which include social network (Scott, 2012), ecological network (Newman, 2012), biological network (Sah et. al., 2014),

DOI: 10.4018/978-1-4666-9964-9.ch011

biochemical network (Bennett et. al., 2014), citation network (Chen and Redner, 2010), web network (Xiaodong et. al., 2008) and ego network (Biswas and Biswas, 2015) etc are very complex. Analysis of such data with network representation eases the understanding of complex relationships among the objects of the data. The core of such analysis is to understand the relationships through different properties of networks such as network transitivity (Han et. al., 2015), power-law degree distribution (Dorogovtsev and Mendes, 2013), and community structure (Fortunato and Castellano, 2012). In this chapter, we limit our discussion only to community structure property. Incorporation of community structure property in the analysis of such complex networks requires detection of communities. The community detection problem is closely related to the clustering problem that is basically an unsupervised learning of groups based on some similarity measures (Schaeffer, S. E., 2007). Therefore, often community detection problem is also referred as a graph clustering.

Numerous approaches have been developed for detecting communities efficiently. These approaches can be categorized broadly into four categories: Node centric, Group centric, Network centric and Hierarchy centric community detection. In node centric community detection, each node or object of a community has to follow certain properties. Clique percolation method is a node centric approach that is based on complete mutuality of nodes. In group centric community detection, group as a whole has to follow certain properties without looking into details of nodes. One such property is group-density (Pattillo et. al., 2013)that must be greater than certain threshold. In network centric community detection, whole network is partitioned into various groups by considering connections of whole network. A function is defined covering entire network and optimized that function. Popular methods such as modularity maximization approaches (Newman, 2004; Clauset et.al., 2004; Blondel et. al., 2008; Medus et. al., 2005; Duch and Arenas, 2005) and spectral clustering (Chauhan et. al., 2009; Arenas et. al., 2006; Shen and Cheng, 2010; Richardson et. al., 2009)are fall under this category. In hierarchy centric community detection, hierarchical structure of communities is formed by analyzing network at different resolution, where hierarchy is represented with a dendrogram. Agglomerative clustering approaches and divisive clustering approaches (Schaeffer, S. E., 2007) are the examples of hierarchy centric community detection approaches. Among these approaches, the network centric approaches are the essence of this chapter where requires optimization of a function bound to the network.

The function that is defined in network centric approaches has to be optimized efficiently to get effective communities. Here, two major questions needed to be resolved. First question is about how to design a suitable function for obtaining better communities. Follow-up second question is about how to optimize the defined function. One approach for resolving the first question is through rigorous study of network and required communities. Another alternative, easy, and widely utilized approach is simply use the quality metrics. Numerous quality metrics such as modularity (Newman and Girvan, 2004), conductance (Kannan et. al., 2004), Silhouette Index (Tan et. al., 2006), cut ratio (Fortunato, 2009), community score (Pizzuti, 2008) are already proposed. These quality metrics are actually defined for measuring the quality of communities detected with any algorithm. Newman is the first to utilize these metrics directly for optimization. He has proposed a greedy approach that optimizes the quality metric modularity (Newman, 2004). Such optimization has been proved as NP-hard problem (Brandes et. al., 2006). Thus for resolving second question several approximation methods(Newman, 2004; Blondel et. al., 2008) has been proposed to detect communities efficiently. Evolutionary computation techniques are in the forefront to solve NP-hard problem. These approaches are competent to detect comparatively better quality communities then other approaches in less time (Tasgin et. al., 2007; Xiaodong et. al., 2008). We consider two of such techniques namely Genetic Algorithm (GA) and Particle Swarm Optimization (PSO) for our study. Both these techniques are very popular not only for community detection but also to the domains where applications require optimization. The study covers the issues associated with community detection problem and these techniques. In addition, the fundamental issues that are relevant to community detection and the applicability of any other optimization techniques are also discussed in detailed manner.

Rest of the chapter is organized as follows. Section 2 explains the basic community detection problem, GA and PSO with suitable examples. Section 3 discusses ongoing research associated with the evolutionary computation techniques for community detection. Section 4 addresses applicability issues while incorporate GA and PSO or any other such techniques. Section5presents a generalized model where any population based evolutionary computation technique can be fit easily. Section 6 discusses the various issues that pop up while applying evolutionary computation techniques into community detection problem both from the view point of community detection problem and optimization problem along with possible solutions. Section 7 expresses the concluding remarks and future research directions.

2. BACKGROUND

2.1 Community Detection Problem Definition

Community detection is a process to detect various communities exists in a network, where community is a group of closely connected nodes. A group is considered as closely connected if among the nodes of the have higher number edges. There has no rigorous definition for communities as far as community detection is concerned. However, connectivity patterns among nodes are often considered detecting communities from a network. Nodes within the communities should be connected *densely* while connectivity with the nodes of other communities should be *minimal*. Hence, community detection problem in general has two objectives that have to be optimized to obtain good quality communities.

Considering a network represented in the form of a graph $G(V, E)$, where V is a set of nodes E and a function $E : V \times V \rightarrow \{0,1\}$ is defined on, here 0 represents presence of connection while 1 represents absence of connection. Community detection is process of finding anon-empty finite set of k communities $C = \{C_1, C_2, ..., C_k\}$ on graph G such that

- Any $C_i \in C$ is a subgraph $C_i = (V_i, E_i)$ with $V_i \in V$ nodes and $E_i \in E$ connections,
- for all $u, v \in V_i$, if there exists a connection $(u, v) \in E$ then $(u, v) \in E_i$,
- $\bigcup_{i=1}^{k} V_i = V$ and,
- $V_i \cap V_j = \varnothing$ if and only if $V_i = V_j$, for all $C_i, C_j \in C$.

2.2 Genetic Algorithm

Genetic algorithm (GA) has been proposed by Bremermann (Bremermann, 1958).In field of computer science this concept is further extended by John Holland (Holland, 1975). This strategy is based on Darwin's principle of survival of the fittest and evolution theory. GAis used to solve optimization problems over both types of search spaces continuous and discrete where a fitness function needs to be optimized. It is a stochastic population based search method, which means, it starts with initial set of random solutions. Flow of GA process is presented in Figure 1. In GA, solutions are encoded in the form of binary or integer, which are known as chromosomes. GA improves the fitness value of function over each generation by applying variation operators and selection technique on chromosomes. Variation operators are used to provide solution diversity over search space by producing offspring population and, selection techniques are used to preserve quality of solutions in next generation. There are two variation operators used to produce offspring population: crossover and mutation. These operators are applied on selected parent solutions by selection technique from population. There are number of selection techniques available such as fitness-proportional selection (Neumann et. al., 2009), tournament selection method (Noraini and Geraghty, 2011). Crossover operator is a binary operator that produces offspring solutions by exchanging parts oftwo solutions from current generation. There are various variants of crossover operators are available such as k-point crossover (De Jong et. al., 1992) and uniform crossover (Burjorjee, 2013). Some variants also have been proposed which treat crossover as ternary operator or, n-ary operator where more than two parents are used to produce offspring population (Elsayed et. al., 2011). Mutation operator is a unary operator, which produces offspring population by modifying on average a random gene of each solution from current generation. Variation operators are controlled by parameter p_c (crossover probability) and p_m (mutation probability) to handle exploitation and exploration of search space (Srinivas and Patnaik, 1994; Meng et. al., 1999; Eiben and Smith, 2003).

A simple example to illustrate the basic process of GA is presented as follows. Suppose we are maximizing a function $f(x) = x^2$ in range 0 to 31. Here, we can use binary encoding to represent a solution. Let population is of size 2 and random.

$Chromosome1 = 00100$

$Chromosome2 = 10001$

The fitness of chromosomes is computed by decoding those as shown below:

$f(Chromosome1) = f(00100) = f(4) = 16$
$f(Chromosome2) = f(10001) = f(17) = 289$

Figure 1. Procedure of GA algorithm

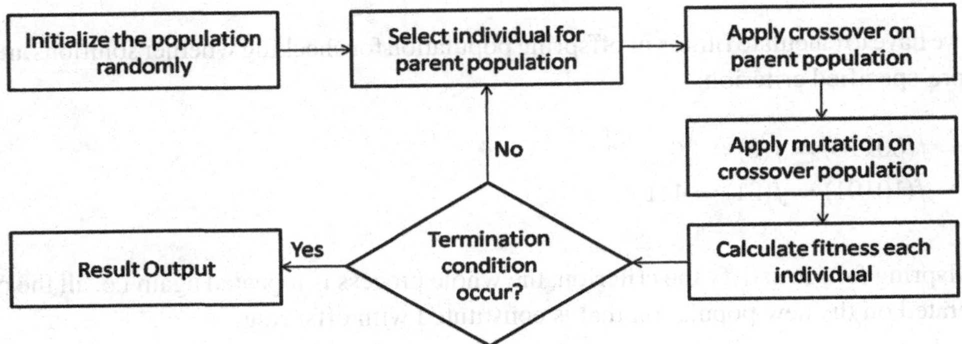

Here, population is of size 2 so both are selected to obtain parent population otherwise we have to apply any selection technique. Now, we apply crossover operator on these parents.

- **Single Point Crossover:** Randomly choose where to give spaces:

001 00 = 00101

100 01 = 10000

- **Multi Point (Two) Crossover:** Randomly choose where to give *k* spaces:

00100 = 00000

10001 = 10101

- **Uniform Crossover:** Any gene value can exchange:

00100 = 00101

10001 = 10000

After this mutation is applied, where any gene value can be changed. But it is practical to mutate only one gene from a chromosome.

Before mutation:

$Child1 = 00101$

$Child2 = 10000$

After mutation:

$Child1 = 00110$

$Child2 = 10101$

Again, we have to calculate fitness of offspring population for checking whether solutions are achieved as per the pre-specified criterion:

$f(Child1) = f(00110) = f(6) = 36$
$f(Child2) = f(10101) = f(21) = 441$

If the offspring fails to satisfy the criterion, the whole process is repeated again i.e. all the operations will be operated on the new population that is constituted with offspring.

Initially fixed size chromosomes were used to represent a solution as shown above. Kotani has proposed a variable size chromosome scheme, which increases the final fitness value of function (Kotani et. al., 2001). There are many variants of GA such as steady state GA, where only two parents are selected for replacement with best fitness solutions out of these parents and offsprings generated by these parents (Agapie and Wright, 2014), multi-objective GA, where more than one fitness functions need to be optimized (Konak et. al., 2006). Chaotic theory is also successfully incorporated into GA for further improvement (Ebrahimzadeh and Jampour, 2013).

2.3 Particle Swarm Optimization

Particle Swarm Optimization (PSO) is also a population based search optimization algorithm based on animal social behavior such as birds flocking. This algorithm was introduced by Eberhart and Kennedy using only velocity vector without inertia (Eberhart and Kennedy, 1995). To improve the efficiency of PSO, concept of inertia is introduced by Eberhart & Shi (Eberhart and Shi, 2000). This variant of PSO is considered as standard PSO. It is easy to implement and quickly converge to good solution. Each solution is known as particle that is composition of position vector and velocity vector. Each particle adjusts position according to its own experience and its neighbor's experience. The flow of PSO is presented in the Figure 2.PSO combines local search method with global search method and attempt to balance exploration and exploitation of search space for optimized solution. Each particle stores its known best position vector and current position vector with velocity vector.

Position vector of ith particle in d-dimensional space at time t is represented as $X_i(t) = (x_{i1}, x_{i2}, \ldots, x_{id})$ and velocity vector is represented as $V_i(t) = (v_{i1}, v_{i2}, \ldots, v_{id})$. At time t, best position tracked so far for each particle i is stored in a vector $P_i(t)$ and, global best position tracked so far for all the particle is stored in vector $G(t)$

$$V_i(t+1) = w.V_i(t) + c_1.r_1(P_i(t) - X_i(t)) + c_2.r_2(G(t) - X_i(t))$$
$$X_i(t+1) = X_i(t) + V_i(t+1)$$

Here, r_1,r_2 are two random variables in range [0,1] and w is inertia weight and, c_1 is known as cognitive coefficient and c_2 is known as acceleration coefficient in range [0,1].

Figure 2. Procedure of PSO algorithm

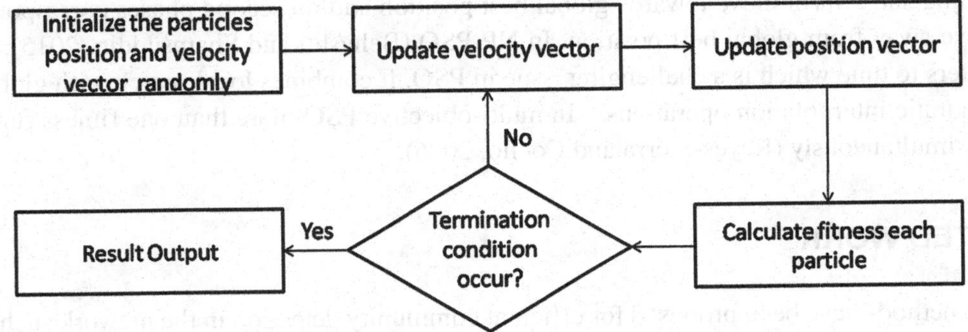

First component in this equation "velocity vector with inertia" is used to search in nearby space, second component helps to move along best position of particle and, last component is used to move along best position among all particles which leads to global optimum value of fitness function.

Same simple example as used above for GA is also used here to illustrate the PSO procedure. Suppose we are maximizing the function $f(x) = x^2$ in range 0 to 31. Let, we choose real encoding for representing particle as position and velocity vector and, we also assume each particle has velocity vector value zero initially, $V(0) = 0$. Let, swarm size is 2, $w = 0.5, c_1 = 2, c_2 = 2, r_1 = 0.5$, and $r_2 = 0.5$

$$Particle1 = 5 \ f(Particle1) = 25$$

$$pbest(Particle1) = 5$$

$$Particle2 = 2 \ f(Particle2) = 4$$

$$pbest(Particle2) = 2$$

$$gbest = 5$$

$$V(Particle1) = 0.5 * 0 + 2 * 0.5 * (5 - 5) + 2 * 0.5 * (5 - 5) = 0$$
$$V(Particle2) = 0.5 * 0 + 2 * 0.5 * (2 - 2) + 2 * 0.5 * (5 - 2) = 3$$
$$Particle1 = 5 + 0 = 5$$
$$Particle2 = 2 + 3 = 5$$

If fitness of particle satisfies necessary criterion, the process ends otherwise it continues.

There are lot of improvements takes place on PSO such as constriction factor method (Chen et. al., 2011), use of chaotic theory with PSO so that search space become more distributed (Masuda and Kurihara, 2007) and by adding one component called cognitive avoidance to PSO so that particle can move against its worst position (Biswas et. al., 2013). There are many variants of PSO also available such as binary PSO, which operate on binary search space (Khanesar et. al., 2007). Multi-start PSO where particle position and velocities are reinitialized based on some probability to enhance the exploration of search space (Talukder, 2011). Inmulti-phase PSO (Al-kazemi and Mohan, 2002), the main swarm of particles is partitioned into two sub swarms and, algorithm executes in two phases. In first phase, corresponding sub swarm move towards global best position and, in second phases corresponding sub swarm move away from global best position. In NP-PSO (Beheshti and Shamsuddin, 2015), there are no parameters to tune which is a challenging issue in PSO. It combines local search with global search by two quadratic interpolation operations. . In multi-objective PSO more than one fitness function are optimized simultaneously (Reyes-Sierra and Coello, 2006).

3. RELATED WORK

Numerous methods have been proposed for efficient community detection in the network such as graph partitioning methods which are based on minimum cut and number of communities must be known prior (Fortunato, 2010), hierarchical clustering methods which can be categorized into agglomerative and divisive methods (Han et. al., 2006),spectral methods which compute vertex similarity using matrix algebra to detect communities (Chung, 1997) and so on; for full review of clustering algorithms follow (Schaeffer, 2007).Agglomerative method is based on bottom-up approach where, each node is considered as unique communities initially after those new communities are formed by combining previously observed communities based on some similarity measures. On the contrary, divisive method is based on top-down approach where whole network is considered as a community initially after that new communities are formed by dividing previously observed communities based on some similarity measure. Girvan introduces a divisive approach based on edge betweenness as a similarity measure but this algorithm has high computational complexity (Girvan and Newman, 2002). In spectral methods, communities are detected using eigenvector of matrices such as adjacency matrix (Chauhan et. al., 2009), Standard Laplacian matrix (Arenas et. al., 2006), Normalized Laplacian matrix (Shen and Cheng, 2010), and correlation matrix (Shen et. al., 2010).Nowadays, evolutionary computation techniques are utilized to solve community detection problem more effectively. The community detection problem is transformed into a combinatorial optimization problem defining objective function, which is solved with popular evolutionary techniques such as GA and PSO. Community detection, in terms of optimization problem, can be defined as division of network into such *k*(*unknown*) communities that best satisfy $f(c_1, c_2, \ldots, c_k)$ where $c_1, c_2, \ldots, c_k$ are *k* communities and *f* is a fitness function to optimize.

In recent years, lot of research has been done to detect communities using GA. Tasgin and his colleagues is the first to use GA into community detection (Tasgin et. al., 2007). As explained above, important steps of GA are: choosing an encoding scheme, defining a fitness function and applying variation operators effectively to produce good solutions. In this scheme, modularity is used as a fitness function and, straight forward representation is used for chromosome. Traditional crossover cannot work properly so a new crossover operator is introduced with point mutation operator. This introduction of evolutionary computation was very successful in community detection. In same line of work, Pizzuti develops a new fitness function, the community score to overcome the problems in modularity (Pizzuti, 2008). Traditional variation operators can be effectively used with locus based representation. For very large networks, a new GA has been introduced which provides better accuracy and, efficiency (Liu et. al. 2007). In this algorithm, crossover operator is not used and mutation operator similar to simulated annealing is used with local hill climbing operation. The search capability of this approach is not effective so new GA with ensemble learning proposed (He et. al., 2009). Here, multi-individual crossover operator is used based on traditional crossover with an ensemble learning using edge join strength and, edge structural similarity. Specialized mutation operator is used in this approach to reduce search space of solution so that algorithm can converge quickly. To overcome the problems of mutation operator new mutation techniques with local search strategy has been introduced in GA for community detection (Jin et. al., 2010). This mutation technique is based on marginal gene concept. To improve efficiency all above algorithm, new coding scheme is used which exhibits more features of modularity (Li et. al., 2014). Result of this algorithm shows it provide better result in each iteration continuously. These approaches consider only topological information to detect community. A new algorithm (He and Chan, 2014) has been developed which is not only based on topological information but also attributes of vertices and edges of network. It consists of special crossover and mutation operators to speed up the convergence. All above discussed approach partition the network into various communities. However, sometimes it is interesting to identify that a node belongs to several communities. Bello-Orgazhas proposed a GA based approach for same (Bello-Orgaz and Camacho, 2014). Here, new coding scheme is followed, where chromosomes are represented as set of vectors of binary values with traditional crossover operators. Various quality metrics density, centralization, clustering coefficient, heterogeneity and neighborhood are combined to develop a fitness function. The results are comparable to heuristic based approaches.

PSO is also another evolutionary computation technique that is used widely for community detection problem. It has some advantages over GA such as fast convergence and simple procedure. Use of PSO in community detection is introduced by Xiaodong and his colleagues, where network divides iteratively into two communities (Xiaodong et. al., 2008). Particles are generated randomly and a function is applied on random values to associate either of two community ids with particles. The approach has a chance of getting isolated nodes because of stochastic nature of PSO. To solve the problem two repairing strategies are proposed for absolute isolated node and flexible isolated node. The resultant communities are better and fast than some previous methods. Qu has proposed another repairing strategy based on edge betweenness on same previous approach (Qu, 2013). The results are more effective. A similarity based clustering with PSO algorithm is proposed by Chen and Qui,where PSO is applied on new weighted graph (Chen and Qui, 2013). Applying PSO in this new weighted graph is equivalent to applying on original graph. This new weighted graph is formed by applying clustering on original graph. This approach uses locus based representation to represent particles on which modified PSO is applied with modularity as fitness function. As we know, modularity is not a best fitness function (Almeida et.al., 2011). New fitness functions is proposed by Yahia and his colleagues that combines modularity and inter class inertia, with standard PSO (Yahia et. al., 2013). This function is proved very effective for community detection. Community detection in multi featured network using PSO is proposed in (Biswas et. al., 2014). Here, a novel encoding scheme is used where each particle is encoded in terms instances. To assign instance to a community, similar approach to k-means is used without re-evaluation. This approach use Davies-Bouldin index to calculated fitness value. To find overlapping communities using PSO spectral based approach is discussed in (Shi et. al., 2009).

4. APPLICABILITY OF EVOLUTIONARY COMPUTATION

Evolutionary computation techniques are very effective in solving both optimization problems: continuous and combinatorial. Combinatorial optimization problems are NP - complete in nature. In that case, approximation methods such as evolutionary techniques are becoming very useful solution. As mentioned earlier, community detection problem can be treated as a combinatorial optimization problem where various quality metrics and others can be used as a function to be optimized. Therefore, it is quite reasonable that evolutionary computation techniques can be effectively used to solve community detection problem.

There are various issues in applying evolutionary computation on different kind of problems. Some of the massive problems are as follows: encoding scheme to represent solution, handling different operators effectively in collaboration with encoding scheme, develop a fitness function and choosing values of various parameters of approach. Setting the value of these parameter need much of skill. Other issues such as encoding scheme and effective use of different operators in collaboration with encoding scheme is handled in various ways; discussed in detail in previous section (section 3). Most commonly, quality metrics such as modularity is used as fitness function. Nevertheless, no quality metric behaves best in all situations. All quality metrics are biased about one or other factors such as number of community more or less, community size and others (Almeida et. al., 2011).

Evolutionary computation based approaches provide various advantage in community detection than other optimization approaches and, heuristics approaches. Networks on which community detection is applied are very large so that detection of communities takes much time. On the contrary, evolutionary computation based approach reduces this time. These approaches are easy to implement. Moreover, evolutionary computation based approaches do not need arbitrary convergence criteria.

5. GENERALIZED APPROACH

For community detection using any evolutionary approach, we have to follow some steps and applying evolutionary approach is one-step of this. Whole process of community detection is presented in the following algorithm:

Algorithm:

Step 1: Choose a representation to represent communities in a network.
Step 2: Develop a fitness function that needs to be optimized.
Step 3: Randomly initialize the population of solution.
Step 4: Calculate fitness of each solution in population.
Step 5: Apply any evolutionary approach to create new population using its operators.
Step 6: Calculate fitness of each solution in new population.
Step 7: Check whether stopping criteria met to stop the condition.

a. If yes, return the resultant communities with optimized fitness function and stop.
b. If no, go to Step.5

Step 1: *Choose a representation for describing community.* We are free to choose any representation scheme for representing communities in the form of a solution. There are some well-known representations to represent communities in a network (Tasgin et. al., 2007; Pizzuti, 2008). First, a number is assigned to each community and an array of integers with size number of nodes in the network is maintained. This is known as straight forward representation where element of array corresponds to one node in network and, contained value is an integer which represents the community number of nodes. Second, another array of integers with size number of nodes in the network is maintained, where each element corresponds to one node in the network. The integer value contained in the array is the identities of nodes that belong to same community. This approach is known as locus based representation. This approach does not need pre knowledge of number of communities so it is a better approach for representing communities. An example is shown in the Figure 3.

Here, array location is the node id. Elements of the array represent community id in representation 1, node id in representation 2.

Step 2: *Develop a fitness function.* There are various predefined quality metrics, which can be used as fitness functions for community which needs to be optimized. One of widely used fitness function is modularity, which needs to be maximized for finding better communities. This optimization approach will choose an individual with highest modularity among all population. There is no

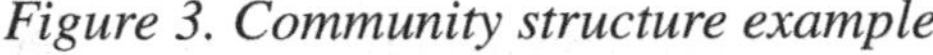

Figure 3. Community structure example

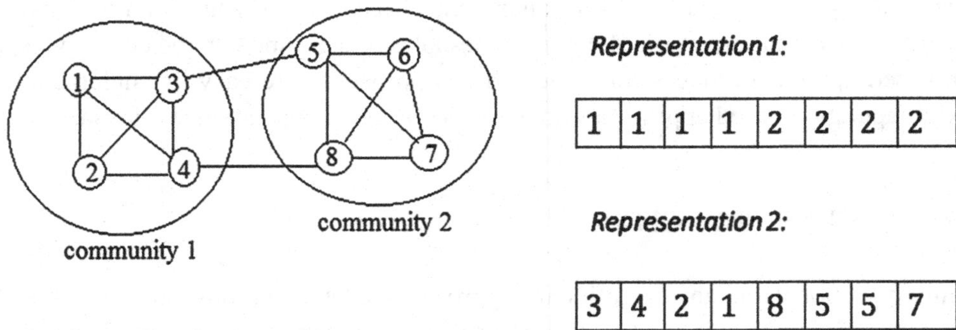

available best fitness function yet for this problem because every quality metric is biased about some factors (Almeida et.al., 2011).

Step 3: *Initialization of population.* Population is consists of many individuals. The entries of individual solution are filled randomly. However, such random entries may result in invalid solutions when there has no exist of any path to reach any node to other node using nodes of same community. In the representation, below of Figure 3is an example of invalid entries for the Representation 1. The Representation 1.has no path exist between node 1 and node 6 in community 1. in . To be in same community nodes must be connected. Same invalid entries between node 1 and node 6 and exist below in Representation 2.

Any heuristic technique can be used to resolve the problem so that mostly individuals are become valid. Reason behind giving emphasize on valid individuals is that they helps in converging the algorithm fast. For representation 1, community identity is assigned to each node of individual and, select some of nodes randomly after assigning same community identity to neighbors of those randomly selected nodes. Nevertheless, this approach cannot claim validity of safe individual but results may better. For representation 2, corresponding entries in individual solution are filled with each node randomly from its neighbor nodes. This always results in valid individuals. Some approaches follows division of network into two iteratively where representation 1 is a prominent strategy.

Step 4: *Apply Evolutionary computation technique.* There are various approaches to solve combinatorial optimization problems. In this generic approach any evolutionary technique can be used for optimizing the function designed for community detection. Evolutionary computation techniques give comparable results to approximation method but in less time. Evolutionary strategies are also very simple to implement. In this chapter, only GA and PSO are discussed as evolutionary computation techniques. Both are population based techniques to solve optimization problems.

Step 5: *Check stopping criteria met or not.* There are many stooping criteria to stop the execution of the algorithm. Generally, the limit of iteration of algorithm is completed or expected allowable error in the solution is considered for stopping.

5.1 Genetic Algorithm as an Evolutionary Technique

GA can be effectively used to detect communities in a large network, which use two kinds of operator selection technique and, variation operators such as crossover and mutation. There are number of variants of variation operators have been proposed to match the encoding scheme or to improve the efficiency. In this chapter, two variants will be discussed based on previous two representations.

For traditional crossover operator, majorly used uniform crossover, representation 1 is not a good choice but can be used on representation 2 easily. It is because in representation 1, same communities can be represented by various different chromosomes. It means there is usually no relation between two chromosomes by this representation. Here, crossover operator is used to combine two or more chromosomes. Thus, a new variant of cross-over is proposed called single sided crossover where one chromosome for crossover is identified as a source and other chromosome identified as destination. Then, randomly select one community id from source and search for nodes having this community id in source after that transfer the community id of these nodes in source to destination chromosome.

For mutation, mostly point mutation operator is applied. In this, initially a chromosome is randomly selected to mutate. Then two vertices are selected randomly, say v_i and v_j. Community id of node v_j is is set to community id of node v_i. And, simple approach can be change community id of node v_i to v_j to, where v_j is one neighbor of v_i, in randomly selected chromosome. This results in safe individual so convergence is fast.

There are various selection operators are available in GA. For community detection, traditional selection operators such as tournament based selection, fitness proportional selection are used frequently, which follows elitism strategy.

5.2 Particle Swarm Intelligence as an Evolutionary Technique

PSO is effectively used in community detection because of its fast convergence. Here, most important component is to update position and velocity vectors with effective value of algorithmic parameters. There are various variants of PSO, which can be used interchangeably in this problem too. One of variant is cognitive avoidance PSO which take less time to converge but quality is little bit degraded than other variants which takes high processing time (Biswas et. al., 2015).

Same standard PSO formula can be used to update the velocity and position vector. Some researchers also allow traditional updating method where, particle encoded in a range of values. This traditional updation technique can also be used with representation 1 for position vector with choice of two communities. And, it looks more effective. Same updating strategy with modular operation has also been applied with representation2 with This modular operation is followed to result values in range.

Isolated nodes occur while applying PSO in most cases. There are various strategy to tackle it such as Absolute isolated node repairing strategy, Flexible isolated node repairing strategy, extremal optimization strategy and so on. Absolute isolated node is an isolated whose neighbors belong to same community. Flexible isolated node is an isolated node whose neighbors may not belong to same community. In absolute isolated node, neighbor's community id is given to isolated node. In flexible isolated node, most occurred community id in neighbor is given to isolated node. Flexible isolated node strategy converges fast than flexible isolated node strategy.

6. DISCUSSION

In this section, various issues of evolutionary computation and community detection problem are discussed. It is followed with issue arises while applying evolutionary techniques to community detection and find what is the advantage of using evolutionary computation. Most of the issues addressed here with possible solutions. Following are the issues solely related to community detection problem:

1. There has no exact definition on which similarity of nodes to be defined. Therefore, most commonly topological intuition is used as similarity measure which stated a community as a collection of node with dense connection and sparse with others.
2. The computation complexity of mentioned definition is NP hard. Thus, different quality metrics are used which are computationally better.
3. These quality metrics are biased about situation so resultant communities are not necessarily accurate but better.
4. Number of communities is unknown. It is automatically less effective as effective quality metric is developed.

Several issues that must be taken care-off during the implementation of evolutionary computation techniques into community detection problem, which are as following:

1. The first issue faced while applying any evolutionary technique is representation of solution. There are various representation are used such as straight forward representation, locus based representation and so on.
2. Other issue faced is development of computationally efficient fitness function. There are various quality metrics which are used as a fitness function because function based on actual definition of community, density and sparsity, takes high computation time.
3. Initialization of population is also a problem because of existence of unsafe individual which make convergence slow. There are several approach has been discussed to make safe population.
4. Same problem existence of unsafe individuals may also arise with algorithmic operators. To handle this different approaches have been proposed.

Evolutionary computation techniques are used to find global optimum solution. Incorporation of these techniques in any application including community detection faces following general issues that are consequences of these approaches itself:

1. These techniques repeatedly calculate the fitness value of solution. If fitness function is expensive as case with many real world application, it takes lot of time to solve.
2. Stopping criterion is another hurdle of these techniques since it is highly dependent on application . Improper stopping criterion may result in degraded solutions.
3. There has a chance of solutions being stuck into local minimum.
4. There is no internal procedure to handle the different constraints of given problem.

There are various heuristic approaches to solve community detection problems. After resolving issues with evolutionary computation while applying to community detection, the results are comparable to heuristic approaches but in less time. The time is a highly important constraint in community detection problem because usually real world networks are very large. Another advantage of using evolutionary computation technique is it does not need to know number of communities in prior as the case with some heuristic algorithms.

7. CONCLUSION AND FUTURE RESEARCH DIRECTIONS

Efficient community detection is a necessity for modern day networks that are diverse in nature and very large. Classical approaches, mostly the heuristics are not sufficient due to the time complexity. Moreover, community detection problem is NP-hard problem. Hence, treatment of the problem with approximation methods such as evolutionary computation techniques would be handy. Primary focus of this chapter is to address the issues associated with these techniques while accumulate those in community detection problem, particularly GA and PSO. Numerous difficulties have to be resolved during incorporation these techniques into community detection. Solution representation and designing of objective function are the two major issues. Despite of these issues incorporation of evolutionary computation techniques into community detection is gaining popularity and success in efficient community detection.

Though community detection has great importance in most of the complex network analysis, still there has much space for research to solve several issues. The definition of community itself is not clear that exactly what would be the best properties that can constitute communities irrespective of the domain. Dealing with real world diverse network of huge sizes is another end of the research. Evaluation of communities detected with any algorithm is also very important for ensuring the quality of communities. Development of good metrics for measuring quality of communities would be very beneficial for the applications of different domains.

REFERENCES

Agapie, A., & Wright, A. H. (2014). Theoretical analysis of steady state genetic algorithms. *Applications of Mathematics*, *59*(5), 509–525. doi:10.1007/s10492-014-0069-z

Al-kazemi, B., & Mohan, C. K. (2002, May). Multi-phase generalization of the particle swarm optimization algorithm. In *Computational Intelligence, Proceedings of the World on Congress on* (*Vol. 1*, pp. 489-494). IEEE. doi:10.1109/CEC.2002.1006283

Almeida, H., Guedes, D., Meira, W. Jr, & Zaki, M. J. (2011). Is there a best quality metric for graph clusters? In *Machine Learning and Knowledge Discovery in Databases* (pp. 44–59). Springer Berlin Heidelberg. doi:10.1007/978-3-642-23780-5_13

Arenas, A., Díaz-Guilera, A., & Pérez-Vicente, C. J. (2006). Synchronization reveals topological scales in complex networks. *Physical Review Letters*, *96*(11), 114102. doi:10.1103/PhysRevLett.96.114102 PMID:16605825

Beheshti, Z., & Shamsuddin, S. M. (2015). Non-parametric particle swarm optimization for global optimization. *Applied Soft Computing*, *28*, 345–359. doi:10.1016/j.asoc.2014.12.015

Bello-Orgaz, G., & Camacho, D. (2014, July). Evolutionary clustering algorithm for community detection using graph-based information. In *Evolutionary Computation (CEC), 2014 IEEE Congress on* (pp. 930-937). IEEE. doi:10.1109/CEC.2014.6900555

Bennett, L., Kittas, A., Liu, S., Papageorgiou, L. G., & Tsoka, S. (2014). Community Structure Detection for Overlapping Modules through Mathematical Programming in Protein Interaction Networks. *PLoS ONE*, *9*(11), e112821. doi:10.1371/journal.pone.0112821 PMID:25412367

Biswas, A., & Biswas, B. (2015). Investigating Community Structure in Perspective of Ego Network. *Expert Systems with Applications*, *42*(20), 6913–6934. doi:10.1016/j.eswa.2015.05.009

Biswas, A., Gupta, P., Modi, M., & Biswas, B. (2014).Community Detection in Multiple Featured Social Network using Swarm Intelligence. In *International Conference on Communication and Computing*.

Biswas, A., Gupta, P., Modi, M., & Biswas, B. (2015). An Empirical Study of Some Particle Swarm Optimizer Variants for Community Detection. In *Advances in Intelligent Informatics* (pp. 511–520). Springer International Publishing. doi:10.1007/978-3-319-11218-3_46

Biswas, A., Kumar, A., & Mishra, K. K. (2013, August). Particle Swarm Optimization with cognitive avoidance component. In *Advances in Computing, Communications and Informatics (ICACCI), 2013 International Conference on* (pp. 149-154). IEEE. doi:10.1109/ICACCI.2013.6637162

Blondel, V. D., Guillaume, J. L., Lambiotte, R., & Lefebvre, E. (2008). Fast unfolding of communities in large networks. *Journal of Statistical Mechanics*, *2008*(10). doi:10.1088/1742-5468/2008/10/P10008

Brandes, U., Delling, D., Gaertler, M., Görke, R., Hoefer, M., Nikoloski, Z., & Wagner, D. (2006). *Maximizing modularity is hard.* arXiv preprint physics/0608255

Bremermann, H. J. (1958). *The evolution of intelligence: The nervous system as a model of its environment.* University of Washington, Department of Mathematics.

Burjorjee, K. M. (2013, January). Explaining optimization in genetic algorithms with uniform crossover. In *Proceedings of the twelfth workshop on Foundations of genetic algorithms XII* (pp. 37-50). ACM. doi:10.1145/2460239.2460244

Chauhan, S., Girvan, M., & Ott, E. (2009). Spectral properties of networks with community structure. *Physical Review E: Statistical, Nonlinear, and Soft Matter Physics*, *80*(5), 056114. doi:10.1103/PhysRevE.80.056114 PMID:20365050

Chen, A. P., Huang, C. H., & Hsu, Y. C. (2011). Particle swarm optimization with inertia weight and constriction factor. In *International Conference on Swarm Intelligence (ICSI)*, (pp. 1-11).

Chen, P., & Redner, S. (2010). Community structure of the physical review citation network. *Journal of Informetrics*, *4*(3), 278–290. doi:10.1016/j.joi.2010.01.001

Chen, Y., & Qiu, X. (2013). Detecting Community Structures in Social Networks with Particle Swarm Optimization. In *Frontiers in Internet Technologies* (pp. 266–275). Springer Berlin Heidelberg. doi:10.1007/978-3-642-53959-6_24

Chung, F. R. (1997). *Spectral graph theory* (Vol. 92). American Mathematical Soc.

Clauset, A., Newman, M. E., & Moore, C. (2004). Finding community structure in very large networks. *Physical Review E: Statistical, Nonlinear, and Soft Matter Physics*, *70*(6), 066111. doi:10.1103/PhysRevE.70.066111 PMID:15697438

De Jong, K. A., & Spears, W. M. (1992). A formal analysis of the role of multi-point crossover in genetic algorithms. *Annals of Mathematics and Artificial Intelligence*, *5*(1), 1–26. doi:10.1007/BF01530777

Dorogovtsev, S. N., & Mendes, J. F. (2013). *Evolution of networks: From biological nets to the Internet and WWW*. Oxford University Press.

Duch, J., & Arenas, A. (2005). Community detection in complex networks using extremal optimization. *Physical Review E: Statistical, Nonlinear, and Soft Matter Physics*, *72*(2), 027104. doi:10.1103/PhysRevE.72.027104 PMID:16196754

Eberhart, R. C., & Kennedy, J. (1995, October). A new optimizer using particle swarm theory. In *Proceedings of the sixth international symposium on micro machine and human science* (Vol. 1, pp. 39-43). doi:10.1109/MHS.1995.494215

Eberhart, R. C., & Shi, Y. (2000). Comparing inertia weights and constriction factors in particle swarm optimization. In *Evolutionary Computation, 2000. Proceedings of the 2000 Congress on* (*Vol. 1*, pp. 84-88). IEEE. doi:10.1109/CEC.2000.870279

Ebrahimzadeh, R., & Jampour, M. (2013). Chaotic Genetic Algorithm based on Lorenz Chaotic System for Optimization Problems. *International Journal of Intelligent Systems and Applications*, *5*(5), 19–24. doi:10.5815/ijisa.2013.05.03

Eiben, A. E., & Smith, J. E. (2003). *Introduction to evolutionary computing*. Springer Science & Business Media. doi:10.1007/978-3-662-05094-1

Elsayed, S. M., Sarker, R. A., & Essam, D. L. (2011, June). GA with a new multi-parent crossover for solving IEEE-CEC2011 competition problems. In *Evolutionary Computation (CEC), 2011 IEEE Congress on* (pp. 1034-1040). IEEE.

Fortunato, S. (2010). Community detection in graphs. *Physics Reports*, *486*(3), 75–174. doi:10.1016/j.physrep.2009.11.002

Fortunato, S., & Castellano, C. (2012). Community structure in graphs. In *Computational Complexity* (pp. 490–512). Springer New York. doi:10.1007/978-1-4614-1800-9_33

Girvan, M., & Newman, M. E. (2002). Community structure in social and biological networks. *Proceedings of the National Academy of Sciences of the United States of America*, *99*(12), 7821–7826. doi:10.1073/pnas.122653799 PMID:12060727

Han, H. J., Schweickert, R., Xi, Z., & Viau-Quesnel, C. (2015). The Cognitive Social Network in Dreams: Transitivity, Assortativity, and Giant Component Proportion Are Monotonic. *Cognitive Science*, n/a. doi:10.1111/cogs.12244 PMID:25981854

Han, J., Kamber, M., & Pei, J. (2006). *Data mining, Southeast Asia edition: Concepts and techniques*. Morgan kaufmann.

He, D., Wang, Z., Yang, B., & Zhou, C. (2009, November). Genetic algorithm with ensemble learning for detecting community structure in complex networks. In *Computer Sciences and Convergence Information Technology, 2009. ICCIT'09. Fourth International Conference on* (pp. 702-707). IEEE. doi:10.1109/ICCIT.2009.189

He, T., & Chan, K. C. (2014, July). Evolutionary community detection in social networks. In *Evolutionary Computation (CEC), 2014 IEEE Congress on* (pp. 1496-1503). IEEE. doi:10.1109/CEC.2014.6900570

Holland, J. H. (1975). *Adaptation in natural and artificial systems: an introductory analysis with applications to biology, control, and artificial intelligence*. U Michigan Press.

Jin, D., He, D., Liu, D., & Baquero, C. (2010, October). Genetic algorithm with local search for community mining in complex networks. In *Tools with Artificial Intelligence (ICTAI), 2010 22nd IEEE International Conference on* (Vol. 1, pp. 105-112). IEEE. doi:10.1109/ICTAI.2010.23

Kannan, R., Vempala, S., & Vetta, A. (2004). On clusterings: Good, bad and spectral. *Journal of the ACM*, *51*(3), 497–515. doi:10.1145/990308.990313

Khanesar, M. A., Teshnehlab, M., & Shoorehdeli, M. A. (2007, June). A novel binary particle swarm optimization. In *Control & Automation, 2007. MED'07. Mediterranean Conference on* (pp. 1-6). IEEE.

Kitchovitch, S., & Liò, P. (2011). Community structure in social networks: Applications for epidemiological modelling. *PLoS ONE*, *6*(7), e22220. PMID:21789238

Konak, A., Coit, D. W., & Smith, A. E. (2006). Multi-objective optimization using genetic algorithms: A tutorial. *Reliability Engineering & System Safety*, *91*(9), 992–1007. doi:10.1016/j.ress.2005.11.018

Kotani, M., Ochi, M., Ozawa, S., & Akazawa, K. (2001). Evolutionary discriminant functions using genetic algorithms with variable-length chromosome. In *Neural Networks, 2001. Proceedings. IJCNN'01. International Joint Conference on* (Vol. 1, pp. 761-766). IEEE. doi:10.1109/IJCNN.2001.939120

Li, X., Gao, C., & Pu, R. (2014, August). A community clustering algorithm based on genetic algorithm with novel coding scheme. In *Natural Computation (ICNC), 2014 10th International Conference on* (pp. 486-491). IEEE. doi:10.1109/ICNC.2014.6975883

Liu, X., Li, D., Wang, S., & Tao, Z. (2007). Effective algorithm for detecting community structure in complex networks based on GA and clustering. In *Computational Science–ICCS 2007* (pp. 657–664). Springer Berlin Heidelberg.

Masuda, K., & Kurihara, K. (2007, September). Global optimization with chaotic particles inspired by swarm intelligence. In *SICE, 2007 Annual Conference* (pp. 1319-1324). IEEE. doi:10.1109/SICE.2007.4421187

Medus, A., Acuna, G., & Dorso, C. O. (2005). Detection of community structures in networks via global optimization. *Physica A: Statistical Mechanics and its Applications, 358*(2), 593-604.

Meng, Q. C., Feng, T. J., Chen, Z., Zhou, C. J., & Bo, J. H. (1999). Genetic algorithms encoding study and a sufficient convergence condition of gas. In *Systems, Man, and Cybernetics, 1999. IEEE SMC'99 Conference Proceedings. 1999 IEEE International Conference on* (Vol. 1, pp. 649-652). IEEE. doi:10.1109/ICSMC.1999.814168

Neumann, F., Oliveto, P. S., & Witt, C. (2009, July). Theoretical analysis of fitness-proportional selection: landscapes and efficiency. In *Proceedings of the 11th Annual conference on Genetic and evolutionary computation* (pp. 835-842). ACM. doi:10.1145/1569901.1570016

Newman, M. E. (2004). Fast algorithm for detecting community structure in networks. *Physical Review E: Statistical, Nonlinear, and Soft Matter Physics*, *69*(6), 066133. doi:10.1103/PhysRevE.69.066133 PMID:15244693

Newman, M. E., & Girvan, M. (2004). Finding and evaluating community structure in networks. *Physical Review E: Statistical, Nonlinear, and Soft Matter Physics*, *69*(2), 026113. doi:10.1103/PhysRevE.69.026113 PMID:14995526

Newman, M. E. J. (2012). Communities, modules and large-scale structure in networks. *Nature Physics*, *8*(1), 25–31. doi:10.1038/nphys2162

Noraini, M. R., & Geraghty, J. (2011). *Genetic algorithm performance with different selection strategies in solving TSP*. Academic Press.

Pattillo, J., Veremyev, A., Butenko, S., & Boginski, V. (2013). On the maximum quasi-clique problem. *Discrete Applied Mathematics*, *161*(1), 244–257. doi:10.1016/j.dam.2012.07.019

Pizzuti, C. (2008). Ga-net: A genetic algorithm for community detection in social networks. In Parallel Problem Solving from Nature–PPSN X (pp. 1081-1090). Springer Berlin Heidelberg.

Reyes-Sierra, M., & Coello, C. C. (2006). Multi-objective particle swarm optimizers: A survey of the state-of-the-art. *International Journal of Computational Intelligence Research, 2*(3), 287-308.

Richardson, T., Mucha, P. J., & Porter, M. A. (2009). Spectral tripartitioning of networks. *Physical Review E: Statistical, Nonlinear, and Soft Matter Physics*, *80*(3), 036111. doi:10.1103/PhysRevE.80.036111 PMID:19905184

Sah, P., Singh, L. O., Clauset, A., & Bansal, S. (2014). Exploring community structure in biological networks with random graphs. *BMC Bioinformatics*, *15*(1), 220. doi:10.1186/1471-2105-15-220 PMID:24965130

Schaeffer, S. E. (2007). Graph clustering. *Computer Science Review*, *1*(1), 27–64. doi:10.1016/j.cosrev.2007.05.001

Scott, J. (2012). Social network analysis. *Sage (Atlanta, Ga.)*.

Shen, H. W., & Cheng, X. Q. (2010). Spectral methods for the detection of network community structure: A comparative analysis. *Journal of Statistical Mechanics*, *2010*(10), P10020. doi:10.1088/1742-5468/2010/10/P10020

Shen, H. W., Cheng, X. Q., & Fang, B. X. (2010). Covariance, correlation matrix, and the multiscale community structure of networks. *Physical Review E: Statistical, Nonlinear, and Soft Matter Physics*, *82*(1), 016114. doi:10.1103/PhysRevE.82.016114 PMID:20866696

Shi, Z., Liu, Y., & Liang, J. (2009, November). PSO-based community detection in complex networks. In *Knowledge Acquisition and Modeling, 2009. KAM'09. Second International Symposium on* (Vol. 3, pp. 114-119). IEEE. doi:10.1109/KAM.2009.195

Srinivas, M., & Patnaik, L. M. (1994). Genetic algorithms: A survey. *Computer*, *27*(6), 17–26. doi:10.1109/2.294849

Talukder, S. (2011). *Mathematical Modelling and Applications of Particle Swarm Optimization.* (Doctoral dissertation). Blekinge Institute of Technology.

Tan, P. N., Steinbach, M., & Kumar, V. (2006). *Introduction to data mining* (Vol. 1). Boston: Pearson Addison Wesley.

Tasgin, M., Herdagdelen, A., & Bingol, H. (2007). *Community detection in complex networks using genetic algorithms.* arXiv preprint arXiv:0711.0491

Xiaodong, D., Cunrui, W., Xiangdong, L., & Yanping, L. (2008, June). Web community detection model using particle swarm optimization. In *Evolutionary Computation, 2008. CEC 2008.(IEEE World Congress on Computational Intelligence). IEEE Congress on* (pp. 1074-1079). IEEE. doi:10.1109/CEC.2008.4630930

Yahia, N. B., Saoud, N. B. B., & Ghezala, H. B. (2013). Evaluating community detection using a bi-objective optimization. In *Intelligent Computing Theories* (pp. 61–70). Springer Berlin Heidelberg. doi:10.1007/978-3-642-39479-9_8

KEY TERMS AND DEFINITIONS

Combinatorial Optimization Problems: These are optimization problems having discrete search space or, have some constraints on search space. Commonly a decision problem is associated with them. A Simple example is to find minimum spanning tree. Search space is discrete because not all combination of vertices and edges are valid.

Gene: A smallest unit of a chromosome. It can be of arbitrary length. Its value is known as Allele.

Genotype: An individual solution which deals with genetic algorithm. It is also known as Chromosome.

Multi-Objective Optimization Problems: These are the optimization problem involving more than one objective functions (fitness functions). Generally objectives are conflicting to each other so, we have to make trade - off among objectives.

NP-Hard Problem: A problem is NP-hard if there does not exist any algorithm to solve it in polynomial time.

Optimization Problems: A problem of finding best solution (either maximum or minimum) from set of all feasible solutions. A simple example is to find maximum value of function $f(x) = x^2$.

Phenotype: An individual solution which is decoded form of a chromosome. It deals with real world domain.

Chapter 12
Differential Evolution Dynamic Analysis in the Form of Complex Networks

Lenka Skanderova
VSB Technical University of Ostrava, Czech Republic

Ivan Zelinka
VSB Technical University of Ostrava, Czech Republic

ABSTRACT

In this work, we investigate the dynamics of Differential Evolution (DE) using complex networks. In this pursuit, we would like to clarify the term complex network and analyze its properties briefly. This chapter presents a novel method for analysis of the dynamics of evolutionary algorithms in the form of complex networks. We discuss the analogy between individuals in populations in an arbitrary evolutionary algorithm and vertices of a complex network as well as between edges in a complex network and communication between individuals in a population. We also discuss the dynamics of the analysis.

1. INTRODUCTION

Differential evolution is a simple yet efficient heuristic originally designed for global optimization over continuous spaces that has been used in many research areas. Thanks to its simple and efficient scheme it is used in many areas of the global optimization research. For example, Kovačević, Mladenović, Petrović, and Milošević (2014) described self-adaptive DE with crossover neighbourhood search for continuous global optimization. Dos Santos Coelho, Ayala, and Mariani (2014) introduced self-adaptive DE based on Gaussian probability distribution, gamma distribution and chaotic sequence. Mlakar, Petelin, Tušar, and Filipič (2015) proposed a novel multi-objective evolutionary algorithm DE for multi-objective optimization based on Gaussian process models.

It is well known, that DE is very sensitive to the choice of the mutation and crossover strategies and their associated control parameters. Tuning of these parameters is time consuming. From this reason, Brest, Greiner, Bošković, Mernik, and Zumer (2006) described DE using self-adaptive control parameters

DOI: 10.4018/978-1-4666-9964-9.ch012

(jDE) where each individual in the population is extended with its own control parameters F_i (mutation constant) and CR_i (crossover rate).

Yang, Tang, and Yao (2008) introduced DE with neighbourhood strategy (NSDE) to adapt the mutation constant (scale factor) F. In the same year, these authors presented self-adaptive NSDE (SaNSDE) to improve NSDE's performance where three self-adaptive mechanisms are incorporated: self-adaptation for two candidate mutation strategies (DE/rand/1/bin and DE/best/1/bin), self-adaptations for controlling mutation constant (scale factor) F and crossover rate CR, respectively (Yang, Yao, & He, 2008). Das, Abraham, Chakraborty, and Konar (2009) used a neighbourhood-based mutation operator to improve variants of DE/target-to-best/1/bin scheme.

Mallipeddi and Suganthan (2010) proposed a DE with an ensemble of mutation and crossover strategies and their associated control parameters (EPSDE). EPSDE consists of a pool of mutation and crossover strategies along with a pool of values for each of the associated control parameters. JADE (Iorio & Li, 2005) and DE/current-to-rand/1 (Zaharie, 2009) are used as the mutation strategies and binomial and exponential crossover are used as the crossover strategies.

Islam, Das, Ghosh, Roy, and Suganthan (2012) introduced an adaptive DE algorithm with novel mutation and crossover strategies for global numerical optimization where three algorithmic components have been proposed. First, DE/current-to-gr_best/1 has been introduced, then the modification of the conventional binomial crossover scheme of DE by introducing a fitness-induced bias in the selection of parents from the current generation has been described. Third, the authors suggested the schemes to update the values of the mutation constant F and crossover rate CR in each generation.

DE with composite trial vector generation strategies and control parameters (CODE) was proposed by Wang, Cai, and Zhang (2011) where authors use the strategy candidate pool with three variants of DE, DE/rand/1/bin, DE/rand/2/bin and DE/current-to-rand/1/bin. For each target vector three trial vectors are generated and the best one is then selected to the new generation, if it is better than the target vector.

DE with intersect mutation operator called IMDE was introduced by Zhou, Li, and Gao (2013). In this algorithm, the population of the individuals are divided into two parts – better and worse according to their objective function values. Authors described two novel mutation and crossover operations to generate new individuals. The experimental results showed that the IMDE is better, or at least comparable to above mentioned jDE.

Yi, Gao, Li, and Zhou (2015) presented a new DE with hybrid mutation operator and self-adapting control parameters for global optimization (HSDE) where each individual is enhanced by its own mutation constant F_i and crossover rate CR_i similarly as in the case of jDE. For each target vector the mutation vector is created such that five mutually different parents are selected randomly. The classical DE/rand/1/bin strategy is applied to generate mutation vector when the objective function value of the target vector is better than the objective function value of the first two parents, otherwise DE/current-to-best/1/bin is applied.

The most of the above mentioned researches are dealing with three ways how to improve DE. The first one is to propose more efficient mutation operators, the second one is focused on the control parameters settings and the third method deals with the process of the parent selection in the mutation step. In the first part of this chapter, we will deal with the analysis of the complex networks created by the differential evolution dynamics and in the second part, we will focus on the third approach described above – parent selection in the mutation step where the weighted clustering coefficient will be used to improve differential evolution convergence rate.

Many schemes of the parent selections where three, four, and even five parents are selected in the mutation step have been introduced.

As it is mentioned above, despite the fact that the DE is an efficient optimizer, especially for continuous optimization, its structure has some limitations. Many researchers proposed modifications to the original algorithm of DE.

Neri and Tirronen (2010) presented a survey on DE and its recent advances. Eight algorithms have been divided into two groups: algorithms integrating additional components within DE structure (TDE (Neri & Tirronen, 2010), DEahcSPX (Fan & Lampinen, 2003), DESFLS (Noman & Iba, 2008) and DEPSR (Tirronen, Neri, & Rossi, 2009) and algorithms which employ a modified DE (OBDE (Brest & Maucec, 2008), DEGL (Rahnamayan, Tizhoosh, & Salama, 2008), SADE (Chakraborty, Das, & Konar, 2006) and jDE (Brest, Greiner, Bošković, Mernik, & Zumer, 2006). The next comparative study has been provided by Das and Suganthan (2011) where authors presented the detailed review of the basic concepts of DE and a survey of its major variants, its application to multi-objective, constrained, large scale, and uncertain optimization problems. The comparative study of Mezura-Montes, Velázquez-Reyes, and Coello Coello (2006) showed that the DE/best/1/bin where one of three parents in the mutation step is the individual with the best objective function value reached worse results in the case of the non-separable and multi-modal problems than for example DE/rand/2/bin or DE/current-to-rand/1/bin. These results led us to the idea to find out the individual which will be the best from the view of the successful spreading of the high quality genomes. In the other words, the individual is considered to be the most successful (best) if it is used to create the offspring with the better objective function value than the target vector most often. From this reason, in our approach, we map each individual in the generation to the node and the relationships between individuals to the edges of the graph. Thanks to this visualization we are able to observe the dynamics of DE and analyse some properties of the corresponding complex networks (CNs).

In this work, two variants of DE are investigated: DE/best/1/bin and DE/rand/1/bin. We have supposed that there will be differences between the properties of the CNs created on the basis of the DE/best/1/bin and DE/rand/1/bin dynamics. In DE/best/1/bin one parent is not selected randomly in the mutation step. It is the individual with the best objective function value and in our opinion this individual will play the key role in the corresponding CN structure. In the first part of this work, seven properties of the CNs will be analysed: node weighted out-degree, graph distance, global clustering coefficient, local clustering coefficient, weighted clustering coefficient, closeness, and betweenness centrality. In the second part of this work, on the basis of the analysis of the CNs, we have selected the weighted clustering coefficient to be incorporated into the DE/rand/1/bin to improve its convergence rate. The parents in the mutation step are selected on the basis of the weighted clustering coefficient. The higher weighted clustering coefficient means the higher probability to become the parent in the mutation step. This principle is based on the theory that the individual with the genomes of a high quality should spread them more often than the individuals with the genomes of the lower quality.

The connection of the evolutionary algorithms (EAs) and complex networks (CNs) is not unknown. Soleimani-pouri, Rezvanian, and Meybodi (2014) dealt with solving of the maximum clique problem in social networks where ant based particle swarm algorithm is used. Wu and Hao (2015) made a review on algorithms for maximum clique problem. Gong, Cai, Chen, and Ma (2014) described complex network clustering by multi-objective discrete particle swarm optimization based on decomposition. In (Li, Liu, & Liu, 2014), a comparative analysis of evolutionary and memetic algorithms for community detection from signed social networks is described. Since 1999, Ashlock, Smucker, and Walker (1999) described graph-based genetic algorithm using a combinatorial graph to limit choice of crossover partner. Mabu,

Hirasawa, and Hu (2007) described a graph-based evolutionary algorithm and graph-based evolutionary algorithm with reinforcement learning.

In the years 2010 and 2011, Zelinka, Davendra, Snášel, Jašek, Senkeřik, and Oplatková (2010) described the method for visualizing the dynamics of EA by the CNs and investigated the analogy between the individuals in the population and nodes of the CN and the relationships between individuals in the EA and the edges between the nodes in CN. Davendra, Zelinka, Senkerik, and Pluhacek (2014) analysed the development of the CN in the discrete self-organizing migrating algorithm and Davendra, Zelinka, Metlicka, Senkerik, & Pluhacek (2014) introduced the complex network analysis of DE algorithm applied to flow shop with no-wait problem where several properties of the created complex networks (adjacency graph, minimal cut, degree centrality, closeness centrality, betweenness centrality, mean neighbour degree, k-Clique, k-Club and k-Clan) are analysed.

As we will show in the next sections, our approach extends the ideas mentioned in the publications (Zelinka, Davendra, Snášel, Jašek, Senkeřik, & Oplatková, 2010) and (Zelinka, Davendra, Chadli, Senkerik, Dao, & Skanderova, 2013). The way how we construct the CNs reflects the behaviour of individuals during the generations of the DE.

The rest of the paper is organized as follows: The differential evolution is described briefly in Section 2. Section 3 is focused on the CN properties that will be analysed. The goal of Section 4 is to clarify the interpretation of the CNs properties from the view of DE. Section 5 describes the creation of the complex network to reflect the DE dynamics and the role of the weighted clustering coefficient in the enhanced algorithms. Experiments and their results are provided in Section 6 while Section 7 gives the discussion and the conclusion.

2. DIFFERENTIAL EVOLUTION

DE is a powerful evolutionary algorithm introduced by Storn and Price (1995). Here, let us describe the DE/rand/1/bin which is one of the most commonly used strategy of DE. DE works with the population of NP individuals $\vec{x}_i^G$, $I = \{1, \ldots, NP\}$. G denotes one generation. One individual $\vec{x}_i^G$ consists of D parameters. Each parameter is constrained by its search range $[x_{\text{lower},j}, x_{\text{upper},j}]$ where *lower* denotes the lower and *upper* the upper bound for each parameter and $j = \{1, \cdots, D\}$ is the index of the parameter. The first population is generated randomly in the space of possible solutions. Then mutation and crossover are used to generate new offspring. If the offspring reach better objective function value than the original individuals, they will survive to the next generation, else the original individuals survive.

2.1 Mutation

In the mutation step of DE/rand/1/bin, the noise (mutation) vector is created by three mutually different randomly selected parents $\vec{x}_{r_1}^G$, $\vec{x}_{r_2}^G$, and $\vec{x}_{r_3}^G$, and the mutation constant F as follows

$$\vec{x}_i^{G+1} = \vec{x}_{r_3}^G + F\left(\vec{x}_{r_1}^G - \vec{x}_{r_2}^G\right) \tag{1}$$

From Equation (1) it is clear that the population must contain at least 4 individuals (Ronkkonen, Kukkonen, & Price, 2005).

Beside DE/rand/1/bin there are a lot of schemes of the noise vector creation. In this chapter, we will work with DE/rand/1/bin, see Equation (1) and DE/best/1/bin where the noise vector is created according to the following equation:

$$\vec{x}_i^{G+1} = \vec{x}_{r_{best}}^{G} + F(\vec{x}_{r_1}^{G} - \vec{x}_{r_2}^{G}), \tag{2}$$

where $\vec{x}_{r_{best}}^{G}$ is the individual with the best objective function value.

2.2 Crossover

The main role of the crossover is to construct the trial vector $\vec{u}_i^{G+1}$ using the combination of the parameters of the noise vector $\vec{v}_i^{G+1}$ and the actual individual (target vector) $\vec{x}_i^{G}$ such that

$$u_{ij}^{G+1} \begin{cases} v_{ij}^{G+1} & if r(j) \leq CR \; or j = rn(i) \\ x_{ij}^{G} & if r(j) > CR \; and j \neq rn(i) \end{cases} \tag{3}$$

where $CR \in [0,1]$ is the crossover rate and $rn(i) \in \{1,\cdots,D\}$ is an integer selected randomly with the uniform distribution that will ensure that the trial vector $\vec{u}_i^{G+1}$ will have at least one parameter from the noise vector $\vec{v}_i^{G+1}$ (Ronkkonen, Kukkonen, & Price, 2005).

2.3 Selection

In the variants DE/rand/1/bin and DE/best/1/bin, the following selection scheme is used

$$\vec{x}_i^{G+1} = \begin{cases} u_i^{G+1} & iff(\vec{u}_i^{G+1}) \leq f(\vec{x}_i^{G}) (for\ minimization\ problem) \\ x_i^{G}, & otherwise \end{cases}, \tag{4}$$

i.e. the trial vector will replace the target vector only if its objective function value $f(u_i^{G+1})$ is better than the objective function value of the target vector $f(x_i^{G})$.

2.4 Control Parameters Settings

Storn and Price (1995) suggested the values of the control parameters as follows:

- $F \in [0.5,1.0]$
- $CR \in [0.8,1.0]$
- $NP = 10D$

On the other hand, Rahnamayan, Tizhoosh, and Salama (2008) mentioned the following values of the control parameters:

- $F \in [0.5,1.0]$
- $CR \in [0,1]$

Ronkkonen, Kukkonen, and Price (2005) mentioned that for separable functions small values of CR ($CR \geq 0.2$) are adequate and for non-separable functions values greater than 0.9 should be used (Yi, Gao, Li, & Zhou, 2015).

3. COMPLEX NETWORKS PROPERTIES AND THEIR INTERPRETATION FROM THE VIEW OF EVOLUTIONARY ALGORITHMS DYNAMICS

In this work, we investigate the dynamics of differential evolution (DE) using the complex networks (CNs). In this part, we would like to clarify the term complex network and the properties that will be analysed briefly.

The CN can be described as the graph with non-trivial topological features, i.e. features that do not occur in the simple networks but occur in the real networks (Kim & Wilhelm, 2008). CN can be represented by the directed or undirected graph $G = (V, E)$, where $V = v_1, \cdots, v_N$ denotes the set of vertices (nodes) and $E = e_1, \cdots, e_K$ the set of the edges, where edge $e_{i,j}$ connects vertices v_i and v_j (Bavelas, 1948).

From the view of the DE dynamics we will analyse the following properties of the CN:

- Node weighted out-degree k_i^{out}
- Geodesic distance d_{ij}
- Local clustering coefficient c_i of a node
- Global clustering coefficient C
- Node weighted clustering coefficient $\tilde{C}_{i,Z}$
- Node closeness centrality C_C
- Node betweenness centrality b_i

3.1 Node Degree

Number of the edges incident with the node is called *node degree*. We denote it k_i and it is defined in terms of the adjacency matrix A by the following equation

$$\sum_{j \in \mathrm{N}} a_{ij}, \tag{5}$$

where a_{ij} is the member of the adjacency matrix. If the graph is directed, the node degree has two components: in-degree (number of in-going edges) k_i^{in} and out-degree (number of out-going edges) k_i^{out}. Total node degree is then defined as $k_i = k_i^{in} + k_i^{out}$ (Boccaletti, Latora, Moreno, Chavez, & Hwang, 2006). In this paper, we work with the multi-edges. These edges are considered as the edges with the weights. In-degree in the graph G containing multi-edges will be denoted as the *weighted in-degree* and out-degree will be called *weighted out-degree*.

3.2 Shortest Path

Boccaletti, Latora, Moreno, Chavez, and Hwang (2006) state that it is useful to represent all the shortest paths of a graph G as a matrix D, where d_{ij} represents the length of the geodesic from node i to node j. The maximum value of d_{ij} is called *diameter* of the graph and it is indicated by $Diam(G)$. *Average shortest path* is the measure of the typical separation between two nodes in the graph and it is given by the following equation

$$L = \frac{1}{N(N-1)} \sum_{i,j \in \aleph; i \neq j} d_{ij}, \tag{6}$$

where N denotes the number of the vertices. If there are disconnected components in the graph, it will make a problem in the definition from Equation (6), because *average shortest path* diverges. That is the reason to define so-called *efficiency* of the graph G described by the following equation

$$E = \frac{1}{N(N-1)} \sum_{i,j \in \aleph; i \neq j} \frac{1}{d_{ij}}. \tag{7}$$

The efficiency of the graph is considered as an indicator of the traffic capacity of the network (Boccaletti, Latora, Moreno, Chavez, & Hwang, 2006).

3.3 Clustering and Clustering Coefficient

Also known as *transitivity* means the presence of a high number of triangles. Imagine situation: two distinct nodes j and k are connected by the edge and both of them are connected to another node i. They create a triangle. Transitivity can be defined also as the relative number of transitive triples, i.e. the fraction of connected triples of the nodes which also form triangles. The *global clustering coefficient c* is given by the following equation (Boccaletti, Latora, Moreno, Chavez, & Hwang, 2006)

$$C = \frac{3 \times number\ of\ triangles\ in\ G}{number\ of\ connected\ triples\ of\ vertices\ in\ G}. \tag{8}$$

Opsahl and Panzarasa (2009) introduced the generalized clustering coefficient which is consistent with the weighted local clustering coefficient described by Barrat, Barthelemy, Pastor-Satorras, and Vespignani (2004). Equation (8) is then modified to the following equation

$$C = \frac{total\ value\ of\ closed\ triples}{total\ value\ of\ triplets} = \frac{\sum_{\tau\Delta} \omega}{\sum_{\tau} \omega}, \tag{9}$$

where ω denotes the weight of the edge.

The local clustering coefficient c_i of the node n_i is counting the actual number of edges e_i in G_i where G_i is potentially the subgraph of neighbours of the node *i*. The local clustering coefficient is defined as the ratio between the actual number of edges, and the maximum possible number of the edges in G_i, given by $\frac{k_i(k_i - 1)}{2}$, see the following equation

$$c_i = \frac{2e_i}{k_i\left(k_i - 1\right)} = \frac{\sum_{j,m} a_{aj} a_{jm} a_{mi}}{k_i\left(k_i - 1\right)} \tag{10}$$

where a denotes the member of the adjacency matrix A. The clustering coefficient C of the graph G is then given by the average of the local clustering coefficients c_i over all nodes in G according to the following equation (Boccaletti, Latora, Moreno, Chavez, & Hwang, 2006)

$$C = \frac{1}{N}\sum_{i'=1}^{N} c_i . \tag{11}$$

Barrat, Barthelemy, Pastor-Satorras, and Vespignani (2004) were the first who described the weighted clustering coefficient. The Equation (10) has been modified to the following equation

$$\tilde{C}_{i,B} = \frac{1}{s_i(k_i - 1)}\sum_{j,k} a_{ij} a_{ik} a_{jk} \frac{w_{ij} + w_{ik}}{2}, \tag{12}$$

where s_i is the sum of all weights in the graph and $a_{ij} = 1$, if there is an edge between the nodes *i* and *j*, and 0 otherwise.

Onnela, Saramäki, Kertész, and Kaski (2005) defined weighted clustering coefficient based on the concept of subgraph intensity where the edge weights are normalized by the maximum weight of the network $\hat{w}_{ij} = \frac{w_{ij}}{\max(w)}$, see the following equation

$$\tilde{C}_{i,O} = \frac{1}{k_i(k_i - 1)}\sum_{j,k}\left(\hat{w}_{ij}\hat{w}_{ik}\hat{w}_{jk}\right)^{\frac{1}{3}}. \tag{13}$$

Zhang and Horvath (2005) introduced the weighted clustering coefficient as

$$\tilde{C}_{i,Z} = \frac{\sum_{j,k} \hat{w}_{ij}\hat{w}_{ik}\hat{w}_{jk}}{\left(\sum_k \hat{w}_{ik}\right)^2 - \sum_k \hat{w}_{ik}^2}, \tag{14}$$

where the weights of the edges are normalized as well as in the previous case by the maximal weight in the graph. This equation can be also written according to Freeman (1979) as

$$\tilde{C}_{i,Z} = \frac{\sum_{j,k} \hat{w}_{ij}\hat{w}_{ik}\hat{w}_{jk}}{\sum_{j\neq k} \hat{w}_{ij}\hat{w}_{ik}}. \tag{15}$$

Holme, Park, Kim, and Edling (2007) defined the weighted clustering coefficient as

$$\tilde{C}_{i,H} = \frac{\sum_{j,k} w_{ij}w_{jk}w_{ki}}{\max(w)\sum_{j,k} w_{ij}w_{ki}}. \tag{16}$$

In this work, weighted clustering coefficient $\tilde{C}_{i,Z}$ has been selected because it is purely weighted based as well as $\tilde{C}_{i,H}$. According to (Saramäki, Kivelä, Onnela, Kaski, & Kertesz, 2007), $\tilde{C}_{i,Z}$ is not sensitive to additive noise unlike $\tilde{C}_{i,B}$ and $\tilde{C}_{i,O}$.

3.4 Closeness Centrality

The closeness centrality of the vertex *i* is the mean geodesic distance (i.e. the mean length of a geodesic path) from the vertex *i* to each other. It is given by the following equation (Newman, 2008)

$$C_C(i) = \frac{1}{\sum_j d_{ij}}, \tag{17}$$

where *d* denotes the shortest distance between the vertices *i* and *j*.

Bavelas (1948) dealt with the idea of centrality applied to human communication and his work has been followed by Leavitt (1951) and Smith (1950). The main conclusion was that the centrality was related to group efficiency in solving of a problem, perception of leadership and the personal satisfaction of participants (Freeman, 1979). The closeness-based measures of point centrality have been developed by Bavelas (1950), Beauchamp (1965), Sabidussi (1966), Moxley and Moxley (1974), and Rogers (1974) (Freeman, 1979). Sabidussi (1966) introduced the centrality of a point as the sum of the geodesic distances from that point to each other in the graph. Freeman (1974) formalized the closeness, degree and betweenness centrality. Opsahl, Agneessens, and Skvoretz (2010) generalized the degree and shortest paths in degree, closeness and betweenness centrality. They extended the shortest path algorithm by taking into consideration the number of intermediary nodes and transformed the inverted weights by the tuning parameter α, before using Dijkstra's algorithm to find the least costly path. The length of the shortest path between two nodes is then defined as:

$$d^{w\alpha}(i,j) = \min\left(\frac{1}{\left(w_{ih}\right)^{\alpha}} + \ldots + \frac{1}{\left(w_{hj}\right)^{\alpha}}\right), \tag{18}$$

where α is a positive tuning parameter. If $\alpha = 0$, the measure according to Opsahl, Agneessens, and Skvoretz (2010) produces the same outcomes as the binary distance measure. When $\alpha = 1$ the outcome will be the same like the outcome obtained with Dijkstra's algorithm. For $\alpha < 1$ a shorter paths consisted of the edges with the low weights (weak ties) are favoured over a longer paths with the edge with the high weights (strong ties). When $\alpha > 1$, paths with more intermediaries are favoured. The final closeness centrality equation is then defined as

$$C_C^{w\alpha} = \left[\sum_{j=1}^{N} d^{w\alpha}(i,j)\right]^{-1}. \tag{19}$$

3.5 Node Betweenness and Betweenness Centrality

When two nodes j and k communicate their communication is dependent on the nodes that belong to the paths connecting these nodes. The measure of the relevance of a given node obtained by counting the number of geodesics going through it is called *node betweenness*. Number of the shortest paths from all nodes to all others that pass through the given node is called *betweenness centrality* and it is given by the following equation

$$b_i = \sum_{j,k \in \aleph, i \neq k} \frac{n_{jk}(i)}{n_{jk}}, \tag{20}$$

where i denotes the i-th node, n_{jk} is the number of the shortest paths connecting nodes j and k, and $n_{jk}(i)$ is the number of the shortest paths connecting nodes j and k passing through the node i (Boccaletti, Latora, Moreno, Chavez, & Hwang, 2006).

4. INTERPRETATION OF THE CN PROPERTIES FROM THE VIEW OF THE DIFFERENTIAL EVOLUTION DYNAMICS

In this section, we would like to familiarize the reader with the interpretation of the CN properties from the view of the differential evolution dynamics.

- **Node Weighted Out-Degree:** We have mentioned that node in CN represents individual of DE. The weighted out-degree of the node represents how many times the individual became the parent improving another individual.
- **Shortest Path:** The mean shortest path between nodes representing the individuals will demonstrate the diversity of the selected parents. It the case of DE/best/1/bin one parent in the mutation step is not selected randomly. It is the individual with the best objective function value. This individual is selected for generation that means that there will be much more edges leading from the node representing the best individual than from the nodes representing the other individuals in the population. In DE/best/1/bin much more geodesics will go throw the nodes representing the indi-

viduals that have become the best than in the case of DE/rand/1/bin where all parents are selected randomly. We should realize that the best individuals will also influence the weights of the edges.

- **Local Clustering Coefficient:** For the unweighted graph, this metric says how close the nodes are to create the complete graph (clique). In the context of DE, it will say how close the individuals are to be in the relationship with each other and in addition *weighted clustering coefficient* indicates how strong this relationship is.
- **Weighted Clustering Coefficient:** Unlike the local clustering coefficient, the weighted clustering coefficient incorporates the weights of the edges. From the view of DE, we must realize that the individuals will be recorded and then visualized only if they are improved during the generation. This leads us to the idea that the individuals spreading the genomes of the high quality will be modelled by the nodes with the higher weighted clustering coefficient than the others.
- **Global Clustering Coefficient:** The main goal of this analysis is to find out which type of DE (DE/rand/1/bin and DE/best/1/bin) creates more closed triplets. The higher global clustering coefficient of the graph means the stronger relationships between individuals in DE.
- **Closeness Centrality:** This property of the CN will indicate the closeness of the individuals in DE. The closeness centrality will increase with the higher number of the relationships among individuals. It will be influenced by the shortest path between individuals. Inasmuch as the third parent in DE/best/1/bin is the individual with the best objective function value and it is selected for one generation, closeness centrality will be probably higher than in the case of DE/rand/1/bin.
- **Betweenness Centrality:** In the case of the betweenness centrality, we will look at the nodes like at the bridges along the shortest path between two other nodes. From the view of DE the individuals with the high values of the betweenness centrality are the most important because they have been improved very often as well as they have improved other individuals. These individuals spread important information to the population.

5. COMPLEX NETWORK CREATION ON THE BASIS OF DE DYNAMICS

In this subsection, we will describe the way how the corresponding CN is constructed. We will build one graph for each generation of the DE algorithm. Thanks to this mechanism we will be able to track the development of the relationships between members of the population. At the beginning of the algorithm the initial population is generated randomly with the uniform distribution in the space of possible solutions and the empty adjacency matrix A^G (G denotes the actual generation) capturing the adjacency of target vectors and corresponding parents is generated. Then for each target vector $\vec{x}_i^G$ three random parents $\vec{x}_{r_1}^G$, $\vec{x}_{r_2}^G$, and $\vec{x}_{r_3}^G$ are selected and the trial vector $\vec{u}_i^{G+1}$ is created. If $f(u_i^{G+1}) < f(x_i^G)$ the adjacency matrix is recomputed such that

$$A_{r_1,i}^G = A_{r_1,i}^G + 1, \; A_{r_2,i}^G = A_{r_2,i}^G + 1, \text{ and } A_{r_3,i}^G = A_{r_3,i}^G + 1,$$

where r_j denotes the row and i the column of the adjacency matrix A^G. In the other words, the edges are created between each node representing the target vector (, which was improved) and all nodes representing the parents (the weight of the edge is increased, respectively). Next, the target vector is replaced by the trial vector which will be represented (in the next generation) by the same position in the adjacency matrix as the target vector that has been replaced by it. If $f(u_i^{G+1}) \geq f(x_i^G)$, no edge between the target vector and the parents is created and the adjacency matrix A^G is not recomputed for this target vector. For better illustration see the following example:

Example 1: Let the population consists of six individuals $\vec{x}_1^G, \ldots, \vec{x}_6^G$.
Generation 1: Let's say that the individuals $\vec{x}_1$, $\vec{x}_2$, $\vec{x}_4$ and their parents have been recorded such that:

$\vec{x}_1^G\{\vec{x}_2^G, \vec{x}_4^G, \vec{x}_5^G\}$ $\vec{x}_2^G\{\vec{x}_1^G, \vec{x}_3^G, \vec{x}_4^G\}$ $\vec{x}_4^G\{\vec{x}_2^G, \vec{x}_3^G, \vec{x}_5^G\}$

From the recorded individuals and their parents the adjacency matrix A^1 is created. The graph of the first generation is then depicted in Figure 1.

$$A^1 = \begin{bmatrix} 0 & 1 & 0 & 0 & 0 & 0 \\ 1 & 0 & 0 & 1 & 0 & 0 \\ 0 & 1 & 0 & 1 & 0 & 0 \\ 1 & 1 & 0 & 0 & 0 & 0 \\ 1 & 0 & 0 & 1 & 0 & 0 \\ 0 & 0 & 0 & 0 & 0 & 0 \end{bmatrix}$$

Figure 1. The first generation of DE/rand/1/bin

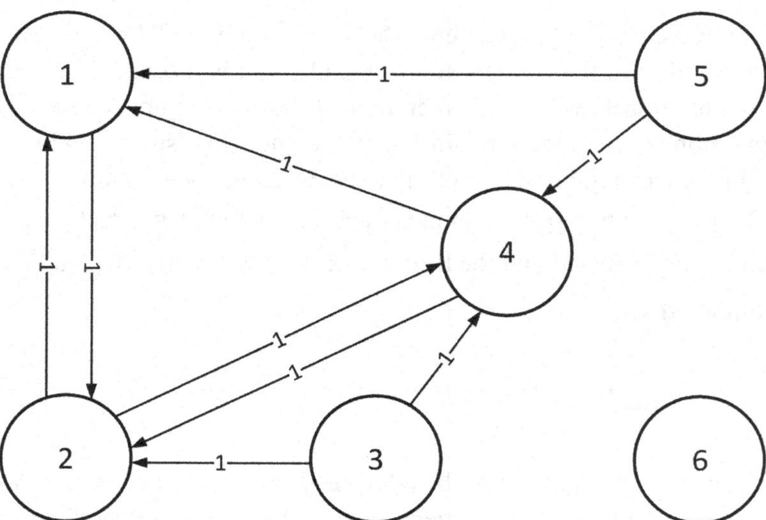

Generation 2: The individuals $\vec{x}_2$, $\vec{x}_4$, $\vec{x}_5$, $\vec{x}_6$ and their parents have been recorded such that:

$\vec{x}_2^G\{\vec{x}_1^G, \vec{x}_3^G, \vec{x}_4^G\}$ $\vec{x}_4^G\{\vec{x}_2^G, \vec{x}_3^G, \vec{x}_5^G\}$ $\vec{x}_5^G\{\vec{x}_1^G, \vec{x}_2^G, \vec{x}_6^G\}$ $\vec{x}_6^G\{\vec{x}_3^G, \vec{x}_4^G, \vec{x}_5^G\}$

$$A^2 = \begin{bmatrix} 0 & 2 & 0 & 0 & 1 & 0 \\ 1 & 0 & 0 & 2 & 1 & 0 \\ 0 & 2 & 0 & 2 & 0 & 1 \\ 1 & 2 & 0 & 0 & 0 & 1 \\ 1 & 0 & 0 & 2 & 0 & 1 \\ 0 & 0 & 0 & 0 & 1 & 0 \end{bmatrix}$$

From the recorded individuals and their parents the adjacency matrix A^1 is recomputed to A^2 The graph of the second generation is visualized in Figure 2.

Generation 3: The individuals $\vec{x}_5^G$, $\vec{x}_6^G$, and their parents have been recorded such that:

$\vec{x}_5^G\{\vec{x}_1^G, \vec{x}_2^G, \vec{x}_4^G\}$ $\vec{x}_6^G\{\vec{x}_3^G, \vec{x}_4^G, \vec{x}_5^G\}$

Figure 2. The second generation of DE/rand/1/bin

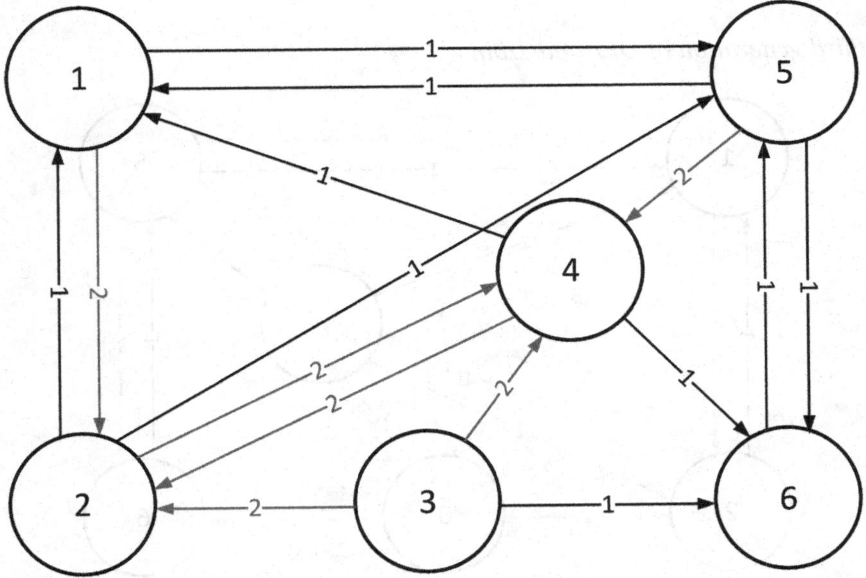

From the recorded individuals and their parents the adjacency matrix A^2 is recomputed to A^3. The graph of the third generation is visualized in Figure 3.

$$A^3 = \begin{bmatrix} 0 & 2 & 0 & 0 & 2 & 0 \\ 1 & 0 & 0 & 2 & 2 & 0 \\ 0 & 2 & 0 & 2 & 0 & 2 \\ 1 & 2 & 0 & 0 & 1 & 2 \\ 1 & 0 & 0 & 2 & 0 & 2 \\ 0 & 0 & 0 & 0 & 1 & 0 \end{bmatrix}$$

The graphs shown in Figures 1-3 are created by the same way.

6. EXPERIMENTS

As we have mentioned above we have selected two types of DE – DE/best/1/bin and DE/rand/1/bin. As the test problems, 6 test functions have been selected: the 1st de Jong's (see Equation (21)), Ackley's (see Equation (22)), Griewangk's (see Equation (23)), Rastrigin's (see Equation (24)), Rosenbrock's (see Equation (25)) and Schwefel's (see Equation(26)). Global minima of these functions are mentioned in Table 1.

$$f_1(x) = \sum_{i=1}^{D} x_i^2; -5.12 \le x_i \le 5.12 \tag{21}$$

Figure 3. The third generation of DE/rand/1/bin

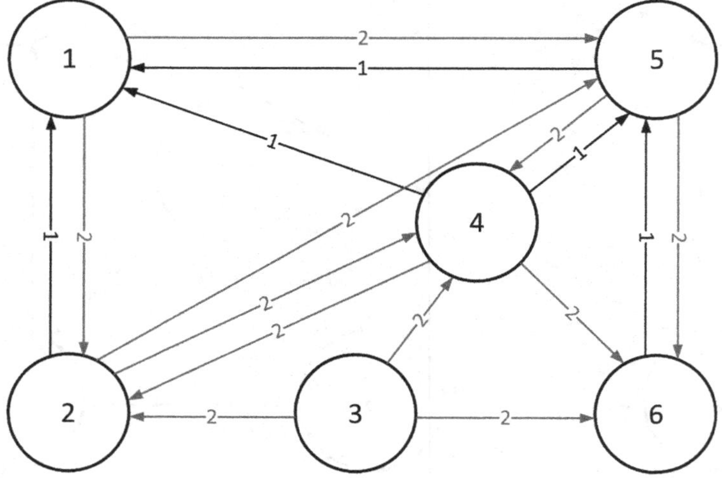

Table 1. Classical test functions, D denotes dimension

Category	Function	Name	Global Min.
Unimodal	f_1	1st de Jong	0.000
	f_2	Rosenbrock	0.000
Multi-modal	f_3	Ackley	0.000
	f_4	Griewangk	0.000
	f_5	Rastrigin	0.000
	f_6	Schwefel	-418.9829 *D*

$$f_2(x) = -20\exp\left(-0.2\sqrt{\frac{1}{n}\sum_{i=1}^{D} x_i^2}\right) - \exp\left(\frac{1}{n}\sum_{i=1}^{D}\cos(2\pi x_i)\right) + 20 + \exp(1); -30 \le x_i \le 30 \quad (22)$$

$$f_3(x) = \sum\nolimits_{i=1}^{D}\frac{x_i^2}{4000} - \prod_{i=1}^{D}\cos\left(\frac{x_i}{\sqrt{i}}\right) + 1; -600 \le x_i \le 600 \quad (23)$$

$$f_4(x) = 10D + \sum_{i=1}^{D}(x_i^2 - 10\cos(2\pi x_i)); -5.12 \le x_i \le 5.12 \quad (24)$$

$$f_5(x) = \sum_{i=1}^{D-1}\left(100\left(x_{i+1} - x_i^2\right) + \left(1 - x_i\right)^2\right); -2.048 \le x_i \le 2.048 \quad (25)$$

$$f_6(x) = \sum_{i=1}^{D} -x_i \sin\left(\sqrt{|x_i|}\right) - 500 \le x_i \le 500 \quad (26)$$

6.1 Experiment 1

The first experiment deals with the analysis of the DE dynamics using the CN. The main goal is to find out whether exists any meaningful connection between the properties of the corresponding CN and DE dynamics. We have selected seven CN characteristics - graph distance, local clustering coefficient, global clustering coefficient, weighted clustering coefficient, node degree, closeness and betweenness centrality. For each characteristic its extreme values are recorded. Each experiment has been repeated 25 times to obtain reliable results.

We must emphasize that in our experiments it is necessary to set number of individuals to the higher values to create the CN structure. Setting is the same for both variants of DE: $D = 20$, $NP = 100$, $G =$

400, $F = 0.5$, $CR = 0.85$, where D denotes dimension, NP number of individuals, F mutation constant, and CR crossover probability.

The results of the DE/best/1/bin and DE/rand/1/bin for the selected six test functions are shown in Tables 2 and 3, where minima, maxima, means, medians and standard deviations are mentioned. The results of the analysis of the complex networks, which have been created by these algorithms are then described in Tables 4 and 5.

6.2 Experiment 2

When we look at Tables 4 and 5, we will see that there is the significant difference between the local clustering coefficients and weighted clustering coefficients of DE/best/1/bin and DE/rand/1/bin. This is logical because in the case of DE/best/1/bin the third parent is not chosen randomly, it is the individual with the best objective function value (high-quality genome). The node representing this individual will have the higher local and weighted clustering coefficient than the others and this will be reflected in the mean local clustering coefficients as well as mean weighted clustering coefficients of the created CNs.

Mezura-Montes, Velázquez-Reyes, and Coello Coello (2006) presented a comparative study of DE variants for global optimization where DE/best/1/bin reached worse results in the case of the non-separable and multi-modal problems than for example DE/rand/2/dir or DE/current-to-rand/1/bin. These results led us to the idea to find out the individual which will be the best from the view of the successful spreading of their genomes. In the other words, the individual is considered to be the most successful (best), if it

Table 2. Results of DE/best/1/bin

Function	Min.	Max.	Mean	Median	Std. Dev.
f1	0.001	0.131	0.038	0.026	0.034
f2	0.021	27.447	15.418	16.189	7.415
f3	0.131	1.738	1.099	1.092	0.371
f4	18.267	53.811	33.520	32.837	9.035
f5	15.028	72.112	27.183	20.103	16.571
f6	-6759.464	-5488.429	-6139.858	-6129.742	353.675

Table 3. Results of DE/rand/1/bin

Function	Min.	Max.	Mean	Median	Std. dev.
f1	0.000	0.000	0.000	0.000	0.000
f2	0.033	0.079	0.051	0.048	0.013
f3	0.007	0.645	0.281	0.312	0.192
f4	88.666	119.936	105.850	108.132	8.977
f5	12.061	14.755	13.838	13.964	0.602
f6	-4505.413	-3835.526	-4130.694	-4079.606	171.375

Table 4. CN analysis, DE/best/1/bin; we have mentioned the average minima and maxima and we have highlighted values of the weighted clustering coefficient to emphasize the differences between results of DE/best/1/bin and DE/rand/1/bin. The results of the weighted clustering coefficient serves as the starting point for Experiment 2.

Property		f1	f2	f3	f4	f5	f6
$\bar{d}_{ij}$	Min	9.724	9.999	9.712	11.033	9.803	10.994
	Max	∞	∞	∞	∞	∞	∞
$\bar{c}_i$	Min	0.005	0.004	0.005	0.000	0.002	0.000
	Max	1.000	1.000	1.000	1.000	1.000	1.000
$\bar{C}$	Min	0.170	0.169	0.173	0.148	0.167	0.132
	Max	1.000	1.000	1.000	1.000	1.000	1.000
$\bar{\tilde{C}}_{i,Z}$	Min	0.008	0.005	0.006	0.007	0.006	0.004
	Max	**0.427**	**0.434**	**0.430**	**0.396**	**0.421**	**0.406**
$\bar{C}_C(v_i)$	Min	0.003	0.003	0.003	0.003	0.003	0.002
	Max	0.104	0.101	0.104	0.092	0.103	0.092
$\bar{k}_i^{out}$	Min	4.633	4.540	4.742	3.678	4.469	2.787
	Max	98.995	98.997	98.997	98.991	98.998	98.992
$\bar{b}_i$	Min	0.005	0.003	0.003	0.009	0.002	0.008
	Max	242.447	240.114	239.135	255.607	251.368	228.755

is used to create the offspring with the better objective function value than the target vectors most often. From this reason, in our approach, we map each improved individual in the generation to the node and the relationships between these individuals and their parents (selected in the mutation step) to the edges of the graph. The success of the individuals is then modelled by the weighted clustering coefficient of the corresponding node. In our enhanced algorithm, the parents are selected on the basis of their weighted clustering coefficient in the mutation step.

6.2.1 Incorporation of the Weighted Clustering Coefficient to the Parent Selection in DE

In this work, weighted clustering coefficient $\tilde{C}_{i,Z}$ has been selected because it is purely weighted based as well as $\tilde{C}_{i,H}$.

As we have mentioned above, the next goal of this work is to find out the way how to select the parents in the mutation step to improve DE convergence rate. In the variant DE/best/1/bin, the best individual is the individual with the smallest (in minimizing problems) or greatest (in maximizing problems) objective function value. As it was described in (Mezura-Montes, Velázquez-Reyes, & Coello Coello, 2006), DE/best/1/bin does not reach the best results in the non-separable and multi-modal functions. This fact led us to search for another criterion of the best individual selection.

Table 5. CN analysis, DE/rand/1/bin; we have mentioned the average minima and maxima and we have highlighted values of the weighted clustering coefficient to emphasize the differences between results of DE/best/1/bin and DE/rand/1/bin. The results of the weighted clustering coefficient serves as the starting point for Experiment 2.

Property		f1	f2	f3	f4	f5	f6
$\bar{d}_{ij}$	Min	34.389	37.360	42.356	128.086	40.065	∞
	Max	∞	∞	∞	∞	∞	∞
$\bar{c}_i$	Min	0.000	0.000	0.000	0.000	0.000	0.000
	Max	0.904	0.879	0.832	0.277	0.853	0.200
$\bar{C}$	Min	0.072	0.070	0.073	0.067	0.067	0.057
	Max	0.991	0.986	0.971	0.480	0.979	0.382
$\bar{\tilde{C}}_{i,Z}$	Min	0.012	0.013	0.011	0.009	0.012	0.009
	Max	**0.243**	**0.212**	**0.208**	**0.083**	**0.212**	**0.072**
$\bar{C}_C(v_i)$	Min	0.003	0.003	0.003	0.003	0.003	0.002
	Max	0.029	0.027	0.024	0.008	0.025	0.007
$\bar{k}_i^{out}$	Min	3.671	3.442	3.591	3.215	3.390	2.589
	Max	89.474	87.020	82.385	27.189	84.495	20.649
$\bar{b}_i$	Min	9.526	11.980	16.615	71.898	14.505	80.131
	Max	204.947	205.278	207.344	202.872	208.530	187.706

From the rules that we have presented above, we know that the edges between nodes representing the individuals are created only if these individuals contributed to the population improvement. The nodes representing the individuals becoming the parents more often will have the greater out-degree (the number of out-going edges). Such parents have the genomes of the high quality and it is important to spread these genomes. The weighted clustering coefficient is one of the most appropriate candidate to be chosen as the criterion of the parent selection in the mutation step from two reasons:

1. It enables to capture spreading of the genomes from the node to another node.
2. Unlike the local clustering coefficient the weights of the edges are took into consideration.

When the adjacency matrix A^G for the generation G is created, the weighted clustering coefficient of each node is computed. Then, for each individual the probability of selection is computed according to the following equation

$$p_i = \frac{\tilde{C}_{i,Z}}{\sum_{j=1}^{NP} \tilde{C}_{j,Z}}, \quad (27)$$

where p_i denotes the probability of the i-th individual selection and $\tilde{C}_{i,Z}$ is the weighted clustering coefficient of the node representing the i-th individual in the population. Individual represented by the node with the higher weighted clustering coefficient has the higher probability to be selected as the parent in the mutation step. The algorithm is described by the pseudo code in Algorithm 1.

Setting of the enhanced DE/rand/1/bin is mentioned in Table 6. We have created eight sets of experiments. We mention the results during 50 independent runs. The results of the comparison of the original version of DE/rand/1/bin and DE/rand/1/bin using weighted clustering coefficient to select parents in the mutation step are mentioned in Tables 7-14.

Algorithm 1. Enhanced DE/rand/1/bin

Input:
***D*:** Problem dimension
***NP*:** Population size
***F*:** Mutation constant
***CR*:** Crossover rate
***Max_G*:** Maximal number of generations
***A*:** Adjacency matrix
***S*:** The set of the individuals and their parents contributing the population
***Sum_W*:** Sum of all weighted clustering coefficients
G = 0
$Sum_W = 0$

Randomly generate *NP* individuals with *D* dimension $p^G = \vec{x}_1^G, \cdots, \vec{x}_{NP}^G$ in the space of possible solutions. Each individual will be enhanced with the parameter W_i corresponding with the weighted clustering coefficient of the corresponding node. Evaluate each individual $\vec{x}_i^G$.

while $G < \mathrm{Max}_G$ **do**
for $i = 1$ to *NP* **do**
Mutation step:
if $SUM_W = 0$ then
Choose three mutually different individuals $\vec{x}_{r_1}^G$, $\vec{x}_{r_2}^G$, and $\vec{x}_{r_3}^G$ from current population
else
Choose three mutually different individuals $\vec{x}_{r_1}^G$, $\vec{x}_{r_2}^G$, and $\vec{x}_{r_3}^G$ on the basis of the parameter $W_l^G, l \neq i$. The individual with higher value of W_l^G has the higher probability to become the parent.
end if
Add the actual individual and its parents to *S*
$\vec{v}_i^{G+1} = \vec{x}_{r_3}^G + F\left(\vec{x}_{r_1}^G - \vec{x}_{r_2}^G\right)$.
Crossover step:
for $\vec{x}_i^G$ generate trial vector $\vec{u}_i^{G+1}$
j_{rand}=int(*rand*[1.*D*])

Table 6. Experimental settings

Parameter	Settings 1	2	3	4	5	6	7	8
D	20	30	30	30	30	50	30	100
NP	100	150	150	150	150	250	150	150
G	200	400	400	400	400	600	400	600
F	0.5	0.5	0.5	0.6	0.6	0.5	0.6	0.5
CR	0.85	0.85	0.75	0.80	0.80	0.85	0.90	0.40

Table 7. Comparison of the results of the DE/rand/1/bin and the enhanced DE/rand/1/bin

Function	Min	Max	Mean	Median	Std. Dev.
DE/rand/1/bin					
f_1	0.006	0.023	0.015	0.014	0.004
f_2	1.271	2.407	1.919	1.901	0.303
f_3	1.021	1.103	1.053	1.054	0.015
f_4	98.157	132.984	117.925	118.384	8.969
f_5	17.923	20.605	19.013	18.907	0.703
f_6	-4202.662	-3538.858	-3899.286	-3929.118	159.293
Enhanced DE/rand/1/bin (the 2nd Half of Generations)					
f_1	0.001	0.014	0.006	0.005	0.003
f_2	0.388	1.956	0.989	0.994	0.398
f_3	0.772	1.044	0.970	0.989	0.068
f_4	82.936	117.745	105.525	107.204	8.311
f_5	16.892	19.770	18.257	18.416	0.739
f_6	-4823.886	-3846.212	-4211.854	-4215.518	219.581
Enhanced DE/rand/1/bin $\left(\sum_{i=1}^{NP} \tilde{C}_{i,Z} > 0\right)$					
f_1	0.002	1.035	0.164	0.031	0.273
f_2	0.106	6.930	1.765	1.526	1.510
f_3	0.550	2.267	1.231	1.156	0.362
f_4	23.641	93.011	62.179	65.541	15.543
f_5	14.454	45.675	22.546	18.802	8.324
f_6	-7830.149	-3667.292	-6652.023	-6697.099	819.007

Notation the 2nd half of generations means the enhanced DE/rand/1/bin has been used in the 2nd half of generations and in the first one, the classical variant of DE/rand/1/bin has been used. The global minimum of the Schwefel's function for $D = 20$ is $f_6(x) = -8379.658$. Setting 1

for $k = 1$ to D **do**
if $rand(j) \leq CR$ or $j = j_{rand}$ **then**
$\vec{u}_{i,k}^{G+1} = \vec{v}_{i,k}^{G+1}$
else
$\vec{u}_{i,k}^{G+1} = \vec{x}_{i,k}^{G}$
end if
end for
Selection step:
if $f(u_i^{G+1}) < f(x_i^G)$ then
$\vec{x}_i^{G+1} = \vec{u}_i^{G+1}$
else
$\vec{x}_i^{G+1} = \vec{x}_i^{G}$
Remove the actual individual and its parents from the set S
end if
end for
Build adjacency matrix A^G on the basis of the S
For each individual $\vec{x}_i^{G+1}$ compute weighted clustering coefficient W_i^{G+1} according to Equation (15)

$$Sum_W = \sum_{i=1}^{NP} W_i^{G+1}$$

For each individual $\vec{x}_i^{G+1}$ compute the probability of selection according to the equation Equation (27)
G $= G + 1$
end while

7. CONCLUSION

This work can be divided into two parts. In the first one, we were dealing with the analysis of DE dynamics with the aim of CNs. We have analysed seven CN characteristics – node distance, local clustering coefficient, global clustering coefficient, weighted clustering coefficient, closeness centrality, betweenness centrality and the node weighted out-degree. In the second part, the enhanced DE/rand/1/bin has been developed to investigate the influence of the weighted clustering coefficient to the DE convergence rate.

In the first part of this work, two types of DE have been selected – DE/best/1/bin and DE/rand/1/bin and the differences between the properties of the established CNs have been observed. As the test problems six difficult functions have been chosen. In Tables 2 and 3, the minimum, maximum, mean, median and standard deviation for DE/best/1/bin and DE/rand/1/bin with the following settings $D = 20$, $NP = 100$, $G = 400$, $F = 0.5$, $CR = 0.85$ are mentioned. In Tables 4 and 5, the analysis of the properties of the corresponding networks created by the DE/best/1/bin and DE/rand/1/bin with above mentioned settings is shown. From these results we can make some conclusions:

Table 8. Comparison of the results of the DE/rand/1/bin and the enhanced DE/rand/1/bin

Function	Min	Max	Mean	Median	Std. Dev.
DE/rand/1/bin					
f_1	0.007	0.023	0.014	0.014	0.004
f_2	1.089	2.171	1.584	1.592	0.288
f_3	1.019	1.090	1.051	1.051	0.017
f_4	184.061	223.307	205.610	204.354	11.621
f_5	27.802	30.813	29.143	29.055	0.732
f_6	-5431.356	-4393.022	-4917.780	-4908.894	200.184
Enhanced DE/rand/1/bin (the 2nd Half of Generations)					
f_1	0.001	0.013	0.004	0.003	0.003
f_2	0.110	1.170	0.397	0.311	0.272
f_3	0.332	1.039	0.672	0.666	0.221
f_4	152.944	196.566	181.135	181.320	10.094
f_5	26.582	29.507	28.165	28.162	0.690
f_6	-6379.518	-5276.288	-5731.317	-5718.013	311.841
Enhanced DE/rand/1/bin $\left(\sum_{i=1}^{NP} \tilde{C}_{i,Z} > 0\right)$					
f_1	0.001	1.524	0.258	0.117	0.350
f_2	0.042	3.118	1.312	1.162	1.041
f_3	0.837	4.083	1.842	1.675	0.801
f_4	42.423	129.087	87.457	88.606	21.604
f_5	27.496	124.206	40.911	33.368	21.483
f_6	-11965.105	-6869.531	-10292.865	-10392.666	1036.395

Notation the 2nd half of generations means the enhanced DE/rand/1/bin has been used in the 2nd half of generations and in the first one, the classical variant of DE/rand/1/bin has been used. The global minimum of the Schwefel's function for $D = 30$ is f_6 (x) =-12569.487. Setting 2.

- **Graph Distance:** The minimal graph distance between nodes are much lower in the case of DE/best/1/bin than in the case of DE/rand/1/bin. This is caused by the third parent (selected in the mutation step), which is not selected randomly in the case of DE/best/1/bin. It is the individual with the best objective function value. In the mutation step, it is selected as the parent for all individuals in the population for one generation. This means that the node representing the best individual in the corresponding CN will be connected with more other nodes (representing the individuals) than the node representing the randomly selected parent in the mutation step. The connections

Table 9. Comparison of the results of the DE/rand/1/bin and the enhanced DE/rand/1/bin

Function	Min	Max	Mean	Median	Std. Dev.
DE/rand/1/bin					
f_1	0.007	0.015	0.009	0.008	0.002
f_2	0.910	1.737	1.359	1.400	0.220
f_3	1.003	1.048	1.032	1.034	0.010
f_4	172.292	209.653	192.665	194.678	10.463
f_5	28.506	31.412	29.620	29.510	0.692
f_6	-6339.260	-4930.969	-5384.633	-5347.144	316.886
Enhanced DE/rand/1/bin (the 2nd Half of Generations)					
f_1	0.000	0.002	0.001	0.001	0.001
f_2	0.171	0.635	0.349	0.323	0.122
f_3	0.301	0.916	0.685	0.699	0.162
f_4	134.704	190.306	162.493	159.450	14.030
f_5	26.565	29.562	27.674	27.708	0.619
f_6	-7226.182	-5667.452	-6269.448	-6283.449	340.914
Enhanced DE/rand/1/bin $\left(\sum_{i=1}^{NP} \tilde{C}_{i,Z} > 0\right)$					
f_1	0.000	0.000	0.000	0.000	0.000
f_2	0.020	0.133	0.056	0.052	0.026
f_3	0.017	0.627	0.175	0.122	0.157
f_4	19.473	126.114	83.403	78.996	28.549
f_5	25.167	28.017	26.891	27.042	0.685
f_6	-12226.605	-9321.386	-10761.269	-10528.585	951.738

Notation the 2nd half of generations means the enhanced DE/rand/1/bin has been used in the 2nd half of generations and in the first one, the classical variant of DE/rand/1/bin has been used. The global minimum of the Schwefel's function for $D = 30$ is f_6 (x) = -12569.487. Setting 3.

of the node representing the best individual and all other nodes will influence the minimal graph distances between nodes.

- **Local Clustering Coefficient:** DE/best/1/bin reached the higher values of the maximum of the local clustering coefficient than DE/rand/1/bin. The higher values of the mean local clustering coefficient mean that the nodes representing the individuals are closer to create a clique, i.e. nodes representing the individuals are connected with each other. The reason of the differences between the local clustering coefficient of DE/best/1/bin and DE/rand/1/bin is the same like in the case of

Table 10. Comparison of the results of the DE/rand/1/bin and the enhanced DE/rand/1/bin

Function	Min	Max	Mean	Median	Std. Dev.
DE/rand/1/bin					
f_1	0.935	2.161	1.270	1.204	0.268
f_2	5.336	6.807	6.153	6.203	0.384
f_3	3.483	6.310	5.350	5.518	0.637
f_4	187.978	245.297	219.168	219.685	12.250
f_5	85.105	199.947	130.981	128.226	24.659
f_6	-5595.789	-4727.268	-5095.292	-5070.100	226.988
Enhanced DE/rand/1/bin (the 2nd Half of Generations)					
f_1	0.283	1.125	0.615	0.599	0.189
f_2	4.019	5.612	4.844	4.861	0.411
f_3	1.678	3.893	3.014	3.108	0.594
f_4	168.456	224.799	195.602	196.687	12.451
f_5	60.041	143.895	97.739	96.351	21.015
f_6	-6779.416	-5544.043	-5969.492	-5925.717	331.000
Enhanced DE/rand/1/bin $\left(\sum_{i=1}^{NP} \tilde{C}_{i,Z} > 0\right)$					
f_1	0.068	0.449	0.157	0.145	0.073
f_2	2.877	4.093	3.353	3.357	0.260
f_3	1.196	2.042	1.501	1.457	0.235
f_4	33.245	152.863	90.095	88.856	30.099
f_5	33.563	60.348	44.288	42.702	6.635
f_6	-12161.414	-8581.606	-10390.349	-10745.368	1015.300

Notation the 2nd half of generations means the enhanced DE/rand/1/bin has been used in the 2nd half of generations and in the first one, the classical variant of DE/rand/1/bin has been used. The global minimum of the Schwefel's function for $D = 30$ is $f_6(x) = -12569.487$. Setting 4.

the mean graph distance. The node representing the best individual selected (in the mutation step) as the parent for one generation in DE/best/1/bin will be connected with more nodes than the node representing the randomly selected parent. This phenomenon will influence the mean local clustering coefficient. The analysis of the local clustering coefficient led us to analyse the weighted clustering coefficient where the weights of the edges are taken into consideration.

- **Weighted Clustering Coefficient:** There are many ways how to compute weighted clustering coefficient. In this work, we have decided to use weighted clustering coefficient computed accord-

Table 11. Comparison of the results of the DE/rand/1/bin and the enhanced DE/rand/1/bin

Function	Min	Max	Mean	Median	Std. Dev.
DE/rand/1/bin					
f_1	8.526	19.822	14.503	14.872	2.547
f_2	10.775	14.539	13.114	13.290	0.860
f_3	33.756	76.237	55.017	56.962	9.394
f_4	229.821	280.932	252.631	254.418	12.691
f_5	332.702	602.217	457.768	469.809	70.965
f_6	-5648.038	-4334.380	-4799.020	-4696.003	272.355
Enhanced DE/rand/1/bin (the 2nd Half of Generations)					
f_1	4.852	10.682	8.526	8.619	1.466
f_2	9.389	12.406	10.861	10.676	0.807
f_3	17.594	42.130	27.111	26.455	4.805
f_4	185.604	248.147	222.781	226.578	16.053
f_5	193.780	397.955	272.536	265.090	42.158
f_6	-6652.027	-4824.304	-5563.555	-5489.674	382.952
Enhanced DE/rand/1/bin $\left(\sum_{i=1}^{NP} \tilde{C}_{i,Z} > 0\right)$					
f_1	0.231	2.391	1.268	1.062	0.642
f_2	3.745	7.516	5.643	5.674	1.004
f_3	2.087	8.196	4.884	4.501	1.862
f_4	32.477	145.000	95.324	90.615	30.679
f_5	32.443	141.047	61.525	58.426	21.127
f_6	-11812.150	-5822.881	-10241.146	-10187.419	834.867

Notation the 2nd half of generations means the enhanced DE/rand/1/bin has been used in the 2nd half of generations and in the first one, the classical variant of DE/rand/1/bin has been used. The global minimum of the Schwefel's function for $D = 30$ is f_6 (x) = -12569.487. Setting 5.

ing to Zhang and Horvath (2005) (see Equation (15)) because it is purely weighted based. From the results mentioned in Tables 4 and 5 we can see that there are significant differences between weighted clustering coefficients of CNs created by DE/best/1/bin and DE/rand/1/bin as well as in the case of the local clustering coefficient. DE/best/1/bin reached higher values of both for all test functions. In DE/best/1/bin, the average maximal values of the local clustering is equal to 1. This means that all individuals are in relationship with each other at the end of the algorithm. So numerous relationships between individuals are also projected into the values of the weighted

Table 12. Comparison of the results of the DE/rand/1/bin and the enhanced DE/rand/1/bin

Function	Min	Max	Mean	Median	Std. Dev.
DE/rand/1/bin					
f_1	0.379	0.943	0.661	0.677	0.126
f_2	3.723	4.946	4.327	4.313	0.258
f_3	2.396	3.553	3.069	3.070	0.315
f_4	381.758	438.436	412.876	413.488	15.285
f_5	77.487	149.272	104.418	99.078	18.157
f_6	-7081.120	-6106.458	-6687.477	-6716.839	271.175
Enhanced DE/rand/1/bin (the 2nd Half of Generations)					
f_1	0.015	0.217	0.057	0.041	0.041
f_2	0.998	2.661	1.870	1.824	0.470
f_3	1.076	1.856	1.193	1.140	0.147
f_4	351.627	417.561	395.823	395.055	16.76
f_5	49.434	70.718	53.595	52.719	4.043
f_6	-8361.759	-6808.304	-7523.347	-7513.978	425.748
Enhanced DE/rand/1/bin $\left(\sum_{i=1}^{NP} \tilde{C}_{i,Z} > 0\right)$					
f_1	0.025	4.599	1.042	0.601	1.178
f_2	0.123	3.349	1.541	1.397	0.698
f_3	1.094	13.079	4.198	2.388	3.503
f_4	68.758	249.595	154.492	146.888	45.979
f_5	47.366	110.447	68.106	63.712	18.985
f_6	-18914.083	-14192.625	-16814.957	-16809.638	1385.797

Notation the 2nd half of generations means the enhanced DE/rand/1/bin has been used in the 2nd half of generations and in the first one, the classical variant of DE/rand/1/bin has been used. The global minimum of the Schwefel's function for $D = 50$ is f_6 (x) = -20949.145 Setting 6.

clustering coefficients, where the weights of the edges are reflected. The results of the weighted clustering coefficient analysis led us to investigate the influence of the weighted clustering coefficient to the DE convergence rate.

- **Global Clustering Coefficient:** According to Equation (8) the global clustering coefficient is the ratio of the number of closed triplets and number of connected triplets of vertices. The global clustering coefficient can be also understood as the probability of the existence of the third edge between arbitrary three vertices where two of them are already connected by the edge. It is well

Table 13. Comparison of the results of the DE/rand/1/bin and the enhanced DE/rand/1/bin

Function	Min	Max	Mean	Median	Std. Dev.
DE/rand/1/bin					
f_1	1.120	2.018	1.557	1.548	0.216
f_2	5.443	7.362	6.616	6.611	0.432
f_3	4.825	9.526	6.826	6.640	1.172
f_4	218.659	262.996	236.556	235.872	12.300
f_5	77.467	159.774	110.841	105.143	23.692
f_6	-5706.980	-4243.727	-4830.711	-4777.877	290.794
Enhanced DE/rand/1/bin (the 2nd Half of Generations)					
f_1	0.081	0.579	0.239	0.212	0.103
f_2	3.577	5.797	4.677	4.754	0.525
f_3	1.360	2.859	1.882	1.804	0.398
f_4	163.517	223.455	193.527	188.395	17.687
f_5	37.031	74.840	48.904	46.625	9.317
f_6	-7461.195	-5330.444	-5982.792	-5999.620	450.195
Enhanced DE/rand/1/bin $\left(\sum_{i=1}^{NP} \tilde{C}_{i,Z} > 0\right)$					
f_1	0.014	0.126	0.044	0.032	0.029
f_2	0.959	3.494	2.400	2.603	0.750
f_3	1.038	1.395	1.157	1.121	0.100
f_4	42.992	133.825	96.071	92.022	25.709
f_5	25.763	43.333	31.067	29.903	3.561
f_6	-11589.007	-8582.344	-10129.953	-10292.377	719.136

Notation the 2nd half of generations means the enhanced DE/rand/1/bin has been used in the 2nd half of generations and in the first one, the classical variant of DE/rand/1/bin has been used. The global minimum of the Schwefel's function for $D = 30$ is f_6 (x) = -12569.487 Setting 7.

known that the global clustering coefficient of the complete network is equal to 1 in contrast with the tree network where the global clustering coefficient is equal to 0 (Dorogovtsev & Mendes, 2002). In the case of DE/best/1/bin, the maximal global clustering coefficient reached value 1 for all test functions. This means that the individuals created the complete network at the end of the algorithm DE/best/1/bin for each test function. DE/rand/1/bin is very close to create the complete network in the most of test functions at the end of the algorithm but in the case of the Rastrigin's function, the maximal global clustering coefficient reached value 0.480 and in the case of the

Table 14. Comparison of the results of the DE/rand/1/bin and the enhanced DE/rand/1/bin

Function	Min	Max	Mean	Median	Std. Dev.
DE/rand/1/bin					
f_1	9.144	14.997	12.141	12.042	1.356
f_2	8.343	9.046	8.692	8.621	0.183
f_3	35.355	48.339	42.467	42.352	3.224
f_4	854.356	910.657	883.142	883.246	14.737
f_5	1515.673	2091.829	1761.872	1751.918	165.305
f_6	-13749.620	-12374.444	-12959.868	-12836.84	413.893
Enhanced DE/rand/1/bin (the 2nd Half of Generations)					
f_1	7.374	11.090	9.037	8.850	1.065
f_2	7.530	8.520	7.982	7.908	0.291
f_3	25.212	39.905	32.000	32.552	3.857
f_4	749.651	835.016	803.332	808.476	23.882
f_5	1432.976	1807.029	1631.522	1623.642	107.138
f_6	-16545.443	-13331.483	-14862.325	-14807.773	695.962
Enhanced DE/rand/1/bin $\left(\sum_{i=1}^{NP} \tilde{C}_{i,z} > 0\right)$					
f_1	4.273	7.307	6.135	6.234	0.752
f_2	6.561	7.611	6.995	6.894	0.283
f_3	18.099	29.439	22.512	22.184	2.92
f_4	408.875	763.203	654.043	673.971	88.602
f_5	900.682	1482.012	1181.326	1192.822	139.263
f_6	-39195.642	-19552.334	-26964.935	-24744.665	6169.382

Notation the 2nd half of generations means the enhanced DE/rand/1/bin has been used in the 2nd half of generations and in the first one, the classical variant of DE/rand/1/bin has been used. The global minimum of the Schwefel's function for $D = 100$ is $f_6(x) = -12569.487$ Setting 8.

Schwefel's function even 0.382, which indicates that the algorithm spent a long time in the local extremes of the functions. There are fewer improved individuals which influence the number of edges between nodes modelling these individuals in the graph.

- **Closeness Centrality:** The values of the closeness centrality in the case of DE/best/1/bin are much higher than in the case of DE/rand/1/bin. It is the next confirmation that the best individual selecting as the third parent in DE/best/1/bin influences the properties of the created CNs. Thanks to the best individual there are more edges between the node representing this individual and the nodes representing the other ones. These connections affect the distances between nodes in the graph which are projected into the values of the closeness centrality.

- **Betweenness Centrality:** DE/best/1/bin reached the higher values of the maximal betweenness centrality. We assume that the higher values in the case of DE/best/1/bin is again caused by the best individual selected as one from three parents in the mutation step.
- **Weighted Out-Degree:** The values of the mean maximal weighted out-degree are higher in the experiments using DE/best/1/bin. The results are influenced by the principle of the parent selection. The weighted out-degree of the individual which has been selected as the best one and becomes the parent for one generation in DE/best/1/bin will be logically much higher than the weighted out-degree of the nodes representing the other individuals. This phenomenon influences the values of the weighted out-degree of the established CN.

In the first experiment we have showed that our strategy of the CNs creation has been designed correctly. The differences between the properties of the created CNs correspond with the differences of the properties of both algorithms (DE/best/1/bin and DE/rand/1/bin). We have shown the influence of the best individual selecting as the parent for all generation in the strategy DE/best/1/bin and our analysis led us to the question - how can the weighted clustering coefficient of the corresponding CN influence the DE convergence rate.

In the second part of this work, we have incorporated the weighted clustering coefficient to the mutation step in the DE/rand/1/bin algorithm. The motivation of this experiment is the idea that the individuals with the higher weighted clustering coefficient have the genomes of the high quality and from this reason they should be used more frequently in the process of mutation to spread their genomes to the population. To verify our hypothesis the enhanced DE/rand/1/bin has been devised. This algorithm looks at the individuals as at the nodes and the relationships between individuals as at the edges of the graph. Each individual is enhanced by the new property – weighted clustering coefficient computed according to Equation (15). The probability of selection is computed for each individual according to Equation (27). In the process of the noise vector creation, parents are selected randomly on the basis of their probabilities.

We have selected eight settings of DE and we have compared the convergence rate of the classical DE/rand/1/bin and our enhanced DE/rand/1/bin. Two experimental sets have been created. In the first one, DE/rand/1/bin is used in the first half of generations and then our enhanced DE/rand/1/bin is used. In the second experimental set, the enhanced DE/rand/1/bin is used when the sum of all weighted clustering coefficients are greater than zero. Otherwise the classical DE/rand/1/bin is used. As we can see in Tables 7 – 13 the enhanced DE/rand/1/bin reached higher convergence rate than the classical DE/rand/1/bin in all cases when the DE/rand/1/bin is used in the first half of generations.

In the second experimental set, the enhanced DE/rand/1/bin is used when the sum of all clustering coefficients is greater than zero. The enhanced DE/rand/1/bin reached significantly higher convergence rate than the classical DE/rand/1/bin in the most of cases. In few cases, the enhanced DE/rand/1/bin reached worse results than the classical DE/rand/1/bin. We assume that the reason is an insufficient number of the edges between nodes representing the individuals at the beginning of the enhanced DE/rand/1/bin.

The results of the second experiment show that the incorporation of the complex network property – weighted clustering coefficient into the DE can positively influence the DE convergence rate.

In the future, we would like to incorporate other CN properties (closeness centrality, degree centrality etc.) into the DE algorithm. The next goal is to improve the convergence rate of the DE using low number of individuals because our approach is now appropriate for the large population (70 and more individuals).

REFERENCES

Ashlock, D., Smucker, M., & Walker, J. (1999). Graph based genetic algorithms. In *Evolutionary Computation, 1999. CEC 99. Proceedings of the 1999 Congress on* (*Vol. 2*). IEEE.

Barrat, A., Barthelemy, M., Pastor-Satorras, R., & Vespignani, A. (2004). The architecture of complex weighted networks. *Proceedings of the National Academy of Sciences of the United States of America*, *101*(11), 3747–3752. doi:10.1073/pnas.0400087101 PMID:15007165

Bavelas, A. (1948). A mathematical model for group structures. *Human Organization*, *7*(3), 16–30. doi:10.17730/humo.7.3.f4033344851gl053

Bavelas, A. (1950). Communication patterns in task-oriented groups. *The Journal of the Acoustical Society of America*, *22*(6), 725–730. doi:10.1121/1.1906679

Beauchamp, M. (1965). An improved index of centrality. *Behavioral Science*, *10*(2), 161–163. doi:10.1002/bs.3830100205 PMID:14284290

Boccaletti, S., Latora, V., Moreno, Y., Chavez, M., & Hwang, D. U. (2006). Complex networks: Structure and dynamics. *Physics Reports*, *424*(4), 175–308. doi:10.1016/j.physrep.2005.10.009

Brest, J., Greiner, S., Bošković, B., Mernik, M., & Zumer, V. (2006). Self-adapting control parameters in differential evolution: A comparative study on numerical benchmark problems. *Evolutionary Computation. IEEE Transactions on*, *10*(6), 646–657.

Brest, J., & Maučec, M. S. (2008). Population size reduction for the differential evolution algorithm. *Applied Intelligence*, *29*(3), 228–247. doi:10.1007/s10489-007-0091-x

Chakraborty, U. K., Das, S., & Konar, A. (2006, September). Differential evolution with local neighborhood. In *Evolutionary Computation, 2006. CEC 2006. IEEE Congress on* (pp. 2042-2049). IEEE. doi:10.1109/CEC.2006.1688558

Das, S., Abraham, A., Chakraborty, U. K., & Konar, A. (2009). Differential evolution using a neighborhood-based mutation operator. *Evolutionary Computation. IEEE Transactions on*, *13*(3), 526–553.

Das, S., & Suganthan, P. N. (2011). Differential evolution: A survey of the state-of-the-art. *Evolutionary Computation. IEEE Transactions on*, *15*(1), 4–31.

Davendra, D., Zelinka, I., Metlicka, M., Senkerik, R., & Pluhacek, M. (2014, December). Complex network analysis of differential evolution algorithm applied to flowshop with no-wait problem. In *Differential Evolution (SDE), 2014 IEEE Symposium on* (pp. 1-8). IEEE. doi:10.1109/SDE.2014.7031536

Davendra, D., Zelinka, I., Senkerik, R., & Pluhacek, M. (2014). Complex Network Analysis of Discrete Self-organising Migrating Algorithm. In Nostradamus 2014: Prediction, Modeling and Analysis of Complex Systems (pp. 161-174). Springer International Publishing.

Dorogovtsev, S. N., & Mendes, J. F. (2002). Evolution of networks. *Advances in Physics*, *51*(4), 1079–1187. doi:10.1080/00018730110112519

dos Santos Coelho, L., Ayala, H. V. H., & Mariani, V. C. (2014). A self-adaptive chaotic differential evolution algorithm using gamma distribution for unconstrained global optimization. *Applied Mathematics and Computation*, *234*, 452–459. doi:10.1016/j.amc.2014.01.159

Fan, H. Y., & Lampinen, J. (2003). A trigonometric mutation operation to differential evolution. *Journal of Global Optimization*, *27*(1), 105–129. doi:10.1023/A:1024653025686

Freeman, L. C. (1979). Centrality in social networks conceptual clarification. *Social Networks*, *1*(3), 215–239. doi:10.1016/0378-8733(78)90021-7

Gong, M., Cai, Q., Chen, X., & Ma, L. (2014). Complex network clustering by multiobjective discrete particle swarm optimization based on decomposition. *Evolutionary Computation. IEEE Transactions on*, *18*(1), 82–97.

Holme, P., Park, S. M., Kim, B. J., & Edling, C. R. (2007). Korean university life in a network perspective: Dynamics of a large affiliation network. *Physica A: Statistical Mechanics and its Applications*, *373*, 821-830.

Iorio, A. W., & Li, X. (2005). Solving rotated multi-objective optimization problems using differential evolution. In *AI 2004: Advances in artificial intelligence* (pp. 861–872). Springer Berlin Heidelberg.

Islam, S. M., Das, S., Ghosh, S., Roy, S., & Suganthan, P. N. (2012). An adaptive differential evolution algorithm with novel mutation and crossover strategies for global numerical optimization. *Systems, Man, and Cybernetics, Part B: Cybernetics. IEEE Transactions on*, *42*(2), 482–500.

Kalna, G., & Higham, D. J. (2006, April). Clustering coefficients for weighted networks. In *Symposium on Network Analysis in Natural Sciences and Engineering* (p. 45).

Kim, J., & Wilhelm, T. (2008). What is a complex graph?. *Physica A: Statistical Mechanics and its Applications*, *387*(11), 2637-2652.

Kovačević, D., Mladenović, N., Petrović, B., & Milošević, P. (2014). DE-VNS: Self-adaptive Differential Evolution with crossover neighborhood search for continuous global optimization. *Computers & Operations Research*, *52*, 157–169. doi:10.1016/j.cor.2013.12.009

Leavitt, H. J. (1951). Some effects of certain communication patterns on group performance. *Journal of Abnormal and Social Psychology*, *46*(1), 38–50. doi:10.1037/h0057189 PMID:14813886

Li, Y., Liu, J., & Liu, C. (2014). A comparative analysis of evolutionary and memetic algorithms for community detection from signed social networks. *Soft Computing*, *18*(2), 329–348. doi:10.1007/s00500-013-1060-4

Mabu, S., Hirasawa, K., & Hu, J. (2007). A graph-based evolutionary algorithm: Genetic network programming (GNP) and its extension using reinforcement learning. *Evolutionary Computation*, *15*(3), 369–398. doi:10.1162/evco.2007.15.3.369 PMID:17705783

Mallipeddi, R., & Suganthan, P. N. (2010). Differential evolution algorithm with ensemble of parameters and mutation and crossover strategies. In Swarm, Evolutionary, and Memetic Computing (pp. 71-78). Springer Berlin Heidelberg. doi:10.1007/978-3-642-17563-3_9

Mezura-Montes, E., Velázquez-Reyes, J., & Coello Coello, C. A. (2006, July). A comparative study of differential evolution variants for global optimization. In *Proceedings of the 8th annual conference on Genetic and evolutionary computation* (pp. 485-492). ACM. doi:10.1145/1143997.1144086

Mlakar, M., Petelin, D., Tušar, T., & Filipič, B. (2015). GP-DEMO: Differential evolution for multiobjective optimization based on Gaussian process models. *European Journal of Operational Research, 243*(2), 347–361. doi:10.1016/j.ejor.2014.04.011

Moxley, R. L., & Moxley, N. F. (1974). Determining point-centrality in uncontrived social networks. *Sociometry, 37*(1), 122–130. doi:10.2307/2786472

Neri, F., & Tirronen, V. (2010). Recent advances in differential evolution: A survey and experimental analysis. *Artificial Intelligence Review, 33*(1-2), 61–106. doi:10.1007/s10462-009-9137-2

Newman, M. E. (2008). The mathematics of networks. *The New Palgrave Encyclopedia of Economics, 2(*2008), 1-12.

Noman, N., & Iba, H. (2008). Accelerating differential evolution using an adaptive local search. Evolutionary Computation. *IEEE Transactions on, 12*(1), 107–125.

Onnela, J. P., Saramäki, J., Kertész, J., & Kaski, K. (2005). Intensity and coherence of motifs in weighted complex networks. *Physical Review E: Statistical, Nonlinear, and Soft Matter Physics, 71*(6), 065103. doi:10.1103/PhysRevE.71.065103 PMID:16089800

Opsahl, T., Agneessens, F., & Skvoretz, J. (2010). Node centrality in weighted networks: Generalizing degree and shortest paths. *Social Networks, 32*(3), 245–251. doi:10.1016/j.socnet.2010.03.006

Opsahl, T., & Panzarasa, P. (2009). Clustering in weighted networks. *Social Networks, 31*(2), 155–163. doi:10.1016/j.socnet.2009.02.002

Qin, A. K., & Suganthan, P. N. (2005, September). Self-adaptive differential evolution algorithm for numerical optimization. In *Evolutionary Computation, 2005. The 2005 IEEE Congress on* (Vol. 2, pp. 1785-1791). IEEE. doi:10.1109/CEC.2005.1554904

Rahnamayan, S., Tizhoosh, H. R., & Salama, M. (2008). Opposition-based differential evolution. *Evolutionary Computation. IEEE Transactions on, 12*(1), 64–79.

Rogers, D. L. (1974). Sociometric analysis of interorganizational relations: Application of theory and measurement. *Rural Sociology.*

Ronkkonen, J., Kukkonen, S., & Price, K. V. (2005, September). Real-parameter optimization with differential evolution. In *Proc. IEEE CEC* (Vol. 1, pp. 506-513).

Sabidussi, G. (1966). The centrality index of a graph. *Psychometrika, 31*(4), 581–603. doi:10.1007/BF02289527 PMID:5232444

Saramäki, J., Kivelä, M., Onnela, J. P., Kaski, K., & Kertesz, J. (2007). Generalizations of the clustering coefficient to weighted complex networks. *Physical Review E: Statistical, Nonlinear, and Soft Matter Physics*, *75*(2), 027105. doi:10.1103/PhysRevE.75.027105 PMID:17358454

Smith Sidney, L. (1950). *Communication pattern and the adaptability of task-oriented groups: an experimental study*. Cambridge, MA: Group Networks Laboratory, Research Laboratory of Electronics, Massachusetts Institute of Technology.

Soleimani-pouri, M., Rezvanian, A., & Meybodi, M. R. (2014). An ant based particle swarm optimization algorithm for maximum clique problem in social networks. In *State of the art applications of social network analysis* (pp. 295–304). Springer International Publishing. doi:10.1007/978-3-319-05912-9_14

Storn, R., & Price, K. (1995). *Differential evolution-a simple and efficient adaptive scheme for global optimization over continuous spaces* (Vol. 3). Berkeley, CA: ICSI.

Tirronen, V., Neri, F., & Rossi, T. (2009, May). Enhancing differential evolution frameworks by scale factor local search-part i. In *Evolutionary Computation, 2009. CEC'09. IEEE Congress on* (pp. 94-101). IEEE. doi:10.1109/CEC.2009.4982935

Wang, Y., Cai, Z., & Zhang, Q. (2011). Differential evolution with composite trial vector generation strategies and control parameters. *Evolutionary Computation. IEEE Transactions on*, *15*(1), 55–66.

Wu, Q., & Hao, J. K. (2015). A review on algorithms for maximum clique problems. *European Journal of Operational Research*, *242*(3), 693–709. doi:10.1016/j.ejor.2014.09.064

Yang, Z., Tang, K., & Yao, X. (2008, June). Self-adaptive differential evolution with neighborhood search. In *Evolutionary Computation, 2008. CEC 2008. (IEEE World Congress on Computational Intelligence). IEEE Congress on* (pp. 1110-1116). IEEE.

Yang, Z., Yao, X., & He, J. (2008). Making a difference to differential evolution. In *Advances in metaheuristics for hard optimization* (pp. 397–414). Springer Berlin Heidelberg. doi:10.1007/978-3-540-72960-0_19

Yi, W., Gao, L., Li, X., & Zhou, Y. (2015). A new differential evolution algorithm with a hybrid mutation operator and self-adapting control parameters for global optimization problems. *Applied Intelligence*, *42*(4), 642–660. doi:10.1007/s10489-014-0620-3

Zaharie, D. (2009). Influence of crossover on the behavior of differential evolution algorithms. *Applied Soft Computing*, *9*(3), 1126–1138. doi:10.1016/j.asoc.2009.02.012

Zelinka, I., Davendra, D., Snášel, V., Jašek, R., Senkeřik, R., & Oplatková, Z. (2010, October). Preliminary investigation on relations between complex networks and evolutionary algorithms dynamics. In *Computer Information Systems and Industrial Management Applications (CISIM), 2010 International Conference on* (pp. 148-153). IEEE. doi:10.1109/CISIM.2010.5643674

Zelinka, I., Davendra, D. D., Chadli, M., Senkerik, R., Dao, T. T., & Skanderova, L. (2013). Evolutionary dynamics as the structure of complex networks. In *Handbook of Optimization* (pp. 215–243). Springer Berlin Heidelberg. doi:10.1007/978-3-642-30504-7_9

Zhang, B., & Horvath, S. (2005). A general framework for weighted gene co-expression network analysis. *Statistical Applications in Genetics and Molecular Biology*, *4*(1). doi:10.2202/1544-6115.1128 PMID:16646834

Zhou, Y., Li, X., & Gao, L. (2013). A differential evolution algorithm with intersect mutation operator. *Applied Soft Computing*, *13*(1), 390–401. doi:10.1016/j.asoc.2012.08.014

Chapter 13
On Mutual Relations amongst Evolutionary Algorithm Dynamics and Its Hidden Complex Network Structures:
An Overview and Recent Advances

Ivan Zelinka
VSB Technical University of Ostrava, Czech Republic

ABSTRACT

In this chapter, we do synthesis of three partially different areas of research: complex networks, evolutionary computation and deterministic chaos. Ideas, results and methodologies reported and mentioned here are based on our previous results and experiments. We report here our latest results as well as propositions on further research that is in process in our group (http://navy.cs.vsb.cz/). In order to understand what is the main idea, lets first discuss an overview of the two main areas: complex networks and evolutionary algorithms.

1. INTRODUCTION

In this chapter synthesis of two partially different areas of research is done: complex networks and evolutionary algorithms dynamics. The possibility to convert evolutionary dynamics of various evolutionary algorithms into complex network structure is discussed in this chapter (the case study on differential evolution is done in the next chapter), as well as possibilities of its analysis (via complex networks math. tools) and control. Ideas, results and methodologies reported and mentioned here are based on our previous results and experiments that are fully reported here for detailed study in case of reader's interest. Therefore this chapter is proposed as an overview-survey of this research. We report here our latest results as well as propositions on further research that is in process in our group (http://navy.cs.vsb.cz/).

DOI: 10.4018/978-1-4666-9964-9.ch013

It is clear that topic discussed here is a fusion of two significantly distinct areas, thus for better understanding of evolutionary algorithms and dynamics it is recommended to read Zelinka I. et.al. 2010. In order to understand what the main idea is, let's first discuss an overview of the two contributing areas: complex networks and evolutionary algorithms. Because this book is devoted to complex networks, we will focus more attention on evolutionary algorithms.

Large-scale networks, exhibiting complex patterns of interaction amongst vertices exist in both nature and in man-made systems (i.e., communication networks, genetic pathways, ecological or economical networks, social networks, networks of various scientific collaboration, Internet, World Wide Web, power grid etc.). The structure of complex networks thus can be observed in many systems. The title "complex networks" (Dorogovtsev S. N., 2002; Boccaletti S., et. al., 2006) comes from the fact that they exhibit substantial and non-trivial topological features with patterns of connection between vertices that are neither purely regular nor purely random. Such features include a heavy tail in the degree distribution, a high clustering coefficient and hierarchical structure, amongst other features. In the case of directed networks, these features also include reciprocity, triad significance profile and other features. Amongst many studies, two well-known and much studied classes of complex networks are the scale-free networks and small-world networks (see examples in Figure 1 and Figure 2), whose discovery and definition are vitally important in the scope of this research. Specific structural features can be observed in both classes i.e. so called power-law degree distributions for the scale-free networks and short path lengths with high clustering for the small world networks. Research in the field of complex networks has joined together researchers from many areas, which were outside of this interdisciplinary research in the past like mathematics, physics, biology, chemistry computer science, epidemiology etc. Complex networks, in general, are exhibiting complex patterns of interaction amongst vertices exist in both nature and man-made systems (i.e., communication networks, genetic pathways, ecological or economical networks, social networks, networks of various scientific collaboration etc.) and are a part of our daily life.

For more recent details about research on complex networks and its applications it is recommended to read for example (Broom M., et. al. 2010; Barrat A., et. al. 2008).

For long time complex networks are studied for their dynamics and structure as for example reported in (Broom M., et. al. 2010; Szabo G., 2007). In all those research papers dynamics of complex networks is described as an "evolutionary" dynamics, but in this sense it is mentioned as a time development of complex networks structure and dynamics. The question is, whether dynamics of an evolutionary algorithm can be transformed into complex network and its growth.

Evolutionary computation is a sub-discipline of computer science belonging to the bio-inspired computing area. Since the end of the Second World War, the main ideas of evolutionary computation have been published (Turing, A., 1969) and widely introduced to the scientific community (Holland, J., 1975). Hence, the golden era of evolutionary techniques began when Genetic Algorithms (GA) by J. Holland, Evolutionary Strategies (ES), by Schwefel (Schwefel, H., 1977) and Rechenberg (Rechenberg, I., 1971) and Evolutionary Programming (EP) by Fogel (Fogel,D.B., 1998) were introduced, as reported in (Zelinka I., et. al., 2010). All these designs were favored by the forthcoming of more powerful and more easily programmable computers, so that for the first time interesting problems could be tackled and evolutionary computation started to compete with and became a high quality alternative to other optimization methods.

As a representative example of evolutionary algorithms we can mention for example Genetic algorithm (GA). This algorithm is one of the first successfully applied EAs methods (Holland J., 1975), (Goldberg D., 1989). In GAs the main principles of EAs are applied in their purest form. The individu-

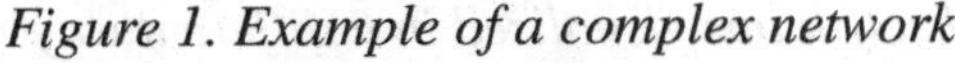

Figure 1. Example of a complex network

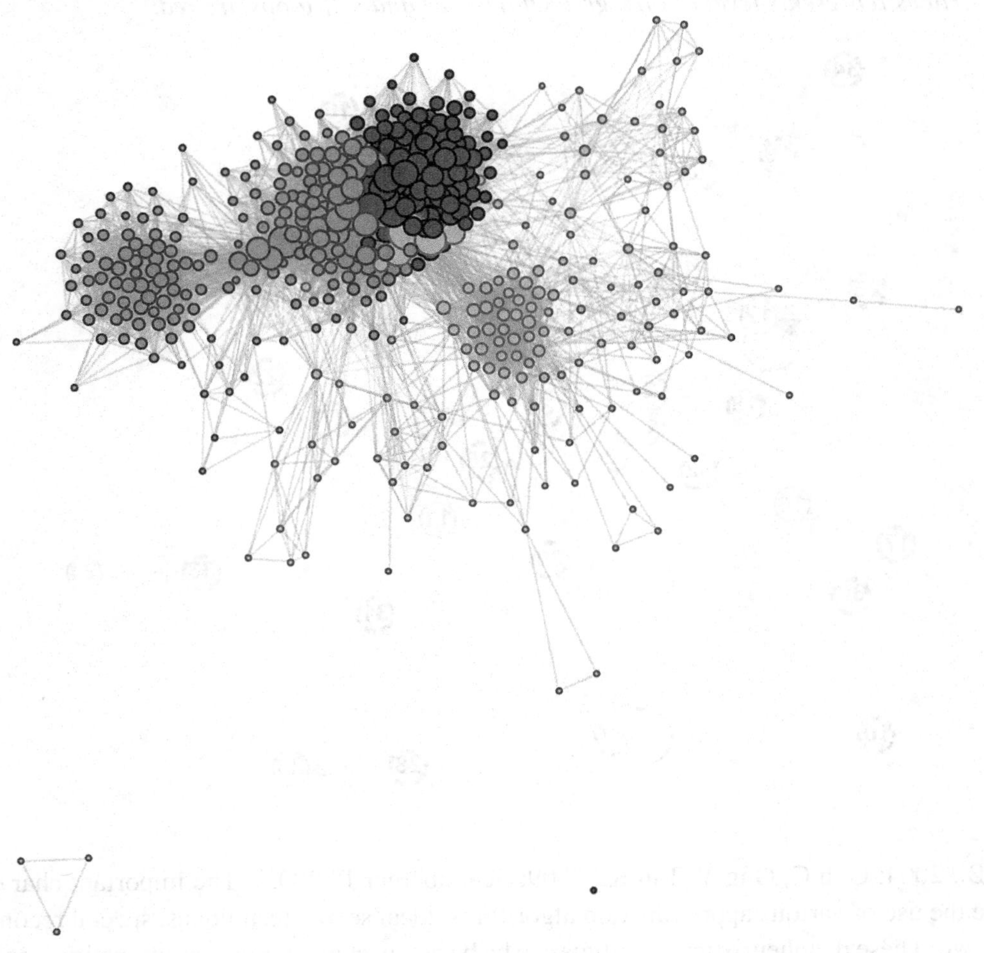

als are encoded as binary strings and represent possible solutions to the optimization problem under study. Another, similar, and in fact historically older algorithms are Evolutionary strategies (ES). This algorithm also belongs to the first successful stochastic algorithms in history. It was proposed at the beginning of the sixties by Rechenberg (Rechenberg I., 1971) and Schwefel (Schwefel H., 1974). It is based on the principles of natural selection similarly as the genetic algorithms. More modern and swarm based algorithm, that mimics natural behavior of swarm colonies with very good performance in combinatorial problems is Ant Colony Optimization (ACO), (Dorigo M., Suttzle T., 2004). This is an algorithm whose action simulates the behavior of ants in a colony and is one of the first swarm based algorithms as well as Particle Swarm (PS) or SOMA (Self-Organizing Migrating Algorithm). SOMA is a stochastic optimization algorithm that is modeled on the social behavior of cooperating individuals (Zelinka I., 2004). SOMA works on a population of candidate solutions in loops called migration loops. It is vector-oriented algorithm based on central individual called Leader that influences behavior of the whole population. SOMA is in fact swarm based algorithm, too, however it can be also cataloged as the Memetic Algorithms (MA) that represents a broad class of metaheuristic algorithms (Onwubolu

Figure 2. Another example of complex network with edges and self-loops visualized in a different way; color of vertices represents level of InDegree/OutDegree and self-loops are red.

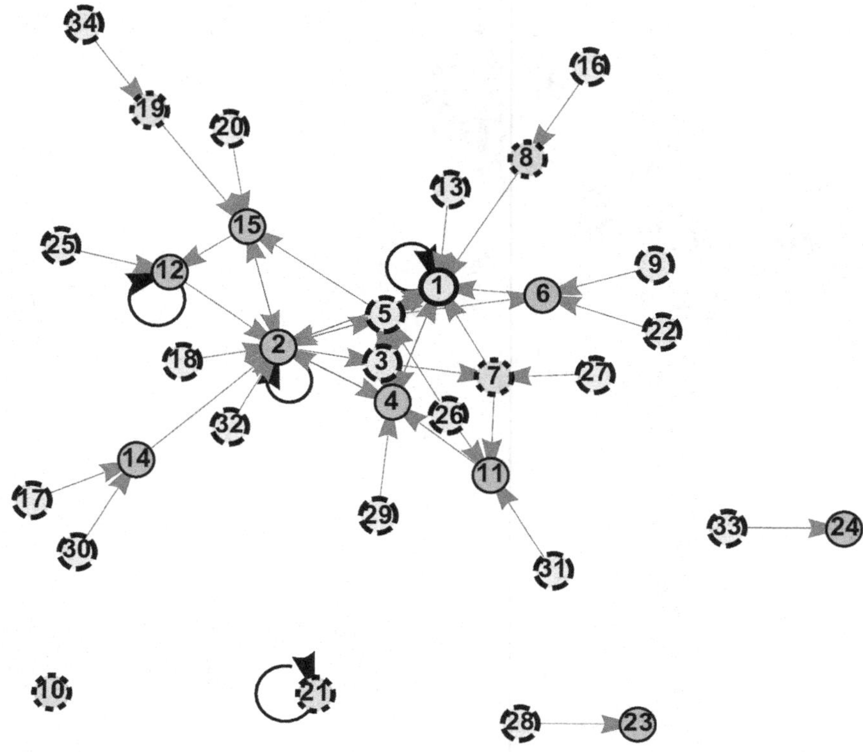

G, Babu B., 2004; Goh C, Ong Y, Tan K., 2009; Schonberger J., 2005). The important characteristics of MA are the use of various approximation algorithms, local search techniques, special recombination operators, etc. These metaheuristic algorithms can be basically characterized as competitive-cooperative strategies featuring attributes of synergy. One of the last mentioned here is Differential Evolution (DE). Differential Evolution (Price, K., 1999) is a population-based optimization method that works on real-number coded individuals. Differential Evolution is robust, fast, and effective with global optimization ability. It does not require that the objective function is differentiable, and it works with noisy, epistatic and time-dependent objective functions. Along with those well known algorithms also exist another (sometimes similar in principle) algorithms like Firefly (Yang, X. S., 2009), CoCoo algorithm, Bat algorithm (Yang X. S., 2010) amongst the others.

Evolutionary algorithms are capable of hard problem solving. A number of examples on evolutionary algorithms can be easily found. Evolutionary algorithms (EA) use with chaotic systems is done for example in (Richter H. and Reinschke K. J., 2000) where EAs have been used on local optimization of chaos, (Richter H., 2002) for chaos control with use of the multi-objective cost function or in (Richter H., 2006; Richter H., 2006), where evolutionary algorithms have been studied on chaotic landscapes. Slightly different approach with evolutionary algorithms is presented in (Zelinka I., 2008) where selected algorithms were used to synthesize artificial chaotic systems. In (Zelinka, I., 2008; Zelinka, I., 2006), EAs have been successfully used for real-time chaos control and in (Senkerik R., et. al. 2006) and for optimization of Chaos Control, see also (Zelinka I, et. al. 2010).

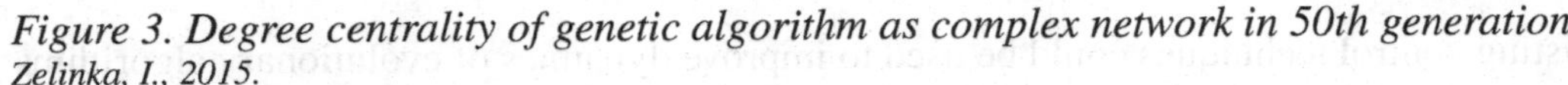

Figure 3. Degree centrality of genetic algorithm as complex network in 50th generation
Zelinka, I., 2015.

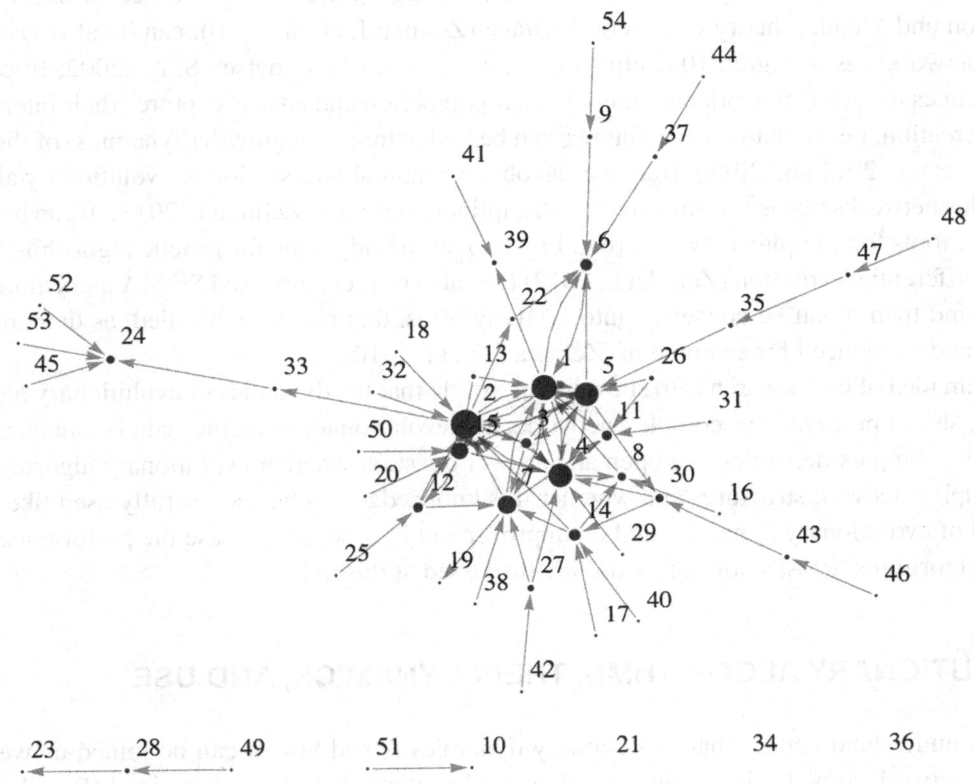

Other examples of evolutionary algorithms application can be found in (Dashora, Y., et al., 2007), which developed statistically robust evolutionary algorithms, alongside research conducted by (Li L., et. al. 2007). Parameters of permanent magnet synchronous motors have been optimized by PSO and experimentally validated on the servomotor. Another research was focused on swarm intelligence, which has been used for many complex tasks, co-evolutionary particle swarm optimization approach for the design of constrained engineering problems, particularly for pressure vessel, compression spring and welded beam, etc. Different problems solved by EAs are solved with different performance and results quality. One of theoretical research directions is how to improve EAs performance. A lot of research papers have been written on that topic.

In this chapter, we would like to demonstrate our continuous research on mutual intersection of complex networks, evolutionary algorithms (dynamics) and so called CML (Coupled Map Lattices) system (i.e. systems that exhibit spatiotemporal chaos and patterns and can be analyzed and/or controlled, (Zelinka I, et. al. 2010; Schuster H. G., 1999; Zelinka I., 2005; Zelinka, I., 2008; Zelinka I., 2006; Zahra R.Ch., 2007).

The main motivation (as well as question) is whether it is possible to visualize and simulate underlying dynamics of evolutionary process like complex network (Dorogovtsev S. N., 2002; Boccaletti S., 2006; Zelinka I., et. al., 2012). Reason for this is that today various techniques for analysis and control of complex networks exist and if complex network structure is hidden behind EA dynamics, then we believe, that existing control techniques could be used to improve dynamics of evolutionary algorithms (EAs). We demonstrate that dynamics of evolutionary algorithms, that are based on Darwin theory of evolution and Mendel theory of genetic heritage (Zelinka I, et. al. 2010), can be also visualized as complex networks, as in Figure 10 (Zelinka I., et. al., 2012), (Dorogovtsev S. N., 2002; Boccaletti S., 2006). Vertices in such a network are individuals of population and edges "capture" their interactions in offspring creation, i.e. evolutionary dynamics can be understood as a growth (dynamics) of the network (Zelinka I., et. al., 2011 and 2013). Here we can observe mutual intersection of evolutionary algorithms and complex networks that is a promising interdisciplinary research (Zelinka I., 2013). It can be analyzed by classical tools for complex networks (e.g. Figure 5. as already done for genetic algorithms (Zelinka, I., 2014), differential evolution (Zelinka I., 2012) (see also next chapter) and SOMA algorithm (Zelinka I., 2012)) and then it can be converted into CML systems, that can be controlled, as demonstrated in Figure 18 and introduced for example in (Zelinka I, et. al. 2010).

The main idea of our research is to show in this article that the dynamics of evolutionary algorithms, in general, shows properties of complex networks and evolutionary dynamics can be analyzed and visualized like complex networks. We open and answer question whether evolutionary algorithms really create complex network structures and whether this knowledge can be successfully used like feedback for control of evolutionary dynamics and its improvement in order to increase the performance of evolutionary algorithms. Possibilities of its use are discussed at the end.

2. EVOLUTIONARY ALGORITHMS, THEIR DYNAMICS, AND USE

In order to understand better what evolutionary dynamics is and how it can be joined-converted into a complex network some basics about evolutionary algorithms have to be explained (for all necessary details, see (Zelinka I, et. al. 2010), Chapter 2). Evolutionary algorithms are based on ideas of Darwin and Mendel theory of evolution uses some building blocks, which the diagram in Figure 4 illustrates. The evolutionary principles are transferred into computational methods in a simplified form that will be outlined now. If the evolutionary principles are used for the purposes of complicated calculations (in accordance with Figure 4), the following procedure is used:

1. **Specification of the Evolutionary Parameters:** For each algorithm, parameters must be defined so that they control the run of the algorithm or terminate it regularly, if the termination criterions defined in advance are fulfilled (for example, the number of cycles - generations). Part of this point is the definition of the cost function (objective function) or, as the case may be, what is called fitness - a modified return value of the objective function). The objective function is usually a mathematical model of the problem, whose minimization or maximization leads to the solution of the problem. This function with possible limiting conditions is some kind of "environmental equivalent" in which the quality of current individuals is assessed.
2. **Generation of the Initial Population:** (Generally $N \times M$ matrix, where N is the number of parameters of an individual - D is used hereinafter in this publication - and M is the number of individuals in the population) Depending on the number of optimized arguments of the objective function and the user's criterions, the initial population of individuals is generated. An individual is a vector of numbers having such a number of components as the number of optimized parameters

Figure 4. The evolutionary algorithm principle, for more see (Zelinka I, et. al. 2010).

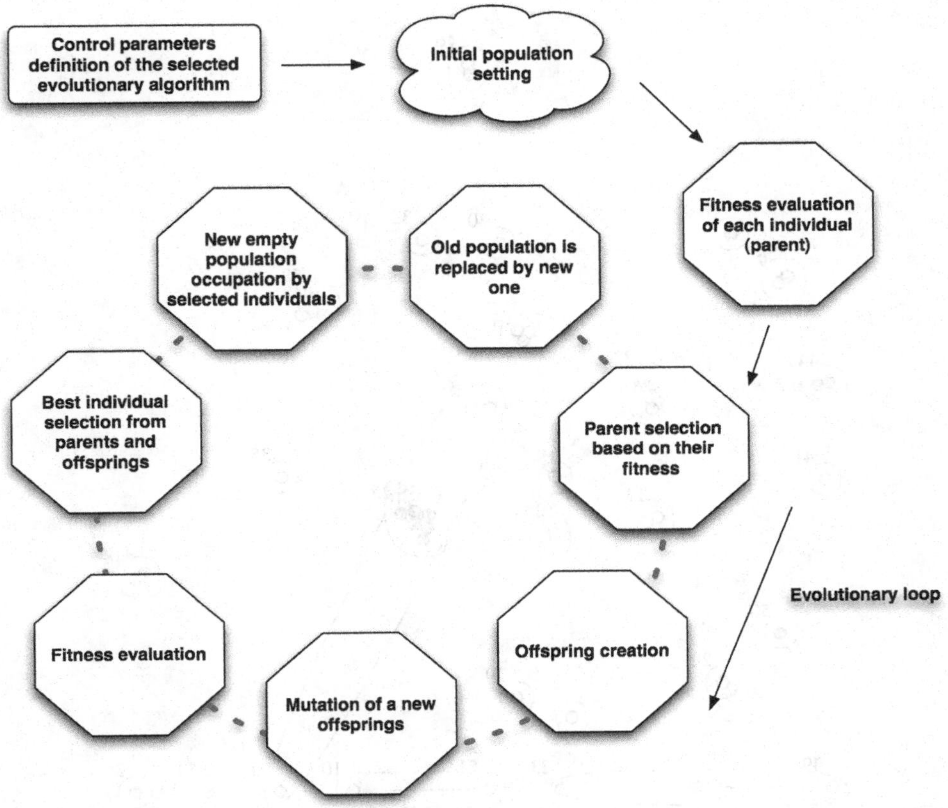

Control parameters definition of the selected evolutionary algorithm

Initial population setting

Fitness evaluation of each individual (parent)

Parent selection based on their fitness

Offspring creation

Mutation of a new offsprings

Fitness evaluation

Best individual selection from parents and offsprings

New empty population occupation by selected individuals

Old population is replaced by new one

Evolutionary loop

of the objective function. These components are set randomly and each individual thus represents one possible specific solution of the problem. The set of individuals is called population.

3. All the individuals are evaluated through a defined objective function and to each of them is assigned:
    a. Either a direct value of the return objective function, or
    b. A fitness value, which is a modified (usually normalized) value of the objective function.
4. Now parents are selected according to their quality (fitness, value of the objective function) or, as the case may be, also according to other criterions.
5. Descendants are created by crossbreeding the parents. The process of cross-breeding is different for each algorithm. Parts of parents are changed in classic genetic algorithms, in a differential evolution, crossbreeding is a certain vector operation, etc.
6. Every descendant is mutated. In other words, a new individual is changed by means of a suitable random process. This step is equivalent to the biological mutation of the genes of an individual.
7. Every new individual is evaluated in the same manner as in step 3.
8. The best individuals are selected.
9. The selected individuals fill a new population.
10. The old population is forgotten (eliminated, deleted, dies,..) and is replaced by a new population; step 4 represents further continuation.

Figure 5. Community graph of genetic algorithm as complex network in 50th generation
Zelinka, I., et. al., 2014.

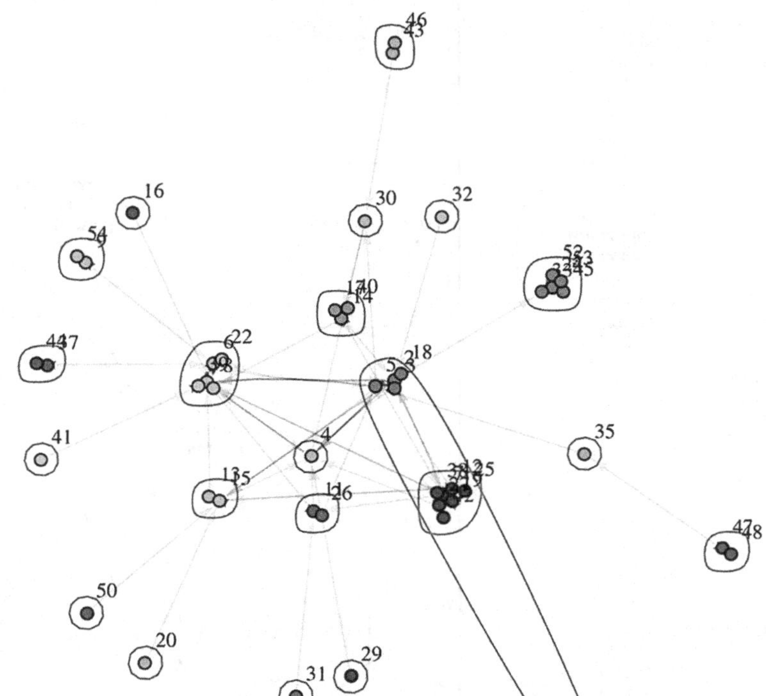

Steps 4 - 10 are repeated until the number of evolution cycles specified before by the user is reached or if the required quality of the solution is achieved. The principle of the evolutionary algorithm outlined above is general and may more or less differ in specific cases.

The new approach reported in this chapter is based on EAs individuals interactions and their recording as a complex network. Evolutionary algorithms, based on their canonical central dogma (following Darwinian ideas) clearly demonstrate intensive interaction amongst individual in the population, which is, in general, one of the important attributes of complex networks (intensive interaction amongst the vertices/in the case of the evolutionary algorithm the interaction between individuals).

The main idea of our research reported in this chapter, is to show how EAs dynamics can be converted into a complex network, then interpret tools of complex networks analysis on complex networks that are given by evolutionary dynamics. The first steps (i.e. conversion of the EA dynamics to the complex network and to CML system) have been done in the (Zelinka I., et. al., 2011; Zelinka I., et. al., 2010; Zelinka I., et. al., 2012).

3. CONVERSION AND VISUALIZATION

Based on above mentioned principles and algorithms, we believe that there is no universal approach, but rather a personal one, based on the knowledge of algorithm principle. Lets take as an example DE, e.g. DERand1Bin in which each individual is selected in each generation to be a parent. Thus in DE, we have recorded only those individuals-parents that have been replaced by better offspring (like vertex with added connections). In the DE class of algorithms we have omitted the philosophy that a bad parent is replaced by a better offspring, but accepted philosophical interpretation, that individual (worse parent) is moving to the better position (better offspring in original DE philosophy). Thus no vertex (individual) has to be either destroyed or replaced in the philosophical point of view. If, for example, DERand1Bin has a parent replaced by offspring, then it was considered as an activation (new additional links, edges) of vertex-worse parent from three another vertices (randomly selected individuals, see the next chapter or (Zelinka I., 2011, 2010 and 2012). In fact, such general approach can be used also in another algorithms. If interaction amongst *N* individuals leads to the improvement of another arbitrary one, say Mth, then it is equivalent to the situation that *N* vertices gives incoming edges to the Mth vertex and vice versa. Edges can be weighted by integer numbers (+1 = successive support of the Mth vertex, -1 = nonsuccesses support) or simply by differences in fitness before interaction and after interaction.

Similar approach can be used for another algorithms. The general rule that positive and/or negative interaction between individuals has to be recorded as a weighted connection between individuals/nodes. Its weights can be assigned according to algorithm structure (e.g. SOMA versus DE, PSO, etc…) and preferred information that has to be captured. Also importance of in-coming/out-coming edges can be different. In one case No. of in-coming edges can play major role (as the most progressive individual/node) or out-coming from node (as the most successive individual that successfully spread its genome through the population/another nodes). Also fitness difference of improved node/individual can be used as a weight. Those and another approaches has been successfully tested in our previous papers (Zelinka I., 2011, 2010, 2012 and 2014), (Davendra D., 2014, 2015; Zelinka I., 2015) and (Pluhacek M., 2015) for example.

Again, this very general idea has to be adopted for each used algorithm. As reported in (Metlicka M., 2014; Davendra D., et.al., 2014; Davendra D., et.al., 2015; Zelinka I., 2015), we have tried this conversion for SOMA, DE, PSO, ABC (Artificial Bee Colony) and GA. A few selected results from ABC and DE algorithms are reported at the end of chapter. Complex networks can be then visualized as for example in Figure 3 or Figure 5. From both figures it is visible that different algorithm dynamics produce different complex networks structure whose attributes can be calculated. Another visualizations can be found in (Metlicka M., 2014; Davendra D., 2015).

3.1. Used Test Problems

The test function applied in (Zelinka I., et. al. 2012) was selected from the test bed of 17 well-known test functions like Schwefels, Rastrigin's, Rana's function amongst the others as demonstrated in Equation 1-3. Evolution was searching for global extreme in 50 dimensions, i.e. individual has 50 parameters. Dimension is in the used test functions represented by variable D, so as one can see, it is easy to calculate selected functions for an arbitrary dimension. A test function has been selected due to their various complexity and mainly for the fact that these functions are widely used by researchers working with evolutionary algorithms. Another reason was that speed of convergence and thus evolutionary dynamics itself is different on that function, compared to simple test functions. Results in more details are reported in (Metlicka M., 2014; Davendra D., et.al., 2014).

$$f(x) = \sum_{i=1}^{D-1} \left(20 + e - \frac{20}{e^{0,2\sqrt{\frac{(x_i^2 + x_{i+1}^2)}{2}}}} - e^{0,5(\cos(2\pi x_i) + \cos(2\pi x_{i+1}))} \right) \quad (1)$$

$$f(x) = \sum_{i=1}^{D-1} \left(\begin{array}{l} -x_i \sin\left(\sqrt{\left|x_i - x_{i+1} - 47\right|}\right) - \\ \left(x_{i+1} + 47\right) \sin\left(\sqrt{\left|x_{i+1} + 47 + \frac{x_i}{2}\right|}\right) \end{array} \right) \quad (2)$$

$$f(x) = \sum_{i=1}^{D-1} \left(\begin{array}{l} x_i \sin\left(\sqrt{\left|x_{i+1} + 1 - x_i\right|}\right) \cos\left(\sqrt{\left|x_{i+1} + 1 + x_i\right|}\right) + \\ \left(x_{i+1} + 1\right) \cos\left(\sqrt{\left|x_{i+1} + 1 - x_i\right|}\right) \sin\left(\sqrt{\left|x_{i+1} + 1 + x_i\right|}\right) \end{array} \right) \quad (3)$$

Figure 6. Example of a network based on PSO
Pluhacek M., et. al., 2015.

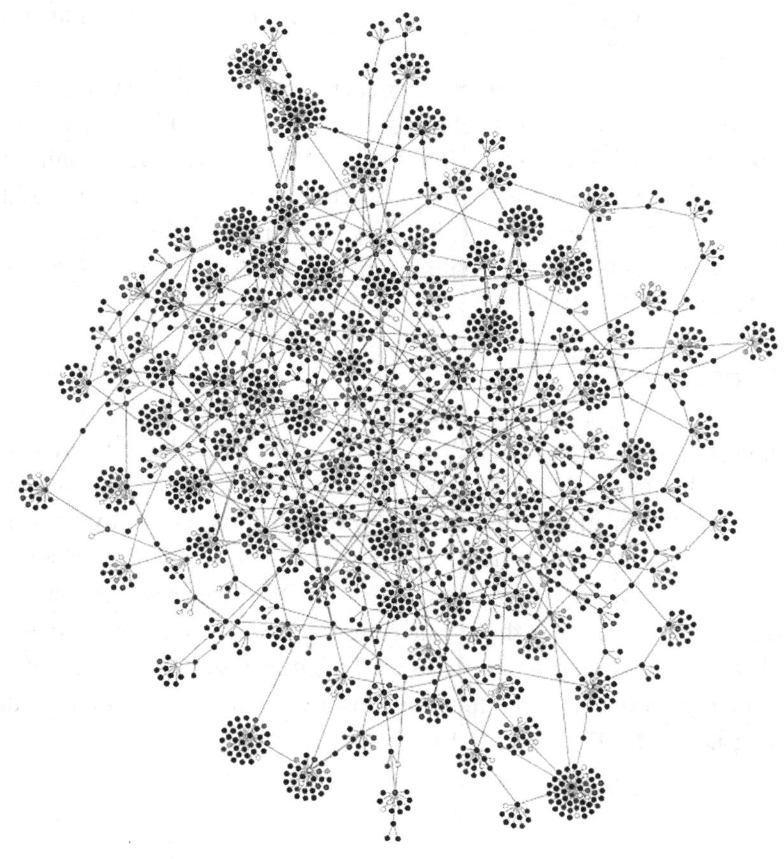

Figure 7. Example of a network based on SOMA
Zelinka I., et. al. 2012.

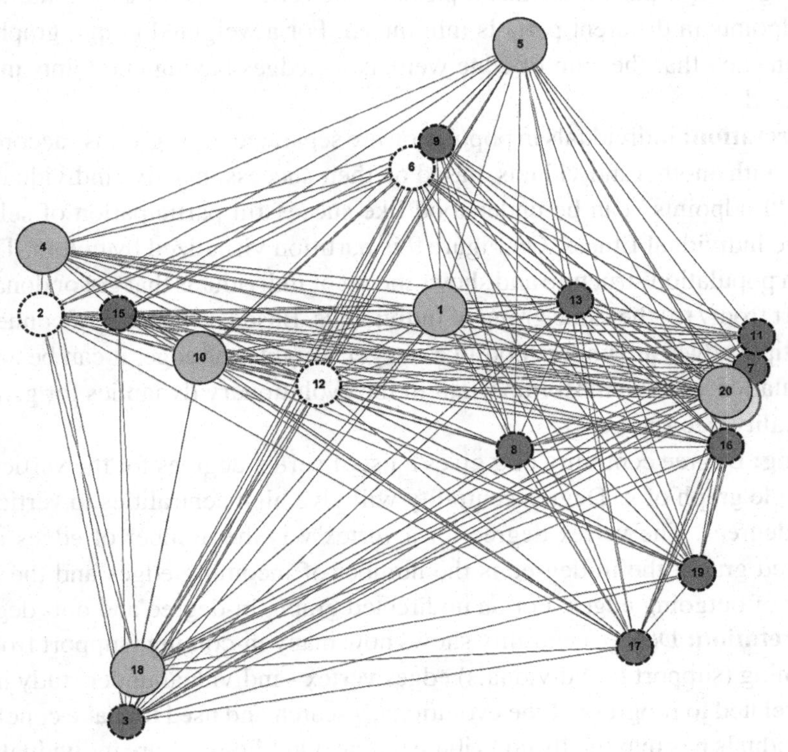

3.2. Interpretation

As reported in (Zelinka I., et. al. 2012) test function with constant level of test function dimensionality (i.e. individual length) has been used. All data have been processed numerically (network attributes) as well as graphically. Visual emergence of complex network structure behind evolutionary dynamics depends on many factors. However some special versions of used algorithms did not visually show complex network structure despite the fact that the number of generations was quite large, see (Zelinka I., 2011, 2010 and 2012). The main tools of *Mathematica* software were used on basic analysis and are proposed here. Visualized and analyzed graphs have multiple edges that can be understand like weight of single edge. Attributes of proposed analysis are represented by subgraph colors and vertices size in graphs. Our proposed interpretation (Zelinka I., 2014), based on terms and command from Wolfram *Mathematica* used for all of our experiments is following:

1. Adjacency graph, see Figure 8.
    a. **Meaning:** Graph with vertices and oriented edges.
    b. **Interpretation:** Visualization of evolutionary dynamics in the form of so called graph. Each vertex represent one individual in the population and each edge (oriented of course) represent successful offspring creation (i.e. fitness improvement of active parent in this philosophy) between parents connected by that edge. The direction of the edge can have different meanings.

2. Graph partition, see Figure 9.
    a. **Meaning:** Graph partition finds a partition of vertices such that the number of edges having endpoints in different parts is minimized. For a weighted graph, graph partition finds a partition such that the sum of edge weights for edges having endpoints in different parts is minimized.
    b. **Interpretation:** Individuals in population are separated into "groups" according to their interactions with another individuals, based on their success in active individual fitness improvements. "Endpoints" can be understood like successful participation of selected individuals in active individual fitness. On Figure 9 is partition visualized by colors. This analysis gives view on population structure and shows the set of individuals that got or donate oriented edges (support from / to) the same group of individuals. Based on number of connections or weights (if multiple edges are understood like integer weights) of edge, it can be analyzed what part of population was the most important in the evolutionary dynamics for given case.
3. Degree centrality, see Figure 11.
    a. **Meaning:** Degree centrality of g gives a list of vertex degrees for the vertices in the underlying simple graph of g. Degree centrality will give high centralities to vertices that have high vertex degrees. The vertex degree for a vertex v is the number of edges incident to *v*. For a directed graph, the in-degree is the number of incoming edges and the out-degree is the number of outgoing edges. For an undirected graph, in-degree and out- degree coincide.
    b. **Interpretation:** Degree centrality shows how many in-coming (support from individuals) or out-coming (support to individuals) edges vertex - individual under study has. This quantity can be related to progress of the evolutionary search and used to make conclusion of what set of individuals has maximally contribute to that. On Figure 11 are individuals sized according to that degree.
4. Community, see Figure 10.
    a. **Meaning:** Community graph plot attempts to draw the vertices grouped into communities.
    b. **Interpretation:** Community graph plot showing the individuals grouped into communities. Communities (with border are individuals that communicate amongst themselves (higher density of edges in community, multi edges are not visualized here, rather than between communities) and community are then joined by connections that are "one-way" and shows flow of information between communities). This kind of visualization can be interesting also in the case of parallel EAs, where islands of subpopulations are formed.

For more comprehensive overview and interpretations of complex network properties and EAs parameters and structure it is recommended to read (Zelinka I., 2014).

4. CASE STUDIES

In following case studies we show our first results on performance improvement of selected EAs. In those experiments was dynamics of EA converted into complex network, its attributes like degree centrality etc. were measured and then used to improve algorithm performance.

Figure 8. Adjacency graph

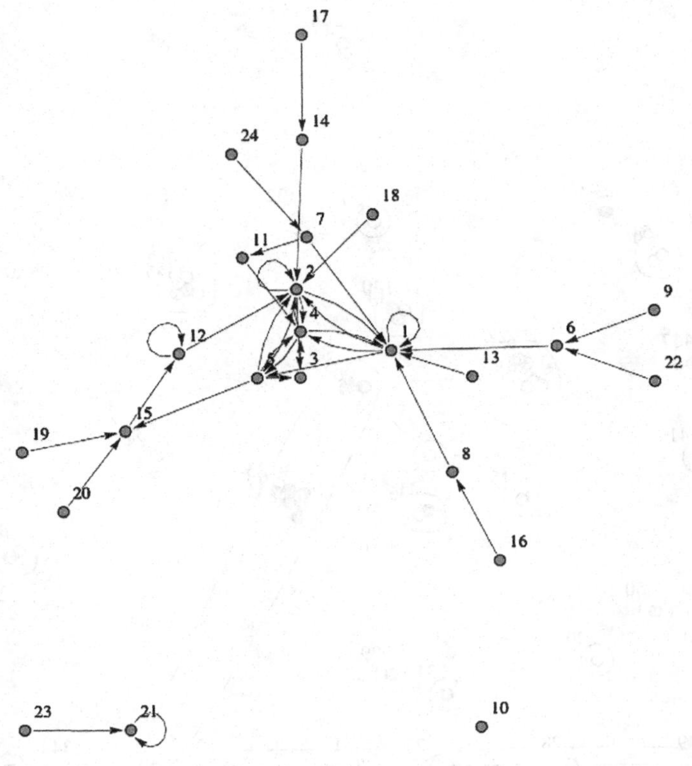

Figure 9. Graph partition

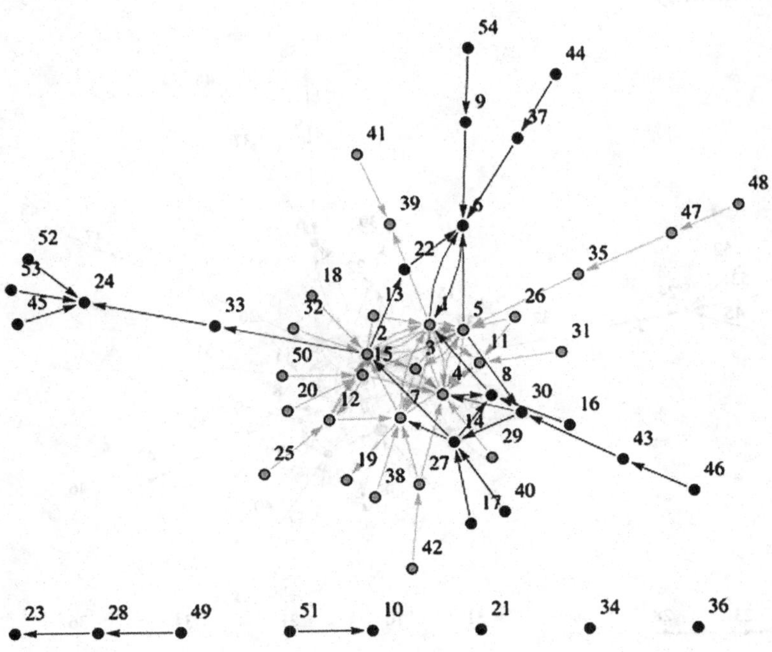

Figure 10. Community graph

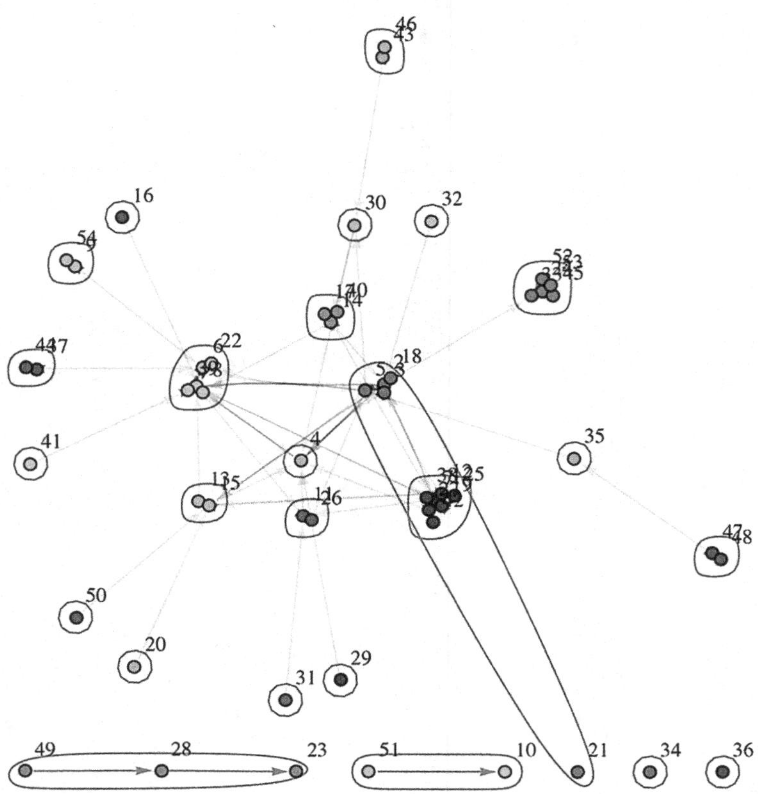

Figure 11. Degree centrality

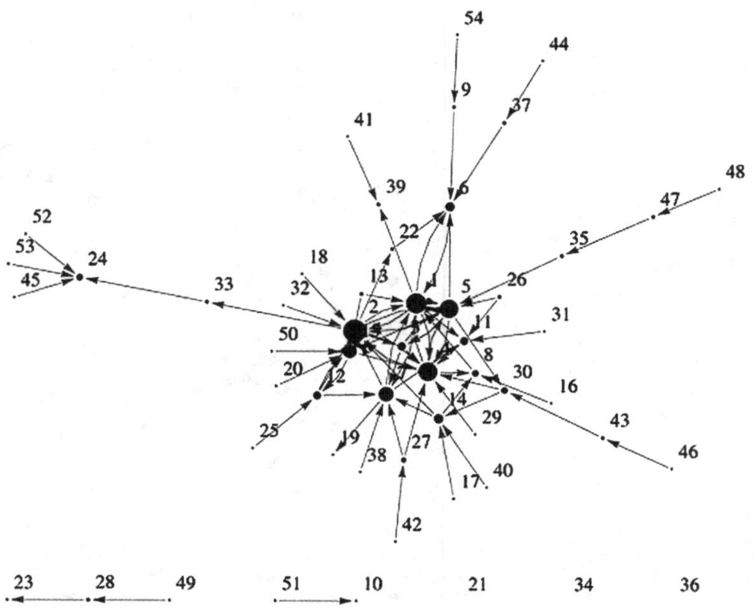

4.1. Artificial Bee Colony

Proposed approach has been tested on Artificial Bee Colony algorithm (ABC) and presented in (Metlicka M., 2014; Davendra D., et.al., 2014; Davendra D., et.al., 2015). The main idea was to test ABC on scheduling problems as well as on continuous test problems. The complex network analysis was used for adaptive control of the population. The structure of the algorithm was as follows: firstly, the weighted adjacency matrix was created throughout the algorithm iterations, for some fixed number of iterations, a fraction of the total expected number of iterations before algorithm termination. The complex network recorded this way is then analyzed, and this information was subsequently used to identify the nodes (solutions) that don't play a significant role in the population dynamics. In this algorithm, such nodes are replaced by the new randomly generated ones, although different schemas of the replacements generation could also be used.

The measures used to identify the nodes that do not contribute significantly to the population improvement were chosen to be the three types of vertex centrality, the weighted degree centrality (strength), closeness and betweenness centrality, as described in (Metlicka M., 2014; Davendra D., et.al., 2014; Davendra D., et.al., 2015). The vertices representing solutions were ranked according to these measures, and the fixed ratio of the solutions corresponding to the lowest ranking nodes was removed and regenerated. The adjacency matrix was then reset. The entire procedure of network recording and the nodes ranking and replacement is repeated until the algorithm terminates. This concept is illustrated in Figure 12-Figure 14.

Figure 12. The network with labeled nodes ranked by centrality; the larger centrality nodes are marked in bigger size and different colors. This smallest blue nodes have the lowest centrality, the largest red node has the highest centrality value.

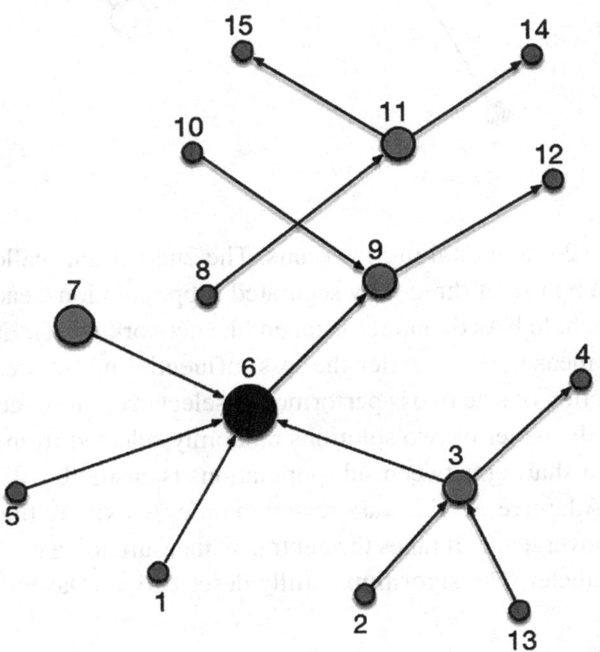

Figure 13. The nodes are sorted according to their centrality score in ascending order. The first Cutoff NS nodes will be removed.

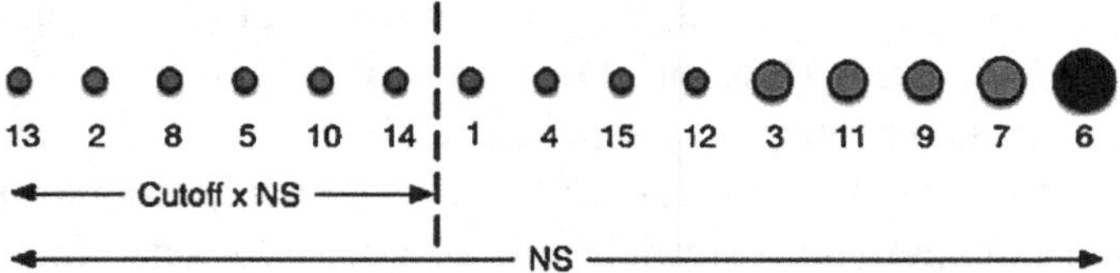

Figure 14. The network after the low centrality nodes removal; the most important nodes are preserved.

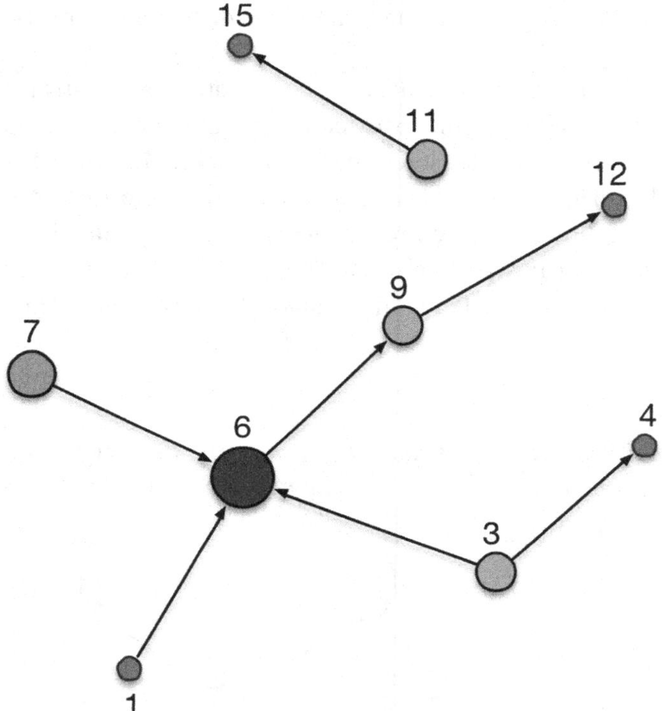

ABC was used in other 2 (so in total in 3) variants. The 2nd variant (called in (Davendra D., 2015) Adaptive ABC 2) is based on use of three fully separated subpopulations, each with their own network (or better sub-network, if whole EAs dynamics is taken like network itself). Each of them was evaluated using different centrality measure type. After the less influential nodes are pruned and the networks reset, the tournament selection of size two is performed to select every next-generation solution of every sub-population, choosing the better of two solutions randomly selected from all three sub-populations. In this way the information sharing between sub-populations is ensured.

Third version, named Adaptive ABC 3 was created in order to explore the influence of distinct centralities on the speed of convergence. It takes the centrality measure to be used for network analysis and nodes evaluation as a parameter. The algorithm is fully described in (Davendra D., 2015).

Based on results reported referenced papers, it can be stated that concept proposed here was successful and has improved ABC performance significantly (Davendra D., 2015).

4.2. Differential Evolution

In the next chapter, use of the weighted clustering in the connection with DE and its conversion into complex network and improvement of the DE performance are discussed. One of the main goals of this experiment is to find out the way to select the parents in the mutation step to improve DE convergence rate. In the variant DE/best/1/bin, the best individual is the individual with the smallest (in minimizing problems) or greatest (in maximizing problems) fitness value. As it was described in former research, DE/best/1/bin does not reach the best results in the non-separable and multimodal functions. This fact led us to search for another criterion of the best individual selection. From the rules that we have presented, we know that the edges between nodes representing the individuals are created only if the individuals represented by these nodes contributed to the population improvement. The nodes representing the individuals becoming the parents more often will have the greater out-degree (the number of out-going edges will be greater) and the weights of the edges leading from these nodes will be higher. Such parents have the genomes of the high quality and it is important to spread these genomes. The weighted clustering coefficient is one of the most appropriate candidates to be chosen as the criterion of parent selection in the mutation step from two reasons:

1. It enables to capture spreading of the genomes from the node to another node/individual.
2. Unlike the local clustering coefficient the weights of the edges are took into consideration.

When the adjacency matrix A_G for the generation G is created, the weighted clustering coefficient of each node is computed. Then, for each individual the probability of selection is computed according to the following equation:

$$p_i = \frac{\tilde{C}_{i,Z}}{\sum_{j=1}^{NP} \tilde{C}_{j,Z}}, \tag{4}$$

where p denotes the probability of the i-th individual selection and C_z is the weighted clustering coefficient of the node representing the i-th individual. Individual represented by the node with the higher weighted clustering coefficient has higher probability to be selected as the parent in the mutation step. The principle of how was complex network created based on DE is in principle captured in the Figures 15-17.

Fully detailed report on this research can be found in next chapter.

5. CONCLUSION AND FUTURE DIRECTIONS

In this chapter we refer possible interpretation of selected well known tools and terminology from complex networks analysis to the evolutionary algorithms dynamics converted to the complex network structures and its consequent control (Zelinka I., et. al., 2012; Zelinka I., et. al., 2011; Zelinka I., 2013;

Figure 15. The first generation of DE/rand/1/bin

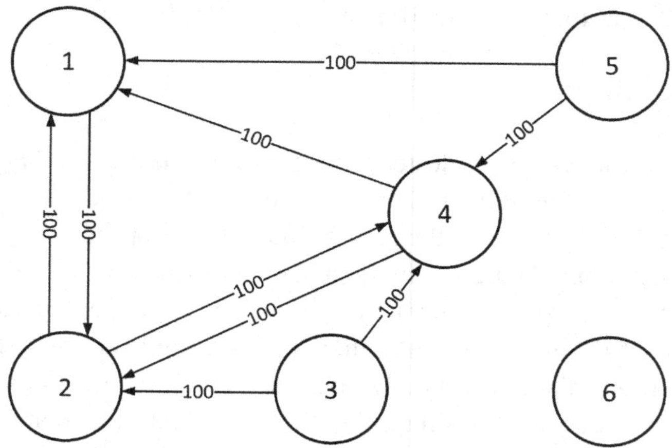

Figure 16. The second generation of DE/rand/1/bin

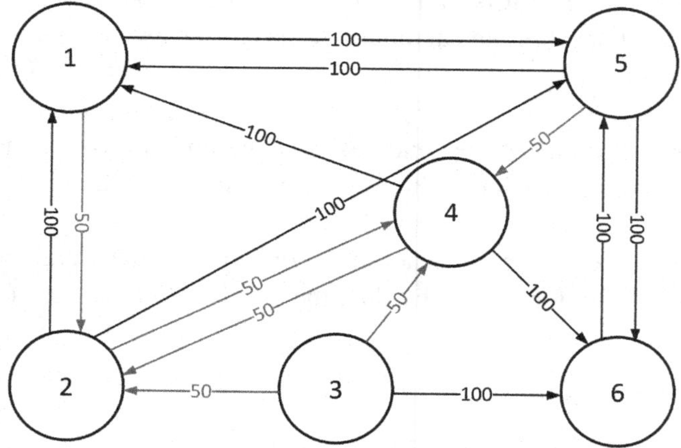

Figure 17. The third generation of DE/rand/1/bin

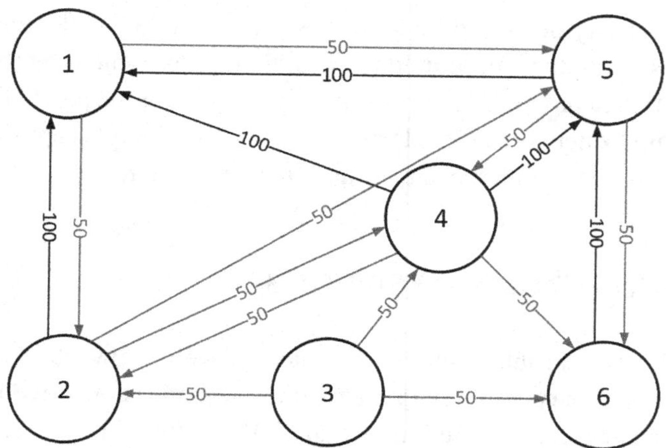

Zelinka I., 2014). This chapter is an extension of our previous research presented in above mentioned papers and latest research reported in (Zelinka, I., et. al., 2014), where we proposed all necessary steps joining evolutionary dynamics, complex networks and CML systems (Zelinka I, et. al. 2010; Schuster H. G., 1999). In this chapter we will discuss new observations, results and interpretations for wider spectra of algorithms and its impact on its performance.

Our contemporary and future aim is to join together evolutionary dynamics, complex networks (Dorogovtsev S. N., 2002; Boccaletti S., 2006; Broom M., et. al., 2010; Tan S., et. al., 2014; Lieberman E., et. al., 2005; Olfati-Saber et. al., 2007; Szabo G., et. al. 2007, Meyn, S., 2007; Maarten van Steen 2010; Chen G., et. al., 2015; Barrat A., 2008) and (Bornholdt S., 2003) and CML systems (Schuster H. G., 1999; Zelinka I., et. al., 2011) in a straightforward way. In a "feedback" loop, as depicted in Figure 18. It is then (independently of each other) possible to analyze complex network as well as evolutionary dynamics via CML tools and also its control (Zelinka I., 2011).

For already mentioned CML systems there are techniques for analysis of chaos and routes to chaos behavior, so it is obvious that this is also an open field of another research that join EAs, complex networks and CML systems. We have already published main parts of feedback system at Figure 18, i.e. evolutionary dynamics => complex network (Zelinka I., et. al., 2011) => CML system (Zelinka I., 2014), and also at (Zelinka I., 2013, 2012) => control CML by means of EAs (Zelinka I, et. al. 2010, 2005, 2008, 2006). The main and remaining part to control evolutionary dynamics or complex networks is now under investigation.

Based on our research papers more or less mentioned here it is clear that for EAs applications as well as in EAs dynamics itself a lot of open research questions can be raised. It is clear that EAs are nothing else than a kind of discrete dynamical systems exhibiting complex structures and dynamics that can be studied by means of various tools of mathematics as classical statistics or/an by tools of complex networks and chaotic systems (Zelinka I., et. al., 2011, 2010, 2012), (Zelinka I, et. al. 2010). It is clear that there is a lot of interesting questions like (for example) what is impact of specific dynamic regimes in EAs dynamics on its performance? What are limitations of EAs performance when complex network methodology proposed here is used? And many others. Concerning on performance tuning of evolutionary algorithm via its complex network it is clear that in the dynamical regimes of EAs and networks, that are highly nonlinear, can be trapped in specific regimes like in the so called hidden chaotic attractors, as it has already been reported in (Zelinka I, et. al. 2010) and in pioneer paper (Wright A., Agapie A., 2001).

Hidden attractors are special kind of attractors, that are hidden in the system structure and if ignored (undiscovered), they can cause serious damages, as already observed in the real world. If the hidden attractor is present in the system dynamics and if coincidently reached, then device (airplane, el. circuit, etc...) starts to show quasi-cyclic behavior, that can, based on kind of device, cause real disasters. As an example we can take Gripen jet fighter crash or F-22 raptor crash landing caused by computer malfunction that lead into oscillations (called also windup in control theory). Hidden attractors as a part of deterministic chaos, can be studied in (Leonov G.A., Kuznetsov N.V., 2013, 2013a; Leonov G.A., et. al., 2012; Bragin V.O., 2011; Leonov G.A., et. al., 2011) and deterministic chaos itself for example in (Hilborn R., 1994; Kantz H, Schreiber T., 1997), (Schuster H. G., 1999).

If EA (or network dynamics) is trapped in chaotic regime, then definitely its performance and information processing is changed.

In this paper we have suggested possible interpretation of selected well-known tools and terminology from complex networks analysis to the evolutionary algorithms dynamics converted to the complex network structures. The volume of this chapter is too small to mention and explain all the possible in-

Figure 18. The schematic principle of proposed feedback control EAs and CNS: evolutionary dynamics complex network CML system control CML control evolutionary dynamics

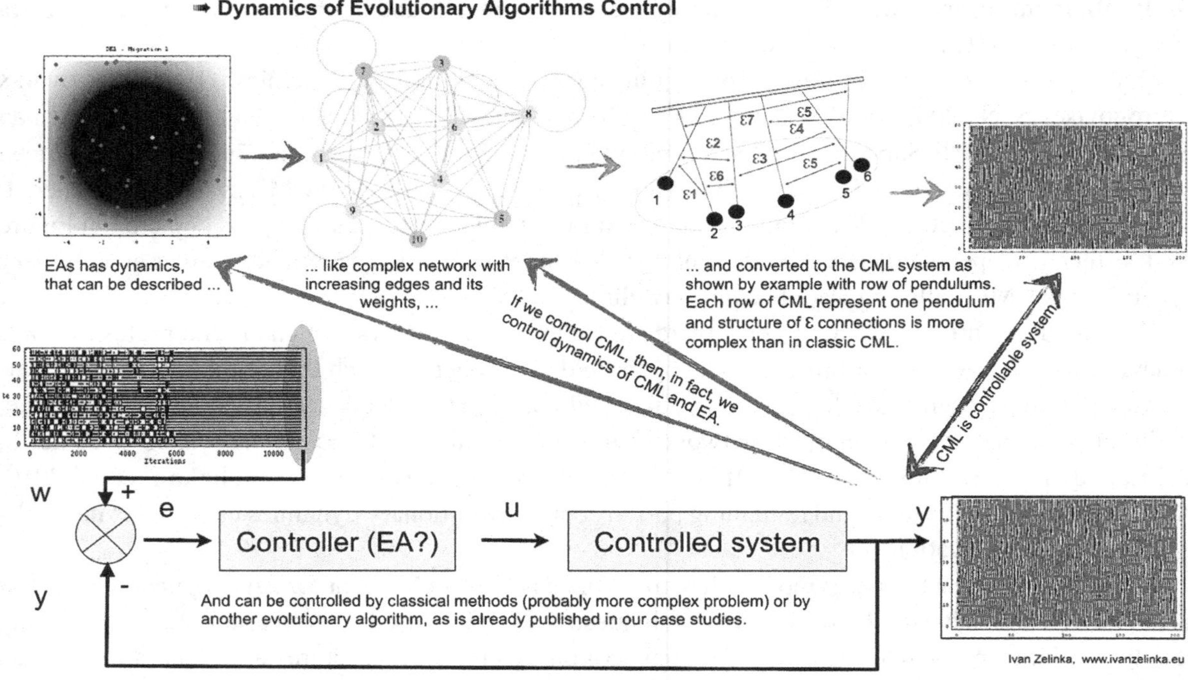

terpretations and tools. This is only a mid-step in our research presented for example in (Zelinka I., et. al., 2011, 2010, 2012) or (Davendra D., et. al., 2014; Davendra D., et. al., 2015; Zelinka I., 2015) where we proposed all necessary steps joining evolutionary dynamics, complex networks and CML systems.

ACKNOWLEDGMENT

The following grants are acknowledged for the financial support provided for this research: Grant Agency of the Czech Republic - GACR P103/15/06700S and partially supported by Grant of SGS No. SP2015/142, VSB-Technical University of Ostrava.

REFERENCES

Barrat, A., Barthélemy, M., & Vespignani, A. (2008). *Dynamical Processes on Complex Networks*. Cambridge University Press.

Boccaletti, S. (2006). Complex Networks: Structure and Dynamics. *Physics Reports*, *424*, 175–308.

Bornholdt, S. (2003). Handbook of Graphs and Networks: From the Genome to the Internet. Wiley-VCH.

Bragin, V. O., Vagaitsev, V. I., Kuznetsov, N. V., & Leonov, G. A. (2011). Algorithms for Finding Hidden Oscillations in Nonlinear Systems. The Aizerman and Kalman Conjectures and Chua's Circuits. *Journal of Computer and Systems Sciences International*, *50*(4), 511–543. doi:10.1134/S106423071104006X

Broom, M., Hadjichrysanthou, C., Rychtar, J., & Stadler, B. T. (2010). Two results on evolutionary processes on general non-directed graphs. *Proc. Royal. Soc. A*, *466*(2121), 2795–2798. doi:10.1098/rspa.2010.0067

Chen, G., Wang, X., & Xiang, L. (2015). *Fundamentals of Complex Networks: Models, Structures and Dynamics*. Wiley.

Dashora, Y., Kumar, S., Shukla, N., & Tiwari, M. K. (2007). Improved and generalized learning strategies for dynamically fast and statistically robust evolutionary algorithms. *Engineering Applications of Artificial Intelligence*. doi:10.1016/j.engappai.2007.06.005

Davendra, D., & Metlicka, M. (2015). Ensemble Centralities based Adaptive Artificial Bee Algorithm. *IEEE Congress on Evolutionary Computation.*

Davendra, D., Zelinka, I., Metlicka, M., Senkerik, R., & Pluhacek, M. (2014). *Complex network analysis of differential evolution algorithm applied to flow- shop with no-wait problem. IEEE Symposium on Differential Evolution*, Orlando, FL.

Dorigo, M., & Stützle, T. (2004). *Ant Colony Optimization.* MIT Press.

Dorogovtsev, S. N., & Mendes, J. F. F. (2002). Evolution of Networks. *Advances in Physics*, *51*(4), 1079–1187. doi:10.1080/00018730110112519

Fogel, D. B. (1998). Unearthing a Fossil from the History of Evolutionary Computation. *Fundamenta Informaticae*, *35*(1-4), 1–16.

Goh, C., Ong, Y., & Tan, K. (2009). *Multi-Objective Memetic Algorithms*. Springer-Verlag. doi:10.1007/978-3-540-88051-6

Goldberg, D. (1989). *Genetic Algorithms in Search, Optimization, and Machine Learning*. Addison-Wesley Publishing Company Inc.

Hart, W., Krasnogor, N., & Smith, J. (2005). *Recent Advances in Memetic Algorithms*. Springer-Verlag.

Hilborn, R. (1994). *Chaos and Nonlinear Dynamics*. Oxford University Press.

Holland, J. (1975). *Adaptation in natural and artificial systems*. Ann Arbor, MI: Univ. of Michigan Press.

Kantz, H., & Schreiber, T. (1997). *Nonlinear time series analysis*. Cambridge, UK: Cambridge University Press.

Kuznetsov, N., Kuznetsova, O., Leonov, G., & Vagaitsev, V. (2013). Analytical-numerical localization of hidden attractor in electrical Chua's circuit. Lecture Notes in Electrical Engineering, 174, 149-158.

Leonov, G. A., Andrievskii, B. R., Kuznetsov, N. V., & Pogromskii, A. Yu. (2012). Aircraft control with anti-windup compensation. *Differential Equations*, *48*(13), 1700–1720. doi:10.1134/S0012266112130022

Leonov, G. A., & Kuznetsov, N. V. (2013). Hidden attractors in dynamical systems. From hidden oscillations in Hilbert-Kolmogorov, Aizerman, and Kalman problems to hidden chaotic attractor in Chua circuits. *International Journal of Bifurcation and Chaos in Applied Sciences and Engineering*, *23*(1), 1330002. doi:10.1142/S0218127413300024

Leonov, G. A., Kuznetsov, N. V., Kuznetsova, O. A., Seledzhi, S. M., & Vagaitsev, V. I. (2011). Hidden oscillations in dynamical systems. *Transaction on Systems and Control*, *6*(2), 54–67.

Li, L., Wenxin, L., & David, A. C. (2007). Particle swarm optimization-based parameter identification applied to permanent magnet synchronous motors. *Engineering Applications of Artificial Intelligence*. doi:10.1016/j.engappai.2007.10.002

Lieberman, E., Hauert, C., & Nowak, M. A. (2005). Evolutionary dynamics on graphs. *Nature*, *433*(7023), 312316. doi:10.1038/nature03204 PMID:15662424

Meyn, S. (2007). *Control Techniques for Complex Networks*. Cambridge University Press. doi:10.1017/CBO9780511804410

Olfati-Saber, R. (2007). Evolutionary dynamics of behavior in social networks. In *Proc. 46th IEEE Conf. Decis. Contr.*

Onwubolu, G., & Babu, B. (2004). *New Optimization Techniques in Engineering* (pp. 167–218). New York: SpringerVerlag. doi:10.1007/978-3-540-39930-8

Pluhacek, M., Janostik, J., Senkerik, R., Zelinka, I., & Davendra, D. (2015). PSO as Complex Network - Capturing the Inner Dynamics – Initial Study. In *Proceedings of Nostradamus 2015: International conference on prediction, modeling and analysis of complex systems*. Springer.

Price, K. (2007). In D. Corne, M. Dorigo, & F. Glover (Eds.), *An Introduction to Differential Evolution, New Ideas in Optimization*. London, UK: McGraw-Hill.

Rechenberg, I. (1973). *Evolutionsstrategie - Optimierung technischer Systeme nach Prinzipien der biologischen Evolution*. (PhD thesis). Fromman-Holzboog.

Richter, H. (2002). An evolutionary algorithm for controlling chaos: The use of multi-objective fitness functions, in Parallel Problem Solving from Nature-PPSN VII. Lecture Notes in Computer Science, 2439, 308-317.

Richter, H. (2005). A study of dynamic severity in chaotic fitness landscapes. *Evolutionary Computation. The IEEE Congress*. doi:10.1109/CEC.2005.1555049

Richter, H. (2006). Evolutionary Optimization in Spatio- temporal Fitness Landscapes. *Lecture Notes in Computer Science, 4193*, 1-10.

Richter, H., & Reinschke, K. J. (2000). Optimization of local control of chaos by an evolutionary algorithm. *Physica D. Nonlinear Phenomena*, *144*, 309–334.

Schonberger, J. (2005). *Operational Freight Carrier Planning, Basic Concepts, Optimization Models and Advanced Memetic Algorithms*. Springer-Verlag.

Schuster, H. G. (1999). *Handbook of Chaos Control*. New York: Wiley-VCH. doi:10.1002/3527607455

Schwefel, H. (1974). *Numerische Optimierung von Computer-Modellen.* (PhD thesis). Birkhuser.

Senkerik, R., Zelinka, I., & Navratil, E. (2006). Optimization of feedback control of chaos by evolutionary algorithms. *1st IFAC Conference on Analysis and Control of Chaotic Systems*, Reims, France

Szabo, G., & Fath, G. (2007). Evolutionary games on graphs. *Physics Reports*, *446*(4-6), 97216. doi:10.1016/j.physrep.2007.04.004

Tan, S., Lu, J., Chen, G., & Hill, D. (2014). When structure meets function in evolutionary dynamics on complex networks. *IEEE Circ. Syst. Mag.*, *14*(4), 3650. doi:10.1109/MCAS.2014.2360790

Turing, A. (1969). Intelligent machinery, unpublished report for National Physical Laboratory. *Machine Intelligence, 7.*

Turing, A. M. (Ed.). The Collected Works (vol. 3). North-Holland.

van Steen, M. (2015). Graph Theory and Complex Networks: An Introduction. In *Chaos-driven Discrete Artificial Bee Colony, IEEE Congress on Evolutionary Computation.*

Wright, A., & Agapie, A. (2001). Cyclic and Chaotic Behavior in Genetic Algorithms. In *Proc. of Genetic and Evolutionary Computation Conference (GECCO).*

Yang, X. S. (2009). Firefly algorithms for multimodal optimization". Stochastic Algorithms: Foundations and Applications, SAGA 2009. *Lecture Notes in Computer Science*, *5792*, 169–178. doi:10.1007/978-3-642-04944-6_14

Yang, X. S. (2010). A New Metaheuristic Bat-Inspired Algorithm. In Nature Inspired Cooperative Strategies for Optimization (NISCO 2010). Springer. doi:10.1007/978-3-642-12538-6_6

Yang, X. S., & Deb, S. (2009). Cuckoo search via Levy flights. *World Congress on Nature and Biologically Inspired Computing (NaBIC 2009).* IEEE Publications. doi:10.1109/NABIC.2009.5393690

Zahra, R. Ch., & Motlagh, M. R. J. (2007). Control of spatiotemporal chaos in coupled map lattice by discrete-time variable structure control. *Physics Letters. [Part A]*, *370*, 3–4, 302–305.

Zelinka, I. (2004). SOMA - Self Organizing Migrating Algorithm. In B. B. Onwubolu (Ed.), *New Optimization Techniques in Engineering* (pp. 167–218). New York: Springer-Verlag. doi:10.1007/978-3-540-39930-8_7

Zelinka, I. (2005). *Investigation on Evolutionary Deterministic Chaos Control*. Prague: IFAC.

Zelinka, I. (2006). Investigation on Realtime Deterministic Chaos Control by Means of Evolutionary Algorithms. *1st IFAC Conference on Analysis and Control of Chaotic Systems*, Reims, France

Zelinka, I. (2006). Investigation on real-time deterministic chaos control by means of evolutionary algorithms. *Proc. First IFAC Conference on Analysis and Control of Chaotic Systems.*

Zelinka, I. (2008). Real-time deterministic chaos control by means of selected evolutionary algorithms. *Engineering Applications of Artificial Intelligence*. doi:10.1016/j.engappai.2008.07.008

Zelinka, I. (2012). *On Close Relations of Evolutionary Dynamics, Chaos and Complexity*. Keynote at International Workshop on Chaos-Fractals Theories and Applications, Dalian, China.

Zelinka, I. (2013). *Mutual Relations of Evolutionary Dynamics, Deterministic Chaos and Complexity*. IEEE Congress on Evolutionary Computation 2013, Mexico.

Zelinka, I. (2014). Hidden Complexity of Evolutionary Dynamics – Analysis. In *ISCS 2013: Interdisciplinary Symposium on Complex Systems, Emergence, Complexity and Computation* (*Vol. 8*). Springer.

Zelinka, I. (2015). *Evolutionary Algorithms as a Complex Dynamical Systems*. Tutorial at IEEE Congress on Evolutionary Computation 2015, Sendai.

Zelinka, I., Celikovsky, S., Richter, H., & Chen, G. (2010). Evolutionary Algorithms and Chaotic Systems. Springer.

Zelinka, I., Chen, G., & Celikovsky, S. (2008). Chaos Synthesis by Means of Evolutionary Algorithms. *International Journal of Bifurcation and Chaos in Applied Sciences and Engineering*, *18*(4), 911–942. doi:10.1142/S021812740802077X

Zelinka, I., Davendra, D., Chadli, M., Senkerik, R., Dao, T. T., & Skanderova, L. (2012). Evolutionary Dynamics and Complex Networks. In *Handbook of Optimization*. Springer.

Zelinka, I., Davendra, D., Lampinen, J., Senkerik, R., & Pluhacek, M. (2014). *Evolutionary Algorithms Dynamics and its Hidden Complex Network Structures*. Congress on Evolutionary Computation, WCCI 2014 IEEE Congress, Beijing, China. doi:10.1109/CEC.2014.6900441

Zelinka, I., Davendra, D., Senkerik, R., & Jasek, R. (2011). Do Evolutionary Algorithm Dynamics Create Complex Network Structures? *Complex Systems*, *2*, 127–140.

Zelinka, I., Davendra, D., Snasel, V., Jasek, R., Senkerik, R., & Oplatkova, Z. (2010). Preliminary Investigation on Relations Between Complex Networks and Evolutionary Algorithms Dynamics. CISIM 2010, Poland.

Zelinka, I., Snasel, V., & Ajith, A. (2012). *Handbook of Optimization*. Springer.

Chapter 14
Wireless Body Area Network for Healthcare Applications

Danda B. Rawat
Georgia Southern University, USA

Sylvia Bhattacharya
Georgia Southern University, USA

ABSTRACT

Wireless Body Area Network (WBAN) is an emerging field of research which has been progressing rapidly in recent years. WBAN is a network utilized for continuous monitoring of physiological state of the subject, where the patient can perform his regular activities while his body parameters get measured continuously and are accessed by the physician remotely. This chapter provides a thorough survey of current WBAN technologies in the healthcare sector. Besides the recording of physiological parameters, discussions have been provided on remote data transmission to a server called Virtual Doctor Server (VDS). During this transmission, WBAN network uses various technologies namely Ultra Wide Band WBAN, Technology Enabled Medical Precision Observation 3.1 (TEMPO 3.1), J2ME and Bluetooth. Details of several existing WBAN related projects have been discussed along with their applications. The next section of the chapter deals with the use and design of medical sensors in WBAN. Performance comparison between WBAN and WSN (Wireless Sensor Network) has also been provided.

1. INTRODUCTION

WBAN is the joint application of biomedical science and wireless communication systems. The development of this technology will have the impact of drastically reducing the time a patient has to spend in his house or in a medical care center for treatment. This technology utilizes the principles of wireless communication to relay data (such as heart rate, ECG) continuously to remote areas (Mundt et. Al., 2005). The data are measured by sensors in a person's body. Besides drastic development in medical instrumentation, it is now also important to have compact machines like portable blood pressure measurement kits that can be attached to a body and be able to measure the parameters round the clock.

DOI: 10.4018/978-1-4666-9964-9.ch014

WBAN has a wide range of applications in medical science. Gait analysis, asthma detection, cancer detection, physiotherapy, brain activity analysis, etc. are some of the applications. In these applications, sensors are installed either inside or outside the body to determine the pattern of movement, to compare the result with standard data and to keep records of the physiological parameters of the patient. In this paper, it has been explained thoroughly how each of these physiological parameters are measured with the help of WBAN round the clock.

The recorded data are sent to a server where they are analyzed. These servers are the point from where the physician get access to the report of the patient round the clock. This server is called the Virtual Doctor Server (VDS). VDS performs a number of important responsibilities which includes maintaining records of patient data to build up the history of the patient, keeping track of patients' medicine timing and giving alarm to the patient to take the pills on time, giving advice to the patients assistant according to the physiological performance of the patient's body recorded by the sensors, alerting doctor or calling ambulance in time of emergency, maintaining confidentiality and privacy of patients' data records (Sghaier, et al., 2011).Patient can input his clinical feelings to the VDS system and then the VDS can give instant suggestion or advice based on the patients' history and vital signs. During this transmission, WBAN network uses various technologies namely Ultra Wide Band WBAN, Technology Enabled Medical Precision Observation 3.1 (TEMPO 3.1), ZigBee, J2ME and Bluetooth. Details of several existing WBAN related projects have been discussed in this paper along with their applications. The projects that have been discussed are Life Guard, Code Blue, Medisn, Wriscare, Mob health, WiMoCA, and Care Net (He et. al., 2013).

Biomedical sensors form a huge part of the patient monitoring system. A biomedical sensor is such an electronic device that senses, processes, sends or receives biomedical data. It has three main parts, the sensing unit, the processing unit and the receiving unit. There are micro controller units at the sensor node and a memory (RAM, ROM) to store the data (Lee et. al., 2006).The function of the sensor is controlled by software consisting of operating system. There are large varieties of biomedical sensors having separate functionalities such as electrocardiogram, electroencephalograph, etc. These sensors can be classified into in-body sensors and on-body sensors. Characteristics of each type of sensors are discussed in detail in this paper. Sensor networks have also been discussed extensively. They comprise of a large number of sensors and sink nodes and all of them are connected to each other wirelessly with the help of multi-hop or single hop communication systems. The data flows from the sensor node to the sink node which finally communicates the data to a gateway. The capabilities of the nodes vary with size, cost, battery lifetime, etc.

The security of WBAN is extremely important since it contains recorded data of patients and mishandling of such data may even cause death of the patient. The main factors affecting data security are confidentiality, dynamic integrity assurance, dependability. Security requirement is applicable to each device or communication link as data integrity, data confidentiality, authentication, availability, privacy, access control and non-repudiation. Each of these factors have been discussed in detail in this paper.

The remaining sections are organized as follows. Section II gives a brief idea about the background of WBAN along with a complete description of the process of WBAN. Section III describes the virtual doctor server which is the master server that works on the results obtained from patients body. Section IV describes the various technologies that are used in WBAN and the various ongoing projects in WBAN. Section V describes the sensors used in WBAN followed by a table showing the differences between the general sensor network and the wireless body network. Section VI is very important as it deals with the privacy and security of the whole system and at the end of this section the requirements for security

Figure 1. Schematic diagram of a wireless body area network

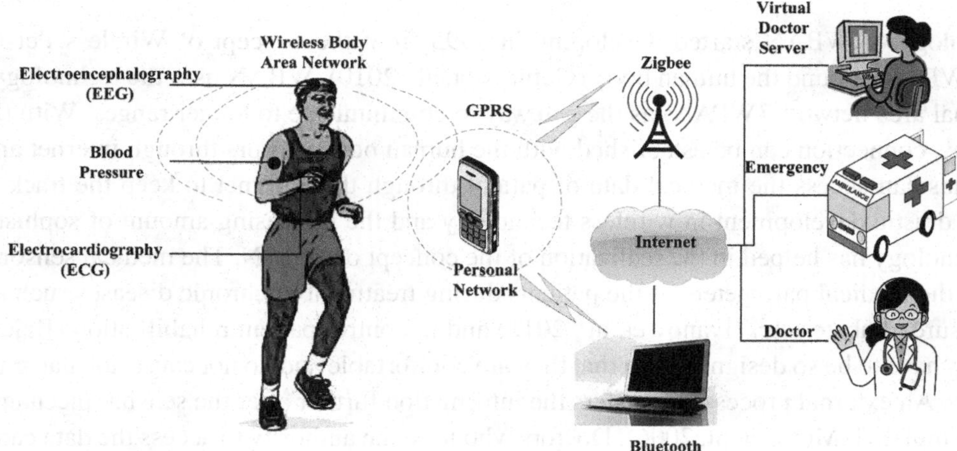

in this type of network is stated. Section VII concludes the paper and presents the future goals in the commercialization of WBAN.

Figure 1 shows the whole mechanism of body area network. It shows how the personal area network records the physiological signals from the various sensors attached to the body and transmits the information to the virtual remote server or physician or emergency center.

The WBAN uses different wireless networks and access technology that leads to complex network as shown in Figure 1. One can easily see the difference in terms of data rate and average power consumption for WBAN applications. We note that Wireless USB and Wi-Fi based technologies offer high data rate but consume high power as shown in Figure 2.

Figure 2. Data rate vs. power profile of different wireless technologies

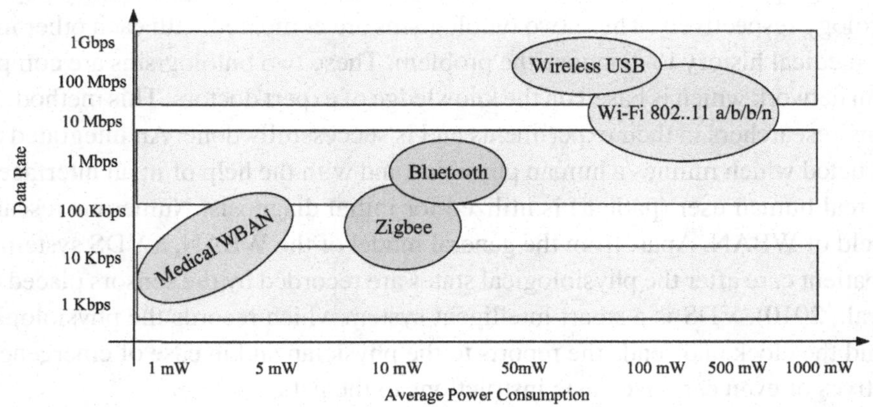

2. BACKGROUND

The technology of WBAN started developing in 1995 from the concept of Wireless Personal Area Network (WPAN) around the human body (Gafurov et. al., 2010). WBAN uses the technology of Wireless Personal area network (WPAN) as the gateway to communicate to longer ranges. With the help of this gateway, connection can be established with the human body sensors through internet and doctors or physicians can access the medical data of patient through this internet to keep the track round the clock. The drastic development in wireless technology and the increasing amount of sophistication in sensor technology has helped in the realization of the concept of WBAN. The medical sensors are used to monitor the medical parameters of the patients during treatment of chronic diseases such as asthma, blood pressure, diabetes etc. (Ivanov et. al., 2012) and to control patient rehabilitation (Bajcsy, 2007). The sensors have to be so designed such that they are comfortable and do not cause any harmful impacts on the body. An external processor transfers the information further after the sensing mechanism of the sensor is completed (Motoi et. al. 2006). Doctors who have the authority to access the data can visualize the result from any part of the world. The doctor can send messages to the patient instantly through this system if he figures out any abnormalities or in emergency situations. Therefore, WBAN can be used to alert the hospital that a patient may experience a heart attack soon by measuring changes in their vital signs. WBAN can also be programmed to perform certain tasks in case of emergency conditions. For example, insulin can be injected in the body when blood sugar levels drops out. Other applications of WBAN can be extended to include sports, military and security services.

3. VIRTUAL DOCTOR SERVER (VDS)

VDS is an intelligent system that is designed in such a way that it can assist a physician in diagnosis of the medical parameters that are functioning abnormally. VDS also collects medical information about the patient from the medical history available from the doctor in order to understand and better diagnose the problem of the patient. They have a virtual doctor construction like a robot which mimics the physician. This robotic doctor interacts with the patient through their voice and examines the various physiological parameters of the patient in order to detect the problem in the health of the patient (Smith et. al., 2013). Diagnosis comprises of both physical and mental state of the patient namely physical ontology and mental ontology respectively. These two ontologisms are compared with each other in order to find similarity with medical history to diagnose the problem. These two ontologisms are compared with the help of Bayesian network which is based on the knowledge of expert doctors. This methodology has been verified by many researchers in their experiments and is successfully done. An integrated computerized model is constructed which mimics a human physician and with the help of it; an interface between that model and the real human user (patient) is utilized for initial diagnosis. Numerous research is already going on the field of WBAN. Apart from the general model of the WBAN, a VDS system is also added to it for better patient care after the physiological states are recorded by the sensors placed on the patient body (Anis et. al., 2010). VDS is a smart intelligent system which records the physiological factors of the patient round the clock and sends the reports to the physician and in case of emergency can call the physician, relatives or even can give basic instructions to the patient.

The system consists of sensors both in body and on body placed in order to record physiological parameters like ECG, EEG etc. The data recorded by the sensors is then sent to a central processor unit in order to analyze and further process the recorded raw data. The mobile phone of the patient can also be used to send the data to the VDS system for further assessment and expert advice. This whole network system is named WBAN where each and every body is assigned an IP address to get distinguished from each other.

The interaction between patient and computer interface is stated in many paper which gives us further detail of the process. Two types of states are described in the research. The first one is the mental state which is the mental behavior of the patient due to a disorder and second is the physical behavior of the patient due to the disorder which is generally the consequence of such a disorder. The two types of bodily states are mapped and described using two software named OWL-S and SWRL which diagnoses the reason to such bodily state. An integrated computerized model is constructed which reflects a diagnostic system for human being as computer model and with the help of it, the patient and the system can interact with each other in order to diagnose the disorder caused to the patient. The VDS system use the knowledge that is obtained from UMLS for testing, and the integrated mapping of the two states of body which is represented through OWL-S framework.

The VDS system performs a variety of responsibilities which are as follows:

- Keeping record of patient data to build up the history of the patient.
- Keeping record of patients medicine timing and giving alarm to the patient to take the pills on time.
- Giving advice to the patients assistant according to the physiological performance of the patient's body recorded by the sensors.
- Calling doctor or ambulance in time of emergency.
- Maintain confidentiality and privacy of patients data records.
- Patient can input his clinical feelings to the VDS system and then the VDS can give instant suggestion or advise based on the patients history and vital signs.

Hence, the VDS is a very important part of the WBAN in terms of data analysis and for providing suggestions based on the medical data. On the other hand when patient is moving from one place to another, it is very important to have this kind of automatic intelligent system to take care of the patient's health giving him important suggestions and reminders.

4. WBAN TECHNOLOGIES

The different existing WBAN Technologies are Ultra Wideband WBAN, TEMPO 3.1, J2ME and Bluetooth. Each of these technologies are discussed in detail in this section.

4.1 Ultra Wideband WBAN (UWWBAN)

Ultra WBAN is used for medical sensing and for in-body tracking and imaging (Khaleghi et. al., 2010). There is an antennae designed for on-body tracking that can communicate with same efficiency as in free space when the distance between the antennae and human body is 16mm (Anis et. al., 2010).

Primary function of UWWBAN is to interface between medical sensors and personal server (PS) in telemedicine systems (Francisco e.t al., 2009). UWWBAN can reduce the probability of detection for protecting patient's data with high security. This can reduce the need to hide the algorithms in sensors which reduces complexity and makes the device smaller in size. Hence the algorithms in the machine are required to be hidden and hence it gives a much smaller handy shape and size. UWWBAN does not interfere with any nearby signals and hence protects security and privacy of patients' data. UWWBAN has no tendency to react with any surrounding network and hence data remains completely protected within the system (Monton et al., 2008). This technology is mostly useful in future for transmitting information over short distance range with a very high speed. The bandwidth of this type is in the range of microwave and it is limited by the Federal Government rules (Takacs, 2006). The UW WBAN transmits data at very low rate pulse and hence it is very suitable for WBAN.

Ultra wide band (USB) radar is designed on the basis of impulse radio and hence it can detect the physiological parameters like blood pressure, insulin level etc. With the development of semiconductors the sensors of UWWBAN are made of low power consumption materials and hence are very efficient for wireless transmission task in WBAN. All the antennas in the system is simulated with the help of a software named Antennae a Simulator (Degli-Esposti, 2014). From all the research literature survey on UWWBAN, the most interesting application of UWWBAN is in Capsule Endoscopy. In this technology a camera is used which is small equivalent to a capsule size and is used to visualize gastrointestinal tract. They are designed in order to record images of digestive tract in order to detect gastrointestinal diseases .Even real time imaging of the gastrointestinal tract is possible (Fabre et. al., 1992).

Depending on their location of operation, there are three sensors associated with UWWBAN namely in- body sensor, on-body sensor and an external sensor (Alvarez-Folgueiras et. al., 2011).The in-body sensors are implanted inside the human body and on body sensors are placed on human skin whereas the external sensor is not in contact at all with the patient skin. Endoscope capsules are the in body sensors and the radars used are the external one. Once their inter connection is established they constitute the WBAN. In-body sensors are very critical and have the hardest structure. Hence an implanted device should be handled carefully as complexity of its circuit and its transmitting power is also very critical. The on body sensors are called gate nodes as their main function is to transmit information from the in body sensors to the WBAN. The circuitry of on body sensor is less complicated and most of its application is seen in Electromyography (EMG). Real time analysis of EMG is not necessary as in case of ECG. The principal component which detects and records all the medical information gathered by the sensors in WBAN is called network coordinator (NC). ECM-368 is the network coordinator which is used for the connection between the NC and P (Rasmussen et. al., 1996). It gives supports to data rate which is very high and also cognitive radio in some of the parts of Europe.

4.2 TEMPO 3.1

TEMPO 3.1 is an acronym for Technology Enabled medical Precision Observation 3.1. It is a third generation sensor which accurately captures and processes six degree of inertial data in a noninvasive factor. The complete system of TEMPO comprises of Hardware and Software part design of TEMPO 3.1, a custom case design and an operating system that manages signal acquisition, processing and management of all data received. The system is then compared to BASN hardware platform (Wu, 2010).

BASN has its application in a number of fields namely healthcare, entertainment, fitness, etc. (Sanchez et. al. 2011). Recent advancement is BASN technology includes noninvasive technology to sense physiological signals and to transmit them across the body by low radio power. BASN should be designed in smaller size with smaller batteries. Many BASN sensors are now being developed for commercial and research use (Vos et. al., 2014). Hardware of BASN is now capable of real time imaging, have lithium batteries, have reduced size of the setup and developed sensor interfacing.

TEMPO 3.1 provides full rotational and translational sensing at the same site. The angular rate is measured by two separate MEMS gyroscope. Functions of TEMPO are data collection, streaming and signal processing. Microcontroller is also used for long term and which is energy efficient. The two networking protocols are Bluetooth and ZigBee which operate in 2.4GHz.

TEMPOS are real time operating system and it carries out signal acquisition, processing and control. They operate under many constraints like such as real time execution, memory utilization and minimum user input. It operates with the help of MSP430 microcontroller and for more efficiency allows access to low level hardware. For processing complex signals new signal processing algorithms are treated as application like Haar wavelet decomposition (Degli-Esposti, 2014). TEMPO3.1 is wearable and non-invasive with plastic and custom casing to allow minimal spatial overhead. There is no hardware user interface in the TEMPO setup except a charger point at the top of the machine. No interface is kept for the following reasons:

- If there are exposed buttons then its body cannot be designed water resistant.
- When it is working on a body, user can impatiently change the buttons in order to change the mode of operation which is not desirable.
- Users do not have to change their habit of wearing TEMPOS regularly as it has no buttons and can function autonomously.

On body sensors have already shown their use to a great extent. TEMPO 3.1 has certain impacts in several areas. There are lots of diseases that are cause due to human movements like Parkinson's disease, Gait disorder, cerebral palsy. Monitoring these diseases carefully can prevent, diagnose and treat these kinds of diseases. When a patient reports on his own by self-assessment, it does not give an accurate result and hence we should rely on sophisticated tools. Hence such self-reports are considered as under sampled, unnatural and unreliable. BASNs such as TEMPO 3.1 can correct such data by continuous monitoring all over the patient's body for a long period of time. Tremor suppressing deep brain stimulation and prosthetic control can be detected by motion capture feedback derived on body from TEMPO 3.1. TEMPO is now IRB approved for four clinical researches involving gait, tremor and akathisia. It has also its function in fitness. It is exclusively useful for athletes and amateurs alike. On body inertial sensing fills current niche which exists between pedometers and machine vision system.

4.3 J2ME and Bluetooth

With the continuation of research in wireless body area network, another technology came into prominence named Bluetooth area network which is operated by Bluetooth and Java technology. Smart phone and Java are the central nodes of Bluetooth area network of a patient (Bratchikov, 2007). The general architecture of Bluetooth area network is as follows:

- A low power short range wireless interface medical sensor.
- Central coordinator communicates with sensors and it also performs the function of internet gateway to other networks in order to transmit bio signals from sensors and receive information.

- A central node which stores the sensor signals and detects alarm and sends patients physiological report to doctor via email, SMS, etc.

This technology is hence a monitoring network of Bluetooth biosensors which is connected to a 3G cell phone via WLAN. This setup is designed to perform the following functions:

- Visualizing and analysis of the physiological status of the patient.
- Recording the outdoor location of the patient using the system.
- Gives medical assistance in case of emergency.

There are three basic components of this Bluetooth system:

1. Internet Bluetooth Area Network (I BAN) to monitor the patient remotely,
2. A central control server (CCS), and
3. A mobile control monitoring unit which is carried by the doctor (MCMU. I BAN consists of a commercial pulse oximeter, a GPS and an Intelligent Node (IN).

Wi-Fi or GPRS is used to send information from IN to CCS and to MCMU (Fabre et. al., 1992).To keep the Bluetooth connection alive the device should be in coverage area of IN so that as soon as any emergency occurs the IN can inform the server. The data rate depends on the mode of operation of the BAN. There are two modes, namely Default mode (mode 1) and verbose mode (mode 2). When a MCMU receives an SMS alert, the physician should start the J2ME monitoring application which displays the patient and sensor data. The Java application is incorporated in the system for the IN. It uses the following application program interface (API):

- Bluetooth API JSR-82 which manages the Bluetooth.
- Location API JSR-179 to get more reliable data from GPS.
- Wireless messaging API JSR-205 for sending SMS and MMS.
- File connection API JSR-75 which records patient's data in mobile phone and memory chip.

The MMS sent by the IN is in the form of ordinary MMS which gets directly into the inbox of the cell phone. The doctor can access the network from any place through internet using Remote Method Invocation which is supported by Java application (Alvarez-Folgueiras et. al., 2011).

Some of the popular WBAN projects being undertaken around the world are listed below:

- Lifeguard (Mundt et. Al., 2005) is a set up that was designed for the astronauts and can be used for monitoring vital signals from patient. It is capable of monitoring various kinds of data such as heart rate, blood pressure, respiratory and pulse oximeter. The physiological data are collected by a wearable device called Crew Physiological Observation device (COPD). It is comprised of skin temperature sensors and 3 axis accelerometer. There is a Bluetooth tablet that displays the data and stores it from COPD for further future analysis.
- Code Blue (Sghaier, et al., 2011) is another hardware and software platform that is designed by Harvard University. The hardware includes a design for 2 lead ECG system, pulse oximetry and

a board for motion analysis. The software architecture is based on a routing framework and each end user communicates with this Code Blue system by a specialized program named Pub Subbase.

- Medisn (Lee et. al., 2006) is another example of a set up that monitors the unattended patients in emergency rooms of John Hopkins Hospital. The set up has four parts namely mi Tag, mi Net, mi Store and mi Viewan. mi Tag consists of all the medical information tags and mi Net is the wireless network connection for communicating the in formations from mi Tag. mi Store stores all the in formations regarding the collected patient data and mi View an is used to display the data to some end users who are designated to analysis the patient data.
- WrisCare (Kim et. al., 2009) is a setup for monitoring heart rhythms for a long period of time. It can detect the changes taking place with heart rhythms. It is of two types namely, home system and institutional system. The home system consists of a wrist band and a base station and is used by the people who live independently in their own houses while the institutional system is used by people who are admitted in Hospitals or Nursing home.

5. SENSORS AND WBANs

Any wireless network comprising of sensors connected to each other is called Wireless Sensor Network (WSN). Basically, in WBAN the sensors are of three types, in-body sensor, on-body sensor and network conductor. This wireless communication system relieves from the pain that is caused due to the cables induced in wired medical communication system. Body area Sensor network nodes should have ergonomic design, have small factors and smaller batteries. A third generation body area sensor is also designed called TEMPO (Technology Enabled Medical Precision Observation) that accurately captures data of human movement and transmits it wirelessly. They can process the data continuously as it is a real time operating system that manages signal processing, control acquisition and everything (Shih-Yeh Chen et. al., 2011). In some wireless area networks mobile phone is used for collecting data. A lot of research is done by the scientists where they used android phone as the medium to communicate the whole process (He et. al., 2013). A light weight activity recognition is detected due to data constraint.

WSN is composed of thousands of nodes and each node is connected to each other as a network so that information gets transmitted from one node to the other (Wu, 2010). These nodes again have several parts. They are microcontroller, a circuit that connects with both the sensor and an energy source, a radio transceiver which is either connected to an external antennae or an internal one, and a battery or any other energy source device. The size of sensor node varies from one another. Similarly the cost of sensor nodes also varies depending on the complexity of the node. Depending on the size and cost constraints of sensor nodes resource constraints such as energy, memory, computational speed and communications bandwidth depends. Routing is the propagation technique between the hops of the networks. WSN topology varies from star network to mesh network which advanced and multi hop wireless.

Biomedical sensors are used mainly in three types of places (Rasmussen et. al., 1996). They are hospital, nursing home and patient's residence. Progressive work is done in this field and a lot of demonstrators are found. The demonstrator for emergency is Field care demonstrator, WiSMoS demonstrator is for post-operative monitoring whereas blood glucose demonstrator is mainly used for monitoring patients at home (Polastre et. al., 2005). The working principle of all these demonstrators are same. They use biomedical sensor to collect patient data and the data is sent to a data collector for further processing and then that data is further sent to the hospital monitoring system for final analysis. The person who is responsible for processing and analyzing these data can access them directly. The principle properties of a WSN are as follows:

- Power consumption constraints for nodes using batteries or energy harvesting.
- Ability to cope with node failures (resilience).
- Mobility of nodes.
- Heterogeneity of nodes.
- Scalability to large scale of deployment.
- Ability to withstand harsh environmental conditions.
- Ease of use.
- Cross-layer design.

Cross-layer is becoming an important studying area for wireless communications.

WBAN and WSN are part of each other and have many things similar to each other. But the basic differences of the two network systems are stated in Table 1.

6. SECURITY AND PRIVACY

Not much work has yet been done regarding the privacy and security of the system. Data security means securing a database from unwanted actions of unauthorized users. It is the relation between collection and dissemination of data, technology, privacy and legal and political issues around. While starting with security of WBAN, we should keep in mind the efficiency of the system too. Even if the device is compromised the patient related data should always remain confidential. Medical data is very vital and it will result into disastrous result if it is modified. The three main factors that makes it important for keeping the data secured are:

- **Confidentiality:** The data that is recorded constantly from the patient's body is stored for the consultancy of the physician but it needs to be kept at a secured location in order to prevent unwanted people from accessing them. The data is usually stored at a node or a local server. Here the data does not get leaked during their storage time. The data confidentiality must be resilient to device compromise to attack.

Table 1. Comparison of WSN and WBAN

Factor	WSN	WBAN
Subject	Environment	Human Body
Required Security Level	Low	Higher
Bio Compatibility	Not required	A must
Mobility	Stationery	Moves from one place to another
Data rate	Event based	Continuous data
Power	High	Low
Node Size	Large or Small	Essentially small

- **Dynamic Integrity Assurance:** A patient who has WBAN for detecting his physiological parameters are critical patients and hence their data are very vital. A little bit of modification of the original data might lead to dangerous consequences. Hence data integrity shall be protecting dynamically all the time (He et. al., 2006). This will help to detect the changes made by the end user and also check that during storage periods in order to detect malicious modifications and an alert is sent to the user.
- **Dependability:** WBAN data are very important data and should be retrieved any time. If there is any problem with getting data on time it can be life threatening. Fault tolerance is very useful in order to manage the threats caused by network dynamics. Hence patient data should be managed such a way that it can retrieved anytime even during node failure or some malicious modifications (Huang et al 2013).

Authentication is a very important step for securing data. It prevents false data injection, DoS attacks and also it verifies the identity of the user before letting the person to access the data. Moreover it is very essential to secure data during transfer with in WBAN system. When a person's data is recorded and processed and transferred from one station to another for further analysis, it is handled by more than one user and hence this path is very risky. Any user can hack the data and modify it. So, it is very important to have user authentication at each step of data transfer where user needs to put a password and get into the system to access the actual data (Xuange et. al., 2010).

High efficiency is very important for the security of a WBAN. The sensors used in recording the parameters should be light and efficient in design and if the authentication protocol is not fast enough then DoS can attack easily (Sung-Yuan, 2001). Privacy of the patient data is destroyed if it is accessed publicly and hence security is one of the most important thing of WBAN. It is very difficult to maintain privacy and security of the data together. Hence it is very difficult to design such a system which is practical. Very few studies are done on this and even the one those are done are far from mature. In Code Blue project a sensor network is developed for pre hospital and emergency responses (Sanchez et. al. 2011). In this system an epileptic curve cryptographic based public key is used for authentication. But there is no other security for stored data and even the access cannot be controlled.

Chess a et al. proposed Redundant Residue Number System which is a secured data storage and sharing scheme for wireless mobile networks (Vos et. al., 2014). In Wang's scheme privacy, dynamic integrity and dependability is achieved all together which is important they usually contradict which each other. Pietro et al found out the solution for data survival problem in wireless (Atallah et. al., 2009). Fine-grained distributed control is an important security service in healthcare. It is designed as role based access model. It prevents handling the patient data publicly and restricts its users with authentication according to their roles. There are 3 types of schemes that are proposed namely SKC based, and ABE based (Ivanov et. al., 2012). SKC was proposed by Morchon et al. (2015). In this method patient can establish connection easily with one entity after authentication. But there are certain disadvantages in the SKC scheme. They are as follows:

- Due to high key management complexity, fine gain access control is hard to be achieved.
- User collision can take place.
- Compromising a node may leak the data or information.

ABE is a very effective scheme. Here the cipher text is allowed to be read by only a group of user who satisfy a certain authentication process. It is collision free. Whenever any data is generated by a WBAN an authentication verification goes with the cipher text (Bhoir et. al., 2014), it supports tree like access policy structure and is easily expressive and it is easy to integrate the context related parameters as attributes like time. One point multiplication and pairing operation takes seconds and hence it might not be a good choice on the sensor nodes (Kathuria et. al., 2014). But it is capable than any other technique as far as obtained after research .but none of the schemes satisfactorily support the security and hence further research in this field is required.

Bluetooth is another extremely popular technology which is short range and low power which is used for portable computing and communication devices. Bluetooth establishes connection automatically which is a great advantage but it has some risks too. There is a huge chance of data getting vulnerable with other low power radio waves (Kathuria et. al., 2014). Unwanted people may receive private information and even people can send files or virus without any permission. The weakest part of the blue tooth technology is that, while establishing connection for the first time between two devices, an authentication is done by each other but without encryption and hence if the hacker actually gets to know the password then he can easily guess the initiation keys and can get all the data that is transferred between the two devices. A very common way of attacking through blue tooth is during pairing process. At this time the connection between the devices is forcefully broken by flooding the channels with packets indicating the slave has lost the key. And when the pairing process is repeated, the hacker observes the encryption keys and gets the link. The BD ADDR is globally unique just like the MAC address (Shen et. al., 2013). In 2005, the researchers at CSAIL found that there is a big vulnerability in it (Ramachandran et. al., 2007). An attacker can assemble list of commonly used BD ADDR in a device and can change his Blue tooth module setting and starts getting packets .then he can attack by sniffing packets or injecting packets. Integrity threat and denial of service are very common in blue tooth communication. Some of the reported attacks in Bluetooth are:

- MAC spoofing attack.
- Attack to crack pin.
- Blue jacking attack.
- Blue printing attack.
- Blue snarfing attack.
- Blue bugging attack.
- Blue over attack.
- Cabir attack.
- DOS attack.
- Skull worms attack.
- Lasco worm attack.
- Brute force attack.

GSM is a standard network used worldwide but it is also attacked. GSM uses several cryptographic algorithms are used by GSM for security. Air voice privacy is protected by using A5/1 and A5/2 stream ciphers. Denial of Service attacks are one of the most powerful attacks. They are so dangerous that they hack the patients' medical data and substitute those valuable data with insensible bogus messages. Now a days a new scheme of location signature is introduced. Symmetric or asymmetrical key cryptography is used which encrypts / decrepit to hide the medical data of patient. Biometric encryption is widely used in most of the places but it is very weak. No, method is strong enough to protect the medical data of patient, so, the security should be strengthened for WBAN to be successfully commercialized. The security requirements of each device and communication link are listed below:

- **Data Integrity:** It assures the correctness of data protection against modification, deletion or replication from an unauthorized user. Usually MAC provides data integrity using secret keys.
- **Data Confidentiality:** Encryption and access control links are the main methods that ensure data confidentiality. It protects the data from handling by unauthorized users. Medical data is very vital and hence it is very important to keep it confidential.
- **Authentication:** This is process when a verification is done with a password in order to choose the right user. There are two kinds of authentication namely message authentication and entity authentication. Biometrics is the most trustworthy authentication possible. There is an ID certificate for the user and a device certificate for the WBAN which achieve authentication.
- **Availability:** This protects from the event taking place and impacting the network. There can be many existing attacks and they results in loss of availability. There are some physical actions that are taken for availability in order to make up for the loss of availability.
- **Privacy:** The medical data may consists of some ones routine health checkup or a particular physiological parameter .These data need some privacy and should not be shared with everyone. Privacy is very important for a patient and these data can only be accessed by people who are allowed to do so.
- **Access Control:** As firewall provides access control, there is personal server that works as a part of firewall. This protects from unauthorized user to access the medical data. It remains open to only few people who are part of WBAN to access data of patient.
- **Non Repudiation:** The process which always keeps evidence. When a user sends or receives it always keeps an evidence of the same. This evidence can be presented to a third party in order to prove that such event has taken place in case of any problem.

7. CONCLUSION AND FUTURE GOALS

Wireless body area network (WBAN) is an emerging field of research which has been progressing rapidly in recent years. The development of this technology will have the impact of drastically reducing the time a patient has to spend in his house or in a medical care center for treatment. This technology has numerous advantages and is very safe helpful if proper security system is incorporated. This technology can get even more popular in use once its privacy and security section is built high. With this development, it can be one of the most successful innovations in medical science. The security issue of this system is very important and from the survey that is performed it can be seen that there is awareness of the importance of these patients' data but not sufficient work has been done yet on this topic. Many scientists have built some models to protect a part of the system. But, the patient monitoring system consists of several process and each and every step should be highly secured so that the information doesn't get leaked at any point of the network. The main focus of this paper has been to draw attention of the researchers to this technology to develop it to make it more commercialized. The future goal includes making it more cheap, safe and popular.

REFERENCES

Alvarez-Folgueiras, M., Minana-Maiques, M., Moreno-Piquero, E., Jorge-Barreiro, F., Lopez-Martin, E., & Ares-Pena, F. (2011, April). Experimental system forthe study of multi-frequency dosimetry. In *Proceedings of the 5th european conference on antennas and propagation* (pp. 1296-1299).

Anis, M., Ortmanns, M., & Wehn, N. (2010, May). Fully integrated uwb impulse transmitter and 402-to-405mhz super-regenerative receiver for medical implant devices. In *Proceedings of 2010 ieee international symposium on circuits and systems* (pp. 1213-1215). doi:10.1109/ISCAS.2010.5537294

Atallah, L., Lo, B., Ali, R., King, R., & Yang, G.-Z. (2009, November). Real-time activity classification using ambient and wearable sensors. *IEEE Transactions on Information Technology in Biomedicine*, *13*(6), 1031–1039. doi:10.1109/TITB.2009.2028575 PMID:19726267

Bhoir, S., & Vidhate, A. (2014, Jan). An improved wban mac protocol. In *International conference on computer communication and informatics* (pp. 1-6).

Bratchikov, A. (2007, Sept). Unified biophysical model for interaction of low intensity laser and ehf electromagnetic fields with cell biosystems and integral organizm. In *17th international Crimean conference microwave telecommunication technology* (pp. 774-775). doi:10.1109/CRMICO.2007.4368937

Chen, S.-Y., Lee, W.-T., Chao, H.-C., Huang, Y.-M., & Lai, C.-F. (2011, Nov). Adaptive reconstruction of humanmotion on wireless body sensor networks. In *First international conference on wireless communications and signal processing* (pp. 1-5).

de Francisco, R., Huang, L., & Dolmans, G. (2009, Sept). Coexistence of wban and wlan in medical environments. In *IEEE 70th vehicular technology conference fall* (pp. 1-5). doi:10.1109/VETECF.2009.5378807

De Vos, J., Flandre, D., & Bol, D. (2014, May). Switchedcapacitor dc/dc converters for empowering internet-of-things socs. In IEEE faible tension faible consummation (FTFC) (pp. 1-4).

Degli-Esposti, V. (2014, April). Ray tracing propagation modelling: Future prospects. In *8th European conference on antennas and propagation* (pp. 2232-2232).

Fabre, J., Camart, J., Prevost, B., Chive, M., & Sozanski, J. (1992, Oct). 915 mhz interstitial hyperthermia: Dosimetry from heating pattern reconstruction based on radiometric temperature measurements. In *14th annual international conference of the IEEE engineering in medicine and biology society* (Vol. 1, pp. 231-231).

Gafurov, D., Snekkenes, E., & Bours, P. (2010, April). Improved gait recognition performance using cycle matching. In *24th international conference on advanced information networking and applications workshops (waina)* (pp. 836-841). doi:10.1109/WAINA.2010.145

He, Z., Luo, Y., & Liang, G. (2013, April). Runking: A mobile social persuasion system for running exercise. In Computing, communications and it applications conference (pp. 74-78).

Huang, C.-W., Kuo, S.-W., & Chang, C.-J. (2013, July). Embedded 8-bit aes in wireless bluetooth application. In *International conference on system science and engineering (ICSSE)* (pp. 87-92). doi:10.1109/ICSSE.2013.6614638

Ivanov, S., Foley, C., Balasubramaniam, S., & Botvich, D. (2012a, November). Virtual groups for patient wban monitoring in medical environments. *IEEE Transactions on Bio-Medical Engineering*, *59*(11), 3238–3246. doi:10.1109/TBME.2012.2208110 PMID:22801487

Ivanov, S., Foley, C., Balasubramaniam, S., & Botvich, D. (2012b, Nov). Virtual groups for patient wban monitoring in medical environments. *IEEE Transactions on Biomedical Engineering, 59*(11), 3238-3246.

Kathuria, M., & Gambhir, S. (2014, Feb). Quality of service provisioning transport layer protocol for wban system. In *International conference on optimization, reliabilty, and information technology* (pp. 222-228). doi:10.1109/ICROIT.2014.6798318

Khaleghi, A., Chavez-Santiago, R., & Balasingham, I. (2010, October). Ultra-wideband pulse-based data communications for medical implants. *Communications, IET*, *4*(15), 1889–1897. doi:10.1049/iet-com.2009.0692

Kim, K., Lee, I.-S., Yoon, M., Kim, J., Lee, H., & Han, K. (2009, Dec). An efficient routing protocol based on position information in mobile wireless body area sensor networks. In *First international conference on networks and communications* (pp. 396-399). doi:10.1109/NetCoM.2009.36

Kim, T.-Y., Youm, S., Jung, J.-J., & Kim, E.-J. (2015, Jan). Multi-hop wban construction for healthcare iot systems. In *International conference on platform technology and service* (pp. 27-28). doi:10.1109/PlatCon.2015.20

Lee, D.-S., Lee, Y.-D., Chung, W.-Y., & Myllyla, R. (2006, Oct). Vital sign monitoring system with life emergency event detection using wireless sensor network. In *5th IEEE conference on sensors* (pp. 518-521).

Monton, E., Hernandez, J., Blasco, J., Herve, T., Micallef, J., Grech, I., & Traver, V. et al. (2008, February). Body area network for wireless patient monitoring. *Communications, IET*, *2*(2), 215–222. doi:10.1049/iet-com:20070046

Motoi, K., Ikeda, K., Kuwae, Y., Yuji, T., Higashi, Y., Nogawa, M., & Yamakoshi, K. et al. (2006, Aug). Development of an ambulatory device for monitoring posture change and walking speed for use in rehabilitation. In *Proceedings of the 7th IEEE international conference on engineering in medicine and biology society* (pp. 5940-5943). doi:10.1109/IEMBS.2006.259364

Mundt, C., Montgomery, K., Udoh, U., Barker, V., Thonier, G., Tellier, A., & Kovacs, G. et al. (2005, September). A multiparameter wearable physiologic monitoring system for space and terrestrial applications. *IEEE Transactions on Information Technology in Biomedicine*, *9*(3), 382–391. doi:10.1109/TITB.2005.854509 PMID:16167692

Polastre, J., Szewczyk, R., & Culler, D. (2005, April). Telos: enabling ultra-low power wireless research. In *Fourth international symposium on information processing in sensor networks,* (pp. 364-369). doi:10.1109/IPSN.2005.1440950

Ramachandran, A., Zhou, Z., & Huang, D. (2007, May). Computing cryptographic algorithms in portable and embedded devices. In IEEE international conference on portable information device (pp. 1-7). doi:10.1109/PORTABLE.2007.47

Rasmussen, J., Scholl, B., Gellekum, T., & Schmitt, H. J. (1996, Oct). Fiber-optic polarimetric temperature sensor for characterizing a 900 mhz tem cell used in bioeffects dosimetry studies. In *Proceedings of the 18th annual international conference of the IEEE engineering in medicine and biology society, bridging disciplines for biomedicine*. (Vol. 5, pp. 1875-1876). doi:10.1109/IEMBS.1996.646298

Sanchez, A., Blanc, S., Yuste, P., & Serrano, J. (2011, June). A low cost and high efficient acoustic modem for underwater sensor networks. In IEEE - Spain oceans (pp. 1-10). doi:10.1109/Oceans-Spain.2011.6003428

Sghaier, N., Mellouk, A., Augustin, B., Amirat, Y., Marty, J., Khoussa, M., . . . Zitouni, R. (2011, July). Wireless sensor networks for medical care services. In *7th international conference on wireless communications and mobile computing conference* (pp. 571-576). doi:10.1109/IWCMC.2011.5982596

Shen, Q., Liu, J., Yu, H., Ma, Z., Li, M., Shen, Z., & Chen, C. (2013, Aug). Adaptive cognitive enhanced platform for wban. In IEEE/CIC international conference on communications in China (pp. 739-744). doi:10.1109/ICCChina.2013.6671208

Smith, D., Miniutti, D., Lamahewa, T., & Hanlen, L. (2013, October). Propagation models for body-area networks: A survey and new outlook. *Antennas and Propagation Magazine, IEEE, 55*(5), 97–117. doi:10.1109/MAP.2013.6735479

Sung-Yuan, K. (2001). The embedded bluetooth ccd camera. In Tencon 2001. Proceedings of IEEE region 10 international conference on electrical and electronic technology (Vol. 1, pp. 81-84). doi:10.1109/TENCON.2001.949556

Takacs, B. (2006, July). A portable ultrasound guidance and raining system using high fidelity virtual human models. In *International conference on medical information visualisation - biomedical visualisation* (pp. 77-81). doi:10.1109/MEDIVIS.2006.2

Wu, P. (2010, Nov). The perspective of biomedical electronics. In IEEE conference on sensors (pp. 1187-1187). doi:10.1109/ICSENS.2010.5690645

Xuange, P., & Ying, X. (2010, March). An embedded electric meter based on bluetooth data acquisition system. In *Second international workshop on education technology and computer science* (Vol. 1, pp. 667-670). doi:10.1109/ETCS.2010.624

Chapter 15
Application of Biomedical Image Processing in Blood Cell Counting using Hough Transform

Manali Mukherjee
Government College of Engineering and Ceramic Technology, India

Kamarujjaman
Government College of Engineering and Ceramic Technology, India

Mausumi Maitra
Government College of Engineering and Ceramic Technology, India

ABSTRACT

In the field of biomedicine, blood cells are complex in nature. Nowadays, microscopic images are used in several laboratories for detecting cells or parasite by technician. The microscopic images of a blood stream contain RBCs, WBCs and Platelets. Blood cells are produced in the bone marrow and regularly released into circulation. Blood counts are monitored with a laboratory test called a Complete Blood Count (CBC). However, certain circumstances may cause to have fewer cells than is considered normal, a condition which is called "low blood counts".This can be accomplished with the administration of blood cell growth factors. Common symptoms due to low red blood cells are:fatigue or tiredness, trouble breathing, rapid heart rate, difficulty staying warm, pale skin etc. Common symptoms due to low white blood cells are: infection, fever etc. It is important to monitor for low blood cell count because conditions could increase the risk of unpleasant and sometimes life-threatening side effects.

INTRODUCTION

In biomedicine field, blood cells with complex behavior are very important. Nowadays, microscopic images are used in several laboratories for detecting cells or parasite by technician. The microscopic

DOI: 10.4018/978-1-4666-9964-9.ch015

images of a blood stream contain Red Blood Cells (RBCs), White Blood Cells (WBCs) and Platelets. In medical field, the number of red blood cells is used as an indication factor for detecting the type of diseases such as malaria, anemia, leukemia etc. Pathological examination of an infected cell by disease, is only dependent on subjective assessment which usually leads to particular inter-observer variation in gradation and results delay in diagnosis. The problems using manual counting of RBC under the microscope tend to give inaccurate result and errors (Mazalan, S.M. et.al, 2013), (Tangsuksant, W. et.al, 2013). However, automatic cell count assessment still remains a challenging task as many of the cells are clumped in an image where segmentation is the primary aspect as well. Hari, J.; Prasad, A.S.et.al., 2014 worked on Separation and counting of blood cells using geometrical features and distance transformed watershed. Because of cell's complex nature, it is difficult to segment cells from its background and count them automatically. Dwi Anoragaingrum et.al, showed cell segmentation with median filter and mathematical morphology operation. Keng Wu et al. worked on live cell image segmentation. Mark B. Jeacocke and Brian C. Lovell proposed a Multi-resolution algorithm for Cytological image segmentation. Blood is unique among all tissues of the body because it exists as the only fluid tissue. According to H Elaine & N. Marieb (2006), a blood cell can be any type of cell normally found in blood which falls into four categories which are red blood cell, white blood cell, platelet and plasma. The differences between these groups lie on the texture, color, size, nucleus morphology and cytoplasm. In blood cells, number of red cells is many more than white blood cells. For example an image may contain up to 100 red blood cells and only 1 to 3 white blood cells. Platelets are small particles and are not clinically important (Fatemeh Zamani, et.al. 2006*)*. Blood cells form in the bone marrow, the soft material in the center of maxium bones. WBCs (Leukocytes) are cells involved in defending the body against infective organisms and unknown substances. Leukocytes or white blood cells containing granules are called granulocytes (composed by neutrophil, basophil, eosinophil). Lymphocyte and monocyte Cells are called agranulocytes i.e., without granules cells. These cells provide major defense against infections in organisms and their specific concentrations can help specialists to discriminate the presence or the absence of very important families of pathologies (Vincenzo Piuri et.al., 2004).

Blood counting is synonym with the complete blood count or CBC which refers to combination of Red Blood Cell (RBC), White Blood Cell (WBC), platelet, hemoglobin and hematocrit. They have their own role in the body system and the counting result is important to determine the deficiency or the capability of the body system. In short, any abnormal reading of CBC can give a sign of infection or disease. For example, the presence of bacterial infection is diagnosed from increasing WBC count. On the other hand, specific low vitamin may come from a decreased RBC and thrombocytopenia is referring to low platelet count. The result can influence physician to make the best response and monitor the drug effectiveness from the blood count (Miswan, M. F., et al., 2011).

Complete blood count (CBC) consists of several counting of the main component in the blood cell. Each of the components have a standard quantity range as a reference for a healthy women and man. Out of the range values are considered to be abnormal and physician interprets the result for further action. As the manual counting method is not very accurate, nowadays, computer based technology is used to count the cells more accurately. Usually, there are four steps involved in counting the blood cells. These are acquisition, pre-processing, segmentation, feature extraction and estimation. The first step involves the acquisition of blood sample images. Pre-processing is done for image enhancement. The segmentation and feature extraction are done by using morphological techniques in order to distinguish the RBC, WBC and Platelets blood cells from background and other cells. The segmentation and classification of the RBCs are the most important stages. Due to the large RBC shape variations, a shape independent framework for identification and segmentation is required (Deb, N. & Chakraborty, S., 2014).

Segmentation is an implementation of automated counting for blood cell which is manually done by hematocytometer by using counting chamber. In the segmentation process, morphological technique is mainly used because the mathematical morphology offers a powerful tool for segmenting images and useful to describe the region shape, such as skeletons, textures and boundaries. The main idea of the image segmentation is to form group of pixels in homogeneous regions and the usual approach to do this is by 'common feature'. Different methods and algorithms have been developed for image segmentation. Image segmentation techniques are categorized into three classes: Clustering, edge detection, region growing. Some popular clustering algorithms like k-means are often used in image segmentation. In the present work, estimation of the number of blood cells is implemented by using Hough Transform technique (Duda, R. O. and P. E. Hart, 1972).

The organization of the chapter is as follows: Section 2 discusses related work and motivation behind the present work. It describes limitation of manual method of blood cell counting and it also describes the need for automated blood cell counting from medical images using image pre-processing and segmentation techniques. Section 3 describes the structural and functional properties of different blood cells e.g. Red Blood Cell (RBC), White Blood Cell (WBC) and Platelets. This domain knowledge is very important for analyzing the blood cell images for developing the algorithm to isolate the particular type of blood cells from the rest of the image and to count them. It also describes some diseases where blood cell counting is very important. Section 4 describes the historical importance as well as the detailed methodology of Hough Transform, which is the key algorithm for the present study. Section 5 discusses the detailed methodology of the proposed work. Section 6 discusses the method of segmentation of blood cells using Hough Transform and section 7 discusses the method of counting of the cells per cumm which is the most important data for the analysis of the related diseases. Section 8 describes the results of our study. We have considered five different blood cell images for our study and a comparison of data has been made between the manual counting method and our proposed method. Finally in section 9 we have concluded that this chapter presents a methodology to achieve an automated detection and counting of red blood cells in microscopic images using Hough Transform. Results show that the counting of red blood cell in microscopic images offer remarkable accuracy. Citometers, based on laser, are available to count blood cells but they are very costly and also they are not based on images and the blood samples are destroyed during the analysis. Our proposed method is very cost-effective and can be implemented easily in medical centers anywhere with a very low investment in infrastructure.

RELATED WORK AND MOTIVATION

Content-based image indexing and retrieval is an important research area in computer science for the last few decades. Many digital images are captured and stored everyday such as medical images, architectural, advertising, design and fashion images, etc. As a result large image databases are created and used in many applications. In this work, the medical images are the focus of our study. A large database of medical images in digital format is generated every day by hospitals and medical institutions. Therefore, it is becoming a challenging problem (Lehmann T.M.et.al., 2000) to make use of this huge amount of images effectively. In the field of biomedicine, because of cell's complex nature, it still remains a challenging job to segment cells from their backgrounds and count them automatically (Dwi Anoragaingrum et.al., 1999; Keng Wu et al., 1995; Mark B. Jeacocke et.al. 1994; Choi H et.al., 2001). Counting problem arises in many real world applications which includes cell counting in microscopic images, monitoring crowds in surveillance systems and performing wildlife census or counting the number of trees in an aerial image of a forest (O. Barinovaet.al., 2010; B. Leibe, 2008). The inspection of blood slides under microscope provides important qualitative and quantitative information concerning the presence of hematic pathologies. Experienced operators performed these operations from decades which includes mainly two analyses. The first method is the qualitative study of the morphology of the cells and it gives information of degenerative and tumoral pathologies. The second method is quantitative and it consists of differential counting of the blood cells. Laser-based citometers, which are the examples of automated cell counter systems, are available in the market, but they are not image based or morphological and the blood samples are destroyed during the analysis (Abbott Diagnostics Website. http://www.abbott.com/products/diagnostics.htm/; Beckman Coulter Website, http://www.coulter.com/coulter/Hematology/). Few approaches of partial / full automated systems based on image processing systems are present in literature and they are still at prototype stage. Vincenzo Piuri et.al. (2004) showed the classification and counting of white blood cells in microscopic images for the assessment of a wide range of important hematic pathologies. Testing in urine sediment is very important for the patients with abnormal urinary tract. Constantly, the appearance of red blood cells, white blood cells, bacteria, crystals and other microorganisms in urine sediment's patients is more important information for diagnosis (Tangsuksant et.al. 2013).

According to American Cancer Society (2009), the red blood cells in our body is divided into four categories of ages, which are men, women, children and new born. Red blood is measured by the amount of hemoglobin. We suffered short of breath and fatigue when the level of hemoglobin is too low due to insufficient oxygen supply. The high count of red blood cells in our blood can be indication of an undetected heart or lung problems. Therefore, count of red blood cell is very important in diagnosis of many diseases. Malaria is one of the most serious parasitic infections of human. The accurate as well as timely diagnosis of malaria infection is essential to control and cure the disease. Some image processing algorithms are developed for automatic diagnosis of malaria using thin blood smears, but the percentage of parasitaemia is often not very precise compared to manual count. One reason resulting in this error is ignoring the cells at the borders of images. Various health hazards are caused by anemia. Anemia decreases and also alters the shape of red blood cells (RBCs) present in blood. Different type of RBC shapes account for different type of anemia. Automated blood cell analyzers can provide RBC, WBC and platelet count and can detect anemia but anemia type identification, which requires classification of RBCs, is carried out manually. The RBC classification provides invaluable information to pathologists for diagnosis and treatment of different types of anemia. The manual visual inspection is tedious, time consuming, repetitive and prone to human error. So automated classification of RBCs are an important zone.

Vinutha H Reddy (2014) introduced an automatic RBC and WBC counting using computer vision. The estimation of red blood cells involves several steps. These are image acquisition, preprocessing of acquired image, segmentation, feature extraction, counting. The pre-processing step includes the conversion of the original blood smear image into saturation image. Histogram thresholding and morphological operations are used for segmentation. Feature extraction is done with the help of morphological operations to differentiate between RBCs, WBCs, Platelets and background. Last step is to measure number of Red Blood Cell by using Hough Transform on the blood cell image.

Venkatalakshmi. B et al. (2013) presented a method for automatic red blood cell counting using Hough transform. The algorithm for estimating the red blood cells consists of five major steps: input image acquisition, pre-processing, segmentation, feature extraction and counting. In pre-processing step, original blood smear is converted into HSV image. As bright components are clearly obtained in saturation image, it is further used for analysis. Detection of the lower and upper threshold from histogram information is the first step of segmentation. Based on this information the saturation image is then divided into two binary images. Morphological area closing is applied to lower pixel value image and area closing as well as morphological dilation is applied to higher pixel value image. Morphological XOR operation is applied to two binary images and RBCs are extracted by applying Circular Hough Transform.

Siti Madihah Mazalan et al. (2013) also presented an approach for automatic RBC counting using circular Hough transform technique. It contains two major steps: finding out maximum and minimum radius of RBC and Hough transform. For measurement of maximum and minimum radius, the steps are carried out that include: cropping the image, RBG to gray conversion, morphological processing, thresholding, noise removing and then measuring mean, standard deviation and tolerance. Finally, Circular Hough Transform is applied to count RBCs in peripheral blood smear image with the help of known radius.

The purpose of our work in this area was also to focus on the problem of identification and counting of red blood cells by microscopic images. We (M. Maitra et.al. 2012) introduced a method for automatic segmentation and counting of red blood cells in microscopic image using Hough Transform. Preprocessing techniques include edge detection, spatial smoothing filtering and adaptive histogram equalization. Hough Transform is used for feature extraction to find out the red blood cells based on their sizes and their shapes. This isolates the red blood cells from the rest of the image of the blood sample and finally counting can be applied exclusively on them.

BLOOD CELLS

Red Blood Cell (RBC)

The major focus of clinical laboratory is to produce an accurate result for every test especially in the area of RBC count. Red blood cells, also known as enthrocytes are the most important and numerous blood cells in human body. Main function of RBCs is to carry oxygen and to deliver it to the cells in the body. They are minute disc shaped. They do not contain nucleus but a protein called hemoglobin. Both outer and inner layers of cell are made of protein that gives red color to blood. Actually hemoglobin does the work of grabbing and carries oxygen. In blood test, the level of hemoglobin is tested usually and the decrease in level may cause severe diseases including anemia, blood loss, leukemia and malnutrition. The life span of RBC is of around 120 days. The production of red blood cells takes place in the bone marrow. Typical red blood cell count (RBC) levels are: 2.6 to 4.8 million cells per micro liter for children, 4.2 to 5.4 million cells per micro liter for women and 4.5 to 6.2 million cells per micro liter of blood for men.

The main importance of the number of red blood cell is to detect as well as to follow the treatment of many diseases like anemia, leukemia etc. Red blood cell count is responsible for important information that helps diagnosis of many of the patient's sickness. The conventional method of RBC counting under microscope gives an unreliable and inaccurate result because it depends on the performance of clinical laboratory technician. This method puts a lot of strain on the technician. Another method for RBC counting uses the automatic hematology analyzer. As this machine is very costly, it is not possible for all the hospital's clinical laboratory to install such an expensive machine to count the blood cell in their laboratory. Attempts are being made to solve this problem using medical image processing. There are six major steps involved in the process of estimating the red blood cells. These are input image acquisition, preprocessing, enhancement, segmentation, feature extraction and finally RBC counting.

The first step in the process is image acquisition. Before any video or image processing, an image must be captured by a camera and converted into a manageable entity. This is the process known as image acquisition. The image acquisition process consists of three steps; energy reflected from the object of interest, an optical system which focuses the energy and finally a sensor which measures the amount of energy. Usually it is microscopic image that can be obtained from online medical library or hospital blood sample images. These images are in RGB color format.

Image pre-processing is a technique of adjusting images suitable for the next step of computational process. It is done in such a way that image quality is improved for the success of the other processes. Pre-processing techniques usually include contrast enhancing, noise removal, region isolation and use of different color models. Original blood cell images are in color. Acquired images have low contrast as all blood element colors are close to background color. Clustered white blood cells are also a factor for noise inclusion.

After pre-processing, image enhancement is done. The principal goal of image enhancement is to process a given image so that the result is more suitable than the original image for a particular application. It sharpens image features such as edges, boundaries, or contrast to make a graphical presentation more helpful for display and analysis. The enhancement doesn't increase the inherent information, but it increases the dynamic range of the chosen features so that they can be detected easily. The greatest difficulty in image enhancement is quantifying the criterion for enhancement and, therefore, a large number of image enhancement techniques are empirical and require interactive procedures to obtain satisfactory results. Image enhancement methods are based on either spatial or frequency domain techniques. These techniques include image negation, histogram plotting, image subtraction and filtering.

The next stage deals with image segmentation. Segmentation partitions an input image into foreground and background region. There are various approaches for segmentation e.g. segmentation by using histogram and thresholding, Otsu adaptive thresholding and watershed transform, Hough transform technique as well as segmentation by K Means clustering. The objective of segmentation is the extraction of desired objects from the background. Segmentation is very complex and requires more processing time in comparison with other methods. However it is important and more challenging step because the feature extraction and counting depends on the correct segmentation of RBC.

Feature extraction includes morphological operations. It extracts features that contain quantitative information of specified objects. Shape features are areas of cell and nucleus, cell perimeter, ratio of nucleus to overall cell area, boundary of the nucleus and circularity factor. Texture features include contrast, homogeneity and entropy derived from the gray-level co-occurrence matrix.

White Blood Cells

Another cellular component of the blood is White blood cells (WBCs). They are also called leukocyte or white corpuscle which lacks hemoglobin, has a nucleus, is capable of motility, and protect the body against infection and disease by ingesting foreign materials and cellular debris, by destroying infectious agents and cancer cells, or by producing antibodies. A healthy adult human has between 4,500 and 11,000 white blood cells per cubic millimeter of blood. Different mode of fluctuations in white cell number occurs during the day; lower values are obtained during rest and higher values are obtained during exercise. An abnormal increase in white cell number is known as leukocytosis, whereas decrease in number is known as leukopenia. White cell count may increase in response to intense physical exertion, convulsions, acute emotional reactions, pain, pregnancy, labour, and certain disease states, such as infections and intoxications. The count may decrease in response to certain types of infections or drugs or in association with certain conditions, such as chronic anemia, malnutrition, or anaphylaxis. Like all blood cells, white blood cells are produced in the bone marrow that developed from stem (precursor) cells which mature into one of the five major types of white blood cells: Neutrophil, Eosinophil, Basophile, Lymphocyte, Monocytes.

Neutrophils are the most abundant white blood cell, constituting 60-70% of the circulating leukocytes (Bruce Albertset.al., 2002). They defend against bacterial or fungal infection.

Eosinophils compose about 2-4% of the WBC total. This count fluctuates throughout the day, seasonally. It rises in response to allergies, parasitic infections, collagen diseases, and disease of the spleen and central nervous system. They are rare in the blood, but numerous in the mucous membranes of the respiratory, digestive, and lower urinary tracts. They primarily deal with parasitic infections.

Basophils are basically responsible for allergic and antigen response by releasing the chemical histamine causing the dilation of blood vessels. Because they are the rarest of the white blood cells (less than 0.5% of the total count) and share physicochemical properties with other blood cells, they are difficult to study (Falcone et.al., 2000).They excrete two chemicals that help in the body's defenses: histamine and heparin. Histamine is responsible for widening blood vessels and maximizing the flow of blood to injured tissue. It also makes blood vessels more permeable so neutrophils and clotting proteins can get into connective tissue more easily.

Lymphocytes are much more common in the lymphatic system than in blood. Lymphocytes are diverse in nature and they have a deeply staining nucleus that may be eccentric in location, and a relatively small amount of cytoplasm.

Monocytes share the "vacuum cleaner" (phagocytosis) function of neutrophils, but they have an extra role: they present pieces of pathogens to T cells so that the pathogens may be recognized again and killed. This causes an antibody response to be mounted.

Platelets

Platelets are the cells that circulate within our blood and bind together when they recognize damaged blood vessels. Platelets have no cell nucleus: they are fragments of cytoplasm which are derived from the mega karyocytes (Machlus KR et.al, 2014) of the bone marrow and then enter the circulation. Platelets, the smallest of our blood cells, are literally shaped like small plates in their non-active form. A blood vessel will send out a signal when it becomes damaged. When platelets receive that signal, they'll respond by traveling to the area and transforming into their "active" formation. To make contact with the broken blood vessel, platelets grow long tentacles and then resemble a spider or an octopus. A normal platelet count ranges from 150,000 to 450,000 platelets per micro liter of blood. Having more than 450,000 platelets is a condition called thrombocytosis; having less than 150,000 is known as thrombocytopenia. Thrombocytosis has two types. One is Primary or essential thrombocytosis – Abnormal cells in the bone marrow cause an increase in platelets, but the reason is unknown and another is Secondary thrombocytosis – The same condition as primary thrombocytosis, but may be caused by an ongoing condition or disease such as anemia, cancer, inflammation, or infection. When there are symptoms, they include spontaneous blood clots in the arms and legs, which if untreated can lead to heart attack and stroke. In severe cases, the patient might have to undergo a procedure called a platelet pheresis. This lowers the platelet count by removing the blood, separating out the platelets, and returning the red blood cells back to the body. When we don't have enough platelets, it's called thrombocytopenia. Symptoms include easy bruising, and frequent bleeding from the gums, nose, or GI tract. Platelet count drops when something is preventing our body from producing platelets.

HOUGH TRANSFORM

The Hough transform was primarily developed to detect analytically defined shapes (e.g., line, circle, ellipse etc.). In these cases, we have knowledge of the shape and want to find out its location and orientation in the image. The method as it is universally used today was invented by Richard Duda and Peter Hart in 1972, who called it a "generalized Hough transform" after the related 1962 patent of Paul Hough.

The transform was popularized in the computer vision community by Dana H. Ballard in 1981. The Hough transform is a feature extraction technique used in image analysis, computer vision, and digital image processing. In automated analysis of digital images, a sub problem often arises of detecting simple shapes, such as straight lines, circles or ellipses. In many cases an edge detector can be used as a pre-processing stage to obtain image points or image pixels that are on the desired curve in the image space. Due to imperfections in either the image data or the edge detector, however, there may be missing points or pixels on the desired curves as well as spatial deviations between the ideal line/circle/ellipse and the noisy edge points as they are obtained from the edge detector. For these reasons, it is often non-trivial to group the extracted edge features to an appropriate set of lines, circles or ellipses. The purpose of the Hough transform is to address this problem by making it possible to perform groupings of edge points into object candidates by performing an explicit voting procedure over a set of parameterized image objects. This voting procedure is carried out in a parameter space, from which object candidates are obtained as local maxima in a so-called accumulator space that is explicitly constructed by the algorithm for computing the Hough transform.

Detection of Straight Line

Knowledge about the lines in an image is useful in many applications. The simplest case of Hough transform is detecting straight lines. To manually extract the line information from an image can be very tiring and time-consuming especially if there are many lines in the image. An automatic method is preferable, but is not as trivial as edge detection since one has to determine which edge point belongs to which line, if any. The Hough-transform makes this separation possible and, is a powerful global method for detecting edges. It transforms between the Cartesian space and a parameter space in which a straight line (or other boundary formulation) can be defined.

Let's consider the case where we have straight lines in an image. We first note that for every point (x_i, y_i)in that image, all the straight lines passing through that point satisfy the $y_i = mx_i + c$ (Equation 1) for varying values of line slope and intercept (m,c) as shown in Figure 1.

Now if we reverse our variables and look instead at the values of (m,c) as a function of the image point coordinates (x_i,y_i) then Equation 1 becomes:

$$c = y_i - mx_i \tag{2}$$

Figure 1. Lines through a point in the Cartesian domain

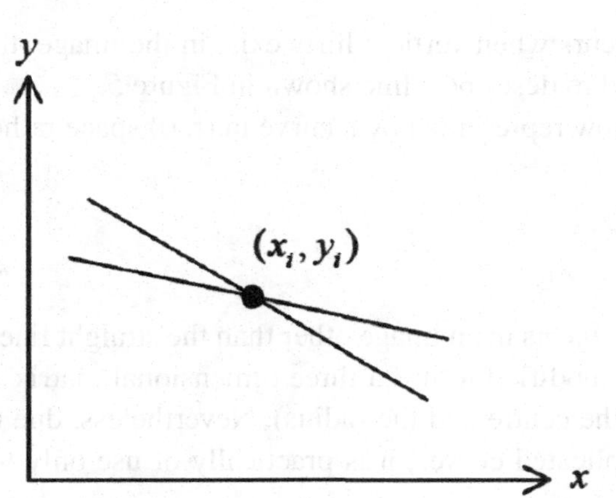

Figure 2. The (m,c) domain

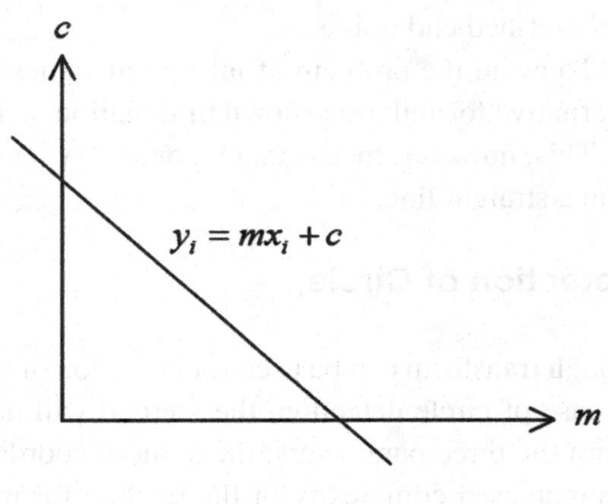

Equation 2 describes a straight line on a graph of c against m as shown in Figure 2.

At this point, it is easy to see that each different line through the point (x_i, y_i) corresponds to one of the points on the line in the (m,c) space.

Now, consider two pixels P1 and P2, which lie on the same line in the(x, y) space of an image. For each pixel, we can represent all the possible lines through it by a single line in the (m,c) space. Thus a line in the (x, y) space that passes through both pixels must lie on the intersection of the two lines in the (m,c) space, which represent the two pixels. This means that all pixels which lie on the same line in the (x, y) space are represented by lines which all pass through a single point in the (m,c) space, see Figure 3 and Figure 4.

The advantage of the Hough transform is that the pixels lying on one line need not all be contiguous. This can be very useful when trying to detect lines with short breaks in them due to noise, or when objects are partially occluded. As for the disadvantages of the Hough transform, one is that it can give misleading results when objects happen to be aligned by chance. This clearly shows another disadvantage

Figure 3. Points on the same line

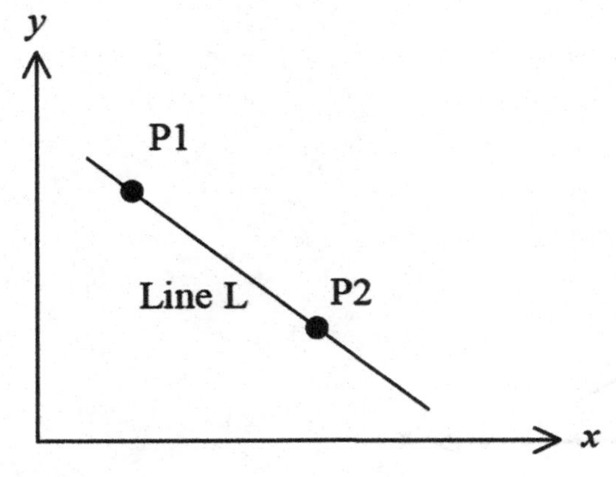

Figure 4. The mapping of P1 and P2 from Cartesian space to the (m,c) space

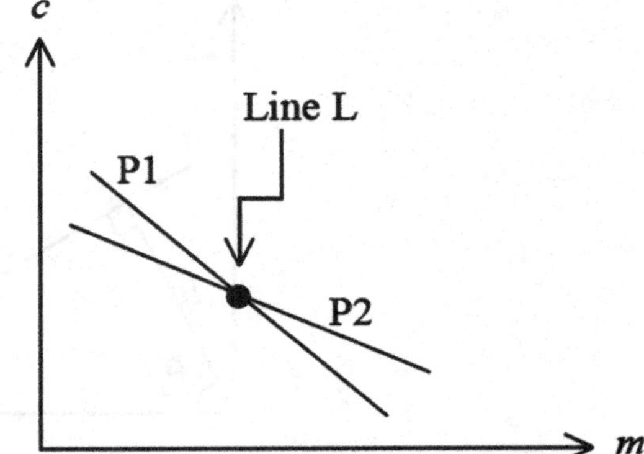

which is that the detected lines are infinite lines described by their (m,c) values, rather than finite lines with defined end points.

To avoid the problem of infinite m values which occurs when vertical lines exist in the image, the alternative formulation shown in Equation 3 can be used to describe a line shown in Figure 5.

This, however, means that a point in (x, y) space is now represented by a curve in (r, θ) space rather than a straight line.

Detection of Circle

Hough transform can be used for detection of shapes of objects in an image other than the straight lines. In case of circle detection, the method will have to be modified to use a three dimensional matrix H (with the three parameters: the x and y coordinates of the centre and the radius). Nevertheless, due to the increased complexity of the method for more complicated curves, it is practically of use only for simple ones.

Here the parameter space can be defined by θ and R, where the values of θ have finite sizes, depending on the resolution of θ. The distance to the line ρ will have a maximum size which is equal to two times the diagonal length of the image [3]. The representation of circle is actually simpler in parameter space, compared to the representation of a line, because the parameters of the circle can be directly transfer to the parameter space.

In a two dimensional space a circle can be described by

$$(x-a)^2 + (y-b)^2 = r^2$$

where (a,b) is the center of the circle, and r is the radius. If a 2D point (x,y) is fixed, then the parameters can be found according to the above equation. The parameter space would be three dimensional, (a, b, r). And all the parameters that satisfying (x, y) would lie on the surface of an inverted right-angled cone whose apex is at (x, y, 0).

The parametric representation of the circle is

$$x = a + r \cos(\theta)$$

Figure 5. The representation of a line in the (x, y) space using (r_i, θ_i)

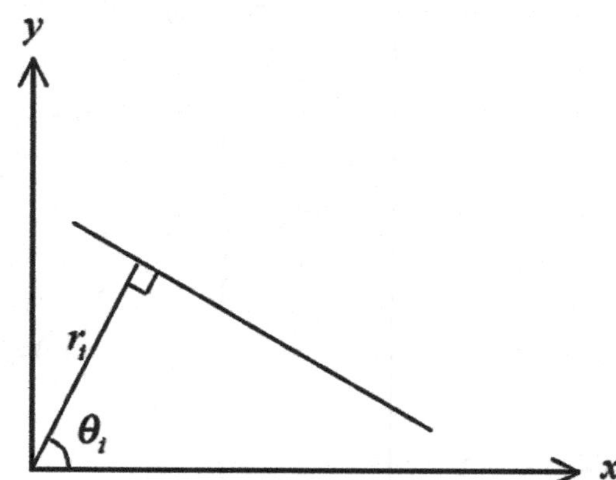

y= b + r sin (θ)

When the angle sweeps through the full 360⁰ range the points (x, y) trace the parameter of a circle. Thus the parameter space for a circle will belong to 3r whereas the line only belong to 2r.The parameter space used for circular Hough transform are shown in Figure 6 and Figure 7. As the number of parameters to describe the shape of circular Hough transform increases, as well as the dimension of the parameter space 'r' increases, so do the complexity of the Hough transform. Therefore, the Hough transform in general is only considered for simple shapes with parameters belonging to 2r or at most 3r. In order to simplify the parametric representation of the circle, the radius can be considered as a constant or it may be limited to number of known radii.

The process of finding circles in an image using CHT is: First the edges in the image are found. For this step any edge detection technique like Canny, Sobel or Morphological operations can be used as it has nothing to do with Hough Transform.

At each edge point we draw a circle with center in the point with the pre-calculated radius. This circle is drawn in the parameter space, such that the z axis is the radii while the x axis is the a-value and the y axis is the b value. At the coordinates, which belong to the perimeter of the circle, we increase the value in our accumulator matrix, which essentially has the same size as the parameter space. In this way, we move around every edge point in the input image drawing circles with the desired radii and increasing the values in the accumulator. The accumulator will now contain numbers corresponding to the number of circles passing through the individual coordinates. Therefore, the highest numbers (selected in an intelligent way, in relation to the radius) correspond to the center of the circles in the image.

Figure 6. The parameter space used for CHT

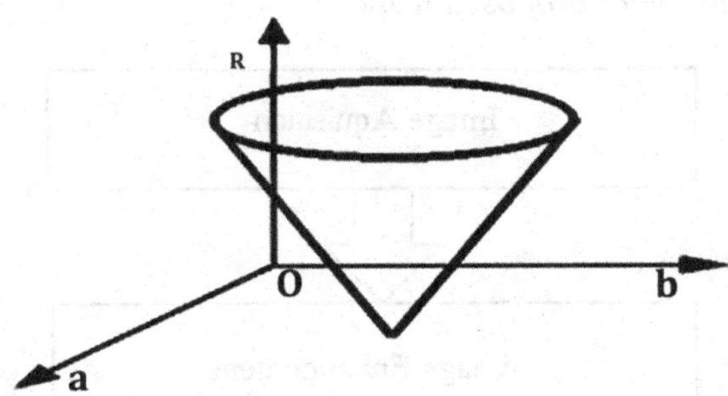

Figure 7. Circular HT from the x, y-space (left) to the parameter space (right), for a constant radius

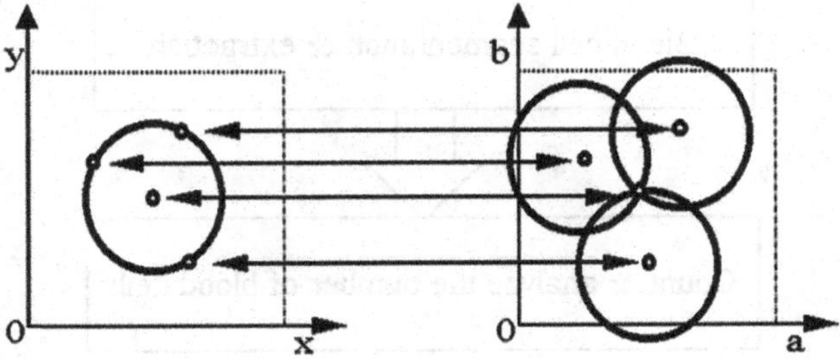

Hough transform can be used to detect shapes in an image other than straight lines such as circles. In that case, the only difference is that the method will have to be modified to use a three dimensional matrix H (with the three parameters: the radius, the x and y coordinates of the centre). Nevertheless, due to the higher complexity of the method for further complicated curves, it is practically of use only for simple ones.

METHODOLOGY

Numerous image processing algorithms and methods have been developed to segment Red Blood Cells (RBC), White Blood Cells (WBC) and counting the same. Generally, blood cell segmentation and counting methods include image acquisition, preprocessing to enhance the quality of the image and to remove noisy information and further to segment and count the number of various blood cells present in the image. The steps are as in Figure 8.

Preprocessing

The purpose of preprocessing of the images is to improve the quality of the image being processed. In the present work three preprocessing steps are used viz. grayscale conversion, histogram equalization and filtering to remove the noise from the input images.

Grayscale Conversion - RGB is a true color image, specified as 3-D numeric array whereas grayscale image, returned as a numeric array. Input image is read in RGB format. But for post processing, this image has to be converted into grayscale format.

Figure 8. Heuristic representation of proposed work

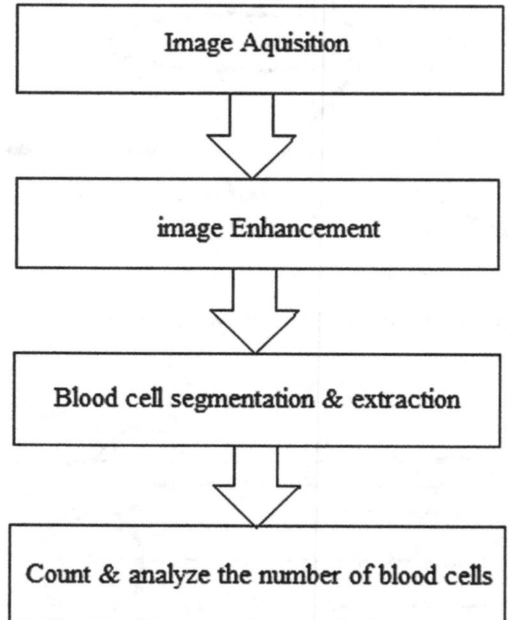

Histogram Equalization - The global contrast of images are usually increased by using histogram equalization, especially when the usable data of the image is represented by close contrast values. The intensities can be better distributed on the histogram through this adjustment. This allows to convert the areas of lower local contrast into gain a higher contrast. Histogram equalization accomplishes this by effectively spreading out the most frequent intensity values. In this section, we have used histogram equalization which enhances the contrast of the grayscale image.

Filtering - One of the important steps of preprocessing is noise filtering. Noise in input images may be added at the time of capturing the microscopic blood images. This noise may be due to the dust particles present on the blood slide during the preparation of the slides. During the preparation of the blood slidesThe blood slides While preparing the slides Here we have used adaptive median filtering method which removes noises from the input images (see Figure 10).

Image Segmentation

In the field of computer vision, image segmentation is a process of partitioning a digital image into set of pixels (i.e., multiple segments, also known as super pixels). The goal of segmentation is to represent the image in a more meaningful way and/or to simplify the analysis. Image segmentation is typically used to locate objects and boundaries such as lines, curves, etc. More precisely, in image segmentation process every pixel in an image have been assigned a label where same label share similar visual characteristics. The result of image segmentation is a multiple segments that collectively cover the entire image, or a set of contours extracted from the image. In a region each of the pixels is similar with respect to some characteristic or computed property, such as color, intensity, or texture.

SEGMENTATION OF BLOOD CELL IMAGES USING HOUGH TRANSFORM

The purpose of the present section is to describe a method to count the number of red blood cells in a given blood sample. For this we have applied various pre-processing techniques like edge detection, spatial smoothing filtering and adaptive histogram equalization for detection and extraction of the red blood cells from the images. Feature extraction has been done by using Hough Transform method which has been used to locate the red blood cells based on their sizes and their shapes. The advantages of the Hough transform over other segmentation techniques makes it attractive for the present application. Hough transform is very efficient to detect with short breaks in them due to noise, or when objects are partially occluded. This step isolates the red blood cells from the rest of the image of the blood sample so that further processes like counting can be applied exclusively on them.

Figure 11 shows the identification of RBCs by Hough Transform.

COUNTING

In the image field, after successful isolation of red blood cells we have applied a counter that has counted the number of RBCs. In medical terms blood count means the number of blood cells (RBC or WBC or Platelets) in a cubic millimeter of blood volume. Hence we have derived a formula to calculate the number of red blood cells per cumm based on the number of cells in the area of the given image of the

Figure 10. Pre-processed gray level images

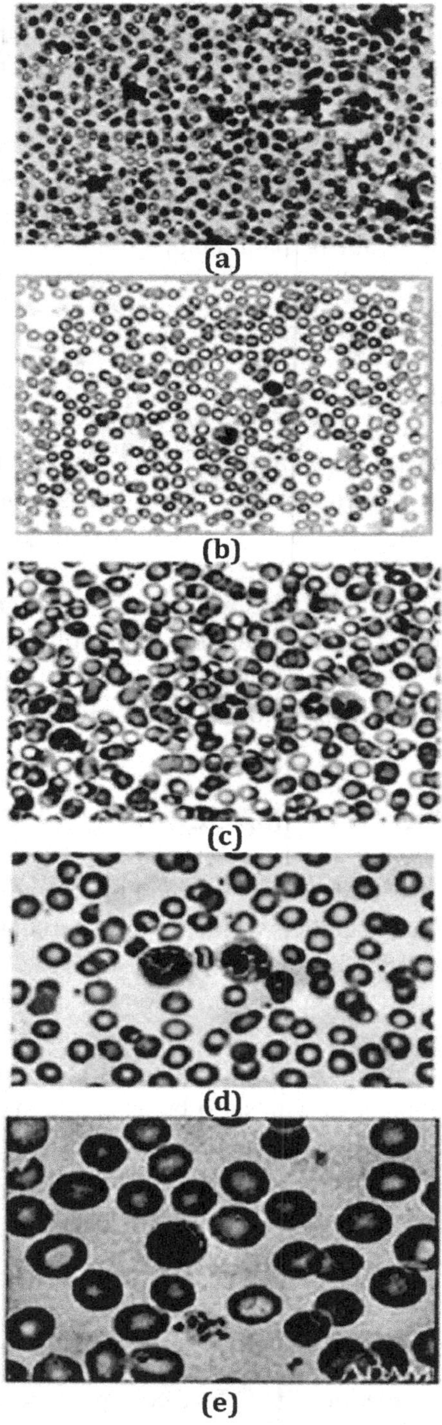

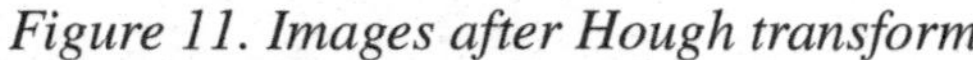

Figure 11. Images after Hough transform

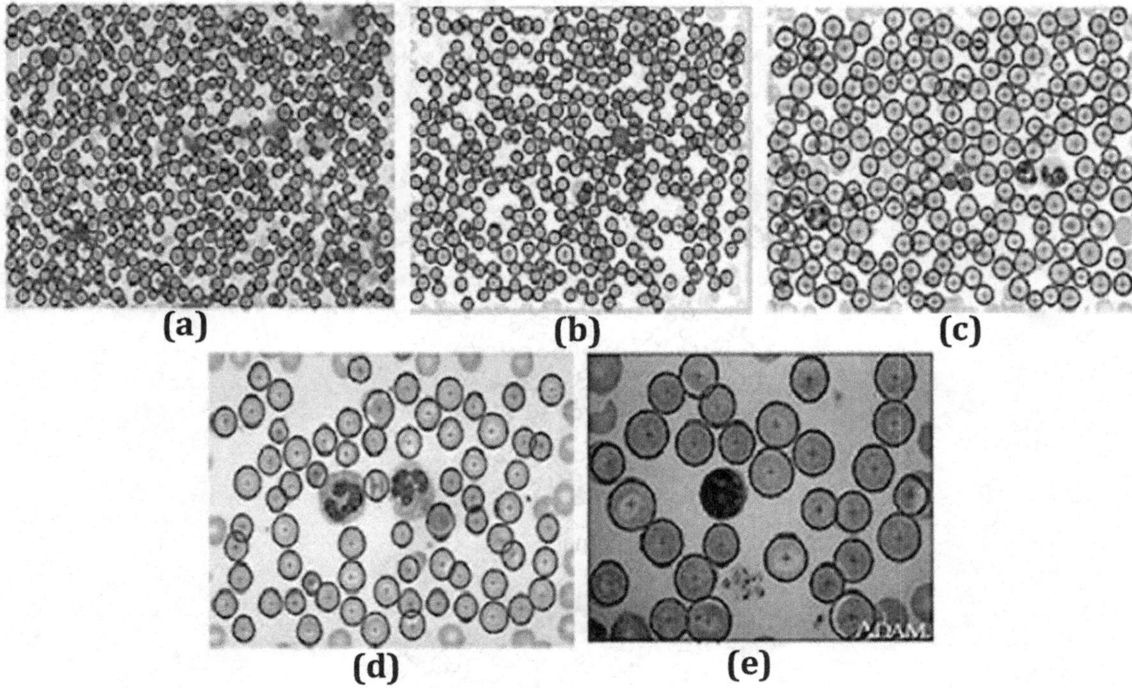

blood sample. We have assumed that the thickness of the blood sample film is 0.1 mm as standard medical practice. This allows for an overlapping of maximum two layers in thickness which is the common practice in the images provided in Figure 9. This formula requires an input for providing the magnification factor which is the magnification level under the microscope at which the image has been taken.

Volume of the blood sample is actually calculated with proper magnification factor (X and Y directions). Now such samples are usually diluted with an anticoagulant liquid to separate the cells to decrease overlapping. In such cases we have to multiply the count by the dilution factor. Considering these factors the formula for RBC count becomes:

Actual RBC count per cumm = (RBC counted by Hough Transform / ((input image area/(magnification * magnification)*film thickness))*dilution factor

RESULTS AND DISCUSSION

We have taken five blood cell images for our study. Each of the images is pre-processed by the above mentioned techniques. Finally the number of red blood cells were identified and counted in each of these images using Hough Transform. The results of our study have been discussed in Table 1 along with the different parameters used for each of the images. Table 2 shows the performance measurement comparing with the manual method and its graphical representation in Figure 12 shows the comparison performance very clearly.

Figure 9. Original blood cell

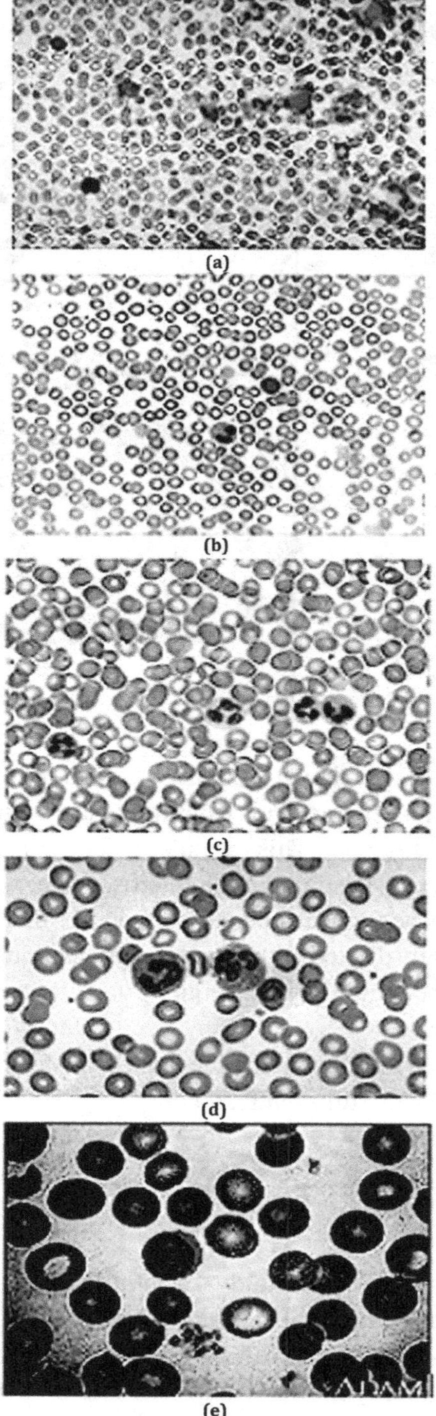

Table 1. Calculation of RBC using the proposed method

Image Samples	Magnification	Radius Range (in Pixel)	Dilution Factor	RBC Count by the Proposed Method per cumm (in Millions)
a	200*200	[2-14]	10	2.38
b	300*300	[5-18]	10	5.00
c	300*300	[5-14]	10	3.02
d	800*800	[5-25]	10	6.22
e	1000*1000	[5-18]	10	9.12

Table 2. Comparison of the result between the proposed method and the manual counting method

Image Samples	Radius Range (in Pixel)	Blood Counted Manually per cumm (in Millions)	Blood Counted Methodically per cumm (in Millions)
a	[2-14]	2.80	2.38
b	[5-18]	5.82	5.00
c	[5-14]	3.12	3.02
d	[5-25]	6.40	6.22
e	[5-18]	9.30	9.12

It is observed that the results obtained by the proposed method offer a good conformity with the manual counting method. In our method, we have ignored the cells that are not totally in the image field. However, in a real blood test where manually blood count is done, the practice is to count the cells on two adjacent edges of the image field and take each cell as one irrespective of how much of it is in the image field. It is assumed that two opposite sides have same number of such cells. As this edge correction has not been considered, by the proposed method in each of the samples the count values are slightly less than the count values obtained manually. The software must be modified to count those RBCs to obtain more accurate result.

Figure 12. Graphical representation of the results

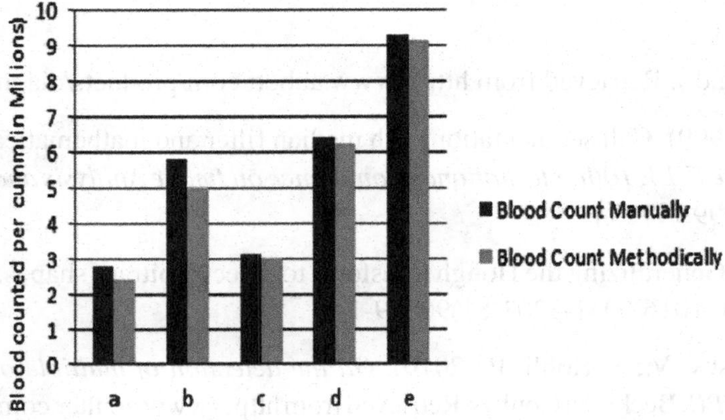

CONCLUSION

In medical diagnosis blood cell count plays a very important role. Increment or decrement in the count of blood cell causes many diseases to occur in the human body. There are different techniques of blood cell counting which involves conventional as well as automatic techniques. The conventional method of manual counting under microscope is time consuming and yields inaccurate results. The main problem arises when massive amounts of blood samples are required to be processed by the hematologist or Medical Laboratory Technicians. The time and skill required for the task limits the speed and accuracy with which the blood sample can be processed.

This chapter presents a methodology to achieve an automated detection and counting of red blood cells in microscopic images using Hough Transform. The advantage of the Hough transform over other segmentation techniques makes it attractive for the present application. Hough transform can detect the object in an image where the pixels lying on one line need not all be contiguous. This can be very useful when trying to detect lines with short breaks in them due to noise, or when objects are partially occluded. It is conceptually simple and can be easily implemented. It can handle missing and occluded data very gracefully and can be adapted to many types of forms, not just lines. Moreover, it is relatively unaffected by noise.

Results of the present study indicates that the counting of red blood cell in microscopic images offer remarkable accuracy. It can also identify overlapping blood cells and count them separately. However, the software must be modified to count the effective number of red blood cells which are partly in the image fields to obtain more accurate result. Further studies will be focused on complete blood cell count i.e. a total count of the number of red blood cells, white blood cells and platelets in the blood sample. This can be easily done by modifying the present software to take into account their different shapes and sizes.

Although there are hardware solutions such as the Automated Hematology Counter, they are not image based and destroy the blood samples during the analysis. Moreover, developing countries are not capable of organizing such unaffordable expensive machines in every hospital laboratory in the country. Proposed method is very cost-effective and can be easily implemented in medical facilities anywhere with minimal investment in infrastructure.

Therefore, this article aims to provide a user-friendly software based technique allowing for quick user interaction with a simple tool for the segmentation and identification of blood cells from a provided image.

REFERENCES

Abbott Diagnostics. (n.d.). Retrieved from http://www.abbott.com/products/diagnostics.htm/

Anoragaingrum, D. (1999). Cell segmentation with median filter and mathematical morphology operation. *Proceedings of the IEEE 10th International Conference on Image Analysis and Processing (ICIAP).* doi:10.1109/ICIAP.1999.797734

Ballard, D. H. (1981). Generalizing the Hough transform to detect arbitrary shapes. *Pattern Recognition, 13*(2), 111–122. doi:10.1016/0031-3203(81)90009-1

Barinova, O., Lempitsky, V., & Kohli, P. (2010). *On the detection of multiple object instances using Hough Transforms, CVPR*. Beckman Coulter. Retrieved from http://www.coulter.com/coulter/Hematology/

Bruce, A., Johnson, A., Lewis, J., Raff, M., Roberts, K., & Walter, P. (2002). *Leukocyte functions and percentage breakdown. In Molecular Biology of the Cell* (4th ed.). New York: Garland Science.

Choi, H., & Baraniuk, R. (2001). Multiscale: Image segmentation using wavelet-domain hidden Markov models. *IEEE Transactions on Image Processing*, *10*(9), 1309–1321. doi:10.1109/83.941855 PMID:18255546

Complete Blood Count. (n.d.). Retrieved from http://www.aidsinfonet.org/fact_sheets/view/121

Deb, N., & Chakraborty, S. (2014). A noble technique for detecting anemia through classification of red blood cells in blood smear. *Recent Advances and Innovations in Engineering*, *2014*, 1–9.

Duda, R. O., & Hart, P. E. (1972). Use of the Hough Transformation to Detect Lines and Curves in Pictures. *Communications of the ACM*, *15*(1), 11–15. doi:10.1145/361237.361242

Elaine, H., & Marieb, N. (2006). *Essentials of Human Anatomy & Physiology* (8th ed.). Pearson Benjamin Cummings.

Falcone, F., Haas, H., & Gibbs, B. (2000). The human basophil: A new appreciation of its role in immune responses. *Blood*, *96*(13), 4028–4038. PMID:11110670

Hari, J., & Prasad, A. S., & Rao, S.K. (2014). Separation and counting of blood cells using geometrical features and distance transformed watershed. *2nd International Conference on Devices, Circuits and Systems (ICDCS)*. doi:10.1109/ICDCSyst.2014.6926205

Hough, P. V. C. (1962). *Method and means for recognizing complex patterns*. U.S. Patent 3,069,654.

Jeacocke, & Lovell. (1994). A Multi-resolution algorithm for Cytological image segmentation. *The second Australian and New Zealand conference on intelligent information systems*.

Lehmann, T. M., Wein, B., Dahmen, J., Bredno, J., Vogelsang, F., & Kohnen, M. (2000). Content based image retrieval in medical applications: A novel multi step approach. *International Society for Optical Engineering*, *3972*, 312–320.

Leibe, B., Leonardis, A., & Schiele, B. (2008). Robust object detection with interleaved categorization and segmentation. *International Journal of Computer Vision*, *77*(1), 259–289. doi:10.1007/s11263-007-0095-3

Li-hui, Z., Chen, J., Zhang, J., & Garcia, N. (2010). Malaria Cell Counting Diagnosis within Large Field of View. *International Conference on Digital Image Computing: Techniques and Applications (DICTA)*.

Machlus, K. R., Thon, J. N., & Italiano, J. E. Jr. (2014). Interpreting the developmental dance of the megakaryocyte: A review of the cellular and molecular processes mediating platelet formation. *British Journal of Haematology*, *165*(2), 227–236. doi:10.1111/bjh.12758 PMID:24499183

Maitra, M., Gupta, R. K., & Mukherjee, M. (2012). Detection and Counting of Red Blood Cells in Blood Cell Images using Hough Transform. *International Journal of Computer Applications, 53*(16), 0975 – 8887.

Mazalan, S. M., Mahmood, N. H., & Mohd, A. A. R. (2013). Automated Red Blood Cells Counting in Peripheral Blood Smear Image Using Circular Hough Transform. *First IEEE International Conference on Artificial Intelligence, Modeling & Simulation*. doi:10.1109/AIMS.2013.59

Mazalan, S. M., Mahmood, N. H., & Razak, M. A. A. (2013). Automated Red Blood Cells Counting in Peripheral Blood Smear Image Using Circular Hough Transform. *1st International Conference on Artificial Intelligence Modelling and Simulation (Anaheim), 2013*, 320–324.

Medicine Health. (n.d.). Retrieved from http://www.medicinehealth.com/leukemia/article.html

Miswan, M. F. (2011). An Overview: Segmentation Method for Blood Cell Disorders. *5th Kuala Lumpur International Conference on Biomedical Engineering 2011*. Berlin: Springer. doi:10.1007/978-3-642-21729-6_148

Panda, D. P., & Rosenfeld, A. (1978). Image Segmentation by Pixel Classification in (Gray Level, Edge Value) Space. *IEEE Transactions on Computers*, *C-27*(9), 875–879. doi:10.1109/TC.1978.1675208

Piuri, V., & Scotti, F. (2004). Morphological classification of blood leucocytes by microscope images. *IEEE International conference on Computational Intelligence for Measurement Systems and Applications*.

Rosenfeld, A., & Davis, L. S. (1979). Image segmentation and image models. *Proceedings of the IEEE*, *67*(5), 764–772. doi:10.1109/PROC.1979.11326

Saladin & Kenneth. (2012). *Anatomy and Physiology: the Unit of Form and Function* (6th ed.). New York: McGraw Hill.

Shapiro, L., & Stockman, G. (2001). Computer Vision. Prentice-Hall, Inc.

Tangsuksant, W., Pintavirooj, C., Taertulakarn, S., & Daochai, S. (2013). Development algorithm to count blood cells in urine sediment using ANN and Hough Transform. *6th International Conference (BMEiCON) on Biomedical Engineering, 2013*. doi:10.1109/BMEiCon.2013.6687725

Venkatalakshmi, B., & Thilagavathi, K. (2013). Automatic Red Blood Cell Counting Using Hough Transform. *Proceedings of IEEE Conference on Information and Communication Technologies*. doi:10.1109/CICT.2013.6558103

Vinutha, H., & Reddy. (2014). Automatic Red Blood Cell and White Blood Cell Counting For Telemedicine System. *International Journal of Research in Advent Technology*, *2*(1).

Wu, K et al. (1995). Live cell image segmentation. *IEEE Transactions on Bio-Medical Engineering*, 1–12. PMID:7851922

Zamani, F., & Safabakhhsh, R. (2006). An Unsupervised GVF Snake Approach for White Blood Cell Segmentation Based on Nucleus. *The 8th International Conference on Signal Processing*.

Chapter 16
A Hybrid Complex Network Model for Wireless Sensor Networks and Performance Evaluation

Peppino Fazio
University of Calabria, Italy

Salvatore Marano
University of Calabria, Italy

Mauro Tropea
University of Calabria, Italy

Vincenzo Curia
University of Calabria, Italy

ABSTRACT

This chapter proposes a new approach, based on Complex Networks modeling, to alleviate the limitations of wireless communications. In fact, many recent studies have demonstrated that telecommunication networks can be well modeled as complex ones, instead of using the classic approach based on graph theory. The study of Complex Networks is a young and active area of scientific research, inspired largely by the empirical study of real-world networks, such as computers and social networks. The chapter contributes to the improvement of distributed communication, quantifying it in terms of clustering coefficient and average diameter of the entire network. The main idea consists in the introduction of Hybrid Data Mules (HDMs) that are able to enhance the whole connectivity of the entire network. The considered HDMs are equipped by "special" wireless devices, using two different transmission standards. The introduction of special nodes contributes to the improvement of network scalability, without substantial changes to the structure of the network.

1. INTRODUCTION AND BACKGROUND

The Internet architecture is today part of everybody's life, thanks to the great progress done in the technologies that allow the use of networks through different type of devices. Despite their different nature, technologies are born with the purpose of ensuring connectivity every-where and every-time: to send information, for example, we can use electromagnetic radiations in infrared frequency band, electric transmission lines or wireless devices, which take advantage of the ether. Since the ether is present everywhere in the world, it is reasonable to exploit the potentiality of this medium in order to use it as a mean of communication, on which information can travel.

DOI: 10.4018/978-1-4666-9964-9.ch016

This is a very good choice, although there are some limitations, due to its intrinsic nature and physical barriers to be overcame. It is a still open challenge for modern engineering: the limited coverage radius that the current IEEE's standards fail to ensure and the supply management of these devices give the majority of limitations. Other important issues are strictly related to higher-level management, such as data link and network operations (Fazio, 2012), that inherently are subject to interference and physical undesired phenomena. Reasonably, Wireless Sensor Networks (WSNs) (De Rango, 2013) are the subject to some kind of recent studies, given that they are applied for many kinds of applications in real life (Fazio, 2013).

Many recent research efforts have confirmed that, given the natural evolution of telecommunication systems, they can be approached by a new modeling technique, not based yet on traditional approach of graphs theory. The branch of complex networking (Yan, 2010), although young, is able to introduce a new and strong way of networks modeling, nevertheless they are social, telecommunication or friendship networks. Each network present in nature, whether artificial (as the national water supply network) or based on telecommunications, natural (such as brain synapses network) or relative to molecular interactions can be seen as a Complex Network (CN), if appropriately modeled. CNs represent a new paradigm to which the world (seen in its various disciplines of humanities, physical and scientific studies) is shifting.

It is necessary to find a modeling technique which allows us to model a real network as a Small World Network (SWN, a particular branch of CNs) (Guidoni, 2008; Huang, 2012; Xiaojuan & Huiqun, 2010), while maintaining a low network diameter and a high *CC*. Such networks are highly connected, because of their largest connected sub-graph contains a huge proportion of the vertices. For example, the Internet represents a SWN: we know that IP-packets cannot use more than a precise amount of physical links (equal to the value of their Time-To-Live field), thus the structure of the Internet has evolved in a graph with relatively small distances, even though it is rather large.

In this chapter, we propose a new approach, based on CN modeling, able to alleviate the limitations of wireless communications. In fact, many recent studies have demonstrated that telecommunication networks can be well modeled as complex ones, instead of using the classic approach based on graph theory. The study of CNs is a young and active area of scientific research, inspired largely by the empirical study of real-world networks such as computers and social networks. Our proposed modeling technique is applied to Wireless Sensor Networks (WSNs). The proposal has the main purpose of ensuring an improvement of the distributed communication, quantifying it in terms of clustering coefficient and average diameter of the entire network. The main idea consists in the introduction of Hybrid Data Mules (HDMs), able to enhance the whole connectivity of the entire network. As known from literature (Jiang, 2008), a Data MULE (DM) is a node (generally a vehicle with a storage-equipped computer) dedicated to the creation of a link among couple of remote nodes. The term MULE has initially born from the acronym Mobile Ubiquitous LAN Extension. In fact, the main DMs application consists in offering network connectivity to last-mile villages (Pentland, 2004). Our idea starts from this approach: computers with storage and Wi-Fi link (DMs) are attached to public vehicles (generally buses on bus routes) and, when the DM stops to pick-up or leave passengers, the data is exchanged from the on-board router to the infrastructure router, via Wi-Fi connection (let us think to e-mail downloading and uploading). This approach is typical of Delay Tolerant Networks (DTNs) (De Rango, 2014; De Rango, 2008). In this way, DMs can be thought as cost-effective mechanisms for rural connectivity, because they use inexpensive hardware, which can be quickly installed and piggybacked on existing transportation infrastructure. The use of DMs is extensively employed also in environmental monitoring, which represents a class of applications that can benefit from sensor networks (Mainwaring, 2002). In these scenarios, there is no need to have a dense sensor network, so a sparse network would be enough (with related low costs, due to the lower number of needed devices). On the other side, the distance among neighbor sensors may become too high and the communication may require a lot of energy to be done. DMs can help data collection, carrying data from sensors to the main infrastructure router. DMs can move randomly in time or following deterministic (predictable) routes. They are assumed power renewable, while static sensors are typically energy-constrained. Referring to a telecommunication network with dynamic topology, DMs are usually used to create shortcuts the position where data gets on the mule is the beginning of the shortcut, while the position where data gets off the mule is the end of the shortcut. The concept of DM shortcut is different from the traditional (wired) one: DMs carry data on-demand, that is to say when data needs to be forwarded; traditional shortcuts have fixed length and position, while DMs are moving nodes. As explained later, we consider hybrid nodes for obtaining a SWN, since we suppose that they are equipped by two radio interfaces.

The Milgram's approach, introduced in the sixties and largely proved in many experiments, gave a big contribution to the spread of CN theory. There are different modeling methods and we have chosen and tested the one proposed by D. Watts and S. Strogatz in the nineties (Erdős, 1960; Watts, 1998) and then spread by A.L. Barabasi in the first years of the new century (Albert, 2002), that allows to transform a WSN into a CN, by the re-wiring technique. This method provides the random deletion of some links of the network, between couple of adjacent nodes and, then, the connections are created again by randomly linking not adjacent and far nodes. So, the average communication distance between two nodes decreases, linking directly a smaller group of nodes. In our simulations, in order to reconsider really these links, we have equipped the public urban transporting vehicle (a bus) with a modem/router in 3G (or LTE) technology, creating long-range links between transportation vehicles, which represent shortcuts for far nodes. So, the proposed scheme is based on the utilization of public transport means (such as buses, trams and subways), used as DMs in our approach, in order to carry data within the network, interconnecting various network clusters, relatively far one from each other. The considered HDMs are equipped by "special" wireless devices, using two different transmission standards, guaranteeing a "double" action range, which permit to expand the scope of the entire SWN. The introduction of special nodes within the network, contributes to the improvement of network scalability, allowing the addition of new sensors nodes, without substantial changes to the structure of the network. The distribution degree of individual nodes in the network will follow a logarithmic trend, meaning that the most of the nodes are not necessarily adjacent but, for each pair of them, there exists a relatively short connecting path. The effectiveness of the proposed idea has been validated thorough a deep campaign of simulations, proving also the power of complex and small-world networks.

This chapter is structured as follows: in paragraph 2 the main contributions and related works on CNs, SWNs and HDMs are introduced, then in paragraph 3 the proposed idea is illustrated in all the main aspects. Paragraph 4 shows the simulation environment and the performance evaluation, while paragraph 5 summarizes the main conclusions and future trends.

2. STATE OF THE ART AND CONTRIBUTION

The concepts related to CNs have been deeply studied in the modern literature, in fact there are many works focusing their attention on some theories and applications of CNs. Many models have been proposed, as the one introduced by Albert and Barabasi in (Albert, 2002), in which an analogy with the structures of biological and social systems has been made. The authors studied the associations between ideas and concepts and with some artificial networks, including Internet and air routes; the model is famous for its ability to explain the evolution of these systems in terms of adding, removing and editing nodes (Boyd, 2007; Petrou, 2009).

The SWN concept has been investigated in (Verma, 2011), in which the authors deals also with the addition of a few Long-ranged Links (LLs), to significantly bring down the Average Path Length (APL) of the network. The authors introduced a more realistic small-world model, considering the real constraints of wireless networks such as the limited transmission range of LLs, and the limited available bandwidth for wireless links. At the end, they propose the Constrained Small-World Architecture for Wireless Network, evaluating the performance when adding LLs for reducing average APL. They shown that in moderately large WMNs, a 43% reduction in APL can be achieved.

Erdös-Rényi and Watts-Strogatz (Erdős, 1960; Watts, 1998) treated the problem of SW modeling: authors found that many already studied networks and systems (such as biological oscillators, excitable media, neural networks, spatial games, genetic control networks and many other self-organizing systems) can be highly clustered, like regular lattices, with a small characteristic path length, as for random graphs. These kind of networks are called SWNs (by analogy with the small-world phenomenon, popularly known as *six degrees of separation*).By the empirical experiments on CNs of the pioneers Euler and Milgram (Milgram, 1967), it has been shown that, in a network of any kind and form, the communication between two random nodes occurs (with information forwarding) through an average of six nodes before reaching its destination (small-world phenomenon). This is a useful concept, which allows us to analyze and evaluate the performance of a telecommunication network, in terms of efficiency and speed of data exchange. In (Guidoni, 2008), authors demonstrated how a WSN can be well approached by a SWN with two different approaches; as known, in a WSN there is a special node, called sink node, that is either the origin or the destination of a message, while the other types of data communications (relay activities for example) happen between arbitrary communicating entities. Authors found that sink node exhibits the most interesting tradeoff between energy and latency, allowing the design of strict applications that demand a small latency and energy consumption.

The Communications Letters (Guidoni, 2012) proposes to design heterogeneous sensor network topologies with Kleinberg's Small World (SW) model. The authors consider a model to create network shortcuts toward the sink node in order to optimize the communication flow between sink and sensor nodes. The considered end-points, in this model, are equipped with more powerful hardware, forming a heterogeneous sensor network. Many simulation campaigns are led-out in order to show that, the shortcuts toward the sink node, the network presents better small world features and a reduced latency in the data communication compared with the original Kleinberg model.

In (Androutsos, 2006), authors applied the concept of SW Indexing Method (SWIM) for image retrievals in a SW distributed media index. In their studies, they considered that each media object is only responsible for a small portion of the overall index, so the loss of portions of the overall network of data objects accounts for a small degradation in the retrieval procedure. They also introduced SW user agents on a large variety of MPEG-7 images. In (Jiang, 2008) authors investigated the effects of DM insertion in MANETs, instead of wire-lines, that are expensive and cannot be determined a-priori when dealing with mobile nodes. Authors have shown the main advantages reachable with the creation of shortcuts by DMs introduction. In this work, a novel approach for modeling WSNs as SWNs is introduced. It is based on the concept of DMs (called also ferries), that act as special nodes for the enhancement of the SW properties of the considered network. In particular, the authors made a simulation of the relationship between path-length and the numbers of added DMs.

In (Banerjee, 2012) the authors propose a self-organization framework for wireless ad hoc networks. The use of directional beam-forming for creating long-range short-cuts between nodes are investigated. Throughout simulation campaigns for randomized beam-forming the authors have individuated crucial design issues for algorithm design. They have proven that their proposal allows important path length reduction even if the problem of asymmetric paths between nodes is still present. In order to face with this issue they propose a distributed algorithm for small-world creation that achieves path length reduction while maintaining connectivity. These results are proven by a detailed simulation campaigns.

In (Chakraborty, 2014) the authors based their study on the Barabasi observation that states "the scale-free network is formed by preferential attachment of new nodes in the existing network". Therefore, a new node is more likely to make a connection with a node having higher neighbor degree in the network. They find that "greedy decision-making" is one of the key characteristics for the transformation of a regular network to a scale-free network. Moreover, they show that pure random addition of new links in a regular network does not result in a scale-free network.

The DM concept has been also used for addressing the problem of energy-efficient data collection in sparse WSNs. In fact, in (Jain, 2006), the authors investigate the impact on the data success rate, latency, and energy cost of a large set of operating parameters (such as data generation rate, sensor buffer size, etc.). In certain application scenarios, different DMs may be required to meet performance requirements. In (Jea, 2005), the authors research about the benefits of using load balancing techniques to assign sensors to DMs when different DMs are used, founding out that the used communication protocol plays an important role in energy management. In (Chakrabarti, 2003)a new protocol is proposed, relying on the assumption of circular transmission range, negligible message loss rate within the transmission range, and predictable DM arrival times.

Another key issue in CNs is related to scalability: different studies in literature investigate the dependence of this characteristic on network topology or, if we consider telecommunication systems, on adopted protocols or architecture. In particular in (Zhou, 2006; De Rango, 2006) the authors investigate about the scalability of wireless ad-hoc networks in terms of protocols. The same analysis is made in (De Rango 2009), with particular emphasis to vehicular networking, while in (Molinaro, 2005) an architectural analysis is carried on. Nowadays, the fundamental issue of network scalability is investigated in terms of dynamics and topology. It has been discovered that scalability depends on dynamical properties and network size. Scale-free networks are scalable for certain types of node dynamics.

As said before, starting from the empirical experiments on CNs by the Euler and Milgram, it can be concluded that "in a network of any kind and form, the communication between two random nodes occurs with information forwarding through an average of 6 nodes before reaching its destination". This is a useful concept, which allows us to analyze and evaluate the performance of a telecommunications networks, in terms of efficiency and speed of data exchange.

With the research activity introduced in this chapter, a new idea applied to a urban WSN is evaluated, increasing the range of action and the communication efficiency. In particular, the chapter contains the following contributions:

- Analysis of the main advantages arising from the introduction of DMs for a WSN;
- Proposal of a hybrid approach, focusing the attention on a double coverage (long and short) for the DM nodes; the traditional shortcut method of DM insertion is extended by the definition of double coverage devices, as illustrated in the next section;

- Implementation of real mobility patterns, instead of synthetic ones (random walk, random waypoint, etc.) which may lead to unrealistic results;
- Performance analysis on a real scenario and analysis of the trend of the main parameters related to a SWN.

3. SCENARIO AND HYBRID MODEL (HM) PROPOSAL

This paragraph is completely dedicated to the proposal of our HM. The idea is illustrated, after a brief set of definitions and a description of the main issues and parameters that have to be taken into account for the argumentation. In order to understand the advantages that can be gained by using HDM nodes, it is necessary to study different parameters and learn about the distribution degree of nodes within the network, with a complete understanding of the functionality of a generic network. As stated before, our main idea consists in the introduction of special nodes (instead of traditional ones), equipped with a long-range and short-range coverage devices. As known from literature, the parameters that have to be taken into account for CNs are three:

- **Average Network DIameter (ANDI):** Following the classical treatment about networks modeling, a network $G = (V, E)$ can be seen as a graph G, that consists of a set of n nodes $V = \{v_1, \ldots, v_n\}$, $||V||=n$ and a set of m edges E, $||E||=m$. Since the network might not be connected, following the definitions of (Chung, 2002; Chung, 2002.2), the average distance in the network can be considered as the average across pairs of path-connected nodes. If $n_l(i,j)$ is the number of links in the shortest path connecting nodes v_i and v_j (its value is infinity if no path exists between v_i and v_j). At this point, the AVerage DIstance (AVDI) of the network is defined as:

$$AVDI(E) = \frac{\sum_{\{v_i,v_j\}/n_l(i,j)\neq\infty} n_l(i,j)}{\{v_i,v_j\}/n_l(i,j)\neq\infty} \tag{1}$$

while the ANDI is:

$$ANDI(E) = \max_{\{i,j\}|n_l(i,j)\neq\infty} n_l(i,j) \tag{2}$$

- **Clustering Coefficient:** (*CC*, conceptually it is the probability of a node *A* to be connected to the node *B*, having as common neighbor a node *C*) By definition, it measures the tendency of two nodes adjacent to a common node to be connected each other, and it represents another important parameter when observing network properties. In practice, it indicates (locally) the connection ability of network nodes and it increases significantly the ANDI. The *CC* of the *i-th* node (indicated with cc_i) is:

$$c_i = \frac{e_i}{k_i(k_i-1)/2} \tag{3}$$

where e_i is the number of edges which interconnect *i's* neighbors and k_i is the number of *i's* neighbors. So, the *CC* of the entire network is defined as the average of all cc_i:

$$CC = \frac{1}{N}\sum_i cc_i C = \frac{1}{N}\sum_i c_i \tag{4}$$

- **Degree Distribution (*DD*):** In the study of networks and their related graphs, the degree of a node v_i, indicated with $\delta(v_i)$, is the number of connections, or edges, it has to other nodes. It can be indicated as:

$$\delta\left(v_i\right) = \sum_{v_j \in V} e_{v_i,v_j}, with\ e_{v_i,v_j} = \begin{cases} 1\ if \left\{v_i, v_j\right\} \in E \\ 0\ else \end{cases} \tag{5}$$

and *DD* is the probability distribution of these degrees over the whole network. The *DD(k)* of a network, generally indicated also with *P(k)*, is then defined to be the fraction of nodes in the network with degree *k*. Thus if $||V||=n$ and n_k nodes have degree *k*, then $DD(k) = n_k/n$. Generally *DD(k)* can be represented by a probability distribution or a pdf. The term $\delta(v_i)$provides an estimation of the importance of node *v* (it is called also degree centrality), related to the analyzed system domain and based on the number of nodes directly related with it. This concept is strictly related to *DD*. Generally, distributions like the Normal one are used but, from many studies, it has been shown that many real networks cannot follow this trend.

A SWN can contain billions of nodes, as an Internet connection: in order to move from one node to another, few intermediate nodes should be crossed. SWNs are called Random SWNs (*R-SWNs*) when the pdf of *DD(k)* is approximately Poissonian. So, it can be modeled by an exponential function ($pdf_{DD(k)} \sim exp(k)$). SWNs are also called Scale-Free (*SF*), if the pdf can be modeled by a power function ($pdf_{DD(k)} \sim k^c$), where *c* is a constant value. Figure 1 conceptually shows the difference between random and scale-free SWNs: humans often form scale-free networks where some people are very connected and then others are not. The more connected nodes in a SWN are called hubs or authorities.

Figure 1. An intuitive representation of random and scale-free SWNs

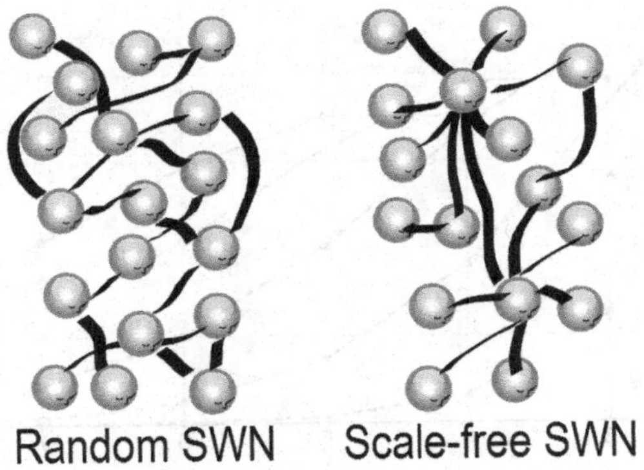

In (Albert, 2002) it is shown that a network can be classified as CN, more precisely SWN, if it has a high *CC* (necessary condition) and a small ANDI, with a consequent average path length equal, approximately, to six (quantified in hops number). Figure 2 shows the trend of the Poisson pdf for Random Networks, while Figure 3 shows the trend of the Power law, with c=2.6.

Regarding the Euler and Milgram's rule about the six degrees of separation, many discussions about the intrinsic meaning of that rule have been made, as in (Backstrom, 2012), showing that in some particular cases, four degrees are enough to describes the particular relationship existing among two nodes. In fact, in (Backstrom, 2012) it is stated that we have to think of the two points as being not five persons apart, but 'five circles of acquaintances' apart—five 'structures' apart." In this sense, people are in fact only four world apart, and not six: on the average, when considering another person in the world, a friend of your friend knows a friend of their friend.

To the aim of our proposal, since $0 \leq CC \leq 1$, a value near to 1 indicates a high connection between neighboring nodes (obviously in a fully connected network this value is exactly equal to 1). Therefore, the first step is to develop a mathematical model with some statistical properties "similar" to the ones of SWN; in this way, it is possible to obtain a platform on which it is possible to perform some mathematical analysis. For the proposed HM, we start from a real regular network (already existing) and, then, we model it in order to consider the obtained topology as a CN (SWN in particular). It will have an average path length L near to six (we based our idea on the classical Milgram's theory) and an average clustering coefficient near to one (as desired). As stated before, natural systems (regular or random) presents complex properties related to internal connections of nodes: traditional network models are not able to express the "complexity" of their connections, so CNs are chosen to do that, by modifying the layout of the starting network. The modeling technique suggested in this chapter has the purpose of shaping

Figure 2. Different trends of DD pdf for random network with different parameter values

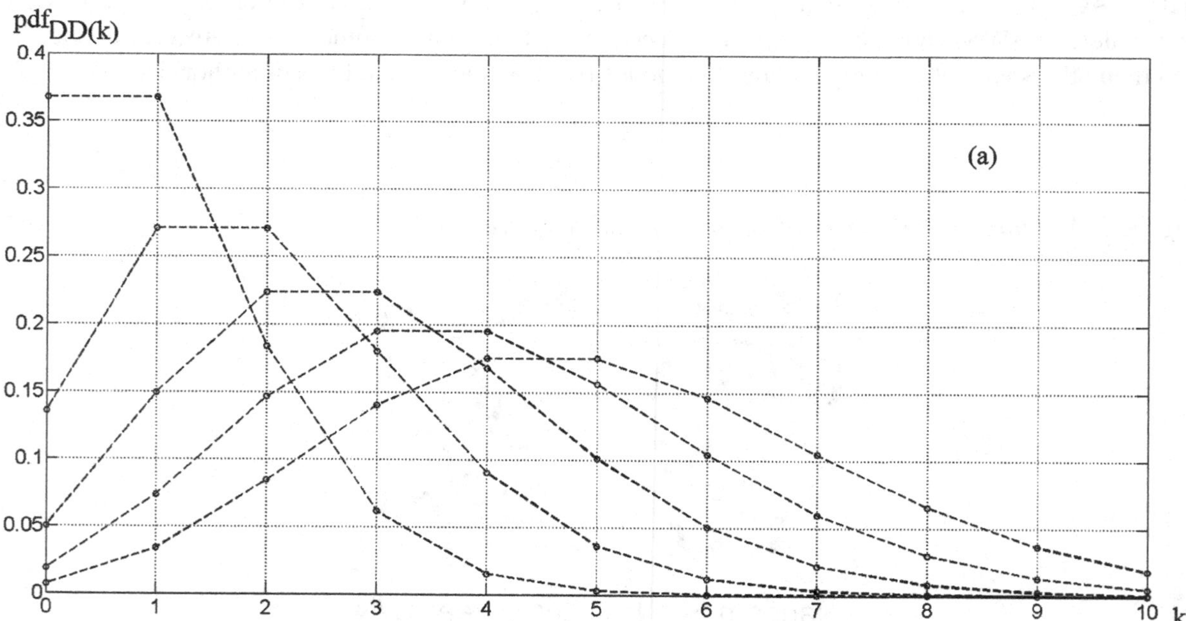

Figure 3. Different trends of DD pdf for scale-free network with different parameter values

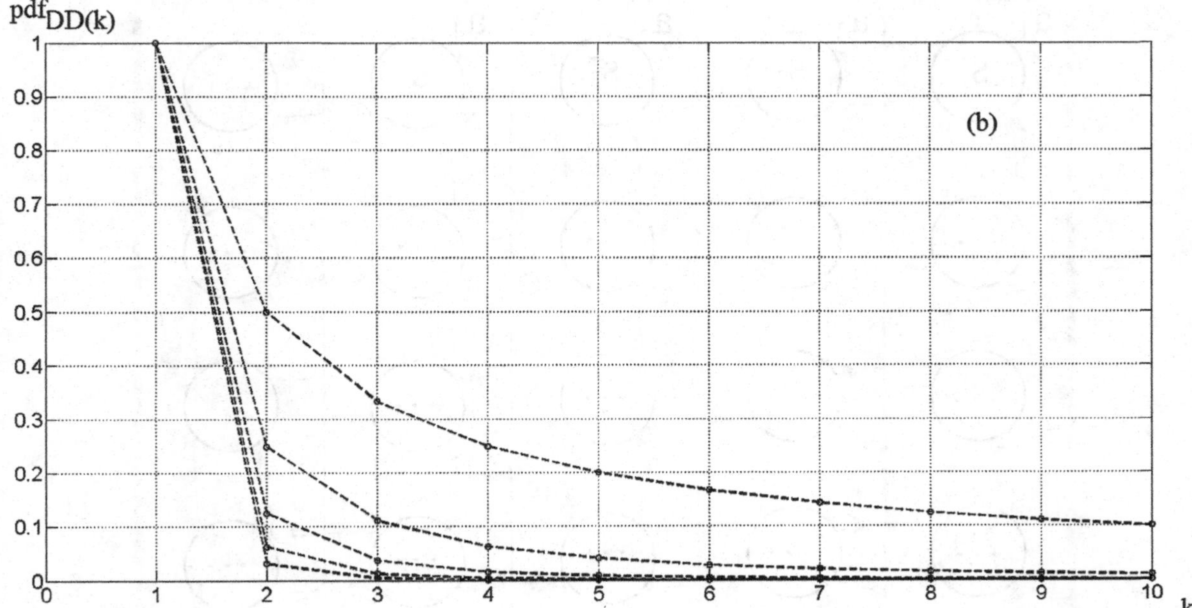

a real WSN in a CN with the SW property, with all the benefits that this kind of modeling can carry to the network, in terms of safety, speed and connection stability.

In this chapter, we describe a HM. It is based on DMs insertion (Jiang, 2008) and it considers two types of nodes. One node composed by traditional DMs (urban buses, metropolitan vehicles for example) and the second one composed by nodes with double coverage range (for example, based on two interfaces with different power or two different technologies); we demonstrate that, in this way, it is possible to increase *CC*, with a consequent decrease in the average path length. Depending on the considered mobility model, there are two ways to realize the DM insertion.

If we are considering "deterministic" networks in which, for example, urban buses and sensors follow standard roads, we can decide what route these nodes should follow in order to obtain a complex structure (without deleting routes casually). In this way, DM routes are known and deterministic.

If we are considering a "non-deterministic" network in which, for example, accidents or fires happen in random points or in which sensors are deployed casually, we should investigate on the number (and/or the position) of mules to insert, for reducing battery consumptions (De Rango, 2012; De Rango, 2013) and coverage radius. In this last case, a markovian process (Fazio & Tropea, 2012; Fazio, 2013 November) can describe DMs movements, for example. In particular, Discrete Markov Chain Models (DMCMs) can be considered for this purpose. First of all the geographical area is subdivided in a discrete number of regions, then a state of the chain is associated to each region. That is, given a geographical area A, it can be described as $A=\{a_1, a_2, ..., a_Z\}$, where a_i, $i=1,..,z$, are the considered adjacent zones, as illustrated in Figure 4.

Figure 4. Geographical map subdivision and the associated Markov states

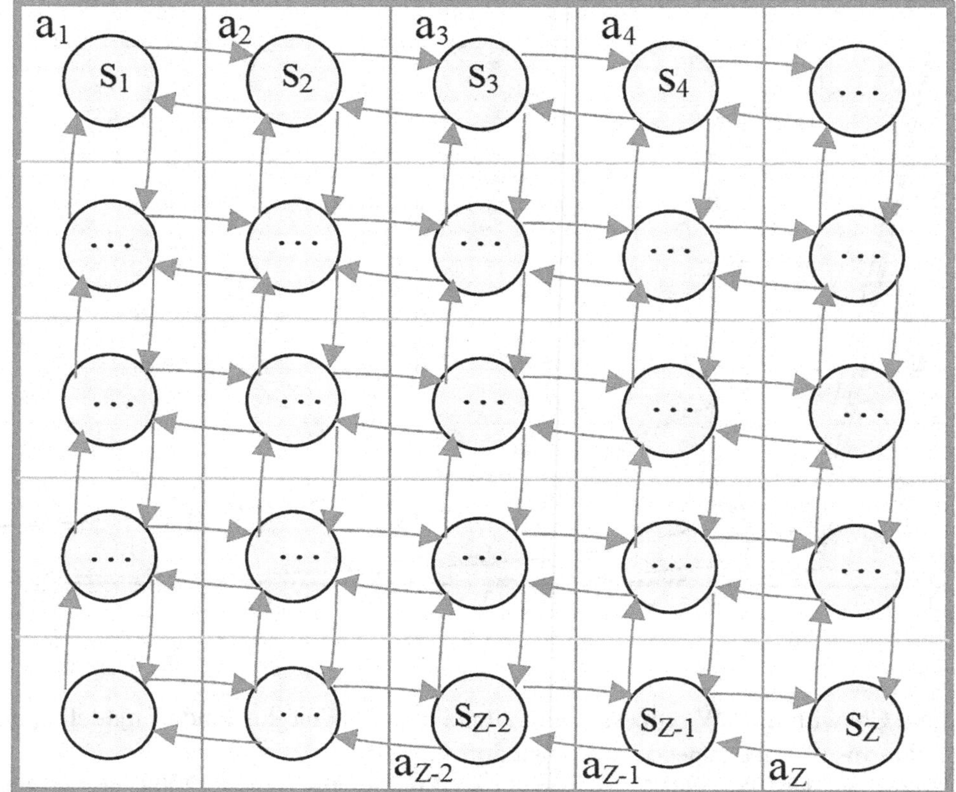

Associating a state $s_i \in S$, where $S=\{s_1,...,s_z\}$ is the set of the considered Markov chain states, to a zone $a_i \in A$, then it is possible to define the DM transition probability p_{ij}, from state s_i to state s_j (the probability of movement of DM from a_i to a_j):

$$p_{ij} = \begin{cases} \dfrac{1}{q_i}, & \text{If } s_i \text{ and } s_j \text{ are adjacent} \\ 0, & \text{Otherwise} \end{cases} \tag{6}$$

where q_i is the number of adjacent areas of a_i and each state $s_i \in S$ represents the condition related to the presence of a DM in a specific area.

By the application of Watts-Strogatz's algorithm, it is possible to reduce the average path-length from $L=n$ to $L'=log(n)$, where n is the number of nodes. So, considering a sensor network composed by n nodes, with an average DD equals to k, with $n>>k>>ln(n)>>1$, the related graph $G=<V,E>$ with nk/2 edges ($||E||=nk/2$) can be obtained by following the Watts-Strogatz's algorithm. Each node is connected until a regular ring network is obtained, where the n nodes are linked to k neighbors, so $k/2$ for each side. Remembering that $V=\{v_1,\ldots,v_n\}$, with $||V||=n$, then the edge $e_i=(v_i,v_j)$ will exist if and only if:

$$0 < \left|i-j\right| \bmod \left(n-\frac{k}{2}\right) \leq \frac{k}{2} \tag{7}$$

At this point, for each node v_i, the edge $e_i=(v_i,v_j)$ with $i<j$ is removed and rewired with a certain probability β, where $0<\beta<1$. If the rewiring is made, the old link e_i is replaced by link $e_t=(v_i,v_t)$, where t is chosen uniformly, in order to avoid loops and link duplications.

During the analysis of real cases, it is possible to achieve the goal of path-length reduction by exploiting the urban buses and the mobile routers (as HDMs), equipped with a double radio coverage system. As shown later, it is possible to reach high values of *CC* and lower values of *L*. Intuitively, the number of mobile nodes to insert within the network has an upper bound, which varies according to the physical size of the entire network.

So, HDMs are means that allow to rewire links, adding new shortcuts, without removing any existing node. The main objective of the HM proposal is to model any existing network as a SWN, with CC $\rightarrow$ 1 and route's average length L$\approx$6, as learned from Milgram's experiences (Milgram, 1967). HDMs, in fact, are not only mobile nodes, but are transmission devices with an increased range: this additional condition makes possible to create some long-range links between different DMs added in the network, drastically reducing the average path length *L*, bringing it at the right condition (near to 6). The special nodes can be implemented by Wi-Fi router with MIMO standard, which use different IEEE standard transmissions as IEEE 802.11n for short-range links (coverage radius *r*) and UMTS for long-range links (coverage radius r_u).

4. PERFORMANCE ANALYSIS AND SIMULATION RESULTS

Different simulation campaigns have been carried on in order assess the effectiveness of the proposed idea. First of all a Java simulator has been implemented, able to describe the behavior of a network and to verify the described proposal. It consists of a multi-thread system, based on real maps, extracted from OpenStreetMap (Open Street Map, 2015) and SUMO (SUMO, 2015). In this way, node movements are forced to follow real roads, giving the possibility to obtain more realistic results. We considered two different maps regarding Cosenza (south Italy) and Paris (France), with the same maximum size of 630x1150 m^2. Figure 5 shows the couple of considered maps. Given the maps, we considered "deterministic" networks.

In our Java tool, the Graph class has been created, recording every movement of each node and saving the information in a matrix adjacency structure. The pattern is based on one or more objects, called observers (or listeners) that are registered to handle an event that could be generated by the "observed" object. The simulation results are shown before and after the DMs insertion. Simulations have been performed for:

1. Density calculation,
2. Calculation of the average path length with only sensor nodes,
3. Calculation of the average path length by varying the number of special nodes,
4. Evaluation of the trend of the clustering coefficient.

Figure 5. Geographical map subdivision and the associated Markov states

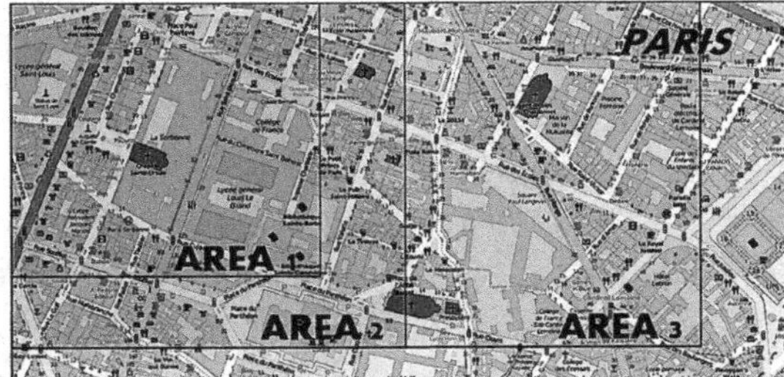

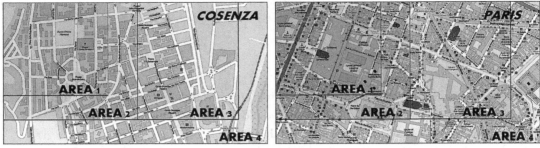

A short coverage range of [70, 100] meters has been considered (we do not specify a particular technology):we assume that fixed sensor nodes can extend their coverage within those values, also on the basis of the path-loss and fading phenomena. As DMs we assumed that public transportation vehicles (such as buses) can be equipped with a standard interface (the same of the sensor nodes) and an extended one (such as 3G or 4G connection). In this way, as shown in the curves, isolated islands of sensors can be connected with a lower number of hops, obtaining a gain in terms of energy consumption. A preliminary campaign has been carried out in order to evaluate the density of the graph for different map dimensions, avoiding considering scattered networks in the whole campaign. In particular, we considered four different areas of simulation: Area 1 of 400x400 m^2 (minimum extension), Area 2 of 550x550 m^2, Area 3 of 550x900 m^2 and Area 4 of 630x1150 m^2 (maximum extension). For the preliminary campaign, the coverage range has been set to 90m.

From Figure 6, it is possible to see, only as example, the typical values of the average shortest path length L for different area extensions, without the corrections introduced by DMs. When special nodes are inserted into the system, we can observe that we get the expected gains since we have a substantial decrease in the average length of the shortest path. In fact, from Figure 7, it can be seen how there is huge decrease in the L value. In addition, we can notice how there exists an upper bound of the number of DMs to be included within the considered network. It has no sense adding a number of special nodes higher than 9 or 10. It is clear, furthermore, that the variation of L, is very similar in the different scenarios.

Let now see what happens to the system in terms of *CC* (Figure 8). It represents another key feature in CNs, indicating the ability of a network to create a certain number of SWs. Special HM, once applied, tends to slightly increase this value compared to the one of the original network.

The maximum gain is about two percentage points. As stated before, a value of *CC* near to 1 indicates a high connection between neighboring nodes (obviously, in a fully connected network, such value is equal to 1).

Figure 9 shows a comparison among the traditional DM insertion method and the proposal of HDMs. In particular, we fixed the map (Paris), the number of added DMs to 10, as suggested by Figure 7, the short coverage range (R_1) to 100meters (the same range for all fixed sensors). We analyzed what happens to the system in terms of L and *CC* when the long coverage range (R_2) is varied into the set [100, 400] meters.

It is clear that, in respect of the traditional ferries insertion, there is no dependence on R_2. In fact, for both L and *CC* there is a constant trend: the average value are 16.1 (hops number) and 0.512 respectively. For the HDM case, the trend of the curves is heavily affected by R_2: for higher values of R_2, each added

Figure 6. Average shortest path length in the network without special hubs

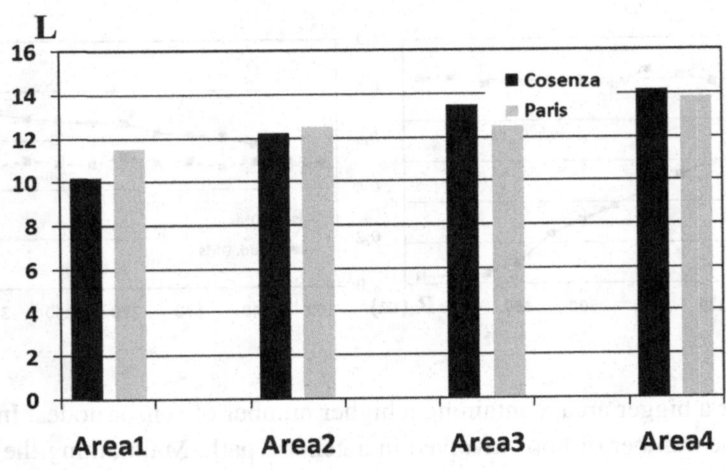

Figure 7. Average shortest path length in the network with special hubs
Cosenza and Paris cases.

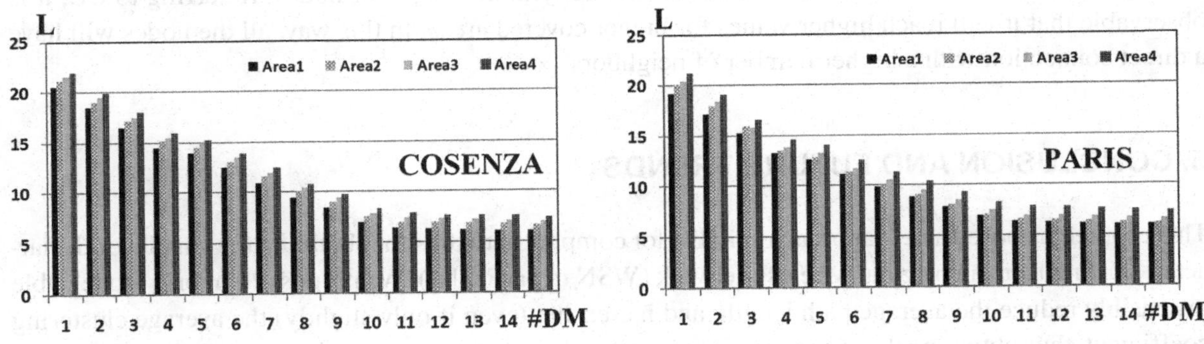

Figure 8. The trend of the average CC with and without HDMs for Cosenza (CS) and Paris (PA)

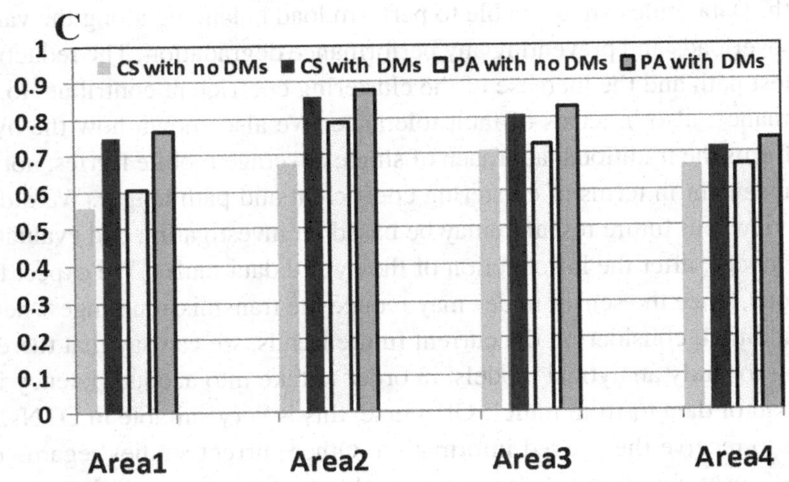

Figure 9. The trend of the average of L and CC in function of R_2

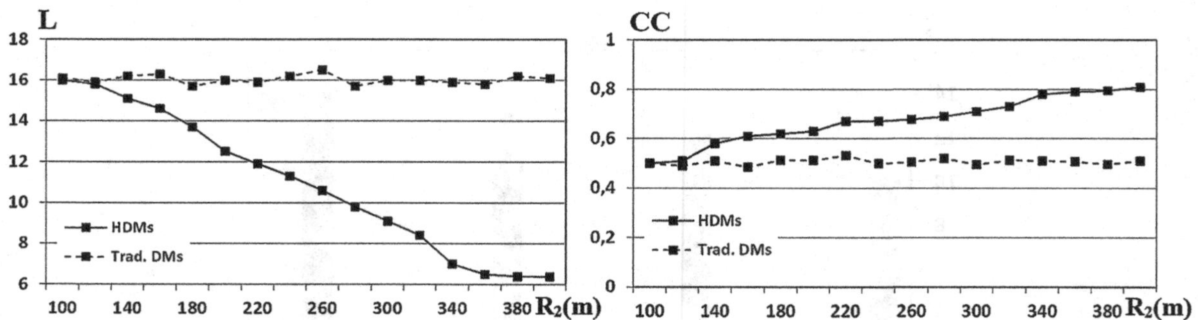

HDM is able to cover a bigger area, containing a higher number of sensor nodes. In this way, there is a heavy reduction of the number of hops involved in a generic path. Maintaining the same map size and increasing more the value of R_2 (over the value of 400 meters) the system will reach a value of L equal to 2, because each HDM will be able to connect directly source and destination nodes. The decreasing trend will also reflect on the energetic point of view: all the nodes can decrease the transmission power, because the HDM nodes will be able to connect directly more couple of nodes. Referring to *CC*, it is observable that it will reach higher values for bigger covered areas. In this way, all the nodes will have a direct connection with a higher number of neighbors.

5. CONCLUSION AND FUTURE TRENDS

This chapter proposed a new approach suitable for complex networks for obtaining the small world character, starting from an original wireless network (WSN in particular). We proposed a hybrid model, able to sensibly reduce the average path length, and increasing (even if only slightly) the average clustering coefficient, thus obtaining those characteristics that mark the complex networks as small-world. The core idea consists of the introduction of hybrid nodes, that is to say data mules equipped with a dual coverage interface. Gaining the small world property may be advantageous, especially for the reduction of the shortest path length. Data mules are also able to perform load balancing along the various paths of the network, avoiding overloads and preventing any performance degradation. The reduction of the average length of the shortest path and the increase of the clustering coefficient contribute to the enhancement of network performance, also in terms of fault tolerance. We also shown how the hybrid behavior of data mules outperforms the traditional approach of single coverage mobile ferries, not able to introduce an additional enhancement in terms of clustering coefficient and path length. We did not consider the energetic point of view, but future research may be based on investigating and evaluating the energetic behavior of sensor nodes, after the introduction of the hybrid data mules. We expect that batteries will have longer durations, since the sensor nodes may reduce the transmission range when under coverage of data mules. In addition, considering the current future trends, we can say that there are many works in literature tending to study analytical models, in order to take into account latency issues, due to the upload and download of data to/from mules. Of course, this is very suitable in DTNs, where nodes are able to spend time to receive the needed information. Other current studies regards the possibility of implementing peer-2-peer communication protocols, able to give the possibility to mobile data mules to exchange some signaling messages, aimed at the optimization of upload/download operations. Additional works regards the possibility to increase the sensor sleep time, without the needing of staying continuously in listening mode to find-out if a mule is under coverage.

REFERENCES

Albert, R., & Barabási, A.-L. (2002). Statistical mechanics of complex networks. *Reviews of Modern Physics*, *74*(1), 47–97. doi:10.1103/RevModPhys.74.47

Androutsos, P., Androutsos, D., & Venetsanopoulos, A. N. (2006). A distributed fault-tolerant MPEG-7 retrieval scheme based on small world theory.Multimedia. *IEEE Transactions on*, *8*(2), 278–288.

Backstrom, L., Boldi, P., Rosa, M., Ugander, J., & Vigna, S. (2012, June). Four degrees of separation. In *Proceedings of the 4th Annual ACM Web Science Conference* (pp. 33-42). ACM. doi:10.1145/2380718.2380723

Banerjee, A., Agarwal, R., Gauthier, V., Yeo, C. K., Afifi, H., & Lee, F. B. (2012). A self-organization framework for wireless ad hoc networks as small worlds.Vehicular Technology. *IEEE Transactions on*, *61*(6), 2659–2673.

Boyd, D., Ellison, N. (2007). Social Network Sites: Definition, History, and Scholarship. *Journ. of Computer-Mediated Comm., 13*, article 11.

Chakrabarti, S. A., & Aazhang A. (2003). Using PredictableObserver Mobility for Power Efficient Design of Sensor Networks. *Proc. IPSN 200.*

Chakraborty, A., & Manoj, B. S. (2014). The Reason Behind the Scale-Free World. *Sensors Journal, IEEE*, *14*(11), 4014–4015. doi:10.1109/JSEN.2014.2351414

Chung, F., & Lu, L. (2002). The average distances in random graphs with given expected degrees. *Proceedings of the National Academy of Sciences of the United States of America*, *99*(25), 15879–15882. doi:10.1073/pnas.252631999 PMID:12466502

Chung, F., & Lu, L. (2002). Connected components in random graphs with given expected degree sequences. *Annals of Combinatorics*, *6*(2), 125–145. doi:10.1007/PL00012580

De Rango, F., Amelio, S., & Fazio, P. (2013). Enhancements of epidemic routing in delay tolerant networks from an energy perspective. *9th International Wireless Communications and Mobile Computing Conference, IWCMC 2013*. doi:10.1109/IWCMC.2013.6583647

De Rango, F., Amelio, S., & Fazio, P. (2014). Epidemic Strategies in Delay Tolerant Networks from an Energetic Point of View: Main Issues and Performance Evaluation. Journal of Networks, 10(1), 4-14.

De Rango, F., Gerla, M., & Marano, S. (2006). A scalable routing scheme with group motion support in large and dense wireless ad hoc networks. *Computers & Electrical Engineering*, *32*(1), 224–240. doi:10.1016/j.compeleceng.2006.01.017

De Rango, F., Guerriero, F., & Fazio, P. (2012). Link-stability and energy aware routing protocol in distributed wireless networks.Parallel and Distributed Systems. *IEEE Transactions on*, *23*(4), 713–726.

De Rango, F., Tropea, M., Laratta, G. B., & Marano, S. (2008). Hop-by-Hop Local Flow Control over InterPlaNetary Networks Based on DTN Architecture. In *Communications, IEEE International Conference on*. doi:10.1109/ICC.2008.368

De Rango, F., Veltri, F., Fazio, P., & Marano, S. (2009). Two-level trajectory-based routing protocol for vehicular ad hoc networks in freeway and Manhattan environments. *Journal of Networks*, *4*(9), 866–880. doi:10.4304/jnw.4.9.866-880

Erdős, P., & Rényi. (1960). *On the evolution of random graphs*. Mathematical Institute of the Hungarian Academy of Sciences.

Fazio, P., De Rango, F., & Sottile, C. (2012). An on demand interference aware routing protocol for VANETS. *Journal of Networks*, *7*(11), 1728–1738. doi:10.4304/jnw.7.11.1728-1738

Fazio, P., De Rango, F., Sottile, C., & Santamaria, A. F. (2013). Routing optimization in vehicular networks: A new approach based on multiobjective metrics and minimum spanning tree. *International Journal of Distributed Sensor Networks*, *2013*, 1–13. doi:10.1155/2013/598675

Fazio, P., & Tropea, M. (2012). A new markovian prediction scheme for resource reservations in wireless networks with mobile hosts. *Advances in Electrical and Electronic Engineering*, *10*(4), 204–210. doi:10.15598/aeee.v10i4.716

Fazio, P., Tropea, M., Marano, S., & Sottile, C. (2013, November). Pattern prediction in infrastructured wireless networks: Directional vs temporal statistical approach. In *Wireless Days (WD), 2013 IFIP* (pp. 1-5). IEEE.

Guidoni, D. L., Mini, R. A., & Loureiro, A. A. (2012). Applying the small world concepts in the design of heterogeneous wireless sensor networks. *Communications Letters, IEEE*, *16*(7), 953–955. doi:10.1109/LCOMM.2012.052112.120417

Guidoni, D. L., Mini, R. A. F., & Loureiro, A. A. F. (2008). Creating small-world models in wireless sensor networks. *Personal, Indoor and Mobile Radio Communications, PIMRC, IEEE 19th International Symposium on*. doi:10.1109/PIMRC.2008.4699823

Huang, J., Xie, Q., & Huang, B. (2012). Creating Small-World Model for Homogeneous Wireless Sensor Networks. *Wireless Communications, Networking and Mobile Computing (WiCOM), 8th International Conference on*. doi:10.1109/WiCOM.2012.6478470

Jain, S., Shah, R., Brunette, W., Borriello, G., & Roy, S. (2006). ExploitingMobility for Energy Efficient Data Collection in Wireless Sensor Networks. ACM/Springer. *Mobile Networks and Applications*, *11*(3), 327–339. doi:10.1007/s11036-006-5186-9

Jea, D., Somasundra, A., & Srivastava, M. (2005). Multiple ControlledMobile Elements (Data Mules) for Data Collection in SensorNetworks. *Proc. IEEE DCOSS 2005*.

Jiang, C. J., Chen, C., Chang, J. W., Jan, R. H., & Chiang, T. C. (2008, June). Construct small worlds in wireless networks using data mules. In *Sensor Networks, Ubiquitous and Trustworthy Computing, 2008. SUTC'08. IEEE International Conference on* (pp. 28-35). IEEE. doi:10.1109/SUTC.2008.93

Luo, X., & Yu, H. (2010). Constructing wireless sensor network model based on small world concept. *Advanced Computer Theory and Engineering (ICACTE), 3rd International Conference on*.

Mainwaring, A., Polastre, J., Szewczyk, R., Culler, D., & Anderson, J. (2002). Wireless Sensor Networks for Habitat Monitoring. *Proc. ACM WSNA*. doi:10.1145/570738.570751

Milgram, S. (1967). The small world problem. *Psychology Today*, *2*(1), 60–67.

Molinaro, A., De Rango, F., Marano, S., & Tropea, M. (2005). A scalable framework for in IP-oriented terrestrial-GEO satellite networks. *Communications Magazine, IEEE*, *43*(4), 130–137. doi:10.1109/MCOM.2005.1421916

Open Street Map. (2015). Retrieved from https://www.openstreetmap.org/

Pentland, S. A., Fletcher, R., & Hasson, A. (2004). DakNet: Rethinking Connectivity in Developing Nations. *IEEE Computer*, *37*(1), 78–83. doi:10.1109/MC.2004.1260729

Petrou, M., & Tabacchi, M. E. (2009). Networks of concepts and ideas. *The Computer Journal*.

SUMO Mobility Manager. (2015). Retrieved from http://sourceforge.net/projects/sumo/

Verma, C. K., Tamma, B. R., Manoj, B. S., & Rao, R. (2011). A realistic small-world model for wireless mesh networks. *Communications Letters, IEEE*, *15*(4), 455–457. doi:10.1109/LCOMM.2011.020111.100266

Watts, D. J., & Strogatz, S. H. (1998). Collective dynamics of 'small-world' networks. *Nature*, *393*(6684), 440–442. doi:10.1038/30918 PMID:9623998

Yan, C., & Qiao. (2010). Application analysis of complex adaptive systems for WSN. *Computer Application and System Modeling (ICCASM), International Conference on* (vol. 7).

Zhou, B., Lee, Y. Z., Gerla, M., & De Rango, F. (2006). Geo-LANMAR: A scalable routing protocol for ad hoc networks with group motion. *Wireless Communications and Mobile Computing*, *6*(7), 989–1002. doi:10.1002/wcm.433

Chapter 17
A Network Analysis Method for Tailoring Academic Programs

Luis Casillas
University of Guadalajara, Mexico

Thanasis Daradoumis
University of the Aegean, Greece & Open University of Catalonia, Spain

Santi Caballe
Open University of Catalonia, Spain

ABSTRACT

Producing or updating an academic program implies a significant effort: involving people, academic units, knowledge elements, regulations, institutions, industry, etc. Such effort entails a complexity related to the volume of elements involved, the diversity of the origins of contributions, the diversity of formats, the representation of information, and the required granularity. Moreover, such effort is a common task performed by humans who collaborate for long periods of time participating in frequent meetings in order to achieve agreement. New educational approaches are heading to adaptive, flexible, ubiquitous, asynchronous, collaborative, hyper-mediated, and personalized strategies based on modern Information and Communication Technologies (ICT). We propose an approach for tailoring academic programs to provide a practical and automated method to discover and organize milestones of knowledge through the use of Complex Networks Analysis (CNA) techniques. Based on indicators from CNA, the act of tailoring an academic program acquires meaning, structure and even body elements.

INTRODUCTION

As most people would agree, there is a continuous digital revolution due to advances in computational capabilities, effective communication protocols, new understanding on data managing/mining/sharing as well as distributed programming approaches; which have allowed achieving standardize new ways to carry out common computer tasks, all over the world. As a consequence, societies nowadays have specific demands on digital services, so significant amounts of knowledge elements have been digitalized. In

DOI: 10.4018/978-1-4666-9964-9.ch017

the same way, current web-infrastructure is able to support new approaches in scientific and academic developments (Isaila, 2012). In educational institutions, academic programs are the mechanism to manage and lead scientific and academic efforts. Such programs require regular updating in order to provide certainty to students, institutions, industry, and even to society.

Updating an academic program implies a significant effort, involving people, academic units, knowledge pieces, regulations, institutions, industry, and etcetera. Such effort entails a complexity related to the volume of elements involved, the diversity of the origins of contributions, the diversity of formats and representation of information, and the required granularity. Moreover, such effort is a common task performed by humans who collaborate for long periods of time participating in frequents meetings in order to achieve agreement. A preliminary work that aimed to develop an automated method for tailoring academic programs was performed in (Casillas & Castillo, 2012). Here, the authors extend this previous work, by including new formalizations and features that leaded to a more integrated and effective approach to model and customize academic programs.

Indeed, the new educational approaches are heading to adaptive, flexible, ubiquitous, asynchronous, collaborative, hyper-mediated, and personalized strategies based on modern information and communication technologies (ICT). This approach for tailoring academic programs, focuses on providing a practical and automated method to discover and organize milestones of knowledge, through the use of Complex Networks Analysis (CNA) techniques (Newman, 2003; Aldana, 2008). In the past, the authors had worked with complex interaction scenarios using neural nets (Daradoumis & Casillas, 2006); then the authors found out by 2008, that complex networks are better suited to model the dynamics and interactions among entities. From that very moment, the research efforts are mainly guided by CNA; due to its functional capabilities.

The CNA is a fresh strategy to view and understand diverse phenomena in nature, societies, physics and any other occurrence in the universe; that includes diverse elements interacting with each other. The main promoters of this so called *new science of networks* are Barabasi (2003), Newman (2003), and Watts & Strogatz (1998). The authors believe that milestones of knowledge populating the traditional syllabuses are inherently organized as scale-free networks, due to its selective binding among concepts, as established by Reka & Barabasi (2002). This proposal is oriented to define a method for building academic programs and will follow up the principles underlying complex-networks, which enables the discovery and construction of educational nuclei. Such nuclei represent the backbone of every academic program.

In current scientific context, the technological advances and the socialization of ICT (social nets, blogs, video repositories, augmented reality, etc.) constitute the basic premises for the development of modern academic programs for present and future higher-education institutions (HEI). Present proposal aims at discovering the pieces of knowledge supporting an academic program, using practical and/or automated steps. The collected knowledge represents the semantic essence of academic programs in HEI. Popolo (2010) and Martin (2003) argue that such collection provides context and trajectory in Bayesian approaches for reality. This perspective agrees with the approach to academic-corpus[1] configuration. Besides, the authors are looking for automating many of the steps from this process. Due to the natural complexity of this challenge, and believe that computers are not able to perform the whole task and complete every known step by themselves. Nevertheless, a creative use of computational capabilities would be very helpful. By modeling the problem elements as a complex network, some automated analysis could be performed on this structure, allowing humans to promptly discover the main aspects and simplifying the discussion. This team has previously dealt with this kind of problem, as described in (Casillas & Daradoumis, 2012) and (Casillas, Daradoumis & Caballé, 2013).

In an effort to discover the body of knowledge that conforms to the training core of an academic program, this study will try to unfold the essential branches of education for the analyzed programs, as well as their cognitive infrastructure. In order to use expert-system techniques for the discovery and extraction of knowledge stored in humans, a group of professors has been invited to collaborate in the study. The results produced are discussed and prove to be interesting and meaningful.

RELATED WORK

Since the 1960's, computers have been used in scientific fields. The use of computers at that time was limited to tasks involved with calculations in: iterative, recurrent, and concurrent contexts. More recently, advances in computer graphics allowed improved simulations from reality. Nowadays, computers are not the actor that uses *brute force* anymore. Of course, they will make the calculations as needed; however, the main goals have been indeed changed. One of current goals for computers, in this context, is to support collaboration among professionals or scientists, as it is shown in the field of e-science (Casillas & Daradoumis, 2012).

The report from Atkins, et al. (2003) is highly focused in the exploitation of the available cyber-infrastructure. According to them, there is a revolution in science due to advances in information and communication technologies. This revolution is based on the innovative capabilities to successfully emulate reality in the digital dimension. Specifically, these authors argue "...the classic two approaches to scientific research, theoretical / analytical and experimental / observational, have been extended to in silico [sic] simulation and modeling to explore new possibilities and to achieve new precision..."; with important achievements in Forestry, Ocean Science, Environmental Science and Engineering, Space Weather, Computer Science and Engineering, Information Science and Digital Libraries, Biology / Bioinformatics, Medicine, Physics, Astronomy, Engineering, Materials Science & Engineering, and Social & Behavioral Sciences.

Throughout the use of Topic Maps (Garshol, 2004), academic researchers, teachers, and students are truly enabled to construct learning scenarios from diverse kind of resources. This method is aimed at collecting knowledge elements from specialists, connect such elements as complex networks, and finally provide students a set of resources. The amounts of knowledge elements to be managed by this approach are defined through the capacity of humans to handle information (Miller, 1956). The resulting global map will represent the course syllabus and the tools for selecting and automatically organize the milestones that students will follow throughout their experience when following a course. Hence, diverse paths over the very same contents are enabled. Each formative nucleus (path) is highly compatible both with the specific student and the global perspective of the course syllabus. These paths are mixed up to integrate a complex network, which represents a synthetic ontology (Gruber, 1993). By the use of specific techniques, the elements in such ontology could be bound to people, and be related to the managing and/or collecting of these elements. In this sense, even Social Networks Analysis (SNA) (Wasserman & Faust, 1994) could be used as a means to analyze and represent these knowledge elements.

Syllabus design, in educational scopes, is mainly bound to language teaching or processing (Horrigan & Haag, 2008) (Taghizadeh, 2013). Thus, most of consulted sources are focused in such approach for syllabus design. Even though there are many ties from syllabus design with language courses; it is possible to admit that learners in any course are *learning a language*, e.g. the students from a Calculus course are learning the symbols (vocabulary) and rules to manage and handle such symbols (grammar), i.e. students are learning a language called *calculus*. Thus, syllabus design could be aimed for course designing. As Kang (2012) has elegantly developed a multipurpose mechanism for syllabus design. A common machinery based on CNA and SNA might imply an infrastructure for academic programs' design. The present study as such goal in the long-term.

Throughout the use of Topic Maps and Ontology, academic programs could be assembled from scratch management (Garshol, 2004; Kannan, 2010; Soori & Ghaderi, 2015; Huang & Chen, 2013), based on minimal pieces of knowledge and the discovered relationships among them. By controlling some elements as: vocabulary, concepts, relationships, and clustering; the body of knowledge acquires a meaningful topology, and eventually satisfies the demands for an academic program.

The study from Long & Crookes (1992), makes an assertion about the importance of task based analysis when syllabus are designed. These authors refer to avoid an analysis based only on words in vocabulary, and include the active perspective involving the concepts. Trough out the inclusion of concepts as: relationships, critical paths among concepts, and the notion of clustering; it will be implied an active perspective, by producing structure and functionality.

Discovering minimal pieces of knowledge, relationships, and supervising rules; becomes the main source of complexity for present effort. Dealing with this complexity is the foremost goal of this work. The authors understand and admit *complexity*, as the resultant-vector from collateral constraints such as: soundness, completeness and decidability; thus, current challenge is to satisfy these constraints while providing a general approach for tailoring academic programs. Regarding *soundness*, current efforts are oriented to provide certainty for every piece of knowledge or awareness, by setting the trust on professionals collaborating. The selection process for professionals must be carefully undertaken. Regarding *completeness*, current efforts are oriented to warrant that every piece of knowledge or awareness in every step of the process; can be followed up to its origins and/or implications along the whole model. Finally, regarding the *decidability* aspect; current efforts are oriented to have the conviction of knowing all the time, what is the following step in procedure.

A CNA/SNA METHOD FOR TAILORING OF ACADEMIC PROGRAMS

Most of the activities developed by humans are based on sets of concepts and the relationships among such knowledge elements. The humans' understanding of the environment is defined by the concepts and ideas acquired before. These previous elements are organized as nets of perceptions in which the relationships are modeled by links of proximity. Hence, humans have a natural tendency to organize understanding as complex networks.

The authors believe that CNA could become a general algorithm to solve problems from diverse nature, even those phenomena that fall away from regular and *computable* treatment, such as social studies, economical matters, personal and/or ethical values, and etcetera. As long as a phenomenon can be modeled as a network, CNA algorithms are enabled to act over such phenomenon and produce some solution indicators. Nevertheless, and inspired by Gödel's Incompleteness[2], modeling a problem as a network cannot guarantee finding the optimal solution; although finding a representation inspired by a network may enhance the chances to solve the problem.

On the one hand, let us consider the scenario presented in Figure 1. In this Figure, it is characterized a situation when humans capture signals from reality through their sensory frontier, and the common sense (at the bottom of understanding) produces an internal image for the captured reality. As the reader

Figure 1. A representation for humans capturing and interpreting reality; the dark 'R' at left is Reality manifesting at full and bold tone. Unfortunately, humans will not capture that fullness and only will be able to interpret a constrained representation to reality: gray 'R' at right. The cause are constraints in sensory frontier and lack of expertise when applying common sense.

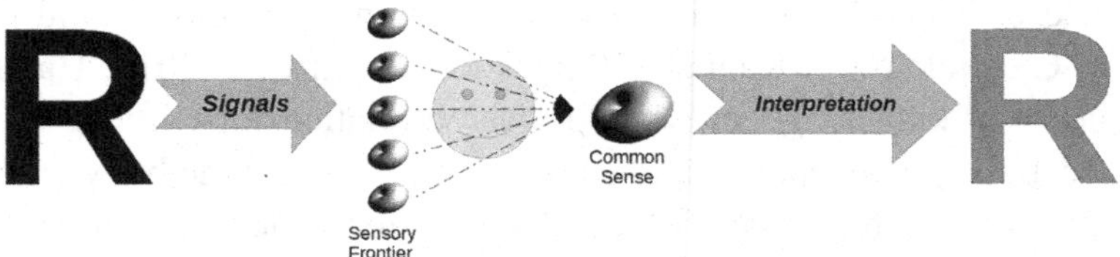

can notice in Figure 1, the interpreted reality ('R' at the right) has a lighter intensity in color; this refers to the loss of meaning and/or semantics during interpretation. This is a normal issue, caused by natural constraints in humans' sensory frontier and the induced constraints is common sense.

On the other hand, let us consider the scenario presented in Figure 2. In this Figure it is characterized a situation when computers capture signals from reality throughout a sophisticated sensory frontier; but in absence of common sense, machine produces an internal image of the captured reality by using only a synthetic version of common sense (which is usually, some sort of programs processing signals creatively). As the reader can notice in Figure 2, the interpreted reality ('R' at the right) has a much lighter intensity in color; this refers to the significant loss of meaning and/or semantics during interpretation. Although machines could include a wide range of sensors, as well as high sensibility for such inputs, constraints bound to a simulation for common sense will restrict the capability to interpret reality considering its richness.

Such frustrating loss of meaning, when machines collect and manage reality by themselves, inspired us to search for a creative approach for cyber-interpretation of meaning from reality. Considering that common sense cannot be described by a computable algorithm, machines are currently unable to perform many reality processing tasks. There are diverse efforts aiming at allowing machines to have a *human*

Figure 2. A representation for machines capturing and interpreting reality; the dark 'R' at left is Reality manifesting at full and bold tone. Unfortunately, computers will not capture most of that that fullness, and only will be able to interpret a very constrained representation to reality: light gray 'R' at right. Although machines could be enabled with highly sensitive frontier, the absence of common sense will break down any possible interpretation of reality.

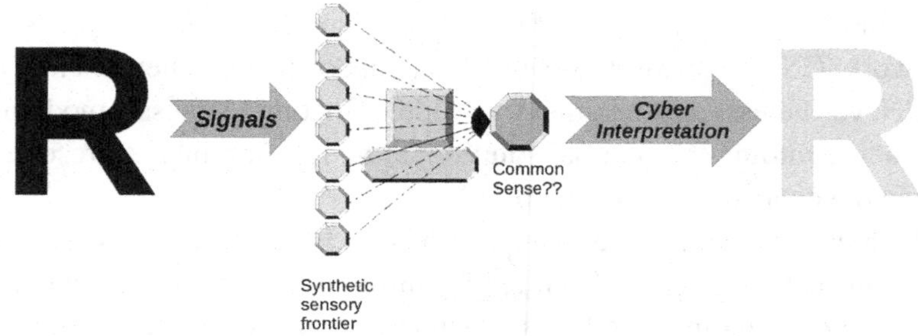

understanding, but there are always loose ends cracking such efforts. The *von Neumannian*[3] essence in machines' operation is the main responsible for all constraints in the *humanization* of computers.

Among diverse options, one strategy to improve machine understanding over reality; is to *help* machines in the interpretation process. Humans are certainly enabled to *preprocess* reality, and produce the bases for machine interpretation. Present strategy consists in using humans' capabilities to identify and bind the main aspects of the studied reality. Figure 3 shows a scheme for this approach. Dark 'R' at upper left corner is interpreted by humans' common sense. The upper right corner in Figure 3 shows the discolored 'R', bound to humans' interpretation for reality. Under the bagel shaped common sense, there is the cyber-interpretation, made by humans. Such act produces a lighter 'R'. Cyber-interpretation made by humans produces a lighter 'R' due to the production of computable structures, which have less strength than conceptual structures in humans' brains. The human-made cyber-interpretation is fed to machines. Then machines produce an interpretation to reality just by combining inputs through a semantics catalyst. The reader can compare the 'R' produced by combining inputs in Figure 3, and the 'R' at the right of Figure 2.

Figure 3. A representation for machines capturing an already interpreted reality, and the production of improved machine interpretation; the dark 'R' at upper-left is Reality manifesting at full and bold tone. As shown in Figure 1, humans could partially interpret reality. Besides, humans could produce an attempt of interpretation for machines; grasping the most significant matters. The magnifying glass, in the middle, is showing the networked essence achieved for the cyber-interpretation.

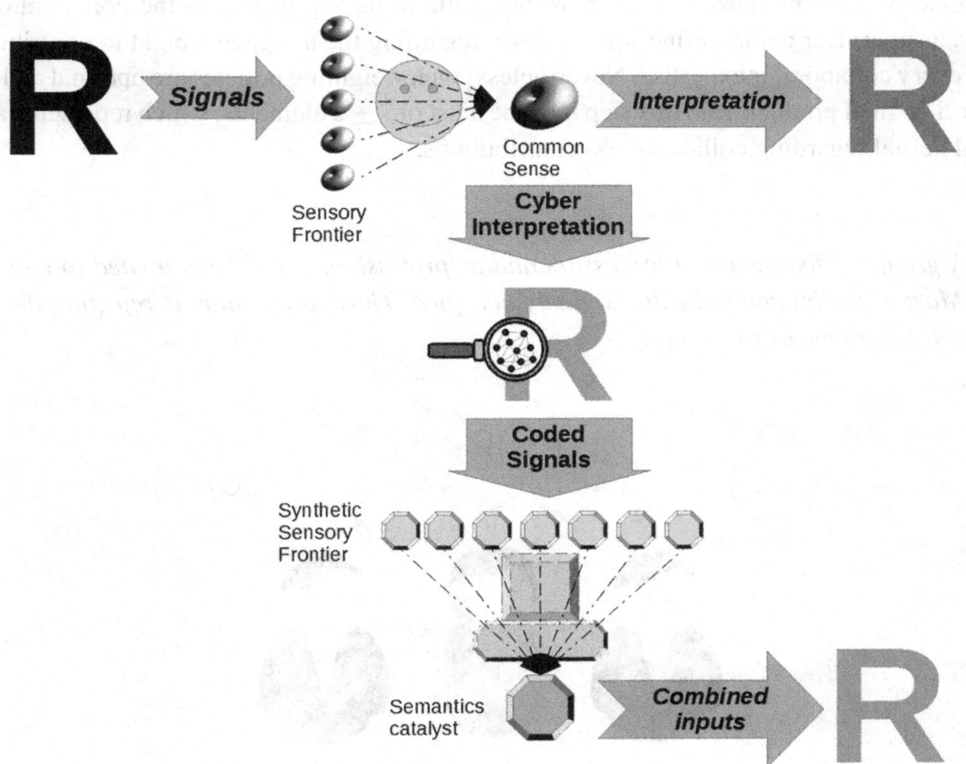

When machines interpret reality using some of their own means, there is a significant loss of meaning; but when machines use a cyber-interpretation made by humans, they produce a lesser amount of loss of semantics. Complex-networks and their analyzing algorithms could be used to achieve this human-made cyber-interpretation. Such approach is the axis for present effort described in this work.

Inspired in such strategy; the authors based this method for tailoring academic programs, on humans' expertise. To this end, the first step consists in identifying professors and specialists who would be collaborators in the study. Authors agreed that these professionals should be individuals possessing a deep understanding of the syllabus studied, both in the pedagogical dimension, and in research or professional areas; reaching approximately 10% of faculty staff and researchers from the program studied (Figure 4). This study could be conducted through electronic means (email, forums, wikis, and etcetera), so collaborators could be in remote locations and continue to participate asynchronously through internet access.

Once the teamwork was formed, collaborators were asked to identify the main areas of knowledge related to the academic program studied, preferably a list of 7 ± 2 items (Miller, 1956), containing only the name of each branch. In this study, collaborators' effort was drove to update an already existing program; so the new knowledge branches were expected to be different from knowledge branches in the actual program, as shown in Figure 5. At this point, collaborators had to look at the program curriculum as a critical mass of knowledge that is fragmented into its parts. After finishing this challenging step, collaborators were requested to send the main branches they individually reached.

The following step consists in collecting the names of branches defined by each collaborator. These branches had some already expected differences in name, and they needed to be somehow merged, combined, unified, and refined into a common nomenclature that meets all collaborators' proposals, as sketched in Figure 6. The weight assigned to contributions is initially democratic, that is, the knowledge engineer reviews only the names of the branches without having access to the collaborators' name. Eventually, a supervisor could define some criteria regarding the assigned weight to contributions, according to every collaborator expertise. Nevertheless, such weighting policies are optional and subject to discussion. The final product from this step must be a list of 7 ± 2 elements, which represents a common ideological kernel regarding collaborators' contributions.

Figure 4. A group of distinguished professors and/or professionals has been invited to collaborate in the study. Most of the invited individuals gladly accepted. Those professionals rejecting the invitation argued they had no time or availability.

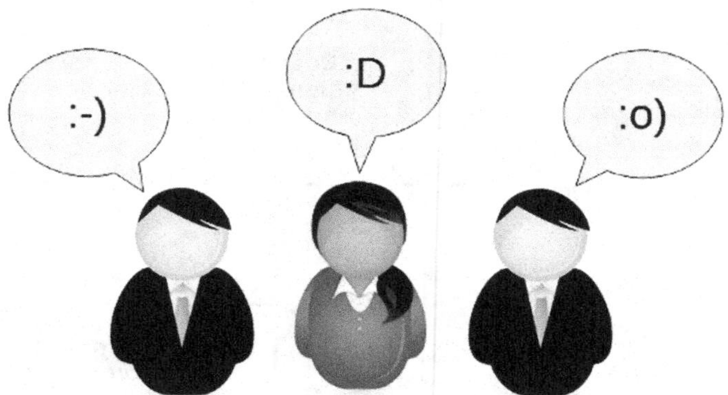

Figure 5. Every collaborator produces a list of knowledge items for the academic program in which he/she is participating. Different colors in message-bubbles are used to denote diverse perspectives or proposals from collaborators.

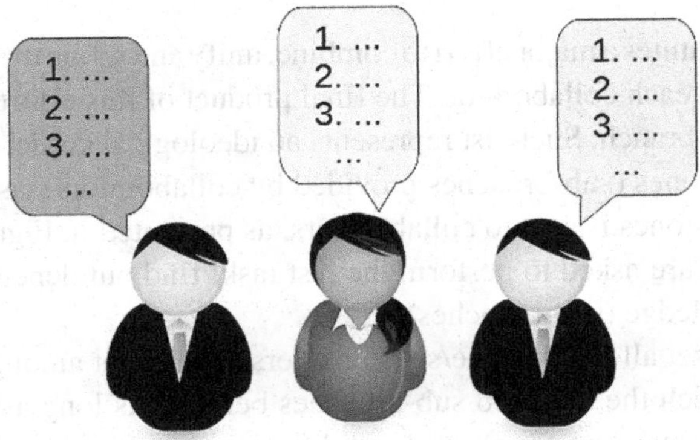

Figure 6. The knowledge engineer proceeds to collect the lists of knowledge items (branches) produced by professors. At this point, the challenge for this engineer is to produce a compact list (7 ± 2 items) which merges the branches proposed. The engineer needs to discover those elements which are common, similar or opposite of each other, without missing the valuable awareness provided by collaborators. Different colors in rolled up papers are used to denote diverse approaches.

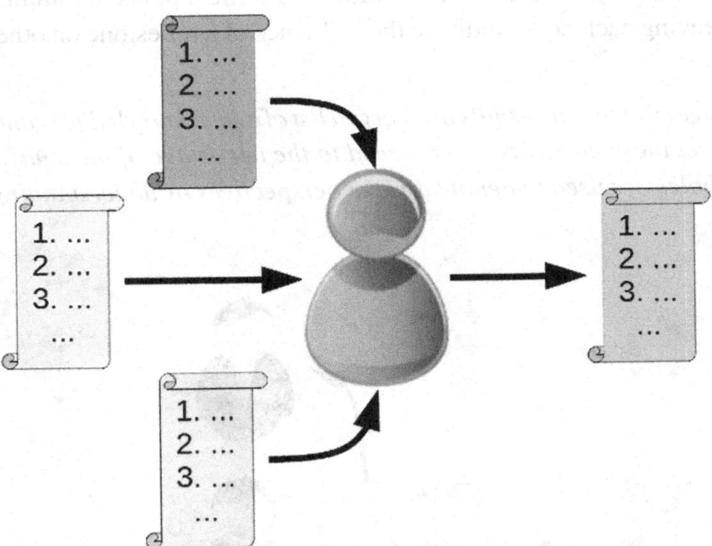

It is important to note that these steps involving professionals crumbling huge knowledge-corpus into branches, weighting policies, and definition of a common list of names for branches; are strictly human tasks. Although some automatic support could be provided, involving natural language processing to identify and bind knowledge names; final decisions must be made by humans.

The next step consists in distributing the already consolidated list of branches among collaborators, as shown in Figure 7. Once the list is distributed and unified, collaborators have to divide each branch into sub-branches or milestones of knowledge. This is sketched in Figure 8. Again, the number of sub-branches should be around 7 ± 2 elements. So far collaborators usually perform a classical decomposition of knowledge, based on the hierarchical approach; humans make this kind of decomposition almost inherently.

The following step constitutes a major effort to combine, unify and refine the milestones (sub-branches) that have been provided by each collaborator. The final product of this effort is, once again, a common list of 7 ± 2 milestones per branch. Such list represents an ideological kernel of contributors, but now it has been made from milestones (sub-branches provided by collaborators), as shown in Figure 9.

The unified list of milestones is sent to collaborators, as presented in Figure 10. Once collaborators have received the list, they are asked to perform the last task: find out dependencies and/or influences among milestones of knowledge (sub-branches).

Every collaborator can set all the links he/she considers as relevant among sub-branches, regardless of the parent-branch to which the involved sub-branches belong. As long as influences are rational or consistent links and collaborators are people with solid experience, this should not be a cause of concern. Once the information from relationships is collected, the authors can proceed with building a directed graph containing all the information. The nodes of this graph are the sub-branches (milestones), and the edges represent the relationships of influence or dependence among them. By doing this, the authors now pass to follow a networked approach to deal with the problem (rather than a hierarchical one followed before), as shown in Figure 11.

As seen in Figure 11, a networked construction enables the search of training core items from the academic program under study, as well as the definition of critical paths in training. The output degrees (the number of arcs leaving each node) indicate the influence of a milestone on others. The input degrees

Figure 7. The knowledge engineer transmits the merged list of items (knowledge branches) to collaborating professors. They collect these elements and proceed to the next stage of the study. Different colors and order in message-bubbles are used to denote diverse perspectives or understanding from collaborators.

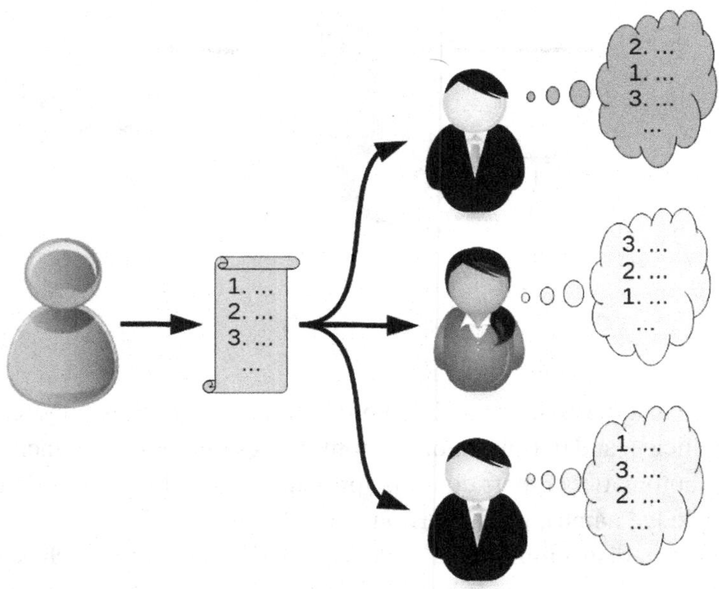

Figure 8. At this point, every collaborating professor produces coherent sub-branches for each branch received. These sub-branches are the milestones he/she considers as the individual concepts composing every knowledge branch. Different colors for message-bubbles are used to denote diverse perspectives or proposals from collaborators.

Figure 9. Once again the knowledge engineer performs a collection of lists coming from collaborating professors. These lists contain the knowledge milestones they considered as sub-branches. Now, the knowledge engineer proceeds to merge, unify and bind all the milestones produced. This task was implemented by electronic worksheets and their formulae, filters and macros. Different colors for rolled up papers are used to denote diverse approaches.

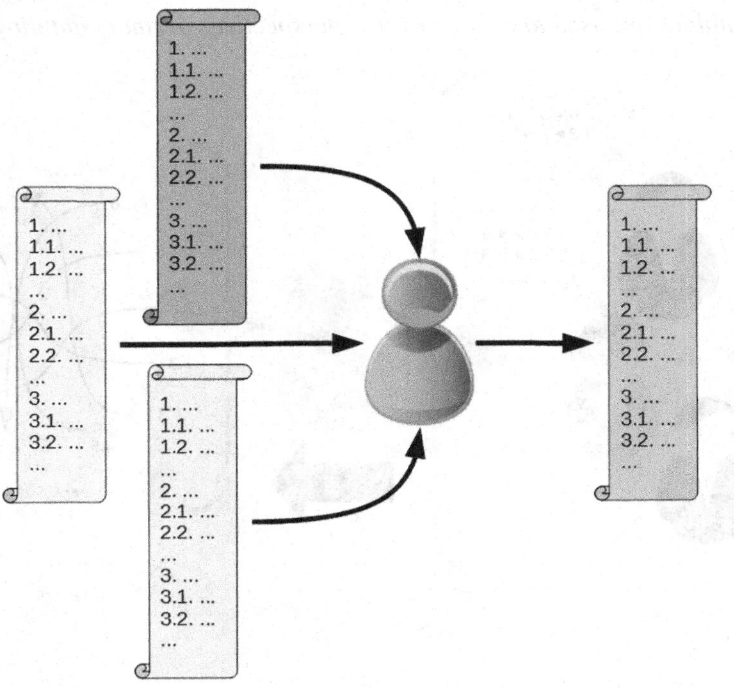

Figure 10. The resulting merged list of sub-branches is now forwarded to collaborating professors in order to start their last task. Different colors for message-bubbles are used to denote diverse perspectives or proposals from collaborators.

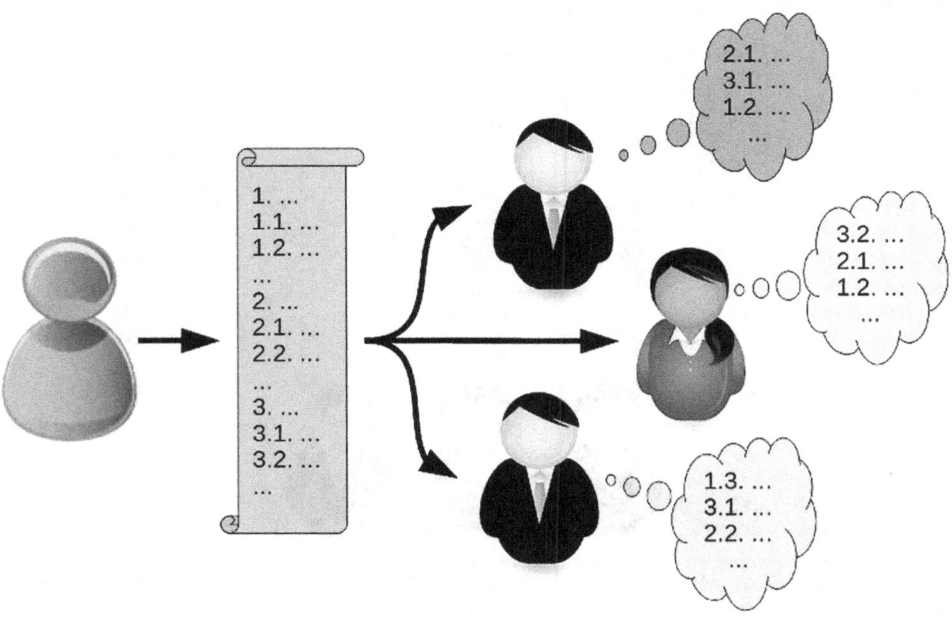

Figure 11. Every collaborating professor establishes influences and dependencies among the knowledge milestones provided in a unified list. These binary relations can be combined into a complex network structure. All the assertions provided by collaborators are used in the network. Different colors and order in message-bubbles are used to denote diverse perspectives or understanding from collaborators.

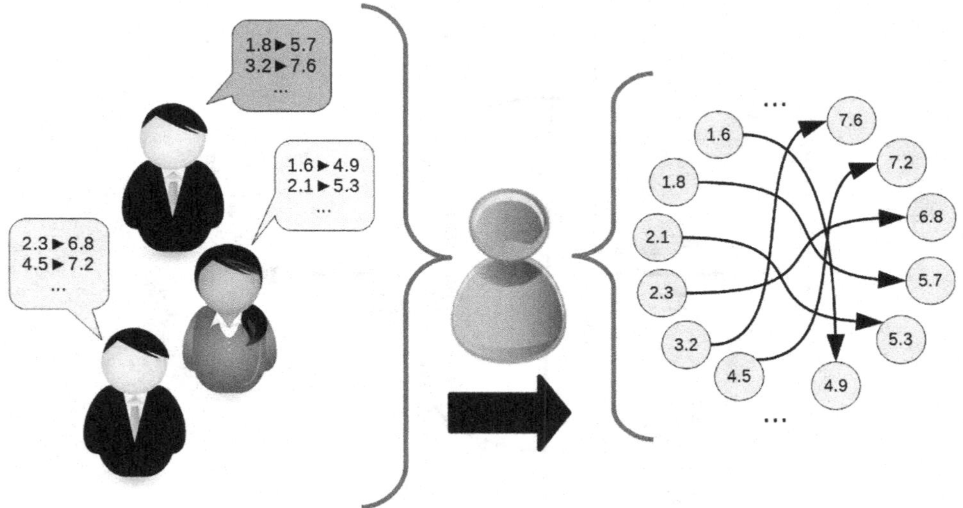

(the number of arcs entering each node) indicate the dependence from other milestones. At a first sight, the most influential milestones, as well as the less dependent ones, constitute the main aspects that shape every training core item in the academic program.

Input and output degrees may incidentally acquire magnitudes which are disconnected from the rules that explain the studied reality. In fact, this network tends to match the form of a scale-free network (Barabasi, 2003). Thus, it is possible to complement these results with the discovery of hub nodes in the graph. By discovering hub nodes, the authors found out relationships among families of nodes in the same neighborhood; which share access to common nodes. This neighborhood is called *cluster*. The clustering coefficient (Watts & Strogatz, 1998) is calculated locally (for each node), whereas the global clustering coefficient is based on the average of all the coefficients calculated for each node locally.

Based on the arguments of Watts & Strogatz (1998), the formula for clustering coefficient in directed graphs is:

$$Cn = pn / (vn (vn-1)),$$

and the formula for undirected graphs is

$$Cn = pn / vn,$$

where Cn is the clustering coefficient for a node n, p is the number of pairs formed between the observed node neighbors, vn is the observed number of neighbors of node. Figure 12 presents a simple example for undirected graphs.

Figure 12. Different cases for calculating the clustering coefficient in undirected graphs; black solid lines denote actual links among the involved nodes. Light gray dotted lines denote possible, but not present links among the involved nodes. Darker circle is the observed node and clearer ones are its neighbors, which could be or not bounded among themselves. The case for (a) denotes a zero clustering coefficient, due to the absence of links among neighbors. In (b) there is only one bound between two of the neighbors, hence the clustering coefficient is 1/3. Finally, in (c) all possible links among neighbors are set; therefore the clustering coefficient is 3/3 or 1.

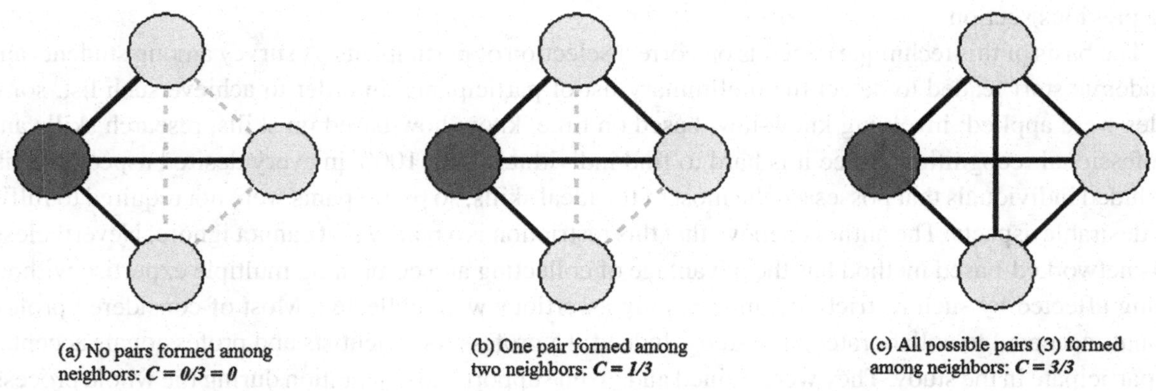

(a) No pairs formed among neighbors: C = 0/3 = 0
(b) One pair formed among two neighbors: C = 1/3
(c) All possible pairs (3) formed among neighbors: C = 3/3

The clustering coefficient is measured within the interval [0, 1] ∈ R, and indicates the strength of the group which maintains a common node as its center. The local coefficient speaks of the capacity of a specific node to be a hub node; the global ratio refers to the cohesion of the entire structure. A good level in the overall coefficient (0.51 to 1) as well as the discovery of sub-networks involving hub nodes, lead to the threshold definition for training corpus.

The networked stages of this strategy could be supported by a tool made specifically for such goal. As concerns the experiments that were carried out with this method, the tailoring of the network structure was performed using *Cytoscape*, which is a tool made specifically for biological networks. Besides, the rest of the analysis for these networks has been performed using software tools developed, from scratch, by the authors. Such analysis consists in measuring input and output degrees, detecting functional dependencies, isolating critical paths, calculating clustering coefficients for every node and the whole network, sorting the nodes based on these coefficients, and finally defining hub-nodes. These steps in the analysis process are automatic.

The knowledge engineer must compare the information about the influences and dependencies between milestones as well as the awareness regarding hub nodes to form groups among them. This process should be carried out among the knowledge engineer and the experts.

Regarding the opportunity to automate some additional steps in the model the authors are presenting here; just as they did in (Garshol, 2004) and (Kannan, 2010), by the use of topic maps and ontology processing emerge some changes. Authors are familiar with Natural Language Processing Techniques (NLP) (Casillas & Daradoumis, 2009). Topics, milestones, branches, and sub-branches could be automatically be: unified, bound, related or unrelated throughout the use of NLP. In order to discover the semantics linkable to every element in discourse, all the branches and sub-branches provided by collaborators would be processed. Tables with synonyms and antonyms can be used over substantives in sentences. Besides, a set of verbs would be considered. All these elements allow grasping the common semantics in contributions from collaborator. Further works in this line will include the automation of such stages.

APPLYING THE METHOD ON A REAL ACADEMIC PROGRAM

In order to verify the convenience and effectiveness of this method, the authors applied it during the curricular redesign of the *Computers Engineering* academic program, following the steps explained in the previous section.

The basis of this technique depends on correct selection of participants. A survey among students and academic staff leaded to detect the preliminary list of participants. In order to achieve such list, some rules were applied: involving know-how based on time, know-how based on skills, research skills and professional recognition. Since it is hard to find individuals with 100% in every desired aspect, the list included individuals that possessed the most of the ideal skills, so participants were not required to fulfill all desirable aspects. The authors believe that this restriction is a reality that cannot ignore. Nevertheless, this networked-based method has the advantage of collecting and combining multiple expertise without being affected by such restrictions; in fact, only assertions were collected. Most of considered professionals accepted to collaborate in the study. Indeed, 15 professors, scientists and professionals accepted to participate in the study. They were trained and given support and orientation during the whole process.

The list containing the first decomposition for knowledge corpus was refined in the first interactions. The knowledge engineer was able to achieve a list of knowledge milestones.

Knowledge Milestones

1. Sciences supporting computers science,
2. Networking, Communications, Distribution, and Parallelism,
3. Intelligent Systems,
4. Base software and hardware programming,
5. Computer architecture,
6. Deployment of Information and Communication Technologies (ICT).

This list of knowledge branches was distributed among collaborators, and every participant found the sub-branches. The knowledge engineer managed to collect all collaborations and unify perspectives. The sub-branches achieved and unified after all this process are set in a list.

Branches and Sub-branches of Knowledge

1. **Sciences Supporting Computers Science:**
    1.1. Calculus,
    1.2. Mechanics,
    1.3. Numerical analysis,
    1.4. Probability and Statistics,
    1.5. Waves physics,
    1.6. Optics,
    1.7. Electromagnetism,
    1.8. Logics and Sets,
    1.9. Discrete mathematics,
    1.10. Computers theory.
2. **Networking, Communications, Distribution, and Parallelism:**
    2.1. Tele-informatics,
    2.2. Computers networks,
    2.3. Multitask systems,
    2.4. Parallel systems,
    2.5. Multi-core programming,
    2.6. Distributed systems,
    2.7. Pervasive computing,
    2.8. Redundancy and fault tolerance,
    2.9. Network management and networking services.
3. **Intelligent Systems:**
    3.1. Knowledge based systems,
    3.2. Inference machines,
    3.3. Machine learning,
    3.4. Artificial neural networks,
    3.5. Fuzzy logic,
    3.6. Automatic control,
    3.7. Evolutive computing,

   3.8. Automatic optimization,
   3.9. Industrial robotics,
   3.10. Mobile robotics,
   3.11. Ludic robotics,
   3.12. Robotics.
4. **Base Software and Hardware Programming:**
   4.1. Programming paradigms,
   4.2. Virtual machines,
   4.3. Assembly programming,
   4.4. Programming languages and tools,
   4.5. Software engineering,
   4.6. Embedded software programming,
   4.7. Language translators: assemblers, compilers, etc.,
   4.8. Operating systems: use and development,
   4.9. Projects management.
5. **Computer Architecture:**
   5.1. Digital systems,
   5.2. Hardware architectures,
   5.3. Firmware development,
   5.4. Computers organization,
   5.5. Human-computer interaction,
   5.6. Low level communications.
6. **Deployment of Information and Communication Technologies (ICT):**
   6.1. Operating systems deployment,
   6.2. Technology management,
   6.3. e-Commerce, e-Government,
   6.4. ERPs (Enterprise Resource Planning),
   6.5. Information security,
   6.6. IT services,
   6.7. Business intelligence,
   6.8. Decision support systems.

The unified sub-branches were sent to participants, so they could perform the influence-dependence definition among these sub-branches. According to his/her expertise, every collaborator made a list of ordered pairs. Every pair contained the sub-branch influencing and the sub-branch influenced. The first element in ordered pair, influencing the second one. Using the accumulated list of pairs, including all contributions and without any removals; an influence-dependence network is built. Figure 13 shows a simplified representation for the resulting complex-network.

The availability of this network is the foundation supporting this study. Different software modules collected and mixed the contributions from participants. When the network is completed; input and output degrees per node, imply the order traceable by different critical paths in the academic program. The clustering coefficient allowed the detection of hubs. These hubs represent the knowledge milestones on which the academic program is built. The clustering coefficient for the whole network presented in Figure 13 is 0.4. A specific analysis regarding clustering coefficients on every node is shown in Table 1.

Figure 13. Complex network modeling the influence-dependence relations among knowledge sub-branches from an academic program; in this case, the academic program is Computers Engineering of the University of Guadalajara. This model is presented in order to allow the reader to have a clear view of complexity achieved by modeling such situation and when including multiple sources of knowledge. The real model presents many more details, but they are not shown in order to simplify the picture of the model.

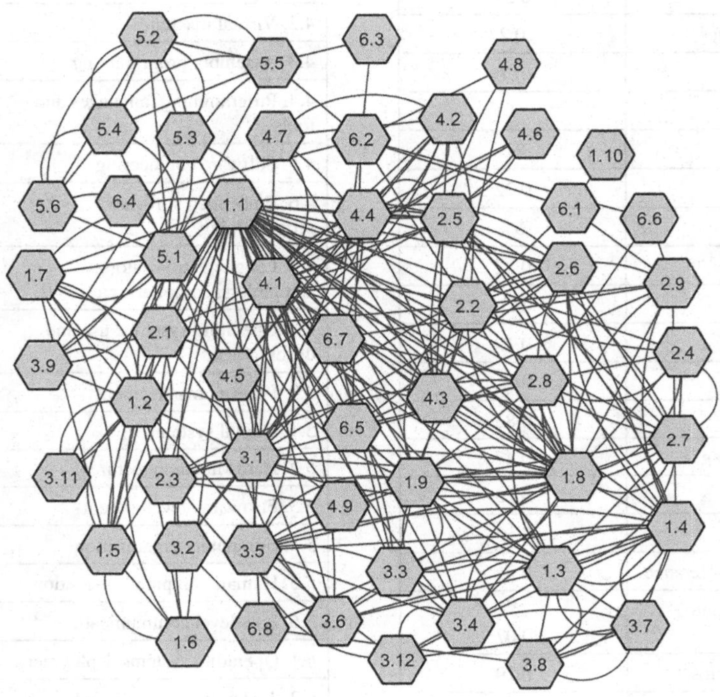

A final meeting was planned. This seminar included professors and knowledge engineers. Participants reviewed the achieved results. From these results and some additional assertions from collaborators, the structure of the academic program was finally redefined. Such structure is described by the list of academic corpuses.

Academic Corpuses Discovered

- Science supporting computing,
- Systems programming and embedded software,
- Computers architecture and organization,
- Cloud computing and networking services,
- Intelligent and robust systems.

In fact, the order presented in academic corpuses tries to represent the value and advantages of every knowledge corpus, as well as the recommended sequence for them. Both aspects (value and sequence)

Table 1. Clustering coefficient per node of the computers engineering academic program

Sub-Branch	Clustering Coefficient
1.1. Calculus	0.26
1.2. Mechanics	0.21
1.3. Numerical analysis	0.36
1.4. Probability and Statistics	0.2
1.5. Waves physics	0.7
1.6. Optics	1
1.7. Electromagnetism	0.5
1.8. Logics and Sets	0.22
1.9. Discrete mathematics	0.4
1.10. Computers theory	0.32
2.1. Tele-informatics	0.3
2.2. Computers networks	0.19
2.3. Multitask systems	0.5
2.4. Parallel systems	0.83
2.5. Multi-core programming	0.47
2.6. Distributed systems	0.25
2.7. Pervasive computing	0.52
2.8. Redundancy and fault tolerance	0.25
2.9. Network management and networking services	0.07
3.1. Knowledge based systems	0.19
3.2. Inference machines	0.33
3.3. Machine learning	0.3
3.4. Artificial neural networks	0.52
3.5. Fuzzy logic	0.4
3.6. Automatic control	0.5
3.7. Evolutive computing	0.5
3.8. Automatic optimization	0.3
3.9. Industrial robotics	0.18
3.10. Mobile robotics	0.23
3.11. Ludic robotics	0.12
3.12. Robotics	0.33
4.1. Programming paradigms	0.26
4.2. Virtual machines	0.6
4.3. Assembly programming	0.4
4.4. Programming languages and tools	0.39
4.5. Software engineering	0.83
4.6. Embedded software programming	1
4.7. Language translators: assemblers, compilers, etc.	1
4.8. Operating systems: use and development	0.15
4.9. Projects management	0.2
5.1. Digital systems	0.18
5.2. Hardware architectures	0.5
5.3. Firmware development	0.2
5.4. Computers organization	0.83
5.5. Human-computer interaction	0.35
5.6. Low level communications	1
6.1. Operating systems deployment	0.22
6.2. Technology management	0.39
6.3. e-Commerce, e-Government	0.21
6.4. ERPs (Enterprise Resource Planning)	0.2
6.5. Information security	0.2
6.6. IT services	0.33
6.7. Business intelligence	0.36
6.8. Decision support systems	0.23

result from the proposed CNA/SNA method. Consequently, the available and already known sub-branches were slightly adjusted and reorganized in order to fit the new schema of academic corpuses. The *Computers Engineering* academic program was finally completed using the results from this model. Table 2 shows the current structure for the *Computers Engineering* academic program. This structure was widely influenced by the results from this study. Building an academic program remains a human responsibility; nevertheless this method has provided significant data and information in order to achieve an effective, robust and useful academic program.

Table 2. Current structure of the computers engineering academic program

Semester	Subjects					
1	Mathematical methods I	Programming	Seminary for problems solution: Programming	Discrete mathematics	Philosophical Foundations of Computer Science	*Open Optional*	
2	Mathematical methods II	Seminary for problems solution: Mathematical methods I	Data structures I	Seminary for problems solution: Data structures I	Computers Theory	*Open Optional*	
3	Mathematical methods III	Seminary for problems solution: Mathematical methods II	Statistics and stochastic processes	Data structures II	Seminary for problems solution: Data structures II	Algorithms	Seminary for problems solution: Algorithms
4	Seminary for problems solution: Mathematical methods III	Databases	Seminary for problems solution: Databases	Software engineering I	Seminary for problems solution: Software engineering I	Networking and communication protocols	Seminary for problems solution: Networking and communication protocols
5	Language translators I	Seminary for problems solution: Language translators I	Computers Architecture	Seminary for problems solution: Computers Architecture	Security	*Specializing Subject*	*Specializing Subject*
6	Language translators II	Seminary for problems solution: Language translators II	**Internships**				
7	Artificial Intelligence I	Seminary for problems solution: Artificial Intelligence I	Operating systems	Seminary for problems solution: Operating systems	Fault tolerance computing	Internet Programming	
8	Artificial Intelligence II	Seminary for problems solution: Artificial Intelligence II	Networking operating systems	Seminary for problems solution: Networking operating systems	Distributed and concurrent systems	Computer simulation	

FUTURE RESEARCH DIRECTIONS

The following efforts over this experiment will be aimed at including, as mentioned in section 3 of this work, automated mechanisms with NLP; when producing common lists of branches and sub-branches from collaborators' responses. This would be possible is a controlled thesaurus, built from official definitions for the academic program. A group of professionals in the area could always recheck this thesaurus, as well as the synonyms and antonyms stored. When branches for knowledge-corpus are presented from collaborators, a NLP could work over the concepts in order discover: unions, intersections, complements and contractions.

In fact, this system will tend to become a web-based application that could be fed with diverse documents describing the knowledge field supporting the academic program that will be constructed. The list of professionals selected, as well as their contact information. The system, by itself would build the thesaurus and knowledge engineer supervises the results. When knowledge engineer approves thesaurus, emails are automatically sent to professionals. They crumble into branches the knowledge corpus, based on their expertise, and capture the branches names in the web. Now, system would use NLP to produce a common list. This common list should be reviewed and approved by knowledge engineer. Now professionals would crumble branches in common list, into sub-branches. Once again they are capture in web application. The system would arrange these sub-branches into a new common list of sub-branches. This new list should be reviewed and approved by knowledge engineer. Finally professionals will work over the common list of sub-branches, presented in web and they would define all the influences they detect. From this point system, by itself, will produce the complex network and the whole set of indicators as: input and output degrees, clustering coefficients, critical paths, and etcetera. From this point, humans must coordinate in meeting in order to analyze results and build the final definition for academic program. The authors are preparing the human resources to build the web-based automated representation for this model.

CONCLUSION

Updating an academic program remains a task demanding significant efforts. Such endeavor involves: people, academic units, knowledge fragments, regulations, institutions, industry, etcetera, and usually entails a specific form of complexity; related to the quantity of elements involved, the diversity of origins from contributions, the diversity of formats and representations of information, and the required granularity.

Along this work, the authors are offering a method for: discovering, handling, and exploiting the knowledge available in academic curricula. Due to nature of such knowledge construction, the awareness is stored in mixed deposits. Besides, persons responsible to stored or manage those deposits are not always aligned to deal with new and different approaches; when handling the expertise under their charge. Hence most of the efforts when dealing with collaborators, were aimed to persuade them to produce knowledge elements in the required terms. There was no struggle, because they wanted to cooperate. The problem came from the common misunderstanding of computers' capabilities and their real skills to capture arguments presented as inputs. Thus, the knowledge engineer has to crumble those *non-crumbled* responses; without missing the essential arguments from collaborators.

Although this proposal is not fully computerized; the automatic parts from this method, provide elements to improve the agreement when looking for consensus. When the collaborating group reviewed the numbers from input and output degrees, the clustering coefficients, and the critical paths along milestones in curricula; the defensive position in *everyone's castle*, was released. The benefit of representing phenomena as complex networks, is that all ideas are incorporated. When collaborators see the structure, they can find out their contributions in the model. Actually, in the real scenario, where the authors applied this method, the relaxed atmosphere drove situation to achieve agreement among participants with opposing positions. Every participant can see his/her contribution in the final result.

The complex network is a democratic model that maintains all contributions, with the same weight, from either collaborator. Nevertheless preemptive notions might be included, if it is required to work with weighted contributions from collaborators; based on collaborators expertise. The whole model could be easily adapted to include such approach a give a different understanding to indicators involved, so that contributions from best weighted collaborators will have a bigger influence in results.

REFERENCES

Aldana, M. (2008). *Complex Networks*. Cuernavaca, Mexico: UNAM.

Atkins, D. E., Droegemeier, K. K., Feldman, S. I., Garcia-molina, H., Klein, M. L., Messerschmitt, D. G., . . . Wright, M. H. (2003). *Revolutionizing science and engineering through cyberinfrastructure: Report of the National Science Foundation blue-ribbon advisory panel on cyberinfrastructure*. Arlington, VA: National Science Foundation, NSF.

Barabasi, A. L. (2003). *Linked: How Everything Is Connected to Everything Else and What It Means*. Cambridge, MA: Perseus Publishing.

Casillas, L., & Daradoumis, T. (2009). Constructing a Multi-agent System for Discovering the Meaning over Natural-Language Collaborative Conversations. In T. Daradoumis, S. Caballé, & J. M. Márquez (Eds.), *Intelligent Collaborative e-Learning Systems and Applications* (pp. 99–112). Berlin: Springer-Verlag. doi:10.1007/978-3-642-04001-6_7

Casillas, L., & Daradoumis, T. (2012). An ontology structure for gathering and sharing knowledge among scientists. In *Collaborative and Distributed-Research: Innovations in Technologies, Strategies and Applications* (pp. 165–179). Hershey, PA: IGI Global. doi:10.4018/978-1-4666-0125-3.ch008

Casillas, L., Daradoumis, T., & Caballé, S. (2013). A network analysis method for selecting personalized content in e-Learning programs. *Seventh International Conference on Complex, Intelligent, and Software Intensive Systems* (pp. 407-411). Taichung, Taiwan: IEEE. doi:10.1109/CISIS.2013.74

Casillas, L. A., & Castillo, A. (2012). Discovering epistemological axes for academic programs in computer science through network analysis. *ReCIBE*. Retrieved from http://recibe.cucei.udg.mx

Daradoumis, T., & Casillas, L. (2006). A Neural Approach for Modeling the Inference of Awareness in Computer-Supported Collaboration. In N. Wolfgang & K. Tochtermann (Eds.), Innovative Approaches for Learning and Knowledge Sharing (LNCS), (vol. 4227, pp. 464–469). Hannover, Germany: Springer. doi:10.1007/11876663_37

Garshol, L. M. (2004). *Metadata? Thesauri? Taxonomies? Topic Maps! Making sense of it all*. Retrieved from http://www.ontopia.net/topicmaps/materials/tm-vs-thesauri.html

Gruber, T. R. (1993). *A Translation Approach to Portable Ontology Specifications*. Palo Alto, CA: Knowledge Systems Laboratory, Stanford University.

Horrigan, M., & Haag, R. (2008). *Syllabus Design*. Oxford, UK: Oxford University Press.

Huang, T.-C., & Chen, C.-C. (2013). Animating Civic Education: Developing a Knowledge Navigation System using Blogging and Topic Map Technology. *Journal of Educational Technology & Society*, *16*(1), 79–92.

Isaila, N. (2012). The Technology in New Learning Environments. *International Journal of Academic Research in Accounting, Finance and Management Sciences, 2*(Special Issue 1), 128-131.

Kang, S. (2012). *From Curriculum to Syllabus Design: AATK Workshop*. Stanford University.

Kannan, R. (2010). Topic Map: An Ontology Framework for Information Retrieval. *National Conference on Advances in Knowledge Management (NCAKM'10)*.

Long, M. H., & Crookes, G. (1992). Three Approaches to Task-Based Syllabus Design. *TESOL Quarterly*, *26*(1), 27–56. doi:10.2307/3587368

Martin, K. (2003). Epistemic Motion. In *Quantum Searching*. Oxford, UK: Oxford University Computing Laboratory.

Miller, G. A. (1956). The Magical Number Seven, Plus or Minus Two: Some Limits on Our Capacity for Processing Information. *Psychological Review*, *101*(2), 343–352. doi:10.1037/0033-295X.101.2.343 PMID:8022966

Newman, M. (2003). The Structure and Function of Complex Networks. *Society for Industrial and Applied Mathematics: SIAM Rev*, 167–256.

Popolo, D. (2010). *A New Science of International Relations*. Lancaster, UK: Ashgate.

Reka, A., & Barabasi, A. L. (2002). *Statistical mechanics of complex networks*. (Doctoral Dissertation). University of Notre Dame, South Bend, IN.

Soori, A., & Ghaderi, M. (2015). A Topic-Based Syllabus Design for a Conversation Course. *Language in India, 15*(1), 538-546.

Taghizadeh, M. (2013). EAP Syllabus and Course Design. *International Research Journal of Applied and Basic Sciences, 4*(12), 3791-3797.

Wasserman, S., & Faust, K. (1994). *Social Network Analysis: Methods and Applications*. New York, NY: Cambridge University Press. doi:10.1017/CBO9780511815478

Watts, D. J., & Strogatz, S. H. (1998). Collective dynamics of 'small-world' networks. *Nature*, *393*(6684), 440–442. doi:10.1038/30918 PMID:9623998

ENDNOTES

1 Regarding the term *corpus*: this concept refers, along this chapter, to a set of knowledge-elements bound by certain conditions.

2 Stanford Encyclopedia of Philosophy. "Gödel's Incompleteness Theorems". First published Nov 11, 2013; substantive revision Jan 20, 2015. [online] Retrieved April 29, 2015 from http://plato.stanford.edu/entries/goedel-incompleteness/

3 The *von Neumannian* essence refers to a collateral effect, produced by the operation of computers; which based on John von Neumann's architecture. This effect consist in a rigid sequential operation when executing instructions and processing data, because of machine's cycle followed up by computers with this architectural approach, i.e. nearly every computer.

Compilation of References

Abbott Diagnostics. (n.d.). Retrieved from http://www.abbott.com/products/diagnostics.htm/

Abou-Rjeili, A., & Karypis, G. (2006). Multilevel Algorithms for partitioning power-law graphs. In *Proceedings of the 20th International Conference on Parallel and Distributed Processing* (pp. 124-124). Washington, DC: IEEE.

Acar, E., Dunlavy, D. M., & Kolda, T. G. (2009). *Link prediction on evolving data using matrix and tensor factorizations.* ICDM Workshops. doi:10.1109/ICDMW.2009.54

Adamic, L. A., & Glance, N. (2005). The political blogosphere and the 2004 US election: divided they blog. In *Proceedings of the 3rd international workshop on Link discovery* (pp. 36-43). ACM. doi:10.1145/1134271.1134277

Adamic, L., & Adar, E. (2003). Friends and neighbors on the Web. *Social Networks*, *25*(3), 211–230. doi:10.1016/S0378-8733(03)00009-1

Agapie, A., & Wright, A. H. (2014). Theoretical analysis of steady state genetic algorithms. *Applications of Mathematics*, *59*(5), 509–525. doi:10.1007/s10492-014-0069-z

Aggarwal, C. C., Xie, Y., & Philip, S. Y. (2012). *On dynamic link inference in heterogeneousnetworks. In SDM* (pp. 415–426). SIAM.

Airoldi, E., Blei, D., Fienberg, S., Xing, E., & Jaakkola, T. (2006). Mixed membership stochastic block models for relational data with application to protein-protein interactions.*Proceedings of the International Biometrics Society Annual Meeting.*

Al Hasan, M., & Zaki, M. J. (2010). In C. C. Aggarwal (Ed.), *A survey of link prediction in social networks.* Social Network Data Analysis.

Albert, I., & Albert, R. (2004). Conserved network motifs allow protein–protein interaction prediction. *Bioinformatics (Oxford, England)*, *20*(18), 3346–3352. doi:10.1093/bioinformatics/bth402 PMID:15247093

Albert, R., & Barabasi, A.-L. (2002). Statistical mechanics of complex networks. *Reviews of Modern Physics*, *74*(1), 47–97. doi:10.1103/RevModPhys.74.47

Albert, R., Jeong, H., & Barabasi, A.-L. (2000). Error and attack tolerance of complex networks. *Nature*, *406*(6794), 378–382. doi:10.1038/35019019 PMID:10935628

Aldana, M. (2008). *Complex Networks.* Cuernavaca, Mexico: UNAM.

Al-kazemi, B., & Mohan, C. K. (2002, May). Multi-phase generalization of the particle swarm optimization algorithm. In *Computational Intelligence,Proceedings of the World on Congress on* (*Vol. 1*, pp. 489-494). IEEE. doi:10.1109/CEC.2002.1006283

Almeida, H., Guedes, D., Meira, W. Jr, & Zaki, M. J. (2011). Is there a best quality metric for graph clusters? In *Machine Learning and Knowledge Discovery in Databases* (pp. 44–59). Springer Berlin Heidelberg. doi:10.1007/978-3-642-23780-5_13

Alon, U. (2012). *Collection of complex networks.* Retrieved from http://www.weizmann.ac.il/mcb/UriAlon/

Alon, U. (2006). *An introduction to systems biology: design principles of biological circuits.* CRC press.

Alon, U. (2007). Network motifs: Theory and experimental approaches. *Nature Reviews. Genetics*, *8*(6), 450–461. doi:10.1038/nrg2102 PMID:17510665

Alvarez-Folgueiras, M., Minana-Maiques, M., Moreno-Piquero, E., Jorge-Barreiro, F., Lopez-Martin, E., & Ares-Pena, F. (2011, April). Experimental system forthe study of multi-frequency dosimetry. In *Proceedings of the 5th european conference on antennas and propagation*(pp. 1296-1299).

Alvarez-Hamelin, J. I., Dall'Asta, L., Barrat, A., & Vespignani, A. (2005). Large scale networks fingerprinting and visualization using the k-core decomposition. In *Proceedings of Advances in Neural Information Processing Systems 18* (pp. 41–50). Vancouver, Canada: MIT Press.

Androutsos, P., Androutsos, D., & Venetsanopoulos, A. N. (2006). A distributed fault-tolerant MPEG-7 retrieval scheme based on small world theory.Multimedia. *IEEE Transactions on*, *8*(2), 278–288.

Anis, M., Ortmanns, M., & Wehn, N. (2010, May). Fully integrated uwb impulse transmitter and 402-to-405mhz super-regenerative receiver for medical implant devices. In *Proceedings of 2010 ieee international symposium on circuits and systems* (pp. 1213-1215). doi:10.1109/ISCAS.2010.5537294

Anoragaingrum, D. (1999). Cell segmentation with median filter and mathematical morphology operation.*Proceedings of the IEEE 10th International Conference on Image Analysis and Processing (ICIAP).* doi:10.1109/ICIAP.1999.797734

Arenas, A., Díaz-Guilera, A., & Pérez-Vicente, C. J. (2006). Synchronization reveals topological scales in complex networks. *Physical Review Letters*, *96*(11), 114102. doi:10.1103/PhysRevLett.96.114102 PMID:16605825

Aron, J. L., O'Leary, M., Gove, R. A., Azadegan, S., & Schneider, M. C. (2002). The Benefits of a Notification Process in Addressing the Worsening Computer Virus Problem: Results of a Survey and a Simulation Model. *Computers & Security*, *21*(2), 142–163. doi:10.1016/S0167-4048(02)00210-9

Artzy-Randrup, Y., Fleishman, S. J., Ben-Tal, N., & Stone, L. (2004). Comment on "Network motifs: Simple building blocks of complex networks" and" Superfamilies of evolved and designed networks. *Science*, *305*(5687), 1107–1107. doi:10.1126/science.1099334 PMID:15326338

Ashlock, D., Smucker, M., & Walker, J. (1999). Graph based genetic algorithms. In *Evolutionary Computation, 1999. CEC 99.Proceedings of the 1999 Congress on* (*Vol. 2*). IEEE.

Aslam, J. A., & Montague, M. (2001). Models for metasearch.*Proceedings of the 24th annual international ACM SIGIR conference on Research and development in information retrieval*(pp. 276-284). New York: ACM.

Atallah, L., Lo, B., Ali, R., King, R., & Yang, G.-Z. (2009, November). Real-time activity classification using ambient and wearable sensors. *IEEE Transactions on Information Technology in Biomedicine*, *13*(6), 1031–1039. doi:10.1109/TITB.2009.2028575 PMID:19726267

Atay, N., & Bayazit, B. (2010). Mobile wireless sensor network connectivity repair with *k*-redundancy. *Algorithmic Foundation of Robotics*, *8*, 35–49.

Atkins, D. E., Droegemeier, K. K., Feldman, S. I., Garcia-molina, H., Klein, M. L., Messerschmitt, D. G., . . . Wright, M. H. (2003). *Revolutionizing science and engineering through cyberinfrastructure: Report of the National Science Foundation blue-ribbon advisory panel on cyberinfrastructure.* Arlington, VA: National Science Foundation, NSF.

Backstrom, L., Boldi, P., Rosa, M., Ugander, J., & Vigna, S. (2012, June). Four degrees of separation. In *Proceedings of the 4th Annual ACM Web Science Conference* (pp. 33-42). ACM. doi:10.1145/2380718.2380723

Bailey, N. T. (1987). *The Mathematical Theory of Infectious Diseases* (2nd ed.). Oxford University Press.

Bai, X., Xuan, D., Yun, Z., Lai, T. H., & Jia, W. (2008). Complete optimal deployment patterns for full-coverage and *k*-connectivity ($k \leq 6$) wireless sensor networks.*Proceedings of the 9th ACM international symposium on Mobile ad hoc networking and computing* (pp. 401-410). ACM.

Balakrishnan, H., & Deo, N. (2006). Discovering Communities in Complex Networks.*Proceedings of the ACM Southeast Regional Conference*. ACM Press.

Ballard, D. H. (1981). Generalizing the Hough transform to detect arbitrary shapes. *Pattern Recognition*, *13*(2), 111–122. doi:10.1016/0031-3203(81)90009-1

Banerjee, A., Agarwal, R., Gauthier, V., Yeo, C. K., Afifi, H., & Lee, F. B. (2012). A self-organization framework for wireless ad hoc networks as small worlds.Vehicular Technology. *IEEE Transactions on*, *61*(6), 2659–2673.

Bao, Z., Zeng, Y., & Tay, Y. C. (2013). SonLP: Social network link prediction by principal component regression. *I Advances in Social Networks Analysis and Mining*, 364-371.

Barab'asi, A.-L., & Bianconi, G. (2001). Competition and multiscaling in evolving networks. *Europhysics Letters*, *54*(4), 436–442. doi:10.1209/epl/i2001-00260-6

Barabasi, A. L. (2002). Linked: The New Science of Networks. Academic Press.

Barabasi, A. L. (2003). *Linked: How Everything Is Connected to Everything Else and What It Means*. Cambridge, MA: Perseus Publishing.

Barabasi, A. L. (2009). Scale-Free Networks: A Decade and Beyond. *Science*, *325*(5939), 412–413. doi:10.1126/science.1173299 PMID:19628854

Barabási, A., Albert, R., & Jeong, H. (2000). Scale-free characteristics of random networks: The topology of the World-Wide Web. *Physica A. Statistical Mechanics and Its Applications*, *281*(1-4), 69–77. doi:10.1016/S0378-4371(00)00018-2

Barabasi, A.-L., & Albert, R. (1999). Emergence of scaling in random networks. *Science*, *286*(5439), 509–512. doi:10.1126/science.286.5439.509 PMID:10521342

Barinova, O., Lempitsky, V., & Kohli, P. (2010). *On the detection of multiple object instances using Hough Transforms, CVPR*. Beckman Coulter. Retrieved from http://www.coulter.com/coulter/Hematology/

Barrat, A., Barthelemy, M., Pastor-Satorras, R., & Vespignani, A. (2004). The architecture of complex weighted networks. *Proceedings of the National Academy of Sciences of the United States of America*, *101*(11), 3747–3752. doi:10.1073/pnas.0400087101 PMID:15007165

Barrat, A., Barthélemy, M., & Vespignani, A. (2008). *Dynamical Processes on Complex Networks*. Cambridge University Press.

Bar-Yehuda, R., & Even, S. (1981). A linear-time approximation algorithm for the weighted vertex cover problem. *Journal of Algorithms*, *2*(2), 198–203. doi:10.1016/0196-6774(81)90020-1

Bastian, M., Heymann, S., & Jacomy, M. (2009). *Gephi: An Open Source Software for Exploring and Manipulating Networks*. Association for the Advancement of Artificial Intelligence.

Bastian, M., Heymann, S., & Jacomy, M. (2009). Gephi: An open source software for exploring and manipulating networks. *ICWSM*, *8*, 361–362.

Batagelj, V., & Brandes, U. (2005). Efficient generation of large random networks. *Physical Review E: Statistical, Nonlinear, and Soft Matter Physics*, 71. PMID:15903499

Batagelj, V., & Zaversnik, M. (2011). An O(m) algorithm for cores decomposition of networks. *Advances in Data Analysis and Classification*, *5*(2), 129–145. doi:10.1007/s11634-010-0079-y

Battiston, F., Nicosia, V., & Latora, V. (2013). *Metrics for the analysis of multiplex networks*. arXive:1308.3182

Bavelas, A. (1948). A mathematical model for group structures. *Human Organization*, *7*(3), 16–30. doi:10.17730/humo.7.3.f4033344851gl053

Bavelas, A. (1950). Communication patterns in task-oriented groups. *The Journal of the Acoustical Society of America*, *22*(6), 725–730. doi:10.1121/1.1906679

Beauchamp, M. (1965). An improved index of centrality. *Behavioral Science*, *10*(2), 161–163. doi:10.1002/bs.3830100205 PMID:14284290

Beheshti, Z., & Shamsuddin, S. M. (2015). Non-parametric particle swarm optimization for global optimization. *Applied Soft Computing*, *28*, 345–359. doi:10.1016/j.asoc.2014.12.015

Bello-Orgaz, G., & Camacho, D. (2014, July). Evolutionary clustering algorithm for community detection using graph-based information. In *Evolutionary Computation (CEC), 2014 IEEE Congress on* (pp. 930-937). IEEE. doi:10.1109/CEC.2014.6900555

Benchettara, N., Kanawati, R., & Rouveirol, C. (2010). *Supervised machine learning applied to linkprediction in bipartite social networks.International Conference on Advances in Social Network Analysis and Mining, ASONAM 2010*. doi:10.1109/ASONAM.2010.87

Benevenuto, F., Rodrigues, F., & Cha, M. (2009). Characterizing User Behaviour in Online Social Networks.*Proceedings of ACM IMC.*

Bennett, L., Kittas, A., Liu, S., Papageorgiou, L. G., & Tsoka, S. (2014). Community Structure Detection for Overlapping Modules through Mathematical Programming in Protein Interaction Networks. *PLoS ONE*, *9*(11), e112821. doi:10.1371/journal.pone.0112821 PMID:25412367

Berlingerio, M., Bonchi, F., Bringmann, B., & Gionis, A. (2009). Mining graph evolution rules. In W. L. Buntine, M. Grobelnik, D. Mladenic, & J. Shawe-Taylor (Ed.), ECML/PKDD (vol. 5781, pp. 115-130). Springer. doi:10.1007/978-3-642-04180-8_25

Berlingerio, M., Coscia, M., Giannotti, F., Monreale, A., & Pedreschi, D. (2011). Foundations ofMultidimensional Network Analysis. *Advances in Social Networks Analysis and Mining*, *2011*, 485–489.

Bettstetter, C. (2002). On the minimum node degree and connectivity of a wireless multihop network. *Proceedings of the 3rd ACM international symposium on Mobile ad hoc networking & computing* (pp. 80-91). ACM. doi:10.1145/513800.513811

Beygelzimer, A., Grinstein, G., Linsker, R., & Rish, I. (2005). Improving network robustness by edge modification. *Physica A*, *3*(3-4), 593–612. doi:10.1016/j.physa.2005.03.040

Bhoir, S., & Vidhate, A. (2014, Jan). An improved wban mac protocol. In *International conference on computer communication and informatics* (pp. 1-6).

Biswas, A., Kumar, A., & Mishra, K. K. (2013, August). Particle Swarm Optimization with cognitive avoidance component. In *Advances in Computing, Communications and Informatics (ICACCI), 2013 International Conference on* (pp. 149-154). IEEE. doi:10.1109/ICACCI.2013.6637162

Biswas, A., & Biswas, B. (2015). Investigating Community Structure in Perspective of Ego Network. *Expert Systems with Applications*, *42*(20), 6913–6934. doi:10.1016/j.eswa.2015.05.009

Biswas, A., Gupta, P., Modi, M., & Biswas, B. (2014).Community Detection in Multiple Featured Social Network using Swarm Intelligence. In *International Conference on Communication and Computing*.

Biswas, A., Gupta, P., Modi, M., & Biswas, B. (2015). An Empirical Study of Some Particle Swarm Optimizer Variants for Community Detection. In *Advances in Intelligent Informatics* (pp. 511–520). Springer International Publishing. doi:10.1007/978-3-319-11218-3_46

Black, D., Newing, R., McLean, I., McMillan, A., & Monroe, B. (1998). The Theory of Committees and Elections (2nd ed.). Kluwer Academic Publishing.

Blondel, V. D., Guillaume, J., & Lefebvre, E. (2008). Fast unfolding of communities in largen etworks. *Journal of Statistical Mechanics*, *2008*(10), P10008. doi:10.1088/1742-5468/2008/10/P10008

Board on Army Science and Technology, Division on Engineering and Physical Sciences, & National Research Council. (2005). Network Science. Washington, DC: The National Academies Press.

Boccalettia, S., Latorab, V., Morenod, Y., Chavezf, M., & Hwanga, D.-U. (2006). Complex networks: Structure and dynamics. Elsevier. *Physics Reports*, *424*(4-5), 175–308. doi:10.1016/j.physrep.2005.10.009

Boccaletti, S. (2006). Complex Networks: Structure and Dynamics. *Physics Reports*, *424*, 175–308.

Bollobas, B. (2001). *Random Graphs*. Cambridge Univ. Press. doi:10.1017/CBO9780511814068

Bonato, A. (2005). A survey of models of the web graph,Combinatorial and algorithmic aspects of networking (LNCS), (vol. 3405, pp. 159–172). Berlin: Springer. doi:10.1007/11527954_16

Borda, J. D. (1781). *Mémoire sur les Elections au Scrutin*. Academic Press.

Bornholdt, S. (2003). Handbook of Graphs and Networks: From the Genome to the Internet. Wiley-VCH.

Bornholdt, S., & Schuster, H. G. (Eds.). (2006). *Handbook of graphs and networks: from the genome to the internet*. John Wiley & Sons.

Bounova, G., & de Weck, O. (2012). Overview of metrics and their correlation patterns for multiple-metric topology analysis on heterogeneous graph ensembles. *Physical Review E: Statistical, Nonlinear, and Soft Matter Physics*, *85*(1), 016117. doi:10.1103/PhysRevE.85.016117 PMID:22400635

Boyd, D., Ellison, N. (2007). Social Network Sites: Definition, History, and Scholarship. *Journ. of Computer-Mediated Comm.*, *13*, article 11.

Boyd, D. M., & Ellison, N. B. (2007). Social network sites: Definition, history, and scholarship. *Journal of Computer-Mediated Communication*, *13*(1), 210–230. doi:10.1111/j.1083-6101.2007.00393.x

Bragin, V. O., Vagaitsev, V. I., Kuznetsov, N. V., & Leonov, G. A. (2011). Algorithms for Finding Hidden Oscillations in Nonlinear Systems. The Aizerman and Kalman Conjectures and Chua's Circuits. *Journal of Computer and Systems Sciences International*, *50*(4), 511–543. doi:10.1134/S106423071104006X

Brandes, U., Delling, D., Gaertler, M., Görke, R., Hoefer, M., Nikoloski, Z., & Wagner, D. (2006). *Maximizing modularity is hard.* arXiv preprint physics/0608255

Bratchikov, A. (2007, Sept). Unified biophysical model for interaction of low intensity laser and ehf electromagnetic fields with cell biosystems and integral organizm. In *17th international Crimean conference microwave telecommunication technology* (pp. 774-775). doi:10.1109/CRMICO.2007.4368937

Bremermann, H. J. (1958). *The evolution of intelligence: The nervous system as a model of its environment.* University of Washington, Department of Mathematics.

Brest, J., Greiner, S., Bošković, B., Mernik, M., & Zumer, V. (2006). Self-adapting control parameters in differential evolution: A comparative study on numerical benchmark problems. *Evolutionary Computation. IEEE Transactions on*, *10*(6), 646–657.

Brest, J., & Maučec, M. S. (2008). Population size reduction for the differential evolution algorithm. *Applied Intelligence*, *29*(3), 228–247. doi:10.1007/s10489-007-0091-x

Broder, A., Kumar, R., Maghoul, F., Raghavan, P., Rajagopalan, S., Stata, R., & Wiener, J. et al. (2000). Graph structure in the web. *Computer Networks*, *33*(1-6), 309–320. doi:10.1016/S1389-1286(00)00083-9

Broom, M., Hadjichrysanthou, C., Rychtar, J., & Stadler, B. T. (2010). Two results on evolutionary processes on general non-directed graphs. *Proc. Royal. Soc. A*, *466*(2121), 2795–2798. doi:10.1098/rspa.2010.0067

Brouard, C., D'Alché-Buc, F., & Szafranski, M. (2011). Semi-supervised penalized output kernel regression for link prediction.*Proceedings of the 28th International Conference on Machine Learning (ICML-11)*.

Bruce, A., Johnson, A., Lewis, J., Raff, M., Roberts, K., & Walter, P. (2002). *Leukocyte functions and percentage breakdown. In Molecular Biology of the Cell* (4th ed.). New York: Garland Science.

Burda, Z., Krzywicki, A., Martin, O. C., & Zagorski, M. (2011). Motifs emerge from function in model gene regulatory networks. *Proceedings of the National Academy of Sciences of the United States of America*, *108*(42), 17263–17268. doi:10.1073/pnas.1109435108 PMID:21960444

Burjorjee, K. M. (2013, January). Explaining optimization in genetic algorithms with uniform crossover. In *Proceedings of the twelfth workshop on Foundations of genetic algorithms XII* (pp. 37-50). ACM. doi:10.1145/2460239.2460244

CAIDA. (2014). *AS Relationships.* Retrieved July 24, 2015, from http://www.caida.org/data/as-relationships

Caldarelli, G. (2007). *Scale-Free Networks: Complex Webs in Nature and Technology.* Oxford Univ. Press. doi:10.1093/acprof:oso/9780199211517.001.0001

Carmi, S., Havlin, S., Kirkpatrick, S., Shavitt, Y., & Shir, E. (2007). A model of Internet topology using k-shell decomposition. *Proceedings of the National Academy of Sciences of the United States of America*, *104*(27), 11150–11154. doi:10.1073/pnas.0701175104 PMID:17586683

Casillas, L. A., & Castillo, A. (2012). Discovering epistemological axes for academic programs in computer science through network analysis. *ReCIBE.* Retrieved from http://recibe.cucei.udg.mx

Casillas, L., & Daradoumis, T. (2009). Constructing a Multi-agent System for Discovering the Meaning over Natural-Language Collaborative Conversations. In T. Daradoumis, S. Caballé, & J. M. Márquez (Eds.), *Intelligent Collaborative e-Learning Systems and Applications* (pp. 99–112). Berlin: Springer-Verlag. doi:10.1007/978-3-642-04001-6_7

Casillas, L., & Daradoumis, T. (2012). An ontology structure for gathering and sharing knowledge among scientists. In *Collaborative and Distributed-Research: Innovations in Technologies, Strategies and Applications* (pp. 165–179). Hershey, PA: IGI Global. doi:10.4018/978-1-4666-0125-3.ch008

Casillas, L., Daradoumis, T., & Caballé, S. (2013). A network analysis method for selecting personalized content in e-Learning programs.*Seventh International Conference on Complex, Intelligent, and Software Intensive Systems* (pp. 407-411). Taichung, Taiwan: IEEE. doi:10.1109/CISIS.2013.74

Chakrabarti, S. A., & Aazhang A. (2003). Using PredictableObserver Mobility for Power Efficient Design of Sensor Networks. *Proc. IPSN 200.*

Chakraborty, U. K., Das, S., & Konar, A. (2006, September). Differential evolution with local neighborhood. In *Evolutionary Computation, 2006. CEC 2006. IEEE Congress on* (pp. 2042-2049). IEEE. doi:10.1109/CEC.2006.1688558

Chakraborty, A., & Manoj, B. S. (2014). The Reason Behind the Scale-Free World. *Sensors Journal, IEEE, 14*(11), 4014–4015. doi:10.1109/JSEN.2014.2351414

Chatterjee, A., Das, D., Naskar, M. K., Pal, N., & Mukherjee, A. (2013). Heuristic for maximum matching in directed complex networks. *International Conference on Advances in Computing, Communications and Informatics (ICACCI).* doi:10.1109/ICACCI.2013.6637339

Chauhan, S., Girvan, M., & Ott, E. (2009). Spectral properties of networks with community structure. *Physical Review E: Statistical, Nonlinear, and Soft Matter Physics, 80*(5), 056114. doi:10.1103/PhysRevE.80.056114 PMID:20365050

Chawla, N. V., Bowyer, K. W., Hall, L. O., & Kegelmeyer, W. P. (2002). SMOTE: Synthetic minority over-sampling technique. *Journal of Artificial Intelligence Research, 16*(1), 321–357.

Chebotarev, P., & Shamis, E. (1997). The matrix-forest theorem and measuring relations in small social groups. *Automation and Remote Control, 58*(9), 1505–1514.

Chen, S.-Y., Lee, W.-T., Chao, H.-C., Huang, Y.-M., & Lai, C.-F. (2011, Nov). Adaptive reconstruction of humanmotion on wireless body sensor networks. In *First international conference on wireless communications and signal processing* (pp. 1-5).

Chen, A. P., Huang, C. H., & Hsu, Y. C. (2011). Particle swarm optimization with inertia weight and constriction factor. In *International Conference on Swarm Intelligence (ICSI)*, (pp. 1-11).

Chen, G., Wang, X., & Xiang, L. (2015). *Fundamentals of Complex Networks: Models, Structures and Dynamics.* Wiley.

Chen, P., & Redner, S. (2010). Community structure of the physical review citation network. *Journal of Informetrics, 4*(3), 278–290. doi:10.1016/j.joi.2010.01.001

Chen, Y., & Qiu, X. (2013). Detecting Community Structures in Social Networks with Particle Swarm Optimization. In *Frontiers in Internet Technologies* (pp. 266–275). Springer Berlin Heidelberg. doi:10.1007/978-3-642-53959-6_24

Chevalier, C., & Safro, I. (2009). Comparison of coarsening schemes for multilevel graph partitioning. In *Including Subseries Lecture Notes in Artificial Intelligence and Lecture Notes in Bioinformatics)* (pp. 191–205). Springer. doi:10.1007/978-3-642-11169-3_14

Chiang, M., Low, S. H., Calderbank, A. R., & Doyle, J. C. (2007). Layering as optimization decomposition: A mathematical theory of network architectures. *Proceedings of the IEEE*, *95*(1), 255–312. doi:10.1109/JPROC.2006.887322

Choi, H., & Baraniuk, R. (2001). Multiscale: Image segmentation using wavelet-domain hidden Markov models. *IEEE Transactions on Image Processing*, *10*(9), 1309–1321. doi:10.1109/83.941855 PMID:18255546

Cho, K. (2012). Internet measurement and Big Data. *Internet Infrastructure Review*, *15*, 31–34.

Chung, F. R. (1997). *Spectral graph theory* (Vol. 92). American Mathematical Soc.

Chung, F., & Lu, L. (2002). Connected components in random graphs with given expected degree sequences. *Annals of Combinatorics*, *6*(2), 125–145. doi:10.1007/PL00012580

Chung, F., & Lu, L. (2002). The average distances in random graphs with given expected degrees. *Proceedings of the National Academy of Sciences of the United States of America*, *99*(25), 15879–15882. doi:10.1073/pnas.252631999 PMID:12466502

Clarkson, K. L. (1983). A modification of the greedy algorithm for vertex cover. *Information Processing Letters*, *16*(1), 23–25. doi:10.1016/0020-0190(83)90007-8

Clauset, A., Moore, C., & Newman, M. (2008). Hierarchical structure and the prediction of missinglinks in networks. *Nature*, *453*(7191), 98–101. doi:10.1038/nature06830 PMID:18451861

Clauset, A., Newman, M. E., & Moore, C. (2004). Finding community structure in very large networks. *Physical Review E: Statistical, Nonlinear, and Soft Matter Physics*, *70*(6), 066111. doi:10.1103/PhysRevE.70.066111 PMID:15697438

Clauset, A., Shalizi, C. R., & Newman, M. E. J. (2009). Power-Law Distributions in Empirical Data. *SIAM Review*, *51*(4), 661–703. doi:10.1137/070710111

Cohen, R., Erez, K., ben-Avraham, D., & Havlin, S. (2000). Resilience of the internet to random breakdowns. *Physical Review Letters*, *85*(21), 4626–4628. doi:10.1103/PhysRevLett.85.4626 PMID:11082612

Colizza, V., Flammini, A., Serrano, M. A., & Vespignani, A. (2006). Detecting rich-club ordering in complex networks. *Nature Physics*, *2*(2), 110–115. doi:10.1038/nphys209

Complete Blood Count. (n.d.). Retrieved from http://www.aidsinfonet.org/fact_sheets/view/121

Cooke, R. J. (2006). *Link prediction and link detection in sequences of large social networks using temporal and local metrics*. (Master Thesis). University of Cape Town.

Cooke, K. L., & van den Driessche, P. (1996). Analysis of an SEIRS epidemic model with two delays. *Journal of Mathematical Biology*, *35*(2), 240–260. doi:10.1007/s002850050051 PMID:9008370

Cornejo, A., & Lynch, N. (2010). *Fault-tolerance through k-connectivity*. Workshop on Network Science and Systems Issues in Multi-Robot Autonomy.

Costa, L., Rodrigues, F., Travieso, G., & Villas Boas, P. (2007). Characterization of complex networks: A survey of measurements. *Advances in Physics*, *56*(1), 167–242. doi:10.1080/00018730601170527

Costa, L., Villas Boas, P., Silva, F., & Rodrigues, F. (2010). A pattern recognition approach to complex networks. *Journal of Statistical Mechanics*, *2010*(11), P11015. doi:10.1088/1742-5468/2010/11/P11015

Costanzo, M. C., Crawford, M. E., Hirschman, J. E., Kranz, J. E., Olsen, P., Robertson, L. S., & Garrels, J. I. et al. (2001). YPD™, PombePD™ and WormPD™: Model organism volumes of the BioKnowledge™ Library, an integrated resource for protein information. *Nucleic Acids Research*, *29*(1), 75–79. doi:10.1093/nar/29.1.75 PMID:11125054

Cowan, N. J., Chastain, E. J., Vilhena, D.A., Freudenberg J. S., & Bergstrom, C. T. (2012). *Nodal dynamics, not degree distributions, determine the structural controllability of complex networks*. Academic Press.

Crucitti, P., Latora, V., Marchiori, M., & Rapisarda, A. (2004). Error and attack tolerance of complex networks. *Physica A, 340*(1-3), 388–394. doi:10.1016/j.physa.2004.04.031

Cui, N., & Li, J. (2012). An SEIRS Model with a Nonlinear Incidence Rate. *Procedia Engineering, 29*(0), 3929–3933. doi:10.1016/j.proeng.2012.01.596

Curia, V., Tropea, M., Fazio, P., & Marano, S. (2014). Complex networks: Study and performance evaluation with hybrid model for Wireless Sensor Networks. *IEEE 27th Canadian Conference on Electrical and Computer Engineering* (CCECE), (pp. 1-5). IEEE.

Cutillo, L. A., & Molva, R. (2009) Privacy Preserving Social Networking Through Decentralization. In *Proceedings of the Sixth International Conference on Wireless On-Demand Network Systems and Services*. doi:10.1109/WONS.2009.4801860

Dagdeviren, O., & Akram, V. K. (2014). An Energy-Efficient Distributed Cut Vertex Detection Algorithm for Wireless Sensor Networks. *The Computer Journal, 57*(12), 1852–1869. doi:10.1093/comjnl/bxt128

Daradoumis, T., & Casillas, L. (2006). A Neural Approach for Modeling the Inference of Awareness in Computer-Supported Collaboration. In N. Wolfgang & K. Tochtermann (Eds.), Innovative Approaches for Learning and Knowledge Sharing (LNCS), (vol. 4227, pp. 464–469). Hannover, Germany: Springer. doi:10.1007/11876663_37

Das, D., Chatterjee, A., Bandyopadhyay, B., & Ahmed, S. J. (2014). Characterizing behaviour of Complex networks against perturbations and generation of Pseudo-random networks. *India Conference (INDICON), 2014Annual IEEE*. doi:10.1109/INDICON.2014.7030428

Das, D., Chatterjee, A., Pal, N., Mukherjee, A., & Naskar, M. (2014). A degree-first greedy search algorithm for the evaluation of structural controllability of real world directed complex networks. *Network Protocols and Algorithms, 6*(1), 1–18. doi:10.5296/npa.v6i1.4756

Dashora, Y., Kumar, S., Shukla, N., & Tiwari, M. K. (2007). Improved and generalized learning strategies for dynamically fast and statistically robust evolutionary algorithms. *Engineering Applications of Artificial Intelligence*. doi:10.1016/j.engappai.2007.06.005

Das, S., Abraham, A., Chakraborty, U. K., & Konar, A. (2009). Differential evolution using a neighborhood-based mutation operator. *Evolutionary Computation. IEEE Transactions on, 13*(3), 526–553.

Das, S., & Suganthan, P. N. (2011). Differential evolution: A survey of the state-of-the-art. *Evolutionary Computation. IEEE Transactions on, 15*(1), 4–31.

Davendra, D., Zelinka, I., Metlicka, M., Senkerik, R., & Pluhacek, M. (2014, December). Complex network analysis of differential evolution algorithm applied to flowshop with no-wait problem. In *Differential Evolution (SDE), 2014 IEEE Symposium on* (pp. 1-8). IEEE. doi:10.1109/SDE.2014.7031536

Davendra, D., Zelinka, I., Senkerik, R., & Pluhacek, M. (2014). Complex Network Analysis of Discrete Self-organising Migrating Algorithm. In Nostradamus 2014: Prediction, Modeling and Analysis of Complex Systems (pp. 161-174). Springer International Publishing.

Davendra, D., & Metlicka, M. (2015). Ensemble Centralities based Adaptive Artificial Bee Algorithm. *IEEE Congress on Evolutionary Computation*.

Davendra, D., Zelinka, I., Metlicka, M., Senkerik, R., & Pluhacek, M. (2014). *Complex network analysis of differential evolution algorithm applied to flow- shop with no-wait problem.IEEE Symposium on Differential Evolution*, Orlando, FL.

Davis, D., Lichtenwalter, R., & Chawla, N. V. (2013). Supervised methods for multi-relational link prediction. *Social Network Analysis and Mining*, 1-15.

Davis, J., & Goadrich, M. (2006). The relationship between Precision-Recall and ROC curves.*Proceedings of the 23rd international conference on Machine learning.* doi:10.1145/1143844.1143874

De Finetti, B. (1931). *Funzione caratteristica di un fenomeno aleatorio.* Academic Press.

de Francisco, R., Huang, L., & Dolmans, G. (2009, Sept). Coexistence of wban and wlan in medical environments. In *IEEE 70th vehicular technology conference fall* (pp. 1-5). doi:10.1109/VETECF.2009.5378807

De Jong, K. A., & Spears, W. M. (1992). A formal analysis of the role of multi-point crossover in genetic algorithms. *Annals of Mathematics and Artificial Intelligence*, *5*(1), 1–26. doi:10.1007/BF01530777

De Rango, F., Amelio, S., & Fazio, P. (2014). Epidemic Strategies in Delay Tolerant Networks from an Energetic Point of View: Main Issues and Performance Evaluation. Journal of Networks, 10(1), 4-14.

De Rango, F., Tropea, M., Laratta, G. B., & Marano, S. (2008). Hop-by-Hop Local Flow Control over InterPlaNetary Networks Based on DTN Architecture. In *Communications, IEEE International Conference on.* doi:10.1109/ICC.2008.368

De Rango, F., Amelio, S., & Fazio, P. (2013). Enhancements of epidemic routing in delay tolerant networks from an energy perspective.*9th International Wireless Communications and Mobile Computing Conference, IWCMC 2013.* doi:10.1109/IWCMC.2013.6583647

De Rango, F., Gerla, M., & Marano, S. (2006). A scalable routing scheme with group motion support in large and dense wireless ad hoc networks. *Computers & Electrical Engineering*, *32*(1), 224–240. doi:10.1016/j.compeleceng.2006.01.017

De Rango, F., Guerriero, F., & Fazio, P. (2012). Link-stability and energy aware routing protocol in distributed wireless networks.Parallel and Distributed Systems. *IEEE Transactions on*, *23*(4), 713–726.

De Rango, F., Veltri, F., Fazio, P., & Marano, S. (2009). Two-level trajectory-based routing protocol for vehicular ad hoc networks in freeway and Manhattan environments. *Journal of Networks*, *4*(9), 866–880. doi:10.4304/jnw.4.9.866-880

De Vos, J., Flandre, D., & Bol, D. (2014, May). Switchedcapacitor dc/dc converters for empowering internet-of-things socs. In IEEE faible tension faible consummation (FTFC) (pp. 1-4).

Deb, N., & Chakraborty, S. (2014). A noble technique for detecting anemia through classification of red blood cells in blood smear. *Recent Advances and Innovations in Engineering*, *2014*, 1–9.

Degli-Esposti, V. (2014, April). Ray tracing propagation modelling: Future prospects. In *8th European conference on antennas and propagation* (pp. 2232-2232).

Delbot, F., Laforest, C., & Rovedakis, S. (2014). Self-stabilizing algorithms for Connected Vertex Cover and Clique decomposition problems. *Principles of Distributed Systems*, 307-322.

Demirci, E., & Unal, A., & Zalp, N. (2011). A fractional order Seir model with density dependent death rate. *Hacettepe Journal of Mathematics and Statistics*, *40*(2), 287–295.

Dey, P., Sinha, A., & Roy, S. (2015). Social Network Analysis of Different Parameters Derived from Realtime Profile. Distributed Computing and Internet Technology. *Lecture Notes in Computer Science*, *8956*, 452–455. doi:10.1007/978-3-319-14977-6_50

Dhamdhere, A., & Dovrolis, C. (2011). Twelve years in the evolution of the Internet ecosystem. *IEEE/ACM Transactions on Networking*, *19*(5), 1420–1433. doi:10.1109/TNET.2011.2119327

Didimo, W., Liotta, G., & Montecchiani, F. (2014). Network visualization for financial crime detection. *Journal of Visual Languages and Computing*, *25*(4), 433–451. doi:10.1016/j.jvlc.2014.01.002

Diekmann, O., & Heesterbeek, J. A. P. (2000). *Mathematical epidemiology of infectious diseases: Model building, analysis and interpretation*. Chichester, UK: John Wiley & Sons Ltd.

Dorigo, M., & Stützle, T. (2004). *Ant Colony Optimization*. MIT Press.

Dorogovtsev, S. N., & Mendes, J. F. (2002). Evolution of networks. *Advances in Physics*, *51*(4), 1079–1187. doi:10.1080/00018730110112519

Dorogovtsev, S. N., & Mendes, J. F. (2013). *Evolution of networks: From biological nets to the Internet and WWW*. Oxford University Press.

Dorogovtsev, S. N., & Mendes, J. F. F. (2003). *Evolution of Networks: From Biological Nets to the Internet and WWW*. Oxford Univ. Press. doi:10.1093/acprof:oso/9780198515906.001.0001

Dorogovtsev, S., Goltsev, A., & Mendes, J. (2006). K-core organization of complex networks. *Physical Review Letters*, *96*(040601), 1–4. PMID:16486798

dos Santos Coelho, L., Ayala, H. V. H., & Mariani, V. C. (2014). A self-adaptive chaotic differential evolution algorithm using gamma distribution for unconstrained global optimization. *Applied Mathematics and Computation*, *234*, 452–459. doi:10.1016/j.amc.2014.01.159

Duch, J., & Arenas, A. (2005). Community detection in complex networks using extremal optimization. *Physical Review E: Statistical, Nonlinear, and Soft Matter Physics*, *72*(2), 027104. doi:10.1103/PhysRevE.72.027104 PMID:16196754

Duda, R. O., & Hart, P. E. (1972). Use of the Hough Transformation to Detect Lines and Curves in Pictures. *Communications of the ACM*, *15*(1), 11–15. doi:10.1145/361237.361242

Dunlavy, D. M., Kolda, T. G., & Acar, E. (2011). Temporal link prediction using matrix and tensor factorizations. *ACM Transactions on Knowledge Discovery from Data*, *5*(2), 10. doi:10.1145/1921632.1921636

Dwork, C., Kumar, R., Naor, M., & Sivakumar, D. (2001). Rank aggregation methods for the web.*Proceedings of the 10th international conference on World Wide Web.*ACM.

Eberhart, R. C., & Shi, Y. (2000). Comparing inertia weights and constriction factors in particle swarm optimization. In *Evolutionary Computation, 2000.Proceedings of the 2000 Congress on* (*Vol. 1*, pp. 84-88). IEEE. doi:10.1109/CEC.2000.870279

Eberhart, R. C., & Kennedy, J. (1995, October). A new optimizer using particle swarm theory. In *Proceedings of the sixth international symposium on micro machine and human science* (Vol. 1, pp. 39-43). doi:10.1109/MHS.1995.494215

Ebrahimzadeh, R., & Jampour, M. (2013). Chaotic Genetic Algorithm based on Lorenz Chaotic System for Optimization Problems. *International Journal of Intelligent Systems and Applications*, *5*(5), 19–24. doi:10.5815/ijisa.2013.05.03

Edmonds, J. (1965, April-June). Maximum matching and a polyhedron with0,1 vertices. *J. Res. NBS*, *698*, 125–130.

Eiben, A. E., & Smith, J. E. (2003). *Introduction to evolutionary computing*. Springer Science & Business Media. doi:10.1007/978-3-662-05094-1

Elaine, H., & Marieb, N. (2006). *Essentials of Human Anatomy & Physiology* (8th ed.). Pearson Benjamin Cummings.

Elsayed, S. M., Sarker, R. A., & Essam, D. L. (2011, June). GA with a new multi-parent crossover for solving IEEE-CEC2011 competition problems. In *Evolutionary Computation (CEC), 2011 IEEE Congress on* (pp. 1034-1040). IEEE.

Erciyes, K. (2013). *Distributed graph algorithms for computer networks*. London: Springer. doi:10.1007/978-1-4471-5173-9

Erdős, P., & Rényi. (1960). *On the evolution of random graphs*. Mathematical Institute of the Hungarian Academy of Sciences.

Erdos, P., & R&WI, A. (1959). On random graphs I. *Publ. Math. Debrecen*, *6*, 290–297.

Erdős, P., & Rényi, A. (1960). On the evolution of random graphs. *Publ. Math. Inst. Hung. Acad. Sci.*, *5*, 17–61.

Eronen, L., & Toivonen, H. (2012). Biomine: Predicting links between biological entities using network models of heterogeneous databases. *BMC Bioinformatics*, *13*(1), 119. doi:10.1186/1471-2105-13-119 PMID:22672646

Evans, T. S., (2004). Complex Networks. *Contemporary Physics*.

Even, S. (1975). An algorithm for determining whether the connectivity of a graph is at least *k*. *SIAM Journal on Computing*, *4*(3), 393–396. doi:10.1137/0204034

Even, S., & Tarjan, R. E. (1975). Network flow and testing graph connectivity. *SIAM Journal on Computing*, *4*(4), 507–518. doi:10.1137/0204043

Fabre, J., Camart, J., Prevost, B., Chive, M., & Sozanski, J. (1992, Oct). 915 mhz interstitial hyperthermia: Dosimetry from heating pattern reconstruction based on radiometric temperature measurements. In *14th annual international conference of the IEEE engineering in medicine and biology society* (Vol. 1, pp. 231-231).

Falcone, F., Haas, H., & Gibbs, B. (2000). The human basophil: A new appreciation of its role in immune responses. *Blood*, *96*(13), 4028–4038. PMID:11110670

Faloutsos, M., Faloutsos, P., & Faloutsos, C. (1999). On power-law relationships of the internet topology. *Computer Communication Review*, *29*(4), 251–262. doi:10.1145/316194.316229

Fan, H. Y., & Lampinen, J. (2003). A trigonometric mutation operation to differential evolution. *Journal of Global Optimization*, *27*(1), 105–129. doi:10.1023/A:1024653025686

Faragó, A. (2007). On the fundamental limits of topology control in ad hoc networks. *Algorithmica*, *49*(4), 337–356. doi:10.1007/s00453-007-9078-6

Faragó, A. (2009). Scalability of node degrees in random wireless network topologies. Selected Areas in Communications. *IEEE Journal on*, *27*(7), 1238–1244.

Faragó, A. (2011). Asymptotically optimal trade-off between local and global connectivity in wireless networks. *Performance Evaluation*, *68*(2), 142–156. doi:10.1016/j.peva.2010.08.024

Fazio, P., Tropea, M., Marano, S., & Sottile, C. (2013, November). Pattern prediction in infrastructured wireless networks: Directional vs temporal statistical approach. In *Wireless Days (WD), 2013 IFIP* (pp. 1-5). IEEE.

Fazio, P., De Rango, F., & Sottile, C. (2012). An on demand interference aware routing protocol for VANETS. *Journal of Networks*, *7*(11), 1728–1738. doi:10.4304/jnw.7.11.1728-1738

Fazio, P., De Rango, F., Sottile, C., & Santamaria, A. F. (2013). Routing optimization in vehicular networks: A new approach based on multiobjective metrics and minimum spanning tree. *International Journal of Distributed Sensor Networks*, *2013*, 1–13. doi:10.1155/2013/598675

Fazio, P., & Tropea, M. (2012). A new markovian prediction scheme for resource reservations in wireless networks with mobile hosts. *Advances in Electrical and Electronic Engineering*, *10*(4), 204–210. doi:10.15598/aeee.v10i4.716

Filkov, V., Saul, Z., Roy, S., D'Souza, R., & Devanbu, P. (2009). Modeling and verifying a broad array of network properties. *Europhysics Letters*, *86*(2), 28003. doi:10.1209/0295-5075/86/28003

Fire, M., Tenenboim, L., Lesser, O., Puzis, R., Rokach, L., & Elovici, Y. (2011). Link prediction in social networks using computationally efficient topological features.*Proceedings of the 3rd IEEE Int. Conference on Social Computing*. doi:10.1109/PASSAT/SocialCom.2011.20

Fogel, D. B. (1998). Unearthing a Fossil from the History of Evolutionary Computation. *Fundamenta Informaticae*, *35*(1-4), 1–16.

Fortunato, S., &Castellano, C. (2007). *Community Structure in Graphs*. Physics Report.

Fortunato, S. (2010). Community detection in graphs. *Physics Reports*, *486*(3-5), 75–174. doi:10.1016/j.physrep.2009.11.002

Fortunato, S., & Castellano, C. (2012). Community structure in graphs. In *Computational Complexity* (pp. 490–512). Springer New York. doi:10.1007/978-1-4614-1800-9_33

Franceschetti, M., & Meester, R. (2008). *Random networks for communication: from statistical physics to information systems* (Vol. 24). Cambridge University Press. doi:10.1017/CBO9780511619632

Freeman, L. C. (1978/1979). Centrality in social networks: Conceptual clarification. *Social Networks*, *1*(3), 215–239. doi:10.1016/0378-8733(78)90021-7

Freeman, L. C., Borgatti, S. P., & White, D. R. (1991). Centrality in valued graphs: A measure of betweenness based on network flow. *Social Networks*, *13*(2), 141–154. doi:10.1016/0378-8733(91)90017-N

Fretter, C., Müller-Hannemann, M., & Hütt, M. T. (2012). Subgraph fluctuations in random graphs. *Physical Review E: Statistical, Nonlinear, and Soft Matter Physics*, *85*(5), 056119. doi:10.1103/PhysRevE.85.056119 PMID:23004833

Fruchterman, T. M. J., & Reingold, E. M. (1991). Graph drawing by force-directed placement. *Software, Practice & Experience*, *21*(11), 1129–1164. doi:10.1002/spe.4380211102

Gafurov, D., Snekkenes, E., & Bours, P. (2010, April). Improved gait recognition performance using cycle matching. In *24th international conference on advanced information networking and applications workshops (waina)* (pp. 836-841). doi:10.1109/WAINA.2010.145

Galil, Z. (1980). Efficient Algorithms for finding Maximum Matching in Graphs. *ACM Computing Surveys*.

Galil, Z. (1980). Finding the vertex connectivity of graphs. *SIAM Journal on Computing*, *9*(1), 197–199. doi:10.1137/0209016

Gao, S., Denoyer, L., & Gallinari, P. (2011*)*. Temporal link prediction by integrating content and structure information. *Proceedings of the 20th ACM international conference on Information and knowledge management - CIKM '11* (p. 1169). New York: ACM Press. doi:10.1145/2063576.2063744

García-Robledo, A., Díaz-Pérez, A., & Morales-Luna, G. (2013). Correlation analysis of complex network metrics on the topology of the Internet. In *Proceedings of the 10th International Conference and Expo on Emerging Technologies for a Smarter World* (pp.1-6). *Melville, NY*. IEEE Society. doi:10.1109/CEWIT.2013.6713749

Garshol, L. M. (2004). *Metadata? Thesauri? Taxonomies? Topic Maps! Making sense of it all*. Retrieved from http://www.ontopia.net/topicmaps/materials/tm-vs-thesauri.html

Gehrke, J., Ginsparg, P., & Kleinberg, J. (2003). Overview of the 2003 KDD Cup. *ACM SIGKDD Explorations Newsletter*, *5*(2), 149–151. doi:10.1145/980972.980992

Getoor, L., Friedman, N., Koller, D., & Taskar, B. (2003). Learning probabilistic models of link structure. *Journal of Machine Learning Research*, *3*, 679–707.

Gilpin, S., Eliassi-Rad, T., & Davidson, I. (2013). Guided learning for role discovery (glrd): Framework, algorithms, and applications. In *Proceedings of the 19th ACM SIGKDD international conference on Knowledge discovery and data mining* (pp. 113-121). ACM. doi:10.1145/2487575.2487620

Girvan, M., & Newman, M. E. (2002). Community structure in social and biological networks. *Proceedings of the National Academy of Sciences of the United States of America*, *99*(12), 7821–7826. doi:10.1073/pnas.122653799 PMID:12060727

Goh, C., Ong, Y., & Tan, K. (2009). *Multi-Objective Memetic Algorithms*. Springer-Verlag. doi:10.1007/978-3-540-88051-6

Goldberg, D. (1989). *Genetic Algorithms in Search, Optimization, and Machine Learning*. Addison-Wesley Publishing Company Inc.

Gong, M., Cai, Q., Chen, X., & Ma, L. (2014). Complex network clustering by multiobjective discrete particle swarm optimization based on decomposition. *Evolutionary Computation. IEEE Transactions on*, *18*(1), 82–97.

Grandoni, F., Könemann, J., & Panconesi, A. (2005). Distributed weighted vertex cover via maximal matchings. *Computing and Combinatorics*, 839-848.

Gruber, T. R. (1993). *A Translation Approach to Portable Ontology Specifications*. Palo Alto, CA: Knowledge Systems Laboratory, Stanford University.

Guidoni, D. L., Mini, R. A., & Loureiro, A. A. (2008). Creating small-world models in wireless sensor networks. *IEEE 19th International Symposium on Personal, Indoor and Mobile Radio Communications. PIMRC 2008* (pp. 1-6). IEEE. doi:10.1109/PIMRC.2008.4699823

Guidoni, D. L., Mini, R. A., & Loureiro, A. A. (2012). Applying the small world concepts in the design of heterogeneous wireless sensor networks. *Communications Letters, IEEE*, *16*(7), 953–955. doi:10.1109/LCOMM.2012.052112.120417

Guillaume, J.-L. (2004). *MatthieuLatapy*. Bipartite Graphs as Models of Complex Networks. CAAN.

Guo, L., Zuo, W., Peng, T., & Adhikari, B. K. (2015). Attribute-based edge bundling for visualizing social networks. *Physica A: Statistical Mechanics and its Applications*, *438*, 48-55.

Hanckowiak, M., Karonski, M., & Panconesi, A. (1998). *On the Distributed Complexity of Computing Maximal Matchings*. ACM-SIAM SODA.

Hanckowiak, M., Karonski, M., & Panconesi, A. (2001). On the distributed complexity of computing maximal matchings. *SIAM Journal on Discrete Mathematics*, *15*(1), 41–57. doi:10.1137/S0895480100373121

Han, H. J., Schweickert, R., Xi, Z., & Viau-Quesnel, C. (2015). The Cognitive Social Network in Dreams: Transitivity, Assortativity, and Giant Component Proportion Are Monotonic. *Cognitive Science*, n/a. doi:10.1111/cogs.12244 PMID:25981854

Han, J., Kamber, M., & Pei, J. (2006). *Data mining, Southeast Asia edition: Concepts and techniques*. Morgan kaufmann.

Hari, J., & Prasad, A. S., & Rao, S.K. (2014). Separation and counting of blood cells using geometrical features and distance transformed watershed.*2nd International Conference on Devices, Circuits and Systems (ICDCS)*. doi:10.1109/ICDCSyst.2014.6926205

Hart, W., Krasnogor, N., & Smith, J. (2005). *Recent Advances in Memetic Algorithms*. Springer-Verlag.

Hasan, M. A., Chaoji, V., Salem, S., & Zaki, M. (2006). *Link prediction using supervised learning*. Workshop on link analysis, Counter-terrorism and security, SIAM Data Mining Conference.

He, D., Wang, Z., Yang, B., & Zhou, C. (2009, November). Genetic algorithm with ensemble learning for detecting community structure in complex networks. In *Computer Sciences and Convergence Information Technology, 2009. ICCIT'09. Fourth International Conference on* (pp. 702-707). IEEE. doi:10.1109/ICCIT.2009.189

He, T., & Chan, K. C. (2014, July). Evolutionary community detection in social networks. In *Evolutionary Computation (CEC), 2014 IEEE Congress on* (pp. 1496-1503). IEEE. doi:10.1109/CEC.2014.6900570

He, Z., Luo, Y., & Liang, G. (2013, April). Runking: A mobile social persuasion system for running exercise. In Computing, communications and it applications conference (pp. 74-78).

Henderson, K., Gallagher, B., Eliassi-Rad, T., Tong, H., Basu, S., Akoglu, L., & Li, L. et al. (2012). Rolx: structural role extraction & mining in large graphs. In *Proceedings of the 18th ACM SIGKDD international conference on Knowledge discovery and data mining* (pp. 1231-1239). ACM. doi:10.1145/2339530.2339723

Hennessey, D., Brooks, D., Fridman, A., & Breen, D. (2008). A simplification algorithm for visualizing the structure of complex graphs. In *Proceedings of the IEEE 12th International Conference on Information Visualisation* (pp. 616-625). London. doi:10.1109/IV.2008.37

Henzinger, M. R., Rao, S., & Gabow, H. N. (2000). Computing vertex connectivity: New bounds from old techniques. *Journal of Algorithms*, *34*(2), 222–250. doi:10.1006/jagm.1999.1055

Hethcote, H. W. (1976). Qualitative analyses of communicable disease models. *Mathematical Biosciences*, *28*(3–4), 335–356. doi:10.1016/0025-5564(76)90132-2

Hilborn, R. (1994). *Chaos and Nonlinear Dynamics*. Oxford University Press.

Hoepman, J. H. (2004). *Simple distributed weighted matchings.* arXiv preprint cs/0410047

Holland, J. (1975). *Adaptation in natural and artificial systems*. Ann Arbor, MI: Univ. of Michigan Press.

Holland, J. H. (1975). *Adaptation in natural and artificial systems: an introductory analysis with applications to biology, control, and artificial intelligence*. U Michigan Press.

Holme, P., Park, S. M., Kim, B. J., & Edling, C. R. (2007). Korean university life in a network perspective: Dynamics of a large affiliation network. *Physica A: Statistical Mechanics and its Applications, 373*, 821-830.

Hopcroft, J. E., & Karp, R. M. (1973). An n5/2 algorithm for maximum matchings in bipartite graphs. *SIAM Journal on Computing*, 2.

Horrigan, M., & Haag, R. (2008). *Syllabus Design*. Oxford, UK: Oxford University Press.

Hough, P. V. C. (1962). *Method and means for recognizing complex patterns*. U.S. Patent 3,069,654.

Huang, J., Xie, Q., & Huang, B. (2012). Creating Small-World Model for Homogeneous Wireless Sensor Networks. *Wireless Communications, Networking and Mobile Computing (WiCOM), 8th International Conference on*. doi:10.1109/WiCOM.2012.6478470

Huang, C.-W., Kuo, S.-W., & Chang, C.-J. (2013, July). Embedded 8-bit aes in wireless bluetooth application. In *International conference on system science and engineering (ICSSE)* (pp. 87-92). doi:10.1109/ICSSE.2013.6614638

Huang, T.-C., & Chen, C.-C. (2013). Animating Civic Education: Developing a Knowledge Navigation System using Blogging and Topic Map Technology. *Journal of Educational Technology & Society*, *16*(1), 79–92.

Huang, Z., & Lin, D. K. (2008). The time-series link prediction problem with applications in communication surveillance. *INFORMS Journal on Computing, 21*(2), 286–303. doi:10.1287/ijoc.1080.0292

Iorio, A. W., & Li, X. (2005). Solving rotated multi-objective optimization problems using differential evolution. In *AI 2004: Advances in artificial intelligence* (pp. 861–872). Springer Berlin Heidelberg.

Isaila, N. (2012). The Technology in New Learning Environments. *International Journal of Academic Research in Accounting, Finance and Management Sciences,* 2(Special Issue 1), 128-131.

Islam, S. M., Das, S., Ghosh, S., Roy, S., & Suganthan, P. N. (2012). An adaptive differential evolution algorithm with novel mutation and crossover strategies for global numerical optimization. *Systems, Man, and Cybernetics, Part B: Cybernetics. IEEE Transactions on, 42*(2), 482–500.

Ivanov, S., Foley, C., Balasubramaniam, S., & Botvich, D. (2012b, Nov). Virtual groups for patient wban monitoring in medical environments. *IEEE Transactions on Biomedical Engineering, 59*(11), 3238-3246.

Ivanov, S., Foley, C., Balasubramaniam, S., & Botvich, D. (2012a, November). Virtual groups for patient wban monitoring in medical environments. *IEEE Transactions on Bio-Medical Engineering, 59*(11), 3238–3246. doi:10.1109/TBME.2012.2208110 PMID:22801487

J.-L. Guillaume, M. Latapy, & C. Magnien, (2005). Comparison of failures and attacks on random and scale-free networks. In *OPODIS* (LNCS), (pp. 186 – 196). Berlin: Springer.

Jaccard, P. (1901). Étude comparative de la distribution florale dans une portion des alpes et des jura. *Bulletin de la Société Vaudoise des Sciences Naturelles, 37*, 547–579.

Jacomy, M., Heymann, S., Venturini, T., & Bastian, M. (2010). Force Atlas2, A Continuous Graph Layout Algorithm for Handy Network Visualization. *PLoS ONE, 9*(6).

Jain, S., Shah, R., Brunette, W., Borriello, G., & Roy, S. (2006). ExploitingMobility for Energy Efficient Data Collection in Wireless Sensor Networks. ACM/Springer. *Mobile Networks and Applications, 11*(3), 327–339. doi:10.1007/s11036-006-5186-9

Jamakovic, A., & Uhlig, S. (2008). On the relationships between topological measures in real-world networks. *Networks and Heterogeneous Media, 3*(2), 345–359. doi:10.3934/nhm.2008.3.345

Jeacocke, & Lovell. (1994). A Multi-resolution algorithm for Cytological image segmentation. *The second Australian and New Zealand conference on intelligent information systems.*

Jea, D., Somasundra, A., & Srivastava, M. (2005). Multiple ControlledMobile Elements (Data Mules) for Data Collection in SensorNetworks.*Proc. IEEE DCOSS 2005.*

Jiang, C. J., Chen, C., Chang, J. W., Jan, R. H., & Chiang, T. C. (2008, June). Construct small worlds in wireless networks using data mules. In *Sensor Networks, Ubiquitous and Trustworthy Computing, 2008. SUTC'08. IEEE International Conference on* (pp. 28-35). IEEE. doi:10.1109/SUTC.2008.93

Jin, D., He, D., Liu, D., & Baquero, C. (2010, October). Genetic algorithm with local search for community mining in complex networks. In *Tools with Artificial Intelligence (ICTAI), 2010 22nd IEEE International Conference on* (Vol. 1, pp. 105-112). IEEE. doi:10.1109/ICTAI.2010.23

Jolliffe, I. (2002). *Principal Component Analysis*. New York, NY: Springer.

Jorgic, M., Goel, N., Kalaichevan, K. A. L. A. I., Nayak, A., & Stojmenovic, I. (2007). Localized detection of *k*-connectivity in wireless ad hoc, actuator and sensor networks. *Proceedings of 16th International Conference on Computer Communications and Networks, ICCCN 2007* (pp. 33-38). IEEE. doi:10.1109/ICCCN.2007.4317793

Kafai, Y. (2008). Understanding Virtual Epidemics: Children's Folk Conceptions of a Computer Virus. *Journal of Science Education and Technology*, *17*(6), 523–529. doi:10.1007/s10956-008-9102-x

Kallenberg, O. (2006). *Probabilistic symmetries and invariance principles*. Springer Science & Business Media.

Kalman, R.E., (1963). Mathematical description of linear dynamical systems. *J. Soc Indus. Appl. Math Ser., A1*, 152-192.

Kalna, G., & Higham, D. J. (2006, April). Clustering coefficients for weighted networks. In *Symposium on Network Analysis in Natural Sciences and Engineering* (p. 45).

Kang, S. (2012). *From Curriculum to Syllabus Design:AATK Workshop*. Stanford University.

Kannan, R. (2010). Topic Map: An Ontology Framework for Information Retrieval.*National Conference on Advances in Knowledge Management (NCAKM'10).*

Kannan, R., Vempala, S., & Vetta, A. (2004). On clusterings: Good, bad and spectral. *Journal of the ACM*, *51*(3), 497–515. doi:10.1145/990308.990313

Kantz, H., & Schreiber, T. (1997). *Nonlinear time series analysis*. Cambridge, UK: Cambridge University Press.

Kashima, H., Kato, T., Yamanishi, Y., Sugiyama, M., & Tsuda, K. (2009). Link propagation: A fast semi-supervised learning algorithm for link prediction. *SDM*, *9*, 1099–1110.

Kathuria, M., & Gambhir, S. (2014, Feb). Quality of service provisioning transport layer protocol for wban system. In *International conference on optimization, reliabilty, and information technology* (pp. 222-228). doi:10.1109/ICROIT.2014.6798318

Katz, L. (1953). A new status index derived from socimetric analysis. *Psychmetrika*, *18*(1), 39–43. doi:10.1007/BF02289026

Kavalci, V., Ural, A., & Dagdeviren, O. (2014). Distributed Vertex Cover Algorithms For Wireless Sensor Networks. *International Journal of Computer Networks & Communications*, *6*(1), 95–110. doi:10.5121/ijcnc.2014.6107

Kelly, F. P., Maulloo, A. K., & Tan, D. K. H. (1998). Rate control for communication networks: Shadow prices, proportional fairness and stability. *The Journal of the Operational Research Society*, *49*(3), 237–252. doi:10.1057/palgrave.jors.2600523

Kermack, W. O., & McKendrick, A. G. (1927). A Contribution to the Mathematical Theory of Epidemics. *Proc. R. Soc., 115*, 700-721.

Khaleghi, A., Chavez-Santiago, R., & Balasingham, I. (2010, October). Ultra-wideband pulse-based data communications for medical implants. *Communications, IET*, *4*(15), 1889–1897. doi:10.1049/iet-com.2009.0692

Khanesar, M. A., Teshnehlab, M., & Shoorehdeli, M. A. (2007, June). A novel binary particle swarm optimization. In *Control & Automation, 2007. MED'07. Mediterranean Conference on* (pp. 1-6). IEEE.

Kim, J., & Wilhelm, T. (2008). What is a complex graph?. *Physica A: Statistical Mechanics and its Applications, 387*(11), 2637-2652.

Kim, K., Lee, I.-S., Yoon, M., Kim, J., Lee, H., & Han, K. (2009, Dec). An efficient routing protocol based on position information in mobile wireless body area sensor networks. In *First international conference on networks and communications* (pp. 396-399). doi:10.1109/NetCoM.2009.36

Kim, T.-Y., Youm, S., Jung, J.-J., & Kim, E.-J. (2015, Jan). Multi-hop wban construction for healthcare iot systems. In *International conference on platform technology and service* (pp. 27-28). doi:10.1109/PlatCon.2015.20

Kiniwa, J. (2005). Approximation of self-stabilizing vertex cover less than 2. In *Self-Stabilizing Systems* (pp. 171–182). Springer Berlin Heidelberg. doi:10.1007/11577327_12

Kitchovitch, S., & Liò, P. (2011). Community structure in social networks: Applications for epidemiological modelling. *PLoS ONE, 6*(7), e22220. PMID:21789238

Kleinberg, J. M., Kumar, S. R., Raghavan, P., Rajagopalan, S., & Tomkins, A. (1999). The Webas a graph: Measurements, models and methods. In *Proceedings of the International Conference on Combinatorics and Computing* (LNCS), (vol. 1627, pp. 1–18). Springer.

Kleinberg, J. (1998). Authoritative sources in a hyperlinked environment.*Proceedings of 9th ACM-SIAM Symposium on Discrete Algorithms.*

Klemm, K., & Bornholdt, S. (2005). Topology of biological networks and reliability of information processing. *Proceedings of the National Academy of Sciences of the United States of America, 102*(51), 18414–18419. doi:10.1073/pnas.0509132102 PMID:16339314

Konak, A., Coit, D. W., & Smith, A. E. (2006). Multi-objective optimization using genetic algorithms: A tutorial. *Reliability Engineering & System Safety, 91*(9), 992–1007. doi:10.1016/j.ress.2005.11.018

Kotani, M., Ochi, M., Ozawa, S., & Akazawa, K. (2001). Evolutionary discriminant functions using genetic algorithms with variable-length chromosome. In *Neural Networks, 2001. Proceedings. IJCNN'01. International Joint Conference on* (Vol. 1, pp. 761-766). IEEE. doi:10.1109/IJCNN.2001.939120

Kovačević, D., Mladenović, N., Petrović, B., & Milošević, P. (2014). DE-VNS: Self-adaptive Differential Evolution with crossover neighborhood search for continuous global optimization. *Computers & Operations Research, 52*, 157–169. doi:10.1016/j.cor.2013.12.009

Krapivsky, P. L., & Redner, S. (2001). Organization of Growing Random Networks. *Physical Review E: Statistical, Nonlinear, and Soft Matter Physics, 63*(6), 066123. doi:10.1103/PhysRevE.63.066123 PMID:11415189

Krishnamurthy, V., Faloutsos, M., Chrobak, M., Cui, J., Lao, L., & Percus, A. (2007). Sampling large Internet topologies for simulation purposes. *Computer Networks, 51*(15), 4284–4302. doi:10.1016/j.comnet.2007.06.004

Kubat, M., & Matwin, S. et al. (1997). Addressing the curse of imbalanced training sets: One-sided selection. *ICML, 97*, 179–186.

Kuhn, F., Schmid, S., & Wattenhofer, R. (2005). A self-repairing peer-to-peer system resilient to dynamic adversarial churn. *LNCS, 3640*, 13–23.

Kunegis, J., De Luca, E. W., & Albayrak, S. (2010). The Link Prediction Problem in Bipartite Networks. *Computational Intelligence for Knowledge Based Systems Design, 10.*

Kuznetsov, N., Kuznetsova, O., Leonov, G., & Vagaitsev, V. (2013). Analytical-numerical localization of hidden attractor in electrical Chua's circuit. Lecture Notes in Electrical Engineering, 174, 149-158.

L, L., & Zhao, T. (2011). Link prediction in complex networks: A survey. *Physica A: Statistical Mechanics and its Applications, 390*(6), 1150-1170

Latapy, M. (2008). Main-memory triangle computations for verylarge (sparse (power-law)) graphs. *Theoretical Computer Science, 407*(1-3), 458-473.

Leavitt, H. J. (1951). Some effects of certain communication patterns on group performance. *Journal of Abnormal and Social Psychology, 46*(1), 38–50. doi:10.1037/h0057189 PMID:14813886

Lee, D.-S., Lee, Y.-D., Chung, W.-Y., & Myllyla, R. (2006, Oct). Vital sign monitoring system with life emergency event detection using wireless sensor network. In 5th *IEEE conference on sensors* (pp. 518-521).

Lehmann, T. M., Wein, B., Dahmen, J., Bredno, J., Vogelsang, F., & Kohnen, M. (2000). Content based image retrieval in medical applications: A novel multi step approach. *International Society for Optical Engineering, 3972*, 312–320.

Leibe, B., Leonardis, A., & Schiele, B. (2008). Robust object detection with interleaved categorization and segmentation. *International Journal of Computer Vision, 77*(1), 259–289. doi:10.1007/s11263-007-0095-3

Leonov, G. A., Andrievskii, B. R., Kuznetsov, N. V., & Pogromskii, A. Yu. (2012). Aircraft control with anti-windup compensation. *Differential Equations, 48*(13), 1700–1720. doi:10.1134/S0012266112130022

Leonov, G. A., & Kuznetsov, N. V. (2013). Hidden attractors in dynamical systems. From hidden oscillations in Hilbert-Kolmogorov, Aizerman, and Kalman problems to hidden chaotic attractor in Chua circuits. *International Journal of Bifurcation and Chaos in Applied Sciences and Engineering, 23*(1), 1330002. doi:10.1142/S0218127413300024

Leonov, G. A., Kuznetsov, N. V., Kuznetsova, O. A., Seledzhi, S. M., & Vagaitsev, V. I. (2011). Hidden oscillations in dynamical systems. *Transaction on Systems and Control, 6*(2), 54–67.

Leskovec, J., & Krevl, A. (2014). *SNAP Datasets: Stanford Large Network Dataset Collection*. Retrieved from http://snap.stanford.edu/data

Leskovec, J., Kleinberg, J., & Faloutsos, C. (2005). Graphs over time: densification laws, shrinking diameters and possible explanations. In *Proceedings of the eleventh ACM SIGKDD international conference on Knowledge discovery in data mining* (pp. 177-187). ACM. doi:10.1145/1081870.1081893

Li, X., Gao, C., & Pu, R. (2014, August). A community clustering algorithm based on genetic algorithm with novel coding scheme. In *Natural Computation (ICNC), 2014 10th International Conference on* (pp. 486-491). IEEE. doi:10.1109/ICNC.2014.6975883

Li, Y., Xiaogang, J., Kong, F., & Li, J. (2009). *Linking via social similarity: The emergence of community structure in scale-free network.*1st IEEE Symposium on WebSociety, SWS '09. doi:10.1109/SWS.2009.5271769

Liben-Nowell, D., & Kleinberg, J. (2007). The link-prediction problem for social networks. *JASIST, 58*(7), 1019–1031. doi:10.1002/asi.20591

Li, C., Wang, H., de Haan, W., Stam, C., & Van Mieghem, P. (2011). The correlation of metrics in complex networks with applications in functional brain networks. *Journal of Statistical Mechanics, 2011*(11), P11018. doi:10.1088/1742-5468/2011/11/P11018

Lichtenwalter, R., & Chawla, N. (2012). Link Prediction: Fair and Effective Evaluation. *Advances in Social Networks Analysis and Mining* (ASONAM), 376-383.

Lichtenwalter, R. N., Dame, N., Lussier, J. T., & Chawla, N. V. (2010). New perspectives and methods in link prediction.*Proceedings of the 16th ACM SIGKDD international conference on Knowledge discovery and data mining.* doi:10.1145/1835804.1835837

Lieberman, E., Hauert, C., & Nowak, M. A. (2005). Evolutionary dynamics on graphs. *Nature, 433*(7023), 312316. doi:10.1038/nature03204 PMID:15662424

Li-hui, Z., Chen, J., Zhang, J., & Garcia, N. (2010). Malaria Cell Counting Diagnosis within Large Field of View.*International Conference on Digital Image Computing: Techniques and Applications (DICTA).*

Li, L., Wenxin, L., & David, A. C. (2007). Particle swarm optimization-based parameter identification applied to permanent magnet synchronous motors. *Engineering Applications of Artificial Intelligence*. doi:10.1016/j.engappai.2007.10.002

Lin, C. T. (1974, June). Structural controllability. *IEEE Transactions on Automatic Control*, *19*(3), 201–208. doi:10.1109/TAC.1974.1100557

Ling, Q., & Tian, Z. (2007). Minimum node degree and *k*-connectivity of a wireless multihop network in bounded area. *IEEE Global Telecommunications Conference. GLOBECOM'07* (pp. 1296-1301). IEEE. doi:10.1109/GLOCOM.2007.249

Liu, Z., Zhang, Q.-M., L, L., & Zhou, T. (2011). Link prediction in complex networks: A local naïve Bayes model. *EPL*, *96*(4).

Liu, B., Chu, T., Wang, L., & Xie, G. (2008). Controllability of a Leader–Follower Dynamic Network With Switching Topology. *IEEE Transactions on Automatic Control*, *53*(4), 1009–1013. doi:10.1109/TAC.2008.919548

Liu, X., Li, D., Wang, S., & Tao, Z. (2007). Effective algorithm for detecting community structure in complex networks based on GA and clustering. In *Computational Science–ICCS 2007* (pp. 657–664). Springer Berlin Heidelberg.

Liu, Y. Y., Slotine, J. J., & Barabasi, A. L. (2011). Controllability of complex networks. *Nature*, *473*(7346), 167–173. doi:10.1038/nature10011 PMID:21562557

Li, Y., Liu, J., & Liu, C. (2014). A comparative analysis of evolutionary and memetic algorithms for community detection from signed social networks. *Soft Computing*, *18*(2), 329–348. doi:10.1007/s00500-013-1060-4

Lloyd, A. L., & May, R. M. (2001). How Viruses Spread Among Computers and People. *Science*, *292*(5520), 1316–1317. doi:10.1126/science.1061076 PMID:11360990

Lombardi, A., & Hornquist, M. (2007). Controllability analysis of networks. *Physical Review E: Statistical, Nonlinear, and Soft Matter Physics*, 75. PMID:17677136

Long, M. H., & Crookes, G. (1992). Three Approaches to Task-Based Syllabus Design. *TESOL Quarterly*, *26*(1), 27–56. doi:10.2307/3587368

Luenberger, D. G. (1979). *Introduction to Dynamic Systems: Theory, Models, & Applications*. Wiley.

Luo, X., & Yu, H. (2010). Constructing wireless sensor network model based on small world concept. *Advanced Computer Theory and Engineering (ICACTE), 3rd International Conference on.*

Luo, X. U., & Yu, H. (2010). Constructing wireless sensor network model based on small world concept.*3rd International Conference on Advanced Computer Theory and Engineering (ICACTE)*, (Vol. 5, pp. V5-501). IEEE.

Mabu, S., Hirasawa, K., & Hu, J. (2007). A graph-based evolutionary algorithm: Genetic network programming (GNP) and its extension using reinforcement learning. *Evolutionary Computation*, *15*(3), 369–398. doi:10.1162/evco.2007.15.3.369 PMID:17705783

Machlus, K. R., Thon, J. N., & Italiano, J. E. Jr. (2014). Interpreting the developmental dance of the megakaryocyte: A review of the cellular and molecular processes mediating platelet formation. *British Journal of Haematology*, *165*(2), 227–236. doi:10.1111/bjh.12758 PMID:24499183

Madduri, K. (2008). *A high-performance framework for analyzing massive complex networks*. (PhD thesis). Georgia Institute of Technology.

Mainwaring, A., Polastre, J., Szewczyk, R., Culler, D., & Anderson, J. (2002). Wireless Sensor Networks for Habitat Monitoring.*Proc. ACM WSNA*. doi:10.1145/570738.570751

Maitra, M., Gupta, R. K., & Mukherjee, M. (2012). Detection and Counting of Red Blood Cells in Blood Cell Images using Hough Transform. *International Journal of Computer Applications, 53*(16), 0975 – 8887.

Mallipeddi, R., & Suganthan, P. N. (2010). Differential evolution algorithm with ensemble of parameters and mutation and crossover strategies. In Swarm, Evolutionary, and Memetic Computing (pp. 71-78). Springer Berlin Heidelberg. doi:10.1007/978-3-642-17563-3_9

Mangan, S., & Alon, U. (2003). Structure and function of the feed-forward loop network motif. *Proceedings of the National Academy of Sciences of the United States of America, 100*(21), 11980–11985. doi:10.1073/pnas.2133841100 PMID:14530388

Martin, K. (2003). Epistemic Motion. In *Quantum Searching*. Oxford, UK: Oxford University Computing Laboratory.

Masuda, K., & Kurihara, K. (2007, September). Global optimization with chaotic particles inspired by swarm intelligence. In *SICE,2007 Annual Conference* (pp. 1319-1324). IEEE. doi:10.1109/SICE.2007.4421187

Mayeda, H., & Yamada, T. (1979). Strong structural controllability. *SIAM Journal on Control and Optimization, 17*(1), 123–138. doi:10.1137/0317010

Mazalan, S. M., Mahmood, N. H., & Mohd, A. A. R. (2013). Automated Red Blood Cells Counting in Peripheral Blood Smear Image Using Circular Hough Transform.*First IEEE International Conference on Artificial Intelligence, Modeling & Simulation*. doi:10.1109/AIMS.2013.59

Mazalan, S. M., Mahmood, N. H., & Razak, M. A. A. (2013). Automated Red Blood Cells Counting in Peripheral Blood Smear Image Using Circular Hough Transform. *1st International Conference on Artificial Intelligence Modelling and Simulation (Anaheim), 2013*, 320–324.

Medicine Health. (n.d.). Retrieved from http://www.medicinehealth.com/leukemia/article.html

Medus, A., Acuna, G., & Dorso, C. O. (2005). Detection of community structures in networks via global optimization. *Physica A: Statistical Mechanics and its Applications, 358*(2), 593-604.

Meng, Q. C., Feng, T. J., Chen, Z., Zhou, C. J., & Bo, J. H. (1999). Genetic algorithms encoding study and a sufficient convergence condition of gas. In *Systems, Man, and Cybernetics, 1999. IEEE SMC'99 Conference Proceedings. 1999 IEEE International Conference on* (Vol. 1, pp. 649-652). IEEE. doi:10.1109/ICSMC.1999.814168

Menon, A. K., & Eklan, C. (2011). Link prediction via matrix factorization. Machine Learning and Knowledge Discovery in Databases, 6912, 437-452. doi:10.1007/978-3-642-23783-6_28

Meyn, S. (2007). *Control Techniques for Complex Networks*. Cambridge University Press. doi:10.1017/CBO9780511804410

Mezura-Montes, E., Velázquez-Reyes, J., & Coello Coello, C. A. (2006, July). A comparative study of differential evolution variants for global optimization. In *Proceedings of the 8th annual conference on Genetic and evolutionary computation* (pp. 485-492). ACM. doi:10.1145/1143997.1144086

Milgram, S. (1967). The small world problem. *Psychology Today, 2*(1), 60–67.

Miller, G. A. (1956). The Magical Number Seven, Plus or Minus Two: Some Limits on Our Capacity for Processing Information. *Psychological Review, 101*(2), 343–352. doi:10.1037/0033-295X.101.2.343 PMID:8022966

Milo, R., Itzkovitz, S., Kashtan, N., Levitt, R., Shen-Orr, S., Ayzenshtat, I., & Alon, U. et al. (2004). Superfamilies of evolved and designed networks. *Science, 303*(5663), 1538–1542. doi:10.1126/science.1089167 PMID:15001784

Milo, R., Shen-Orr, S., Itzkovitz, S., Kashtan, N., Chklovskii, D., & Alon, U. (2002). Network motifs: Simple building blocks of complex networks. *Science*, *298*(5594), 824–827. doi:10.1126/science.298.5594.824 PMID:12399590

Mirzasoleiman, B., Babaei, M., Jalili, M., & Safari, M. (2011). Cascaded failures in weighted networks. *Physical Review E: Statistical, Nonlinear, and Soft Matter Physics*, *84*(4 Pt 2), 046114. doi:10.1103/PhysRevE.84.046114 PMID:22181234

Mishra, B. K., & Saini, D. K. (2007). SEIRS epidemic model with delay for transmission of malicious objects in computer network. *Applied Mathematics and Computation*, *188*(2), 1476–1482. doi:10.1016/j.amc.2006.11.012

Miswan, M. F. (2011). An Overview: Segmentation Method for Blood Cell Disorders.*5th Kuala Lumpur International Conference on Biomedical Engineering 2011*. Berlin: Springer. doi:10.1007/978-3-642-21729-6_148

Mlakar, M., Petelin, D., Tušar, T., & Filipič, B. (2015). GP-DEMO: Differential evolution for multiobjective optimization based on Gaussian process models. *European Journal of Operational Research*, *243*(2), 347–361. doi:10.1016/j.ejor.2014.04.011

Molinaro, A., De Rango, F., Marano, S., & Tropea, M. (2005). A scalable framework for in IP-oriented terrestrial-GEO satellite networks. *Communications Magazine, IEEE*, *43*(4), 130–137. doi:10.1109/MCOM.2005.1421916

Montague, M., & Aslam, J. A. (2002). Condorcet fusion for improved retrieval.*Proceedings of the eleventh international conference on Information and knowledge management.*ACM.

Monton, E., Hernandez, J., Blasco, J., Herve, T., Micallef, J., Grech, I., & Traver, V. et al. (2008, February). Body area network for wireless patient monitoring. *Communications, IET*, *2*(2), 215–222. doi:10.1049/iet-com:20070046

Moreira, J. A. J. A. A., Herrmann, H., & Indekeu, J. (2009). How to make a fragile network robust and vice versa. *Physical Review Letters*, 102. PMID:19257248

Morris, J. F., O'Neal, J. W., & Deckro, R. F. (2013). A random graph generation algorithm for the analysis of social networks. J. Defence Model. Simulation Appl. Methodology. *Technology (Elmsford, N.Y.)*, 1–12.

Motoi, K., Ikeda, K., Kuwae, Y., Yuji, T., Higashi, Y., Nogawa, M., & Yamakoshi, K. et al. (2006, Aug). Development of an ambulatory device for monitoring posture change and walking speed for use in rehabilitation. In *Proceedings of the 7th IEEE international conference on engineering in medicine and biology society* (pp. 5940-5943). doi:10.1109/IEMBS.2006.259364

Motter, A. (2004). Cascade control and defense in complex networks. *Physical Review Letters*, 93. PMID:15447153

Moxley, R. L., & Moxley, N. F. (1974). Determining point-centrality in uncontrived social networks. *Sociometry*, *37*(1), 122–130. doi:10.2307/2786472

Mundt, C., Montgomery, K., Udoh, U., Barker, V., Thonier, G., Tellier, A., & Kovacs, G. et al. (2005, September). A multiparameter wearable physiologic monitoring system for space and terrestrial applications. *IEEE Transactions on Information Technology in Biomedicine*, *9*(3), 382–391. doi:10.1109/TITB.2005.854509 PMID:16167692

Neri, F., & Tirronen, V. (2010). Recent advances in differential evolution: A survey and experimental analysis. *Artificial Intelligence Review*, *33*(1-2), 61–106. doi:10.1007/s10462-009-9137-2

Neumann, F., Oliveto, P. S., & Witt, C. (2009, July). Theoretical analysis of fitness-proportional selection: landscapes and efficiency. In *Proceedings of the 11th Annual conference on Genetic and evolutionary computation* (pp. 835-842). ACM. doi:10.1145/1569901.1570016

Newman, M. (2003). The Structure and Function of Complex Networks. *Society for Industrial and Applied Mathematics: SIAM Rev*, 167–256.

Newman, M. E. (2001). Scientific collaboration networks. II. Shortest paths, weighted networks, and centrality. Physics Review E, 64(1).

Newman, M. E. (2008). The mathematics of networks. *The New Palgrave Encyclopedia of Economics, 2*(2008), 1-12.

Newman, M. E. J. (2012). *Network Data*. Retrieved from http://www-personal.umich.edu/~mejn/netdata/

Newman, M., Barabasi, A.-L., & Watts, D. J. (2006). The Structure and Dynamics of Networks. Princeton Univ. Press.

Newman, M. (2002). Assortative mixing in networks. *Physical Review Letters*, *89*(20), 208701. doi:10.1103/PhysRevLett.89.208701 PMID:12443515

Newman, M. E. (2003). The structure and function of complex networks. *SIAM Review*, *45*(2), 167–256. doi:10.1137/S003614450342480

Newman, M. E. (2004). Coauthorship networks and patterns of scientific collaboration.(PNAS). *Proceedings of the National Academy of Science of the United States*, *101*(Supplement 1), 5200–5205. doi:10.1073/pnas.0307545100 PMID:14745042

Newman, M. E. (2004). Fast algorithm for detecting community structure in networks. *Physical Review E: Statistical, Nonlinear, and Soft Matter Physics*, *69*(6), 066133. doi:10.1103/PhysRevE.69.066133 PMID:15244693

Newman, M. E. J. (2012). Communities, modules and large-scale structure in networks. *Nature Physics*, *8*(1), 25–31. doi:10.1038/nphys2162

Newman, M. E., & Girvan, M. (2004). Finding and evaluating community structure in networks. *Physical Review E: Statistical, Nonlinear, and Soft Matter Physics*, *69*(2), 026113. doi:10.1103/PhysRevE.69.026113 PMID:14995526

Newth, D., & Ash, J. (2005). Evolving cascading failure resilience in complex networks. *Complexity International*, *11*, 125–136.

Noman, N., & Iba, H. (2008). Accelerating differential evolution using an adaptive local search. Evolutionary Computation. *IEEE Transactions on*, *12*(1), 107–125.

Noraini, M. R., & Geraghty, J. (2011). *Genetic algorithm performance with different selection strategies in solving TSP*. Academic Press.

Olfati-Saber, R. (2007). Evolutionary dynamics of behavior in social networks. In *Proc. 46th IEEE Conf. Decis. Contr.*

Onnela, J. P., Saramäki, J., Kertész, J., & Kaski, K. (2005). Intensity and coherence of motifs in weighted complex networks. *Physical Review E: Statistical, Nonlinear, and Soft Matter Physics*, *71*(6), 065103. doi:10.1103/PhysRevE.71.065103 PMID:16089800

Onwubolu, G., & Babu, B. (2004). *New Optimization Techniques in Engineering* (pp. 167–218). New York: SpringerVerlag. doi:10.1007/978-3-540-39930-8

Open Street Map. (2015). Retrieved from https://www.openstreetmap.org/

Opsahl, T., Agneessens, F., & Skvoretz, J. (2010). Node centrality in weighted networks: Generalizing degree and shortest paths. *Social Networks*, *32*(3), 245–251. doi:10.1016/j.socnet.2010.03.006

Opsahl, T., & Panzarasa, P. (2009). Clustering in weighted networks. *Social Networks*, *31*(2), 155–163. doi:10.1016/j.socnet.2009.02.002

Ou, Q., Jin, Y. D., Zhou, T., Wang, B. H., & Yin, B. Q. (2007). Power-law strength-degree correlation from resource-allocation dynamics on weighted networks. *Physical Review E: Statistical, Nonlinear, and Soft Matter Physics*, 75. PMID:17358308

Ouzienko, V. A. (2010). Prediction of Attributes and Links in Temporal Social Networks. *ECAI*, 1121-1122.

Özalp, N., & Demrc, E. (2011). A fractional order SEIR model with vertical transmission. *Mathematical and Computer Modelling*, *54*(1–2), 1–6. doi:10.1016/j.mcm.2010.12.051 PMID:21076663

Panda, D. P., & Rosenfeld, A. (1978). Image Segmentation by Pixel Classification in (Gray Level, Edge Value) Space. *IEEE Transactions on Computers*, *C-27*(9), 875–879. doi:10.1109/TC.1978.1675208

Parnas, M., & Ron, D. (2007). Approximating the minimum vertex cover in sublinear time and a connection to distributed algorithms. *Theoretical Computer Science*, *381*(1), 183–196. doi:10.1016/j.tcs.2007.04.040

Pastor-Satorras, R., Vázquez, A., & Vespignani, A. (2001). Dynamical and correlation properties of the Internet. *Physical Review Letters*, *87*(25), 258701. doi:10.1103/PhysRevLett.87.258701 PMID:11736611

Pastor-Satorras, R., & Vespignani, A. (2001). Epidemic spreading in scale-free networks. *Physical Review Letters*, *86*(14), 3200–3203. doi:10.1103/PhysRevLett.86.3200 PMID:11290142

Pattillo, J., Veremyev, A., Butenko, S., & Boginski, V. (2013). On the maximum quasi-clique problem. *Discrete Applied Mathematics*, *161*(1), 244–257. doi:10.1016/j.dam.2012.07.019

Penrose, M. (2003). *Random geometric graphs* (Vol. 5). Oxford, UK: Oxford University Press. doi:10.1093/acprof:oso/9780198506263.001.0001

Pentland, S. A., Fletcher, R., & Hasson, A. (2004). DakNet: Rethinking Connectivity in Developing Nations. *IEEE Computer*, *37*(1), 78–83. doi:10.1109/MC.2004.1260729

Perdisci, R., Lanzi, A., & Lee, W. (2008). Classification of packed executables for accurate computer virus detection. *Pattern Recognition Letters*, *29*(14), 1941–1946. doi:10.1016/j.patrec.2008.06.016

Perer, S. (2006). Balancing systematic and flexible exploration of social networks. *Visualization and Computer Graphics. IEEE Transactions on*, *12*(5), 693–700.

Petrou, M., & Tabacchi, M. E. (2009). Networks of concepts and ideas. *The Computer Journal*.

Piuri, V., & Scotti, F. (2004). Morphological classification of blood leucocytes by microscope images. *IEEE International conference on Computational Intelligence for Measurement Systems and Applications*.

Pizzuti, C. (2008). Ga-net: A genetic algorithm for community detection in social networks. In Parallel Problem Solving from Nature–PPSN X (pp. 1081-1090). Springer Berlin Heidelberg.

Pluhacek, M., Janostik, J., Senkerik, R., Zelinka, I., & Davendra, D. (2015). PSO as Complex Network - Capturing the Inner Dynamics – Initial Study. In *Proceedings of Nostradamus 2015: International conference on prediction, modeling and analysis of complex systems*. Springer.

Polastre, J., Szewczyk, R., & Culler, D. (2005, April). Telos: enabling ultra-low power wireless research. In *Fourth international symposium on information processing in sensor networks*, (pp. 364-369). doi:10.1109/IPSN.2005.1440950

Polishchuk, V., & Suomela, J. (2009). A simple local 3-approximation algorithm for vertex cover. *Information Processing Letters*, *109*(12), 642–645. doi:10.1016/j.ipl.2009.02.017

Pons, P., & Latapy, M. (2006). Computing Communities in Large Networks Using Random Walks. *J. Graph Algorithms Appl., 10*(2), 191–218. doi:10.7155/jgaa.00124

Popolo, D. (2010). *A New Science of International Relations*. Lancaster, UK: Ashgate.

Price, K. (2007). In D. Corne, M. Dorigo, & F. Glover (Eds.), *An Introduction to Differential Evolution, New Ideas in Optimization*. London, UK: McGraw-Hill.

Prill, R. J., Iglesias, P. A., & Levchenko, A. (2005). Dynamic properties of network motifs contribute to biological network organization. *PLoS Biology, 3*(11), e343. doi:10.1371/journal.pbio.0030343 PMID:16187794

Pujari M & Kanawati R. (n.d.). Link prediction in multiplex networks. *AIMS Networks & Heterogeneous Media Journal, 10*(1), 17-35. 782-789.

Pujari, M., & Kanawati, R. (2012). *Link prediction in Complex Networks by Supervised Rank Aggregation*. ICTAI 2012: 24th IEEE International Conference on Tools with Artificial Intelligence. doi:10.1109/ICTAI.2012.111

Pujari, M., & Kanawati, R. (2012). *Tag Recommendation by link prediction based on supervised Machine Learning*. ICWSM.

Puzis, R., Elovici, Y., & Fire, M. (2013). Link Prediction in Highly Fractional Data Sets. Handbook of Computational Approaches to Counterterrorism, 283-300.

Qin, A. K., & Suganthan, P. N. (2005, September). Self-adaptive differential evolution algorithm for numerical optimization. In *Evolutionary Computation, 2005. The 2005 IEEE Congress on* (Vol. 2, pp. 1785-1791). IEEE. doi:10.1109/CEC.2005.1554904

Rahman, M., Bhuiyan, M. A., & Al Hasan, M. (2014). GRAFT: An efficient graphlet counting method for large graph analysis. *IEEE Transactions on Knowledge and Data Engineering, 26*(10), 2466–2478. doi:10.1109/TKDE.2013.2297929

Rahnamayan, S., Tizhoosh, H. R., & Salama, M. (2008). Opposition-based differential evolution. *Evolutionary Computation. IEEE Transactions on, 12*(1), 64–79.

Ramachandran, A., Zhou, Z., & Huang, D. (2007, May). Computing cryptographic algorithms in portable and embedded devices. In IEEE international conference on portable information device (pp. 1-7). doi:10.1109/PORTABLE.2007.47

Rasmussen, J., Scholl, B., Gellekum, T., & Schmitt, H. J. (1996, Oct). Fiber-optic polarimetric temperature sensor for characterizing a 900 mhz tem cell used in bioeffects dosimetry studies. In *Proceedings of the 18th annual international conference of the IEEE engineering in medicine and biology society, bridging disciplines for biomedicine*. (Vol. 5, pp. 1875-1876). doi:10.1109/IEMBS.1996.646298

Rattigan, M. J., & Jensen, D. (2005). The case for anomalous link discovery. *ACM SIGKDD Explorations Newsletter, 7*(2), 41–47. doi:10.1145/1117454.1117460

Ravasz, E., & Barabási, A. (2003). Hierarchical organization in complex networks. *Physical Review E: Statistical, Nonlinear, and Soft Matter Physics, 67*(2), 026112. doi:10.1103/PhysRevE.67.026112 PMID:12636753

Rechenberg, I. (1973). *Evolutionsstrategie - Optimierung technischer Systeme nach Prinzipien der biologischen Evolution*. (PhD thesis). Fromman-Holzboog.

Reif, J. H., & Spirakis, P. G. (1985). *k*-connectivity in random undirected graphs. *Discrete Mathematics, 54*(2), 181–191. doi:10.1016/0012-365X(85)90079-2

Reka, A., & Barabasi, A. L. (2002). *Statistical mechanics of complex networks*. (Doctoral Dissertation). University of Notre Dame, South Bend, IN.

Reyes-Sierra, M., & Coello, C. C. (2006). Multi-objective particle swarm optimizers: A survey of the state-of-the-art. *International Journal of Computational Intelligence Research, 2*(3), 287-308.

Richardson, T., Mucha, P. J., & Porter, M. A. (2009). Spectral tripartitioning of networks. *Physical Review E: Statistical, Nonlinear, and Soft Matter Physics, 80*(3), 036111. doi:10.1103/PhysRevE.80.036111 PMID:19905184

Richter, H. (2002). An evolutionary algorithm for controlling chaos: The use of multi-objective fitness functions, in Parallel Problem Solving from Nature-PPSN VII. Lecture Notes in Computer Science, 2439, 308-317.

Richter, H. (2006). Evolutionary Optimization in Spatio- temporal Fitness Landscapes. *Lecture Notes in Computer Science, 4193*, 1-10.

Richter, H. (2005). A study of dynamic severity in chaotic fitness landscapes. *Evolutionary Computation. The IEEE Congress*. doi:10.1109/CEC.2005.1555049

Richter, H., & Reinschke, K. J. (2000). Optimization of local control of chaos by an evolutionary algorithm. *Physica D. Nonlinear Phenomena, 144*, 309–334.

Rieder, B. (2013). *Studying Facebook via Data Extraction: The Netvizz Application*. ACM.

Rodriguez, J. A., & Yebra, J. L. A. (1999). It bounding the diameter and the mean distance of a graph from its Eigenvalues: Laplacian versus adjacency matrix methods. *Discrete Mathematics, 196*(1-3), 267–275. doi:10.1016/S0012-365X(98)00206-4

Rogers, D. L. (1974). Sociometric analysis of interorganizational relations: Application of theory and measurement. *Rural Sociology*.

Ronald, S. B. (1987). Social contagion and innovation: Cohesion versus structural equivalence. *American Journal of Sociology, 92*(6), 1287–1335. doi:10.1086/228667

Ronkkonen, J., Kukkonen, S., & Price, K. V. (2005, September). Real-parameter optimization with differential evolution. In *Proc. IEEE CEC* (Vol. 1, pp. 506-513).

Rosenfeld, A., & Davis, L. S. (1979). Image segmentation and image models. *Proceedings of the IEEE, 67*(5), 764–772. doi:10.1109/PROC.1979.11326

Rosvall, M., Axelsson, D., & Bergstrom, C. T. (2009). The map equation. *The European Physical Journal. Special Topics, 178*(1), 13–23. doi:10.1140/epjst/e2010-01179-1

Roy, S., & Filkov, V. (2009). Strong associations between microbe phenotypes and their network architecture. *Physical Review E: Statistical, Nonlinear, and Soft Matter Physics, 80*(4), 040902. doi:10.1103/PhysRevE.80.040902 PMID:19905265

Sabidussi, G. (1966). The centrality index of a graph. *Psychometrika, 31*(4), 581–603. doi:10.1007/BF02289527 PMID:5232444

Sah, P., Singh, L. O., Clauset, A., & Bansal, S. (2014). Exploring community structure in biological networks with random graphs. *BMC Bioinformatics, 15*(1), 220. doi:10.1186/1471-2105-15-220 PMID:24965130

Saladin & Kenneth. (2012). *Anatomy and Physiology: the Unit of Form and Function* (6th ed.). New York: McGraw Hill.

Sanchez, A., Blanc, S., Yuste, P., & Serrano, J. (2011, June). A low cost and high efficient acoustic modem for underwater sensor networks. In IEEE - Spain oceans (pp. 1-10). doi:10.1109/Oceans-Spain.2011.6003428

Saramäki, J., Kivelä, M., Onnela, J. P., Kaski, K., & Kertesz, J. (2007). Generalizations of the clustering coefficient to weighted complex networks. *Physical Review E: Statistical, Nonlinear, and Soft Matter Physics*, *75*(2), 027105. doi:10.1103/PhysRevE.75.027105 PMID:17358454

Schaeffer, S. E. (2007). Graph clustering. *Computer Science Review*, *1*(1), 27–64. doi:10.1016/j.cosrev.2007.05.001

Schonberger, J. (2005). *Operational Freight Carrier Planning, Basic Concepts, Optimization Models and Advanced Memetic Algorithms*. Springer-Verlag.

Schuster, H. G. (1999). *Handbook of Chaos Control*. New York: Wiley-VCH. doi:10.1002/3527607455

Schwefel, H. (1974). *Numerische Optimierung von Computer-Modellen.* (PhD thesis). Birkhuser.

Scott, J. (1998). Social Network Analysis. *Sociology*, *22*(1), 109–127. doi:10.1177/0038038588022001007

Scott, J. (2012). Social network analysis. *Sage (Atlanta, Ga.).*

Senkerik, R., Zelinka, I., & Navratil, E. (2006). Optimization of feedback control of chaos by evolutionary algorithms. *1st IFAC Conference on Analysis and Control of Chaotic Systems*, Reims, France

Serrano, M. A., Boguñá, M., & Vespignani, A. (2009). Extracting the multiscale backbone of complex weighted networks. *Proceedings of the National Academy of Sciences of the United States of America*, *106*(16), 6483–6488. doi:10.1073/pnas.0808904106 PMID:19357301

Sghaier, N., Mellouk, A., Augustin, B., Amirat, Y., Marty, J., Khoussa, M., . . . Zitouni, R. (2011, July). Wireless sensor networks for medical care services. In 7th *international conference on wireless communications and mobile computing conference* (pp. 571-576). doi:10.1109/IWCMC.2011.5982596

Shapiro, L., & Stockman, G. (2001). Computer Vision. Prentice-Hall, Inc.

Shavitt, Y., & Shir, E. (2005). DIMES: Let the Internet measure itself. *SIGCOMM Computer Communication Review*, *35*(5), 71–74. doi:10.1145/1096536.1096546

Shen, Q., Liu, J., Yu, H., Ma, Z., Li, M., Shen, Z., & Chen, C. (2013, Aug). Adaptive cognitive enhanced platform for wban. In IEEE/CIC international conference on communications in China (pp. 739-744). doi:10.1109/ICCChina.2013.6671208

Shen, H. W., & Cheng, X. Q. (2010). Spectral methods for the detection of network community structure: A comparative analysis. *Journal of Statistical Mechanics*, *2010*(10), P10020. doi:10.1088/1742-5468/2010/10/P10020

Shen, H. W., Cheng, X. Q., & Fang, B. X. (2010). Covariance, correlation matrix, and the multiscale community structure of networks. *Physical Review E: Statistical, Nonlinear, and Soft Matter Physics*, *82*(1), 016114. doi:10.1103/PhysRevE.82.016114 PMID:20866696

Shen-Orr, S. S., Milo, R., Mangan, S., & Alon, U. (2002). Network motifs in the transcriptional regulation network of Escherichia coli. *Nature Genetics*, *31*(1), 64–68. doi:10.1038/ng881 PMID:11967538

Shi, Z., Liu, Y., & Liang, J. (2009, November). PSO-based community detection in complex networks. In *Knowledge Acquisition and Modeling, 2009. KAM'09. Second International Symposium on* (Vol. 3, pp. 114-119). IEEE. doi:10.1109/KAM.2009.195

Slotine, J.-J., & Li, W. (1991). *Applied Nonlinear Control.* Prentice-Hall.

Small, M., Xu, X., Zhou, J., Zhang, J., Sun, J., & Lu, J. A. (2008). Scale-free networks which are highly assortative but not small world. *Physical Review E: Statistical, Nonlinear, and Soft Matter Physics*, *77*(6 Pt 2), 066112. doi:10.1103/PhysRevE.77.066112 PMID:18643341

Smith Sidney, L. (1950). *Communication pattern and the adaptability of task-oriented groups: an experimental study*. Cambridge, MA: Group Networks Laboratory, Research Laboratory of Electronics, Massachusetts Institute of Technology.

Smith, D., Miniutti, D., Lamahewa, T., & Hanlen, L. (2013, October). Propagation models for body-area networks: A survey and new outlook. *Antennas and Propagation Magazine, IEEE*, *55*(5), 97–117. doi:10.1109/MAP.2013.6735479

Soleimani-pouri, M., Rezvanian, A., & Meybodi, M. R. (2014). An ant based particle swarm optimization algorithm for maximum clique problem in social networks. In *State of the art applications of social network analysis* (pp. 295–304). Springer International Publishing. doi:10.1007/978-3-319-05912-9_14

Song, H. H., Cho, T. W., Dave, V., Zhang, Y., & Qiu, L. (2009). Scalable proximity estimation and link prediction in online social networks.*Proceedings of the 9th ACM SIGCOMM conference on Internet measurement conference*. doi:10.1145/1644893.1644932

Soori, A., & Ghaderi, M. (2015). A Topic-Based Syllabus Design for a Conversation Course. *Language in India, 15*(1), 538-546.

Soundarajan, S., & Hopcroft, J. (2012). Using community information to improve the precision of link prediction methods.*Proceedings of the 21st international conference companion on World Wide Web*. doi:10.1145/2187980.2188150

Sporns, O., & Kötter, R. (2004). Motifs in brain networks. *PLoS Biology*, *2*(11), e369. doi:10.1371/journal.pbio.0020369 PMID:15510229

Srikant, R. (2004). *The Mathematics of Internet Congestion Control (Birkhauser)*. American Mathematical Society. doi:10.1007/978-0-8176-8216-3

Srinivas, M., & Patnaik, L. M. (1994). Genetic algorithms: A survey. *Computer*, *27*(6), 17–26. doi:10.1109/2.294849

Storn, R., & Price, K. (1995). *Differential evolution-a simple and efficient adaptive scheme for global optimization over continuous spaces* (Vol. 3). Berkeley, CA: ICSI.

Stoyanov, J. M. (2013). *Counterexamples in probability*. Courier Corporation.

Strogatz, S. H. (2001). Exploring complex networks. *Nature*, *410*(6825), 268–276. doi:10.1038/35065725 PMID:11258382

Subbian, K., & Melville, P. (2011). Supervised rank aggregation for predicting influence in networks.*Proceedings of the IEEE Conference on Social Computing (SocialCom-2011)*.

SUMO Mobility Manager. (2015). Retrieved from http://sourceforge.net/projects/sumo/

Sung-Yuan, K. (2001). The embedded bluetooth ccd camera. In Tencon 2001. Proceedings of IEEE region 10 international conference on electrical and electronic technology (Vol. 1, pp. 81-84). doi:10.1109/TENCON.2001.949556

Sun, X., & Wandelt, S. (2014). Network similarity analysis of air navigation route systems. *Transportation Research Part E, Logistics and Transportation Review*, *70*, 416–434. doi:10.1016/j.tre.2014.08.005

Sun, Y., Barber, R., Gupta, M., Aggarwal, C., & Han, J. (2011). *Co-author relationship prediction in heterogeneous bibliographic networks. In Advances on social network Analysis and mining*. Kaohsiung, Taiwan: ASONAM.

Szabo, G., & Fath, G. (2007). Evolutionary games on graphs. *Physics Reports*, *446*(4-6), 97216. doi:10.1016/j.physrep.2007.04.004

Szczytowski, P., Khelil, A., & Suri, N. (2012). *DKM: Distributed k-connectivity maintenance. In Wireless On-demand Network Systems and Services (WONS)* (pp. 83–90). IEEE.

Taghizadeh, M. (2013). EAP Syllabus and Course Design. *International Research Journal of Applied and Basic Sciences, 4*(12), 3791-3797.

Takacs, B. (2006, July). A portable ultrasound guidance and raining system using high fidelity virtual human models. In *International conference on medical information visualisation - biomedical visualisation* (pp. 77-81). doi:10.1109/MEDIVIS.2006.2

Talukder, S. (2011). *Mathematical Modelling and Applications of Particle Swarm Optimization.* (Doctoral dissertation). Blekinge Institute of Technology.

Tan, F., Xia, Y., & Zhu, B. (2014). Link prediction in complex networks: A mutual information perspective. *PLoS ONE, 9*(9), 1–8. doi:10.1371/journal.pone.0107056 PMID:25207920

Tangsuksant, W., Pintavirooj, C., Taertulakarn, S., & Daochai, S. (2013). Development algorithm to count blood cells in urine sediment using ANN and Hough Transform.*6th International Conference (BMEiCON) on Biomedical Engineering, 2013.* doi:10.1109/BMEiCon.2013.6687725

Tanner, H. G. (2004). On the controllability of nearest neighbor interconnections. *43rd IEEE Conference on Decision and Control (CDC)*, 3. doi:10.1109/CDC.2004.1428782

Tan, P. N., Steinbach, M., & Kumar, V. (2006). *Introduction to data mining* (Vol. 1). Boston: Pearson Addison Wesley.

Tan, S., Lu, J., Chen, G., & Hill, D. (2014). When structure meets function in evolutionary dynamics on complex networks. *IEEE Circ. Syst. Mag., 14*(4), 3650. doi:10.1109/MCAS.2014.2360790

Tao, S., & Yue, X. (2010). The attributes similar-degree of complex networks. *2nd International Conference on Future Computer and Communication (ICFCC).* doi:10.1109/ICFCC.2010.5497519

Tarjan, R. (1972). Depth-first search and linear graph algorithms. *SIAM Journal on Computing, 1*(2), 146–160. doi:10.1137/0201010

Tasgin, M., Herdagdelen, A., & Bingol, H. (2007). *Community detection in complex networks using genetic algorithms.* arXiv preprint arXiv:0711.0491

Taskar, B., Wong, M., Abbeel, P., & Koller, D. (2003). Link prediction in relational data. In S. Thrun, L. K. Saul, & B. Schölkopf (Eds.), *NIPS. MIT Press.*

The Great Telecoms Market Crash. (2002, July 18). *The Economist.* Retrieved from http://www.economist.com

Tirronen, V., Neri, F., & Rossi, T. (2009, May). Enhancing differential evolution frameworks by scale factor local search-part i. In *Evolutionary Computation, 2009. CEC'09. IEEE Congress on* (pp. 94-101). IEEE. doi:10.1109/CEC.2009.4982935

Turau, V., & Hauck, B. (2009). A self-stabilizing approximation algorithm for vertex cover in anonymous networks. *Stabilization, Safety, and Security of Distributed Systems*, 341-353.

Turing, A. (1969). Intelligent machinery, unpublished report for National Physical Laboratory. *Machine Intelligence, 7.*

Turing, A. M. (Ed.). The Collected Works (vol. 3). North-Holland.

University of Michigan. (2002). *INET-3.0: Internet topology generator.* Technical report. Author.

Valiant, & Leslie, G. (1990). A bridging model for parallel computation. *Communications of the ACM, 33*(8), 103-111.

van Steen, M. (2015). Graph Theory and Complex Networks: An Introduction. In *Chaos-driven Discrete Artificial Bee Colony, IEEE Congress on Evolutionary Computation.*

Varshney, L. R., Chen, B. L., Paniagua, E., Hall, D. H., & Chklovskii, D. B. (2011). Structural properties of the Caenorhabditis elegans neuronal network. *PLoS Computational Biology*, *7*(2), e1001066. doi:10.1371/journal.pcbi.1001066 PMID:21304930

Venkatalakshmi, B., & Thilagavathi, K. (2013). Automatic Red Blood Cell Counting Using Hough Transform.*Proceedings of IEEE Conference on Information and Communication Technologies*. doi:10.1109/CICT.2013.6558103

Verma, C. K., Tamma, B. R., Manoj, B. S., & Rao, R. (2011). A realistic small-world model for wireless mesh networks. *Communications Letters, IEEE*, *15*(4), 455–457. doi:10.1109/LCOMM.2011.020111.100266

Vinutha, H., & Reddy. (2014). Automatic Red Blood Cell and White Blood Cell Counting For Telemedicine System. *International Journal of Research in Advent Technology*, *2*(1).

Wang, T., Chen, Y., Zhang, X. T., Jin, L., Hui, P., Deng, B., & Li, X. (2011). Understanding Graph Sampling Algorithms for Social Network Analysis. Simplex'11. IEEE.

Wang, C., Satuluri, V., & Parthasarathy, S. (2007). Local probabilistic models for link prediction. In Y. Shi, & C. W. Clifton (Ed.), *Seventh IEEE International Conference on Data Mining (ICDM)*. doi:10.1109/ICDM.2007.108

Wang, J. C., & Chiu, C. C. (2008). Recommending trusted online auction sellers using social network analysis. *Expert Systems with Applications*, *34*(3), 1666–1679. doi:10.1016/j.eswa.2007.01.045

Wang, P., Li, J., & Ji, B. (2015). Online fraud detection model based on social network analysis. *Journal of Information and Computational Science*, *12*(7), 2553–2562. doi:10.12733/jics20105690

Wang, S., Mao, X., Tang, S. J., Li, M., Zhao, J., & Dai, G. (2011). On "Movement-Assisted Connectivity Restoration in Wireless Sensor and Actor Networks". *IEEE Transactions on Parallel and Distributed Systems*, *22*(4), 687–694. doi:10.1109/TPDS.2010.102

Wang, X., & Sukthankar, G. (2013). Link prediction in multi-relational collaboration networks.*Proceedings of the 2013 IEEE/ACM International Conference on Advances in Social Networks Analysis and Mining*. doi:10.1145/2492517.2492584

Wang, Y., Cai, Z., & Zhang, Q. (2011). Differential evolution with composite trial vector generation strategies and control parameters. *Evolutionary Computation. IEEE Transactions on*, *15*(1), 55–66.

Wasserman, S. (1994). *Social network analysis: Methods and applications*. Cambridge University Press. doi:10.1017/CBO9780511815478

Watts, D. J., & Strogatz, S. H. (1998). Collective dynamics of 'small-world' networks. *Nature*, *393*(6684), 440–442. doi:10.1038/30918 PMID:9623998

Wayne, G., & Oellermann, R. O. (2011). *Distance in Graphs, structural Analysis of Complex Networks*. Springer.

Wilson, R. E., Gosling, S. D., & Graham, L. T. (2012). A Review of Facebook Research in the Social Sciences Perspectives. *Psychological Science*, *7*(3), 203–220.

Winkler, M. (2015). *On the Role of Triadic Substructures in Complex Networks*. Berlin: epubli.

Winkler, M., & Reichardt, J. (2013). Motifs in triadic random graphs based on Steiner triple systems. *Physical Review E: Statistical, Nonlinear, and Soft Matter Physics*, *88*(2), 022805. doi:10.1103/PhysRevE.88.022805 PMID:24032881

Winkler, M., & Reichardt, J. (2014). Node-Specific Triad Pattern Mining for Complex-Network Analysis. In *ICDMW, 2014 IEEE International Conference on Data Mining* (pp. 605-612). IEEE. doi:10.1109/ICDMW.2014.36

Wright, A., & Agapie, A. (2001). Cyclic and Chaotic Behavior in Genetic Algorithms. In *Proc. of Genetic and Evolutionary Computation Conference (GECCO).*

Wu, P. (2010, Nov). The perspective of biomedical electronics. In IEEE conference on sensors (pp. 1187-1187). doi:10.1109/ICSENS.2010.5690645

Wu, K et al. (1995). Live cell image segmentation. *IEEE Transactions on Bio-Medical Engineering*, 1–12. PMID:7851922

Wu, Q., & Hao, J. K. (2015). A review on algorithms for maximum clique problems. *European Journal of Operational Research, 242*(3), 693–709. doi:10.1016/j.ejor.2014.09.064

Xiaodong, D., Cunrui, W., Xiangdong, L., & Yanping, L. (2008, June). Web community detection model using particle swarm optimization. In *Evolutionary Computation, 2008. CEC 2008.(IEEE World Congress on Computational Intelligence). IEEE Congress on* (pp. 1074-1079). IEEE. doi:10.1109/CEC.2008.4630930

Xing, X. Wang, G., Wu, J., & Li, J. (2009). Square region-based coverage and connectivity probability model in wireless sensor networks. *5th International Conference on Collaborative Computing: Networking, Applications and Worksharing,* (CollaborateCom 2009) (pp. 1-8). IEEE.

Xuange, P., & Ying, X. (2010, March). An embedded electric meter based on bluetooth data acquisition system. In *Second international workshop on education technology and computer science* (Vol. 1, pp. 667-670). doi:10.1109/ETCS.2010.624

Xu, X., Zhang, J., & Small, M. (2010). Rich-club connectivity dominates assortativity and transitivity of complex networks. *Physical Review E: Statistical, Nonlinear, and Soft Matter Physics, 82*(4), 046117. doi:10.1103/PhysRevE.82.046117 PMID:21230355

Yahia, N. B., Saoud, N. B. B., & Ghezala, H. B. (2013). Evaluating community detection using a bi-objective optimization. In *Intelligent Computing Theories* (pp. 61–70). Springer Berlin Heidelberg. doi:10.1007/978-3-642-39479-9_8

Yahoo Research. (2004). Finding good nearly balanced cuts in power law graphs. Technical report. Pasadena, CA: Author.

Yakoubi, Z., & Kanawati, R. (2014). LICOD: A Leader-driven algorithm for community detection in complex networks. *Vietnam Journal of Computer Science*, 241-256.

Yan, C., & Qiao. (2010). Application analysis of complex adaptive systems for WSN. *Computer Application and System Modeling (ICCASM), International Conference on* (vol. 7).

Yan, C., & Ji-Hong, Q. (2010). Application analysis of complex adaptive systems for WSN.*International Conference on Computer Application and System Modeling (ICCASM 2010)* (Vol. 7).

Yang, X. S. (2010). A New Metaheuristic Bat-Inspired Algorithm. In Nature Inspired Cooperative Strategies for Optimization (NISCO 2010). Springer. doi:10.1007/978-3-642-12538-6_6

Yang, Z., Tang, K., & Yao, X. (2008, June). Self-adaptive differential evolution with neighborhood search. In *Evolutionary Computation, 2008. CEC 2008. (IEEE World Congress on Computational Intelligence). IEEE Congress on* (pp. 1110-1116). IEEE.

Yang, X. S. (2009). Firefly algorithms for multimodal optimization". Stochastic Algorithms: Foundations and Applications, SAGA 2009. *Lecture Notes in Computer Science, 5792*, 169–178. doi:10.1007/978-3-642-04944-6_14

Yang, X. S., & Deb, S. (2009). Cuckoo search via Levy flights. *World Congress on Nature and Biologically Inspired Computing (NaBIC 2009).* IEEE Publications. doi:10.1109/NABIC.2009.5393690

Yang, Z., Yao, X., & He, J. (2008). Making a difference to differential evolution. In *Advances in metaheuristics for hard optimization* (pp. 397–414). Springer Berlin Heidelberg. doi:10.1007/978-3-540-72960-0_19

Yan, P., & Liu, S. (2006). SEIR epidemic model with delay. *The ANZIAM Journal*, *48*(01), 119–134. doi:10.1017/S144618110000345X

Yin, D., Hong, L., & Davison, B. (2011). Structural link analysis and prediction in microblogs. *Proceedings of the 20th ACM international conference on Information and knowledge management - CIKM '11* (p. 1163). doi:10.1145/2063576.2063743

Yi, W., Gao, L., Li, X., & Zhou, Y. (2015). A new differential evolution algorithm with a hybrid mutation operator and self-adapting control parameters for global optimization problems. *Applied Intelligence*, *42*(4), 642–660. doi:10.1007/s10489-014-0620-3

Young, H., & Levenglick, A. (1978). A consistent extension of Condorcet's election principle. *SIAM Journal on Applied Mathematics*, *35*(2), 285–300. doi:10.1137/0135023

Youssef, B., & Hassan, H. (2014). IASM: An Integrated Attribute Similarity for Complex Networks Generation. In *Proceedings of the 28th IEEE International Conferenceon Information Networking (ICOIN)*. doi:10.1109/ICOIN.2014.6799745

Yu, X., Gu, Q., Zhou, M., & Han, J. (2012). Citation Prediction in Heterogeneous Bibliographic Networks. *SDM*, 1119-1130.

Zaharie, D. (2009). Influence of crossover on the behavior of differential evolution algorithms. *Applied Soft Computing*, *9*(3), 1126–1138. doi:10.1016/j.asoc.2009.02.012

Zahra, R. Ch., & Motlagh, M. R. J. (2007). Control of spatiotemporal chaos in coupled map lattice by discrete-time variable structure control. *Physics Letters. [Part A]*, *370*, 3–4, 302–305.

Zamani, F., & Safabakhhsh, R. (2006). An Unsupervised GVF Snake Approach for White Blood Cell Segmentation Based on Nucleus. *The 8th International Conference on Signal Processing*.

Zdeborova, L. & Mezard, M., (2006). *The number of matchings in random graphs*. Academic Press.

Zelinka, I. (2012). *On Close Relations of Evolutionary Dynamics, Chaos and Complexity*. Keynote at International Workshop on Chaos-Fractals Theories and Applications, Dalian, China.

Zelinka, I. (2013). *Mutual Relations of Evolutionary Dynamics, Deterministic Chaos and Complexity*. IEEE Congress on Evolutionary Computation 2013, Mexico.

Zelinka, I. (2014). Hidden Complexity of Evolutionary Dynamics – Analysis. In *ISCS 2013: Interdisciplinary Symposium on Complex Systems, Emergence, Complexity and Computation* (*Vol. 8*). Springer.

Zelinka, I. (2015). *Evolutionary Algorithms as a Complex Dynamical Systems*. Tutorial at IEEE Congress on Evolutionary Computation 2015, Sendai.

Zelinka, I., Celikovsky, S., Richter, H., & Chen, G. (2010). Evolutionary Algorithms and Chaotic Systems. Springer.

Zelinka, I., Davendra, D., Lampinen, J., Senkerik, R., & Pluhacek, M. (2014). *Evolutionary Algorithms Dynamics and its Hidden Complex Network Structures*. Congress on Evolutionary Computation, WCCI 2014 IEEE Congress, Beijing, China. doi:10.1109/CEC.2014.6900441

Zelinka, I., Davendra, D., Snasel, V., Jasek, R., Senkerik, R., & Oplatkova, Z. (2010). Preliminary Investigation on Relations Between Complex Networks and Evolutionary Algorithms Dynamics. CISIM 2010, Poland.

Zelinka, I., Davendra, D., Snášel, V., Jašek, R., Senkeřik, R., & Oplatková, Z. (2010, October). Preliminary investigation on relations between complex networks and evolutionary algorithms dynamics. In *Computer Information Systems and Industrial Management Applications (CISIM), 2010 International Conference on* (pp. 148-153). IEEE. doi:10.1109/CISIM.2010.5643674

Zelinka, I. (2004). SOMA - Self Organizing Migrating Algorithm. In B. B. Onwubolu (Ed.), *New Optimization Techniques in Engineering* (pp. 167–218). New York: Springer-Verlag. doi:10.1007/978-3-540-39930-8_7

Zelinka, I. (2005). *Investigation on Evolutionary Deterministic Chaos Control*. Prague: IFAC.

Zelinka, I. (2006). Investigation on Realtime Deterministic Chaos Control by Means of Evolutionary Algorithms. *1st IFAC Conference on Analysis and Control of Chaotic Systems*, Reims, France

Zelinka, I. (2006). Investigation on real-time deterministic chaos control by means of evolutionary algorithms. *Proc. First IFAC Conference on Analysis and Control of Chaotic Systems.*

Zelinka, I. (2008). Real-time deterministic chaos control by means of selected evolutionary algorithms. *Engineering Applications of Artificial Intelligence*. doi:10.1016/j.engappai.2008.07.008

Zelinka, I., Chen, G., & Celikovsky, S. (2008). Chaos Synthesis by Means of Evolutionary Algorithms. *International Journal of Bifurcation and Chaos in Applied Sciences and Engineering*, *18*(4), 911–942. doi:10.1142/S021812740802077X

Zelinka, I., Davendra, D. D., Chadli, M., Senkerik, R., Dao, T. T., & Skanderova, L. (2013). Evolutionary dynamics as the structure of complex networks. In *Handbook of Optimization* (pp. 215–243). Springer Berlin Heidelberg. doi:10.1007/978-3-642-30504-7_9

Zelinka, I., Davendra, D., Chadli, M., Senkerik, R., Dao, T. T., & Skanderova, L. (2012). Evolutionary Dynamics and Complex Networks. In *Handbook of Optimization*. Springer.

Zelinka, I., Davendra, D., Senkerik, R., & Jasek, R. (2011). Do Evolutionary Algorithm Dynamics Create Complex Network Structures? *Complex Systems*, *2*, 127–140.

Zelinka, I., Snasel, V., & Ajith, A. (2012). *Handbook of Optimization*. Springer.

Zhang, B., & Horvath, S. (2005). A general framework for weighted gene co-expression network analysis. *Statistical Applications in Genetics and Molecular Biology*, *4*(1). doi:10.2202/1544-6115.1128 PMID:16646834

Zhang, H., Zhao, H., Cai, W., Liu, J., & Zhou, W. (2010). Using the k-core decomposition to analyze the static structure of large-scale software systems. *The Journal of Supercomputing*, *53*(2), 352–369. doi:10.1007/s11227-009-0299-0

Zhang, J., & Philip, S. (2014). *Link prediction across heterogeneous social networks: A survey*. Chicago: University of Illinois.

Zhao, J., Yagan, O., & Gligor, V. (2014). *Results on vertex degree and k-connectivity in uniform s-intersection graphs*. Technical Report CMU-CyLab-14-004. CyLab, Carnegie Mellon University.

Zhao, J. (2014). Minimum node degree and *k*-connectivity in wireless networks with unreliable links.*IEEE International Symposium on Information Theory (ISIT)*, (pp. 246-250). IEEE. doi:10.1109/ISIT.2014.6874832

Zhao, K., Kumar, A., Harrison, T., & Yen, J. (2011). Analyzing the resilience of complex supply network topologies against random and targeted disruptions. *IEEE Systems Journal*, *5*(1), 28–39. doi:10.1109/JSYST.2010.2100192

Zhao, L., Park, K., Lai, Y.-C., & Cupertino, T. (2007). Attack induced cascading breakdown in complex networks. *Journal of the Brazilian Computer Society*, *13*(3), 67–76. doi:10.1007/BF03192546

Zhou, B., Lee, Y. Z., Gerla, M., & De Rango, F. (2006). Geo-LANMAR: A scalable routing protocol for ad hoc networks with group motion. *Wireless Communications and Mobile Computing*, *6*(7), 989–1002. doi:10.1002/wcm.433

Zhou, F., Mahler, S., & Toivonen, H. (2012). Simplification of networks by edge pruning. In *Bisociative Knowledge Discovery* (pp. 179–198). Springer-Verlag Berlin. doi:10.1007/978-3-642-31830-6_13

Zhou, S., & Mondragón, R. (2004). The rich-club phenomenon in the Internet topology. *IEEE Communications Letters*, *8*(3), 180–182. doi:10.1109/LCOMM.2004.823426

Zhou, S., & Mondragón, R. (2007). Structural constraints in complex networks. *New Journal of Physics*, *9*(6), 173–173. doi:10.1088/1367-2630/9/6/173

Zhou, Y., Li, X., & Gao, L. (2013). A differential evolution algorithm with intersect mutation operator. *Applied Soft Computing*, *13*(1), 390–401. doi:10.1016/j.asoc.2012.08.014

Zhu, X. (2005). *Semi-supervised learning literature survey. Tech Report, Computer Sciences*. University of Wisconsin-Madison.

About the Contributors

Natarajan Meghanathan is a tenured Full Professor of Computer Science at Jackson State University, Jackson, MS. He graduated with a Ph.D. in Computer Science from The University of Texas at Dallas in May 2005. Dr. Meghanathan has published more than 150 peer-reviewed articles (more than half of them being journal publications). He has also received federal education and research grants from the U. S. National Science Foundation, Army Research Lab and Air Force Research Lab. Dr. Meghanathan has been serving in the editorial board of several international journals and in the Technical Program Committees and Organization Committees of several international conferences. His research interests are Wireless Ad hoc Networks and Sensor Networks, Graph Theory and Network Science, Cyber Security, Machine Learning, Bioinformatics and Computational Biology. For more information, visit http://www.jsums.edu/nmeghanathan.

* * *

Vahid Khalilpour Akram received the BSc and the MSc degrees in Computer Eng from IAU University. He is currently a Ph.D candidate at Ege University, International Computer Institute.

Sylvia Bhattacharya is a Graduate Students at Georgia Southern University.

Anupam Biswas received M.Tech. degree in Computer Science and Engineering from Motilal Nehru National Institute of Technology Allahabad. He received B.E. degree in Computer Science and Engineering from Jorhat Engineering College affiliated to Dibrugarh University. He is working toward the Ph.D. in Computer Science and Engineering from Indian Institute of Technology (BHU), Varanasi. His research interests include Data Mining, Social Computing, Evolutionary Computation and Optimization.

Bhaskar Biswas has obtain his PhD degree from department of computer science & engg, Indian Institute of Technology (BHU), Varanasi.His research interest includes Data mining, Social Network Analysis. Bhaskar Is currently working as Assistant Professor in the CSE department, IIT (BHU) VAranasi.

Santi Caballe has a PhD, Masters and Bachelors in Computer Science from the Open University of Catalonia (Barcelona, Spain). Since 2003 he has been an Assistant Professor and in 2006 he became Associate Professor at the Open University of Catalonia in the area of Software Engineering and Web-applications for Collaborative Work. He has been involved in the organization of several international conferences, conference tracks and workshops, and has published over 200 research contributions as books, book chapters, international journal and conference papers. He has also acted as editor for books and special issues of leading international journals. His research focuses on e-Learning and Collaborative and Mobile Learning, Distributed Technologies and Software Engineering.

Luis Casillas holds a Ph.D. and a Master's Degree in Information and Knowledge Societies, as well as a Master's Degree in Information Systems and a B.Sc. in Informatics. He has been working as full-time professor for more than 20 years in the Computer Science Department from the University of Guadalajara (Mexico). He has published various papers and scientific chapters in diverse journals and books. He serves as member of the editorial board for a couple of journals, and reviewer for diverse journals and other scientific publications about: knowledge engineering, computer science and ICT in education. His research interests are: knowledge gathering and representation, bio-inspired systems, expert systems, complex networks analysis, and soft-computing.

Ayan Chatterjee did his B.E. from the department of Electronics and Telecommunication Engineering, Jadavpur University, India. Currently he is pursuing Master's degree. His interest lies in the field of complex networks and his research mainly centers around structural control theory, study of network breakdown and architectural analysis.

Orhan Dagdeviren received the BSc and the MSc degrees in Computer Eng from Izmir Institute of Technology. He received Ph.D. degree from Ege University, International Computing Institute. He is an associate professor in International Computing Institute in Ege University. His interests lie in the computer networking and distributed systems areas. His recent focus is on graph theoric middleware protocol design for wireless sensor networks, mobile ad hoc networks and grid computing.

Thanasis Daradoumis is Assistant Professor at the Department of Cultural Technology and Communication, University of the Aegean, Greece. He is also Joint Professor at the department of Computer Science, Multimedia and Telecommunications at the Open University of Catalonia, Spain, and Collaborating Professor at the Hellenic Open University. He holds a PhD in Computer Science from the Polytechnic University of Catalonia-Spain. His research focuses on e-learning, e-collaboration, e-learning communities, creative e-learning content-design, creative e-course design, synchronous and asynchronous communication, interaction analysis, e-assessment, e-monitoring and scaffolding, computer supported collaborative learning (CSCL), adaptive learning, emotional and affective learning. He has written over 130 papers, serves in the editorial board of several international conferences and journals, whereas he has coordinated or participated in various European R & D projects.

Debayan Das was born in India on February 3, 1993. He is currently a senior undergraduate student in the Dept. of Electronics and Telecommunication Engg., Jadavpur University, Kolkata, India. His research interests mainly include complex networks, wireless body area networks, and analog circuit design.

Paramita Dey is currently an Assistant Professor in the Department of Information Technology, Govt. College of Engineering and Ceramic Technology, Kolkata, India. She is presently pursuing PhD at Jadavpur University, Kolkata, India. Her research interests are in the areas of Distributed Computing and Social Network Analysis.

Arturo Diaz-Perez is the head of Cinvestav-Tamaulipas, located in Ciudad Victoria, Mexico. Since 1998, Arturo Diaz-Perez joined to Cinvestav as a Full Professor. He received a Ph.D. (1998) degree in Electrical Engineering from Cinvestav. He also holds a M.Sc. (1988) degree in Electrical Engineering from Cinvestav, and a B.Sc. (1987) degree in Computer Science from the University of Puebla, Mexico. Prof. Arturo Diaz-Perez has published one book in the field of reconfigurable computing for cryptographic algorithms, 16 papers in technical refereed journals, more than 40 papers in technical conferences. He has supervised one Ph.D. thesis and 24 M.Sc. thesis. Prof. Diaz-Perez' research interests are in information security and parallel computing for large problems. Since 2006, he is the head of the Cinvestav's IT Lab and his work has focused on promoting information technology developments for the State of Tamaulipas in a join venture initiative between Cinvestav and Government of Tamaulipas.

Peppino Fazio received the master's degree in computer science engineering and telecommunications in May 2004 and Ph.D. in Electronics and Communications Engineering in 2008. He is an assistant professor at DIMES Department of University of Calabria, after many collaborations with the UPV of Valencia and the VSB-Technical University of Ostrava. His research interests include mobile communication networks, QoS architectures and interworking wireless and wired networks, mobility modeling for WLAN environments and mobility analysis for prediction purposes.

Alberto Garcia-Robledo is a Computer Science PhD candidate at the Information Technology Lab of the Center for Research and Advanced Studies (Cinvestav-Tamaulipas) in Mexico. His PhD thesis is related to the design of a high performance computing strategy for the processing of complex networks on hybrid multi/many-core parallel arquitectures. He made his BA in Computer System Engineering at the Higher Technological Institute of Poza Rica (Mexico) and his MSc in Computer Science at Cinvestav-Tamaulipas. Alberto Garcia-Robledo has attended courses, participated in projects, or performed presentations in renowned Mexican and international academic institutions, such as the Monterrey Institute of Technology and Higher Education (Mexico), the National Laboratory of Advanced Informatics (Mexico), Cinvestav-Tamaulipas (Mexico), the University of La Laguna (Spain), the University of Informatics Sciences (Cuba) and the Università della Svizzera Italiana (Switzerland). Recently he was invited to participate in a data anlytics research project involving government, academia and industry at the Geospatial Data Center of the Massachusetts Institute of Technology (USA).

Abhishek Garg received M.Tech. degree in Computer Science and Engineering from Motilal Nehru National Institute of Technology Allahabad. He received B. Tech. degree in Information Technology from Institute of Engineering and Technology Lucknow College affiliated to Gautam Buddha Technical University. He is working toward the Ph.D. in Computer Science and Engineering from Indian Institute of Technology (BHU), Varanasi. His research interests include Data Mining, Community detection in social network, Evolutionary Computation and Optimization.

Can Umut Ileri received his BSc. degrees from Kadir Has University, one in Statistics and Computer Science and the other one in Computer Engineering. He received MSc degrees in Computer Engineering from Politecnico di Milano and Politecnico di Torino. He is currently a PhD candidate in Information Technology and Computer Science joint program between International Computer Institute, Ege University and Izmir University. His research interests are graph theory, distributed algorithms and complex networks.

Kamarujjaman is with Govt. College of Engineering and Ceramic Technology, Kolkata. He is working as JRF in the Department of Information Technology, Govt. College of Engineering & Ceramic Technology. He was born on the 2nd January, 1991 at Radhakantapur. He obtained his B.Tech. Degree fromMurshidabad College of Engineering and Technology in 2012. He is now working under the guidance of Dr. Mausumi Maitra, HOD in the Department of Information Technology, Government College of Engineering and Ceramic Technology.

Rushed Kanawati is an Associate Professor at Université Paris 13, Sorbonne Paris Cité.

Vedat Kavalcı received the BSc. degree in Computer Eng. and MSc. degree in Computer Eng. from Ege University. He is a lecturer in Vocational Higher School in İzmir University. He is currently a Ph.D. student in Computer Science and Information Technology program at Ege University. His interests lie in the computer networking, wireless sensor networks and embedded systems areas.

Mohammad S. Khan received his M.Sc. and Ph.D. in Computer Science and Computer Engineering from the University of Louisville, Kentucky, USA, in 2011 and 2013 respectively. He is currently affiliated with Department of Electrical Engineering and Computer Science at Texas A&M University- Kingsville. His primary area of search is in ad-hoc networks and network tomography. His research interest span several fields including ad-hoc network, mobile wireless mesh network and sensor network, statistical modeling, ODE, wavelets and ring theory. He has been on technical program committee of various international conferences and technical reviewer of various international journals in his field. He serve as editor-in-chief of International Journal of Grid and High Performance Computing.

Mausumi Maitra is with the Information Technology Department, Govt. College of Engineering and Ceramic Technology, University of WBUT, Kolkata WB 700010 India (e-mail: mou1232005@yahoo.com). Mausumi Maitra is presently working as Associate Professor & HOD of the Dept. of Information Technology of Govt. College of Engg. and Ceramic Technology. She obtained her B.Tech., M.Tech. and Ph.D. degree from the Institute of Radiophysics and Electronics, C. U.. She has more than twenty years of research and teaching experiences in different institutes and has more than twenty publications in National / International Journals and Conferences. She has completed / pursuing four projects sponsored by AICTE and UGC. Her current research interest is in VLSI design and Image Processing.

Salvatore Marano (M'97) received the Laurea degree in electronics engineering from the University of Rome, Rome, Italy, in 1973. In 1974, he was with Fondazione Ugo Bordoni. Between 1976 and 1977, he was with the ITT Laboratory, Leeds, U.K. Since 1979, he has been an Associate Professor with the University of Calabria, Arcavacata di Rende, Italy. His research interests include performance evaluation in mobile communication systems, satellite systems, and 3g/4G networks. He has published more than 130 papers in international conference proceedings and journals. Dr. Marano has been a Reviewer for many journals such as the IEEE Communication Letters, the IEEE Journal of Selected Areas in Communications, the IEEE Transactions on Vehicular Technology, the IEEE Transactions on Wireless Communications, and the European Transactions on Telecommunications Journal.

Guillermo Morales-Luna is a Researcher at Cinvestav-IPN since 1985. He received a Ph.D (1984) in Mathematics from the Polish Academy of Sciences, Poland. He also holds an M.Sc. (1978) in Mathematics and a B.Sc. (1976) in Physics and Mathematics from from the National Polytecnic Institute (IPN), Mexico. Prof. Guillermo Morales-Luna has authored more than 19 papers in technical refereed journals related to Theoretical Computer Science, Logic and Cryptography, more than 20 conference papers, 6 technical reports at Cinvestav, one book at IPN, and one chapter in a book published by Springer-Verlag. He has supervised more than 7 Ph.D. thesis, 21 M.Sc. thesis and 3 B.Sc. thesis. He has also refereed texts and books edited by the Sociedad Matemática Mexicana, the Universidad Autónoma Metropolitana and IPN. From 1989 to 1992 he chaired the Cinvestav Computer Science Section. He has received several grants for research and technology projects from Mexican CONACyT, UNESCO, PEMEX and the Mexican Institute of Telecommunications. His research interest areas include Logic (model theory, Peano arithmetic, proof theory) and mathematical foundations of Computer Science (recursive functions, computational complexity and algorithms).

Manali Mukherjee is with Govt. College of Engineering and Ceramic Technology, Kolkata. Manali Mukherjee is working as a project fellow in the Department of Information Technology,Govt. College of Engineering & Ceramic Technology. She was born on the 15th day of August, 1986 at Kolkata. She obtained her B.Tech. degree from Saroj Mohan Institute of Technology and M. Tech. degree from West Bengal University of Technology(in house) in 2009 and 2011 respectively. She is now working under UGC sponsored project under the guidance of Dr. Mausumi Maitra, HOD in the Department of Information Technology.

Manisha Pujari is a PhD graduate from Université Paris 13 working in the computer science research lab LIPN.

Danda B Rawat is an Assistant Professor in the Department of Electrical Engineering at Georgia Southern University. His research focuses on wireless communication networks, cyber-physical systems and cyber security. His current research interests include design, analysis, and evaluation of cognitive radio networks, software defined networks, smart grid security, cyber-physical systems, vehicular/ wireless ad hoc networks, wireless sensor networks, and wireless mesh networks. He has published over 120 refereed scientific/technical articles. He has authored 8 books and over 15 peer-reviewed book chapters. He has been serving as an Editor and Guest Editor for over 15 international journals. He served as a Web-chair for IEEE INFOCOM 2016, Student Travel Grant Co-chair of IEEE INFOCOM 2015, Track-chair for Wireless Networking and Mobility of IEEE CCNC 2016, Track-Chair for Communications Network and Protocols of IEEE AINA 2015, TPC Chair of IEEE SDS, and so on. He served as a program chair, general chair, and session chair for numerous international conferences and workshops, and served as a technical program committee (TPC) member for several international conferences including IEEE GLOBECOM, IEEE CCNC, IEEE GreenCom, IEEE AINA, IEEE ICC, IEEE WCNC, IEEE RWW, IEEE SCAN, IEEE CCAN, IEEE Cloud-CPS, and IEEE VTC conferences. He has received the Best Paper Awards at the International Conferences. He is the recipient Outstanding Research Faculty Award (Award for Excellence in Scholarly Activity) 2015, Allen E. Paulson College of Engineering and Technology, Georgia Southern University in August, 2015. He is the Founder and Director of the Cyber-security, Wireless Systems and Networking Innovations (CWiNs) Research Lab (http://www.CWiNs.org) at GSU. He is a Senior Member of IEEE, and a member of ACM and ASEE. He is serving as a Vice Chair of the Executive Committee of the IEEE Savannah Section since 2013.

Mohamed R. M. Rizk obtained his B.Sc. from Alexandria University and his master's and Ph.D. from McMaster University, Canada. He is an Emeritus Professor in Alexandria University. He worked as an assistant professor at McMaster University, a visiting professor at Sultan Qaboos University, Oman, Beirut Arab University and the Arab Academy for Science and Technology, Egypt. He is the academic coordinator of VTMENA (Virginia Polytechnic and State University, Virginia, U.S.A and Alexandria University, Egypt). He is a Life Senior Member of IEEE. His research interests include Computer Aided Design, Computer Networks, Encryption, Fuzzy Logic, and Image processing.

Sarbani Roy is currently an Associate Professor in the Department of Computer Science and Engineering, Jadavpur University, India. She has received the Ph.D. degree from Jadavpur University, Kolkata, India in July, 2008. Her research interests are in the areas of Cloud Computing, Wireless Sensor Networks and Social Network Analysis.

Lenka Skanderova received her bachelor's degree and master's degree in the field of computer science in 2009 and 2011, respectively. She is currently pursuing her Ph.D degree in the Faculty of Electrical Engineering and Computer Science of VSB - Technical University of Ostrava. Her research interests include evolutionary algorithms in connection with the complex networks, multi-objective optimization and deterministic chaos.

Mauro Tropea was born in 1975 and graduated in computer engineering at the University of Calabria, Italy, in 2003. Since 2003 he has been with the telecommunications research group of Department of Electronics, Computer Science and Systems (DEIS) of University of Calabria. In 2004 he won a regional scholarship on Satellite and Terrestrial broadband digital telecommunication systems. In 2009 he got the Ph.D. student in Electronics and Communications Engineering at University of Calabria. His research interests include satellite communication networks, QoS architectures and interworking wireless and wired networks, mobility model.

Cemil Aybars Ural is a B.Sc. in Mechanical Engineering - METU(1995), B.Sc. in Computer Engineering - Yasar University(2010), Ph.D. Student on Information Technology at Ege University (2010 - Present).

Marco Winkler studied physics at the University of Wuerzburg in Germany and at Boston University in Boston, MA. He received his PhD in physics from the University of Wuerzburg in 2015. His research focuses on complex networks using methodologies from statistical physics, data mining, and machine learning. In 2011, he won the Wilhelm-Conrad-Roentgen students' prize from the physics department of the University of Wuerzburg. He has received scholarships from the German National Merit Foundation (Studienstiftung des deutschen Volkes) and the German Academic Exchange Service (DAAD).

Rupei Xu is a PhD student in Telecommunications Engineering, University of Texas at Dallas.

Ivan Zelinka (born 1965) is currently working at the Technical University of Ostrava (VSB-TU), Faculty of Electrical Engineering and Computer Science. He graduated consequently at Technical University in Brno (1995 – MSc.), UTB in Zlin (2001 – Ph.D.) and again at Technical University in Brno (2004 – assoc. prof.) and VSB-TU (2010 - professor). Before academic career he was an employed like

TELECOM technician, computer specialist (HW+SW) and Commercial Bank (computer and LAN supervisor). He has been invited for numerous lectures at universities in different EU countries plus role of the keynote speaker at the conferences like Global Conference on Power, Control and Optimization in Bali, Indonesia (2009), Interdisciplinary Symposium on Complex Systems (2011), Halkidiki, Greece and IWCFTA 2012, Dalian China and CEC 2013 and 2015 and more. He is and was responsible supervisor of 5 grant of fundamental research of Czech grant agency GAČR, co-supervisor of grant FRVŠ - Laboratory of parallel computing and international granted research about cybersecurity (Czech-Vietnam). He was also working on numerous grants and two EU project like member of team (FP5 - RESTORM) and supervisor (FP7 - PROMOEVO) of the Czech team. He was awarded by Siemens Award for his Ph.D. thesis, as well as by journal Software news for his book about artificial intelligence. Ivan Zelinka is a member of British Computer Socciety, Editor in chief of Springer book series: Emergence, Complexity and Computation, Editorial board of Saint Petersburg State University Studies in Mathematics, Machine Intelligence Research Labs (MIR Labs - http://www.mirlabs.org/czech.php), IEEE (committee of Czech section of Computational Intelligence), a few international program committees of various conferences and international journals (Associate Editor of IJAC, Editorial Council of Security Revue, http://www.securityrevue.com/editorial-council/). He is author of journal articles as well as of books in Czech and English language.

Bassant Youssef is a PhD degree holder from Virginia tech.A Msc. Degree holder from Alexandria University. Bassant is currently an Assistant Professor in the Department of Engineering Mathematics and Physics, Faculty of Engineering, Alexandria University.

Index

A

academic program 396-399, 402-404, 407-408, 410-414
augmenting path 37-40, 99, 106, 109-111, 114

B

backbone formation 1
BA model 218-219, 222, 227, 232, 235

C

CBC 359-360
central algorithm 36, 46-47, 50-51, 54
centrality 80, 221, 238, 243, 262, 287-288, 293-294, 299, 305, 313, 323, 330, 332-334, 385
chaos 319, 322-323, 337
clustering 1, 32-34, 65, 80, 101, 121, 139-144, 184, 193, 215, 217-218, 220-221, 223, 227-228, 230-231, 238, 240-241, 244-248, 267, 273-274, 286-288, 291-293, 299-303, 305, 313, 320, 335, 361, 364, 379-380, 386, 392, 399, 407-408, 410, 414
CML systems 324, 337-338
Combinatorial Optimization Problems 274, 284
community detection 75, 88-89, 244-245, 256, 266-268, 272-275, 277-279, 287
complex network 32, 34, 74, 88, 98-103, 115, 117-119, 121, 127, 215-219, 223, 227, 235, 266, 279, 285, 287-288, 290, 295, 313, 319-324, 326, 329-330, 333, 335, 337-338, 345, 379-380, 397-398, 406, 411, 414-415
complex networks 31-34, 45, 54, 58, 73-75, 83, 88, 92, 98-99, 101, 103, 106, 111, 116-117, 121-122, 125, 127, 144, 180, 215-223, 227, 231, 235, 267, 285-288, 290, 300, 319-320, 323-324, 326-327, 335, 337-338, 379, 392, 396-399, 414
connected vertex cover 2, 25, 27-29
connectivity 30, 32, 34-37, 40-44, 46-48, 50-54, 64, 67, 115, 180-181, 185, 188, 191, 194, 200-201, 208, 232, 234, 247, 255, 268, 379-380, 383
connectivity detection 41, 44, 46
connectivity restoration 50
consensus 48, 414
control 2, 73, 98-103, 105-106, 114-115, 117-119, 121-122, 285-286, 289-290, 319, 322-324, 333, 335, 337-338, 344, 346, 349, 351, 353, 362, 382
counting 129, 292, 294, 359-364, 370-371, 375-376
cut vertex 30, 46, 53, 56

D

Data Mules 379-380, 392
delay differential equations 198
detection 30, 35, 41, 43-46, 49, 51, 53-54, 56, 75, 88-89, 125, 144, 244-245, 256, 259-260, 266-268, 272-275, 277-279, 287, 344, 347, 361, 363, 366, 368-369, 371, 376, 410
disjoint paths 34, 40-43, 49-50, 56
distributed algorithm 5, 10, 13, 15, 18, 27, 45, 49, 51, 54, 383
distributed systems 1, 27, 30
driver node 99, 103, 106, 111, 115-116, 118-119

E

effective driver node density 119
epidemic threshold 197
Erdős-Rényi model 111
evolution 68, 73, 127, 144, 198, 218-219, 222, 225, 231, 238, 268, 285-286, 288, 290, 294, 319, 322, 324, 326-327, 335, 380, 382
evolutionary algorithms 285, 287, 290, 319-320, 322-324, 326-327, 335, 337
evolutionary computation 266-268, 273-275, 278-279, 319-320

F

fault tolerance 392
feedback 100, 324, 337-338, 349
feed-forward loop 127, 135, 137-138, 144

G

gene 99, 269-270, 273, 284
genetic algorithm 266-268, 277, 284, 287, 320, 323, 326
Genotype 284
graph clustering 267
graph connectivity 42
graph matching 5, 29
graph sampling 238, 240, 249
graph theory 30, 37, 99, 101, 216, 243, 379-380
graph topology 62, 125
greedy algorithm 11-13, 38

H

Hough transform 359, 361-364, 366-371, 373, 376

I

image segmentation 360-361, 364, 371

K

k-connected network 30-31, 34, 36, 44, 50, 56
k-connectivity 30, 34-35, 43-45, 47-51, 53-54, 56
k-connectivity detection 30, 35, 43-45, 53-54, 56

L

large networks 54, 66, 71, 180, 273
link monitoring 1-2
link prediction 58-65, 67-68, 70-75, 78-80, 82, 87-89, 92

M

maximum matching 54, 99-101, 105-107, 116-119, 121-122
methodology 125, 127, 140, 337, 346, 361, 370, 376
Min Cut Set 56
minimal vertex cover 1-2, 29
minimum vertex cover 1, 29
minimum weighted vertex cover 2, 10-11, 27, 29
modularity 90, 256-257, 267, 273-274
motifs 125-127, 133, 135, 137-139, 144
Multi-Objective Optimization Problems 284

N

network diameter 33-34, 380
networks analysis 216, 326, 335, 337, 396-398
network topology 180, 219, 238, 383
node-specific pattern mining 127-128, 144
NP-hard problem 1, 267, 279, 284

O

ontology 346, 398-399, 408
optimization problems 268, 274, 284, 287

P

Particle Swarm Optimization 266-267, 271, 287, 323
patterns 75, 125-130, 133-136, 142, 216, 268, 320, 323
PCA 74
performance 32, 45, 60-61, 63, 68, 72-74, 78, 80, 89-90, 131, 240, 286, 321, 323-324, 330, 335, 337, 343-344, 363, 373, 379, 381-383, 389, 392
Phenotype 284
Platelets 359-362, 365-366, 371, 376
preferential attachment 67, 80, 85, 102, 122, 218, 221, 224, 383

R

red blood cell 360-363, 376
restoration 30, 45, 49-51, 53-54, 56
robustness 54, 98, 102, 117-118

S

scale free 33, 196-198, 200-201, 207-210, 217-218, 228, 248
scale free network 198, 201, 207, 209-210, 248
SEIRS model 198, 201-202, 209, 213
Self-Stabilization 27, 29
shortest path 34, 68, 70, 80, 85, 241, 247, 291, 293, 390-392
SIR model 196-202, 210
small world networks 320
social network 32-33, 133-134, 140, 197, 223, 229, 237-238, 240, 243-244, 246-247, 249, 252, 256, 261, 266
social networks 33, 58, 68, 74-75, 99, 121, 139, 197, 208, 216-217, 219, 221, 223, 229, 237-238, 247, 287, 320, 379-380, 398
structural controllability 98-99, 103

subgraphs 46-47, 125-128, 138, 144
supervised machine learning 68-70, 73, 79-80, 82, 89
supervised rank aggregation 58, 75, 77-78, 92

T

tailoring 396-397, 399, 402, 408
triads 128-129
triangles 246, 291

V

vertex cover 1-7, 9-11, 13, 15, 18-19, 21-29

W

WBC 360-362, 365, 370-371
wireless sensor networks 1, 30-31, 379-380

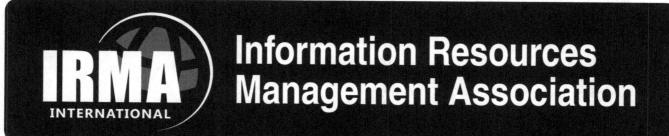

Printed in the United States
By Bookmasters